Rea

G

The Road to Winesburg

A Mosaic
of the Imaginative Life of
Sherwood Anderson

by

William A. Sutton

The Scarecrow Press, Inc.
Metuchen, N.J.   1972

This Book Is Dedicated to

Sherwood Anderson, who survived the tortures of life, derived much satisfaction from it, and left a remark-able record of his experience.

Cornelia Lane Anderson, who gave him his children and compassion, and Eleanor Copenhaver Anderson, who gave him love and extraordinary loyalty.

Libraries, those who create and maintain them, and those who give their lives and talent to their devoted operation.

The citizens of Andersonia, who gave of their knowledge of Anderson, who provided record and commentary on him, who helped in the production of this book in a variety of ways, a group of people approximately large enough to inhabit a Clyde or a Winesburg.

Sherwood Anderson
Elyria, Ohio, ca. 1911

Preface

Sherwood Anderson demonstrated repeatedly his recognition of the close relationship his life bore to his work; he believed his life should be judged in terms of his artistic accomplishment. A careful curator of the facts of his life may make a significant contribution to the understanding of his art, and of all art thereby. That is the ambition of the present writer and of this work. The writer hopes the reader will benefit in terms of understanding gained of an outstanding American artist but even more so of the reader's self. Anderson makes one of his Winesburg inhabitants say, "We are all Christ and we are all crucified." Even the least articulate can participate in the gains and losses of the artist struggling for utterance.

Aside from the great many debts all researchers know, special acknowledgments are always due. First among these to be mentioned is Mrs. Eleanor C. Anderson, whose generosity and encouragement to scholars has in it the quality of her deep love for Sherwood Anderson. Others who knew and loved him and who have made important contributions to this work are Mrs. Cornelia Lane Anderson, John S. Anderson, Karl Anderson, and Miss Marietta D. Finley.

The Newberry Library in Chicago and its dedicated personnel are especially thanked as are the willing assistants at the libraries of Ball State University, The Ohio State University, and the Hayes Memorial Library in Fremont, Ohio. Encouragement and support of every kind has been tendered by officials of the Ball State University and particularly of the English Department there.

Many people, most of whose contributions are documented, gave both time and information in both interviews and letters. One whose consultation was outstandingly helpful was Dr. Peter D. Cacavas, of the Department of Psychology at Ball State University.

Specific thanks are here given for the granting of

v

permission by the Saturday Review to reproduce quotations
from Karl Anderson's "My Brother, Sherwood Anderson"
and Little, Brown, and Company, Publishers, for use of
material from Letters of Sherwood Anderson, edited by
Howard Mumford Jones and Walter B. Rideout. These
letters are noted in the book by the symbol (JR) following
each citation.

Great appreciation is also extended both to the
Chicago Sun Times/Chicago Daily News and the Chicago
Tribune for their generous permission to reprint articles
relevant to this book.

The writer can only wish for each of the readers of
this book that traveling the road to Winesburg offer as much
insight into the simplicities, bafflements, and satisfactions
of Anderson's existence as the writer has found in negotiating
the frustrations and rewards of book production.

William A. Sutton
Muncie, Indiana
October, 1971

Sources for This Book

The most important factor in supplying sources to make this book possible is the Anderson Collection, which Mrs. Eleanor C. Anderson instituted at The Newberry Library in Chicago. The documents there, some 17,000 of them, provide a rich and unusual storehouse on which to draw.

The author was fortunate enough to get permission of the late Mrs. E. Vernon Hahn (Miss Marietta D. Finley, when the recipient of the letters) to add the 275 letters she received from Anderson between 1916 and 1931 to the Newberry Collection. Much richness is added to this book through the use of these materials. Many other unpublished letters from the Newberry are used in this book.

The writer had as a basic belief that people who knew Anderson should be interviewed and their ideas recorded. To the greatest extent possible, this was done in connection with this segment of Anderson's life. The interviewing was done most intensively in 1941 and 1942, thus saving and making available material otherwise now lost forever.

Various periodicals, such as the Clyde Enterprise and Chicago papers especially, contained useful and previously unnoticed and unusual material. The writer regrets that efforts to find a file of the Clyde Democrat have so far been unsuccessful.

Additional sources used in the compilation of this work may be found in the bibliography appended to the book.

Contents

ix

List of Mosaics

PART ONE

The Road to Winesburg

Mosaic I

"The only road to maturity..."

Writing can be, like the practice of any other art, a way of
    life. It is what we all want, to find a way to live.
                            to George Freitag, Aug. 27, 1938 (JR).

              *   *   *

To make me see something so vividly, the intensity of life
    in you at the moment, makes new life in me.   So that
    I am for the moment no longer blind.
              Isn't that the object of all so-called Art?
                            to Carrow DeVries, Oct. 5, 1939 (JR).

              *   *   *

All the morality then becomes a purely aesthetic matter.
    What is beautiful must bring aesthetic joy; what is ugly
    must bring aesthetic sadness and suffering.
                            from A Story Teller's Story, p. 78.

              *   *   *

As regards human relationships, I suppose I am as muddle-
    headed a man as ever lived.
              How could I be anything else, being both an artist
    and an American?
                            from "It's A Woman's Age"

              *   *   *

To the writer of prose, who loves his craft, there is nothing
    in the world so satisfying as being in the presence of
    great stacks of clean white sheets.   The feeling is in-
    describably sweet and cannot be compared with any re-
    action to be got from sheets on which one has already
    scribbled.
                            from A Story Teller's Story, p. 290.

14

The process of writing had been for me purifying and fine.
It had been curative and later I was filled with unholy
wrath when someone said that, during that period of
work, I had been unclean or vile.

from A Story Teller's Story, p. 316.

*   *   *

Put the badge of poet on a man and you crush the poetry in
him.

to Marietta D. Finley, Dec. 10, 1916

*   *   *

I guess we ought to feel that these human relations are
more important than our work.   I don't know.   We are
so often bastards.   We kick anyone aside who gets between us and the job.

to Gilbert Wilson, Feb. 1939.

*   *   *

It is the impotent man who is vile.   His very impotence has
made him vile and in the end I was to understand that
when you take from man the cunning of the hand, the
opportunity to constantly create new forms in materials,
you make him impotent.

from A Story Teller's Story, p. 195.

*   *   *

For it I have sacrificed a lot, life with my own children,
perhaps in the end the respect of that great body of
people, simple and good, much of my work has affected.

to Ferdinand Schevill, Dec. 19, 1923

*   *   *

When I see what is going on in my time, the loose talk of
the arts, the all around misunderstanding, cheapness in
attitude, I feel a rather deep obligation to something
that must always remain dearer to me than any woman.
That I think women only understand intellectually but I
do not blame them.

to M. D. Finley, March 9, 1929.

16 The Road to Winesburg

The Road to Winesburg

Probably I always was, in my outlook on life, an artist,
loving the color of things, words, arrangement of words
and ideas. I might I suppose have been a painter as I
can get excitement out of that too.

to Nelson Antrim Crawford, Oct. 29,
1921

*   *   *

... in taking the risk of trying to create the very feel of
life we take the terrible responsibility.   Let us say that
one of us a little succeeds.   He will hurt others, will
be constantly sending out little darts that wound.   Truth
so often hurts, at least for the time.   It is always,
when approached at all, a little startling, even shocking.

But one must have faith ... that truth, when it
can be got at always, in the end, also heals ... both
the artist and, he hopes, always the others.   It always
seems to him the only road to maturity ... that maturity
we all, knowingly or unknowingly, are seeking.

to Mary Emmett, 1935.

*   *   *

No person seen, met, so insignificant as not to be worth
while looking at, thinking of.   There can be an absorption that is also a way out.

to Mary Emmett, 1935.

*   *   *   *   *

Chapter 1

" A FAIR AND SWEET TOWN"

I guess we all have this other, the hunger back
into childhood and boyhood. . . . [1]

Camden I do not remember at all when my thoughts
turn back to childhood but Clyde, its streets, the
houses, the people there, all of these are very
sharp in my mind. . . . [2]

The town of Clyde is so packed with memories for
me--has been so much a part of my imaginative
life as a writer that it is difficult for me to say
words about it. [3]

I wish it would not sound to[o] silly to say I pour
a dream over it [the town], consciously, intention-
ally, for a purpose.   I want to write beautifully,
create beautifully, not outside but in this thing in
which I am born, in this place where ... I have
always lived, must always live. [4]

But I must hurry through my stories of childhood and
boyhood.   There is the temptation to go on and on
with them.   The impressions gathered by a writer,
let us say, in the first twenty years of his life, ...
are bound to become source materials for him all
his life, and often you have to go far back into the
childhood to recapture some of these impressions
that become materials. [5]

Again I begin the endless game of reconstructing
my own life, jerking it out of the shell that dies,

17

striving to breathe into it beauty and meaning.
A thought comes to me.

When I was a boy I lived in a town in Ohio and
often I wandered away to lie upon my back, thinking, as I am doing now.   I reconstruct and begin
to color and illuminate incidents of my life there.
Words said, shouts of children, the barking of dogs
at night, occasional flashes of beauty in the eyes
of women and old men, are remembered... [6]

Looking back upon boyhood and youth in Clyde, Ohio,
in the days when "the modern world had not come into full
flower," Anderson remembered that Clyde was "a fair
and sweet town."   It had been settled by the New Englanders
who had come to Ohio's Western Reserve.   He tells us in
his Memoirs (page 13) that "There were many little white
frame houses.   All the residence streets were lined with
maples."   It was in this town of 2,500 people surrounded
by farms that raised all sorts of fruits and vegetables,
notably cabbage and berries, that Anderson passed the years
between the time he was seven and perhaps twenty.

Any one who has read A Story Teller's Story[7] will
recall that there "Never was such a family to take the haunts
out of a house" and will remember the episode of collecting
cabbages at Hallowe'en.   "It is true that I remember whole
winters when there was no such thing as white flour in the
house.   There was, during a whole winter, no butter to
spread on bread."[8]   Herman Hurd, his boyhood companion,
did not think the family ever went hungry, though he could
recall that his father, the grocer, did give Sherwood a
bushel of apples "and other seconds" for "driving the wagon."[9]

One of Anderson's two enduring friendships of the
Clyde period was with young Hurd, with whom he went to
school and worked and played.   He stayed at the Hurd home
one whole winter and was always welcome there.   "He liked
them and they liked him."[10]   On his infrequent visits to
Clyde, he always visited Hurd.   One man "... looked for
him in the place where I had heard he would be found and
there he was sitting on a soap box in the back of Herman
Hurd's grocery story where he and Herman were exchanging
reminiscences of the days when each was a youngster in
town."[11]   Anderson wrote, "I spent last evening with my
boyhood friend Herman Hurd ...a very lovable, shrewd

capable man of no pretentions for whom I have a great affection. "[12] Much of the information in this volume about
Anderson in the town of Clyde comes from the recollections
of Herman Hurd in an interview with the present writer on
November 10, 1962.

In many places in his writing heavy emphasis is laid
on the poverty Anderson had known. In Hello Towns he
wrote, "Alas, this editor was born poor. Winter is ahead.
As a child the coming of winter always brought fear of cold
and hunger. The old dread holds. In contemplation of
winter I am always afraid. "[13] In an early autobiographical
sketch he exclaimed, "Lord, but we were poor--too poor. "[14]
A fuller analysis and a more illuminating one is found in
the following passages of A Story Teller's Story:

If our family was poor, of what did our poverty
consist? If our clothes were torn the torn places
only let in the sun and wind. In the winter we
had no overcoats, but that only meant we ran
rather than loitered. Those who are to follow the
arts should have a training in what is called poverty. Given a comfortable middle-class start in
life, the artist is almost sure to end up by becoming a bellyacher, constantly complaining because the public does not rush forward at once to
proclaim him.

The boy who has no warm overcoat throws back
his head and runs through the streets, past houses
where smoke goes up into a clear sky, across
vacant lots, through fields. The sky clouds and
snows come and the bare hands are cold and
chapped. They are raw and red but at night, before the boy sleeps, his mother will come with
melted fat and rub it over the raw places. (Pages
5-6.)

One may gather from this statement that Anderson
felt there was a connection between being poor and being an
artist. Elsewhere he was to make a more overt statement
concerning this matter. "Let us say the average young
American writer comes from a poor family. Most of them
do. I don't know why. They are lucky if they do. They
may get a little real education that way. " "My heavens, "
he exclaimed, if the average American millionaire knew
"what his monetary success cost him... in real contact with

life, " he would "go Bolshevik. " He went on to say that if
he had never tried to rise, "had earned my bread and butter
always with the same hands with which I wrote words I
might not have had something real to say with the words I
wrote. "[15]

What evidence now existing shows that the poverty of
the Anderson family was not abject. A woman who knew
the family well has said that the family was "aristocratically
poor... very clean and respectable. Sherwood was the live-
liest of them, and he was rather quiet, too, well brought
up and not rowdy. "[16] Anderson himself has written, "Although we were poor there were always plenty of books in
our house and Mother always managed to get materials to
make cookies. "[17] Hurd commented: "I don't think they
had lots of books. They didn't have much of a library at
the school. Sherwood absorbed all that the school had. Mr.
Ginn, the principal, gave Sherwood the privilege of using
his books, which Sherwood did. Few homes had many books. "

The soundest view of the position of the Anderson
family in Clyde seems to be that conditions, though at times
difficult, were seldom if ever desperate. The children do
not seem to have known plenty, and life was linked with toil
from childhood. It was assuredly a hard life, but it was
not so hard that Sherwood's imagination could not harden it
still more. The statement that the family lived in haunted
houses can not be substantiated. Mrs. Winfield Adare recalled that the family lived in the Piety Hill district [Race
Street] on Spring Avenue, Vine Street, Mechanic Street, and
Duane Street. [18] Late in life Anderson was able to pick out
"six different houses we had lived in" when driving about
Clyde. [19] Whatever the reason for perhaps half-a-dozen
moves in a dozen years, it is more likely than not that the
rent was paid. After all, the family has been called "respectable. " Furthermore, however negligent a provider the
father may have been, the boys all worked as soon as they
were able, and Stella Anderson taught school between 1892
and 1894. [20]

The necessity of constant work on the part of the
children, caused by the lack of a strong sense of responsibility on the part of the father, seems to have built up tensions which caused, among other things, a strong sense of
resentment against the father. [See Appendix I.] Another
way in which tensions were expressed is reflected in an
episode recalled by Herman Hurd. "The boys always used

to, at Easter, think they had to have something to wear.
This Easter most of us had new straw hats.   This one
Sunday we were in Whitehead's barn.   Someone knocked
his [Sherwood's] hat off, and he went all to pieces and
jumped up and down and smashed the hat. "

     Perhaps some of the earliest work the boys did was
to help their father with his painting.   The group of boys,
at least two of whom were considered "smart," attracted
quite a lot of attention.   The "tribe" might be seen indus-
triously working on a building with their father, ignoring
the gallery below.   Their father used to say every one
should learn a trade. [21]

     Anderson further remarks his willingness to take on
work:

> As early as I can remember, I was on the streets
> of our town, sweeping out stores, mowing the
> lawns before houses, selling newspapers, taking
> care of horses belonging to families where there
> were no men, selling popcorn and peanuts to the
> crowds on Saturday afternoon--perpetually busy.
> I became known in town as "Jobby" Anderson,
> because of my keenness for any job that presented
> itself. [22]

Other known jobs he held while in Clyde were water boy,
cow-driver, groom, delivery boy, errand boy, corn-cutter,
worker in the cabbage fields, worker in the bicycle factory,
laborer, printer's devil, painter, and sweeper in a doctor's
office.   "The truth is that...[he] did anything and everything
to earn an honest penny. "[23]

     Several people recalled Anderson as most energetic
and a good salesman.   As a newsboy, Sherwood would retail bits of news to any gathering until he had made his
sale, overcoming all sales resistance with genial witticisms. [24]
Karl recalled that his brother was proud that he could sell
more copies of the paper than any boy in town.   "Once he
boasted of his persuasiveness in inducing a farmer, in a
barroom, to buy more than one copy of the Enquirer. "[25]
"I was strong, cheerful, and willing.   I wasn't afraid of
work.   I have become lazier since. "[26]

     The aggressive quality of his action, so widely noted
in Clyde, was a natural reaction to a lack of parental leader-

ship on the part of the father. [See Appendix C.] The almost unconscious desire this driving activity created in him
is identified in this comment:

> It may be, after all, just the sense of security,
> or assurance of warmth, food, and leisure--most
> of all leisure--the boy wanted on that evening,
> that, for some reason I cannot explain, marked
> the end of boyhood for him. [27]

Possibly his preoccupation with work is at least
partly responsible for the fact that Sherwood's school record
is only average. The first record of any of the Anderson
children in the Clyde schools is for September, 1884. [28]
Karl and Stella, listed as ten and nine years old, respectively,
were in school in September, 1884. Sherwood, aged eight,
started his attendance in the second grade, then called C
Primary, on October 1, 1884.

The school records in Clyde are chiefly those of
attendance. In the third grade Sherwood's attendance was
good. In the next year he was in the fifth grade, apparently having skipped a grade. During this year his attendance declined, he being present only three days of the third
year, 1887-1888, in which he was excused from attendance
often and withdrawn entirely for nine weeks of the second
term. His attendance record for 1888-89 is missing but
he is on the roll of the sixth grade for that year. Much
tardiness occurred in 1889-90, but attendance was normal
while he was in the eighth grade, 1890-91. [29] One friend
said Sherwood's absences from school were due to his work
outside school rather than to illness or mere "hookey."
He had so many jobs his schoolmates teased him about
them.

But Anderson has written, "The school was a kind of
prison. How you hated it! What was the good of all this
parsing sentences to one who was going to be a railroad
engineer, a driver of race-horses, or...."[31] But the
"teachers all liked him."[32] And Karl recalled him as an
effortless student who "took no honors."

> One day the principal of the school, the one man
> in town who owned books, a patriarch with a long,
> white beard, invited Sherwood and me to his
> home to discuss our futures. He appeared more
> interested in Sherwood than in me, and offered

to try to get him a scholarship if he was interested
in going to college.   But Sherwood was somehow
in a hurry for life, and he shrugged the idea
off. [33]

In one account Anderson suggests that "necessity"
made him turn to "books and to the men and women directly
about him. ... What a life the people of the books had! They
were for the most part respectable people, with problems I
did not have at all or they were such keen and brainy vil-
lains as I could never hope to become. "[34] To this may be
added, "What education I got was picked up in the barrooms,
in the stores, in the street, and by the grace of certain
lovable characters in our place who took me in hand, loaned
me books, and talked to me through the evening about the
old poets and story tellers. "[35]

Trace has been found of one of these "certain lovable
characters. " The impact of John Telfer on the young Sam
McPherson in Windy McPherson's Son[36] is well indicated by
this passage:

> John Telfer's friendship was a formative influence
> upon Sam McPherson.   His father's worthlessness
> and the growing realization of the hardship of his
> mother's position had given life a bitter taste in
> his mouth, and Telfer sweetened it.   He entered
> with zeal into Sam's thoughts and dreams, and
> tried valiantly to arouse in the quiet, industrious,
> money-making boy some of his own love of life and
> beauty.   At night, as the two walked down country
> roads, the man would stop and waving his arms
> about, quote Poe or Browning or, in another mood,
> would compel Sam's attention to the rare smell of
> a hayfield or to a moonlit stretch of meadow.   Be-
> fore people gathered on the streets he teased the
> boy, calling him a little money grubber and say-
> ing, "He is like a little mole that works under-
> ground. "

Thinking of Telfer, the present writer in the 1962
interview asked Herman Hurd the following question: "Was
there a man who might have taken a special interest in
books and radical subjects, talking to Sherwood about them?
He might have had a wife who was a milliner and no children?" Hurd's answer, given with no hesitation, deserves
full quotation:

John Tichenor. He was a character. He was an
artist. Mother took lessons from him. The picture of grandpa [a pencil sketch] up there [in the
living room of the Hurd home at 144 W. Forest
St. , Clyde] is by him. He did the carvings for
the Clyde Armory. His wife did run a millinery
shop. In later life he did a lot of the kind of
painting which later became popular. He was interested in spiritualism. Very much interested in
him [Sherwood]. Sherwood's brother, Karl, took
lessons from John. He was very much interested
in young people. Sherwood was a friend of his.
She [Mrs. Tichenor] really supported him. He had
a race horse. Tichenors were an old Clyde family. He was just a natural painter.

The Clyde Director for 1887, on page 55, lists "Tichenor,
Jno. B. , crayon artist. " The linkage is made more secure
through the references in the Clyde Enterprise to the presentation of the play, Allatoona, 37 which involved the only
known appearance of Sherwood Anderson on the stage. The
first reference, on page 2, February 24, 1892, points out
that "the many friends of Mr. and Mrs. Jno. B. Tichenor
will no doubt appreciate the pleasure of again witnessing
their admirable rendition of characters in amateur performances. They are both endowed with rare talent and splendid
stage presence.... " They are to have leading roles in
Allatoona, which give them "a better opportunity than ever
before to display their talents. "

The next day, the 25th, the full list of characters
appears on page three of the Enterprise, including Sherwood
Anderson, then 15 years old, as "Little Jimmy. " An advertisement appearing the same day on the same page proclaims that "an excellent performance of the five-act Military
Comedy Drama" will be given at the "Opera House" on Friday and Saturday nights, February 26 and 27, by a "carefully selected cast of characters of well-known local talent
assisted by and under the direction of Mr. H. L. Widner
for the benefit of Co. I [a Local National Guard unit]. "

Examination of the published edition of Allatoona
reveals the disappointing but interesting fact that the play
does not contain a character known as "Little Jimmy. "
Otherwise the cast is as in the original. This allows the
surmise that a special part was written in for Sherwood because of the interest in him by the Tichenors, the leading

players. It is tantalizing to note that Anderson never referred to this episode, particularly in view of his comment
on his father's home-town theatrics. Or possibly it was
because of them that he allowed himself not to recall this
episode. Significant, too, may be the fact that the play, a
Civil War melodrama, was not a success, "both Co. I and
Mr. Widner" being "out of pocket on the venture. " The
newspaper did mention plans to "make up the deficit by giving the play at Oak Harbor in the near future. "[38] All considered, it is surprising that Anderson either forgot or
suppressed this dramatic fling, as he certainly did not forget
Tichenor and his experience with him and the other more
unconventional and artistic-minded people in the community.

However many Tichenor-Telfers there were and whatever they meant to him in terms of specific incidents, it is
clear that Anderson thought of Clyde as the place of the
dawning of his artistic consciousness. "In our house, even
when we were children, we talked constantly of painting. "[39]
Karl, Irwin, and Earl, of the Anderson brothers, all showed
ability in painting. But, for Sherwood, "the curse that is to
lie heavily [on him]... through... life... has its grip on
him.... I am the tale-teller, " he says, "the man who sits
by the fire waiting for listeners, the man whose life must
be led in the world of his fancies. "[40] Hurd said he was
not surprised when Sherwood turned to writing. "He had a
very vivid imagination and was a very good story-teller. "

Both the painting (which he was later to attempt, seriously enough to have an exhibition and for paintings to survive) and the story-telling depended upon the establishment
in his mind of vivid images. Two examples of persistent
images from that time may be mentioned. In a letter in
1938, he recalled an incident of his boyhood in which Hal
Ginn, son of the school superintendent, asked him to hold
his topcoat while he skated on the waterworks pond. "I
still remember what seemed to me the extraordinary fine-
ness of the cloth... and with what sharp pleasure I caressed
the fabric. "[41] When this episode is used in Tar, [42] particulars are changed and the emphasis placed on it is to
indicate the low social and economic status of the Moorehead
family. Doubtless the boy who could still recall the fine
fabric nearly fifty years after the event had a strong sense
of its significance.

One of the main characteristics of Anderson's art,
however, is well identified by a comment made by the

narrator of Tar, which he says was an attempt to recreate
his childhood, of course fictionally.   Anderson devotes Chapter XII (pages 199-222) of Tar to an episode he uses also in
"Girl by the Stove" and for one of his best short stories,
"Death in the Woods": finding a woman's partially-nude body
lying in the snow in a woods.   The central theme of "Death
in the Woods" is that the aroused artistic mind is continually
returning to arresting scenes, working out gradually the destiny of their meaning.   "The scene in the forest had become
for Tar, without his knowing it, the foundation for a story
a child could not understand and it needed understanding.
The fragments had to be picked up slowly long afterwards"
(page 220).   Just which events and how many there were
which later caused his life to focus on artistic productivity
will always have to remain a matter of speculation, but
continuing study makes it increasingly clear that Clyde was
the most important source of those fragments which he
fitted into his finished artistic mosaic.

In the more formal aspects of his education, the record of Anderson's scholastic achievement while in grammar
school is very brief.   For 1886-7, when he was in the fifth
grade, there is a record that contains only a few marks,
all of which are good.   This is the year his attendance was
so poor as to cause him to repeat.   There is a fuller record for the seventh grade.   It shows him making good and
average marks in such subjects as geography, practical
arithmetic, mental arithmetic, music, and history.   He was
weaker than average in spelling and stronger in reading.

His high school career included nine months in all.
He attended September through March of 1891-92 and January
and February in 1893.   In those months he attended a total
of 144 days out of a possible 176.   His grades were average
to a little less than good in algebra, physical geography,
Latin, music, and physics.   He got one 89 in rhetoric, and
his grades in deportment and "workmanship" were in the
90's.   One may assume that his record would have been
better if he had been undistracted by outside work.   The two
months of attendance in 1893 may be taken as evidence of an
attempt to get more schooling, but this was the last schooling he was to have in Clyde.

It should be mentioned that in those days it was unusual for the average boy to be graduated from high school.
By no means was it abnormal that Karl had about a year
and a half of high school and Sherwood not a complete year,

while only Stella was graduated from the Clyde high school (in 1891).   Further it should be noted that she had only 27 days of absence during her four years in high school.   Perhaps the reason for her being allowed to finish school was that she was an excellent student, the class valedictorian with an average of 92.1 for all subjects.   The Anderson family in Clyde could never be denied a certain prestige while the boys worked so hard and the daughter was such a good student.

Anderson recalls in his Memoirs (page 150) that when he asked "a boyhood companion" what impression he had of him as a boy

> he told me that he remembered me only as a lazy fellow, sitting on the curb on the main street or before the little frame hotel at evening, listening to the tales told by traveling men.   Or I sat with my back against a barn wall listening to men talking within a barn or to women gossiping in the kitchen of a nearby house. ... I would come out of the house.   I wanted you to go play ball with me or to go with me to bring home the cows.   I remember your sitting there, your eyes glassy, and that I walked over and stood before you.   I shouted but you did not hear.   I had to lean over and hit you before I could get your attention.   With a book in your hands you were ten times worse.

When Anderson protested that he had been called "Jobby," the man replied:

> You were both a hustler and bone lazy. ... I do, now that you speak of it, remember periods of intense activity, when you worked feverishly at any job you could get.   You used to go about at such times declaring your determination to be a rich man, the most powerful man in the state, and when we others laughed you wanted to fight.

Hurd remembered, "He had as much ambition as any boy."

In spite of his preoccupation with work, Sherwood found time to play, to day-dream, to accumulate (in his Memoirs, page 360) such memories as this: "I used to crawl in [the cornfield] and lie under the corn.   It was warm and close in there.   On the ground, under the tall corn, pumpkins grew.   There was the singing of the insects.   Little insects flew about my head or crawled along the warm ground. "   The episode (pages 12-18) in A Story Teller's Story which tells how Anderson and his brother, Irwin, lived the parts of La Longue Carabine and Uncas, respectively, is a fine monument to the imaginative play of childhood.   A playmate recalls the "pirate's cave" on Spring Avenue behind Anderson's house that Sherwood and his companions had.   "It was Sherwood's idea that each boy must sign his name with his own blood, on a large rock, before he could become a real pirate. "[43]   Hurd still recalled this vividly in 1962, saying that the boys dug a cave into a hill behind the Anderson home on Spring Avenue, each signing a compact in his own blood and putting the agreement in a box, which was buried in the cave.

Both Herman Hurd and another Clyde resident   agreed that "Sherwood used to eat more meals at Hurd's than he did at home. "[44]   The memory of his visits in the Hurd home was a pleasant one, as the Memoirs show (pages 53-54).   As Hurd recalls it, "It was nothing to have an extra one sit down at the table. "   The relaxed generosity of the Hurd home evidently was an important change from the tensions reflected in Sherwood's memory of his own home.

The tendency to lapse into silence was mentioned by the friend whom Anderson questioned.   Another friend recalls going fishing with him.   To this man Anderson seemed very moody and changeable.   On some occasions he would be "quite genial"; on others he would only grunt when spoken to. [45]   What was happening within Anderson in these times when he was hard to rouse, could only grunt in answer? Perhaps this statement is a clue:

> I sat under a tree alone on the summer afternoon and it seemed to me that I held my own life in the palm of my hand.   Periods of a strange weakness had been coming upon me for weeks and now another came.   I felt faint and ill.   It seemed to me that I held my own life in my hand and that it slipped out of my grasp. [46]

From what evidence there is, it seems quite possible that Anderson was able as a youth to lose contact completely with his material surroundings, to become lost in some such vision as the one above, a day-dream, an imaginative flight.

A related phenomenon, referred to with special emphasis in Tar (page 104), involves a "going away" of the real elements of life.

> I would listen for a time to their talk and then
> their voices would seem to go far away. The
> things I was looking at would go far away too.
> Perhaps there would be a tree, not more than a
> hundred yards away, and it would just come out
> of the ground and float away like a thistle. It
> would get smaller and smaller, away off there in
> the sky, and then suddenly--bang, it would be back
> where it belonged, in the ground, and I would be-
> gin hearing the voices of the men talking again. 47

Akin to his tendency to lose contact with reality was his power to concentrate on the reading of a book, which Anderson's friend also mentioned. Miss Kintner concluded:

> We may picture him "hanging out" at Becker's
> tailor shop with his nose in a good book. He was
> always reading good books, the tailor remembers,
> as does his friend Mr. Hurd. His ability to con-
> centrate was a source of amusement to his friends;
> they had to shake him to get his attention when he
> was reading. 48

To Herman Hurd, "That was the most peculiar thing you ever heard of. If he got hold of something he was reading, if you got ready to go, it wasn't enough to tell him you were ready to go. You had to shake him. " Story Teller indicates (on pages 155-56) that this was probably because "... books--any books--have always fed my dreams and I am one who has always lived by his dreams... books like life itself are only useful to me in as much as they feed my own dreams or give me a background upon which I can construct new dreams. " To this may be added Anderson's own statement.

> I read... any books I could get my hands on. I
> went fishing with a book under my arm, went to
> ball games and read in a book between innings.
> There being few books in our house, [a contradic-
> tion of a statement quoted earlier] I went book
> borrowing through the town [Hurd agreed]. 49

The townspeople, he has related, were sympathetic to his

quest and lent him many books.

But one must not think Anderson was always reading, having spells of concentration, or busy working. One Clyde resident has said Sherwood was always full of pranks, such as playing practical jokes whenever the occasion offered. "I wouldn't call him a steady home boy. He was in for a lark. "[50]

It may be wondered if the church had any influence on Anderson during this period. As far as can be ascertained, whatever influence there may have been was indirect. Mrs. Anderson and Stella joined the First Presbyterian Church in Clyde in March, 1892. The only other members of the family to join were brothers Ray (on February 11, 1893) and Earl (on April 12, 1896, after Mrs. Anderson's death). [51] There is no record that Sherwood had any connection with the church, but he may have attended Sunday school as a child. Certainly the connection of the family with this church began before Anderson and Stella actually joined, for Stella gave recitations in exercises on Children's Day and at Christmas in 1886. [52] Too, it must be remembered that Mrs. Anderson has been described as a "devout Christian, "[53] and it seems very likely that she would have insisted on the enforcement of her standards in the upbringing of her children. Anderson himself bore testimony to her firmness of character. One church interest that all Clyde boys had, according to Herman Hurd, was that of meeting girls after church on Sunday night to ask to take them home. Anderson made an incident out of this custom for Tar (pages 316-17).

As one looks about for other evidence of influence on Anderson's life in Clyde, one should not fail to consider that Clyde was basically a farm town. Though none of the Andersons in Clyde were farmers, what Sherwood saw and did in Clyde gave him an understanding of the farmer that was to be useful to him later when he was earning his living in the field of agricultural advertising. Anderson remembered his days as a field-worker.

> The cabbage fields grew larger and larger and, as we grew older, my brothers and I went every spring and fall to work in the fields. We crawled across the fields, setting out cabbage plants in the spring, and in the fall went out to cut cabbages. [54]

His observation of farmers helped him to develop a sympathy
for their problems:

> ... I remember a sight I saw when I was a small
> boy.   There had been a heavy hailstorm and a
> large wheat field, almost ready for the harvest,
> was destroyed.   I happened to be fishing in a near-
> by stream on that day and had got under a tree.
> The farmer who owned the field came down after
> the storm and knelt in a fence corner.   I heard
> his prayer.   He was praying for strength not to
> give up.   "Give me courage to plant again next
> year," he prayed. [55]

It would have been a little unnatural for Anderson to
have grown up when he did in a small town without an appreciation of horses.   Partly, that was because

> Almost every boy and man hanging over the fences
> along the home stretch at the big mile tracks, at
> the state fairs where the fastest sometimes came,
> at the little dusty half-mile tracks at the county
> fairs, knew his horses.   He could recite for you
> the blood lines of his favorites.   In every Ameri-
> can town there were a few men, owning a few good
> ones, colts they hoped might come on, get in the
> big time.   It was the sport of the small town men,
> the farmer. [56]

Herman Hurd recalls Anderson spent much time at the Clyde
racetrack. [57] His interest in track activities was sufficient
for the Enterprise to record on August 2, 1895 that Anderson
had gone with two others to Cleveland on July 31 "to see the
big races. " Years later Anderson, in his Memoirs could
write in lyric vein of the hours when he watched the horses.

> There was a boy, myself, hanging over the low
> fence in the infield by the judges' stand.   How his
> heart beat.   There was something in the sustained
> rhythmic swing of the legs and bodies of the
> horses going at speed that touched some secret
> hunger in him.   And morning after morning, when
> the horses were in training, he cut away from his
> father's house alone and raced through the corn
> fields past the water works and the engine house
> to the fair grounds to catch what he could of the
> glorious sight before he was compelled to go off

to school. He stood by the low fence trembling. He leaned far over the fence. Tears sometimes came into his eyes and a lump into his throat. It was his first love. Oh, how the beautiful, the courageous and the aristocratic creatures stirred him. He grew sick with envy of the drivers in their high-wheeled carts whirling about the half-mile track, their hands on the reins. With all his heart he longed to hold the reins over some beautiful beast and a heavy sadness came into his heart when the first school bell rang and he had to go, with dragging, reluctant feet, away from the racing track and toward the distant schoolhouse (page 35.)

Elsewhere he explains:

My race track experience must have been when I was about fifteen and sixteen. There was a man named Tom Whitehead who owned a string of race horses. I went to county fairs with him in the lowly position of "swipe" or groom. [58]

"In my own boyhood I went to them, lived with them, was a groom to running and trotting horses, now I know, because they were the most beautiful thing about me. "[59]

This experience working for Thomas C. Whitehead, who was one of the directors of the Clyde Fair in 1887, [60] and the man whom the Enterprise characterized on March 14, 1891 as having "the finest lot of horses ever seen together in this country, " should not be confused with Anderson's later experience as a groom in a livery stable in Clyde. According to Anderson, he was living at the livery stable at the time of his mother's death in 1895. [61]

Probably it was through his race-track connection that he met the two prize-fighters he says he knew personally, "Bill McCarthy, a lightweight, and Harry Walters, a heavy. "[62] Hurd reported he saw McCarthy, who worked for a Clyde livery stable, fight in the livery barn one night. At the racetracks Anderson must have seen many characters who fascinated and educated him. He has told of his observation of "flash men, " sharpshooters, touts, gamblers, politicians, and

most of all a strange kind of sensitive and

> foot-loose man or woman, unfitted for the life of
> a hustler, not shrewd, usually lovable and per-
> plexed, feeling themselves out of touch with the
> mood of the times and often spending life getting
> drunk, wandering about and loving to talk away
> long hours on bridges in cities, on country roads
> and in the back rooms of saloons, which for all
> the evil they are presumed to have brought upon
> us I thank my gods existed during my youth. 63

The chief fruit of Anderson's interest in, and observation of, horses and track life was Horses and Men.   Just as
direct a connection may be seen between Poor White and
Anderson's experience with the industrial revolution in Clyde.
Poor White is a chronicle of the changes wrought by the
coming of mass production and big business in the imaginary
town of Bidwell. 64

> There was something strange happening to our town
> that must have been happening at about the same
> time to thousands of American towns: a sudden and
> almost universal turning of men from the old
> handicrafts toward our modern life of the machine.
>
> I was to see it happen.   I was to be part of it.
> It meant the end of the old craftsmen of the towns,
> the shoemakers, the harness, wagon, buggy, fur-
> niture, and clothing makers.   All the little shops
> scattered through the towns, shops in which men
> fashioned things with their hands directly out of
> raw materials furnished by nature, were to dis-
> appear with amazing rapidity.   It was a strange
> time and, as I now look back upon it, it seems to
> have happened almost in a day.   It was a kind of
> fever, an excitement in the veins of the people,
> and later when I tried to write of it, using not a
> particular individual but rather an American town
> as the central character of my story, it became
> to me strangely dramatic.
>
> There was a kind of blind faith in what we were
> all doing, a belief that the machine would solve an
> old, old problem for men, lifting the load of heavy
> brutal toil off men's shoulders, making a new life
> of ease and comfort for all.   This, however, all
> mingled with a feeling of doubt and fear among the
> elder men of the towns.

> This feeling of change was in our own little house.
> It was in all houses along the street.   It was in
> all the houses in every street of every town.   Men
> proclaimed it while others protested.   It was the
> end of the old workman.
>
> It ran all through our Middle West.   Here and
> there, in towns nearby, oil and gas began to spurt
> out of the ground. 65

Clyde was not as greatly affected as some of the other towns, because its gas wells never produced, to the great
disappointment of the town's leading citizens. 66   But it was
this same movement that was perhaps partly responsible for
the rocky economic road the family had to travel.   Irwin
Anderson had to abandon his craft, presumably because there
was no longer a need to pay more to have one's harness
made by hands when it could be done for less by machine.
Although the evidence shows that Irwin Anderson drank and
was not generally a good provider, part of the reason for
his drinking may have been his frustration at having to give
up his trade.

The big industry that did come to Clyde was the bicycle factory.   Just when Anderson worked there is not
clear; his statements about it are confusing.   Already mentioned is the statement that he was "about fifteen and sixteen" when he had his "race track experience. "   This can
not be reconciled with the following:

> As for my factory experience, I began as an em-
> ployee in a bicycle factory in my native town of
> Clyde.   Afterwards, I worked for a year or two
> around race tracks.   I drifted for a time from
> town to town.   I worked in an iron foundry in
> Erie, Pennsylvania. 67

However, it is not necessary to know precisely when
he worked in the factory.   It is enough to note that this experience started a train of reflection and investigation which
was to last all his life.   He was particularly interested in
the reaction of the factory worker to work in the factory.
In A Story Teller's Story he spoke of the constant vile talk
in the factories, an unconscious adjustment, he thought, to
the impotence induced by mechanical standardization.

> In the many [?] factories where I worked most men

talked vilely to their fellows and long afterward I
was to understand that a little. It is the impotent
man who is vile. His very impotence has made
him vile and in the end I was to understand that
when you take from man the cunning of the hand,
the opportunity to constantly create new forms in
materials. you make him impotent. (Page 195.)

The same theme is developed in the Memoirs (pages
84-89) through the presentation of Rice, the boss of the bicycle factory, whom Hurd recalled as coming from Elmore,
Ohio. (Hurd did not think Sherwood worked in the bicycle
factory very long.) This man had formerly been a carriage
painter and despised the methods of mass-production. He
expressed his frustration in fits of running and crying. Perhaps this is the same "old carriage painter" whom he worked
beside and who striped wheels. "As he bent over his task
he muttered, 'Ladede! The wind roughened her long bare
hands. '"68 The Elmore bicycle works moved to Clyde in
the summer of 1894. By that December it had forty men
working and was making plans for 100 the next month. In
March, 1896, it had "1,500 wheels crated and ready to go"
and was "running at full force and till ten o'clock at
night. "69

It was a bicycle factory where I was employed as
an assembler. With some ten or twelve other men
I worked at a bench in a long room facing a row
of windows. We assembled the parts that were
brought to us by boys from other departments of
the factory and put the bicycles together. There
was such and such a screw to go into such and
such a screw hole....

In the bicycle factory I had repeatedly told the
other men that I was subject to sick headaches
and I used to go to a window, throw it open and
lean out, closing my eyes and trying to create in
fancy a world in which men lived under bright
skies, drank wine, loved women and with their
hands created something of lasting value and
beauty and seeing me thus, white and with trembling hands, the men dropped the talk that so
sickened me. 70

Anderson's concern with the effect of machines on men continued through the rest of his life and was manifested

particularly in <u>Dark Laughter</u>, <u>Perhaps Women</u>, and <u>Beyond Desire</u>.

As good a view as one can expect to get of what Anderson learned about sex in Clyde may be obtained from the <u>Memoirs</u>.   Anderson has related in that book three episodes which may be taken, for lack of better evidence, as indicative.   One (pages 61-66) tells how he has ridicule heaped upon him when his first adventure with one of the town tarts is interrupted.   Another (pages 66-74) tells of his first "real adventure" when he was a "slender boy of fourteen. "   The third episode (page 247) is mentioned in connection with his finding a mutilated volume of Walt Whitman.   It concerns the young lady who was willing to have intercourse with him but insisted on pretending she was asleep and knew nothing of what had happened.   After relating that incident he wrote:

> No.   I do not think that any of us at the time [approximately 1919] wanted to over-play sex.   But we wanted in our stories and novels to bring it back into real relation to the life we lived and saw others living.   We wanted the flesh back in our literature, wanted directly in our literature the fact of men and women in bed together, babies being born.   We wanted the terrible importance of the flesh in human relations also revealed again. (Page 247.)

From what one may gather Anderson had seen his first view of that "terrible importance" in Clyde.   (Certainly the episode related in Appendix D and probably Chapter XV of <u>Tar</u> (pages 254-268) are also relevant to his initiatory experiences.)   Hurd noted that Sherwood was very much interested in girls and they in him.   "He had a way with him that took with the young ladies. "

While Anderson was absorbing information about these various facets of life in Clyde, he was constantly being indoctrinated with the chief American philosophy of the time. Although Anderson's father advised his sons to learn some craft with care, he and all the rest soon took up the cry, "Money makes the mare go. "[71]   The meaningfulness of America's "industrial progress" was preached at him from every side.

> We were all taught that there is a certain kind of disgrace in being poor.   How sharply I remember

how the men of my town spoke to me when I was
a lad. The mayor of the town did it, the merchants did it, the judge spoke to me, a preacher
spoke to me. I was a rather energetic, hustling
boy. . . .

There it was, right from the beginning. You have
to make money to rise in the world, to be a bigger, showier man than others in order to respect
yourself. . . . 72

Later, as he has said, ". . . I was to take up the cry
myself and become one of the most valiant of the hustlers. . . "
but still later he came to be one of its strongest opponents.
It was to move him to a kind of satiric brilliance in a piece
called "Ohio, I'll Say We've Done Well. "73 In the Clyde
period, though, "I made great plans for my life. I was going to be a business man and grow rich. "74

In 1895 occurred two events which were to have far-
reaching consequences. The first was his joining Company
I. Sixteenth Infantry Regiment, Ohio National Guard, known
in Clyde as the McPherson Guards. 75 The record of his
enlistment on March 28, 1895, states that he was 5 feet
8 3/4 inches tall, had black eyes, black hair, and fair
complexion (see Figures 1 and 2). Aged 18, he enlisted for
a five-year period. 76 He gave his occupation as painter
when he enlisted. 77

The assumption is that he joined up because "The
better class of fellows generally joined the National Guard.
It was a boost socially. "78 The McPherson Guard met
usually once a week on Thursday evening to drill and learn
certain military fundamentals. A five-day encampment was
held for more realistic drill every summer. The company
turned out in force for parades and such events as Memorial
Day and the dedication of the monument to General McPherson, Clyde's Civil War hero. 79 Occasionally the militia
men attended church in a body. And sometimes they had to
perform more serious duties, such as quieting disorders at
strikes and guarding jails against lynch mobs. Apparently
Company I was not called to do any such duty while Anderson was in Clyde, but on one occasion in 1894 the mayor
ordered the captain of the company to use his men to protect the town against the demands of an "industrial army"
and "160 foreigners. " The guard unit moved "'Count' By-
lakorrski" and his followers, who provided no "material

Figure 1.
Anderson during Spanish-American War

resistance" but "many threats of an anarchistic nature, " out of town and saw to it that they stayed there. [80]

The fact that Sherwood had been in the performance of "Allatoona, " put on hopefully to benefit Company I, proves that he had been conscious of the unit since 1892 and doubt-less before.   So he would have known of such action as the foregoing as well as perhaps taking part in a riot call to Tiffin on Sunday, October 27, 1895, when the guardsmen caught colds standing duty at night. [81] In July of 1895 and 1896 the company went to Bryan and Cleveland, Ohio, re-spectively, for a week of camp.   They were in Cleveland for the first week of that city's centennial celebration, "and there will be plenty of amusement for the boys. "   Unfortun-ately, it rained all the time, and the camp was a "mud-hole. "[82]   Probably the man enjoyed much more the invitation they accepted in June, 1895, to take part in the parade "in honor of the G. A. R. boys, " who were holding their annual encampment in Sandusky. [83]

The most intriguing of all the notes found on this subject are two dealing with striking miners.   On January 14, 1894, the Enterprise reported that part of Company I went to southeastern Ohio to protect property against striking miners.   Some of the men went to "Wheeling Creek, the center of the miner's disturbance. "   Though Anderson was not in Company I, he must have heard about the experiences of those who went.   The next January the men of the compa-ny were collecting "provisions and supplies" for starving miners and their families in the Hocking Valley. [84]   The reader of Marching Men (1917) can readily see in Wheeling Creek a suggestion for the Coal Creek of the novel.   And Anderson could have gained the beginning of his conscious-ness, so vividly portrayed in his fiction, of the problems of the miners from his continuing association with the men of Company I.   There is, at least on record so far, no ex-perience before 1917 which brought him closer to the life of the miners.   And in Marching Men (Chapter III, pages 48-50) he specifically depicts relationships between striking miners and guardsmen brought in for duty in keeping the peace, just as Company I was.

This enlistment was to be of considerable importance to Anderson at the outbreak of the Spanish-American War. For by that time he had been working in the warehouse in Chicago a little over a year and was quite tired of it.   He was quite eager to go into service with his company when

Figure 3. Clyde Stars baseball team, probably summer 1894. Herman Hurd second from left, standing; Anderson second from right, sitting.

the time came.   And it was his service in the army that enabled him to make the break from manual labor; after coming back from the war, he did not strike out immediately
for a job but made his last bid for formal education at Wittenberg Academy, from which he went to Chicago and the
advertising business, where he first had a chance to explore
his ability to handle words.

The other important event of 1895 was the death of
his mother on May 10.   With that death began the gradual
disintegration of the family, which process was slowed by
the efforts of Stella, who apparently tried to carry on where
her mother had left off.   By the time Stella left to get
established in Springfield in 1899 she had found family duties
to be troublesome.

But for the three older boys life was good.

We were getting along.   We were working.   A little money was coming in.   We could buy new suits
of clothes, usually on the installment plan, five or
ten dollars down, a dollar a week.   We could go
to parties, walk about through the streets at night
with gangs of boy friends, stopping to sing before
the house in which some girl lived.   It was a
custom among us in our town in that time.

We could go in the winter to sleigh-ride parties,
to spellings-down in some country school house.
Some of the prosperous parents of. . . the boys. . .
would own horses and surreys.   We could go. . . on
a moonlight summer night for drives in the country
with girls.   Life having for each of us young males
a certain gaiety--youth--what did having to work
matter. 85

But in spite of this pleasant life, Sherwood was soon
to leave Clyde and enter the drudgery of hard labor in a
cold storage warehouse in Chicago.   Even though the date
remains a conjecture, certain pieces of evidence enable one
to fix the date of Anderson's leaving for Chicago within certain limits.   Mr. John Becker is certain that Sherwood played
right field for and helped manage Clyde's junior baseball
team, the Clyde Stars, in 1896 (see Fig. 3).   Mr. Becker
might well be in a position to know, for he says his tailor
shop was "baseball headquarters. "   Mr. Hurd assigned 1894
as the date of Fig. 3, in which both he and Sherwood appear.

Articles about the Clyde Stars appear in the <u>Enterprise</u> for
1894, 1895, and 1896, none mentioning Anderson. In the
pictures, it will be noted, he is one of the two managers.
On June 19, 1896, the following note appeared in the <u>Enter-</u>
<u>prise</u>: "The Clyde Star [sic] baseball nine has been resur-
rected and will play a game this afternoon with the Ivys of
Bellevue at Ames' Park. " An inference from the attendance
record of the encampment of Company I at Camp Moses
Cleveland, Ohio, for July 20-25, 1896, agrees with Mr.
Becker's recollection that Anderson was in Clyde that summer.   Herman Hurd's recollection also agreed with this impression.   Anderson was, of course, on the company's
roster.   The attendance record for Company I states that
every one of the three officers and 55 men in it attended
camp. 86   Presumably Anderson had left Clyde for Chicago
by the time the next encampment was held; the attendance
record in the adjutant general's report for 1897 shows that
one man from Company I did not attend camp.   Anderson's
enlistment ran five years from 1895, it will be recalled.

The effect of his life in Clyde on the susceptible Sherwood Anderson was intense and continued for years to grow
in its power.   Some suggestions of the relationship of his
Clyde experiences to his artistic achievement have already
been made.   Particularities will be explored later.   One or
two generalized factors seem appropriate now.

Elizabeth Prall Anderson, his third wife, thought of
him as a neurotic whose condition was complicated by being
an artist.   She thought he lacked the discipline of formal
education and the benefit of contact with people who could
help develop his character.   She thought he always had to
meet the problem of getting enough to eat as well as he
could. 87   One may accept her view or think in Anderson's
terms, such as these: "... I am still the country boy, a
little astonished and frightened..." (on being in New York). 88

Anderson remembered his Clyde life as a time when:

> I began to gather these impressions.   There was
> a thing called happiness toward which men were
> striving.   They never got to it.   All of life was
> amazingly accidental.   Love, moments of tender-
> ness and despair, came to the poor and the miser-
> able as to the rich and successful.
>
> It began to seem to me that what was most wanted

by all people was love, understanding. Our writers, our storytellers, in wrapping life up into neat
little packages were only betraying life. It began
to seem to me that what I wanted for myself most
of all, rather than so-called success, acclaim, to
be praised by publishers and editors, was to try
to develop, to the top of my bent, my own capacity to feel, see, taste, smell, hear. I wanted,
as all men must want, to be a free man, proud
of my own manhood, always more and more aware
of earth, people, streets, houses, towns, cities.
I wanted to take all into myself, digest all I could. 89

The statement carries him far beyond the time of his
leaving Clyde. He had evidently begun to assess life, but
there is no evidence that he had developed the conscious
artistic conception here enunciated. That was to come, as
will be seen, some years later. The Clyde experience was
the necessary first stage for the realizations and ambitions
he was eventually to recognize.

If the impact of Clyde on Anderson was great, his
impression on Clyde has, so far, been something less.
General McPherson is still the town hero, though Anderson
is recognized. His books were sufficiently uncomfortable
and frank in their analysis of life as he saw it to draw such
unfavorable response as to have the town librarian burn them
in the 1920's. 90 A Clyde native interested in Anderson has
recently written the present writer that in conversation in
the town a certain lady "promptly told me what she thought
of Sherwood, which was unprintable--concerning both his life
and writing. Unfortunately that is typical of all I can learn
from old Clyde citizens. " This is in spite of the fact that,
around 1927, its editor wrote in the Enterprise:

It matters little to the world whether Clyde accepts
Sherwood Anderson's genius or not but the fact
still remains that he is a product of this village
and is not nearly so ashamed to put the names of
his boyhood playmates into his stories and give
Clyde the recognition as the village itself is loathe
to give him.

Two of Anderson's reactions seem to contribute to the
picture of his overt relationship with Clyde. In 1940 he prepared a short anecdote for possible use by the Reader's Digest. It told of how he went back to his "native Ohio town

[meaning Clyde rather than Camden] after twenty-five years. "
Needing a haircut, he went for this service to a "man who
had been one of my closest boyhood friends. " They had
played baseball together and been in the army together, he
related. "I presume that I had rather hoped that, in coming
back to my native town, I would be recognized as a genius. "
The barber questioned him, Anderson thought accusingly, as
to whether he had become a writer. Anderson denied it, and
"a look of relief spread over his face. " "Well, I heard the
story, " he said, "but I never believed it. I never thought
you would turn out to be that kind of guy. "[91]

In 1941 Anderson wrote to Hurd wondering if the story
of "an old-maid librarian" burning his books had been true.
(Hurd said it was.) He had also read a report that later the
Clyde library wrote and asked him for copies of all his
books to put on the shelves of the library. This request he
was supposed to have answered "by writing a rather imper-
tinent letter telling them that if they wanted my books they
should buy them. I wonder, Herman, if this story is also
true as I have certainly forgotten the incident.... If they
still want the books, find out which ones they have, so that
I can check up and furnish the books they have not got. "[92]

Notes

1.   Letter to John Paul Cullen, Oct. 28, 1937 (JR).

2.   Letter to Mrs. Oliver Kuhn, July 20, 1938.

3.   Letter to editor of the Clyde Enterprise, "Mr. Kastorp";
undated clipping, prob. 1927.

4.   Letter to Paul Rosenfeld, Fall, 1921.

5.   Anderson, Sherwood Anderson's Memoirs, New York,
Harcourt, Brace, 1942, p. 40.

6.   Anderson, "From Chicago, " Sherwood Anderson's Notebook, New York, Boni and Liveright, 1926, p. 43.

7.   Anderson; New York, Huebsch, 1926. The quoted portion is from p. 6, the cabbages episode, p. 50-53.

8.   Memoirs, p. 59.

9. Interview with Herman Hurd, Nov. 10, 1962. All other quoted remarks of Mr. Hurd in this volume are from this interview unless specified otherwise.

10. Undated Clyde Enterprise clipping.

11. Ibid.

12. Letter to Mrs. L. L. Copenhaver, Jan. 7, 1939.

13. Anderson; New York, Boni and Liveright, 1929, p. 301.

14. "Who's Who, " Chicago Tribune, May 31, 1919.

15. Anderson, Harlan Miners Speak, New York, Harcourt, 1932, p. 306-7.

16. Mrs. Winfield Adare, Clyde, Ohio; reported in Evelyn Kintner, "Sherwood Anderson: Small Town Man, " unpub. M. A. thesis. Bowling Green, Ohio, Bowling Green State Univ. , Aug. 1942, p. 39.

17. "In a Box Car, " Vanity Fair, Oct. 1928, vol. 31, p. 76.

18. Kintner, p. 34-5.

19. Mary H. Dinsmoor, "An Inquiry Into the Life of Sherwood Anderson as Reflected in His Literary Works, " unpub. M. A. thesis. Athens, Ohio, Ohio University, Aug. 1939, p. 71; from an Anderson Letter of Jan. 7, 1939.

20. Kintner, p. 39-40.

21. From a letter by Mr. F. Lauriston Bullard, Boston, Mass; letter of March 22, 1942.

22. "Who's Who, " Chicago Tribune, May 31, 1919.

23. Interview with Miss Jeanette Paden, Clyde.

24. From a note by Harry Heffner, Clyde; Nov. 10, 1962.

25. "My Brother, Sherwood Anderson, " Saturday Review of Literature, Sept. 4, 1948, vol. 31, p. 6.

26. Anderson, "Please Let Me Explain, " The Sherwood

Anderson Reader. Boston, Houghton Mifflin, p. 659-660.

27. A Story Teller's Story, p. 130.

28. Records for 1883-1884 exist and have been examined.

29. For this complete analysis of the grammar school attendance I am indebted to Kintner, p. 44-46.

30. Mr. Herman Hurd, Clyde, according to Kintner, p. 46.

31. Anderson, "The American Small Town, " Sherwood Anderson Reader, p. 805.

32. Hurd interview, Nov. 10, 1962.

33. "My brother, Sherwood Anderson, " Saturday Review, Sept. 4, 1948, p. 6.

34. A Story Teller's Story, p. 153.

35. "Who's Who, " Chicago Tribune, May 31, 1919.

36. Anderson; London, John Lane, 1916; see especially Chapter IV, p. 56-73; passage quoted is from p. 56.

37. Judson Kirkpatrick and J. Owen Moore, Allatoona, New York, French, 1875, French's Standard Drama Series, No. 376.

38. Enterprise, March 3, 1892, p. 3.

39. Letter to Otto Kahn, Jan. 26, 1929 (JR).

40. A Story Teller's Story, p. 20.

41. Letter to L. P. Jones, Gates Mills, Ohio, June 1938.

42. Anderson; New York, Boni and Liveright, 1926, p. 278.

43. Herman Hurd interview of Sept. 1, 1938, reported by Dinsmoor, p. 15.

44. Hurd Interview, Nov. 10, 1962; also interview with Miss Jeanette Paden.

45. Interview with Mr. Albert Hayden, Tiffin, Ohio.

46.   Memoirs, p. 39.

47.   "The Man Who Became a Woman, " Sherwood Anderson
      Reader, p. 135-6.   Such an hallucinatory experience, also
      referred to in Memoirs and A Story Teller's Story, might
      confirm the subconscious pressures he encountered in this
      period, to become more intense in Elyria.

48.   Kintner, p. 39.

49.   Memoirs, p. 57.

50.   Interview with Judge S. S. Richards, Clyde, Ohio.

51.   From church records in possession of Mrs. John Beck-
      er, Clyde, Ohio.

52.   Reported in the Clyde Enterprise, June 13, 1886, and
      December 23, 1886.

53.   Judge Richards interview.

54.   A Story Teller's Story, p. 49.

55.   Hello Towns, p. 323.

56.   Anderson, "Here They Come, " Esquire, March, 1940,
      voL 13, p. 80.

57.   Kintner, p. 62.

58.   Letter of June 26, 1939, in Dinsmoor, p. 72.

59.   Letter to Alfred Stieglitz, Aug. 6, 1923 (JR).

60.   Clyde Directory for 1887.

61.   Memoirs, p. 75-77.

62.   A Story Teller's Story, p. 193.

63.   Ibid. , p. 157.

64.   There is a Bidwell, Ohio, but it is near the Ohio River
      between Gallipolis and Pomeroy.   Anderson's Bidwell has
      the same general geographical location as Clyde.

65. Memoirs, p. 79-80.

66. The Clyde Enterprise, 1886-1890, passim, chronicles both the attempts and the disappointments.

67. Letter of June 24, 1938; in Dinsmoor, p. 64.

68. Letter to Marietta D. Finley, Dec. 10, 1916.

69. The Clyde Enterprise, June 1894, and March 18, 1896.

70. A Story Teller's Story, p. 198-200.

71. Ibid. , p. 83-6.

72. Anderson, Puzzled America. New York, Scribner, 1935, p. 162.

73. Nation, Aug. 9, 1922, vol. 115, p. 146-8.

74. Memoirs, p. 73.

75. In honor of Gen. James Birdseye McPherson, a Clyde native, who "gave up his young life on the field of battle at Atlanta, booted and spurred. " When Grant heard "that McPherson was no more of earth, he went into his tent and wept like a child. " Enterprise, Oct. 16, 1896. Clyde now has the McPherson Cemetery and the adjacent stretch of U. S. Route 20 known as McPherson Highway. In Nov. 1962, the Sandusky County Historical Society requested the issuance of a McPherson stamp.

76. Adjutant General's Department, State of Ohio, Columbus; Letter to author dated December 11, 1941.

77. Photostat of discharge papers in Anderson Collection in Newberry Library, Chicago.

78. Mr. Ira H. Squire, Clyde; interview.

79. Anderson wrote: "The Civil War was not so far away. On all sides one found men who had taken part in it. Something of the flavor of life in all of our town in Civil War days... clung to the life I saw and led" ("Father Abraham: A Lincoln Fragment, " The Sherwood Anderson Reader, (p. 532-3). And "I am going to write a history of the Civil War. Have been aching to get at the job

since I was a boy.... Have been traveling and reading all
my life for this... " (letter to Gertrude Stein, late 1934).

80. Report of Capt. W. E. Gillett, Co. I, in James C.
Howe, Annual Report of the Adjutant General... to the
State of Ohio for... the Year Ending November 15, 1894.
Columbus, Ohio, Westbote, 1895, p. 211.

81. Enterprise, Nov. 1, 1895.

82. Ibid., July 3 and 28, 1896.

83. Ibid., May 24, 1895.

84. Ibid., Jan. 22, 1895.

85. Memoirs, p. 92.

86. Henry A. Axline, Adjutant General's Report for November 15, 1896. Norwalk, Ohio, Laning, 1897, p. 264
(roster), p. 54 (attendance record).

87. From a letter from Elizabeth Prall Anderson to Hans
W. Poppe, Sept. 15, 1947.

88. Letter to Charles H. Funk, Oct. 23, 1938 (JR).

89. Letter to George Freitag, Aug. 27, 1938 (JR).

90. Herman Hurd interview, Nov. 10, 1962.

91. Letter to DeWitt Wallace, May 23, 1940 (JR).

92. Letter to Herman Hurd, Jan. 7, 1941.

Mosaic II

"To become intense individualists... "

I am trying to live from day to day, work from day to day.
I am what my experiences of life make me.
                    to M. D. Finley, 1927.

*   *   *

One thing is certain. The world is ill and our illness is a
part of something universal.
                    to M. D. Finley, 1920.

*   *   *

The mystery has to be solved. In some way we have got to
come to an understanding of the shrillness and empti-
ness of our times.
                    to Waldo Frank, Nov. 1918.

*   *   *

These last days I drive bare-headed through this golden land,
looking at brown-eyed negroes and at the color and
wonder of the country where I have been more free,
more alone and at the same time closer to all people
than ever before in my hurried life.
                    to M. D. Finley, 1920.

*   *   *

I should have liked to see you in order to tell you how much
of what you told me that summer at the lake I have
found to be true and how much you helped me by giving
my mind new slants. The difficulty with me is that I
cannot learn things by being taught but have to get them
in my own way out of life.
                    to Trigant Burrow, New Year's Eve,
                                    1918.

What things books are, painting, sculpture, poems.   Men
     write, carve, paint.   It is a way of dodging the issue.
     They do so like to think no issue exists.   Look at me.
     I am the center of life, the creator--when I have
     ceased to exist, nothing exists.
               Well, isn't that true, for me at least?
                    from Dark Laughter, p. 252.

               *   *   *

The idea I try to express is perhaps sound enough, that the
     protection we must always seek is that inner laughter
     ... that is to say, I presume, to try to take it also as
     a part of the total picture, this damn fastinating [sic]
     thing. . . life.
                    to Miriam Phillips, Fall 1935.

               *   *   *

And so you can see I want a body of healthy, young men and
     women to quit working--to loaf, to refuse to be hurried,
     or try to get on in the world--in short, to become in-
     tense individualists.   Something of the kind must hap-
     pen if we are ever to bring color and a flair into our
     modern life.   Naturally I believe that the growth of
     such a class would do more than anything else to make
     this a better world to live in.
                    to Paul A. Kellogg, Dec. 14, 1920 (JR).

               *   *   *

I get nothing out of anything in life except as it affects the
     lives of men and women.
                    from "It's a Woman's Age, " Jan. 15,
                                             1931.

               *   *   *

There was a violent dangerous man, said to be a killer.   One
     night he walked and talked to me and became suddenly
     tender.   I was forced to realize that all sorts of emo-
     tions went on in all sorts of ways.
                    to George Freitag, Aug. 18, 1938.

               *   *   *

I and my kind told the story of repressed life.   I have never
    thought of myself as a profound thinker.   I was the
    story teller.
                        to Robert L. Anderson, 1929 (JR).

                *   *   *

I guess what I think is that, if you start to write of your
    own life experiences you will find yourself more and
    more, as you go along with it, stopping to think about
    this or that situation you have been in.   This is pretty
    likely to get you to thinking more and more of others,
    involved with you in the damned difficult business of
    living, this all the time leading you more and more
    out of yourself and into others.   Damn it, there is
    something to be said here.
                        to Gilbert Wilson, Feb. 17, 1939 (JR).

                *   *   *

If our youth is to get into his consciousness that love of
    life--that with the male comes only through the love of
    surfaces, sensually felt through the fingers--his prob-
    lem is to reach down through all the broken surface
    distractions of modern life to that old love of craft out
    of which culture springs.
                        from A Story Teller's Story, p. 81.

                *   *   *

Was it grown up to come to the realization that oneself did
    not matter, that nothing mattered but a kind of con-
    sciousness of the wonder of life outside oneself?
                        from A Story Teller's Story, p. 250.

                *   *   *

I can't make out about people--why they want to be as they
    are.   Mostly I sympathize with them.
                        to Charles Bockler, fall 1935.

            *   *   *   *

Chapter 2

A CALLOW YOUTH

"When I was sixteen or seventeen years old I came to the city of Chicago, and there for four or five years I worked as a common laborer. The Spanish American War saved me from this. "[1] It was a period in which Anderson recalled being "caught in that vicious circle of things when a man cannot swagger before his fellows, is too tired to think, and too pitifully ashamed of his appearance to push out into the world. "[2] Karl Anderson had gone to Chicago to art school in 1894 and recalled "I had been boarding with a family on the West Side of Chicago for about two years when Sherwood followed me there to share my room. "[3]

Other facts have shown that Anderson was in Clyde during the summer of 1896. Karl says that Sherwood was "nineteen then, a callow youth. " Thus this period he spent in Chicago must have been between the end of the summer of 1896 (on September 13 he was twenty that year) and the spring of 1898, when he went back to Clyde and Company I as it went off to war, a matter of about eighteen months.

Karl says that in later years Sherwood "placed the blame for his having gone off to be a writer at my feet. 'Your going off to study art, ' he said, 'that set a bad example for me. '"[4] Whether or not Sherwood went to Chicago to be a writer, a matter which seems highly doubtful in view of no evidence of his doing any writing till considerably later, he was to say of Karl's studying art:

> I can well remember how proud we all were at the thought of this older brother of ours living the artist's life. In fact, so much did the life he had taken up influence ours, that all, at one time or another, tried to be artists. [5]

By going to Chicago he placed himself in an environment

where it was more likely he could think of himself as a writer or one who wanted to become one. But Herman Hurd's analysis seems sound: "He had a brother there. The Padens were there. Lots of people from Clyde were there. Plenty of work to be had. He was doing what a lot of other people were doing."

Clifton Paden[6] was the second of the important life-long friends Sherwood found in his boyhood in Clyde. Anderson long after thought of him as "my oldest friend, both born on the same street of the same town [inaccurate], peddled papers together, went off to the city together...."[7] Clifton and his family, whose head, Henry F. Paden, had been the editor of the Enterprise and the mayor of Clyde before his death about 1890, actually left to live in Chicago in May, 1893.[8] But it was certainly natural that, after, as Hurd noted, "playing ball in the road together and growing up together," Anderson would have found the Paden boarding house at 708 Washington Boulevard, Chicago, the place to stay, just as Karl was doing.

According to Miss Jeanette Paden,[9] who lived at that address with her sister, Carrie, and her brothers, Clifton and Alexander, Sherwood lived with her family and Karl all the time he was in Chicago. Miss Paden had no specific recollection of the length of time he lived with her family, but she did remember his leaving the house to go to war. And it was from that address that Anderson wrote to his militia captain of his eagerness to get into the war that was brewing.[10]

Karl was to recall:

> At once he captured the hearts of the family with whom we were staying by his good-natured assurance. He told everyone on the day of his arrival that he would first get a job as a grocery clerk and then progress upwards in a short time.
>
> The following evening Sherwood appeared at dinner with the exalted announcement that he, that day, had landed ten grocery jobs. "I'm going to work at one of them tomorrow morning," he told us. "I haven't made up my mind which one. I'll flip a coin. See which fellow is to have my services."[11]

When Sherwood referred in his <u>Memoirs</u> (pages 107-8) to his going to Chicago at this time, the focus he gave the experience was that of fear. "I was a raw boy just out of my Ohio town when I first came to Chicago. " He said Karl, who had been first in Cleveland and then in Chicago, seemed unimpressed. "The bigness did not overwhelm him. " Though he was nearly twenty, Sherwood said of himself, "I was little more than a boy. It was too big for me, too terrible. " He thought of himself as being on his brother's hands. He recalled, "Brutal murders going on. Everything unfinished. Hope--hopelessness. Nothing to do but get drunk as often as possible. " That Karl thought of Sherwood as engagingly assured and that he was uncomfortable enough to think later, doubtless exaggeratedly, of himself as fearful and raw, is perhaps typical and similar to the reactions of many who lived with Sherwood throughout his life. There was an outward bravado to him which often masked an inner unhappiness or insecurity. Just as typical of Anderson was that he made a great difficulty out of what should have been a relatively simple transaction. He was living with his brother and a whole family of hometown people whom he had known and liked for years. He could hardly have had better auspices for the move into the big city. When Sherwood was not working, he shared in the home activities of the Paden family. "He had little money to do otherwise. " He was not remembered as having read much. "He used to come home so dog-tired at night that he was just all to pieces, " recalled Miss Paden.

Most accounts indicate that Anderson's job in Chicago was in a cold-storage warehouse. Karl has written that a girl who happened to be visiting where they lived was so impressed by Sherwood's self-confidence that she took him to her father, who owned a large cold-storage plant. "Sherwood spent the next two years wheeling meat in and out of the frigid vaults. "[12] Hurd said he knew of his working nowhere but the cold-storage plant. Miss Paden recalled his "rolling barrels, " and Anderson refers to himself as:

> rolling kegs of nails out of a great sheet-iron warehouse and onto a long platform, from where they were to be carted by trucks, down a short street, out to a wharf and aboard a ship. The kegs were heavy but they were not large, and as they were rolled down a slight incline to the platform the rolling could be done with the foot. [13]

Twenty years after the fact he was to write from Chicago to a friend:

> It was cold and snowy last night and I went for a
> walk.   I wandered into a district where I worked
> as a laborer nearly twenty years ago.   Uh.   I
> shiver when I think what I endured there.   The
> foreman over me was a German.   The superinten-
> dent understood I was a boy and could not do any
> hard tasks.   He gave me only light tasks but when
> he had gone away the German gave me only heavy
> work.
>
> I did not dare complain.   It was a year of hard
> times and I knew no other place where I could get
> work.   The German sent me out on the lake front
> where the company was laying the foundation for a
> new warehouse.   It was bitter cold and the wind
> blew the spray of the lake over us.   With me it
> became a struggle of life and death.   Every night
> I was proud to think I had not been overcome by
> the cold. [14]

Dissatisfaction was the basic mood of Anderson while
he was in the Paden home; "He simply despised the work he
was doing, " Miss Paden remembered.   Anderson recalled in
A Story Teller's Story that, "Like practically all modern
workmen my body had plenty to do but my mind was idle.
There was no planning of the work, no scheming to make the
day's work fit the plan" (page 133).   "In the midst of it all, "
he was to report, "I continued to dream.   In some way I
knew I would survive--say my say.   How strange it is that
in a life the purpose of which cannot be told there should be
the idea of surviving. "[15]

The last reference might foster the surmise that Sherwood was thinking about writing, but Miss Paden recalled
that he was simply filled with a desire to "do something bigger, " "spread his wings, " improve his condition, but that he
had no specific aim in mind.   Another indication of his ambition was his attendance at a night school session of Lewis
Institute, now a division of the Illinois Institute of Technology.
in Chicago, from September, 1897, to December, 1897.   He
was registered for a course called New Business Arithmetic,
receiving a "final estimate" of 90. [16]   In addition to the fact
that this subject could hardly be more diametrically opposed
to the interests of an aspiring writer, it may be observed

that Anderson never referred to this business training in any
of his writings or records, and his long-time friend, Herman
Hurd, could not recall having knowledge of it.

That was the only course he took, and probably he
had no other schooling then.   But he had other interests and
experiences.   It has been suggested that he was impressed
(put as being overwhelmed) by the city, and Windy McPherson's Son and Marching Men both show the impact of the
metropolitan experience, as will be seen.   In addition, according to Miss Paden, Sherwood was engaged briefly to a
girl named Mabel Harper while he was in Chicago.   This
may be what he had in mind when he wrote: "I was a young
man in Chicago. ... There I saw the first woman who rejected me--felt what men feel when they are rejected. "[17]
Too, he could recall, "I arose and went to walk in the silent
streets and twice during that summer I was stopped by hold-
up men who took a few dollars from me. "[18]   Another kind
of encounter involved "all sorts of love adventures in Jackson
Park, a good many of which I have written about. "[19]

Whatever the total of his experiences in big city was,
he "talked about his dissatisfaction and unhappiness all the
time. "[20]   It is not surprising that he was writing of his
eagerness for action with Company I six weeks before war
broke out.   Nonetheless, the local newspaper reported that
Sherwood Anderson was leaving a "lucrative position in
Chicago to rush to his country's defense. "[21]

Notes

1.   Quoted in Bookman, May, 1917, p. 307.

2.   "Who's Who, " Chicago Tribune, May 31, 1919.

3.   "My Brother, Sherwood Anderson, " p. 6.   A substantiating reference is in the Clyde Enterprise of Aug.
9, 1894, mentioning Karl, "who has been in Chicago
attending the art school, " at home for a few weeks' vacation.

4.   "My Brother, Sherwood Anderson, " p. 6.

5.   Letter to Newlin Price, April 15, 1922.

6.   Later known as a movie producer and husband of Anita

Loos, under the name of John Emerson.

7.   Letter to Mrs. L. L. Copenhaver, Nov. 14, 1939.

8.   Enterprise, May 18, 1893, p. 3.

9.   Interviewed in her home at Clyde in 1942.

10.   Enterprise, March 3, 1898, p. 2.

11.   "My Brother, Sherwood Anderson, " p. 6.

12.   Ibid.

13.   A Story Teller's Story, p. 133.

14.   Letter to Marietta D. Finley, Dec. 21, 1916.

15.   Letter to Finley, note 14.

16.   Letter from Charlene S. Hubacek, Recorder, Illinois
      Institute of Technology, Oct. 9, 1962.

17.   "Chicago--A Feeling, " Vanity Fair, Oct. 1926, p. 53.

18.   A Story Teller's Story, p. 228.

19.   Letter to Roger L. Sergel, March 26, 1928 (JR).

20.   Interview with Miss Paden.

21.   As reported in Memoirs, p. 120.

Mosaic III

"In accordance with my feeling: ... "

I had already, as far as I reacted to the life about me at all, started upon another road, was becoming, a little, the eternal questioner of myself and others. Not for me the standardized little pellets of opinion, the little neatly wrapped packages of sentiment the magazine writers had learned to do up, I told myself.
from A Story Teller's Story, p. 231.

*   *   *

When writing of another being, I have always found it best to do so in accordance with my feeling. Besides, men do not exist in facts. They exist in dreams.
from "Introduction to the Memoirs, "
The Sherwood Anderson Reader,
p. 697.

*   *   *

I write perhaps too much from pure feeling. I am trying to use my head more, perhaps be a little more considerate of my reader. It may be, I think that, to me, writing has always been a little like... striving towards the intense moment of copulation.
to Roger Sergel, Dec. 1925.

*   *   *

If, however, as you lie on the banks of streams and have thoughts, you try to push your thoughts out beyond the immediate things, if you will make yourself little like a bug that looks up at the towering grass stalks you will begin to understand something you haven't yet understood.
to M. D. Finley, April 1918.

I have, almost always, tried to work out of pure feeling,
  having the conviction that if I got the feeling straight
  and pure enough the form I wanted would follow.   I am
  trying to make this job more objective, keep the whole
  story definitely on two or three people, the whole cen-
  tering upon one, in other words being more objective,
  trying, you see, to use the mind as well as feeling.
                      to Maxwell Perkins, Nov. 8, 1935
                                                    (JR).

                *   *   *

I had always been drawn toward horses, dogs and other animals and among people had cared most for simple folk
  who made no pretense of having an intellect, workmen
  who in spite of the handicaps put in their way of modern life still loved the materials in which they worked,
  who loved the play of hands over materials, who followed instinctively a force outside themselves--they
  felt to be greater and more worthy than themselves--
  women who gave themselves to physical experiences
  with grave and fine abandon, all people in fact who
  lived for something outside themselves, for materials
  in which they worked, for people other than themselves,
  things over which they made no claim of ownership.
                      from A Story Teller's Story, p. 269.

                *   *   *

Questions invaded my mind and I was young and skeptical,
  wanting to believe in the power of the mind, wanting to
  believe in the power of intellectual force, terribly
  afraid of sentimentality in myself and in others.
        Was I afraid also of people who had the power
  of loving, of giving themselves?   Was I afraid of the
  power of unasking love in myself and in others?
        That I should be afraid of anything in the realm
  of the spirit, that there should perhaps be a force in
  the world I did not understand, could not understand,
  irritated me profoundly.
                      from A Story Teller's Story, p. 268.

                *   *   *

He was of the type of which American heroes are made, you
  see, and she had, in her young girlhood, read American
  novels.   In American novels, as in American plays--as

everyone knows--a man can, just as well as not, be a
horse thief, a desperado, a child-kidnapper, a gentleman burglar, or a well-poisoner for years and years,
and then, in an instant, become the sweetest and most
amiable fellow possible, and with perfect manners too.
It is one of the most interesting things about us Americans. No doubt it came to us from the English. It
seems to be an Anglo-Saxon trait and a very lovely one
too. All anyone need do is to mention in the presence
of any one of us at any time the word "mother, " or
leave one of us alone in the darkness in a forest in a
lonely cabin on a mountain at night with a virgin.

from A Story Teller's Story, p. 113.

*   *   *

It is because he [Paul Rosenfeld] writes from the head;
whereas, in my case, each book is a kind of love affair. I am always deeply stirred. Often, after a
thousand or fifteen hundred words, I am a wreck.

to Mary Emmett, summer 1936.

*   *   *

It may sound childish, but men will have to go back to nature more. They will have to go back to the fields
and the rivers. There will have to be a new religion,
more pagan, something more closely connected with
fields and rivers.

from "It's a Woman's Age, " Jan. 15,
1931.

*   *   *

The keener critics have always known the Gothic thing in the
old form in me--a simple religious man.

to Eleanor Copenhaver, June 21, 1932.

*   *   *

I was like one tortured by a desire for conversion to something like the love of God, by a desire to love and be
loved and sometimes in the night I lay in my bed like
a very lovelorn maiden and sometimes I grew angry
and walked up and down in the moonlight in my room
swearing and shaking my fist at the shadows that flitted

across the walls in the moonlight.
                    from A Story Teller's Story, p. 268.

*   *   *   *   *

Chapter 3

THE RIGHT WAR

> To the young factory hand [warehouse-worker]...
> it was grand and glorious. There has always been
> a kind of shrewdness and foxiness in me and I
> could not convince myself that Spain... could offer
> much resistance and I could not get over the feel-
> ing that I was going off... on a kind of glorious na-
> tional picnic. Very well, if I was to be given
> credit for being a hero I could not see why I
> should object. [1]

That statement contains the kernel of the attitude displayed by Anderson in his accounts of his Spanish-American
War experiences. [2] He was very calculating about the whole
affair. He did not enlist in Chicago, for there his joining
the cause of freedom would pass unnoticed. He related that
he sent off a wire to the captain of the militia in Clyde and
"beat his way" almost to his destination, being treated with
respect by hoboes. Shrewdly, he stopped at a station "twenty
miles from home" to buy a new outfit and achieved a look
"something between a bank clerk and an actor out of work. "[3]

Karl Anderson recalled that Sherwood wrote him in
New York to say, "I prefer yellow fever in Cuba to living
in cold storage in Chicago. " Karl thought a girlfriend in
Clyde had spread the news of Sherwood's coming, and thus
had let him in for "a demonstration for which he was not
prepared. " "Me, just to duck a rotten job, being made a
fuss over--it was doggone embarrassing!'" was the way Karl
recalled the comment in "My Brother, Sherwood Anderson"
(page 7). But Sherwood was to say in another account:
"I was greeted as a hero--one who had given up a lucrative
position in the city in order to fight for his country. My
natural shrewdness led me to take advantage of this situation,
and I enjoyed it thoroughly. "[4]

    If Anderson had chosen to stay in Chicago and ignore
the fact that his national guard company was going into service, he could have done so.   Going to the colors was quite
voluntary, especially if one were not within range of local
public opinion.   But Anderson was eager to go.   As early
as March 3 he had written the following letter to his militia
captain in Clyde:

> Captain Gillette:
>   Dear Sir: if by any chance this war scare
> amounts to anything, and the company is called,
> please telegraph me 708 Washington Boulevard and
> I will be with you.
>   Sherwood Anderson, Chicago, Ill.

    The letter was printed by the Enterprise (on March 3,
1898) as evidence that, if the boys should be called to war,
"there is no question as to how they would acquit themselves. " It was part of an article surveying the condition of
the town's militia company in case war should break out.
The article described the company as drilling hard, "being
under arms going through the various evolutions for over two
hours, " and listed Anderson as a private in the company
roster.   Perhaps the prospects of the company as seen by
the Enterprise reporter in that article may be useful in picturing the atmosphere Anderson entered when he returned to
Clyde and Company I:

> While the boys of our local military are not exactly
> itching for war, still they entertain the universal
> opinion that if the Spaniards blew up our battleship
> they must pay for it with a fight.   Our boys have
> seen enough service during the Cincinnati riots,
> the Wheeling strikes and at other times to know
> that war means something serious. ... The boys
> have had no orders to prepare for an emergency,
> because they need none. ... Capt. Gillett could re-
> port for duty with a company of fifty or more
> trained soldiers, armed and equipped, for active
> service.

    The Maine had been sunk in Havana harbor on Febru-
ary 15, 1898, and the American board of enquiry had not
made its report when Anderson wrote to the captain.   But
on March 21 the board announced its finding that the explosion which had resulted in the sinking of the Maine had
been caused by an exterior mine.   From then on the

situation continued to become more grave. No doubt Anderson was watching the course of events as President McKinley approved on April 20 a resolution demanding the withdrawal of Spain from Cuba and setting noon of April 23 as the latest date for reply. Before the demand could be delivered to the Spanish government in Madrid by the American minister, he was sent his passports. On April 22 the President declared a blockade of Cuban ports. The Spanish government replied with a declaration of war on April 24. The formalities were concluded when on April 25 the United States Congress declared that a state of war had existed between the United States and Spain since April 21.

It is certain the passage of six weeks and the developments which took place in that time had not abated Anderson's desire to go into service with Company I. An April 28 item in the Enterprise makes that clear:

> Capt. Gillett on Friday [April 22] received a message from E. L. Hildwein, a former Co. I boy who has been at Shreveport, La., stating that he wanted to be notified when the company was called out and would join them immediately. Sherwood Anderson wired to the same effect from Chicago. That's the sort of material Clyde boys are made of.

Anderson remembered his reception in Clyde as that of a hero. "I was received with acclaim. Never before that time or since have I had a personal triumph and I liked it"; he indicated elsewhere that although "I...was looked upon as a local hero.... I am afraid it was bunk. The laborer's job was too hard for me. I wanted the chance to travel, see strange places."[5] He was also to write that his work in Chicago was "damn heavy" and "disagreeable," that the war was "rather a holiday," and that he was neither shot at nor hit.[6]

Doubtless Anderson was in the spotlight with the other fifty or so boys in the company. The countryside saw to it that its boys got a good send-off. According to the local paper, the "long expected and anxiously awaited call to arms came to the boys of Company I, 16th Reg., O. N. G., late Monday evening [April 25, 1898]." The company was directed to report at regimental headquarters in Toledo on the following morning. The Enterprise account of April 28, continued:

The message found the soldier boys enjoying a banquet at Terry's opera house.   For several days
previous it was apparent that at almost any moment
the militia would be called out.   Foreseeing this
event, a citizen's meeting was called at G. A. R.
hall on Monday morning to arrange for a banquet
and reception for the boys, and committees promptly went to work to arrange the details.   Terry's
hall was secured, and the ladies of Clyde on Monday evening had prepared a magnificent banquet to
which the soldier boys and their parents, wives
and ladies were invited, over 150 plates being laid.

After the banquet the tables were taken out of the
hall and the reception and speech-making began.
Addresses were made by the local clergy and at-
torneys.   The hall was crowded to its fullest capacity and hundreds were unable to gain admittance.
The scene was one long to be remembered, and
several ladies were overcome and had to be carried from the hall.

Later on, when the crowd had mostly gone home,
the floor was cleared for a dance, and many of
the boys remained until a late hour to indulge in
this pleasure with the ladies.

Bright and early Tuesday morning came the bugle
call assembling the boys at the armory, and long
before time for them to leave the streets were
crowded with friends eager to bid them farewell
and Godspeed.   A guard of honor, comprising the
old veterans and their wives and led by a drum-
corps, escorted the boys to the morning train on
the Wheeling road, and a crowd numbering thousands gathered to see them start.   There were
many painful scenes at the parting, but the boys
did not feel nearly so badly as those they left behind. ..

The boys reached Toledo in good shape and were
at once sent to the armory with the balance of the
regiment to await a call to Columbus, the state
headquarters.

    It is easy to credit Anderson's statement that he
wanted to get away from the warehouse to travel, but it is

difficult to see how he could have escaped being infused with
at least some of the idealism and enthusiasm of those about
him.   It is at least possible that he allowed what was later
apparently his own opinion and that of his nation concerning
that war to color his accounts, both of which were written
after World War I.   If on the one hand he was not mature
enough to participate in the soberer emotions of his elders,
then it is not likely he had the insight to pronounce the war
a "push-over" from the beginning.

In the Memoirs Anderson alludes to the absorption of
the town with the farewell and the emotion of the old soldiers
and the women.   In the face of this Anderson remembered
that he "tried to appear stern, to maintain an air of indifference.   We, in our little company of local braves, were
for the most part boys.   We kept whispering to each other
as we marched."   They wanted the emotions to be quieted,
to be let alone.   He added, "I think we were all relieved •
when we had got aboard our train" (page 121).

> We were the boys of a Middle-Western country
> town, farmers' sons, merchants' sons, young town
> roughs, gentle, quiet boys.   Our hearts did not
> ache for the people of the island of Cuba.   Our
> hearts ached for adventure (page 122).

Furthermore, Anderson was preoccupied with another
matter at this leave-taking.   Before he left Clyde for Chicago he had proposed to one of the Clyde girls, one far
above him in the social scale.   In a "beautiful moment" she
had said she would wait for him while he went to Chicago to
make good.   After he got to Chicago he used to write to her
from his hall bedroom.   Anderson relates his irritation at
finding when he got back to Clyde that his beloved had become engaged to marry a non-belligerent jewelry clerk.   So
it was that he turned away and laughed scornfully when she
left the others and started toward him as he marched past
to go to war. [7]

The incident, which dominated his account of the
leave-taking of Company I, if true, shows his essential pre-
dilection for the dramatic and romantic incident and lack of
concern for what was happening to the town.   Anderson's
concern was typically for Anderson.   When the company got
to the armory in Toledo, one of the boys sang an inspirational song dealing with the liberation of Cuba.   The singer
was cheered.   Anderson's reaction was that of envy.   He

would have liked to have had the cheers.   He did not think
of the suffering people. [8]

On Thursday, April 28, the Enterprise published a
Wednesday report of its correspondent, a sergeant with Company I:

> It was almost impossible to sleep last night, as
> the boys were singing and yelling, and when one
> would go to sleep they would throw water on him,
> and they kept that going till late in the night.
> Charlie Dennis said he had gone crazy, and that
> there is nothing like a soldier's life.

It does not seem that the boys remembered the evening before when, on the announcement of the time for the
boys to leave Clyde, "sobs and sighs came from those who
were seeing sons, husbands and brothers go forth. . . . "[9]
These boys, like many boys, had not lived long enough to
understand the parental attitude.   They did not realize the
reason for the banquet, the speeches, the guard of honor,
the bunting, the tears.   They seem only to have known
"there is nothing like a soldier's life. "

In Toledo some of the soldiers helped the police control the crowd which was all about the armory.   On the
night of Tuesday, April 26, there was a dress parade.   The
Enterprise correspondent's report continued:

> We have plenty of girls to see us and jolly us
> along; and how the boys do scrap when it is time
> to eat, to see which one is going to get there first.
>
> The boys are all well as yet, but are getting tired
> of staying here in the Armory.   They are not allowed to be away from the Armory very long at a
> time, and they do not seem to like it.
>
> All the companies of the Sixteenth Regiment are
> quartered in the Armory, and there is not much
> room to spare.   Some sleep on the floor with only
> a little straw under them, but we all [Company I]
> have ticks and can make a good bed.

When the boys of the Sixteenth Regiment left Toledo
on the morning of April 29, they got what was described as
a great "sendoff. "   A "presentation ceremony" in the morning

was followed by a "celebration" at the railway depot. After the troops left Toledo, "All the way along the line people were out to meet the boys as they passed through, and the demonstration that had begun at the start of the troops was continued clear to Columbus. " When the troops arrived in Columbus, the paper there stated, they passed along streets lined with "hundreds of people, " while "every window contained its share of patriots, some of whom were provided with flags. Prolonged cheers greeted the boys all along the line of march. "

The Columbus paper said further that preceding regiments had left the field in which the Sixteenth Regiment was to camp "not very presentable" and that there was "considerable kicking" about the fact.

> The boys were hungry and had to depend on haversacks or nearby regimental sutlers for their suppers. The tents, too, were slow in coming, and it was after 10 o'clock before most of them were under cover. They had to put up with just what some of the other regiments had to before them. 10

On May 5 the Enterprise printed its sergeant-correspondent's report that the boys had started in Columbus at 2:30 p. m. on Friday, April 29. After walking the six miles from the point of debarking from the train to Camp Bushnell, which was somewhat out East Broad Street, "The boys were very tired when they got there. "

> We have at last got down to work and are now in full working order. Drills every morning and afternoon for one and a half hours each time. We drill in battle formation and are now learning to drill by bugle calls.... They are very strict here; only 4 men can leave camp at a time.... They started to break us in the first night by not having anything ready for us when we arrived. When we arrived where we were to camp there were no tents and Col. McMaken went to headquarters and told them they would have to fix us out. When we did at last get tents it was about 7:30 p. m. We then went to work putting up the tents. When we had them up we were about as bad off as we were when we did not have any tents, as we had no straw or anything to lay [sic] on and the ground was very damp. At last they did get enough straw

for one tick [apiece?], and O, how the boys did
kick about having to sleep that way.   They did not
seem to like the life of a soldier but would rather
be home in their little beds.

In the same article the following daily routine was
outlined.   In the morning: 5, reveille; 5:30, breakfast; 6:15
surgeon's call; 6:30, cleaning up quarters; 8, mounting
guard; 9, drill for 90 minutes; 11:30, "dinner"; and in the
afternoon: 1, "school"; 2:30, drill for 90 minutes; 4, recall; 5, supper; 8, dress parade followed by sunset retreat;
and 9:30, taps, after which every man must be quiet in his
tent with lights out.

The writer went on to say, "The boys of Co. I do
their share of guard duty and other duties that are required
of them without a murmur, and the new recruits are doing
fine.   We enjoy a band concert every evening.   For one to
come into camp and look around they would think. . . [the
boys] went into camp for pleasure. . . . "   The boys at Camp
Bushnell ate fat pork, "a little beef, " eggs, and pork and
beans.   "Some of the boys do not like the bill of fare but
have to put up with it.   I believe they will soon come to
eating what they get or go hungry. "

Shortly after arriving at Camp Bushnell, Company I
received orders to recruit up to 84 men for United States
service.   The company was called together, and the men
who did not care to go into federal service were given the
opportunity to decline.   "We told them that we wanted to
have those that were going to back out to do so now. "   Six
proved not to be "true blue"; a lieutenant was sent back to
Clyde to get replacements for them and enough other recruits to bring the company up to authorized strength. 11

Anderson told in the Memoirs (pages 124-5) of the
brutality of the company toward the "quitters. "   The treatment he describes is the beating of the buttocks against a
tree.   "It was the first time I knew how cruel men in the
mass could be. "   The right of the men to refuse service
was subjected to heavy pressure everywhere.   When Company H, from the neighboring town of Fremont, "found out
one of their members was not going to war. . . they grabbed
him, clipping his hair, rode him on a rail and had a general
hurrah.   They now say when Stack goes home he will wear
a pair of blue overalls, a yellow coat and a red hat.   He
was detailed at the cook's quarters this morning. "12   The

Enterprise looked down its nose and proclaimed, "It is surprising how many men there are who are anxious to get a
little notoriety or free advertising out of this war without
endangering their own precious hides. A few of them live
right here in Clyde" (May 5, 1898; page 3). Another whack
was given the offenders with the announcement on the same
page that "New men are being recruited to replace seven
'quitters' who have already had enough of war. "

To continue that day's account: on May 4 "A representative of the Enterprise visited Camp Bushnell. . . and found
the boys all well and in good spirits. " The dinner, he was
able to report, consisted of beef steak, boiled potatoes,
bread and butter, gravy, and black coffee. "The Clyde company is one of the best on the grounds, and has excellent
quarters which are kept in fine condition. . . . The 'quitters, '
as they are called, are receiving an immense amount of
chaffing, and some of them don't stand it very well. " The
newspaper declared that any one who thought the boys were
not having a good time should take a visit to the camp and
"dispel the illusion. "

Looking back on his war experience, Anderson wrote:

> I was a soldier and had picked the right war. We
> of the local military companies were taken into
> the national service just as we were. Our local
> companies had been built up on a democratic basis.
> I had got what I wanted. After my experience as
> a laborer the drilling seemed to me play. We
> were well fed. We had warm clothes. [13]

He has reminisced about the fact that the members of
his company were just boys from an Ohio town with officers
from the same town being made soldiers and not taking it
too seriously. The captain had been "the janitor of a public
building, " the first lieutenant, a celery-raiser, and the
second lieutenant, a knife-grinder in a cutlery factory. "The
officers had to remember that they expected to go back to
the same Ohio town; they were not thought of as superiors,
except perhaps in military matters. " An officer might be
beaten up when he got home if he did an injustice. [14]

Corroboration of this account is found in comments
made by a Fremont visitor to Camp Bushnell. He deplored
the lack of discipline:

> The officers are too busy to enforce it. The men
> are too good natured and enthusiastic to make it
> apparent. There are no regular army officers in
> camp, as there are at the state encampments
> and officers and men of the guard mingle on a
> plane of beautiful equality. Privates invade the
> tents of their officers at will, and yell at them
> half the length of the street. The recruits talk
> and smoke cigars in ranks, and officers frequently
> associate in the pastimes of the men. [15]

On May 12, 1898, Sherwood Anderson went out of the
service of the state of Ohio and became a private in Company
I of the Sixth Ohio Regiment of volunteer infantry at Camp
Bushnell. Just a little over a year later, on May 24, 1899,
he was mustered out of the federal service at Camp Mac-
Kenzie, Georgia, a corporal. The time of enlistment had
been for two years unless he was mustered out sooner.

The following tabular presentation of the movements
of Company I may serve the reader as a handy key to the
activities of Anderson during his year in service:

1898   May   12- Mustered into service as a company at
                     Camp Bushnell, Columbus, Ohio.
                 17- Left Camp Bushnell for Chickamauga Park,
                     Georgia.
                 18- Arrived at Chattanooga, Tenn. ; moved to
                     Rossville, Ga. , in the evening.
                 19- Marched 12 miles to Camp George H.
                     Thomas, Chickamauga Park, Ga.
        Aug.   27- Marched from Camp Thomas to Rossville;
                     went by rail to Lonsdale, suburb of Knox-
                     ville, Tenn.
                 28- Marched from Lonsdale to Camp Poland,
                     Lincoln Park, Knoxville.
        Dec.   27- Marched from Camp Poland to Lonsdale;
                     boarded train for Charleston, S. C.
                 29- Arrived Charleston in the morning; em-
                     barked on U. S. T. Minnewaska in the eve-
                     ning.
                 30- Sailed for Cienfuegos, Cuba, in the eve-
                     ning.

1899   Jan.   3- Arrived in the harbor at Cienfuegos.
                  4- Disembarked, marched through Cienfuegos
                     and four miles out to Camp Sixth Ohio.

1899   Jan.   26- Went to Sagua La Grande.
        March 13- Returned to regiment at Camp Sixth Ohio.
               26- Went to Provost Guard Camp at Cienfuegos.
        April 21- Embarked on U. S. T. Sedgewick.
               25- Arrived at the mouth of the Savannah River.
               27- Disembarked at the disinfecting station,
                   went through fumigation, were transported
                   by lighter to detention camp on Dafuski
                   Island.
        May   2- Went by lighter to Savannah and then by
                   rail to Augusta, Ga. , and then to Camp
                   MacKenzie, Ga.
               24- Mustered out at Camp MacKenzie. 16

        The signing of a peace protocol and declaration of an
armistice between the two warring nations took place on
August 12, 1898, just three months after Anderson's company
really entered the war.   At the time Anderson was "sick in
quarters" (August 9 to 19). 17   But this was not before he
had been made a corporal, which promotion took place on
July 1, 1898.

        Newspaper reports, excerpts from letters, and the
comments of comrades have produced more detail of what
happened to Anderson during his army year, only three
months of which were during war-time and a little less than
four of which were spent out of the country and after the
peace.

        The trip from Camp Bushnell to Camp Thomas, which
occupied two full days and was topped off with a twelve-mile
hike, was arduous.

            When we marched to camp last Thursday morning
            the weather was hot and we looked like a lot of
            mudhens when we got there.   It was so dry and
            dusty that the sweat and dust mixed together made
            us look like a lot of darkies.

            Our grub was "on the bum" coming down here.
            All we had was corned beef, a few canned beans,
            a little bread and about one cup of coffee on the
            trip. 18

        Hardtack was substituted for bread and butter.   Some
of the boys, carrying blanket bags and guns, had to fall out
on the march to Camp Thomas because of the heat.   Water

was so scarce that each regiment placed guards over its own water supply. [19]

An anecdote of this time may indicate the trust Anderson was already given by the leaders. "One of the Fremont boys is under arrest for going to sleep on guard, and Sherwood Anderson had the pleasure of guarding him. Sherwood seemed to enjoy it. "[20]

Anderson's sense of humor must have been brought into play when the following took place:

> Joel Elliott said the other day that he was not afraid of a lizard, but when Sherwood Anderson wet his finger and put it on Joel's neck one night the boys thought he was going through the top of the tent.... [21]

The next Clyde read of Anderson was that he and six others had been in Chattanooga on June 4. [22] Another activity in which he undoubtedly engaged was that of visiting Civil War monuments. On June 16, 1898, the Enterprise quoted the recently-elevated Major Gillett as writing:

> The boys derive great pleasure in their sight seeing journeys and at present there is scarcely one but can accurately describe the many movements of Bragg's or Rosecrans' army. They have visited the many monuments, studied tablets and markers, scaled the observation towers and visited the sites of historical points.

It is impossible to resist contemplation of the memories of his father's tales this pursuit may have aroused in Anderson. As a member of the Seventh Ohio Cavalry his father had fought in Tennessee and Georgia. When Anderson was at Camp Thomas and Camp Poland, he must have been near, if not on, some of the scenes his father liked to tell about. It seems odd that Anderson never wanted to write more in detail about his camp experiences.

On June 30, a report from the Enterprise's correspondent was published. "We are still in camp in this ideal park. " The tents were pitched in groves of trees, the shade of which tempered the heat. But the writer had to admit that camp life was "monotonous. " "Jobby Anderson, " he noted, "puts in most of his time at the Y. M. C. A. " The

Y. M. C. A. was the place to write letters, play games, read current publications, play the organ, sing songs, or attend religious services.   A good guess, based on evidence to be presented shortly, is that Anderson was most interested in the reading.

Although the records show that Anderson's promotion, one of six, to the position of corporal took place on July 1, 1898, the story which told about his promotion and others did not appear in The Toledo Blade correspondence from Camp Thomas until July 12.   From it one learns that

> For the best part of a week the colonel has been considering the names which have been recommended by the different captains, and he has required each to send up several more names than would fill the existing vacancies.   In addition to this, he has been watching the work of many of the boys who were not aware that they were having "tab" kept on them, and as a result, some men were called up for examination who were not recommended by their captains.   Maj. Stanberry had some of the candidates turned over to him, and both he and the colonel put in several hours in asking the boys questions of vital importance. 23

It was undoubtedly Camp Poland he was thinking of when he wrote of "the camp at the edge of a southern city under forest trees..." and of "the physical hardening process that I instinctively liked."

> I have always enjoyed with a kind of intoxicating gusto any physical use of my body out in the sun and wind.   In the army it brought me untroubled sleep at night, physical delight in my own body, the drunkenness of physical well-being and often in my tent at night after a long day of drilling and when the others slept, I rolled quietly out under the tent flaps and lay on my back on the ground, looking at the stars seen through the branches of the trees.   About me many thousands of men were sleeping and along a guard line, somewhere over there in the darkness, guards were walking up and down.   Was it a kind of child's play?   The guards were pretending the army was in danger, why should not my imagination play for a time?24

Another recollection seems also to catch the spirit of the camp experience.

> Out from under the trees into a wide field we went,
> the southern sun pouring down on us and presently
> the back tired, the legs tired. One sank into a
> half-dead state. This did not signify battles, kill-
> ing other men. The men with whom one marched
> were comrades, feeling the same weariness, obey-
> ing the same commands, being molded with oneself
> into something apart from oneself. We were being
> hardened, being whipped into shape. For what?
> Well, never mind. Take what is before you! You
> have come out from under the shadow of the facto-
> ry, the sun shines. The tall boys marching with
> you were raised in the same town with yourself.
> Now they are all silent, marching, marching.
> Times of adventure ahead. You and they will see
> strange people, hear strange tongues spoken. [25]

While the company was at Camp Poland, one of its members died. From Camp Poland to Clyde on October 6, 1898, was sent a resolution of respect, one of the signers of which was Corp. Sherwood Anderson. The text:

> Resolution of respect to our late comrade Frank
> W. Craig.
> Whereas, it has pleased the Almighty to with-
> draw from our ranks our dearly beloved friend and
> comrade Frank W. Craig, we bow in submission
> to his divine will.
> Be it resolved, That in his death Co. I. , 6th
> O. V. Infantry, has lost one of its best soldiers
> and a comrade who was always ready to respond
> to the call of duty without hesitation and without
> question of time or place.
> Be it resolved, That we tender our heartfelt
> sympathy to his bereaved family and relatives, and
> that copies of these resolutions be forwarded to
> the family, the Clyde papers and Greensprings pa-
> pers, as a mark of our sympathy with them for
> their great loss. [26]

The only reason for reproducing that document is that one would hardly have expected the Sherwood Anderson of later years to have signed it. It should be pointed out that the resolution was a form used by the soldiers; it was

customary to have half-a-dozen or so soldiers send along a
message of that sort whenever one of the boys died or was
killed.   An identically-worded resolution was sent to Clyde
by an entirely different committee when another soldier died
in November.

At the beginning of 1899 the boys found themselves at
last on the way to Cuba and arrived there on January 4.
The trip was "uneventful and very pleasant. " The company
was described as "enjoying the best of health" and "delighted
to have a change from the dull routine life which they have
followed since they responded to their country's call and left
their homes in northwestern Ohio. "27

Those whose hearts had "ached for adventure" had
done a little traveling and nothing else but become acquainted
with the routine and discomforts of army life.   There was
much sight-seeing to do but even that was not always the
pleasantest occupation.   A letter of January 9, 1899, written
by Lieutenant Jesse A. Douglas from Cienfuegos disclosed
the following incident:

> The other day I went into an old Spanish fort a
> little way from camp for relics, and I found about
> a million.   I was with Harry Sergeant and Sher-
> wood Anderson, and when we came out Harry said,
> "What are those things on me?"   I looked and told
> him that they were fleas.   Then I looked at my-
> self and I will bet I had a million on me. 28

It is not surprising that in February one of the soldiers ended a letter home by saying, "None of the boys are
seriously sick--except of army life. "29   It is likely that out
of the ennui and dissatisfaction felt while in service came
the jocularly cynical tone of the episode Anderson called
"The Capture of Caratura" in the Memoirs. 30   Anderson
never professed that he went into the war idealistically; he
went on the "picnic" for the ride.   But that did not stop him
from being cynical about it later.

Much of the material that has preceded in this account
of Anderson in the army has given just a glimpse of him at
this activity or that, but it is fortunate that there is a rather good picture of Anderson as a reader.   Four of Anderson's comrades in the service have been able to contribute
information which shows clearly that Anderson was reading
with deep interest and constantly.   One soldier wrote to his

sister from Camp Poland that "Jobby, " as Corporal Anderson
was known to his Clyde friends, was reading With Fire and
Sword and that he could not be interrupted. The soldier refers to another soldier coming in for a daily argument, which
at its height made concentration impossible. [31]   Each soldier
in the group, one learns from the letter, had his favorite
author and would argue for him or her.   Obviously Anderson
must have enjoyed the discussions a great deal.

A fellow corporal[32] recalls that the other fellows in
camp made fun of Anderson for reading instead of going
around with them.   He remembers Anderson best as one who
sat around and read.   In addition he says, "We all liked
him. "

Another fellow-soldier agreed that Anderson was always pleasant and agreeable, probably the most agreeable of
all.   He could not think of a time when he was offensive to
the others. [33]

A messmate remembered him as untidy in appearance,
that he was always lying on his bunk reading.   Even if a
dozen others were laughing and talking in the tent, he would
read uninterruptedly, probably in an adventure story. [34]

Another messmate says, "He always had his nose in
a book; if you wanted him to do anything, you might find him
under the sunny side of a pine tree.   If you wanted to talk
to him, you had to pry him loose from a book. "[35]   One day
a trip to Lookout Mountain was proposed.   Anderson was
reading a novel.   "What's the idea of reading?   There is
sunshine and places to go, " his friend argued.   Anderson
replied, "I like the stuff and some day I'm going to write
books. "[36]   Whether this was just an idle remark designed
to ward off an interruption of his reading or something which
was based on ambition that had already taken root can hardly
be determined.   But it does seem certain that Anderson's
constant reading, which began in Clyde and was not interrupted by the war, was the fundamental inspiration of his
ambition to write.

Dr. William Holtz recalls of Anderson that he was
popular and "could always get a girl ...   He could go into
any place or church.   I never saw him drink.   He was a
gentleman in every respect. "   To Dr. Holtz he seemed, "a
little better than average soldier"; and he "didn't talk out of
turn. "

Toward the end of April, 1899, Company I started home from Cuba, and early in May it was back on American soil in Georgia.   On May 24 the men were mustered out, paid off, [37] and started on the way home.   There is no record of what Anderson thought about his army year as he approached Clyde on the train along with the other boys who had been with him.   A comrade found that, in later years, he seemed indifferent to his year in service, that he did not join the United Spanish War Veterans, and seemed not to want any one to know he had been in the Spanish-American War. [38]

Anderson's treatments of the period were not extensive, and his comments were always in terms of later developments and realizations.   One gathers, though, that it must have seemed just another militia encampment many times magnified.   There was the same "roughing it," the same drill, a lot more travel, a lot more scenery, and the only danger was imaginary, just as it was in camp.   He may have had a chance to realize more completely the nature of military life, but he could not have learned anything significant about war.   It was a great national picnic for the group Anderson was in, though they did know boredom and hardship.

But there had been no evidence enabling one to predict the picnic when the war started.   Indeed, there were those in the war who knew danger, disease, and disaster. Anderson at twenty-one could hardly have been so heedless a youth that he was unaware of the dangers of war.   He was brought up in an atmosphere of the Civil War story.   The logical conclusion seems to be that Anderson was so fed up with the situation in which he found himself that he was willing to take a chance on what would happen to him in the army during the war.   He was luckier than he could have guessed he would be.

Company I arrived in Clyde on May 26, 1899, and Clyde had another of its red-letter days.   Browned, ruddy, elastic of step, the boys looked as if their year in service had done them a "world of good."   Every man was conscious of having done his duty, the local newspaper said, "and we are as proud of the boys as if they had seen actual service." Aware that a heroic reception had been accorded men who had done nothing heroic, the paper said further, "It is not their fault that they were not in battle."[39]

Most of the home folks were not too much concerned about that, though; they just wanted to welcome their loved ones. As early as daybreak and in perfect weather, people set about decorating the town. "Every business place and private residence was gaily decorated, and the stars and stripes greeted the eye at every turn." The business of extending a welcome to the returning engaged almost every one in the town and the surrounding areas. The exact time of the arrival of the train was unknown. Queries kept coming into the local station all morning. But a special citizens' committee boarded the train at Tiffin, about twenty miles away, sent word ahead, and Clyde's fire bell gave notice when the train was about to arrive.

The scene at the depot when the train pulled in was, as one might expect, "beyond description." People packed platforms, grounds, tracks, car tops, roof tops, and every other possible view point. Van Doren's drum corps, school children, and the G. A. R. were all there. The Enterprise reported on June 1, 1899, that

> ...there was not a semblance of regular order. There was cheering and shouting; flags and hats were waved, and as the soldiers alighted from the train they were immediately surrounded by relatives and friends, and such kissing and handshaking has not been witnessed for many a day. Dinner was waiting in dozens of homes and travel stained soldiers were soon enjoying a square meal at mother's table.

Who met Corporal Anderson? His father was possibly there, because it is unknown just when in 1899 he moved to Connersville and brother Ray, who is mentioned in the June 1 Enterprise as going on a visit to Springfield, was surely there. Karl and Stella were in Springfield, and it does not appear that Anderson saw them until after the homecoming banquet on the evening of June 6. It seems likely that he waited only to attend the banquet before going to see them in Springfield, for the Enterprise of June 8 said, "Sherwood Anderson left yesterday afternoon for Springfield, where he went to visit his brother and sister" (page 3).

The army year came to a close as it had opened, with a banquet. This was, however, not only a banquet but also a reception and was distinguished by torrid weather, an immense crowd, an exhibition of genuine patriotism, a lavish display of the stars and stripes, and a magnificent supper and flow of oratory. The evening ended, as always, with dancing.

Notes

1.   A Story Teller's Story, p. 278-9.

2.   The accounts appear in Story Teller, p. 272-285, and Memoirs, p. 120-135.

3.   A Story Teller's Story, p. 278.

4.   "Who's Who, " Chicago Tribune, May 31, 1919.

5.   A Story Teller's Story, p. 278; Dinsmoor, p. 71.

6.   Letter to John Paul Cullen, Sept. 16, 1937 (JR).

7.   Memoirs, p. 120-21.

8.   Ibid. , p. 122.

9.   Fremont Daily News, April 28, 1898, p. 2.

10. Columbus Dispatch, April 30, 1898, as quoted in Clyde Enterprise, May 5, 1898, p. 2.

11. Enterprise, May 5, 1898, p. 2.

12. Fremont Daily News, May 6, 1898, p. 2.

13. Memoirs, p. 125.

14. A Story Teller's Story, p. 281-2.

15. Fremont Daily News, May 9, 1898, p. 2.

16. This tabulation is a slight modification of that for Company I in Sixth Ohio Volunteer Infantry War Album [of] Historical Events, Reminiscences and Views of the Spanish-American War, 1898-1899, Comp. and Pub. by Capt. L. W. Howard. Toledo, Ohio, Bee Job Print, n. d.

17. Official Roster of Ohio Soldiers in the War with Spain, 1898-99, Pub. by Authority of the Ohio General Assembly,

1916, p. 471.

18. Material excerpted from a letter by Harry Sergeant in Clyde Enterprise, May 26, 1898, p. 2.

19. Ibid.

20. Ibid.

21. Enterprise, June 2, 1898, p. 2.

22. Ibid., June 9, 1898, p. 2.

23. Quoted in the Fremont Daily News, July 16, 1898, p. 2.

24. A Story Teller's Story, p. 279-80.

25. Ibid., p. 273.

26. Enterprise, Oct. 13, 1898, p. 1.

27. Ibid., Jan. 5, 1899, p. 1.

28. Quoted in the Enterprise, Jan. 19, 1899, p. 2.

29. Enterprise, March 2, 1899, p. 1.

30. Especially see p. 129-135.

31. Letter of Wells D. Ream to sister Leila, in Clyde, from Camp Poland, Dec. 15, 1898. With Fire and Sword is in all probability the historical novel of war between Poland and Russia by Henryk Sienkiewicz, the Polish novelist. A popular edition of the book in English had just come out in 1898.

32. Interview with Mr. William H. Covell, Bellevue, Ohio.

33. Letter of Fred J. Wertel[ewski], Gibsonburg, Ohio; Nov. 6, 1941.

34. Letter of Mr. Harry D. Sergeant, Clearwater, Fla.; Nov. 14, 1942.

35. Interview with Dr. William A. Holtz, Tiffin, Ohio.

36.   This and following recollection also from interview with Dr. Holtz.

37.   Each private had about $100, and the officers had larger sums.   Reported in the Enterprise, June 1, 1899, p. 2.

38.   Letter, Mr. Sergeant (note 34).

39.   Enterprise, loc. cit.

40.

Mosaic IV

"For the most part beyond me..."

It was not until long afterward I came to the conclusion that
    I, at least, could only give myself with complete aban-
    donment to the surfaces and materials before me at
    rare moments, sandwiched in between long periods of
    failure.
                    from A Story Teller's Story, p. 321.

*   *   *

Every artist who goes to pieces and takes the joy of complete
    abandonment from his task, and the joy from his own
    life too, does so because he lets some outside impulse,
    want of fame, want of praise, come between him and
    his materials.
                    from A Story Teller's Story, p. 320.

*   *   *

I rather think that modern life and in fact any life wherein
    most people are compelled to be driven by the profit
    motive makes it impossible for all of us to be anything
    else but grotesque.
                    to Kenneth Davenport, April 14, 1937 (JR).

*   *   *

I suspect that the thing needed is quite simple--a real desire
    on the part of a few people to shake off the success
    disease, to really get over our American mania for
    "getting on." It has got to be pretty deep seated if it
    gets us anywhere.
                    to Waldo Frank, Nov. 1918.

In a sense I have been like one living in a damp dark cellar
     ever since I went back into business after my few
     months of freedom in New York last year.   To think
     straight at all I had to get temporarily out of it.   In
     New York I did. . . .   I found out the old lesson that one
     cannot muddy oneself and be clean.
                         to Waldo Frank, 1920.

                   *   *   *

Of course you may never be able to write anything that is
     worth a whoop.   But then I may not.   No one can tell
     whether he will or not.
                         to M. D. Finley, April 1918.

                   *   *   *

Surely nothing in the modern world has been more destructive
     than the idea that man can live without the joy of hands
     and mind combined in craftsmanship, that men can live
     by the accumulation of monies, by trickery.
                         from A Story Teller's Story, p. 327.

                   *   *   *

In the end I had become a teller of tales.   I liked my job.
     Sometimes I did it fairly well and sometimes I blundered
     horribly.   I had found out that trying to do my job was
     fun and that doing it well and finely was a task for the
     most part beyond me.
                         from A Story Teller's Story, p. 409.

                   *   *   *

I think I am like George Moore in that I write a good deal
     for myself, to give myself more life.   I think a man
     is a fool who does not think well of his own work.   If
     he does not, why do it?   It would probably be as im-
     portant to drive a truck or fix watches.
                         to Helen Dinsmoor, June 24, 1938.

                   *   *   *

You ask what experience in my life has brought me the
     greatest satisfaction and I suppose that I can answer
     that I have got the greatest satisfaction out of working,
     that is to say out of my writing.
                         to Helen Dinsmoor, June 24, 1938.

What purity I have got has come from the contempt of what
    is called being competent in life.   Why should I feel
    that way--that is to say that competence is anything.
            It is all too cheap--too easy.
                    to Charles Bockler, fall 1935.

            *   *   *

When it comes to criticism I like praise and dislike blame.
                    to Dwight Macdonald, June 14, 1939 (JR).

            *   *   *

And most of all I was furiously angry when someone said
    that the people of whom I wrote, being only such people
    as I myself had known, were of a lower, more immoral,
    less healthy order of beings.
                    from A Story Teller's Story, p. 316.

*   *   *   *   *

Chapter 4

INTERIM

As Sherwood Anderson rode from Clyde to Springfield, Ohio, to meet his older brother and sister, Karl and Stella, he may very possibly have been wondering, what next? Except for "about $100" or perhaps a little more he was in almost exactly the same position he had been in when he left Chicago to join his company in Clyde. It is true he had seen many new things and was perhaps a little more mature, though he had been more than a boy when he left. But his army year had done nothing to establish him in life, to give him money and leisure, to gain the "success" he had been taught should be his goal in life.

Karl, on the other hand, was already known to the Enterprise as "Clyde's well known artist"[1] and was soon to have his first cover on the Woman's Home Companion. Stella had gone to Springfield in February, 1899,[2] to work in the office of the same magazine. Of the change she wrote a friend that she was not sorry to be away from the problems related to the family.[3] Earl was already with Karl in Springfield. Ray stayed in Clyde until June 1 and Irwin was in Chicago,[4] where he had gone to take Sherwood's job in the warehouse when Sherwood went into the army.

Apparently Anderson stayed in Springfield about a month, for the Enterprise of July 13 (page 3) reported that "Sherwood Anderson returned last week from Springfield," where he had been "visiting his brother Carl [sic]." In that month one assumes Sherwood was enjoying the pleasures of civilian life and holding a council of war with Karl and Stella as to what he should do next. Anderson had had thoughts of going to college while he was in the army;[5] he said he had tried to study (Lewis Institute) while he was in Chicago. It is quite possible that the subject of education for Sherwood was broached during the Springfield month. Apparently nothing was settled.

The return to Clyde, one supposes, was made in the hope that Anderson could most easily find something to do where he was best known.   On the other hand, he may have had his job before he returned to Clyde.   He went to work that summer on the farm of Wallace Ballard, a good friend of Karl's. [6]   Karl might have written his friend and made arrangements.   Mrs. Ballard remembered there was nothing for Sherwood to do in town and that he came to her husband's farm to cut corn.   Her recollection of him tallies with what had been noticed earlier.

> He was a peculiar fellow.   We were packed up and
> ready to move, ready to go in a short time.   We
> came back from town to find a man sitting on a
> box of books reading.   He hardly looked up.   Sher-
> wood had walked into our house, which was strange
> to him, and started to read a book.

While Sherwood was living with the Ballards, he got a job with a threshing rig. [7]   Mr. Wertel recalled he worked at that until quite late in the summer.   "For one not particularly accustomed to this work he did well, " Mr. Wertel thought.   "He did feeding and cutting and traveled with the rig. "

Besides doing the farm work Anderson also secured his honorable discharge from Company I of the Sixteenth Regiment of the Ohio National Guard.   Although his enlist-ment on March 28, 1895, had been for a period of five years, he received his honorable discharge on September 7, 1899, on his own request by reason of his service as a volunteer in the war with Spain. [8]   If it is recalled that And-erson's absence when he was in Chicago did not affect his standing in the company, it may be wondered why he bothered to withdraw even if he were anticipating going away to col-lege.   His enlistment would have lapsed automatically in another six months.   Probably Company I wanted to re-organize with men who expected to stay in the group.

Notes

1.   Dec. 29, 1898, p. 3.

2.   Enterprise, Feb. 23, 1899, p. 3.

3.   Letter from Springfield to Miss Alice Waugh of Clyde,

March 15, 1899.   Miss Waugh became Mrs. W. H. Covell, Bellevue, Ohio.

4.   Ibid.

5.   Memoirs, p. 125.

6.   Interview with Mrs. Myrtle Ballard, Fremont, Ohio.

7.   Recalled by Mrs. Ballard; Wells D. Ream, Bellevue; and Frank J. Wertel, Gibsonburg, Ohio.

8.   Statement from Adjutant General's Department, State of Ohio, Dec. 11, 1941.

Mosaic V

"As they feed my own dreams..."

The books like life itself are only useful to me in as much
as they feed my own dreams or give me a background
upon which I can construct new dreams.
from A Story Teller's Story, p. 156.

       *   *   *

A passion for reading books had taken possession of me and
I did not work when I had any money at all but often
for weeks spent my time reading any book I could get
my hands on.
from A Story Teller's Story, p. 220.

       *   *   *

The book some man had spent years in composing was often
waded through in a day and then thrown aside. What
a jumble of things in my head! At times the life directly about me ceased to have any existence. The
actuality of life became a kind of vapor, a thing outside
of myself.
from A Story Teller's Story, p. 221-22.

       *   *   *

The lives of the dead men and women had become more real
to me than the lives of the living people about me.
from A Story Teller's Story, p. 222-23.

       *   *   *

So many men you like do not like the old bastard [George
Borrow, author of Lavengro] but I have always liked
his flamboyancy. He is a damned old fraud of course
but Lordy God he can write.
to Glenn Gosling, 1939.

Alas, some of them may have read some of the editor's
   books.   The thought sends a little shiver down his
   back.   "They may have taken them literally," he is
   saying to himself.
            But are books not to be taken so?   Certainly
   not.   Books are books.   They are to be taken as books.
                   from "A Beginning," The Sherwood Anderson
                                             Reader, p. 490.

                  *   *   *

I have always been a great reader and consistently used libraries wherever I go, and I daresay have been deeply
   influenced by my reading, but my deepest interest has
   always been in human beings.
            I spend as much time as I can with human be-
   ings, and really think that this is my library.
                   to Leonard Kirkpatrick, Jan. 25, 1934 (JR).

                  *   *   *

You read, read, read.   You live in the world of boredom.
   It is only after a long time that you know that this is
   a special world, fed out of the world of reality, but
   not of the world of reality.
                   to Roy Jansen, April 1935 (JR).

*   *   *   *   *

Chapter 5

FOR HE WAS STUDIOUS

Karl was to recall Sherwood's visit to Springfield "soon after he was mustered out of the Army." "He was very thin, all skin and bones, and I could see that something was troubling him." Sherwood revealed to his brother that he was in doubt about his future, felt he should have a better education. [1]

Two items in the Clyde Enterprise indicate that Anderson's plans did not become definite until quite late. A page three item of September 7, 1899, noted, "Sherwood Anderson, late of Company I, will leave next week for Springfield where he will enter Wurtemburg [sic] college." But in the next issue, September 14, a somewhat changed account was given (page 1). "Sherwood Anderson, late of Company I, left Monday September 11 afternoon for Springfield where he will visit his brother Karl, the artist. Sherwood has not yet decided whether he will attend Wurtemburg [sic] college, Springfield, or at [sic] the Lewis Institute in Chicago."

Karl suggests that Sherwood's inadequate high school preparation caused some concern and that "several Wittenburg professors" helped "prepare him to matriculate."[2] Regardless of what caused the indecision indicated by the newspaper items, Sherwood Anderson was listed as one of the new students in The Wittenberger for September 16, 1899. At 23 Anderson was enrolled in Wittenberg Academy for what was the equivalent of his senior year in high school. Although Anderson had only parts of three years in high school in Clyde, it is likely that the registrar thought his age and experience would give him enough of an advantage to overcome his insufficient scholastic background. Anderson proved himself equal to his studies. The records of Wittenberg College show that Anderson's grades for 1899-1900 were 11 A's and three B's in Latin, German, English, plane geometry, and physics. [4]

92

Anderson evidently was interested in his studies, anxious to take this opportunity to "get ahead." Those who knew him then agree that this was true. The Anderson of that time was "retiring, good-looking, slender" and possessed of "wavy hair," according to a woman who was a freshman in the college while he was in the academy. She remembered him as someone who had come to the school to study. He had gone to Wittenberg because his brother, an artist on the staff of the Woman's Home Companion, was there. [5]

Anderson seemed "very enthusiastic, very energetic" to one classmate[6] and appeared to another as having an "eager mind." The second classmate recalled, too, that his eagerness to get everything possible out of school would cause him to ask questions when the time for dismissal of the class was near. The physics professor, thus encouraged, would go into detail, holding up the annoyed class. Anderson was older than the rest of the class and more determined to learn. [7]

One of Anderson's teachers remembered Anderson "as an attractive young man." "Even at that time he was plainly superior to most of the students of his age. He was in at least one of my classes and I remember him as a very fine student. "[8]

Anderson's effort is seen as still more serious when it is learned that Anderson was working while he was going to school. Karl and Sherwood shared a room in Springfield at a boarding house known as "The Oaks," operated by Mrs. Louise S. Folger, a widow around whom Anderson centered a story he told in the Memoirs (pages 259-262). Mr. Marco Morrow, who met Sherwood at "The Oaks" and became a life-long friend, recalled that he "worked his way through school" by acting as "house man" for Mrs. Folger. [9] His duties involved tending stoves, filling and cleaning kerosene lamps, mowing grass, and running errands. [10] Mrs. Wade recalled that "he worked hard at shoveling snow... for there was a large yard at 'The Oaks'. "[11]

Karl thought that Sherwood's stay at "The Oaks" was influential in his deciding to become a writer. "For the first time he was with people of quickened mentality who extended their interest beyond his mere geniality. "[12] To Morrow, Anderson was later to write: "Many times I think of our talks in the old days. We both wanted to be writers. "[13] Continuing discussions with teachers, publishers, editors, and artists undoubtedly brought response from the boy who had found stimulation in the more enlightened characters in Clyde. Morrow observed that "He immediately became a great favorite in the house and formed friendships which lasted through his life. "[14]

Doubtless the most important of the Wittenberg friends was one of his teachers, Trillena White, for whom he showed concern, writing to her until her death in 1940.   When she was living in Akron, Ohio, in 1919, he asked Hart Crane to "drop her a note and go see her. "[15]   He visited her several times in 1939, when he knew she was dying, wrote to her affectionably, urged Karl to visit her, and commented in this way about her:

> I want to stop in Springfield, where a woman, an old school teacher, is dying with cancer.   She was a great friend of mine when I was little more than a kid and the first person to really introduce me to literature, for which she had a very fine feeling. [16]

With Miss White to walk with him in the evenings talking about books, and Mrs. Folger to "treat him like a favorite son, helping him with his school work and seeing that he felt at home, "[17] the circumstances of his Wittenberg year were good.

They were good enough that he found time and energy for extra-curricular activities.   Items in The Wittenberger show him to have been quite active in the Athenian Literary Society and to have had at least some connection with what was called the Academic Athletic Association.   Two items in The Wittenberger refer simply to "Anderson" with regard to Athenian Literary Society affairs.   Inasmuch as the students who took part in its affairs were all apparently academy students and since there was another literary society apparently for students in the college, it seems likely Sherwood was meant.   If it were he, he was on the losing affirmative side in a debate on "Resolved, That England is Right in Her War with the Transvaal" at the October 4 meeting of the society. [18]   And he was, on the same likelihood, named "critic" for the society at its November 24 meeting, as reported in the next day's The Wittenberger, page 8.

The conjecture about those items is supported by the fact that two or more items which mention him specifically

prove conclusively that Anderson was active in the society.
In December he presented a declamation, "The Defense of
Dreyfus, " and at the March 3 meeting he read an essay,
"The Mormons. " On a Friday afternoon in March Anderson
was elected secretary of the Academic Athletic Association.[19]
Of the activities of the organization or of Anderson's activ-
ities in it no further record has been discovered.

Anderson's last act as a student in the Wittenberg
Academy was to take part with twenty-five classmates in the
Academy Commencement in the Wittenberg Chapel on the
evening of Monday, June 4, 1900. The exercises were
"lengthy, " a newspaper account commented. Anderson followed a violin solo, a prayer, the class history, and seven
other orations to give his own oration, "Zionism. " He was
described as "certainly the orator of the class. His deep
flexible voice and winning manner completely captivated the
audience. The oration was a plea for the Jew, and was a
finely worded, scholarly address. "[20] Even after one has
allowed for the fact that the newspaper did not comment
adversely on any of the eight orations, he must conclude that
the reporter was favorably impressed with Anderson's presentation. Additional evidence that he did well is provided
by Miss Grace Prince, Wittenberg College Librarian, who
remembered that Anderson's commencement oration was
discussed at the time as being "quite unusual for an academy
student. "

With the conclusion of his year at the academy Anderson was ready for college. According to the Wittenberg College catalogue of the day, "Students who complete the pre-
scribed course in the Academy are well prepared to enter
Wittenberg or any other high-grade college or university. ...
Wittenberg Academy exists primarily as the preparatory school
of Wittenberg College. "[21]

Anderson did not go to any of the colleges or univer-
sities he was prepared for; the reasons are not hard to find.
He was considerably older than the average student and had
no money or resources to enable him to continue. Karl was
still educating himself. Stella was probably hoping Sherwood
would come to Chicago to help with the household she had
established there with Irwin. It is only natural that Sherwood should not have hesitated to take his chance to get into
advertising in Chicago.

Before leaving consideration of the Wittenberg Academy

period, one may note two small curiosities.   In both the college catalogue[22] and in the class roster included in the newspaper account of the commencement, Anderson is given the middle name Berton and has his home address given as Chicago.   These are the only two places where Anderson's middle name has been found recorded.   It is simply a provocative "B. " in the army and militia records.   When he entered Wittenberg Academy, he registered as from Clyde.   But before he was graduated, he had let the authorities know he was from Chicago.   The readiest explanation is that by September, 1899, Stella was established in Chicago with Irwin, Ray, and Earl. [23]   This leads to the supposition that Anderson may have been pointing for Chicago throughout the year in Springfield.

That he did this willingly or regretfully may only be speculated.   He did later write, doubtless out of his experience, "I suppose that if you do not have a college education you have to slowly and painfully get another kind. "[24]   And it is a matter of record that he did show an active interest in the college education of his own three children.

Notes

1.   "My Brother, Sherwood Anderson, " p. 7.

2.   Ibid.

3.   He was years later to refer to Springfield as a place where he spent a part of his "late boyhood. "

4.   Miss Grace N. Hannaford, Registrar, Wittenberg College, in a letter of Oct. 16, 1941.

5.   Letter from Mrs. Helen Burk Patton, Phoenix, Arizona; Nov. 27, 1941.

6.   Mr. Waltz S. Salladay, Columbus, Ohio.

7.   Letter from Mrs. Frank R. (Nellie Wilkerson) Wade, Beaver, Pa. ; Oct. 30, 1942.

8.   Letter from Miss Alice M. Mower, Springfield, Ohio; Oct. 23, 1941.

9. In a letter of Oct. 11, 1941, from Topeka, Kansas.

10. James Schevill, Sherwood Anderson, His Life and Work. Denver, Univ. of Denver Press, 1951, p. 28.

11. See note 7.

12. "My Brother, Sherwood Anderson, " p. 7.

13. Letter of Dec. 1927.

14. See note 9.

15. Letter to Hart Crane, Dec. 3, 1919.

16. Letter to Mary Emmett, Jan. 4, 1939.

17. Schevill, p. 29. (See note 10.)

18. The Wittenberger, Nov. 4, 1899, p. 2.

19. The three items were noted in The Wittenberger, Dec. 9, 1899, p. 6; March 3, 1900, p. 2; and March 21, 1900, p. 3.

20. The Springfield Republican-Times, June 5, 1900, p. 5.

21. Fifty-Fourth Annual Catalogue, Wittenberg College, 1899-1900, Springfield Pub. Co. , 1900, p. 38.

22. Ibid. , p. 73.

23. Clyde Enterprise, Sept. 14, 1899, p. 3; also Evans and Stivers, p. 678.

24. Letter to Miss Grace Ream, Jan. 2, 1935.

Mosaic VI

"To push something out a little beyond the horizon..."

Don't know how long I shall stay here--while my money lasts
and until I want people again.   Now I want only the life
of the imagination and the sea and the pine forests.
           to Hart Crane, March 2, 1920.

                    *   *   *

I want to say that in spite of everything life is a grand show.
I don't think we can ever quit.   I know that sometimes
I myself have had to try and be like a small child
learning to walk again.
           to Burton Emmiett, May 8, 1933 (JR).

                    *   *   *

Again I got in love with America.   What a land--O Charlie--
if we can but begin to love it and treat it decently some
day.   It is so violent and huge and gorgeous and rich
and willing to be loved.
           to Charles Bockler, Jan. 20, 1933 (JR).

                    *   *   *

I belong much more to the submerged than you ever can or
will, Paul, and tried in my own way to get back to the
people I feel at bottom are my own.
           to Paul Rosenfeld, July 14, 1933 (JR).

                    *   *   *

I have hurt so many people Charles--trying to keep some integrity.   Do I dare go on existing.   A few tales, told
at last--to push something out a little beyond the hori-
zon--no one caring much.
           to Charles Bockler, 1929 (JR).

In my generation, as you know--(you kids of mine had partly
    to pay for it) I was a rebel.
            Could there be anything more strange than what
    has happened to me.
            I wanted for people, quite frankly, many things
    my generation did not have. I fought for it in my life
    and work.
            Then the war came. The war did more than
    anything I or my kind could have done to make people
    face life.
                    to Robert L. Anderson, 1929 (JR).

                *   *   *

I have always fought and bit and struck my way through,
    keeping after something. I don't know whether it has
    been right or not. How can I know[?] How can I know
    whether or not it has been worthwhile?
                    to Karl Anderson, undated.

                *   *   *

...and through all the lectures I tried to emphasize the idea
    of smallness as opposed to bigness; that is to say, the
    desirability of being just a man going along rather than
    something outstanding and special.
                    from "A Writer's Conception of Realism,"
                    The Sherwood Anderson Reader, p. 341.

                *   *   *

It is absolutely essential to us to get away from self. In
    others life goes on. When I have no more courage it
    may be that the person sitting next to me or walking
    beside me in the street is full of courage. Why
    shouldn't I ask for it, take it when I can get it. There
    is a curious contradiction, comfort and love from
    another, knowing I do not deserve it, I begin a little
    in others and then I get away from myself.
                    to Burton Emmett, May 8, 1933 (JR).

                *   *   *

And you are most terribly and in a quite unforgivable way
    vain. I sense the thing so keenly because it has been

my own struggle.   I have seen so often the worst, the
most childish side of me in you.
                    to M. D. Finley, April 1918.

*   *   *   *   *

Chapter 6

AN AMERICAN ADVERTISING MAN

A life-time friend, Marco Morrow, recalled that the advertising manager of Crowell Publishing Company, who also lived at "The Oaks," hired Anderson for the Chicago office. After a few months, Morrow hired him for work as a copy writer, with solicitation on the side, for the Frank B. White Company. His work was marked by a tendency to do things in his own way, sometimes being too original for advertisers. Though he did not accept the standard precepts of the advertising of that day, he was successful.[1]

Anderson's account of his getting a chance to go to Chicago closely parallels that of Mr. Morrow. "The little money I had saved was all gone. I had been chosen class orator. I delivered a speech on the Jews." The advertising manager heard him deliver his oration, was impressed, and impulsively offered him the job in the Chicago office. But Anderson's new boss in Chicago had been intending to hire another man for the position Anderson got. "I was in an uncomfortable position."

> But a thing happened--it was amusing. I was sent to the office of a certain manufacturer. He advertised in magazines, it seemed, sold by what was called the "agate" line. I knew very little of that.
>
> I was afraid. I went by train to the Ohio town. The man had written saying that he wanted two hundred lines of space in the magazine, and a mistake had been made by his stenographer. He wanted two thousand lines.
>
> I was afraid and did not dare enter the office. I approached and went away....
>
> At last I did get up courage to enter.... I stood

trembling before the man who had dictated the letter. He must have realized my confusion.

He was very kind, very good-natured. He corrected
the stenographic mistake. I did not have to talk.
I had a rate card in my pocket and laid it, with
trembling hand, on his desk.

He wrote the order and I went away. I breathed
again. . . . I sent a wire, not to the company's
Western manager in Chicago, but to the man, his
superior, in the Ohio town. . . who had hired me.

"I have called on my first man, " I said in the
wire. "The order was raised from two hundred
to two thousand lines. " I returned to Chicago.
There was a wire on my new boss's desk. I had
got a sharp raise. [2]

Later in this section attention will be given to articles
Anderson had published during this Chicago period. [3] But for
now the interest will be focused on one sketch which seems
to be another version of the episode just mentioned. [4] The
background of the scene is that Curtis, the head of Curtis-
Crosby, has repelled the efforts of both the Western representative and the publisher of the "Farmer's Blast" to get
him to advertise in their journal. So they send "the boy"
"down there" to let him have a try. "The boy was a new
comer in the advertising field, a bright young fellow, fresh
from school, who was trying to break into the business. It
was a hot summer and things were dull and the boy was discouraged. " His superiors have been sending him after the
"dead ones" in the dull season. He is sent to get a "thousand lines" and told it means a raise for him. He has been
watching the efforts to land Curtis and knows what he is up
against. On the train "as he lay in his berth, looking out
at the fields, he was nervous, so nervous he couldn't sleep,
and the worst part of it was he couldn't see any way out of
it for him. " After much indecision and hesitation, doing
such things as walking up to the office door and then not entering, he makes his attack. He is, to his surprise, ushered
into Mr. Curtis' office without delay.

"I am the boy, " he said. "I am from the Blast.
I am sent down here to try and get that thousand
line order the other fellows couldn't get. I don't
know what I'm going to say to you. I guess there

isn't anything to say, but any way, I would like to
have the order. "

Curtis looked up at him in a surprised manner a
moment, then laughed and said, "You're a modest
boy any way, only asking for a thousand lines.
Why, see here, I've got the order made out for
five thousand lines. Here it is. "

When the boy got back to the office, he started in
to tell Bradley all about it, but Bradley only
laughed and said, "You're altogether too modest,
my boy. " And so he got his salary raised and he
got the name of a good solicitor, which perhaps
he was. At any rate, he is now, and that's all
the story. [5]

Anderson in the later account made himself shrewd,
a strategist. The boy in the earlier account was going to
tell "all about it" when his boss jumped to the wrong but
happy conclusion. This boy then took advantage of the good
fortune which was thrust upon him, but the other character
had maneuvered his own good fortune. The question may be
asked whether one may assume that Anderson had his own
experience in mind when he wrote the earlier episode. The
personal note at the end, "he is now, " makes it seem more
than likely that he did.

Anderson made rapid progress in Chicago. He has
perhaps indicated something of the character of his experience in the following statement:

And so, of a sudden, I am lifted up into a new
world of well-dressed young men. As it turns out
I couldn't sell advertising but I could write advertisements.

I now advance rapidly. I have twenty-five dollars
a week, then thirty-five, forty, fifty, seventy-five.
I buy new clothes, hats, shoes, socks, shirts. I
walk freely on Michigan Boulevard in Chicago, go
to drinking parties, meet bigger and bigger business men.

I create nothing. I boost, boost. Words of glowing praise for this or that product of some factory
flow from under my pen. [6]

It was during this period in Chicago that Anderson began to feel the need for self-expression.

> Before I began to write and when I lived in Chicago, there were certain days when just walking in the streets exhausted me. On such days just a glance at a passing face was like reading the whole life history of some man or woman. It was too much. I couldn't stand it. When I went home and to bed at night, the faces closing before my eyes. "Tell my story. Tell it honestly, " lips were shouting at me. It was a kind of madness. The only remedy I could find was to get drunk. [7]

Cornelia was asked if she knew when Anderson first considered himself a writer. Her reply was as follows:

> I had the feeling that he always did. When I first met him [1903], he had a lot of stories he'd written. Did you ever come across "Girl in the Snow"? [Doubtless an early version of "Death in the Woods. "] I imagine the Agricultural Advertising items were the first published. He had a scrapbook, it seems to me. [8]

He told Morrow one day, before leaving on a trip, that he would decide while he was away whether he would become a millionaire or an artist. He saw that he had to decide whether to throw his energies into self-expression or into making money. He seemed to feel he had a choice between various arts. He chose writing, began producing reams of manuscript in his free time on the road. He put himself through a strenuous training. [9]

Fortunately, there is available a sampling of the writing Anderson produced, for he had material published in the trade organ of the company he worked for, Agricultural Advertising, and in The Reader, a magazine published by the Bobbs-Merrill Co. [10] Of the twenty-seven items in the bibliography for this period, twenty-five were published in the Agricultural Advertising. Most of those items, twenty, appeared in two "columns" Anderson conducted; "Rot and Reason" (1903) and "Business Types" (1904). Each of the columns ran for ten months. Each represents a substantial body of material and deserves separate analysis.

"Rot and Reason" consisted usually of two or three sketches or essays and was often concluded with a series of five to a dozen epigrams. The focus of the material was business enterprise and often more specifically agricultural advertising. However, the articles were quite varied in subject-matter and treatment. As a result, they have been cast into rough categories for the purpose of more orderly analysis.

In the first group are those statements which show what may be called Anderson's "business philosophy," his basic attitude toward the endeavor in which he was involved. One of the most indicative of these is too long for an epigram and yet not an article. It was published as follows without a title:

> There was a moment when the battle of Waterloo wavered in the balance. There were doubtful hours in the hot grain fields of Gettysburg. There are always shaky days in the successful advertising campaign when the quitter quits and the winner prepares for another charge. [11]

In all seriousness, Anderson brought to the task of expressing his attitude toward the advertising campaign his knowledge of the world's major battles. As one reads this and many other statements, it becomes clear that Anderson was deeply interested in his advertising work. The "Rot and Reason" articles give ample evidence that Anderson was constantly turning over in his mind the vital problems of the business, arriving at answers, writing about them.

One of the prominent problems in the mind of any manufacturer, Anderson thought, was how to sell goods. Anderson had a formula for accomplishing that end:

> Trade is obtained, first, by sowing the proper kind of seed; then it must be gathered just like any crop, and it must be properly cared for after it is gathered. A man might have the best article on earth, but it will do him very little good unless it is pushed. Without push behind it, it is no better than an idle wheelbarrow. Put your shoulder to the wheel, infuse some of that whole-souled energy you have sticking in that frame of yours, and you will find inanimate things will fairly fly. [12]

One perceives in Anderson a generally optimistic
spirit.   One senses that Anderson was content in his work,
felt willing and able to tackle anything that might come along.
In this vein he found himself irked by "the determination of
one or two men among every dozen you meet who persist in
believing you have cards up your sleeve. " The suspicious
business man or advertiser Anderson could not approve.   He
asked,

> Would it not be better to believe that all lawyers
> and all politicians were honestly trying to benefit
> their clients than to believe that even one-half of
> them were grafters?   For the same reason, I
> choose to believe that all men in the advertising
> business are really trying to do the square thing
> and help the man whose money they spend.   Strange
> as it may seem, even our competitor may be a
> rather decent sort of fellow. [13]

One must not misconstrue the fact that Anderson was writing
for an advertising trade journal.   Naturally it is probable
that his writings would not have been published in it if he
were anti-advertising, but there can be no doubt that his
statements were sincere.   The statement just quoted is not
characterized by slickness but rather by naiveté.   But in
another statement may be found a more realistic utterance
of the challenge, despair, and reward he then found in his
work:

> In the first waking sickness of it, how many [are]
> the good men who have felt like dropping the whole
> thing and going out to find a healthy, reasonable
> job as end man on a sewer contract.   A most
> hopeful, cheerful beggar he is, the advertising
> man, seeing his hardest licks go smash, his
> cleverest lines muddled and his finest talk inter-
> rupted. ... Day after day, week after week, year
> after year, he faces his own failures and yet be-
> lieves down in the heart of him that he is in the
> greatest business on earth and that next year will
> set all straight and turn all his penny marbles into
> diamonds.
>
> It makes a man glad he is alive and young now and
> it makes him doubly glad that he is in even such
> an unfinishable business as advertising. [14]

Even more emphatic and enthusiastic is the statement he
quoted elsewhere from an unnamed source:

> "... Give me the man who thanks his God when a
> day begins rather than when it closes, who goes
> eager to his office, who gets as much fun and knowl-
> edge out of to-day's failure as from tomorrow's
> success. I want to love my work because it sup-
> plies me with bread and butter, I want to laugh
> and sing and fight and win and lose, and I want to
> get a lot of good fun out of the whole business. "15

The earnestness of the attitude of Anderson toward
his work can not be doubted when one reads "The Laugh of
Scorn, " an essay which points out that the fellow "who is
earnest about his work" will always find "plenty of people
to make fun of his poor efforts. " "The cynical, the weak,
the incompetent and sometimes the brutally strong, are prone
to laugh long and loud at the earnest conscientious fellow. "
However, "if our earnest fellow has a touch of humor in his
makeup and a quiet twinkle in the corner of his eye, he will
weigh that laugh, judge its effect on his ego and go merrily
on his way toward the goal. " Of course, when "brave,
patient, earnest fellows, fighters for the firm and winners
in the game" do come to the fore, "us poor sightless ones
... are glad indeed to proclaim" them. 16 Even though Anderson classes himself among the "poor sightless ones, " it is
apparent he does not really belong there. He was appreciative of the man persevering in an effort to reach his goal,
fighting "for the firm. " Doubtless Anderson was describing
in that passage a standard of action that might well have
been his own. One may mention in this connection "Packingham, "17 which is a sketch of a man who has a chance to
make himself independently wealthy by letting a rival company
buy him out. But his loyalty is more valuable to him than
money.

When it came to the material of which advertisements
are made, Anderson was a classicist. He was against the
"everlasting effort to say something new" when it led to
"strange freaks. "

> ... To get this newness, men will sometimes sacri-
> fice strength and utility and every other quality
> that makes for the one great end of all advertising;
> that is to say, to put money in the till.... Men
> sometimes seem to forget that they are themselves

> the more easily convinced by well written, plain
> excellent stuff that tells the story in an earnest,
> convincing way and then stops.18

The article as a whole makes the point that each advertising
medium demands its own type of advertising and includes the
statement that a considerable exercise of discretion is necessary.   Anderson was apparently accepted as one who had absorbed a philosophy of advertising and was capable of ex-
pounding such matters.   One other point may be noted.   Mr.
Morrow related that Anderson came to recognize he had to
choose between self-expression and making money.   This
article indicates he was avowedly deeply interested in the
art of putting money in the till.

Another interesting essay is "The New Job," which
is a discussion of the man who is eternally changing from
one job to the next.   Changing from one job to another is
just a case usually of thinking the grass is greener on the
other side of the fence, Anderson pointed out.   He wrote
that, after all, a man should expect to have to work in any
job he might hold.   "The business house that doesn't hoe out
the weeds won't raise the big crops and the man with the
red heart of life in him, don't [sic] want to be planted in the
garden of a careless chief."   Anderson's statements reflect
an undaunted conviction that all one had to do to get his salt
was to be worth it:

> To the end of life Brown and Johnson will require
> that every man earn his salary (and rightly) and
> rightly or not, they will both have days when the
> unsertainties [sic] of business and the incompetence
> of employes will make them surly and disagreeable.
> And neither Brown nor Johnson will be surly to
> me if I am too valuable for Brown and Johnson to
> lose. 19

Anderson apparently accepted the system as he found it and
felt himself competent to deal with it on its own terms.   One
can only conclude that he felt himself successful and capable
after two and a half years in the advertising business.

Because Anderson felt that way, because he was able
to define "American advertising men" as "rather decent,
earnest, clever fellows, who make a good living for themselves, and for those they love, and they know how to work,
better than most," he was accepted as one capable of

commenting on various phases of business and advertising. Consequently, there is a group of articles devoted largely to evaluation and criticism.   One may note how he paid his respects in them to the traveling man, the advertiser, the business man, and the farmer.

Anderson was himself a traveling man, [20] but he was of a new era in business and looked with scorn on the notorious "traveling salesman." Anderson's indictment is fired with indignation.   "Common to the verge of imbecility, dressed as only a fool would dress nowadays, and having as his chief stock of trade a fund of vile and indecent stories, he went forth with his soap, his cigars and his ladies' underwear to smear the path of all decent men who must follow him for years to come." One gathers Anderson felt he was one of those bringing the monster to his downfall.

> And it isn't the house and it isn't his fellows who are causing this welcome death.   It's the new business man, the new manufacturer, the new buyer--clean, well read, clever men are not going to buy goods of fellows like our friend above when they can buy of their equals, of men who can be quiet, earnest and decent, even when away from home and with the eyes of high school girls and waitresses upon them.

> The world moves and to the man whose business sends him forth with bags and baggage, the best and most hopeful sign of its moving is the disappearance of "Noisy Johnny." [21]

It is already evident that Anderson thought well of advertising men as he saw them.   Yet he felt it necessary to deplore the fact that advertising

> ... like every other well established proposition, is gradually accumulating a lot of stock expressions and proverbs that are picked up and used by the thoughtless, regardless of their true meaning.   Of course, the better men know well enough that each particular proposition is a problem in itself and must be analyzed and studied before a decision can be given.   Even then the best of men in closing his year's work can look back to many a spot where they have done the things they ought not to have done, and left undone the things they ought to have

done. [22]

Three statements summarize Anderson's attitude toward the business man in this period.   The first hails him
as the heroic type in American life. [23]

> As a man travels about he realizes more and more,
> that the business man is the very front and center
> of things American.   He is the man on horseback
> in our national life.   He knows, and I pray you,
> doubt not, that he dictates the whole works.
>
> ... And what manner of man is he, this American
> business man?   Is he a better, cleaner and braver
> man than the warriors and scholars who have cast
> their big shadows in the past?   You can be sure
> he is.   He may have occasionally a bad dose of
> dollarism, but he takes care of his family; he edu-
> cates his sons, he loves one woman, and he usually
> knows that honesty is a solid wall, and truth is a
> shining light... the place to look for... truly great
> individuals... is among business men.   They prob-
> ably won't play much to the grand stand, nor make
> epigrams before they die, but they'll be there, and
> the negro question, the labor question and other
> things that do ripple the surface of things will be
> settled quietly and firmly in good time by that great
> force--the American business man.

Anderson used a quotation from Henry George as a
foil for his second statement about the virtues of the business
man.   First, Anderson noted that Henry George had said
twenty years earlier that employees could no longer hope to
be employers, to which Anderson replied that the last twenty
years had seen "more men spring from poverty to affluence
than any other like period in the history of the world."   After
showing George to be wrong in that particular, he went on
in this second statement to compare business men and "reformers":

> There is the labor question and the negro question
> and the ever present money question, to be sure,
> and meanwhile the business men of the world go
> quietly ahead by this and that expedient, doing the
> work of the week and the day, while the reformers
> and the preachers and the politicans talk and mix
> new cure-alls for the ailing body politic.   One

good, clean-minded business man, who gets down
to work cheerfully in the morning, who treats the
people about him with kindness and consideration,
who worries not about world politics, but faces the
small ills of his day and the people about him, who
tries to understand the janitor with his cap in his
hand as well as the corporation manager and who
sees the manhood in both, is probably doing more
downright good than all of the canting moralists
that ever breathed.   Just as truly as the petty
greed and selfishness of individuals and not anarchy
and revolution, work the destruction of nations,
just that surely will cheerfulness and industry in
the individual do their part of the work for the
nation's prosperity.   Every man is a unit in the
nation and a unit in the firm.   The firm is smaller, and one dissatisfied grumbler, or one peevish
back-biter will work more harm, but for the same
reason one strong man, one cheerful, ready worker
can do more good, the more reason for cheerfulness, and to get back to Henry George, the less
reason for individuals to believe the dismal proph-
ets of today. [24]

Two aspects of this statement are to be noticed.   It
is evident that Anderson was expressing with approval the
doctrine of what are now known as the "service" clubs.
More important, though, is the fact that his statements were
not cynical or thoughtless.   Apparently, Anderson felt sincerely that the businessman as he knew him and as he wanted
to be himself might be the nation's problem-solver sooner
than the men he looked upon as "canting moralists, " and
"reformers and the preachers and politicians. "   His attack
on George, for example, is at least in view of something
George had said, not just a blind repudiation without any
thought at all.   Finally, Anderson placed a definite responsibility on the business man.   He really expected him to be
able to settle the nation's problems.

The third of the statements embodies this attitude
succinctly: "When America is the biggest and finest country
on earth, the world is going to look to the manners and
hearts of American business men, and the groan or cheer
depends upon what they see there. "[25]

This view of the business man seems to throw light
on the two accounts mentioned earlier of the young

advertising solicitor.   In the later account, published in the
Memoirs, Anderson pictured himself as a shrewd and con-
scienceless operator from the beginning.   In the earlier account, in which one finds a person who might well have been
Anderson, the honest boy gets a break because of the friendliness and generosity of a business man.   Certainly the atmosphere of the first account is more nearly appropriate to
the Anderson of "Rot and Reason" than is that of the Memoirs
story.

        Like the business man, the farmer was celebrated by
Anderson.   But the farmer was not the "white hope" of
America, the problem-solver; he was a source of revenue.
In "The Golden Harvest Farmer" Anderson's characterization
shows his commercial interest:

                He is a dandy, a winner, a free-holder, a man,
                a farmer, and we who make a living trying to sell
                him goods have got to get up and dust, if we are
                going to keep pace with him.

                Is it to be wondered at that the President of the
                Frank B. White Company is thinking day and night
                of how to improve the quality of the work sent out?

                They have much moneys on the farms in these days
                of 1903, but they are taking care of it, and the
                man who sells to them and starts the golden stream
                flowing his way has got to talk turkey straight from
                the shoulder in his advertisements, his letters and
                his literature. [26]

        In another article Anderson contended that it was the
farmer, not Wall Street, who ruled prosperity.   "Shall we
not now turn our eyes to the western wheat and corn fields
and draw at least a part of our public confidence from
them?"[27]   The importance of the farmer was naturally
primarily commercial to agricultural advertisers.   Consequently, it is not a surprise that Anderson should have continued to sound a note first struck in his first published article:

                Some of the big, general advertisers seem to be
                grasping the fact that the agricultural press is
                tucked up close to the hardest reading, best living
                class of people in the world, the American Farm-
                er.   Still, there are, as one of our friends

remarked a year ago at Milwaukee, "acres of dia-
monds that have never been worked."[28]

Another type of article written by Anderson for the
Agricultural Advertising was that which dealt with what might
be called "business information." In these articles Anderson
presents information considered to be valuable or interesting
to advertising men and advertisers. One article, "Twenty
Years in the West," deals with the way the farmer has
transformed the barrenness of the West in two decades. The
significance of the change for manufacturers of agricultural
implements was doubtless Anderson's chief interest in writing the article.

> From your point and our point, this is the best
> possible kind of a country. When a land is brand
> new, man lives simply, with few tools for his
> trade and few luxuries for his living, but as neigh-
> bors thicken about him, his land becomes fenced
> and his energies are bent toward the higher develop-
> ment of his particular plot of ground. The use of
> fertilizers with their accompanying tools and ma-
> chinery comes into his scheme of things. He re-
> quires more complicated tools for the stirring up
> of his soil, [the] better to pulverize it and fight
> out the weeds. The struggles of the middle states
> farmer becomes [sic] his [the western farmer's]
> struggle and he becomes open for the argument of
> the middle states manufacturers of agricultural
> implements.[29]

Two more technical subjects about which Anderson
wrote informatively were unfinished contracts and inquiries.
Apparently the advertising men were plagued by advertisers
who switched unfinished contracts from one agency to another. Consequently, Anderson cited in one article the fact
that the American Advertising Agents' Association had decided that unfinished contracts made by advertising agencies
could not be transferred to other advertising agencies without the consent of the contracting agency and a statement of
the reasons for the change.[30] Another question among advertising men was the advisability of inviting the consumer
to inquire further after reading an advertisement. The
characteristic way of encouraging inquiry was to invite the
reader to send for a catalogue. Some thought this type of
thing just a waste of money. Anderson very strongly asserted the basic importance of getting the reader to make

further inquiry:

> ...The retail man makes custom by getting people
> in to look at his goods, the mail order advertiser
> makes custom by getting his catalogue into the
> homes of readers of farm papers.   "Give me the
> inquiries and I will manage the sales" is the con-
> stant cry of the advertising manager of the coun-
> try. [31]

From what has been said so far about Anderson's articles, it might be concluded that his writings for Agricultural
Advertising were concerned predominantly with making pro-
fits.   It may be shown that this is far from true.   Several
articles of the "Rot and Reason" group show his interest in
the human side of business endeavor.   These may be considered before the fuller explanation of the same thing in the
"Business Types" articles.

Most interesting is Anderson's concern with what he
calls the "lightweight."   He is the "ordinary, hard-working
fellow with good enough intentions, with no great amount of
will power and very little of the philosopher in his makeup."
"A common man like the rest of us, with a fair amount of
ambition, a sprinkling of good, a shower of vanity, and the
need of a job for his inheritance."   It was this man, almost
any man, Anderson had in mind when he wrote, "The intense
strain of America's pellmell business life is breaking down
the weak men and is, no doubt, the direct cause of many a
good man's downfall."   These words may well have echoed
in Anderson's mind a few years later in Elyria.   But Anderson certainly did not have himself in mind when he described
how this "lightweight" needed a hand when he got depressed
over how others were forging ahead of him.   As one of the
successful ones Anderson was certainly taking the humani-
tarian view in the following combined comment and exhorta-
tion:

> The gleam of light, the saving fact is that there
> be men, quick, hard, strenuous fellows, who don't
> take much stock in the "survival of the fittest"
> proposition and who are in business to better it
> rather then pound a fortune out of it.
>
> Business wants more such spirits, wants more
> newspaper editors, more editors, more workers
> who can shut their eyes to the main chance

occasionally and work for the game itself. Let's
stick to the strenuosity, let's stick to the pound
and the grind and the general hurrah for things,
but let's take a look at the heads we hit and stop
occasionally to engender a little ginger and hope into
the limber-legged fellow beside us, "the lightweight."

We'll balance up all right in the end. We'll do our
share toward making this the biggest and brightest
spot on the whole black earth, and we'll now and
then make a winner out of a possible suicide. It's
all a question of knowing and teaching, for the
average businessman isn't given to hitting his fellows in the face. But you know and I know that
some of the cruelest moves in the day's work are
made by cheerful enough fellows who go whistling
through the market place, totally unconscious of
the wrong they have done. [32]

It is clear that Anderson was analyzing the implications of the power and efficiency of the business-man ideal
he accepted. While he applauded the victorious and effective
man, he was capable of conceiving a deep concern over the
man who was losing out. Anderson sensed the eternal problem of the defeated that goes with every victory. He did
not think the victor entitled to ignore the vanquished. He
reiterated his concern in the following plea:

Let's reconsider Johnson and this smashing business. Not but what we ought to ride hard and
whoop things up--that's what's making winners of
us--but when we're back there in the dark and the
crowd is listening to the band and the judges can't
see, and there isn't a soul looking, let's just
smash Johnson over the rump instead of the nose. [33]

Another very important personal problem to which
Anderson had given thought was that of a person's "finding
his work." Anderson came to some significant conclusions.
"I think it true in the great majority of cases, it isn't so
much a question of finding your work as it is of finding yourself, your faith, your courage." "Your really successful
man...does...things well because he believes the work at
hand is his work and believing gives it his love and throws
about it all of that glamour that comes to any place where a
strong man works...." These considerations were to be of

basic importance in the not-too-distant future, when Anderson
was to have grave doubts about his work, when he was to
undertake what constituted a work-revolution.   Even at this
time of writing Anderson was a little vague in his confidence:

> We are all chasing shadows no doubt, shadows of
> love, shadows of art, shadows of death, but there
> is no need chasing the shadow of my work. ...
>
> Let's save our pining and our moaning for our love
> affairs and be brave and cheerful about the work.
> It takes so much time out of our lives, and then
> perhaps if we are brave and clean and true, our
> work will appear there in the midst of the work
> at hand. [34]

When one contrasts the doubtful conclusions here with
the positive affirmation of the great role of the business men
in American life, one begins to see the first dangerous fis-
sures opening in the road of Anderson's life.

Every one who is familiar at all with the works of
Anderson is also familiar with his frequent voyages back into
the realm of his boyhood and youth.   In the Agricultural Advertising articles there is one unmistakable example of his
having already formed that habit:

> There was an old fellow that hoed corn.   He was
> grim, grey and silent, but because he pleased my
> boyish heart I was glad to hoe beside him for the
> dignity of his presence.   One hot day when we had
> hoed to the end of a particularly long and weedy
> row and were resting in the shade by the fence he
> put his big hand on my shoulder and said, "Don't
> the corn make you ashamed, Sherwood, it's so
> straight?"[35]

Another article in a category by itself shows perfectly
the incongruous blending of the observant and sensitive man
seeking to express himself and the advertising man earning
a living:

> You can imagine a fellow who spends his days in
> the offices and his nights in all sorts of hotels
> looking forward with no little pleasure to a day
> on a country road among the farmers who buy the
> things he helps to advertise.   When that fellow is

fortunate enough to have for companion a man who
understands the country and is full of love of it
and when these two start off at sunrise down a
road that follows the winding course of the Mississippi and have no more to carry than a stout stick
for the chance of knocking down nuts from the trees
along the road; when all these things work out in
this manner, I say, ... a fellow is rather bound to
have a good day ahead of him.   If you want to take
part in a conversation that reaches every kind of
business and life and is in a pleasant and happy
vein withal, try this sort of walking on this sort
of a day with this sort of man.   The road leads
up hill and down, past farm houses and about sharp
turns, over bridges and through marshes and along
the road are many old companions of the catalogue
and farm papers.   Here is a wind mill and there
a wire fence, here a cultivator and there a plow
and up the road rolls the Studebaker wagon in use
by the family going to church, and over all the
quiet of Sunday and Indian summer. [36]

Anderson was in the habit of punching out epigrammatic material which was used to fill up remaining space in
his "Rot and Reason" columns.   Sometimes he would string
a series of items together under a single heading.   For
example, under "Of No Value" he included a series of items,
including "A system in the hands of an unsystematic man"
and "A wife who inspires you to no better work"; and under
"Chicago Inspirations" he mentioned "The morning sun shining on the Field Columbian Museum" with "The view on
Upper State Street at night" and "The new offices of Agricultural Advertising, in the Powers building. "[37]   Under "Men
That Are Wanted" were listed "Men that sleep and eat and
live with the desire to get on in the world tingling through
their whole beings"; "Men that are just a little dissatisfied
with the old, slow, plodding ways"; "Men that can and will
work; work for themselves and others"; and "Men that feel
as though they would like to take hold of the rudder and run
a business for themselves. "[38]   It seems a slight misusage
to describe the items just mentioned as "epigrammatic, "
but Anderson did use the true epigram.   A sampling of those
appearing with "Rot and Reason" (in Agricultural Advertising,
Feb. 1903, p. 16) follows: "The man who fails has all the
fun ahead"; "No man ever finished his work.   He does well
if he finishes his hopings"; and "We are no better advertising
men than we are good citizens"; and (in Aug. 1903, p. 25):

"The fact that financial advertising isn't always crooked is
often put forth as an argument in its favor"; and "The man
who makes a good article and advertises it honestly is helping the progress of the world"; and (in March 1903, p. 20):
"A man's saying that he believes in the world does not necessarily mean he is a credulous fool"; "The successful man is
not wrecked in the wreck.   The unsuccessful man is wrecked
by success"; and "The Spaniard who originated the phrase
'Yankee pig' must have traveled in the spit-besmeared smoking car of one of our passenger trains"; and (in March 1903,
p. 19): "I wish I had a friend honest enough to tell me when
my stuff was 'rotten'. "   "I said this to a Philistine and he
told me it was all 'rotten'"; and finally: "The fear of being
called a knocker keeps many an advertising man from trying
to right known wrongs"; and "When some men shake hands
with you, you feel like asking them to hand it back. "[39]

    In those statements the reader has a kaleidoscopic
view of many facets of Anderson's mind.   The implications
of them are in most cases obvious; one need say only that
they reflect quite strongly earnestness and idealism, definite
standards of business and personal character, a tendency to
reform, and a ready wit.

    Mention should be made of four other articles appear-
ing in the Agricultural Advertising in the period under discussion but not in either series, "Rot and Reason" or "Business Types. "   The first of these other articles, which appeared the month before the first "Rot and Reason" column,
may have been a predecessor as a column, for it had the
major heading "We Would Be Wise" and a sub-heading
"Talking It Out. "   The subject of the article is the value to
the individual of talking "about our schemes and hopes when
we talk together. "   Apparently between January and February
Anderson decided he liked "Rot and Reason" better than "We
Would Be Wise" as a name for his department in the magazine and made the change accordingly.   "Talking It Out" was
done as if addressed to the persons an advertising solicitor
might have to interview; its attempt is to promote more
friendly conversation:

        Let's tell each other about our schemes and our
        hopes when we talk together.   You may get one
        practical suggestion from the solicitor who comes
        in and takes two hours, but if you have talked
        heartily and wholesomely to him of your work, and
        have not wasted time with beating about the bush,

> you will find you have done yourself no end of good
> and strengthened your convictions and your courage
> by the very force of your statements.... How are
> we to grow in power and ability if we are not oc-
> casionally well roasted in the flames of ridicule?
> Let the mistake be a healthy one from a healthy
> mind and the laugh will be just as healthy, and will
> no doubt help us and prevent us taking ourselves
> too seriously. [40]

And after the "Business Types" series ended, Anderson had two articles in Agricultural Advertising during 1905.
The first of these, "The Sales Master," gives a most important insight into Anderson's attitude toward his occupation.
As will be seen, the article is a plan of reform, the articulation of an ideal, a ringing assertation of the true place
of the honest advertising man in the realm of business.   One
who reads the article must feel certain that Anderson was
fully at grips with a job he thought was worth doing.

> The ability to write good copy and buy space at low
> prices, which are and have been the chief claims
> to consideration of many a high priced agency man,
> are all right and very necessary.   But with the
> growth of organizations and organization men there
> has come a demand for sound, practical business
> advice, from the man who handles advertising.
>
> There is a growing demand for the advertising man
> of a quick sympathy and appreciation of the ends
> sought by the sales manager; men who, because of
> their wide acquaintanceship and their study of many
> problems, are able to keep the inside man alive to
> the other side of the story, and who help him to
> see the effects of his work upon the public.
>
> Some years ago a number of young advertising men
> got together and talked these things over.   They
> believed they could see in these conditions the
> possibilities of a great and needed profession, a
> profession that is day by day and year by year be-
> ing more fully developed.   These are the conditions
> that lay before the far-seeing eyes of these men,
> and pointed out to them the road they were trying
> to follow.
>
> There are, in this country, many firms, that

because of their size and limited capital, cannot
afford a high-priced organization man to handle
and develop new ideas for exploiting their goods,
therefore the question arose, "Why should there
not come from the ranks of American Advertising
Men a class of business physicians who can walk
into an office and lay their hands upon diseased
spots in the selling system?" The requirements
for such a position in the business world are many.

Such a man as the business physician, the article goes on
to say, would need to be "unapproachable behind his fortifi-
cation of business honor," and "clean and with soul untainted
by the lust of money," a "proud lover of his profession,"
and a "quick and sure judge of human nature."

You see, it is a sort of compromise between the
corporation lawyer and the advertising man that has
been built up. Let us call him the Sales Master....
Certainly the conception is a noble one, and offers
a working point worthy [of] the effort of every sincere advertising man....

Let me close my argument by predicting again that
the sales master will get into his rightful place,
and that when he does it will be the great much-
needed healthy note in the advertising agency business. The advertising agency would then become
really the agent of the advertiser and the agency
business would go on in its growth until agency
men are what we have called them in this article,
sales masters, and the absurd plan of paying such
a man a commission on his expenditure will be replaced by a system of compensation rated according to the service rendered. [41]

The next month Anderson commented on the advertising
ability of Theodore Roosevelt, then president. Rallying to
his defense against those who thought he did things with too
much fanfare, Anderson continued to be the enthusiastic advertising man:

We believe that the dignity of the office this man
fills is not injured by his appreciation of publicity.
The man who cannot think of the word "Omaha"
without a smile will probably chuckle over our own
joy at this thought of the advertising ability of the

President; but in our conception of the word, good
advertising carries with it good goods, good intentions, making good; and if the present trip of
the President or any of his impulsive actions of
the past may be classed as advertising campaigns,
he has at least carried with him the goods.... [42]

So far all the articles discussed have been those
signed with Anderson's name.   One may wonder whether
some of the unsigned articles in Agricultural Advertising may
not have been written by him.   One article in particular supports this belief.   It is entitled "Letter of an Advertising
Solicitor to His Wife at Home" and is apparently an imaginery
letter from an advertising man who has just lost out in a
deal.   The man expresses to his wife his disappointment and
his determination to show that he has learned a lot from his
experience.   The signature at the end of the imaginery letter
is that of "Bert Sherwood." When one recalls that Anderson's first two names were Sherwood Berton, the signature
seems to be a clear clue to the author.   Anderson was not
married when the article was written but he was an advertising solicitor.

Of the articles published in Agricultural Advertising
there remain eleven to be discussed.   Ten of these were in
the "Business Types" series, and the other one, "The Fussy
Man and The Trimmer," is classed with them because of its
similar nature and chronological contiguity to the series.
These articles are sketches of typical characters Anderson
observed in the course of his activities in the advertising
business.   He was studying carefully the people who were
about him constantly.   These articles represent the first
published fruits of his study of his fellow men, a study which
was to become an increasingly absorbing factor in his life.
They are for the most part not distinguished in character
and bear universally the coloring of experience in the advertising agency, but they all show something of life as Anderson saw it, some of them being of decided importance for
that reason.

"The Solicitor" has been discussed earlier and will
not be recapitulated here.   "The Traveling Man" is a further
vibration of a note struck in the article of the same name
appearing earlier in the "Rot and Reason" series.   In this
later sketch, though, attention is given to the description of
the "loose, big, hearty, tired fellow, who loves his wife and
babies madly and is not always true to them," rather than

to the vulgar "Noisy Johnny" mentioned in the earlier article.
In fact, "About the best thing that can be said here about the
old dyed-in-the-wool, six-months-twice-a-year traveling man,
commonly called 'one of the boys', is that he is passing...."
The new traveling man, Anderson pointed out, was the "average man who has answered the wander call in his breast."
Anderson recalled in this connection the travel dreams of a
country boy who stood in the corn and watched with fascina-
tion as trains roared by. He remembered, too, the boy who
was going away with a shoe-blacking outfit to make his fortune in Cairo, Illinois. 43   The recollection of a boyhood
notion of going to Cairo as a shoeblack was still in Anderson's mind when he wrote the Memoirs (page 65).

Humor is the keynote of "The Discouraged Man," which
is also distinguished by a surprise ending.   Most of the
sketch is devoted to the boasting of a salesman who tells how
a deal he has just completed is going to revolutionize the
sleepy little town in which he finds himself.   He gives the
storekeeper a glowing account of what is to happen as the
result of his negotiations.   At the end the reader learns the
salesman in reality failed to make his deal and his fanciful
talk with the storekeeper had been compensation for his
failure. 44

Plot is very important to "The Liar--A Vacation
Story." Five men on a walking tour in the country are disturbed to find that the sixth member of the party is a know-
it-all and a colossal liar.   The five plot to embarrass the
boor into silence.   A manufacturer of bicycles contrives to
get him to expatiate on that subject.   The "liar" delivers a
dissertation on the subject of bicycles at great length and
never makes a slip.   The five walk off beaten, while the
"liar" has a "satisfied grin upon his lips."45   Everything
hinges on the fact that the man just happened to know about
bicycles.   In writing the story Anderson employed a good
deal of his own specialized knowledge of bicycle manufacture,
knowledge he had gained in the factory in Clyde.   One almost suspects the rest of the story is an excuse to bring in
his knowledge of bicycle manufacture, for it is perhaps the
least successful of his attempts at character portrayal.

Very directly connected with advertising are "The Hot
Young 'Un and the Cold Old 'Un" and "The Undeveloped Man."
The latter presents this scene: "The advertising man sat
upon his upturned grip at a railroad junction.   It was midnight, a drizzle of rain was in the air and close about him

lay the unbroken blackness of a cloudy night. " He hears the
fluent, prolonged, and effective swearing of a brakeman and
is moved to discuss the brakeman's expression with a by-
stander. He concludes the brakeman is an undeveloped advertising man, for he knows the value of words. [46] The first
sketch deals with an old man and a young man who are being
tried out for the job of representative of Bunker's big monthly.
It is arranged to have the men face each other in a meeting
and present their claims to the position. The young man
speaks first, is exceedingly energetic; his behavior and attitude are marked by the utmost conviction in his ability to do
a remarkable job. He impresses the old man so much that
he does not present a plea for himself but instead advises
Bunker to take the younger man. The employer hires neither
man, for both lack balance. Anderson combined a surprise
ending with a moral. The story is most notable for two interesting characters it contains, a barber and a tobacconist,
who are asked to attend the meeting to impress the candi-
dates. These minor characters must have caught Anderson's
imagination, for they are treated with humor and interest;
they live. [47]

    In discussing "Silent Men" Anderson harked back to
Carlyle's admiration for the "Quiet man of work who with
strong hands knew what to do and when to do it. " And then
he commented:

> After all, there are a lot of really good reasons
> for the advertising manager keeping silent on most
> occasions and one who does this well and has in
> him a sense of humor must see sights and hear
> sounds, as a succession of good and bad solicitors
> plow past, to make food for much laughter. Blus-
> tering, pleading, whining, smiling, all are grist
> that come to his mill; and in the quiet evening,
> when men walk home from their day's work, if
> such a one cannot name over any wise or clever
> thing he has said during the working hours, he can
> at least chuckle cannily at the memory of the fool
> things he has left unsaid. [48]

    One gathers from that statement that Anderson was of
a mind to be observant of others and cautious of his own
utterances. The ideas Anderson expressed in "The Fussy
Man and The Trimmer" were closely allied to those in
"Silent Men. " The Fussy Man is one who is everlastingly
busy and produces very little real accomplishment. The

Trimmer trims out all foolishness, works quietly and according to plan, and gets things done. The Trimmer is busy
with his brains instead of his hands. As Anderson sarcasti-
cally pointed out:

> The thing is so unusual that such an excuse [that
> one was thinking and therefore not physically ac-
> tive] offered to the average business man would be
> treated as an absurdity. The Fussy Man may be
> uncomfortable to live with, but he won't get the
> reputation of being queer and indifferent and won't
> be talked about in the newspapers and magazines. [49]

Anderson had nothing but praise for "The Good Fellow," who is "interested in you and your lot. He has a few
helpful suggestions to smooth the road for you. He wants
to make you as happy, as good natured and as useful as himself, and he usually succeeds."

> Off with your hat then to this genial soul, he of
> the smile and the words of cheer, and may the ad-
> vertising game yearly find in its ranks more of
> this good breed who are called good fellows, and
> are in reality only true-born gentlemen after all.

A personal reminiscence may lie behind the encounter of the
"Good Fellow" and "Young Yeager," "quick, earnest and not
afraid of work," who is an advertising solicitor and whose
impersonal boss gives him the most difficult accounts to
solicit. The "Good Fellow" makes "Young Yeager" "feel
like a man again" by talking to him in a kindly way. [50]

The two most significant of the "Business Types"
items have been saved until last. When he wrote "The Boyish Man," it seems obvious Anderson was picturing a type
of man that was very important and pleasant to him.

> Oh, but it is good to write of this man; and it is
> good for you, Mr. Reader, to stop in your day's
> work and think of him--the boyish man; the living
> man; the fellow with something refreshing about
> him; the fellow who, in the midst of life, when
> adversity calls hungry, old shadows up before him,
> keeps in his heart a bit of his boyhood and on his
> lips a laugh at the grimness of the old world.

Anderson was always to keep in his heart a "bit of

his boyhood" and was to write much of the "grimness of the
old world." The piece "The Boyish Man" contains the incident of a city man who trembled at the sight of an injured
man. His hands trembled; his lips moved. When the man
was asked why he reacted so to an ordinary accident, he
replied, "I'm not thinking of that man at all. Say! When
you were a little boy did you ever pretend you were two people? Well, I used to do that, and I've never got over the
habit. Just now I'm that fellow's wife."[51] Certainly this
man, whoever he was and whether or not he ever existed at
all, was a forerunner of the Anderson-to-be, the story-
writer, the man who found a whole new realm of the imagination to inhabit.

This man of the imagination and a very youthful one
who had unbelieved experiences in Africa, Anderson wrote,
were of the type he was trying to write about:

> ...the men who laugh; the men who see life painted
> in the colors of boyhood. We have a lot of them
> in the advertising business? [sic] I think it's the
> kind of men that keep the game alive. The adver-
> tising business calls for unbounded hope, and it's
> only the boy among men who keeps hope ever in
> his heart. For when a man turns forty and there
> are a lot of raw places where his harness doesn't
> fit just right, it takes courage, boyishness and al-
> most heroism to laugh and be a boy; but it's
> worth while--at least, for the rest of us.[52]

Apparently, Anderson was not thinking of himself as one
whose harness was rubbing when he wrote. But the words
seem prophetic when one thinks about the Anderson who left
Elyria less than a decade later. During this period in Chicago Anderson's life was very satisfactory, one can assume.
He had a job in which he obviously was greatly interested
and which paid well. He had been married only a few
months before. But his own comfortable position did not
allow him to become unaware of the life going on about him.
He was observing carefully, absorbing the phenomena of life
about him, feeling deep appreciation, scrutinizing formulas.

One of the formulas he examined was that of the
country boy who went to the city and became rich and powerful. This may have had particular interest for Anderson,
because he had followed it himself in modified fashion.

"The Man of Affairs" is a consideration of the career of
Peter Macveagh, a boy from the Indiana country.   On the
farm "under his rough clothes he was clean, right down
through to his heart....   He was like the fields and the
woods, sort of kept clean by God and the seasons." Then
he went to Chicago and went to work in a downtown coal office, "because he wanted to mix with men, and stretch his
mental muscles."

Peter, the healthy, active country boy, compared his
attitudes with those of the people about him in the city.

> Slowly...the conviction began to creep in on him
> that in this world there are many people who are
> stupid and incompetent, and many more that are
> unclean pretenders.   He wondered the more about
> this because of the miracles in the life about him
> and the great forces that seemed to be always at
> work, moving the life of the city forward...some-
> times...he would pause and take in a quick breath
> at the wonder of it....   Everywhere was work get-
> ting itself done.   Somewhere back of it all was
> another kind of man; his kind; clean, stout of
> heart, clear of mind, square and vigorous.

The minister at home wrote in answer to Peter's
questioning, "The men who made and are making Chicago,
were just the sort of boy you are, Peter, and after a time
when you deserve to know these men, you will."

> So Peter kept on at his work, and he grew; and he
> went forward; and he made money; and by wisely
> investing it, became rich and in time was a very
> powerful man; but he was not the sort of man the
> Indiana minister intended; and, for that matter,
> he was not the sort of man that young Peter had
> dreamed of when he was a solicitor for a coal of-
> fice and walked the streets of Chicago.   It was
> of little use to tell the story of Peter Macveagh
> and his affairs and end it here.   To do so is only
> to repeat what has been said by dozens of men,
> and well said.   Articles have been written, and
> are being written every month, on the careers of
> such men as Peter.   Their shrewdness, boldness
> and success have been bruited forth until our ears
> are filled with the din of it.   But all of them go
> just as far with their man as I have done with

Peter Macveagh, and then they drop him.   He is
clean, he is frugal, his morals are right, he has
made money and, having made money, has suc-
ceeded; is about the tone usually assumed by the
scribe who tackles the problem.

To us Americans this much seems to be taken for
granted and the thought that Peter Macveagh
(strong, rich, and powerful), may be a failure,
never seem [sic] to occur to us.   We never dream
of the possibility of his old friend and well-wisher
(the family minister down in Indiana) having another sort of man in mind when he wrote to Peter
Macveagh.   We lose sight of the fact that in buck-
ling down to his work and building factories... and
forming trusts, Peter was doing about the simplest
task for men like Peter.   Here was a fellow of
unusual vigor, and moral cleanliness, cast down
among the ruck of folk who don't bathe more than
once a week and are not thoroughly awake once in
a year.   How could he help getting rich?   Or, for
that matter, getting about anything else he might
chance to want?

America is the sort of country that breeds strong
men.   It is rich with wonderful opportunities--
opportunities that we, who walk in our sleep, don't
see; and yet, in spite of the fact that it is a
country for strong men, a really powerful man
only appears in about the proportion of one to one
hundred thousand of us common folks; and it is
not to the glory of us who look up to such men,
and who, by our praises, influence them in their
desires that these men bend all of their powerful
energies to the acquisition of a few millions of
dollars.   In extenuation of such men and their
lives it is common for us to say that the strong
men don't care for the money; that it is the power
they seek; but, for my part, I am not able to see
the distinction.   The result to the man is exactly
the same.   Peter, grown in power, is not the
Peter of old days; no more the good books nor the
letters to his friend, the minister.   He has learned
the weaknesses of humanity now and is busy playing upon these weaknesses, and the blood that
hurries through his brain draws warmth from his
once big heart.   Because he despises and sees

the weaknesses of all men, all men hate and fear
him, and he goes on his way, envied by no man
except it be Green, the assistant bookkeeper, or
the dentist on Madison street.   Peter Macveagh is
a product of the time and the opportunities.   His
lust for power is satisfied because most of us are
asleep.   Mere living is so simple a matter for a
man of average energy and intelligence that Peter,
with no more effort comparatively, becomes rich
and works his own ruin, for if we pay for our
stupidity and drowsiness, Peter also pays for his
title, Man of Affairs. 53

Anderson's position is clear.   The accumulation of
wealth and power is not a particularly admirable achievement
when one considers the limitations of the average human.
Furthermore, the man who focuses his life on possessing
money and power loses his own sympathy for, and the sympathy of, humanity.   These are all-important considerations.
The true significance of this attitude may be more fully
realized when the turmoil of the Elyria period is considered.

Perhaps it would be well to summarize briefly the
view one gets of Anderson from what he wrote for Agricultural Advertising.   He was an earnest, interested proponent
of the advertising business and wanted sincerely to raise its
standards and increase its usefulness.   He seems to have
been alert, contemplative, and observant of himself and his
fellow men.   His thinking about his own life and work was
not superficial and caused him to examine fruitfully the lives
of others.   Welling up within him were many plans and ideas
which he was eager to get expressed.   As a result of his
observations and analysis, he became possessed of a very
definite set of ethical standards.   Though possessed of a
satisfactory vocation and a comfortable position in society,
he was eagerly reading and writing about the nature and
problems of mankind as he realized them.

So far consideration has been given only to the material published in Agricultural Advertising.   Attention may now
be turned to the two articles published in The Reader, a
literary publication, in 1903.   Both of these essays deal with
reading and present an interesting insight into the nature of
that part of Anderson's development at that time.   One might
guess from his other writings that he was reading a good
deal.   But these articles are in direct reaction to his reading, written out of a reading response satisfied only by

published utterance.

The first of the essays, "A Business Man's Reading,"
is a message to business men about their reading. It appeals
to "bright, quick-minded fellows," worthy opponents for any
man "in a clash of wordy wits or a plunge into philosophy
on a country road." These men, the article recognizes,
have a store of logic and truth, but they say they are not
readers; they acquire their knowledge "in the great human
grind of the work." But these are some questions Anderson
wants to ask of these bright men who do not read:

> To what purpose do you come to my room with
> your pipe when the lights are lit? You don't love
> me, surely, and I have no wife. Then, I conclude,
> because you storm up and down and look into my
> eyes and dig neck-breaking holes for me in the
> wilderness of argument, that you are here to whet
> your wit, to knock me down and out with a storm
> of your best and strongest thoughts. And you had
> thought you could not fight with Stevenson nor take
> issue with Socrates? That Shakespeare spoke only
> the truth and Johnson was invincible? Where all
> that bravado with which you strutted away after
> your conquest of me? Where all that fire and
> logic? Here are the fellows to shade you. Why
> not rush at Carlyle's conclusions as you did at
> mine? Lay a trap for Browning's unshaken faith.
> Say for me the things that Shakespeare neglected.
> Leave me at peace with my pipe and my book.
> The bookshelf is there. [54]

Two comments on Sherwood's reading by Cornelia may
be interpolated here. She called him an "inveterate reader"
of "particular taste." "When I first knew him, he was reading Stevenson. Stevenson was his god. He bought every
book. Then he went to Carlyle and read every word of
Carlyle." Stevenson was read for his "humor and exquisite
writing" and Carlyle for philosophy. In a note giving further
comment on those remarks, she elaborated:

> We read him [Stevenson] with true appreciation of
> his gallant spirit, his whimsies, and his good
> tales.... Perhaps your generation can't even read
> Stevenson, but we did and profited by it.... The
> fact that Mr. Anderson turned from Stevenson to
> Carlyle, Hazlitt, and Tolstoi, Dostoievsky, Borrow,

etc. shows there was no immaturity there. 55

　　Anderson recognizes that reading done by women's clubs just for the sake of quoting appropriately is silly, and he agrees that the reading for school orations avails little. But he maintains that the average author is wiser than the average man and that even business men can learn from the writers.

> Go to them on the shelf there. . . . If they convince you against your own judgement you had better look to your next deal in corn, or your late shipment to Argentine [sic]. You were not so invincible then, were you? If you find there your own truths much better expressed, ah, much better, than you or I can ever express them, read them, spend more time there and less time keeping me from my work. You will be a better man in the market place, and we shall smoke our pipe in peace. 56

　　Despite the slightly jocular tone of the statement, it seems clear that Anderson was speaking out of his own habit and conviction. If one may assume he followed his own advice, he read much and very thoughtfully, perhaps combatively. One can imagine Anderson examining very carefully each new proposition presented by each author he read, using the wisdom each might have to increase the clarity of his own vision of life. Apparently he felt so much benefit from his own reading that he was moved to try to convince non-readers of what they were missing. It may be noticed, too, that his allusions indicate a familiarity with the classical authors as well as the more recent Stevenson and Browning. One senses he had ranged wide in his reading.

　　The other essay, "The Man and the Book," is a further delineation of the value of reading, this time for "The man in the street, --he who knows the unravelled tale in the sound of music from lighted houses at night, from lovers walking arm and arm in the park, and from wan, tired faces in the drift of the sidewalks. . . . " This is the realistic man who does not read "only for the charm of the unravelled tale" and is not interested in the popular romantic tales "most likely to run into the hundred thousands. " This reader is

> . . . the man, in short, who, having much work to do in a short time, has learned the value of the

> hours given to reading and how to apply the good
> gleaned to the militant game of life as he plays
> it, --this man, believing that the salvation of his
> soul can be worked out in the shoe business or the
> meat business or the hardware business, is apt to
> demand the kind of reading that will make him a
> better man in his work, and often falls into a habit
> of depending upon a few close friends among books.

Anderson appears here as the interpreter of the practical man who draws from his reading sustenance needed in
a "militant life." He tells of the sugar salesman who carries the "lordly Macaulay" with him and often finds strength
in him. Anderson comments on Macaulay's "store of rich
meaty sentences" and "sentences that came back and said
themselves over in his mind in the night time." He tells of
the commercial artist who becomes a reader, finds his heart
"caught and held," and becomes an artist "full of earnest
love of his work." Another example is a "hot, strong-
headed, silent man, from a family whose men had for generations burned the oil of life at a fierce blaze and gone to
their graves loved of women and with the names of bad men
on them." This man found help in his fight to live a "quiet,
sober, and useful life" in spite of his heredity.

> ...he told me of the fight he had fought and how
> the battle went with him.... He had made a game
> fight, that is all we need to know, and when the
> lust of his fathers was strong on him and he was
> near to the sin he fought against, he would go into
> his room alone, and over and over repeat King
> Henry's cry to the English at Harfleur. Once more
> into the breach, dear friends! He told me that at
> such times he forgot even the meaning of the words
> on his lips, but that the rolling music of them
> soothed him and at last made him sleep unbeaten....
>
> It is no difficult thing to find these instances of
> the way in which men call upon their friends among
> books in their hour of need. 57

Americans, Anderson concludes, may sometimes give their
lives to making money, but "there is much of the music of
words in them."

All the reading and writing Anderson had been doing
doubtless played an important part in an episode which

occurred early in 1905.   Cyrus Curtis, who had seen Anderson's work in Agricultural Advertising, stopped in to see
Anderson at the office of the advertising agency but missed
him.   Ten days later Anderson got an invitation to submit a
story with a business background to Saturday Evening Post.
Because the story he wrote did not "glorify" business, it was
not acceptable.   Interest in his work was high enough, however, for the editor to invite him to the magazine's office in
Philadelphia for a conference on their efforts to get business
men to read the Post. 58   But, according to Mr. Morrow,
Anderson would not change his stories.   One can easily believe that to be true, for the articles just discussed certainly
indicate Anderson believed in a man's integrity.   As a serious reader he must have felt strongly that really important
writings come from a man's heart and soul and can not be
written to some one else's pattern.   Furthermore, Anderson
did not need the money; he had a good job.   One should not,
however, ignore Anderson's own statement in the Memoirs
about the matter.   "Just why I did not accept I did not at
that time know.   The Curtis Publishing Company was so big.
It may have terrified me."59   Anderson wrote in the Memoirs
that the Saturday Evening Post offered him a position as an
"editorial writer," which is at variance with Mr. Morrow's
understanding of the matter.   There is no doubt, though, that
Anderson's writing had brought him to the attention of one of
the nation's most powerful magazine publishers.   Unless he
was a complete impostor in his writings, it seems likely
that it was more than just the size of the company that
caused him to decide not to accept what must have been an
attractive offer.

        Even if Anderson were not averse to becoming a hack,
albeit one who would be noted and highly paid, he had to
consider the fact that his position with Long-Critchfield60
was interesting and satisfactory to him.   The Agricultural
Advertising articles indicate that.   He was interested in reform, it is true.   But his attitude was that of making better
something already good.   Concrete evidence of his standing
in the company may be found in an account of a banquet for
Long-Critchfield department heads and assistants held at the
Palmer House on the evening of May 1, 1905.   Anderson,
one of four representatives of the copy and promotion department, was one of twelve speakers chosen from the 36 guests.
His topic was "Making Good," which may be a clue to what
his superiors thought of him. 61

        It has been seen that in the years in Chicago now

under discussion Anderson established himself in the advertising business and started writing.   There remains one important phase of his activities to be discussed, his marriage
on May 16, 1904, to Cornelia Lane of Toledo, Ohio. [62]

Cornelia Platt Lane was only a little younger than
Sherwood Anderson, she having been born on May 16, 1877. [63]
But her background and training were much different from
his.   Her father was Robert H. Lane of R. H. Lane & Co.,
a firm which had been engaged in the wholesale jobbing of
shoes and rubbers in Toledo since 1854. [64]   Miss Lane's
family had been financially secure; when R. H. Lane died
in 1928, he left an estate valued at over $100,000. [65]   The
family had membership in the First Baptist Church in Toledo,
of which R. H. Lane was a sometime deacon and treasurer. [66]

When Cornelia Lane entered the College for Women
of Western Reserve University in 1896, she submitted to the
registrar a certificate of graduation from Toledo High School
and twelve hours of credits, six in French and six in mathe-
matics, earned during a year at Shepardson College. [67]   Her
credits from Shepardson enabled her to take a little less than
full-time work during her four years at College for Women.
A "good but not excellent" student, she received the Ph. B.
degree in June, 1900, after taking the following number of
semester hours of the following subjects: Bible, 7; English,
18; French, 6; history, 15; Latin, 15; philosophy, 6; German, 9; art history, 6; biology, 12; pedagogy, 3; geology,
3. [68]

A college roommate during two years[69] remembers
her as "intelligent, witty, fun-loving, a person of fine integrity, and a leader in her class."   She joined the Sigma
Psi sorority as a sophomore and became that year a member of the Present Day Club, apparently a group organized
for the discussion of current events.   She was one of the
literary editors of the annual published in 1899.   As a senior
she was president of Student's Association, apparently a form
of student council, took part in a farce, "The Peace Conference at the Hague," presented by the Present Day Club, had
membership in the Browning Club, was on the entertainment
committee for the Senior Hop, and wrote an article for the
college literary magazine. [70]

The article for The College Folio, "The Development
of the Mask in English Literature Until the Beginning of the
Seventeenth Century," may perhaps be most accurately

described as an academic exercise.   The tone of the article
may be perceived from its concluding and summarizing paragraph:

> Its [the mask's] whole history may be summed up
> in a few words.   The mask was introduced from
> Italy into England by Henry VIII.   Here on account
> of environment it lost some of its spectacular
> character and developed in a dramatic and literary
> way.   It reached its literary culmination in Milton's
> "Comus. "   Under James and Charles the mask
> flourished with great magnificence until the Puritan
> wars, when it came to an end.   Its only effect
> upon the drama was that, simplified in form it was
> introduced into plays, but unlike the play within a
> play, had no influence on the plot. [71]

Little is known about what Cornelia Lane did between
June, 1900, and May 16, 1904, but it is clear that she spent
the period between June, 1901, and March, 1902, in Europe.[72]
Several acquaintances have recalled that she studied at the
Sorbonne, [73] and it is established that she was "staying in
Paris" in November, 1901. [74]   There was no necessity for
her working, and it is likely that she busied herself before
her marriage with such pursuits as appealed to her.   A
mention of her in the "Alumnae Notes" of The College Folio,
for June, 1903 (page 9), may be suggestive of freedom to
travel about as she wished: "Cornelia Lane, '00, of Toledo,
recently spent several days in Cleveland and attended the
Guilford House dance. "   She was introduced to Sherwood
Anderson by Mrs. Jennie Bemis Weeks, a former Clyde resident and her next-door neighbor, a year before their marriage. [75]

Few details of the romance between the handsome and
successful advertising man and the attractive, intelligent,
and educated daughter of the successful business man are
known.   One may surmise that Anderson felt Cornelia was a
woman of high caliber, of substantial family, of culture, one
who could inspire a man to better work.   Cornelia has referred to his "early years when his charm and warm personality were so much a part of him. "   She understood that
he was from a "very poor family, his mother being the
beautiful, heroic type and his father being irresponsible,
good-natured. "   She knew he had been "the town newsboy. "
She knew that he "was a person of enthusiasm.   He could
convince you of anything. "   Perhaps only later she found

"then he lost interest." She recalled that he "hated advertising from the start. "[76]

In any case, marriage was in the air. The following
letter to Karl Anderson's fiancée is revelatory of at least
one facet of Sherwood Anderson in early 1904:

                                        Sunday, March 6
        My Dear Miss Buell

        Karl told me the good news. I had thought of it
    that night in New York when I met you but I hardly
    went as far as to hope it would come out so fine for
    Karl. You will have a fine life, you two, and do
    great things and the sun shall shine on your wed-
    ding day, the stars declare it and who doubts the
    stars know all about lovers. We at home have
    seen but little of Karl for many years and I have
    almost grown old in the wish that I might some
    day live near him. Your coming to him will
    freshen that wish and I shouldn't be surprised if
    it carried me off east to live.

        I am to be married in May. Miss Cornelia
    Lane of Toledo Ohio is venturing the voyage with
    me. You are invited to the wedding its [sic] May
    10th. It will be a small wedding at home and it
    would be very fine for me and for her if you came.

        I suppose I may safely call myself the head of
    the house of Anderson at home [Irwin lived until
    1919.] and as such I pledge you the heartfelt wish
    of all of them that you and Karl will be very
    happy.
                                    Sincerely yours,
                                    Sherwood Anderson

        The marriage, which Miss Helen Buell evidently
could not attend, took place as the following account describes:

        The marriage of Miss Cornelia P. Lane and Mr.
    Sherwood Anderson of Chicago, will take place at
    8 o'clock this evening at the residence of the
    bride's parents, Mr. and Mrs. Robert H. Lane,
    2428 Robinwood avenue.

        Rev. W. E. Loucks, of the First Baptist Church,

will perform the ceremony.   Just before the entrance of the bridal party, Mrs. Robert C. Miller
will sing Aylward's beautiful composition, "Beloved,
It is Morn," with Mrs. Charles Weeks at the
piano.   Miss Eunice Weeks will play the Lohengrin
and Mendelssohn wedding music.

Miss Margaret Lane, the bride's sister, will be
the bridesmaid, and Mr. Marco Morrow, an editor
of Agricultural Advertising, of Chicago, will serve
Mr. Anderson as best man.   The bridal gown is
a handsome creation of white chiffon, and the
bridesmaid will be attired in white.   The service
of a wedding supper will follow the ceremony, the
bridal table to be laid for ten.

Mr. and Mrs. Anderson will leave this evening for
a wedding journey, Mrs. Anderson to travel in a
dark blue tailored costume.

The out-of-town guests for the wedding will include
the groom's brother and sister, Mr. Karl Anderson
of New York, and Miss Stella Anderson of Chicago;
Miss Mary Wildman, of Norwalk; Miss Anne Mc-
Intyre, of Cleveland; Miss Lucille Trowbridge, of
Hudson; and Mrs. Charles Wicks [Weeks] of Hamilton, Ont. [77]

Another letter relating to Karl's marriage seems to
give a reliable index as to Anderson's attitude toward the
family which the next few years were to bring him in Cleveland and Elyria:

Dear Karl, [78]

You old dog - not to have telegraphed it.   Cornelia is writing from home and I want you to know
how very happy we all are that everything is all
right and that she is here.

I heard an old nurse recite a little verse today.
"First a girl and then a boy, and all their lives
they're full of joy."

That isn't it but that's the sense of it.   I suppose you can't realize your pride but we are all
proud enough.   The little lady monopolized all of

the conversation Sunday at home.

> My love to Helen and I'm so happy that it's all
> over and all safe.
>> With love,
>> Sherwood

Apparently the Andersons set up housekeeping at 5854
Rosalie Court in Chicago. [79]   A friend has described the atmosphere of their home as he knew it.   Mrs. Anderson
seemed, to people who visited frequently in their place on
the south side of Chicago, to be an excellent hostess, one
who could help him to master city ways.   Games were not
of as great interest as reading choice pieces by the light
from the fireplace. [80]   Morrow remembered Anderson's home
life as being pleasant, recalling the evening by the fire, noting that the Andersons did not participate in any "literary
set."[81]   Cornelia was to recall the "good fireplace at Rosalie
Court" and that in their reading circle discussions "Sherwood
always took up the cudgels for Shaw.   I can remember the
battles that used to rage over Shaw."[82]

A paragraph from one of Cornelia's post-marriage
letters to Sherwood gives just a suggestion of some of their
Chicago friends and one aspect of Cornelia herself:

> Do you remember Nan Cutter or Anne Spencer Cut-
> ter of Cleveland, who ate at our house in Chicago?
> Anne Spencer Morrow, Lindberg's [sic] fiancee is
> her niece - I saw the Morrow children at the Cut-
> ters in Chicago so I've evidently seen this most
> important of American girls and am all primmed
> [sic] up with majestick pride.
>
> Perhaps you did too. [83]

Looking back on this marriage from the vantage point
of 1916 (when he was recently divorced), Anderson was able
to write:

> When I was first married a girl came to visit us.
> It was a pretty conventional household.   I made
> money - was a prosperous young businessman in
> those days.   Well on the first evening she came I
> offered her a cigarette as we sat over our coffee.
> She was the first woman I ever saw smoke.   The
> talk drifted to this idea of door-shutting and Marian

said, "I am never in the company of any one but I
am glad when they go.   It does not make any difference how delightful the occasion may have been.
When it is over I stand like a child in a strange
place, fronting new and wonderful possibilities. "

I understand that.   It was so keen and so true that
I remember to have leaned forward and said.   "And
death too.   I would feel that way about the death
of anyone I know except a child. "

I remember the incident vividly because what I said
hurt C [ornelia] as I was always hurting.   She
thought I wanted her to die and I dare say I did.
I have always hurt people who cared for me except
the born adventurers. 84

In spite of hurtful aspects, such as reflected in that
letter, it would appear that Anderson was comfortably married to a woman who gave him intellectual companionship,
who was "a charming hostess" to his friends.   He was comfortable from an economic point of view, too.   Why, then,
did he leave Chicago, take the chance he did when he went
into the mail-order business in Cleveland in the fall of
1906?   Anderson wrote, "I had grown to hate advertising
and returned to Ohio.... "85   The article about the "sales
master" in the April, 1905, Agricultural Advertising contains
the answer.   That article makes it clear that Anderson was
dissatisfied with advertising as it existed, that he had ideals
and ambitions for it, that he would have liked to work
changes.   He told one of his clients that he was disgusted
with the commission-system of payment for advertising
men. 86

Anderson has summarized his reactions during this
period in the following manner:

There was a good deal of talk about the nobility of
business...the big beautiful business man.   The
word service had begun to be used.   I went in
enthusiastically.   There was a side of my nature,
a certain great plausibility, a trick of winning
men's confidence that made me rather succeed
from the first.

I grew sick of it.   I think I was most worried by
my own growing slickness.   I determined to get

out of advertising writing.   There were too many
lies being told.

I didn't so much mind lying.   I was afraid I would
begin to believe the lies I wrote.   I used to get
drunk.   I went to lie with women, not loving them.

It seemed that being a manufacturer would be better.   At least I would be better making something
people could use.... [87]

It may be pointed out, however, that he did not go
into manufacturing when he left Chicago.   His duties with
the company he joined in Cleveland were wholly concerned
with the promotion and selling.   It is most likely that he
got his chance to go to Cleveland when he was deep in his
disillusionment over the difference between what advertising
was and what it could be.   Feeling keenly that ideas and
ideals were impotent before power and money and the lust
for them, he may have sardonically decided to prove that
he, too, could be a money-maker.

Notes

1.   Letter from Mr. Marco Morrow, Topeka, Kansas;
      Oct. 11, 1941.   In a letter of Aug. 20, 1949, to Mrs.
      Eleanor Anderson, Morrow gave a very similar account,
      differing only in saying he hired Anderson as his assist-
      ant on the copy department.   Phillips' account ("Sherwood
      Anderson's Winesburg, Ohio"), based on interviews with
      Morrow and George Daugherty, another Springfield-Chi-
      cago friend, adds that Anderson left Crowell because
      he "tired of the routine of the office. "

2.   Memoirs, p. 137-8.

3.   Marco Morrow, who served in 1904 as the best man at
      Anderson's wedding, told Phillips that Anderson "wrote
      constantly during 1902-1905, discarding most of what he
      wrote. "   Phillips, p. 16.

4.   "The Solicitor, " Agricultural Advertising, Aug. 1904,
      p. 21-24.

5.   Ibid. , p. 23-24.

6.   Memoirs, p. 138. "I Court a Rich Girl," Memoirs,
      p. 136-149, deals with this Chicago period but is taken
      up chiefly with a rather inconclusive account of his being
      engaged to a rich girl and the breaking off of that engage-
      ment.

7.   "Why I Write," The Writer, Dec. 1936, p. 364.

8.   Interview with Mrs. Cornelia Lane Anderson, Oct. 10,
      1946. In the same interview she also said, "He just
      wrote all the time" and "He was writing in a small way
      when I first knew him. "

9.   Morrow letter, Oct. 11, 1941.

10.   See bibliography at end of this chapter, after Notes;
      Anderson publications 1900-1906.

11.   Agricultural Advertising, May 1903, p. 22.

12.   "Push, Push, Push," op. cit. , Feb. 1903, p. 16.

13.   "About Suspicion," op. cit. , Nov. 1903, p. 58.

14.   "Unfinished," op. cit. , May 1903, p. 20.

15.   "Fun and Work," op. cit. , July 1903, p. 23.

16.   Op. cit. , Feb. 1903, p. 14.

17.   Op. cit. , April 1903, p. 12.

18.   "The Old and the New," op. cit. , Dec. 1903, p. 50.

19.   Op. cit. , Feb. 1903, p. 14.

20.   Anderson's name appeared in the Chicago directory for
      the years 1901 to 1907, inclusive. Six of those times he
      was listed as a solicitor and once as a salesman. "He
      soon went on the road as a salesman, but handled his
      own accounts, contact and copy," according to the Morrow
      letter, Oct. 11, 1941. Probably a description of function
      found in "Chest of Drawers," The Sherwood Anderson
      Reader, p. 832, is relevant: "There were... men, ... em-
      ployed by the advertising agency... called 'solicitors. '...
      These men, having to bring in clients, keep them satis-
      fied; convince them that we who wrote their copy were

men of talent... had to put up a front.   They were provided
with private offices, often expensively furnished;   they arrived and departed... did not have to ring time clocks,
went off for long afternoons of golf with some client.... "

21.   This and previous lines from "The Traveling Man, "
op. cit. , Feb. 1903, p. 15-16.

22.   "Knock No. 1, " op. cit. , June 1903, p. 54 and 56.

23.   "Boost No. 1, " op. cit. , June 1903, p. 56-7.

24.   "What Henry George Said Twenty Years Ago, " op. cit. ,
Oct. 1903, p. 18.

25.   "Work in the Dark, " op. cit. , July 1903, p. 26.

26.   Op. cit. , Aug. 1903, p. 22.

27.   "A Christmas Thought, " op. cit. , Dec. 1903, p. 51.

28.   "The Farmer Wears Clothes, " op. cit. , Feb. 1902, p.
6.   This is the first article to appear in Agricultural Advertising signed by Anderson.   Possibly there are earlier,
unsigned contributions of his in the magazine; this prospect is discussed later in this chapter.

29.   "Twenty Years in the West, " op. cit. , Oct. 1903, p.
18.

30.   "Unfinished Contracts, " op. cit. , Feb. 1903, p. 16.

31.   "About Inquiries, " op. cit. , Nov. 1903, p. 56.

32.   "The Lightweight, " op. cit. , March 1903, p. 18.

33.   "The Born Quitter, " op. cit. , March 1903, p. 19-20.

34.   "Finding Our Work, " op. cit. , May 1903, p. 21-22.

35.   Untitled item, op. cit. , April 1903, p. 14.

36.   "About Country Roads, " op. cit. , Nov. 1903, p. 56.

37.   Op. cit. , April 1903, p. 14.

38.   Op. cit. , Dec. 1903, p. 51.

39. These items were not in a "Rot and Reason" column but in
     "We Would Be Wise, " Jan. 1903, p. 47.

40. Op. cit. , Jan. 1903, p. 45-6.

41. April 1905, p. 307-08.

42. "Advertising a Nation, " op. cit. , May 1905, p. 389.

43. Agricultural Advertising, April 1904, p. 39.

44. Op. cit. , July 1904, p. 43-4.

45. Op. cit. , June 1904, p. 27-29.

46. Op. cit. , May 1904, p. 31-2.

47. Op. cit. , Sept. 1904, p. 24-6.

48. Op. cit. , Feb. 1904, p. 9.

49. Op. cit. , Dec. 1904, p. 79, 81-2.

50. Op. cit. , Jan. 1904, p. 36.

51. Op. cit. , Nov. 1904, p. 53.

52. Ibid.

53. Op. cit. , March 1904, p. 36-8.

54. The Reader, Oct. 1903, p. 503-4.

55. Interview with Mrs. Cornelia Lane Anderson, Oct. 10,
     1946; and from a letter from Mrs. Anderson, Oct. 16,
     1946.

56. The Reader, Oct. 1903, p. 504.

57. Ibid. , Dec. 1903, p. 71-73.

58. Letter, Mr. Morrow; Nov. 12, 1941.

59. See Memoirs, p. 264-5, for Anderson's account of the
     whole episode.

60. The Frank B. White Company and its personnel became

a part of the Long-Critchfield Company in Sept. 1903; Agricultural Advertising was continued by Long-Critchfield.

61.   "Long-Critchfield Banquet," Agricultural Advertising, May 1905, p. 421.

62.   Lucas County (Ohio) Marriage Record No. 7022.

63.   Lucas County Record of Births, Vol. 2, p. 262.

64.   Scribner, Harvey Scribner, Memories of Lucas County and the City of Toledo.   Madison, Wisc., Western Hist. Assoc., 1910, vol. 1, p. 580.

65.   Administration Docket No. 21,311, Lucas County (Ohio) Probate Court Records.

66.   Report and Register of the First Baptist Church, Toledo, Ohio, 1898-9, Printed Feb. 2, 1899, p. 4, 8, and 20.

67.   A Baptist college for women since merged with Denison University, Granville, Ohio.

68.   The above information was obtained in an interview with Miss Eleanor R. Wells, registrar of Flora Stone Mather College (formerly College for Women), Western Reserve University, Cleveland.

69.   From an interview with Mrs. Esther Allen Gaw, Dean of Women, The Ohio State University, Columbus.

70.   These items of information were collected from issues of the college annual, Varia Historia, and the college's monthly literary magazine, The College Folio, for 1897-1900.

71.   The College Folio, Jan. 1900, p. 109.   (The whole article is on p. 105-109.)

72.   Items in The College Folio, Nov. 1901, p. 76, and May 1902, p. 326.

73.   Sorbonne officials found in 1962 no record of such study.

74.   The College Folio, Nov. 1901, p. 76.

75. Cornelia Anderson interview, Oct. 10, 1946.

76. Ibid.

77. The Toledo Blade, May 16, 1904, p. 6.

78. On stationery of Hotel St. Charles, Toledo, Thurs., Oct. 23, 1905.

79. The record of the Registrar at Flora Stone Mather College indicates that Mrs. Anderson gave that as her address on July 15, 1904. In the Chicago directory for 1905 and 1906 the address for Sherwood Anderson is "Riverside," at that time one of the more westerly suburbs. The 1907 directory gives 6126 Jackson Park Ave. as his address. Cornelia also gave the Rosalie Ct. address when she registered for French 21 in the autumn of 1904. She took French 22 in the winter of 1905. Cornelia recalled spending one summer at Riverside. Information from letter of Dec. 10, 1946.

80. Letter from Mr. Louis D. Wallace, Nashville, Tenn.; Oct. 17, 1941.

81. Phillips, p. 17.

82. Cornelia Anderson interview, Oct. 10, 1946.

83. Letter ca. Feb. 21, 1929.

84. Letter to Marietta D. Finley, Oct. 24, 1916.

85. Memoirs, p. 151.

86. Interview with Mr. Joseph T. Conkey, Cleveland.

87. Letter of Sept. 14, 1938. Dinsmoor, p. 69.

Chronological Bibliography of Anderson Publications (1900-
1906)

1.   "The Farmer Wears Clothes," Agricultural Advertising,
     Feb. 1902, IX: 6.

2.   "We Would Be Wise," Agricultural Advertising, Jan.
     1903, X: 45-46.

3.   "Rot and Reason" [a column]: "The New Job," "The
     Laugh of Scorn," "The Traveling Man," "Unfinished
     Contracts," and "Push, Push, Push," Agricultural Ad-
     vertising, Feb. 1903, X: 13-16.

4.   "Rot and Reason": "The Lightweight," and "The Born
     Quitter," Agricultural Advertising, March 1903, X:
     18-19.

5.   "Rot and Reason": "Doing Stunts," "Packingham,"
     "Of No Value," and untitled, Agricultural Advertising,
     April 1903, X: 12-14.

6.   "Rot and Reason": "Unfinished," "Finding Our Work,"
     and untitled, Agricultural Advertising, May 1903, X:
     20-21.

7.   "Rot and Reason": "Knock No. 1," "Knock No. 2,"
     and "Boost No. 1," Agricultural Advertising, June
     1903, X: 54, 56-7.

8.   "Rot and Reason": "Office Tone," "Fun and Work,"
     and "Work in the Dark," Agricultural Advertising,
     July 1903, X: 22-23, 26.

9.   "Rot and Reason": "Golden Harvest Farmer," "Golden
     Harvest Manufacturers," and "Golden Fake," Agricul-
     tural Advertising, Aug. 1903, X: 22, 24-25.

10. "Rot and Reason": "Twenty Years in the West, " "What Henry George Said Twenty Years Ago, " "Twenty Years in Figures, " and "Fairs, " Agricultural Advertising, Oct. 1903, X: 17-19.

11. "A Business Man's Reading, " The Reader, Oct. 1903, III: 503-4.

12. "Rot and Reason": "About Country Roads, " "About Inquiries, " "About Cleverness, " and "About Suspicion, " Agricultural Advertising, Nov. 1903, X: 56, 58.

13. "Rot and Reason": "The Old and the New, " "A Christmas Thought, " and "Men That Are Wanted, " Agricultural Advertising, Dec. 1903, X: 50-51.

14. "The Man and the Book, " The Reader, Dec. 1903, III: 71-3.

15. "Business Types" [a column]: "The Good Fellow, " Agricultural Advertising, Jan. 1904, XI: 36.

16. "Business Types": "The Silent Men, " Agricultural Advertising, Feb. 1904, XI: 19.

17. "Business Types": "The Man of Affairs, " Agricultural Advertising, March 1904, XI: 36-8.

18. "Business Types": "The Traveling Man, " Agricultural Advertising, April 1904, XI: 39-40.

19. "Business Types": "The Liar--A Vacation Story, " Agricultural Advertising, May 1904, XI: 31-2.

20. "Business Types": "The Liar--A Vacation Story, " Agricultural Advertising, June 1904, XI: 27-9.

21. "Business Types": "The Discouraged Man, " Agricultural Advertising, July 1904, XI: 43-4.

22. "Business Types": "The Solicitor, " Agricultural Advertising, Aug. 1904, XI: 21-4.

23. "Business Types": "The Hot Young 'Un and the Cold Old 'Un, " Agricultural Advertising, Sept. 1904, XI: 24-6.

24. "Business Types": "The Boyish Man," Agricultural
     Advertising, Oct. 1904, XI: 53.

25. "The Fussy Man and the Trimmer," Agricultural Ad-
     vertising, Dec. 1904, XI: 79, 81-2.

26. "The Sales Master and the Selling Organization," Agri-
     cultural Advertising, April 1905, XII: 306-8.

27. "Advertising a Nation," Agricultural Advertising, May
     1905, XII: 389.

Mosaic VII

"Quite childishly eager..."

I have always thought that I came into writing rather through
the back door as my primary object in the beginning
was not publication but rather if possible, to clear up
things about myself and others, in my mind.
                    to Clarence Gohdes, April 16, 1936 (JR).

                *   *   *

When later I began to write I for a long time told myself I
would never publish, and I remember that I went about
thinking of myself as a kind of heroic figure, a silent
man creeping into little rooms, writing marvelous tales,
poems, novels--that would never be published.
                    from A Story Teller's Story, p. 94.

                *   *   *

When I published my first book I was quite childishly eager
to see what everyone would say. I was so naive as to
suppose that criticism of living writers could be quite
imperson[al] and clear.
        I found it a muddy mess. When Marching Men
was published I paid very little attention.
                    to Waldo Frank, March-April 1918.

                *   *   *

Long ago when I wrote without thought of printing my attitude
toward writing was quite clear. It was a creative thing
I had managed to bring into my own muddle.
        Criticism made me more or less self-conscious.
I lost something of my own innocence. Thats what I
cant afford to loose. [sic]
                    to Waldo Frank, March-April 1918.

I'm grinning now.   I take to myself a wide sense of leisure.
     I'm going to have my own way about the book on which
     I am at work if it never gets itself finished.   We die
     and rot anyway and the author of forty volumes would
     make no better fertilization for the corn.
          Don't let them crowd you brother.   You don't
     have to do the job and I don't have to do it.   When we
     are dead a million fools will survive us.
                    to Waldo Frank, Nov. 1918.

                    *   *   *

It often happens, after the publication of a book.   You must
     know the feeling. . . that you have anyway pounded all
     you know into something and then that it has been rath-
     er like having a child and, taking it in your arms,
     you have gone and dropped it down a deep hole and
     walked away.
                    to Roger Sergel, Dec. 1937 (JR).

                    *   *   *

I am still in a strange state of uncertainty.   As you know I
     am always so after I have published a book.   My inner
     life is for the time perhaps too much invaded.
                    to M. D. Finley, Dec. 14, 1924.

                    *   *   *

For several years the man O'Brien selected stories of mine
     as the top stories of the year.   He wrote me that he
     did it until he got tired of doing it but none of these
     stories so selected, brought me any money.
                    to George Chambrun, Aug. 29, 1938.

                    *   *   *

Winesburg has gone off to Lane.   I wonder if the public will
     really take that book.
                    to Waldo Frank, before June 5, 1918.

                    *   *   *

Is it a good plan to advertise telling people to get Winesburg
     at the public library.   The damn cusses do that anyway.
                    to Ben Huebsch, Nov. 12, 1919.

This I know is true.   Formerly, when I was an advertising
    writer I, from time to time, saved a little money.   I
    went of [sic] to work.   In this way I produced Wines-
    burg, Poor White, A Story Tellers [sic] Story, Mid
    American [sic] Chants and other books.
            They brought little money.   Each time I had to
    go, from such a time of work, back to writing of toilet
    soaps, tooth pastes etc.   It was pretty sickening.   It
    caused in me a kind of decay, [which] even yet, often
    comes back.
                        to Mary Emmett, 1936?

                *   *   *

To tell the truth I would be a happier man if I lived in en-
    tire obscurity.
                        to N. Bryllion Fagin, July 1927.

                *   *   *

You have been made to think you want success, recognition
    when what you want is love of life, to come into you,
    to go out of you.
                        to Luella Williams, June 20, 1930.

                *   *   *

After years of striving to get money, to get power, to be
    successful, I had found in the end well-nigh perfect
    contentment in looking and listening, in sitting lost in
    some little corner, writing, trying to write all down.
                        from A Story Teller's Story, p. 399.

    *   *   *   *   *

Chapter 7

SHERWOOD ANDERSON, PRESIDENT

In the latter part of 1903, Sherwood Anderson had
written into his "Rot and Reason" column[1] under a section
titled "Men That Are Wanted" a category including "Men that
feel as though they would like to take hold of the rudder and
run a business for themselves." When he went to Cleveland
on Labor Day, 1906,[2] to become president of The United
Factories Co., he was on the road to getting a business of
his own.

Anderson was taken into the company as "new life."
He was made president but really shared the power with Mr.
Bottger, who had been general manager. As an advertising
man he was supposed to bring the mail-order concern out of
the doldrums.[3] According to Mr. Bottger, Anderson's special provinces were sales and advertising, in which work he
had had experience while with the Long-Critchfield agency in
Chicago. In fact, the opportunity to join United Factories
had come to Anderson as a result of his work on United
Factories "campaigns" while with Long-Critchfield.[4]

Mrs. Anderson thought he had an "idea of being independent. He was writing copy for Taylor-Critchfield and
was trying to get away from it." "Ed Cray [who had a considerable financial interest in the company] had money; we
didn't have any." Sherwood put in the ideas and Cray the
money.[5]

Mr. Bottger believed that Anderson went to United
Factories with a "$25,000-2-year dream."[6] "He wanted to
come to Cleveland and United Factories. He came at a
sacrifice and just after the company had suffered a considerable loss in an unfortunate venture. He had been paid well
by Long-Critchfield." To understand fully what Anderson
may have had in mind when he went to United Factories, one
has to know a little more of the kind of enterprise it was.

151

The key words in its name, "United Factories," really explain it.   The idea was to make one company the mail-order outlet for a number of factories, producing all types of merchandise.   In a 24-page "Roofing Catalog," which contains a price-list dated October 1, 1906, there are mentioned catalogues for vehicles, buggy tops and repairs, stoves, incubators, agricultural implements, and paints, any of which might be obtained by sending in a card with one's name and address.   That means the company was dealing in products of seven types and perhaps from seven different manufacturers. "We wanted to make of our company in fact what it was in name, a united factories company; Anderson and Ed Cray traveled over quite a territory talking to manufacturers in the hope of interesting a group of manufacturers in this kind of arrangement" and "Anderson had some very big ideas for a factory combine.   The scheme failed for lack of a head. Each factory wanted to be boss."[7]

During the year he was with the company, one gathers, Anderson was in charge of selling the goods made by factories already using the company as an outlet and was helping to promote the company's basic scheme.   One of his duties was to prepare catalogues of merchandise sold by his company.   This he did, if one may take the "Roofing Catalog" mentioned earlier as a fair sample, in such a way as to make himself the symbol and representative of the company in its relation with the customer who read the catalogue.   One whole page in the "Roofing Catalog" is reserved for a picture of Anderson, one which had appeared earlier in Agricultural Advertising, and a statement entitled "My Word to You" and signed by Anderson as president of the company.

In this pledge or "word," Anderson had struck the note he was to continue to use when he started his own business in Elyria.   The approach was to convince the buyer that United Factories was a company that did everything honestly and was designed only to serve the customer:

> I promise as a decent man trying to be square that every man, rich or poor, small or large, shall have a square deal from my company.
>
> Every word of this book was written under my supervision, and for it I am responsible to you.
>
> As you and I may never meet face to face I give you my word now that what is written in this book

is true in spirit and in fact.

I stand ready to do what is right by you, the buyer, and if you at any time buy anything of the
factories whose goods are sold through our catalogues, and if you are not satisfied, you can feel
free about taking the matter up with me personally,
and I promise you that I will not delegate the matter to a clerk or pile up words to confuse you,
but will satisfy you with what you have bought or
return every penny of your money no matter what
we lose by it.

In the above statement Anderson said every word of
the catalogue was written under his supervision. So it seems
reasonable to presume that the statement of the basic selling
argument on the first page of the "catalog" was written by
Anderson.   As such, it seems worth including here.   It has
all the simplicity and candor that became characteristic of
his advertising:

Just let us reason this matter out for a moment.

The average jobber to live must make from 10 to
25 per cent on the goods he buys from the manufacturer.

The average traveling man receives a salary of
from $25.00 to $50.00 per week and from $25.00
to $50.00 per week more, for expenses for selling
the goods handled by the jobber to the dealer.

The average local dealer makes from 25 to 100
per cent on everything he passes over his counter.

It costs us but a very few pennies to put this catalogue into your hands.

For us the catalogue is jobber, traveler and dealer.   It works for us and works so cheaply that
there is no wonder we can give you a better quality of goods and still save money for you.

Local dealers may talk but the fact remains that
the "straight from the factory way" of doing business has come to stay.   It is logical, it is right
and it is economical.

> The United Factories Company, then, is just taking advantage of the situation. We expect to make a living profit on what we sell, but we can do this and give you a bigger dollar's worth than you can get any place else.

The tone of both of the statements quoted was obviously intended to make the customer, usually the farmer, trust the company and look upon it as a beneficial institution doing away with "middle-men" and unnecessary high prices. Naturally, people took Anderson at his word and wrote in when they had complaints. Not the least of his jobs was the handling of the "trouble" correspondence.

> Anderson fired more people than the company could have hired. He had to answer letters of complaints and was constantly firing the person responsible for the customer's complaint. He was really mild-mannered and never would have fired any one. [8]

Perhaps the greatest amount of "complaint" mail was received as the result of a disastrous experience in the spring of 1907 with an incubator "line," which Anderson himself had introduced to the company. While he had worked for Long-Critchfield, he had handled advertising for an incubator-manufacturer in Illinois. When he became associated with United Factories, he induced the incubator-manufacturer to use his company as an outlet. The crux of the matter was that the particular incubator United Factories marketed was defectively manufactured; although this was not Anderson's fault, he did handle the contract with the manufacturer. Of 3,200 sold, 600 were returned. "We lost thousands of dollars and wound up in a law suit. That disturbed his relationship here."[9] Mr. Bottger says this failure, which was really due to bad faith on the part of the manufacturer, was a heavy blow to Anderson. Not only was his dream of success for the business being shattered, but also his mail was unsatisfactory. The correspondence concerning the return of all those incubators must have been both distasteful and interminable. Doubtless a circumstance of this sort may have brought on the condition which led Mr. Schaad to observe, "When I considered the pace he was going and the number of cigarettes he smoked, I didn't think that fellow would last five years. He seemed very nervous."

The preparation of the catalogues and other advertising matter for the company, which appeared chiefly in farm

journals, with his correspondence occasioned Anderson's doing a lot of writing.   Mr. Bottger characterized him as a
"very brilliant writer. "   "He could write on any subject.
It didn't make any difference whether he had any knowledge
of the subject. "   One presumes that would be a handy
achievement for an advertising man.   But Mr. Bottger
thought Anderson was inclined then toward being a story-
teller, too.   Anderson related many of his early experiences
to Mr. Bottger but apparently did not mention anything he
had written in the Chicago period (1900-1906).

        Anderson had been made president of United Factories
for one year.   The assumption is that what occurred during
that year was to form a basis for any new arrangement at
the end of the year.   One can not be sure of all the reasons
for Anderson's leaving to go into business for himself late
in the summer of 1907, but several of them seem apparent.
One recalls the debacle of the incubators.   That "disturbing"
factor was still a fresh memory for Mr. Bottger 35 years
later.   Then, too, all three informants[10] were in agreement
that Anderson's knowledge of office routine was deficient.
As Mrs. Puchta put it, "He could lay out the work but was
not used to being confined to details of office work. "   Finally, Anderson was very likely anxious all along to get a
business of his own.   Apparently he got a chance, just as
his year with the Cleveland company was ending, and took
it. [11]

        Perhaps one should not leave consideration of Ander-
son's business life in Cleveland before recording the impression he made on the office-secretary, Mrs. Puchta.   He
dictated easily and seemed to know and like his work.   A
neat dresser, he seemed well-read and well-educated, always used good language, never forgot to be "gallant. "   A
"good-looking, dark, mature" man, he always had a smile,
no matter how hard the work was.   In fact, his pleasantness
always made the secretary feel willing to work for him.   He
had a good, hearty laugh; he laughed when other men smiled.
"He'd always kid with you when you came to the desk. "

        Of Anderson's home life, a brief but interesting
glimpse may be obtained.   Mr. Bottger has implied that
Mrs. Anderson knew about, was interested in, and helped
with some of the work Anderson had to do.   "Sherwood
gave her credit at that time at least for helping him with
his writing.   I believe she edited some of his stuff, for he
was not well-educated. "   Mrs. Anderson also undertook to

Figures 3 & 4. About 1911 in Elyria, Ohio. Left,
Cornelia Lane Anderson holding John (the younger) and Robert.
Right, Sherwood with Robert, standing, and John on father's lap.

teach Bottger and Anderson French on Sunday mornings. Mr. Bottger could still recall a couplet he learned in one of the limited number of lessons. [12] "She was interested in improving our education. I didn't have much and he [did] not [have much] in that line. " "I thought she was a very capable and well-educated person. "

Mr. Bottger recalled that the "home relationship" of the Andersons was "very pleasant" and that they lived in an "old house on Lamont Avenue, "[13] Of the Lamont Avenue house Mrs. Anderson recalled: "We got moved into this big house and got it fixed up artistically. The roof was just a sieve. Sherwood said, 'I believe we have something that will fix that. ' And that was a triumph. It was Roof-Fix. "[14]

The other, later residence in Cleveland was at 8310 Cedar Avenue. A friend[15] has described the two houses in which they lived as "run down" but having a "pleasant atmosphere. "[16] Anderson's wife, Cornelia, according to Mr. Baxter, was a casual[17] housekeeper, the intellectual side perhaps dominating the domestic a little. One further item concerning the family life of the Andersons in Cleveland may be added: "They were active here in some church. I was there one Sunday morning, and Sherwood was all dolled up in morning clothes and top hat. "[18]

The Cleveland year was a heavy one for Anderson. He was at least titular head of a mail-order business, responsible for a considerable portion of its operation. Doubtless, the experience was very valuable to him when he made preparation to go into his own business at the end of the summer. But his new business was not his only concern as the summer drew to a close. On August 16, 1907, the first child of Sherwood and Cornelia Lane Anderson, Robert Lane Anderson, was born at the Maternity Hospital at 2364 E. 55 Street in Cleveland. [19]

Notes

1.   Agricultural Advertising, Dec. 1903, X:15.

2.   Statement of Mr. George A. Bottger, Cleveland, who was secretary-treasurer of the company during Anderson's year as president. Most of the information about the Cleveland period was obtained in an interview with Mr. Bottger.

3.   Interview with Mrs. William Puchta, Cleveland, Ohio, who was stenographer for the firm during Anderson's stay.

4.   Bottger interview.

5.   Cornelia Anderson interview, Oct. 10, 1946.

6.   In the Memoirs, p. 206, Anderson mentioned the time "when, with a good deal of beating of dreams, I had gone off to Ohio to become a rich man."

7.   Bottger interview.

8.   Interview with Mr. E. O. Schaad, Cleveland, who worked for the company during Anderson's presidency.

9.   Mr. Bottger, who was still in The United Factories Co. in 1942.

10.   Mrs. Puchta, Mr. Schaad, Mr. Bottger.

11.   Karl Anderson's account of this episode, reflecting as it may some defensiveness, is as follows: "He said he left his first advertising job in Chicago to take charge of a failing mail-order house in Cleveland, with the understanding that he would receive an interest in the business if he put it on its feet again. By hard work he increased the business 400 per cent, but the owners reneged on their agreement." From "My Brother, Sherwood Anderson," p. 7.

12.   "I faintly remember having George B. and S. A. as French pupils." Mrs. Cornelia Lane Anderson, letter of Oct. 16, 1946.

13.   9711 Lamont Ave. was the address Mrs. Anderson gave the Alumnae Association of the College for Women at Western Reserve in 1906.

14.   Interview, Oct. 10, 1946.   Roof-Fix was the main product of the forthcoming Elyria operation.

15.   Mr. Edwin C. Baxter, Cleveland.

16.   Both addresses were on the east side of Cleveland in a middle-class neighborhood.

17.   "I was pleased with Edwin Baxter's word <u>casual</u> for
      my housekeeping--it's so much nicer than <u>sloppy.</u>"   Mrs.
      Cornelia Anderson, letter of Nov. 18, 1946.

18.   Mr. Bottger.   Mrs. Cornelia Anderson had said in
      the Oct. 10, 1946 interview, "We never went to church."
      After reading Mr. Bottger's statement, she wrote, "I
      hadn't known that Mr. Anderson ever went to church in
      Cleveland, but evidently he did go once"; letter of Dec.
      10, 1946.

19.   Files of the Department of Health, City of Cleveland.

Mosaic VIII

"And best express my love. . . "

I do feel that by keeping at the task of telling the story of
the common man, trying to see it clearly, I can best
help and best express my love. If you go through all
my writing, I think you will find this impulse in everything I have ever done. . . .
> to Paul Rosenfeld, Aug. 5, 1936.

*   *   *

. . . a kind of a book of memoirs--men and women met[,] seen,
loved, disliked--(don't think I ever did hate). I am
trying to set them all down, the famous, the infamous,
just people.
> Trying thus to catch the flow of a man's life in
people.
> to J. J. Lankes, Sept. 7, 1940.

*   *   *

In your own writing keep trying to make it serve your own
purpose. If you will do that, in case of necessity
whipping yourself a little into the realization it is to
be primarily an instrument for curing yourself, much
will be gained.
> to M. D. Finley, May 1918.

*   *   *

I don't know why I should recommend writing for any other
purpose than this help to self facing. When it comes
to real things the autobiographical note isn't the true
note by any means.
> to M. D. Finley, May 1918.

When I started writing my conception wasn't so clear.   Then
I went only so far as to want health for myself.   I
was a money getter, a schemer, a cronic [sic] liar.
One day I found out that when I sat down to write it
was more difficult to lie.   The lie lay before one on
the paper.   It haunted one at night.
                          to Paul Rosenfeld, Feb. 1921.

         *   *   *

It may be the reason I write, to occasionally escape out of
myself and into others in that way.
                          to Monte Bartlett, Nov. 12, 1939 (JR).

         *   *   *

It seems to me that the duty of the story teller is to study
people as they are and to try to find the real drama
of life just as people live and experience it.
                          to Harriet Martin, Sept. 19, 1939 (JR).

         *   *   *

I guess I really began writing because I wanted to get off
self and found that, sometimes, I could by absorbing
myself in others.
                          to Monte Bartlett, Nov. 9, 1939 (JR).

         *   *   *

...I have never been much concerned with this question of
the value of the work of other men.   I think it must
be because I am so absorbed in trying to get at and
understand a little the lives of so-called ordinary people.
                          to Daniel Lerner, Dec. 19, 1938 (JR).

         *   *   *

To me the world is simply filled with individuals some few
of whom I would like to come to understand a little.
                          to Dwight Macdonald, June 14, 1939 (JR).

*   *   *   *   *

Chapter 8

EXIT TO ELSINORE

Sherwood and Cornelia Anderson were starting anew
in Elyria; they had a new business and a new child and were
in new and different surroundings. But they were not long
in establishing a circle of friends. Cornelia had a college
friend (Mrs. Helen Bowen Garfield) who got her into the
Fortnightly literary club. She prepared papers for presentation and was a "very fine member."[1] She was in the club
"three or four years," even after her second and third children
came.[2] Both Cornelia and Sherwood attended meetings of
the Round Table Club, a discussion group for young married
people founded in 1910.[3] Sherwood was always the center of
discussion. He was the person with the most ideas, and his
ideas were always at variance with those of the group. They
seemed to take it good-naturedly, but Cornelia felt it probably did rankle.[4] Anderson played golf at the Elyria Country
Club, and Cornelia accompanied him there on occasion.[5]
It was also Anderson's habit to go to the Elks Club, of which
he was a member, and "shoot pool" with several regular
cronies.[6]

Cornelia Anderson left the impression in Elyria of
being "dignified, quiet, pleasant"[7] and lovely and cultured.[8]
But the impressions Sherwood Anderson left are quite varied.
To Mrs. Gee, who worked for him, he was "a golf enthusiast
and seldom missed an opportunity to play." Golf had been
too expensive for him to play in Chicago, but he did play on
public courses.[9] To a man who invested in The American
Merchants Co. "Anderson was an eccentric, a dreamer, an
agnostic. He didn't know. . . . He was on the order of a
socialist. The country wasn't being run right. He had views
for its correction. . . . He didn't seem to live in the same
world with us. He had some very rabid views about various
matters."[10] Mr. Wilford's comments are in similar vein:
"His views of life clashed a lot with those of others. There
was a feeling that Anderson was erratic. He was very

162

modernistic in his views of life. He seemed to believe in
'free love'. " His banker remembered him as pleasant, aloof,
moody, self-contained, and rather strange over-all. [11] These
opinions tally with Cornelia's recollection that he was usually
at variance with the conventional attitude but that his relations with the town were good. [12]

His golf partner commented that Anderson, the masculine type, spent most of his time with men. [13] His caddy
at the country club did not consider him a good player but
thought he played for the associations the game gave him.
Cornelia said he went golfing every Sunday "as a refuge from
social pressures. "[14] He drank quite a bit but not too much.
Although he was "happy-go-lucky, " he did not take advice
about playing very readily. Especially jovial "when he'd
had a drink or two, " he could be a "kidder. " He was "easy
to know, ordinary, and a bit on the slouchy side as a
dresser. "[15] One acquaintance thought he was self-centered
and careless of clothes and hair. He was not systematic
about where he kept his money, even on his own person. [16]

A local druggist found he "was very moody, might
hardly answer questions. He was very deliberate, not ex-
citable, not a mixer. He had few close friends. "[17] A
newspaper man noticed, "There was a complete absence of
bluff or self-dramatization in his conversation. He was very
handsome, exceedingly pleasant, modest, rather deferential
in manner. "[18] A friend of the family thought him charming,
hospitable, modest, and inquisitive. [19] Another newspaper
man recalled him as "a fine, upstanding man, a good conversationalist. He always had a good story. "[20] A neighbor
remembered him as playing imaginatively with his children.

> Many a time we'd hear him through open windows
> romping with his children. He would be acting out
> imaginative scenes with them. Imagination ran
> riot. He and the kids had many a set-up with
> imaginary persons. There was quite a little action
> over there. And the children followed right along.[21]

Mrs. Georgia Lane, Cornelia's step-mother, remembered
Sherwood's helping Robert through an account of Robert's experiences as an Arctic explorer. When Mrs. Lane was
puzzled by such activity, Cornelia explained that Sherwood
was training Robert's imagination.

To all these impressions should be added that of

Anderson himself:

> ...during my first year or two as a young company
> promoter and manufacturer in an Ohio city I had
> continually hurried from place to place--walked
> rapidly, even I think set my jaw in a certain way.
> There must have been in my head some notion of
> a part I was to play in life as a successful young
> man.... I talked rapidly, rushed through the
> streets to my office, slammed doors, gave orders
> to my subordinates in sharp tones. I was merely
> trying to enact the part of the pushing, bright,
> successful young American business man. 22

A general view of Anderson's business activity in
Elyria may be gained from the following statement:

> ...I have spoken of myself as having become a
> manufacturer but really I wasn't a manufacturer.
> I was in house paint--as a salesman who had got
> control of a factory.... I was one of the slick
> ones. I dare say I never did make any first-rate
> house paint. There were always traveling men
> coming to my office to show me some substitute
> for the more expensive ingredients I had been using
> and usually I bought. All the time I had a kind of
> pride in my ability as a word slinger and thought
> most people who buy house paint are, like the peo-
> ple who are sold anything else, at bottom probably
> yaps. I was plausible, thought faster than most
> people....
>
> And as I had picked up ideas about selling goods
> by mail by my earlier experience as an advertising
> writer, presently money came rolling in. I do not
> mean to say that I was rich or even on the border-
> line of anything like great riches but I had learned
> how men get rich. 23

His business associate, Purcell, had met him in 1908,
when he was selling Roof-Fix by mail from Elyria. They
consolidated Purcell's paint factory in Lorain with his sales
promotion, which he called Commercial Democracy. Involving the sale of stock to dealers, it was later revised to
interest a group of Elyria business men and called American
Merchants Co. Capitalized for $200,000, it received support
from bankers, doctors, retired men, a druggist, and others.

He was to receive $25,000 in common stock for his share.
What money was paid in was gone by the time the company
collapsed as the result of his amnesia attack in November,
1912. [24]

Anderson's attention was probably first turned to
Elyria when he visited there in the interests of The United
Factories Co. , which had dealings with the Fox Furnace Co.
in Elyria. [25] Two possible sources of capital for The Anderson Manufacturing Co. have been discovered.   Miss Jeanette
Paden thought her brother, Clifton, Anderson's good friend,
had put money in Anderson's business in Elyria; Mr. Purcell
recalled meeting Mr. Paden in Elyria several times. [26]
Another possible backer was Walter E. Brooks, who rented
Anderson factory space.   Mr. Brooks may have given Anderson backing in order to get a tenant for his vacant factory.
Furthermore, Mr. Brooks helped Anderson interest investors
in The American Merchants Co. when it was formed in
November, 1911. [27] Mr. Boynton, who was never connected
with Anderson's business, had the impression that Mr.
Brooks "provided all financial backing for Anderson's enterprise. " Mr. E. O. Schaad, however, has said that Anderson
"kited" checks to build up false credit.   "He told me how to
start a business without money. " So it is possible Anderson
did not have a great deal of financial support from any one.
Cornelia recalled the situation this way: "At first we put
up our money, which was mostly air.   Then there was
stock. "[28]

Whatever the exact machinery for getting started was,
the business was under way by the middle of September,
1907, when an advertisement appeared in at least one farm
weekly.   The advertisement was one inch by one column.
Headed by the injunction in bold capitals to FIX YOUR ROOF,
its text was as follows:

> We will guarantee to put any old leaky, worn-
> out, rusty, tin, iron, steel, paper, felt, gravel or
> shingle roof in perfect condition, and keep it in
> perfect condition for 5¢ per square per year.

> The Perfect Roof Preserver [Roof-Fix] makes
> old, worn-out roofs new.   Satisfaction guaranteed
> or money refunded.   Our free roofing book tells
> you about it.   Write for it today.   The Anderson
> Manufacturing Company, Dept. 16, Elyria, Ohio. [29]

Roof-Fix, Cornelia recalled, had passed its test on Anderson's own house in Cleveland.   Cornelia said, "Roof-Fix
carried us to Elyria. "[30]

No effort has been made to study exhaustively the advertising coming from Anderson's new company but various
items have been collected which reveal his manner of oper-
ating his business.   One of his advertisements makes it
clear that his sales approach was exactly like that used in
the United Factories catalogue:

We will guarantee to put any old leaky, worn-
out, rusty, tin, iron, steel, paper, felt or shingle
roof in perfect condition and keep it in perfect
condition at a cost to you of less than 5 cents per
square per year.

A new roof will cost you from $2. 00 to $5. 00
a square for material alone.

Suppose it lasts 15 years.

That is from 14 cents to 35 cents per square
per year.

Counting repairs and the cost of putting it on,
you can absolutely count on a cost of 25 cents per
square per year.

Now ROOF-FIX will take that old roof just as
it is and make it tight and useful for from three
to eight years longer, at a guaranteed cost of less
than 5 cents per square per year.

Are you planning to spend $100. 00 for a new
roof?

Just figure a moment.

The interest on $100. 00 for three years is
$18. 00.

Spend from $3. 00 to $5. 00 for ROOF-FIX and
keep that $100. 00 for 5 years longer.

WE TAKE THE RISK.   If ROOF-FIX won't fix
that roof of yours, you don't need to pay us one

cent. We won't ask for the goods back. We won't
quibble and fuss. We will simply not ask you to
pay.

Can you afford to let the old roof go? Can you
afford to let the water leak thru and rot the walls
of your building when a few dollars will make it
tight and sound for years?

See what some ROOF-FIX users say.

[Two testimonals follow.]

WRITE FOR THE FREE BOOK.

We will send you absolutely free a book full of
useful information about fixing roofs and how to
save money.

We have men connected with the company who
are practical roof men of long experience. Tell
us about your sick roof.

Our free book and what personal advice and
help we can give you will not cost you a cent.
Don't let the old roof go. Write at once.

The ANDERSON MANUFACTURING Co.

Carrier No. 5, Elyria, Ohio. [31]

Two other advertisements in The Rural New-Yorker
show how Anderson attempted to exploit the personal element,
this time more blatantly than in the United Factories catalogue. One has a heading which asks the reader to "Tell
Me Your Roof Troubles. " It goes on to suggest:

Let me tell you, Free, how to cure your roof
troubles for keeps. ROOF-FIX cures roof troubles
in your felt, gravel, shingle, steel, tin or iron
roofs. The longest-lived roof-dressing made for
sound roofs. Get my new free book about roofs
and roofing. Write to

ANDERSON, "The Roof-Fix Man"

Dept. 35   Elyria, Ohio[32]

Further evidence that Anderson felt strongly about
making the customer feel he was dealing with a person rather than with a company is found in a large advertisement
which appeared in almost every issue of the weekly Elyria
Republican in the months of April, May, June, and July,
1912.   The ad was sub-headed "A PLAIN TALK," in bold
type, and the text took up seven inches of type.   Most of it
is quoted below:

> ... We can save your money on paint and I want to
> tell you why.   We run our business on a coopera-
> tive basis and although we are having[,] as this is
> written, an increase of over one hundred per cent
> in business over last year we still have no sales-
> men on the road and a very low selling cost.   If
> you will come in and see us I am sure we can
> show you where this means a big saving in cost of
> paint to you and also I know that we can convince
> you once and for all of the quality of the goods.
> Wilcoxson Paint is good stuff.   Don't take the word
> of the fellow that has another paint to sell about
> that.   Come in and let us prove it to you.   And
> let me say that whether you come to the factory or
> order through your painter we'll stand back of it.
> If it isn't as good paint as you ever used, you
> know where I am.   Come to me and say so and
> you can have your money back.
>
> Naturally I want to see the business in our home
> town go to a home town paint factory.   Ill [sic]
> try to make it worth your while to look us up if
> you are going to use paint.   We will save our
> people here about twenty cents a gallon on the
> best grade paint.   That's worth while.
>
> ANDERSON'S RED BARN PAINT
>
> We are making a special red barn paint this
> year at one dollar a gallon that is a good one.
> We are putting it out as a sort of advertisement
> of our whole line of paints.   It is sold with a five
> year guarantee.
>
> Varnishes, Stains, Etc. --We have a high grade
> line of these goods but we will willingly supply you
> at just about what the dealer would have to pay
> for the same goods, because the factory is here

and we want your trade.

> I will willingly mail color cards or come to see
> anyone interested in paint. Write or call Phone
> 646. Old Topliff and Ely plant (Opposite Lake
> Shore Railroad Depot.)

> ANDERSON MANUFACTURING Co.
> SHERWOOD ANDERSON, MGR.

Predominantly, it would seem, Anderson's advertising
was in the tone of the above. But the Lorain County Directory for 1910[33] contained advertising that was more impersonal. The main importance of this material is that it
shows that Anderson Manufacturing Co. was handling Roof-
Fix, the Wilcoxson Paints (named after the paint-maker who
entered the firm with the Purcell merger), and Rawhide
Roofing, "a pure wool felt roofing."

The Roof-Fix, which was the first product Anderson
sold, stemmed directly from his experience with United
Factories, which had sold a similar compound. Mr. Bottger
said he traveled to Elyria several times at Anderson's request to help with details of the business. Anderson coined
the name Roof-Fix himself, however. The profit on the roofing compound was great, the cost of manufacture being about
one-fifth of the sale price.[34] At first Anderson had it made
for him in Cleveland. Later it was made by the Purcell
company. According to a man who worked for Anderson as
office boy, the Roof-Fix was brought into the Anderson "factory," put into new containers, and sent out to the custom-
ers. He recalled that results were very good in 1908 and
1909, and lots of money came in.[35]

Anderson has referred to the time "when I worked
rather long hours in a factory office, surrounded by a cloud
of young women stenographers, dictating form letters for
hours at a stretch, getting up very plausible-sounding form
letters that went out in thousands...." And when, "having
been a slow-moving dreamy boy I had made myself into this
crisp thing that hurried to an office, sat at a big desk,
rang bells, got suddenly and sometimes nastily executive.
Do this and do that, I cried to others...."[36]

One of the stenographers, Mrs. Yost, had a memory
of him that agrees with his own. To her he seemed to be
a man of driving ambition. Everyone worked hard. The

girls were not supposed to stretch their fifteen-minute rest
period. He never said more than good morning and not always that. His shrewd, sharp eye was used to "pep the
girls up. " He had "no conception of the time it took to get
out the letters. . . . There were never any words about work
failures; he just gave notice and never said why. He had no
use for any one who didn't work. " The office was very
crude and had long pine benches in it. "He never wanted to
spend money to make the office presentable. He was a
strict economist. " The girls worked from eight till five,
had thirty minutes for lunch, had a fifteen-minute rest period at 10 a. m. , and had to get permission to leave at any
other time. "He was kindly but impersonal and insisted that
the girls give every effort to the work. "

Mrs. Yost also recalled that the business was almost
completely mail order. The business seemed to her to be
prosperous, but there was trouble with the barn paint, which
peeled. The Anderson company sold a glass razor hone for
50 cents but did not use the Anderson name in connection
with it, she remembered further.

The recollections other employees had of Anderson as
an employer are not the same as that of Mrs. Yost. Mr.
McConnell said Anderson was a "swell fellow" to work for.
"He had a soft, pleasing voice and was very considerate. "
He added, "He smoked like the devil. " Another woman
commented, "He was a fine man to work for. I always got
along with him. Any one would. " Her memory added a
knife-sharpener to the list of products sold. 37 Another employee added ironing-board springs to the list. She thought
he was a "grand man" to work for. "Nobody I ever worked
for was any nicer. " In her case, she said, he had an understanding way with a beginner. "There was no sense of
permanency. After all, a novelty business isn't permanent. . . .
I thought we were floating pretty close to the surface most
of the time. I don't know why. "38 That may have been why
Mrs. Yost could recall, "He seemed to have something on
his mind. " He would puff on his pipe and let the dictaphone
run on. The stenographer had to reach over and turn it
off. 39

The first major change in Anderson's business was
the absorption of the Purcell Company of Lorain in 1908.
The next important development was the promotion of what
was called "commercial democracy, " a plan based on the
sale of stock to dealers, which seems to have had its

inception in October, 1909. The first ad mentioning it in
The Rural New-Yorker is of that date:

> LET ME START YOU IN BUSINESS!
>
> I will furnish the capital and advertising. I want
> one sincere, earnest man in every town and town-
> ship. Farmers, Mechanics, Builders, Small busi-
> ness men, any one anxious to improve his condi-
> tion. Address Anderson Mfg. Co. , Dept. d. 35,
> Elyria, Ohio. [40]

With the issue of November 20, 1909, a change was made in
the advertisement. The address was no longer the Anderson
Company. Instead the applicant was to write to "Commercial
Democracy. " Otherwise the statement remained the same
and was in almost every weekly issue of The Rural New-
Yorker through November 12, 1910, when the last advertisement appeared.

     The exact nature of the commercial democracy scheme
is not known, but it might be useful to remember one of
Anderson's statements concerning his business attitude:

> ... I was going to be a rich man. ... We were in
> this respectable house now, the biggest and best
> that, at least up to that time, I had ever lived in;
> but I told myself that it was nothing. "Wait and
> see, " I often said to myself as I walked along the
> street toward my house at evening. "Next year a
> bigger house; and after that presently, a country
> estate. " I had no idea that we would stay in the
> town we were then in. The stopping in that town,
> perhaps for a few years, was but an incident. I
> had to find out how things were done in the Ameri-
> can business world. "Talk a good deal about
> honesty but keep your eyes open and when the
> chance comes slip it over on them, " I often at that
> time said to myself, laughing as I said it. Of
> course this may all be somewhat twisted, but I am
> trying to put down what went on in me at that time.
> I think I did realize that I had a good mind and I
> remember that often, even then, I said to myself
> that it wasn't the stealing, robbing others, cheating
> others, that ruined a man, but that what did ruin
> him was getting to the place where he did not know
> he was stealing. [41]

Perhaps it was in some such ruthless spirit as that expressed above that The Anderson Manufacturing Company, "Commercial Democracy," and The American Merchants Company were manipulated. Part of the commercial democracy scheme was Commercial Democracy, which has been described by an American Merchants stock-holder as an "advertising pamphlet" to be sent to hardware dealers. "It stressed a new plan of retailing, cooperation between manufacturers and retailers. "[42]   Anderson described it this way:

> ...I began publishing a magazine called Commercial
> Democracy, writing the entire magazine myself. I
> spent money circulating it by thousands of copies.
> I went from town to town preaching my idea of
> altruism in manufacturing and retailing to retail
> merchants. [43]

He also wrote:

> Then I started a magazine.   I wrote it all, every
> month, I mailed it out to business men.   I don't
> mean to say that my ideas were clean.   I kept
> thinking up little cheating schemes and putting them
> in operation at the same time I was preaching to
> myself and others against just such schemes.... [44]

No copies of the Commercial Democracy publication have been found, but Karl recalled Sherwood wrote "some semi-autobiographical sketches which he had printed up in pamphlet form and distributed as advertisements. "[45]   Cornelia recalled articles in Commercial Democracy using a picturesque fictional character, based on "Daddy" Wilcoxson, the paint-maker, as a "mouthpiece for Sherwood's philosophy. "   The Wilcoxson character "used words with too many syllables in them, etc. "[46]

The testimony of Mr. Purcell, who went into Anderson's business in 1908, [47] is that commercial democracy was a selling plan.   The evidence of the advertising in The Rural New Yorker is the same.

There is another thing about the commercial democracy plan that should be noted.   Anderson sold "small blocks of stock to dealers. "   One would expect the stock would be in a corporation, but the office of the Ohio Department of State has no record of articles of incorporation for The Anderson Manufacturing Company.   If in actuality Anderson was, as seems likely, issuing stock, it was not in a regular corporation. Any difficulty arising from that fact was eliminated when The American Merchants Company was incorporated on November 20, 1911. The corporation was formed

> ...for the purpose of manufacturing and selling paints, varnishes, oils and chemicals, and all ingredients, compounds and by-products thereof and for the purpose of manufacturing and selling all kinds of wood and metal preservatives and all preparations and articles used in or incident to the paint and roofing business and all things incident to the above mentioned purposes. [48]

The company was capitalized at $200,000, having 1,600 shares of common stock and 400 of preferred, all having a par of $100. Anderson was not one of the signers of the articles of incorporation. Nor was he one of the seventeen men who subscribed for $24,000 in stock. [49] Consequently, the $25,000 in common stock, which Mr. Purcell said was Anderson's share, was purely a potential gain.

According to two stockholders, Mr. Squire and Dr. Saunders, the support of Mr. Brooks, who subscribed to $2,000 worth of stock, was very important to the setting up of the new company, of which Anderson was a director. The impression was that Anderson was a good advertising man and a good salesman. Dr. Saunders said "We thought we had a world-beater. We were going to put Sherwin-Williams out of business." Anderson was apparently in complete charge; Mr. Squire referred to him as "captain, cook, and bottle-washer." Anderson did all the banking business.

Mr. Squire has pointed out that the real function of American Merchants was to serve as the merchandising outlet of the Anderson Company. But actually there was no such straight-forward arrangement. The Anderson Manufacturing Company continued to exist and to advertise, as the items in the Elyria Republican prove. In the Elyria directory for 1913 Anderson styled himself the proprietor of the Anderson Company. "Anderson Mfg. Co." is listed under paint manufacturers; there is no mention of The American Merchants Company. But when Anderson left Elyria, "Anderson Mfg. Co." left with him. American Merchants was left and Purcell undertook its salvage. According to Dr. Saunders:

As a consequence of Anderson's leaving, his investors were faced with the problem of clearing up
the business. The company was heavily in debt.
Available funds were used to pay debts. Then the
assets were liquidated to take care of debts then
unpaid.

Two advertisements in the Elyria Evening Telegram
throw some light on the situation. The first, which appeared
first on April 3, 1913, said The American Merchants Company had sold the Roof-Fix business to the G. E. Conkey
Company, Cleveland, Ohio. American Merchants also announced that the balance of the stock on hand, "including
several thousand gallons of high grade house and barn paint,"
would be sold at once at a great sacrifice. According to
Mr. J. T. Conkey, however, the Roof-Fix business transaction was a deal between the Conkey Company and Anderson.
Coinciding with this is the statement of Anderson's secretary,
Mrs. Howk, that the sale of the Roof-Fix business was the
only thing he did toward clearing up the business before he
left Elyria. On May 1 The Purcell Paint Manufacturing Company inserted an advertisement in the Daily Telegram and
styled itself as the successor to The American Merchants
Company.

A former employee epitomized Anderson's business
career in Elyria by recalling him as a friendly person, a
great talker and not afraid of any transaction he thought
would make money. [50] In his Memoirs Anderson said: "I
have hated every method by which I have ever been able to
get money in America" (page 168).

Cornelia Anderson has supplied an interesting comment on the relationship of the two opposing factors, business and writing, and the struggle of which Anderson was
the center:

As for the business men, it is natural they should
feel as they do. But he was a victim of the catastrophe as much as they were--and more.

Mr. Anderson was trying to build up a business to
support his family and had business ability. He
was an enthusiast and believed in his own ideas,
and his enthusiasm was contagious. The urge to
write came upon him, and I believe the conflict between the two urges caused his mental lapse.

> ... He had no feeling of irresponsibility. When he
> said he was an artist, he was simply giving the
> true explanation and was not excusing himself on
> that score. He had no illusions about himself but
> a strong belief in himself.

For herself she added, "I don't know whether I had enough
acumen to know if the business was going to wreck." As
far as Sherwood was concerned, any setback was temporary. [51]

The process of emphasizing the desire and necessity
of writing and neglecting the duties of business was evidently
protracted and unsystematic, but certain aspects of it can be
identified and partially described. In spite of the fact that
Anderson eventually did separate himself from his family to
follow the destiny of his artistic urge, the decision seems to
have been achieved only gradually through great struggle and
in response to powerful inward pressures. "'The trouble
with you,' I told myself, 'is just the years you spent in
business.'"[52]

> More and more I found I could return to my desk
> and lose myself in the writing of others. I tried
> to put down little sketches of things seen--little
> glimpses out of life given me by others--my writ-
> ing began to have a little form.... If I could not
> think clearly of what seemed to me the false posi-
> tion in life into which I had got I could take some
> imaginary figure... and put him in the same posi-
> tion in life in which I found myself. [53]

He has written also that "I came to writing rather through
the back door, as my primary object in the beginning was
not publication, but rather, if possible, to show up things
about myself and others in my own mind."[54]

As has been discussed, Anderson had written a great
deal in connection with his duties as an advertising man and
perhaps otherwise in the second Chicago period. It is difficult to tell how Anderson later viewed these writings; probably he did not consider them as part of his serious artistic
effort, for he was to write in 1916: "For nearly seven
years now, ever since I began writing--and I count any happiness I have had in life as beginning when I began to
scribble--..."[55] The nature of his first "scribbling" is also
subject to speculation, but there is evidence which is certainly worthy of review. The quotation just above indicates

1909 as the year in which he began to write in Elyria. Anderson's notorious incapacity for concern with dates serves
as a warning about taking that literally, but there are other
indications which point to that year.

> I remember my own first experience as a writer.
> Book on Socialism.   Oh life, I have solved thee.
> Young men everywhere now having the experience.
> Young socialists, communists, having this air...
> the cocksureness of most of it. [56]

In the latter part of 1909, as has been seen, the commercial
democracy scheme was initiated with its attendant magazine.
Cornelia makes a half-serious reference to this socialist
phase.   Perhaps at this time Anderson was really concerned
with Socialism.   Or was it just reforms?   Or was it profit-
sharing?   Certainly there does not seem to have been any
dedication to the cause of socialism, for Windy McPherson's
Son and Marching Men mention socialism but give little consideration or comfort to it.   In any case, if a book on
socialism was really the first of the Elyria books, it has
not survived any more than Commercial Democracy and
possibly other books from the period did.

He was also to say in 1919, that it was an "impulse
for my own salvation" that led him to write his novels:

> One day I sat down and began to write a novel.   I
> liked it.   To my amazement, I found that on paper
> I was entirely honest and sincere--a really like-
> able, clear-headed, decent fellow.   At once, I knew
> that I would write novels the rest of my life, and
> I certainly shall. [57]

Although it is not known what he wrote, some of his
feelings while involved in the process are known:

> My eyes began to be a little opened. ...   I think I
> must have been a little insane.   I was taking long
> walks alone in the woods.   I began drinking again.
> I shut myself up in a room at home.   I think my
> wife thought I was a little insane.
>
> It was then I began to write, sitting often all night
> at my desk in an upper room of our house, with
> the door locked.   I quit wanting to change people.
> I began more and more to want to understand

rather than change.

At the same time I was keeping at my factory.   I
still constantly wrote lies.   It was that made me
drink.

I think the writing too was a kind of drunkenness.
I grew to hate the factory office.   And, at the same
time, I did a lot of woman chasing too.   A man
could forget what he was in the arms of a woman
as well as in drink. [58]

I used to take a lot of long walks alone.   I began
that.   There was a time during which I drank a
good deal, got drunk almost every night.   Drink
helps sometimes.   I got a notion in my head.   I
said to myself, "Look here, " I said, "if you can't
really approach people in the real world, in the
world of nature, there may be another world, " and
I must say the thought jerked a door open for me.
I do not believe that I have ever thought of myself
as a fine writer, that I have ever cared for writing
in that way. . . .

And so naturally I think of writing as a kind of
giving out, a going out.   What is of interest to
me is the fact of how very unimportant my factory,
my achievements, my position in society, became
to me. . . . [59]

    In the Memoirs Anderson devoted two chapters, "The
Italian's Garden" (pages 163-174) and "The Man of Ideas"
(pages 175-185), to a delineation of his reactions in this
transitional stage.   The account is apparently fictional, but
one may assume the spirit of it is accurate.   The Italian
symbolizes a man satisfied by a simple, earthy life.   "The
Man of Ideas, " who is presented under the pseudonym of
Luther Pawsey (a good Winesburg surname) embodies artistic
consciousness, the appreciation of the true beauties in life
and art, the ethical realization of responsibility for the
words he misused as a slick advertiser.   Luther Pawsey is
reminiscent of the late Perry S. Williams, who by all accounts was Anderson's best friend in Elyria.   Pawsey was
a local printer; Williams was managing editor of a newspaper.   Pawsey and Anderson walked and talked a great deal;
so did Williams and Anderson. [60]   But Williams' remark to
Mr. Boynton, "Do you know this man Anderson has an

ambition to be a writer? He told me he spends most of his
nights writing," makes it seem improbable that he was the
Pawsey who patiently argued Anderson into seeing that he
should be a writer. Pawsey, perhaps created in the reminiscent image of Williams, is a character conceived especially
to serve as a foil for the delineation of Anderson's announced
spiritual mutations. Cornelia remembered of Williams that
Sherwood liked him and was always quoting him. 61

Certainly a contribution to Anderson's artistic development was made by the presence in Elyria for some of this
period of Sherwood's youngest brother Earl, who would have
been 22 when Sherwood's move to Elyria was made. Details
of Anderson's accounts of his relationship[62] are demonstrably
inaccurate, but it seems that this quotation points in the direction of truth. This brother had been to art school in
Chicago, wanted to be a painter, "...had a great deal to do
with my becoming a writer and understanding a little the impulses and purposes of the artist man."[63] Karl thought
Sherwood was so in need of "intellectual companionship"
that he made a job for Earl so they could take long
walks and hold conversations about writers, on which
Karl seems to think Earl was the better versed, [64]
though this seems doubtful.

The date Earl was in Elyria is so far impossible to
determine. In March of 1926, Anderson wrote one correspondent that Earl had disappeared fifteen years before (i.e.,
1911). [65] In April of the same year, he told another person
the disappearance had been "about eighteen years ago" (i.e.,
1908). [66] Of the two dates the latter seems more likely.
In any case, the brother, evidently feeling massively in-
ferior and rejected by the rest of the family, only became
reunited with the family when they were notified on the occasion of his having had a stroke.

Helen, Karl's wife, wrote to Sherwood that Earl
thought he had not been wanted by his mother at birth or by
Stella, Sherwood, or Karl later. This factor was the chief
among his "grievances about life."[67] She also thought,
"This is his whole trouble, he can not make the right contacts with his fellow men. And he lays hold of his early
life to excuse himself. And he believes he was spoiled in
the making."[68]

Sherwood's reaction to Earl's attitude, in view
of his other capacity for mystical and intense sympathy, is

interestingly objective:

> This feeling of his about not being wanted, not be-
> ing loved, etc. is part of what has been the matter
> with him all the time.   It is not very sensible
> really as he has had more affection from all of us
> than we have given each other.   He is the one who
> hid himself away.   At least Karl always did for
> him all that an older brother would do. [68]

> I dare say the poor lad was made to feel something
> of what he says when he was a boy and yet, I am
> quite sure we loved him more than we loved each
> other.   We weren't a very tender lot.   A restless
> ambition seemed to drive us all on.   The result
> was that those who got brushed aside by life had a
> tendency to justify themselves by thinking their own
> fate perilously hard and sad. [70]

Sherwood was also to say of this brother, "He... looked
out at life always as from a distance.   He was the stuff
of which poets are made. "[71]   "He was a strange chap, very
talented, rather silent.   He was born to a woman who didn't
want him....   People were always trying to help him.   They
couldn't. "[72]   Karl said that once during his recluse years
Earl had seen Sherwood ahead of him on the street, a
famous, successful man, and scurried out of sight. [73]   Just
after Earl was hospitalized and reunited with his family,
Sherwood wrote him: "Need I tell you that I love you and
want you.   I have wanted you back since you disappeared. "[74]

All the forces at work had plunged Anderson into new
and compulsive patterns, which he recalled:

> When I had been doing my writing, unknown and
> unseen, there was a sort of freedom.   One worked,
> more or less in secret, as one might indulge in
> some secret vice.   There were the bankers and
> others who had put money into my enterprises.
> They had expected I would be giving myself wholly
> to the matter in hand and I had been cheating and
> did not want them to know.   One wrote tales,
> played with them.   One did not think of publication,
> of a public that was to read. [75]

But that account is highly colored.   Actually, it was
rather widely known that Anderson wrote.   It was his habit

to dictate stories into the dictaphone and have his secretary
type them. "I typed his first two books [Windy McPherson's
Son and Marching Men]--and corrected his spelling, " remembers his secretary, Mrs. Frances Howk. She was well
aware of Anderson's determination to "get out of business
and into writing. " He was submitting manuscripts for publication in 1911 and 1912. [76] "I typed up the manuscripts and
got them ready for mailing. He'd send the manuscripts
right from the office, " she said. Mr. Purcell remembered
that "while we were together he spent much of his time
writing short stories--none of which were accepted until after
he left Elyria. " The editor of a local newspaper noted that
Anderson was busy with his efforts to express his observations of the people around him in Elyria. He was working
nights on his writing. The editor recalled seeing Marching
Men in manuscript. [77] One of the stockholders in The American Merchants Company, Mr. Crandall, said "Anderson was
a dreamer and did a lot of writing. He wrote volumes of
stuff instead of attending to business. There was usually a
sheet of manuscript on his desk. " Dr. Saunders, another
stockholder, was aware that "Anderson used to dictate stories to be typed next morning along with the letters. He had
the writing bug in his bonnet. "

It is possible to add a few notes concerning the several novels he told many people he had written before he published and which he took to Chicago with him. The two
which survived to be published were Windy McPherson's Son
(1916) and Marching Men (1917). Of the first he has written
"I had reached near to the middle station of life and was un-
fitted for my place in it. My own nature was in revolt
against money making as an end in life and the history of
Sam McPherson is the history of such a revolt. "[78] He
speaks of the fact that his "mind reached back into childhood"
for material. The stylistic faults of the books he sees as
those of a "badly educated man struggling to tell a story to
his own people in his own way. " (The book is dedicated to
"the living men and women of my own middle western home
town. ") On the occasion of submitting a revised ending, he
points out, "The book was written under rather trying circumstances and all the latter part of it represents my own
floundering about in life. " Also, "the book was written
[when I had] a false conception of what is due the reader of
a novel. "[79]

Although information about his reading in Chicago indicates he had read Dostoevski, he took the trouble to inform

Waldo Frank that he had never heard of Dreiser or Dostoevski when he wrote <u>Windy McPherson's Son</u>.[80]   In view of all
that is known of his active reading and discussing of writers,
this statement may perhaps most agreeably be thought of as
a minor prevarication.   Anderson seems at times to have
wished to present an impression of knowing less than he did
about other writers and their writings.   This was particularly
true of the Russian writers.

    Of <u>Marching Men</u> he wrote as follows:

> ...I wrote it in the midst of the big readjustment
> in my own life.   It was a theme that appealed to
> my rather primitive nature.   The beat and rhythm
> of the thing would come and go; a thousand outside
> things would flow in.   I worked madly; then I threw
> the book away.   Again and again I went back to it.
> In the end I had no idea whether it was good or
> bad.   I only knew that the thing was out of me and
> I could turn to something else. [81]

    Cornelia has recalled that his development as a writer
was random rather than planned, and she seems to have been
quite conscious of his writing.   "Sherwood never went on a
bus or anywhere that he didn't come home with the life story
of some acquaintance.   All these later came out in his stories.   It was interesting to see them come out. "   According
to her, he wrote when he wanted to and he wanted to very
often.   It was true that he was known to write all night, as
several sources have averred.   To her, "The whole idea of
his writing was satisfactory.   I am not practical.   I guess I
never have been practical.   The spirit of adventure was
strong in both of us. "   One day Bob, the older of the two
boys, asked his mother: "What is a novelist?"   The occasion of the question was that the plumber had asked him if
his father were a novelist. [82]

    Newspaper articles on the occasion of Sherwood's
amnesia attack made reference to his writing, and one of
them had detail on this point.   In identifying Anderson, one
article refers to him as "manufacturer and author. "   His
Elyria friends are said to believe he "broke down under the
strain of work on a novel, which was to have been his masterpiece. "   The article points out that "in the last year or
more" he has worked "long days at the office of his paint
factory" and then at night has "toiled over his writing.   He
is the author of a quantity of magazine fiction.   Early last

summer [1912] he began on a larger work, a complete novel which was to climax his work. " His wife is said to have "remonstrated with him gently, warning him that he could not stand the strain. At these times he would put the writing aside and get out on the lawn and play with his wife and their two boys six and four years old. "

> But another night would find him at his work. The long, hot evenings made work impossible indoors, but his ambition could not wait on weather conditions. He built a large screened porch at the back of the house and arranged lights so that he could write outside. There he could be seen toiling in the early hours of the morning. And at 8 o'clock he would again be at the office, wrestling with the problems of manufacture. [83]

Karl's account was that Sherwood had undertaken creative effort as a sideline, making up stories during working hours, writing them by night. "He thought of himself as an amateur who could afford non-conformity; 'I am damn well writing what I like!' he told me. " He also told Karl he had fixed "an enclosed room" in his attic to be alone to write. He went to the "boxed room and wrote deep into the night. "[84]

Anderson's reaction to the enforced interruption of his writing to play on the lawn with the children is reflected in two nearly identical letters in the fall of 1937, referring to a visit by his grandchildren, from whom he has retreated. He says he is allergic to small children and explains: "I think perhaps the trouble, as regards small children, dates back to my life with their mother. She was very determined that I be one kind of man--for the children's sake, etc. -- and I was as determined [to be another]. "[85] And "I think it is left over from the old struggle between the children's mother and myself... she determined I was to stay in business and I determined I'd go my own road. It was all put on the grounds of the children. "[86]

In Chicago Anderson and his wife had apparently belonged to something of a literary group, people who liked to read and discuss reading. The Fortnightly, to which Cornelia belonged in Elyria, was primarily a reading group. Cornelia remembered writing for it. "We were all yearning for culture. "[87] Cornelia's education had been in large part literary. Perhaps one of the bases of rapport between them was their mutual love of reading, which he did voraciously and intelligently, as his Chicago writings show. Yet Anderson has implied that not the least of his difficulties in starting his writing career was with his wife:

> In the first place, my first wife, the mother of my children, had been unable to believe in me as an artist and I could not blame her. She was a woman who, having married one sort of man, had awakened to find she had another. She married a bright young business man, one who might, had he remained as he seemed to be when she had married him, have been a good father, a good provider, one who would have seen to it that her children were brought up in the classic American style-- that is to say the classic style for the well-to-do-- who would have provided them with automobiles, sent them to the best colleges, etc.
>
> However, I was determined [I] would not be turned aside, and there had been a long silent struggle, ending in divorce. [88]

An almost desperate quality is found in his recollections of that period:

> I shall never forget a quite childish thing in the life of [Cornelia] and myself. Just because I was married to her when I did not want to be I imagined terrible things about her. It did not seem to me possible to escape out of marriage into life. I pictured her as my jailer and terrible hate worked in me. At night I even dreamed of killing her.
>
> And all the time I suppose I was a quite normal, quiet-appearing fellow. I used to walk out of the house into the street at night and say to myself: "Great God, she don't [sic] know."
>
> And of course, dear patient woman, she did not know. No one can know what they have not themselves felt. Only by feeling do we come into knowledge and I suspect that it is only by feeling deeply, deeply that we shall come to culture. [89]

Another, less intense aspect was seen in the relationship with their friends the Terrys, mother and daughter, who visited often in each other's homes. He was just beginning

to write and read from <u>Windy McPherson's Son</u> till the Terrys
said they could stand no more and advised him the reading
public would not accept it.   Miss Terry recalled his sitting
up during the night writing, being confident of his ability to
write successful novels, disliking business the more as his
creative ambitions became more intense and well established. [90]

Cornelia remembered that when Miss Terry and her
mother visited the Andersons, Sherwood would read aloud "to
be able to get a better view of his work.   Sherwood never
lost an opportunity to read his work aloud. "[91]

Miss Terry has declared that "it is certainly untrue
that she [Cornelia] ever discouraged Sherwood's writing efforts, but, on the contrary, did all she could to help and
encourage him. " She has also stated "he knew his limitations in a cultural way and expressed great appreciation of
his wife... for her help in diction, rhetoric, and so forth. "[92]
Cornelia, however, has said she did not think she ever helped
her husband with his writing. [93]   Perhaps related to this idea
is Anderson's statement to Karl: "When I was with C[or-
nelia] and T[ennessee] I always had to escape as far as I
could from them to work at all. "[94]

Miss Terry described both Sherwood and Cornelia as
radical on social questions.   Cornelia was open to new ideas,
thought they ought to be given a chance to prove their worth.
She specifically recalled that, when she and her mother crit-
icized Sherwood's ideas and work, Cornelia did not. [95]

Perhaps Cornelia was not always so reserved.   Mrs.
Howk has recalled Mrs. Anderson's commenting favorably
on a book and her remarking, "It isn't anything like those
things Sherwood's writing. " As her husband's ambition to
write became stronger, as he devoted more and more time
to writing, completing at least two novels before 1913, and
as his business affairs became more and more tangled,
events must have indeed been trying for her.   She accepted
passively his ambition to write; she had been educated to
understand literary men.   There is no evidence to show that
she was enthusiastic about what he had written.   But at the
same time that she had her husband's ambitions to consider,
she had also herself and three children to consider.   She
has said of her situation, "I think he felt it was his duty to
be in business and support a family and that it was his inclination to write. "[96]   It is not at all clear that she knew,
or that he did, why he had the inclination.

Anderson made his exit from the physical cause of the struggle that raged within him at the beginning of 1913. As Mr. Purcell wrote, the business collapsed "when he appeared to have suffered from a case of lost identity." The various accounts, oral and written, by Anderson of how he left Elyria would make an interesting separate study. But the gist of the story as he presented it may be found in the Memoirs and A Story Teller's Story.

> What was I to do? It seemed to me impossible to explain to others what was going on within me. It was all too unformed in my own mind. I had had very little schooling. After all I thought of writers as educated men and I had no education. It is perhaps that I had been acquiring education very rapidly during the last two or three years in that place but it did not seem to me the kind of education I could explain to others. I wanted to leave, get away from the business, turn it over to some one else but did not know how to go about it.
>
> Again I resorted to slickness. Already I had got a reputation for a kind of queerness among my acquaintances.... The impression got abroad. I perhaps encouraged it--that I was overworking, was on the point of a nervous breakdown and I encouraged the notion. I have told something of all this in a book of mine called A Story Teller's Story. The thought occurred to me that if men thought me a little insane they would forgive me if I lit out....[97]

It was in A Story Teller's Story that Anderson told of the "pregnant moment" when he left Elyria afoot.

> Whether at that moment I merely became shrewd and crafty or whether I became temporarily insane I shall never quite know. What I did was to step very close to the woman [his secretary] and looking directly into her eyes I laughed gayly. Others beside herself would, I knew, hear the words I was now speaking. I looked at my feet. "I have been wading in a long river and my feet are wet," I said.
>
> Again I laughed as I walked lightly toward the door and out of a long and tangled phase of my life, out

of the door of buying and selling, out of the door
of affairs.

"They want me to be a 'nut,' will love to think of
me as a 'nut,' and why not? It may just be that's
what I am," I thought gayly and at the same time
turned and said a final confusing sentence to the
woman who now stared at me in speechless amazement. "My feet are cold wet and heavy from long
wading in a river. Now I shall go walk on dry
land," I said.... I went along a spur of a railroad
track, out of a town and out of that phase of my
life (pages 312-13).

According to the Memoirs, as he walked eastward along the
railroad track, "toward the city of Cleveland...there were
five or six dollars in my pocket" (page 194).

In Appendix D is reproduced the full text of a cruci-
ally-revealing letter by Anderson, giving an account of the
way the Elyria situation "ended in a convulsion that touched
the edge of insanity." Information from Mrs. Cornelia Anderson, his Elyria secretary (Mrs. Leon Howk, Lakewood,
Ohio, then Miss Frances Shute), manuscript material related
to his actual illness, and newspaper accounts give basic corroboration to the following statement of his letter of 1916:

...When finally the affairs of the company became
desperate and I, seeing the money entrusted in me
by others, slipping away, I could not sleep at
night.... One morning my mind became a blank
and I ran away from Elyria, scurrying across
fields, sleeping in ditches, filling my pockets with
corn from the fields that I nibbled like a beast.
I would have been afraid even of her [his sympathetic secretary] then. I was afraid of everything
in human form...after several days of wandering
my mind came into my body and I dragged myself
weary and yet glad of my final defeat into a hospital in a strange town and slept....98

Anderson's secretary remembered that he came into
the office on a Thursday morning (November 28, 1912) and
"acted queerly." She had never noticed anything erratic in
his behavior before, though she had worked for him since
the summer of 1908. He opened his mail, noted the small
amount of money in it, and went to stand by a gas heater.

He said, "I feel as though my feet were wet, and they keep
getting wetter." Then he wrote a note to his wife, and
leaving it with Mrs. Howk, he said he was going for a walk
and did not know whether he would be back or not. He
walked along the railroad tracks, which went past the office.
The secretary then called Mrs. Anderson and asked her how
Mr. Anderson had felt when he left home. She said he had
seemed to be all right. Mrs. Howk then delivered the note
to Mrs. Anderson. (She never learned what was in it. Mrs.
Cornelia Anderson has not commented on this point.)

After she had got her husband's note, Mrs. Anderson
waited for his return. When he did not come home that
night, she consulted Mr. Walter Brooks, who advised her to
do nothing. On Sunday Mr. Edwin Baxter called to tell Mrs.
Anderson that her husband was in Huron Road Hospital in
Cleveland. According to Mrs. Howk, the police were never
notified that Anderson was missing.

Anderson told Mrs. Howk later that he had amnesia
and could not remember effectively things he wanted to do,
such as call his wife. He would think of something he
wanted to do and then forget it before he could do it. He
said he wandered into a drugstore and attempted to call his
wife, but his memory failed him again. Then he showed his
address book to the druggist, who recognized Mr. Baxter's
name. The druggist called Mr. Baxter, who had Anderson
taken to the hospital and notified Mrs. Anderson. [99]

Information to supplement Mrs. Howk's account is to
be found in Elyria and Cleveland newspapers. Mrs. Howk's
statement that the police were not asked to look for Anderson
is substantiated. No news of Anderson's disappearance was
in the newspapers until he was found, when a considerable
amount of space was given to the story. On Monday, December 2, 1912, the following story, headlined "ELYRIA MAN
IS FOUND DAZED IN CLEVELAND," was on page one of
the Elyria Evening Telegram:

> Sherwood Anderson, head of the Anderson Manu-
> facturing Co., and well known as "the roof-fix
> man" was found in Cleveland last night dazed and
> unable to give his name or address. He was taken
> to the Huron road hospital, where physicians said
> he was suffering from nerve exhaustion. His con-
> dition is not critical and it is expected that a few
> days['] rest will restore his memory.

Mrs. Anderson was notified of her husband's condition and hurried to the hospital. Friends here
say that overwork is the cause of Anderson's sick-
ness.

Anderson left home Thanksgiving day on a business
trip. Since that time nothing has been heard from
him until Monday when news of his condition was
conveyed to his family and his business associates.

Late Sunday afternoon Anderson went into the drug
store of J. H. Robinson, East 152 street and Aspinwall avenue. His clothes were bedraggled and
his appearance unkempt. To the questions asked
by the clerk in the store, Anderson replied in-
coherently. A physician and police who were notified ordered him conveyed to Huron road hospital.

Added to the cares of the Anderson Manufacturing
Co. and other enterprises in which Anderson was
the guiding spirit, for the last several months he
has been working on a novel and at odd times has
been writing short stories for magazines. En-
grossed in writing Anderson worked many a night
until nearly dawn and then attended to business affairs.

Two months ago he was warned by a physician that
he was overworking and should stop writing. A
few days later, however, he was back again at work
on his book. That he has been keeping steadily at
his literary endeavor was known to friends, who
only a week ago remarked his fagged out condition.

It is thought overwork caused a mental breakdown
when he reached Cleveland last Thursday. Anderson's identity was learned through papers found in
his clothes at the hospital.

An article in a Cleveland paper recorded that Anderson had difficulty in recognizing his wife, finally did recognize her, and then fell asleep. This article said the physician's diagnosis was that the patient was suffering from
"severe mental strain and overwork," which "physicians say
will gradually wear off. The patient had not been able to
tell anything of his four days of wandering."[100]

Some additional glimpses, into Anderson's family situation as well, may be seen in this segment of another story
on his hospitalization:

> Four months ago a third boy [Marion, the Ander-
> son's daughter, was born on October 29, 1911]
> was born.   The coming of the baby so busied its
> mother that her warnings to her husband were
> necessarily less frequent, and he worked harder
> at his novel.
>
> When his business took him away for a day or so
> on trips out of Elyria, he had always telegraphed
> to his wife daily.   Often the oldest boy [Robert],
> proud of his limited ability to read, would get a
> telegram or a night letter.   The lad reveled in
> puzzling them out with his nurse or mother.
>
> Friday no messages came and Mrs. Anderson be-
> came worried.   Saturday and Sunday brought no
> word and she called upon friends to locate him. 101

The manner of Anderson's re-entry into the real world
from his state of amnesia was rather carefully described:

> It was shortly after 5 o'clock that Fred W. Ward,
> pharmacist in the drug store of J. H. Robinson,
> E. 152d Street and Aspinwall Avenue, noticed the
> man come in.
>
> Anderson is about thirty-seven years old but looked
> older, with several days' growth of beard on his
> face and haggard lines resulting from his unusual
> fatigue and exposure.   He was dressed in a dark
> grey business suit, the trousers of which were
> splattered with mud to the knees.   The shoes bore
> evidence of a long tramp.
>
> Anderson looked to Ward vacantly for a moment,
> and the latter, seeing he was ill, offered him a
> chair.   Seating himself, the manufacturer fell into
> a brown study.
>
> "I am lost, " he announced finally, rousing himself.
> "Where am I?"
>
> "You are in Collinwood, Cleveland, " he was told.

"Cleveland?   Collinwood? Cleveland--let me see, "
and he pressed a hand over his eyes.

Ward asked where he came from.

"Up that way somewhere, up from the north--I
don't know just where and I can't tell you who I
am, " Anderson said, straining to think.

"Here, " he continued, after another pause, pulling
a notebook from his pocket.   "Take this and see if
you can find out who I am.   See if you can find the
name of any Cleveland person in there. "

Ward looked and found the name of Sherwood Anderson, a number of figures, and at last the name of
Edwin Baxter, assistant secretary of the Chamber
of Commerce [Anderson belonged to the Elyria
Chamber of Commerce].   Anderson arose and made
as if to leave, but Ward asked him to remain while
he telephoned for someone who knew him and he
sat down again.

Baxter came and recognized the man as Anderson,
head of the large paint manufacturing company.   A
physician was summoned and made a superficial
examination for injuries... but found none.

Anderson persisted in silence, answering questions
with nearly incoherent monosyllables.   He told
Baxter he could not say how he happened to be in
Cleveland, nor when, nor why he left Elyria.   He
remembered vaguely riding in an interurban car.
Baxter called an automobile and took Anderson to
the hospital, where the physicians made another
examination.

He was found to be suffering from a nervous ex-
haustion which apparently had been induced by worry of some kind or overwork. [102]

On December 3 the Evening Telegram in Elyria was
able to announce on page 1 that "the many friends of Sherwood Anderson... will be pleased to learn that his mental
condition has improved to such an extent that he will probably
be able to return home Saturday [December 7].   The article
goes on to say that Anderson regained his memory after a

few hours' sleep, talked with his wife, and could not "remember exactly when his memory failed him. . . . Anderson was surprised to awaken and find himself in a hospital and was inclined to consider his four days' wandering a joke. "

One of the investors in The American Merchants Company, Dr. Saunders, said, "We never knew whether he was a victim of amnesia or whether he'd been on a drunk or whether it was a nervous breakdown. His physician, who was my best friend, never told anybody his diagnosis. " The evidence certainly shows that Anderson had been in a state that "touched the edge of insanity, " probably easiest to designate as amnesia.

The best evidence of what was happening to Anderson psychologically is supplied, amazingly enough, by Anderson himself (the "amnesia letter" in Appendix D). As is detailed in that appendix, Anderson wrote and mailed to his wife a letter full of notes on what had been happening to him, though he later did not know what the events were and did not see the notes until long after, as Mrs. Anderson has recorded. Anderson told his brother, Karl, "My mind was a blank until I found myself in a ward of a Cleveland hospital. "[103]

Interpretations of conscientiously-written, objective documents may be expected to vary, so it is certainly appropriate to approach the subjective amnesia letter with caution. Fortunately, certain factors are so well-established as patterns and elements in the letter that they may be pointed out with a secure feeling, one reason for which is that they fit so well the pattern of all else that is known about Anderson.

The most frequently-reiterated element (18 times) in the letter is the word Elsinore (twice misspelled) which will be recognized as the castle of Hamlet, the very type of the person caught between opposing stresses. The first impulse might be to think that Anderson had thus thought of himself as Hamlet on the torture rack identified symbolically as Elsinore (Elyria). Further examination reveals, however, that he is not wanting to leave Elsinore but is rather pointed toward it: "Told her I was going to Elsinore, " "Get to Elsinore, " "went to Elsinore, " "Go to Elsinore, " and finally "To Elsinore. " Juxtaposed against "It was cold at night" is "Think of Elsinore. " Next to "T Powers head hurt also" is "went to Elsinore. " The curative relationship is perhaps seen most clearly in the following sequence: "After while

your head won[']t hurt.   Walk and keep still.   Go to Elsinore.
Hamlet--Elsinore. --"   Almost the last words in the letter
are: "Though it made my head hurt I laughed to Elsinore. "

    The letter, as will be seen, is full of fearsome and
unsatisfactory ugliness, and Elsinore represents the escape
hatch.   As Anderson said in many ways, his basic approach
to literature was therapeutic, to give him release from consciousness of his world, to work out through the manipulation
of imagined life the problems of his own, to find understanding for himself through probing the lives of his imagined
characters.   This is a veritable refrain, as many biographical passages show.   The fantasy-world of the fictional Elsinore, so closely identified with his kindred sufferer, Hamlet, is the doorway to escape, to the pleasant land where the
head no longer hurts.   (Anderson had a strong interest in
Shakespeare and other highly-acclaimed writers.   The symbol
of Elsinore in the "amnesia letter" indicates more knowledge
of literature than Anderson, who protected himself by claim-
ing to be uneducated, normally would admit.)

    If we understand that the realm of Elsinore is the
realm of escape, it is necessary to understand what factors
created the need for escape.   If one uses the understanding
of the psychologist that in such subjective documents as this,
as in dreams, the writer uses objective terms in referring
to himself, a phrase such as "Why do the children cry?"
may be rendered as something like "Why do I feel like crying as though I were a child?"   This in turn simply reflects
the person's feeling of ineffectuality.   Perhaps the central
unsatisfactory elements here may be seen in the sentence,
"The dogs howl and the children cry. "   To the psychologist,
the dogs in this letter represent the animalistic or brutal
aspects of life to this person.   To the Freudian psychologist
they represent dominant or male sexual factors.   A passage
like "There are so many children and so many dogs and so
many long streets filled with dirty houses" will represent a
feeling of rejection of female sex (long streets), which is
characterized by "dirty houses. "   Other factors which suggest a rejection of male sexuality are "a child that cried
looked at a man with a pipe in his mouth who growled like
a yellow dog" and "I tried to drink some beer, " which uses
a child's symbol of masculinity.

    The constant reference to hitting will be easily noticed.
As Anderson wrote to Miss Finley, he was afraid of everything in human form during his amnesia.   In the amnesia

letter, if he asks where Cornelia is, "people will hit [me]. "
Mrs. Leonard, who might have been one of two Elyria neighbors of that name, wants to hit him with a book.   The men
in the bar would have hit him.   Perhaps the most helpful
reference to hitting is "Writing dont [sic] hurt your head
Its [sic] just being hit with things. "   "T Powers" is thought
of in this same relationship.   At the outset of the letter
mention is made of "T Powers Elsinore. "   Later, in a whole
constellation of references, the "head-hurt-Elsinore" pattern
is incorporated: "Elsinore--Elsinore/Elsinore--Elsinore/
Get to Elsinore. /   T Powers Elsinore. / River at Elsinore. /
Bridge at Elsinore. / Elsinore Water Works. / T Powers
head hurt/also. went to Elsinore. / They hit T Powers. One/
after another they hit/him. like you [meaning Anderson]. /
They put his name/on a wall-near Elsinore. "   One is tempted
to assume that "T Powers" was a friend, a kindred, be-
wildered, overwhelmed person.   But so far no information
has been found concerning that person, if the name in fact
represented a real person.

        Related to the feeling of being attacked by arrogant,
brutal forces, whether they are essentially sexual or not, is
the idea represented as follows: "They didn't mean to/hit
you.   Keep thinking of /that and walk.   Dont [sic] talk to
anyone. Dont [sic] hit any one. "   Referring to Robert, his
son, he soon after writes, "Dont [sic] let them hit/him.
After while/your head wont [sic] hurt/Walk and keep still. /
Go to Elsinore. / Hamlet--Elsinore. "   Instead of a violent
reaction to the opposing forces, there is a response that is
informed by passivity.   The hurt is received in silence and
worked off in walking.

        At the same time he recognizes that his assailants
are not his personal attackers and that the negative, unsatisfactory elements in his world are not focused specifically
and antagonistically on him.   He wonders why they do confront him.   "I didnt [sic] want to fish in the river.   Why did
they hit me. "   It might be customary for the psychologist to
interpret the fishing symbol sexually but, however its meaning is taken, it represents the idea that he finds himself in
a situation not of his choosing and wonders why he should be
under pressure because of it.

        The role of Cornelia deserves comment here.   It is
to be remembered that the letter was sent to her, indicating
that she occupied for him a position of benign confidant, that
she is not a part of the antagonistic forces but rather one he

can tell nearly all about it: "If one does ask he could find
Cornelia." Is this an unfulfilled approach to possible ex-
ternalization of his problem, possibly sexual in basis, with
her? The likelihood that this is an accurate rendering is
strengthened by the references: "Why are men so proud of
a house--They walk around it and take pictures" and, closely
following, "Ask Cornelia about the men and the houses."
The house is a very common female sexual symbol. Perhaps
he would like to discuss with his wife their own sexual relationships or his own sexual bases but does not. At any
rate, he does not seem to include her in the besetting forces,
which might well be thought of as including sex.

In making interpretations of this material the writer
has attempted to be wary of pat, if unprovable, conclusions.
Anderson's ciphers on (the final) page 7 of his "amnesia
letter" offer a good opportunity, however, for a general ap-
prehension of his state of mind when he wrote the letter.
He seems to have retreated from the world of fact and routine to one where all the unacceptable requirements of daily
life are forgotten in a blanking out of normal consciousness
and reaction capacity. The curious addition of these numbers, in accord with the normal rules of arithmetic, arrives,
through fanciful arithmetic juggling, at a sum perhaps representative of his desired impossible answer--surcease from
his problems. His real world did not add up the way he
wanted it to. He did not like the disparity between what he
wanted and what he had. His four-day wandering in darkness
between Elyria and Cleveland was a phase of his re-adjust-
ment of the intolerable relationship. But it seems wiser not
to insist on such particularized interpretations, to which this
document can give much stimulation. Doubtless many theories
can develop from this letter and other documents with energy
and conviction. The present writer's effort has been only to
demonstrate that in the main the meaning which Anderson put
into this letter was, unsurprisingly, directly related to the
tremendous insecurity and unrest which he then felt.

As the reader will again be able to see, the hospital
dictation concerns itself mainly with an attempt to remember
"what he did," elements of which are in the "amnesia letter."
In his returned consciousness, however, he has successfully
suppressed those fearful elements which had for a time
wrenched from him the control of his physical actions and
psychic states. Throughout his life Anderson was to be a
man who masked his fears behind an appearance of bravado.
As a salesman, this was, of course, essential, particularly

for an intelligent and sensitive man.   Realizing that he had
to put his fears and regrets behind him as well as he knew
how (and he fought this problem throughout his life) he may
very possibly have made a conscious decision not to examine
the record he had made.   It is unfortunate for his interested
posterity that he never commented on the amnesia record.
The true significance of it seems to be that it helps to complete and verify the picture of the torture Anderson under-
went in Elyria.   His own record of himself is replete with
references to his "slickness. "   It seems to have appealed to
him to present the idea of being devious rather than weak.
At least at some points he seems to have preferred to have
others believe (and perhaps to believe himself) that he was
only pretending to have lost control of his life.   The hallu-
cination propensity described in his Clyde recollections and
the Tar episode based on his childhood can prepare the reader to believe that escape from his actual life was habitual
and perhaps necessary, certainly desired and pleasant, for
Anderson from an early age.   In Elyria it constituted in its
extreme form an illness; in general it was an important part
of his preparation for being an intensely-involved creator of
convincing fiction.   He became, throughout his adult life, a
person who both could not and would not separate the reality
and the make-believe of his life, whether they were caused
by his disappointments or his aspirations.

    An essay called "On Being Published, " in which he
refers to the Elyria experience, contains material which is
very relevant to the problems and processes in Anderson
which resulted in his writing fiction.   He writes of seeing
how orderly the gardens of his neighbors seemed to be.   "I
had a passion for order in myself.   I wanted some sort of a
rhythm, a swing to life--my life and others.   I never got it
in fact.   I have approached it sometimes on the printed
page. "[104]   One of the recognized motivations of the artist is
to impose pattern on life.   Part of leaving Elyria was to
change the pattern of his own existence.   His art will be
seen as showing great concern with both pattern (or rhythm)
and lack of pattern.

    Another interesting aspect of this essay, as it affects
his life in Elyria, is his reference to the publication of the
story Rabbit Pen, which appeared in Harper's in July, 1914.
"Someone brought the letter, accepting the story, or the
magazine with it in, to my bed in the hospital. "[105]   So far,
no substantiating evidence concerning this has been obtained,
but the acceptance of the story that much in advance seems

unlikely, and the story did not actually appear until over a
year later.   It is possible, both because of the scene with
which the story deals and the fact that he was writing stories
and sending them out, that the story was written in Elyria.

        Anderson accumulated experiences in an intense way
and they reverberated through his life and into his future.
The temptation to show how one experiential phase so central
to the exit from Elyria to Elsinore stayed with him can not
be resisted.   The recurrent figure of the person who has had
the very wearing experience of swimming or wading in an un-
friendly river was often in his mind, as it was when he walked
out of the Elyria office.   Not only in his writings but in
his epistolary figures as well one finds represented some
harsh experience, real or vicarious: "I am like a man who
has been swimming a broad cold river in winter and have at
last reached the other shore."[106] And "I had been swimming a long time in winter, in an icy river and had got
ashore only to find your warm friendly house."[107] These
two statements are from the same time period, some time
after the Elyria experience, some time after he wrote about
it in A Story Teller's Story after his swimming experiences
in Clyde and in Lake Chateaugay (1916-17).   A routine physical exercise which he evidently enjoyed quite thoroughly
lent a dramatic setting to his more unhappy states, and did
so repeatedly.

        In spite of the intense strain of the Elyria "amnesia"
experience, the essential health of Anderson's mind and body
were so great that they enabled him to rally quickly.   Before
the end of December, Anderson was able to be active again.
"Mr. and Mrs. Sherwood Anderson returned from a short
visit with [Cornelia's] relatives in Toledo on Thursday of last
week."[108] His illness apparently gave Anderson a chance to
make the desired change from the impossible situation in
Elyria.   The pressures of guiding his rather complicated
business and serving his consuming ambition to write had
been disintegrating him.   During December, 1912, and January, 1913, the arrangements for moving were made.   Early
in February the following announcement was made:

            Sherwood Anderson leaves next week to accept a
            position with the Taylor-Critchfield [formerly Long-
            Critchfield] Advertising Co., of Chicago, [sic]
            He has been for years connected with the Anderson
            Manufacturing Co. and the American Merchants'
            [sic] Co., of this city, as manager, and his many

friends regret his decision to change his activities
to the Chicago field. His family will remain in
Elyria, probably through the summer. 109

A similar announcement was in the Elyria Telegram for February 12 (page 3) with the additional statement that, "His
family will remain in Elyria for some time." Actually,
Anderson had left three days before that issue was published:
"Mr. Sherwood Anderson left Sunday evening [February 9]
for Chicago to take up his work with the Taylor-Critchfield
Co. "110

Anderson's attitude toward his return to the advertising business, the completion of a cycle in his life, may be
accurately stated in the following quotation from the Memoirs,
the context of which, however, may be recognized as inaccurate:

> When I had left my factory, walking down the rail-
> road track that day in 1910 [1912], I had kept on
> walking until I got to the city of Cleveland. It was
> summer and I slept for two nights out of doors.
> One night in a lumber yard and another night in an
> open field. In Cleveland I had borrowed a little
> money from a friend, Mr. Edwin Baxter... and had
> returned to Chicago. The days and nights of walk-
> ing and lying out under the sky had been a time of
> soul wrestling. I had come to a certain conclusion,
> "I cannot change American life, " I told myself.
> "It is not in me to be a leader of men leading them
> into new paths. " I already knew that when I re-
> turned to Chicago there would be but one fate open
> to me. I could again become an advertising writ-
> er. Essentially as an advertising writer I would
> continue indulging in lies. I had a gift for words,
> a gift of statement. Deep within me somewhere
> there was a respect for words. I would be com-
> pelled as an advertising writer, to corrupt these
> words. They were the instruments by which poss-
> ibly men might find each other in the confusion of
> life. "Very well, " I said to myself, "I will stick
> to those dependent upon me. I will be corrupt
> but, God give me this grace, " I cried, "let me in
> some way keep an honest mind. When I am being
> corrupt, perverting the speech of men, let me re-
> main aware of what I am doing. " ...It seemed to
> me then, as it does now, that hypocrisy in this

matter, this believing your own bunk, was the real sin against the Holy Ghost....

It was the advertising agency which formerly had employed me that, after some hesitation, had hired me back.

"I do hope you'll go straight now" (pages 202-03).

Whatever his attitude may have been, however, he lost no time in taking up where he had left off. In February, 1913, there was an article on advertising by him in Agricultural Advertising (page 16).

Every man who makes anything for sale wants expression for his business. He may have manufacture down pat, he may have a fine cost system and everything modern, efficient and high class throughout his offices and plant and if he hasn't found expression, he is nowhere....

That's where the advertising man comes in. If he is a good one he takes those fellows out into the other room and tells them to spread around and enthuse and tell the facts about themselves and what they are making. And then he helps them to find expression, helps them to tell it to thousands as they would tell it to their personal friends.

As the newspaper article said, Mrs. Anderson and the children did not leave Elyria when Anderson did. This last Elyria link was broken only gradually, as the following two items show:

Mrs. Sherwood Anderson and children will leave Elyria on Monday of next week to join Mr. Anderson in Chicago to make their home there.

and

Mrs. Sherwood Anderson and sons and sister, Miss Margaret Lane, left Elyria on Monday [April 21] for Little Point Sable, Mich. , where they will spend the summer before making Chicago their home. 111

In recalling the removal from Elyria, Cornelia

Anderson said: "I suppose I stayed behind till he got a foot-
hold. Stella told Sherwood we could have a cottage which
belonged to her at Little Point Sable, Mich. We went to
Chicago and met Sherwood. Some furniture went by freight
to Chicago. Some was left in Elyria." Cornelia went with
the children to Little Point Sable, and Sherwood, who was
rooming in Chicago, went there for weekends. The family
never went back to Chicago. [112]

Evidently Cornelia did not feel the discontinuation of
her marriage to be near. Its latter stages were entered
when the family left Elyria. Some of Sherwood's retrospective remarks indicate that he was at or near the point of
wishing to be free, but whether he was actually desiring it
or working for it can not now be established.

Notes

1.   Interview with Mrs. C. S. Johnson, Elyria, Ohio.

2.   John Sherwood was born on December 31, 1908, in
the Maternity Hospital, Cleveland; Marion, a girl, was
born in the Elyria Memorial Hospital on October 29, 1911.
Cleveland and Elyria Health Departments.

3.   Interview with Mr. Frank Wilford, Elyria.

4.   Interview, Oct. 10, 1946.

5.   Interview with Mr. Frank Kimbel, Elyria.

6.   Interview with Mr. S. H. Squire, Tiffin, Ohio. Anderson had on his person his "pass book to the Elks" when
hospitalized for amnesia. Cleveland Leader story of Dec.
2, 1912.

7.   Interview with Mrs. Gertrude Yost, Grafton, Ohio.

8.   Letter from Mrs. E. J. Gee, Cleveland Heights,
Ohio; Nov. 8, 1942.

9.   Cornelia Anderson interview, Oct. 10, 1946. See also
"The Golf Ball," Memoirs, p. 112-6.

10.   Interview with Dr. Burton E. Saunders, Elyria.

11.   Letter from Mr. S. H. Squire, Tiffin; Oct. 7, 1941.

12.   Oct. 10, 1946 interview.

13.   Letter from Mr. Starr Faxon, Elyria; Oct. 28, 1942.

14.   Oct. 1946 interview.

15.   Kimbel interview.

16.   Letter from Mr. Waldo E. Purcell, Amherst, Ohio;
Dec. 2, 1942.

17.   Interview with Mr. Harry J. Crandall, Elyria.

18.   Interview with Mr. Henry P. Boynton, Cleveland.

19.   Letter from Miss Florence Terry, Charlotte, N. C.;
Oct. 25, 1942.

20.   Interview with Mr. Charles Lord, Elyria.

21.   Wilford interview.

22.   Memoirs, p. 192-3.

23.   Ibid., p. 151.

24.   Purcell letter of Dec. 2, 1942.

25.   George A. Bottger interview.

26.   Purcell letter.

27.   Dr. Saunders interview.

28.   Oct. 1946 interview.

29.   The Rural New-Yorker, Sept. 14, 1907, p. 719. This
ad appeared in The Rural New-Yorker 28 times in 1907,
1908, and 1909. It also appeared in Collier's (Aug. 28,
1909, p. 26, and Sept. 4, 1909, p. 34, and probably other
issues) and a number of times in Country Gentleman (e. g.,
Feb. 18, 1909, p. 167).

30.   Oct. 1946 interview.

31.   The Rural New-Yorker, March 7, 1908, p. 201.
        Spread over two columns, the ad was four inches deep.

32.   Oct. 2, 1909, p. 868.

33.   Elyria, The Globe Publishing Co. , 1910, p. 4, 20,
        36, etc.

34.   Mr. E. O. Schaad.

35.   Interview with Mr. Winton W. McConnell, Elyria.

36.   Memoirs, p. 187-8, and p. 153.

37.   Interview with Mrs. Frances Howk, Lakewood, Ohio.

38.   Interview with Mrs. Jane Manning, Elyria.

39.   Mrs. Cornelia Anderson commented on this passage:
        "I am pleased that the stenographers who worked for Roof-
        Fix think their employer was a fine person.   I know that
        Frances [Howk] grew perceptibly under his influence, and
        doubtless the others did too.   Mr. Anderson was good for
        people, and they were the better for contact with him.
        The stenographers evidently got his quality. "   Note with
        letter of Oct. 16, 1946.

40.   The Rural New-Yorker, Oct. 30, 1909, p. 944.   Also
        in issues of Nov. 6 and 13.

41.   Memoirs, p. 152.   The first Anderson residence in
        Elyria was a suite in The Gray, a four-family apartment
        still standing on the NW corner of West and Second Sts.
        The other, to which they moved in 1908, was a house at
        229 Seventh St. and was their home the rest of the time
        they were in Elyria.

42.   Interview with Mr. Harry J. Crandall, Elyria.

43.   Memoirs, p. 187.   Of commercial democracy, Cor-
        nelia was to comment: "Oh, yes, I believe we were
        socialists at one period.   Perhaps he did have the idea
        of profit-sharing;" letter of Oct. 16, 1946.

44.   Letter of Sept. 14, 1938.   Dinsmoor, p. 69.

45.   "My Brother, Sherwood Anderson, " p. 7.

46.   Oct. 1946 interview.

47.   In testimony given in defense of a suit filed against the Purcell Paint Co., he said he had been in the business five years before April, 1913. Case No. 13,113, Common Pleas Court, Lorain County, Elyria.

48.   Record of Corporation No. 77,798. Index File No. 167. Office of the Department of State, Columbus.

49.   The stock subscription list of the American Merchants Co. was in the files of R. F. Vandermark, Elyria attorney.

50.   Letter from Mrs. E. J. Gee, Cleveland Heights; Nov. 8, 1942.

51.   Note with letter of Oct. 16, 1946, intended as a considered comment on the interview of Oct. 10, 1946.

52.   "The Sound of the Stream," The Sherwood Anderson Reader, p. 365.

53.   Memoirs, p. 193.

54.   Letter to Clarence Gohdes, April 16, 1936 (JR).

55.   Letter to Marietta D. Finley, Dec. 8, 1916. See Appendix D for full text of the letter.

56.   Ms. fragment to Mary Emmett, dated 1935.

57.   "Who's Who," Chicago Tribune, May 31, 1919.

58.   Letter of Sept. 14, 1938; Dinsmoor, p. 69-70.

59.   "Why Men Write," Story, Jan. 1936, p. 103 and 105.

60.   Information from interview with Mr. Charles Lord; and from Miss Claire A. Williams, Elyria, as reported by Dinsmoor, p. 21.

61.   Oct. 1946 interview.

62.   Notably Memoirs, p. 185-194.

63.   Memoirs, p. 190.

64. "My Brother, Sherwood Anderson, " p. 7.

65. Letter to Charles Connick, early March, 1926.

66. Letter to Alfred Stieglitz, April 19, 1926. Karl said it was thirteen years (i. e. , 1913) in "My Brother, Sherwood Anderson, " p. 27.

67. Letter of April 17, 1926.

68. Letter of April 30, 1926.

69. Letter to Helen Anderson, April 25, 1926.

70. Letter to Karl and Helen, Spring, 1926.

71. A Story Teller's Story, p. 8.

72. Letter to Maxwell Perkins, ca. April, 1935.

73. "My Brother, Sherwood Anderson, " p. 27.

74. Letter to Earl, Feb. 22, 1926 (JR).

75. A Story Teller's Story, p. 316-7.

76. Cornelia remembered his sending manuscripts "everywhere" in his effort to publish; interview, Oct. 10, 1946.

77. Letter from Mr. Rollin T. Reefy, editor of the Elyria Democrat when Anderson was in Elyria, St. Petersburg, Florida; May 5, 1942.

78. Letter to Ben Huebsch, ca. Nov. 22, 1921 (JR).

79. Ibid.

80. Letter Nov. 6, 1916 (JR).

81. Letter to Waldo Frank, Sept. [?] 1917 (JR).

82. Cornelia Anderson interview, Oct. 10, 1946.

83. Undated clipping from Cleveland Leader, in Newberry Library collection, probably Dec. 3, 1912.

84. "My Brother, Sherwood Anderson, " p. 26, and p. 7.

85.   Letter to Ruth Sergel, Aug. 29, 1937.

86.   Letter to Mary Emmett, Sept. 1, 1937.

87.   Oct. 1946 interview.

88.   Memoirs, p. 347. See also p. 157-9, 203.

89.   Letter to Marietta D. Finley, Jan. 12, 1917.

90.   Letter from Miss Florence Terry, Charlotte, N. C.; Oct. 25, 1942.

91.   Oct. 1946 interview.

92.   Letter of Oct. 25, 1942.

93.   Oct. 1946 interview.

94.   Letter ca. Summer 1927.

95.   Letter from Miss Terry; Oct. 31, 1942.

96.   Oct. 1946 interview.

97.   Memoirs, p. 194.

98.   Letter to Marietta D. Finley, Dec. 8, 1916; full text in Appendix D.

99.   The preceding three paragraphs are based on an interview with Mrs. Howk. Mr. Baxter has confirmed the details which relate to his activity. Mrs. Cornelia Anderson read this account and accepted it.

100.   Cleveland Press, Dec. 2, 1912, p. 2.

101.   Cleveland Leader clipping in Newberry Library, probably Dec. 3, 1912.

102.   Ibid. , Dec. 2, 1912.

103.   "My Brother, Sherwood Anderson, " p. 7.

104.   Colophon, 1930, no pagination.

105.   Ibid.

106.   Letter to Marietta D. Finley, Jan. 13, 1929.

107.   Letter to Ferdinand Schevill, Jan. 16, 1929.

108.   Elyria Democrat, Dec. 26, 1912, p. 5.

109.   Ibid. , Feb. 6, 1913, p. 5.

110.   Ibid. , Feb. 13, 1913, p. 8.

111.   Ibid. , April 17, 1913, p. 8; April 24, p. 8.

112.   Interview, Oct. 10, 1946.

Mosaic IX

"Shadowy life striving to take on flesh..."

The imagined figures may well live on and on in the fanciful
    life of others after the man from whose lips it came,
    or whose fingers guided the pen that wrote the tale,
    long after he is forgotten.
                from A Story Teller's Story, p. 122.

                *   *   *

In my own actual work as a tale-teller I have been able to
    organize and tell but a few of the fancies that have
    come to me.   There is a world into which no one but
    myself has ever entered and I would like to take you
    there....
                from A Story Teller's Story, p. 121.

                *   *   *

In any event the whole silly affair has remained in my fancy
    for years.   When I was a lad I played with such fanci-
    ful scenes as other boys play with brightly colored mar-
    bles.   From the beginning there has been, as opposed
    to my actual life, those grotesque fancies.
                from A Story Teller's Story, p. 119.

                *   *   *

Perhaps he did not dare let his fanciful life mature to keep
    pace with his physical life.   He lives in America,
    where as yet to mature in one's fanciful life is thought
    of as something like a crime.
                from A Story Teller's Story, p. 141.

Have you not often read a story when a character has been
    made by the story tellers to do something you knew the
    character could not do [?] We call it bad art.   It is
    more than that.   It is a display of immorality.
            to Carrow DeVries, Aug. 9, 1939 (JR).

                *   *   *

These and many other figures, all having a life of their own,
    all playing forever in the field of my fancy.   The fanci-
    ful shadowy life striving to take on flesh, to live as
    you and I live, to come out of the shadowy world of
    the fancy into the actuality of accomplished art.
            from A Story Teller's Story, p. 121-22.

                *   *   *

You have to pay dearly for being an imaginative person.   You
    see a great deal and feel a great deal but there is
    ugliness to see and feel--as well as beauty--and in
    yourself as well as in others.   I fancy what you have
    to do is to try to learn to give as little time as pos-
    sible to self-pity.
            to John S. Anderson, 1929? (JR).

                *   *   *

The central notion is that one's fanciful life is of as much
    significance as one's real flesh and blood life and that
    one cannot tell where the one cuts off and the other
    begins.   This thing, I have thought, has as much phys-
    ical existance [sic] as the stupid physical act I yesterday
    did.   In fact so strongly has the purely fanciful lived
    in me that I cannot tell after a time which of my arts
    had physical reality and which did not.
            to Alfred Stieglitz, June 30, 1923.

                *   *   *

There is the life of fancy.   In it one sometimes moves with
    an ordered purpose through ordered days, or at the
    least through ordered hours.   In the life of the fancy
    there is no such thing as good or bad.   There are no
    Puritans in that life.... They cannot breathe in the
    life of the fancy.
            from A Story Teller's Story, p. 77.

In the world of fancy, you must understand, no man is ugly.
    Man is ugly in fact only.   Ah, there is the difficulty!
        from A Story Teller's Story, p. 78.

     *   *   *

What an intense study the mind of the man running in the
    field.   My mind can play with it for hours.   I should
    be able to pick a thousand varieties of scenes like that
    from every field.
        to M. D. Finley, Oct. 24, 1916.

     *   *   *

When I deal in facts, at once I begin to lie.   I can't help it.
    I am by nature a story-teller.   No one ever taught me.
        from "Introduction to The Memoirs, " The Sher-
                wood Anderson Reader, p. 696.

     *   *   *

I have been absorbed this summer in a book of memoirs and
    at least [it] has been a pleasure to take my imagination
    away from the present a little.
        to Manuel Komroff, Oct. 10, 1940.

*   *   *   *   *

Chapter 9

A HERO TO HIMSELF

A. The Peculiar Difficulties of My Position

When Anderson left Elyria and went to Chicago, he knew perfectly well that he was not going into the promised fantasy-Elsinore he wanted and needed. There was much ambivalence in his character. Troubled in his mind, he accommodated impulses and capabilities which made him, as Stuart Chase recalled him, a dreamy, aloof business man. [1]

The conflict between the dream and the reality of the advertising business can be traced in his various utterances. "I find that my resentment at having to go back into business is very deepseated and hard to throw off. The queer notion that I am in a prison clings to me and my laugh at it all grows a bit bitter. "[2]

> What I figure is that my reactions take two forms. I ride on a wave above the sordid details of my life spent among cheap little commercial ventures. For days I sit in the boat made of planks borrowed from people who love me. In the boat I sit very quietly writing words.
>
> Then something happens. The planks tears [sic] apart. My boat goes to pieces. I am sucked down into the river, out of sight, and out of sound.
>
> It is also sad that those who have done most for me get the least in return. To the men about me in the office I present myself as a strong swimmer. Hardly a day passes that some business man or woman does not come to me asking a question.
>
> How do you remain so calm and quiet? they ask. . . .

I can't explain to them that I also am tumbled and
tossed out.   I am too much like them. [3]

I keep working in and out of terrible fits of depression followed by times when I am very happy
and work very freely.   Business and business life
is more dreadful than ever.   There are moments
when I even play with the idea of suicide as a way
of escape.

Of course there is no such prospect, as that would
not help and there is so much eager life I want to
find my way into.

And I am not always depressed.   There are days
when I ride like a boat on top of it all. [4]

Those revealing passages were written to his confidant,   Frank,   in 1919, but they are typical of what he felt before,   during,   and after the Chicago period in which Winesburg, Ohio came into being.   The impulse which identified
for him "so much eager life" was always there as an anti-
dote, and he fought back insistently and ingeniously.   In
1916 he instituted this plan:

I have an idea.   Suppose instead of just writing you
letters which may concern themselves with personal
things, a cold in the head etc. , I write you instead
my observations on life and manners as they present themselves to me here and now.   By this
plan I may write to you daily or at times only
once a week.

When these things come to hand type them, putting
on date and making a carbon copy.   At the end of
six months or a year we will see if we haven't
material for a book that would be of interest to
others.

In arriving at this idea I have several things in
mind.   In the first place I think of myself.   Perhaps no man writing has had to meet just the
peculiar difficulties I have.   With me writing has
never been in any sense a science.   There are
days when to save my life I could not write one
good sentence.   I have really no knowledge of
words, no creating of the art... of sentence

structure.

And then the mood comes over me.   The world is
of a sudden all alive with meaning.   Every gesture,
every word of the people about carries significance.
My hand, my eyes, my brain, my ears all sing a
tune.   If I can get to pencil and paper I write
blindly,   scarcely seeing the streets before me.

At such times the terrible feeling of the utter
meaninglessness of life passes.   I am carried
along through hours and days as by a great wind.
I am happy.

Now if you can understand what it means at such
times to have a man come to my office door and
tell me that I am to go into a room with other men
and drone for hours over the advisability of advertising a new kind of hose supporters you will understand what I mean by the peculiar difficulties of
my position.   I go because there are children to
be fed, obligations that I have not the courage to
face down but as I go I often feel that I could take
a revolver from my pocket and begin shooting the
men in the room with the greatest glee.   I don't
want you to misunderstand me.   I don't always
feel this way about the hose-supporter gentlemen.
At times I go with delight and all of their words
strike on my consciousness as just a part of the
inexhaustible drollery of life.

However, here is my thought.   I want to save what
I can of value to me of these destroyed words.
Many times when they are checked they break up
into little words.   As I sit with the men I scribble
little notes about them.   On the street car my
mind plays with little notions about things and
people.   To express these things in even a fragmentary way gives me satisfaction.   If the art of
writing in this way has no value to others it has
at least value to me.

As you well enough know I have on now a big piece
of work [likely Winesburg, Ohio].   It can be completed now only in a twisted and distorted way.   I
shall just write it blindly, pouring myself and my
character into it when I can.   Then when I have

> leisure I will go back at it, eliminating, changing
> and trying to make a book of it.
>
> In a personal way I think I can promise you that
> these notes will have more value to you than any
> formal letters I might write.   There is but one
> way by which you can get value out of your friend-
> ship for me.   If the things I write extend or en-
> large your own horizon they will be of value to
> you.   You will have to be the judge of that. [5]

The next day he wrote:

> I went home in the rain and the car was crowded.
> The working men with their brutal faces climbed
> aboard in droves.   I stood among them breathing
> the air that reeked with the strong scent of their
> bodies.   I thought that I had made too much money.
> In my pocket there was a pouch filled with bills.
> I put down my hand past the shaking body of a fat
> man and felt of the pouch.   I was a little ashamed.
> Not because I had money when others had none but
> because the possession of $73.00 raises me a little
> into the lower middle class.   There is a kind of
> healthy desperation in the utter lack of money.
> Often I have tramped in utter poverty and misery
> through the streets and got something out of my
> misery.   For a moment on the car I was senti-
> mental regarding this matter and then I laughed.
> My mind checked back to the notion that again and
> again saved me, living as I do altogether among
> men of business.   Again I put my hand down past
> the fat man and touched the pouch.   I patted it
> affectionately.   As the car rattled along I had keen
> joy in thinking of myself as an outlaw.   "I have
> stolen the money from a stupid world."   I whis-
> pered to myself and was happy. [6]

Probably most of the time he accepted his work situation.   "Don't you see that my only chance lies in staying in
my own puddle here.   I have got to live as the men right
here in this office live.   I have got to make my living as
they do."[7]   But at times he was grim about the acceptance:

> Last night I sat in a room in a hotel in Minnea-
> polis with two men.   The first was short and fat.
> He had a wart on the nose and a peculiar soft,

child-like smile.   The second man was lean and
hard.   His eyes were clear blue.   He knows how
to make money, is absorbed, is oblivious to everything else in life.

The two men are both employed by an industrial
leader of the northwest.   They came to consult me
about various shrewd projects the man has on foot.
These men are to handle the publicity; to state the
big man's projects to the people.   They came to
me to be told how to do it cleverly, with apparent
frankness and honesty.

We talked until my train left at ten o'clock and my
soul was sick.   I have no conscience.   In such
matters.   The right and wrong of the matters does
not bother me at all.   We are after all nothing but
grey thieves, rats that live in a great barn but the
deadly monotony of this thing wearies me terribly. [8]

Another time he might be rather impishly ebullient:
"I have got me a secretary.   Is that not putting on the dog.
The firm have the wild notion that they can make me work. "[9]

Again he could report: "Have just been through a bad
week.   Last night I felt so unclean that I spent hours walking
by the lake and praying....   You may be sure that I'd like
to quit it all to try to live and think away from it, but I
can't.   It may go on always with me.   I have to face that,
and I have faith that it is better than cheap writing anyway. "[10]

As much pain as his work in advertising gave him,
one of his staunchest friends and admirers was to note that
he did his best work when he was involved in it.   When he
shook off the shackles of making a living, he did not seem
to reach the same plane of work. [11]

The fact that he knew that the pressure of business
could affect him beneficially is demonstrated in this comment
to Frank:

I am having an experience that is always a delight
to me.   The thing is something that I am always
being reminded of and always forgetting.   It is
this--that I always write better and most purely
when conditions for working are the worst.

> I don't know that I clearly understand the reason
> for this but believe I do.   In a business office such
> as ours the mental conditions are at the very worst.
> Men are occupied with matters so trivial and so
> very unimportant that their minds run about in lit-
> tle crazy circles.   In self-defense one is compelled
> to create and maintain in his own mind a world of
> people who have significance.   Day by day as he
> goes on this created world becomes a thing more
> definite. [12]

That he was an extremely competent advertising man
there can be little doubt.   One of his former colleagues
attested to both his ability and his honesty in a magazine
article. [13]   At the same time his friends at the agency knew
he scribbled beginnings of stories on lay out sheets.   He
called himself the "greatest unpublished novelist in America"
in the office. [14]   A business acquaintance who was an aspir-
ant writer, later wrote Anderson: "I am thinking of taking
a leaf from your old practice at Critchfield's and coming
down to the office at the ungodly hour of 7 am!"[15]   Anderson
was to recall that the piece "I'm a Fool" was "written at the
copy desk one morning while I was presumed to be writing
copy for a gas engine company."[16]

He was constantly to feel, "I've been under the wall,
squirming for a week.   Occasionally the business thing lights
down on me like a million ton of brick.   I go about black
and silent.   Then I spread open, squirm out again...."[17]

Often he felt, "It is unfortunate that just as my mind
begins again to swing into the writing I should have to do
violence to it"[18] or "I want two or three weeks steady writing yet and then a week or two for cutting to shape.   I wonder how and where I am to get time for that."[19]   One may
assume Anderson was buoyed up by his feeling

> ...as though I were drifting toward some new and
> to me, strange adventures with life.   Whenever I
> am not actually engaged in the affair of making a
> living my mind goes off to country roads, to
> strange towns and villages.   I dramatize myself as
> a solitary figure tramping, tramping--tramping and
> waiting. [20]

The following portion of a letter shows that exhilarated moments did come to him:

> I am writing again and when I do much goes over
> my head.   Suddenly things thus begin to coordinate
> for me.   All staleness in life floats away.   I find
> myself vitally interested in everything.   I live and
> am strong.
>
> That I allow the affairs of life to in any way inter-
> fere with me at such times is because I am a
> coward.   It must be so.   What should I care if I
> starve?[21]

He was to refer to recurrent "convulsive emotions
against business that always leave me shaken and tired."[22]
He has left us this vivid description of one such attack:

> At times there comes over me a terrible conviction
> that I am living in a city of the dead.   In the of-
> fice dead voices discuss dead ideas.   I go into the
> street and long rows of dead faces march past.
> Once I got so excited and terrified that I began to
> run through the streets.   I had a mad impulse to
> shout, to strike people with my fist.   I wanted
> terribly to awaken them.   Instead I went to my
> room and shut myself in.   I drank whiskey.   Pres-
> ently I slept.   When I awoke I laughed.
>
> Long ago I realized that I must laugh or go insane.
> I go along seeing little things and being amused.   A
> kind of dreadful smartness and alertness takes
> possession of me.   I write smart advertisements[;]
> I do little tricky things to make money.   I laugh
> and grin like a little ape.[23]

He began to think of advertising and business in terms
of prostitution:

> Chicago is horrible.   The living impulses that drive
> the men I meet day by day are materialistic.   They
> want to preserve the respectability of their homes
> and keep alive the institutions of prostitution.   They
> want not beautiful clothes but clothes that represent
> vaguely the idea of money spent.   They are weakly
> sentimental, occasionally coarse beyond your com-
> prehension and for the most part there is no life
> in them.[24]

And then back to the writing of letters--to sell my
goods.   In the city to which I had gone to carouse
I had seen many women of the streets, standing at
corners, looking furtively about.   My thoughts got
fixed upon prostitution.   Was I a prostitute?   Was
I prostituting my life?[25]

In 1933 he began to refer to a novel he called Thanksgiving (which was never completed), "written in the mood rather of a Story Teller's Story....   I had some twenty years
in affairs of advertising agencies--being a little whore there
--and had never used the material.   I had too much hatred. "[26]
He mentions the same book to his long-time friend, Marco
Morrow, wondering "if I am equipped.   Am I enough outside
to do the things clearly[?]   Am I too much outside now[?]"[27]

In 1940 he was to write that he had little enthusiasm
for a proposed radio program because it would plunge him
back into a connection with the business "from which I once
escaped. "[28]   In 1939 he recalled:

For nearly fifteen years I had to spend my own
time as an advertising writer because I felt myself
not strong enough physically to stand day labor and
couldn't make a living by my story telling.   I sincerely believe that all advertising is corrupt. [29]

An episode published in "A Part of Earth"[30] deals
with unethical business tactics, specifically gaining clients
through blackmail.   "Two or three of us dreamt of some day
becoming real writers.   This fellow was, in secret, working
on a play, that fellow on a novel.   Sometimes at lunch in
some little saloon we talked it over among ourselves.   'We
are little male harlots.   We lie with these business men.
Let us at least try keeping our minds a little clear.   Don't
let's fall for this dope that we are doing something worth
doing here. '"   Elsewhere, Anderson related that "The men
employed with me, the businessmen, many of them successful and even rich, were like the laborers, gamblers, soldiers,
racetrack swipes I had formerly known.   Their guard down,
often over drinks, they told me the same stories of tangled,
thwarted lives. "[31]   He could not forget that during his time
in the business five men he had known personally had com-
mitted suicide. [32]

His discontentment over the gulf between his idealism
and the materialism he encountered applied also to publishing:

> I'd say the central difficulty, in all publishing, in
> all its forms, is that there is a pretense of inter-
> est, say in literature, or science, or in truth,
> while there is, at the same time, the fact that the
> whole set-up is a business set-up. ... We have to
> thread our way through it as best we can. ...   It
> confuses, puzzles and defeats writers.   But how
> are you going to change it without changing the
> whole civilization?   That is what you are up against. [33]

It was this realization that endeared his <u>Winesburg</u>
publisher, Ben Huebsch, to him.   "While Ben never has sold
my books much, he has been very, very fine with me in
other ways.   There never has been any lack of moral support.   He published me and gave me his support when no
one else much wanted me"[34] and "I've stuck to Ben because
my years as a businessman cured me so effectively of any
desire to make money that there is almost a satisfaction in
some of Ben's inefficiencies as a publisher. "[35]

Eventually he felt forced to leave Huebsch on the
grounds of his not being aggressive enough in business matters.   The struggle between the idealistic utterance of the
personally-realized truth and the compromise with the ideals
in the interest of money was to rage on for years to come.

When he was forty Anderson wrote "The average man
I see who has passed his fortieth year is a nervous wreck.
He takes some kind of indigestion medicine. "[36]

A few years later he was to note "I do in some way
manage to escape.   If my final escape will only come before
the faculty for flashes of joy goes out of me all will be
well. "[37]

Perhaps all the movements of a person's life are
kinds of escape, if escape is the negative view of change.
Going from Clyde to Chicago could be thought of as an attempt to escape.   It is rather evident that Anderson went into
the Spanish-American War with a sense of relief.   It can
easily be imagined that his attendance at Wittenberg was
motivated by a desire to rise above manual labor.   The episodes in Cleveland and Elyria were focused on the idea of
becoming economically independent.   The whole process of
writing was entered to find relief, by understanding, from
his problem of coming to terms with existence.   It is as
though he had become addicted to "flashes of joy" rather

than the more customary kinds of stimulant. The aggressive-
ly individualistic personality of Anderson the artist demanded
a constant seeking of relief from what it considered the bondage of the business world, a bondage which consisted mainly
in the constant necessity of adhering to patterns and concepts
which were not acceptable to him.

Just how hungry he was for escape from the business
world to a situation in which he had freedom to enjoy the impact of life in his own way, to exploit his gifts as he saw fit
or was able, may be seen through the following fragment:
In April, 1918, he announced, "An opportunity has come up
for me to go live for two or three years in a little interior
Kentucky town. I may decide to do it."[38] This town may
well have been Harrodsburg, of which he was to write later:

> ...Harrodsburg is the oldest of Kentucky towns.
> I used to come here, as an advertising writer 20
> or 25 years ago. My clients were the Bohons.
> The two sons went into the mail order business.
> Dave was the brainy shrewd one.... He used to
> come to see me in Chicago.... One year, on a
> scheme I had thought up, Dave made $100,000....[39]

Of this prospect he was to write the next month to
Waldo Frank, "There is the beginning of a scheme on foot
by which I may go to live for two or three years in a small
Kentucky town. If I do you shall come to visit me."[40] In
the same letter he continued:

> The Kentuckians are the most beautiful people I
> have seen in America. I think it is because they
> love the fleet beautiful thoroughbred horse.
>
> As one walks up and down in the hill country one
> sees flocks of sheep followed by mountain patri-
> archs. There is no war there. On the grassy
> hillside horses graze. In the river bottom men
> and women work in the fields. I am in love with
> Kentucky. I am going out of the city to live for a
> time in that country.

If it were not Harrodsburg he was thinking of in these
pastoral terms, perhaps it was Owensboro (location of another
client, the Owensboro Ditcher and Grader Company), of which
he remembered

> ... sharply the trips we used to take together, the
> place out by the river... the persimmon trees, the
> old hotel... the yellow and gold Ohio, the square at
> the heart of town and how I used to love to come
> there.   Often I went up the river in a little boat,
> getting... my train for Chicago, a train I always
> took with regret. [41]

His most specific explanation of this scheme was:

> The country thing would not take me out of busi-
> ness.   I would merely be living in a small quiet
> place.   Would have to do much the same kind of
> work I do here.   I figure I would not wear myself
> out so much.   Tennessee would stay here.   I would
> take one of my boys along.

Late that year he was still "at work on it. "   He wrote
of a need to escape the city for a year or two, of hungering
for the "quiet of a small place.... It may be that I will
succeed in making the arrangement I want for living in the
country. "[42]   There is no further information about this plan.

After the demise of The Seven Arts, through which he
had met Waldo Frank, in which he had had very helpful publication, and from which he had received important stimulation, he and Frank became very interested in getting another,
perhaps better, magazine started.   It would tell the

> ... story of repression, of the strange and almost
> universal insanity of society.   The story does not
> need to be an unpleasant one to right minded men
> and women but it must be coldly and subtle [sic]
> told and make it's [sic] audience slowly. [43]

The rest of the story of the magazine may be found
in these two installments:

> I am working on a very hot trail here that you will
> be able to help on lately [sic].   There is a woman
> here... who has several millions.   She married an
> old man. ...   The old man is dead and she has no
> children.   She is almost to marry again... a New
> Englander, a gentleman of fine taste and really a
> fully nice fellow.   I have him interested in the
> magazine project and he is working on the widow.
> They will both be in New York in March and I

want you to meet.   and [sic] if you can have Paul
Rosenfeld, Copeau, Gallimard, Ernest Block, Bob-
by Jones and others meet them.

I have played your hand with these people as the
great fellow for the project.

I have talked the idea of you and myself going to
work on the project about June 1st and starting the
magazine in the fall or January 1st, 1920.   My
idea is you, Paul, Van Wyke [sic] and myself.

The fiancee [sic] would be ideal as a business manager.   He has been a teacher in one of the schools
here, is not bull headed, is modest and will not
try to interfere editorially.   He [sic] an old friend
of Tennessee's and she says he would be an ideal
man.

The widow is entirely a possibility.   She is shrewd
but has more money than she knows what to do
with.   Will be anxious, I fancy to do something to
help make a career for [the fiancé] with whom she
is much in love.

[The fiancé] himself is a splendid fellow.   He is
in a sense the kind of man that Tennesse is a
woman.   I can't imagine a better hook-up for us
all. 44

When one recalls Cornelia's comment on Sherwood's
sweeping enthusiasms, one regrets to present the following
obituary:

About the soap lady.   She is a widow.   It turned
out that she hasn't control over her own future.
The thing hung at any rate on her drive to please
her lover.   When it was discovered that her future
was harnessed the lover, I imagined, [sic] thought
of himself instead of the project.   He had accepted
it as an [amusement?], had no real passion for the
notion. 45

The intensity of his hunger to escape to pursue his
art and his self-centered naiveté concerning his prospects
are further exemplified as follows:

All the time in the back of my mind I am working
and working trying to devise some plan by which I
may live and get out of business.   It is going to be
harder than ever for me to face the thing this year.
Everything in me that is worth a dam [sic] draws
away.

One play I have is to try to raise enough money to
buy a good sized track [sic] of land up in Door
County [Wisconsin].   Then start a summer camp
there.   Take in both grown people and children.
Employ a practical carpenter and a farmer and let
the children work with them during the summer
months.   No doubt many grown people, if we get
them up there would be happy in working with the
children also.

The work would be in the nature of building little
log houses for people, clearing the forests, improving the place, doing some farming, etc.   It
would take some money to get it under way but
once under way I should be able to live there six
months a year and have six months to spend in a
room in New York or Chicago writing.   Tennessee
has genius with children and I could handle the
grown ups. . . .

I am wondering if such a plan might not offer a
handle by which I could take hold of a man like
Emerson [presumably his friend, John].   If I could
get some man like him to back me in such a venture I am sure that after a few years I could return his money and have left a means of making a
living entirely outside the world of affairs.

In some ways I have got to come to that.

Always there has been a kind of cunning in me.   I
have been able to sabotage [it] very successfully
but I grow weary of it and I am losing my cunning.
Often I feel that I would rather starve than stay
another day at any occupation other than the occupation of writer.

All of these problems have been at the back of my
mind all summer. . . . [46]

The man who had become the author of Winesburg, Ohio was to write to Huebsch, his publisher, after hoping "you are still getting some sales for Winesburg," that

> Business has rather got on my nerves. I keep wondering why the devil I should have to spend so large a part of my life in writing fool advertisements in order to live. You dont [sic] know of some intelligent man or woman who wants to be a patron for an American artist, do you[?] Seems to me I've got a lot of good books in my system and I would like to get them out. [47]

His travels in search of a better design for living took him to Hooker, Missouri; and Lake Chateaugay, New York; and through, notably, Palos Park, Illinois; Ephraim, Wisconsin; Fairhope, Alabama; and New Orleans. The road led him eventually to an arrangement by which, through the financial aid of his great friend, Burton Emmett, he bought the newspaper in Marion, Virginia, and established himself in that western Virginia mountain country, where he built his only home, Ripshin.

It was Anderson's custom to bring his work and his situation to the attention of friends, and he was full of schemes to harness their interest and funds to artistic endeavors, especially his own. One of the best documented of his efforts to escape, or search out a new way of living, follows on the next few pages.

His boyhood friend, John Emerson (who changed his name from Clifton Paden, as he was known in Clyde)

> ...had given me the movie job, knowing I would be no good at it. He was a successful man, a money-maker, and was always planning out schemes for giving me money and leisure. I went often to the movie studios and watched the men and women at work. [48]

He went to New York at the beginning of August, 1918, to work for Emerson's movie company. "I do little personal news stories for the newspapers concerning John and Anita Loos. One can be done in ten minutes. There is no office to go to, no quibbling. It is amazingly simple."[49]

In anticipation of this opportunity, he had written:

"The very thought of this move has rested me, and I feel as though I could make a place for myself in some new field with real gusto. "[50]

He wrote to Waldo Frank that he lived at first in John Emerson's apartment but, after looking at "a hundred places, " had found "a hole of my own. "[51] In a letter to Miss Finley in August, 1918, he described his pleasure in his new surroundings:

> In town I have found me a delightful place in which to live. The address is 427 West 22nd Street. There is a large room with a fireplace and a high ceiling. The house is neatly kept by an ancient maiden Irish woman of sixty. Her name is Rose McCurran. At daylight she rises and goes to early mass. She is back at 7:30 and brings me up coffee, toast and fruit. I am in an old dressing gown and sit writing until noon. Nothing disturbs me. The room is at the back of the house and the roar of the city is far away. I rise from sleep and step into a created world. If letters arrive they are not opened until noon when I shave, dress and go out on the streets to the town. To one who has had to fight to maintain a mood this is paradise. No more of the necessity of breaking in and out of the affairs of the office.

The letter continues, giving a clear insight to his mental attitude:

> It is all very splendid, the complete release from business. I am happy but I work hard. I want now that the opportunity has come to establish myself as a man of letters so that I may live by that. I shall fight for it but will not make the hurtful kind of compromises....
>
> Already the easement on my mind is making itself felt. A sense of struggle has gone away. A certain long swing of things is going away....
>
> They will be afraid of my becoming a New Yorker. As though my forty years and my struggle to maintain myself and my flare at life all this time has resulted in nothing!...

There is a certain definate [sic] sharpness and
shallowness about the people here that I like just
as I have always known I would like Paris and as
I love aristocrats and ladies in delicate clothes.
I love them perhaps most because they are so little
a part of myself.

Old Chelsea is an overlooked place. . . . It is oddly
apart, a place from which to emerge and look and
to which to retire and ponder. . . .

Just now I am half ill, a cold from staying a long
time in the sea.   It was so easy and delightful to
swim that I went on at it for hours.   Later it
turned cold and I got chilled. . . .

I go to the moving picture studio, write the stuff
there by which I live, get me about with friends
or go by myself into some little restaurant to look
at people. . . .

John is driven like a slave.   We have little half
hour talks and occasionally dine together.   On
Sundays we perhaps go with Miss Loos for a day
in the country. . . .

I eat, smoke, make sacrifice to the gods and go
to work.   Many new impulses flow in me. . . .

If you come here late this fall I shall have many
new people crept out from under my pen to tell
you about. . . .

It is good to have access to men and women of my
own world. . . a thing really lacking in Chicago.   I
begin to sense the fact that I may never really live
there again. . . .

Tennessee will be with me in New York in September and later I shall come west for a month or
two.

In a September, 1918, letter to Miss Finley the following notes were recorded:

The days go marching past.   Fall has come to the
city and the air is like wine.   I am in a disturbed

mood and working steadily at my new book [Poor
White].   The city with its people and its perplex-
ities lies outside me.   Everything does a little now.
Mr. Brooks has published a new book and I have
written an article for the Chicago Tribune about it.
It is called Letters and Leadership.   Get it and
read it.   His is to me the most sustained and
thoughtful mind ,concerned with American criticism. . . .

You will see that I am rather absorbed.   The spirit
of something keeps me rather up to the mark here.
I presume there is here an atmosphere I want.   It
comes out in the air and springs from the fact that
a great many real men of vast significance in
America have walked and thought thoughts in these
streets. . . .

Beside my work I am developing three or four
story themes.   They are delicate things.   I want to
write them as one would sit down to play on a
piano or a violin in the evening. . . .

I have seen almost no one. . . .   Tennessee is here
and we go often in the afternoon on sightseeing
trips.   I plan to write long weekly letters to the
children about the city and get notes during these
trips.   I am also at work on a book of notes covering the impressions of a western man in this town.

In October he wrote to her: "One of the places I have
found a God-send is Central Park.   You can take the bus up
there and sit for hours watching life flow past.   I go there
often to work" and "I should say the test of a man and
woman lay in that--how can they face maturity.   And what is
maturity beyond a realization that life is a trap into which
we are thrown and nobody knows the way out. "

The next information on this episode comes in late
December, when he found the movie sinecure had become
impossible.

Something in me is deeply rested.   I shall have
courage and strength to keep on in the face of the
dullness of the daily grind for a year or two.   One
doesn't need to think further ahead than that. 52

He reported to Burrow at the year's end: "I am back

in Chicago at the old grind after four months of glorious liberty. . . . "[53]

> I was very greatly depressed when I first came home and had to get back into this business but have quite recovered. For one thing the later part of the novel has been going well and it is nearing the end. I find that I got really rested in New York. The physical ugliness of Chicago loses its ability to hurt me when I am really at work. Besides all this I am really well. [54]

And the next month he wrote Waldo Frank: "You know after all I was a guy in New York. The moving picture crowd had an affectionate but patronizing regard for me. "[55]

Even though he had gone to New York full of gusto for a new experience, had worked very well, had developed the feeling that he was never to return to Chicago, he returned "home" reasonably well-adapted to the failure of yet another attempt to find the ideal routine for his purposes.

Notes

1.   Letter of Nov. 25, 1962.

2.   Letter to Waldo Frank, May 1919.

3.   Letter to Waldo Frank, Feb. 1919.

4.   Letter to Waldo Frank, May 1919.

5.   Letter to Marietta D. Finley, Nov. 23, 1916. This letter is one of the first of some 275 which Miss Finley received between 1916 and 1933. They are a very rich source of insight into the mind of Anderson, who felt he could write to her very freely and truly of himself.

6.   Letter to M. D. Finley, Nov. 24, 1946.

7.   Letter to M. D. Finley, Nov. 27, 1916.

8.   Letter to M. D. Finley, Jan. 26, 1917.

9.   Letter to Waldo Frank, April 10, 1918.

10. Letter to Waldo Frank, before Oct. 29, 1917 (JR).

11. Letter from Roger Sergel to Eleanor C. Anderson, Sept. 28, 1962.

12. Letter to Waldo Frank, Sept. 5, 1917.

13. Donald M. Wright, "A Mid-Western Ad Man Remembers," Advertising and Selling, Dec. 17, 1936, p. 35, 68.

14. George Daugherty in interview with William L. Phillips, Sept. 22, 1949.

15. Undated letter from George Daugherty.

16. Letter to Burton Emmett, July 4, 1926.

17. Letter to Waldo Frank, May, 1919.

18. Letter to Waldo Frank, Nov. 5, 1919.

19. Letter to Dr. Trigant Burrow, early 1919.

20. Letter to M. D. Finley, Jan. 8, 1917.

21. To M. D. Finley, 1919.

22. Letter to Waldo Frank, 1919.

23. Letter to M. D. Finley, Nov. 27, 1916.

24. Ibid.

25. A Story Teller's Story, p. 306-7.

26. Letter to Charles Bockler, Feb. 12, 1933.

27. Letter to Marco Morrow, Feb. 1933 (JR).

28. Letter to Mrs. L. L. Copenhaver, Nov. 24, 1940 (JR).

29. Letter to Dwight MacDonald, June 14, 1939 (JR).

30. The Sherwood Anderson Reader, p. 323-4.

31. Letter to George Freitag, Aug. 27, 1938 (JR).

32. "The Sound of the Stream," The Sherwood Anderson Reader, p. 365.

33. Letter to Paul Appel, April 1, 1938.

34. Letter to Horace Liveright, after Nov. 22, 1924 (JR).

35. Letter to Dr. Trigant Burrow, Oct. 12, 1921.

36. Letter to M. D. Finley, Dec. 2, 1916.

37. Letter to Waldo Frank, May 1919.

38. Letter to M. D. Finley, April 1918.

39. Letter to Mrs. L. L. Copenhaver, Sept. 26, 1939 (JR).

40. Letter to Frank, late May, 1918.

41. Letter to W. A. Steele, Aug. 29, 1938.

42. Two letters to Frank, after June 5, 1918 and in Oct. or Nov. 1918.

43. Letter to Dr. Trigant Burrow, early 1919.

44. Letter to Frank, Jan. 29, 1919.

45. Letter to Frank, late Feb. 1919.

46. Letter to Frank, late August 1919.

47. Letter of Sept. 25, 1919.

48. A Story Teller's Story, p. 26.

49. Letter to M. D. Finley, Aug. 1918.

50. Letter to Anita Loos, July 19, 1918.

51. Letter after Aug. 6, 1918.

52. Letter to Paul Rosenfeld, Dec. 28, 1918.

53. Letter of Dec. 31, 1918.

54. Letter to M. D. Finley, a Sunday afternoon, Jan. 1919.

55.   Letter of Feb. 1919.

Mosaic X

"At such times takes possession..."

When the nerves are tired from long thinking and feeling
   there comes often a kind of explosion.   A hundred
   images come--stories tales poems.   None of them
   complete the circle.   They break off and disappear.
                    to M. D. Finley, Dec. 18, 1924.

              *   *   *

Already there creeps back over me the sense of power to
   hurdle long unbroken rhythms as when I worked on my
   long books.   If this truly comes back and I can work
   in the old mood of unlimited power, carrying into it
   also the surge of a greater subtility [sic] of understanding gathered from these years of living and of
   association with such men as you things may yet be
   done.   I was beginning to be afraid.   Now courage
   comes surging back.
                    to Waldo Frank, after Aug. 6, 1918.

              *   *   *

For each man and woman his own reactions to life and life
   happen to be the writer's materials.   If you are to
   have any individuality as a workman you have to go
   alone through the struggle to find expression for what
   you feel.
                    from "What Say," Marion Democrat, un-
                                                      dated.

              *   *   *

...I think that all of the more beautiful and clear--the more
   plangent and radiant writing I have done--has all been
   done by a kind of secondary personality that at such

230

times takes possession of me.
>   to Mary C. Anderson, spring 1934 (JR).

*   *   *

There is, more than likely, some one man you follow slav-
ishly.   How magnificently his sentences march.   It is
like a field being plowed.   You are thinking of the
man's style, his way of handling words and sentences.
>   to Roy Jansen, April 1935 (JR).

*   *   *

Hackett always attacks me by saying my sense of form is
atrocious and it may be true.   However he also com-
mends me for getting a certain large loose sense of
life.   I often wonder, if I wrapped my packages up
more neatly, if the same large loose sense of life
could be attained.
>   to Paul Rosenfeld, March 10, 1921 (JR).

*   *   *

The men employed with me, the business men, many of them
successful and even rich, were like the laborers, gamblers, soldiers, race track swipes, I had formerly
known.   Their guards down, often over drinks, they
told me the same stories of tangled thwarted lives.
>   How could I throw glamour over such lives.   I
couldn't.
>   to George Freitag, Aug. 18, 1938.

*   *   *

In America we have had a bad tradition, got from the British
and the French.   To our tales that are popular in our
magazines one goes for very clever plots, all sorts of
trickery and juggling.   The natural result is that human
life becomes secondary, of no importance.   The plot
does not grow out of the natural drama resulting from
the tangle of human relations, whereas in your Russian
writings one feels life everywhere, in every page.
>   to Peter Tchemenko, late 1922.

As for using him in a novel or a story, I may do it or I
may not.   Sometimes, in thinking about it, I have told
myself that my feeling for him is too keen to be used.
Perhaps I shall get over this later.   It is a matter that
is always in my mind.

to Miss Ella Boese, June 10, 1937.

*   *   *

In my own experiences, for example, and in my work as a
writer I have always attempted to use material that
came out of my own experience of life.

from "A Writer's Conception of Realism,"
The Sherwood Anderson Reader, p. 338.

*   *   *   *   *

B. To Forgive My Idiosyncrasies

> ...Do not ask me to write of the women with whom
> I have lived in marriage. I respect them too much
> to do it. That I have found a woman who, after
> ten years with me, can still laugh at me, who un-
> derstands my wrinkles, who is there beside me,
> smilingly willing to forgive my idiosyncrasies, who
> after seeing through the years we have lived to-
> gether my worst and my best.... When one of us
> makes a failure of marriage, it is, almost inevit-
> ably, his own fault. He is what he is. He should
> not blame the woman.

> The modern woman will not be kicked aside so.
> She wants children, she wants a certain security,
> for herself and for her children, but we fellows do
> not understand the impulse toward security. When
> we are secure, we are dead. There is nothing
> secure in our world out there, and, as for the
> matter of having children, we are always having
> children of our own. [1]

> I've never been able to work without a woman to
> love. Perhaps I'm cruel. They are earth and sky
> and warmth and light to me. I'm like an Irish
> peasant, taking potatoes out of the ground. I live
> by the woman loved. I take from her.

> I know damn well I don't give enough. [2]

> You perhaps know this feeling of being a guest.
> At times it takes a strong hold of me. I am a
> guest in the life of Cornelia, of Tennessee, of
> George, you, M. Curry, John, a hundred people.

In marriage I am a guest and in love too. [3]

When Sherwood Anderson went back to Chicago in February of 1913, he was a partner in a marriage, with Cornelia, which had been considerably transmuted, not to say eroded. A significant part of the concern of both Sherwood and Cornelia for the next several years was deciding on the course of action which was as satisfactory as possible for both persons and for the children. As has been pointed out, Sherwood returned to live in Chicago, and Cornelia took the children to a house in the summer colony at Little Point Sable. [4] The Andersons were still a family unit, with Sherwood assumedly commuting as he found the occasion, and continued to be when they went to the Ozarks the following winter.

Originally, according to Cornelia, the plan had been for the family to be reunited in Chicago in the fall. But a book was sold, and "on the strength of that he threw up his job and went to the Ozarks. I hadn't a practical hair on my head." After they got to the Ozarks, the company reneged. "Then we lived on what we had." [5]

Before going to the Ozarks, the family stayed temporarily in Chicago and had Thanksgiving dinner with a friend, Edith Kenton. Their stay in the Ozarks was supposed to be at a "hunting lodge," lent to them through another friend, George Ann Lillard. [6]

> We did spend the winter of 1913-1914 about a mile from a tiny settlement of perhaps a dozen houses called Hooker, Missouri. The house had three rooms, two downstairs and one up, with a porch. It had the Little Piney River in front and a "branch" at the side, crossed on stepping stones. On that side was a better house owned by our landlord, who used it during the hunting season. We were given the key and Sherwood withdrew there to write. [7]

Sherwood, Cornelia recalled, was a good shot, and he went hunting that winter. On one occasion he threw down a book he was reading, grasped a rifle, and knocked a squirrel out of a tree. [8]

Anderson recalled that he had spent "five or six months" in the Ozarks. [9] Cornelia said he left for Chicago

in March, 1914.[10] She further stated, "By summer our
funds were so depleted that Sherwood went back to Chicago
to seek reinstatement in an advertising agency."[11] When he
did return to Chicago, some time in the spring, accounts
agree[12] that he was a sensational figure, sporting a beard
and wearing his trousers tucked into boots.

According to one account, he had not written much at
Hooker because of the cold.[13] Anderson told Hansen[14] that
he had written a novel but that he threw it out of the window
on the way back to Chicago. Cornelia wrote: "I have no
recollection of what he wrote there. As to him throwing it
out the train window on the way back to Chicago--I never
heard that story. It sounds like one of his."[15]

However vague his writing accomplishments were, a
major adjustment in the marriage did take place. Karl
thought the couple had gone to the Ozarks "in an effort to
reconcile themselves to matrimony"; if so, they were without
success.[16] Cornelia said the separation agreement really
came in the Ozarks.[17] Each of the two parties has written
a comment on this decision to separate.

> You perhaps do not know that I was married and
> the father of three children, that I had to undertake
> the delicate and difficult task of breaking up that
> marriage and of trying to win the real love of that
> woman out of marriage and outside the difficulties
> and complications of sex. . . .
>
> That was the year, Frank, that I went into the
> Ozark Mountains. I took the woman and the chil-
> dren with me. I lived in a separate cabin on a
> hillside, and together the woman and I went through
> poverty, hatred of each other, and all the terrible
> things which come from such a situation.
>
> It is odd now to think that it was misunderstanding
> that brought us through. She came to the con-
> clusion that I was not mentally sound. That awoke
> the mother instinct in her. We began to make
> progress.
>
> No story I will ever write will touch that story,
> and that is one of the keenest pleasures of life to
> me, that I have lived something beyond any power
> of mine to write it.[18]

As Cornelia recalled these events, she thought of "a long period there not free from mental agony. No one had fewer illusions about himself than he did." And further:

> The step he took in giving up his family was not an easy one, but I still think he did the right thing. He wouldn't have been free to develop otherwise. You are worldly-wise enough to know that some marriages don't last forever. Then a separation is the best thing. It is a question whether living in a strained atmosphere would be any better for the children. I am a much better person for having known him so well.
>
> I don't know whether you would agree. I read once that what a genius needs is a mother and not a wife. I do. [19]

Originally the plan had been to go back to Chicago after the sojourn in the Ozarks, but the developing fissure in the marriage worked against that. Too, Anderson's artistic friends[20] had found Union Pier, Michigan, a lake shore community within commuting distance of Chicago, which they resorted to for weekend parties. It was an inexpensive place for Cornelia to live in separation with her children. "Sherwood theoretically came for weekends but came just for parties. After I got settled, we talked pretty frankly. We had been separated for a long time and he had other interests.... We knew perfectly well that we weren't going to live together," but divorce was then of no use because both said they did not want to marry again. Later he did want to marry; then she got the divorce. [21]

By Christmas of 1914 Sherwood's group stopped coming to Union Pier because of the cold. Cornelia turned her attention to getting work so as to support herself and her children, being completely assured that Sherwood felt his writing came before his family responsibility. And it should be noted that she, contrary to convention, accepted her role with a minimum of animosity. Her 1946 statement seems in accord with her complete program of action and reaction. She left her children with the Leatherman family in Union Pier and became a student in the School of Civics and Philanthropy, in Chicago, from January to August, 1915. The preparation was for social work. She found, as the summer wore on, that she could not get such a job. "Thank God I don't have to do that," she thought, and found that a teaching job was open at Union Pier, where she taught from 1915 to 1917. [22] Thereafter she taught at Michigan City, Indiana, which is between Union Pier and Chicago, from 1917 until her retirement in 1943, [23] and it was there the Anderson children were reared to adulthood.

The divorce of Sherwood and Cornelia Anderson took place through court actions of the spring and summer of 1916.   On April 8, Cornelia filed her divorce complaint, which stipulated that the pair had ceased to live together "on or about March, 1914," that he had "willfully deserted and absented himself from the plaintiff, without any reasonable cause, for the space of two years and upwards, and has persisted in such desertion."   It went on to state that Sherwood's salary in Chicago was $50 per week and that "the defendant has at several and various times sent certain sums of money to her for the support of the three children... but that the said sums are not regular and often times for months there will not be anything forwarded to her, and that the said several sums during the course of the year are nowhere near sufficient for the support of the children, and this plaintiff has been obliged to teach school for her own support and to help support the children."

On the order of Circuit Judge George W. Bridgman at St. Joseph, Michigan, the county seat of Berrien County in which Union Pier was located, the marriage was dissolved on July 27, 1916, the custody of the children being given to Cornelia, but no alimony awarded her.   The tenor of the documents pertinent to the action is amicable (though accusative through legal necessity), and it seems likely that it was understood that no alimony was expected. [24]

Of the time in the Ozarks, Anderson was to write:

> There are certain definite things I came to out of that--the ability to be brutal with women, the conclusion that for me there must always be my own place, some hole in the wall into which I could crawl to pray and be alone and to catch and hold my own note out of the jar and jingle of voices. [25]

It has already been suggested that Cornelia dealt with the break-up of her marriage with dignity, courage, and understanding.   Constituted quite differently from the gifted man she married, she tried to see her own course and follow it, being reluctant to mull over the past.   This has made it

difficult to get the kind of information which might fascinate.
The present author wrote in 1941 for information and was
met by polite but resolute refusal.   After an interview in
1946, Mrs. Anderson wrote:

> I felt like Rip Van Winkle awakening from a sleep
> of over thirty years.   During those thirty years I
> had resolutely put Elyria out of my mind from un-
> willingness or fear of that period.
>
> This last month I have been living there again,
> every moment I have not been too busy to think.
> I believe now I can see the whole thing clearly and
> fairly and the none-too-comfortable experience has
> done me good.   Perhaps after this psychiatric
> catharsis I shall be cleansed and happier. [26]

Her daughter-in-law[27] reported that she never made any effort to discuss Sherwood with Mrs. Anderson, even when
they were living together, because she had determined she
did not want to go back over that part of her life.

But if she did not, understandably, want to look back,
she did not avoid the present.   She did not exorcise her
children's father from her own or their lives.   (See Appendix
G for fuller coverage of Anderson's relationship to his children.)   A relationship of deeply interested and frank friendship continued throughout the rest of his life, as the following reveal:

> I was tremendously sorry to hear your news.   I
> had hoped that you were happy and that E. [Eliza-
> beth Prall, his third wife] was.   But evidently
> marriages are but cycles. [28]
>
> I felt that I had to do it and have sent it, that is
> to say half the sum.   When Cornelia divourced
> [sic] me, because she thought I was a little crazy,
> trying to write etc., she was square, never asked
> any money from me.   And she has worked hard
> as a school teacher ever since.   The money must
> mean a lot to her.   I couldn't do less than she
> did. . . . [29]
>
> R's [their son Robert's] plans are all prospering.

You needn't worry about his retrogressing. He
steadily improves--only fortunately the general public has never known how much room for improvement there was. This course of treatment is doing him good. He's behaving very well--has to
earn $40 in order to stay six weeks. He's so
taken up with that he has little time for mischief--
He is also practicing to enter an athletic contest--
pole vaulting and jumping. . . .

Mimi [their daughter Marion] not only sings in the
Episcopal choir but wormed her way into the quin-
tet. I certainly admire the child's nerve. She
can't in the least sing a tune. 30

He [Earl] had several defective teeth but his blood
pressure was high and they were afraid to take
them out. He began to get better but overdid.
Walked around too much and last week had a slight
stroke of appoplexy. [sic] [This letter contains a
very full report on Earl's illness, a health problem
of his brother, Irwin, and then the following:]

Bob is doing splendidly. Everyone likes him and
nowdays he is taking great interest in his work and
advancing rapidly. It seems entirely possible that
he will make a fine reputation as an alert capable
newspaper man down here [New Orleans] and then
can tackle a bigger city job. I hate to leave him
down here but he is doing so well and has such a
charming little apartment and is so interested in
his work that I hate to disturb him. He is planning to come up to the farm with John later. 31

There is no use apologizing for not acknowledging
your book, I suppose, but at any rate I do. I enjoyed reading it, am glad to have it and thank you
for sending it--very much. 32

This appears to be a sequel to part of a previous letter:

In Chicago I discovered you had a new book out,
your Notebook, and tried to negotiate a loan but
failed. If you will send me yours to the Point
soon, I will read it and return it. 33

One of her fellow teachers at Michigan City recalled
that Cornelia encouraged contact between the children and
their father.   There were casual contacts with him, as when
he took Mimi to Europe, helped John with his art studies,
or established Robert with the newspapers.   She had respect
for talent in anyone.   Perhaps still loving him, she displayed
no bitterness toward him, showing only occasional amusement
when he encountered other marital problems. [34]

As one considers all the other ways that Cornelia
could have acted and that perhaps the wife is traditionally
expected to act under such circumstances, it becomes very
clear that Sherwood Anderson had in his first wife a truly
remarkable woman, one perhaps ideally suited for the trials
to which his ordeal subjected her.   It must be recognized
that his artistic success owes something to her capability of
disciplining herself to a cooperative, understanding role rather than an understandably destructive or vindictive one.

*   *   *

I only mean that poor E. is very, very nice--much
nicer than I will ever be--and I do not want her
any more.   C[ornelia] and T[ennessee] were nice
too.   Why should I not face myself--a wanderer. [35]

It may seem a terrible pronouncement that woman,
although she accept work and make of herself a
sturdy figure in the world is yet unworthy of love
if she be not physically beautiful and have not that
daring fling at life that belongs to the artist but it
is true. [36]

I am also not sentimental enough to think that by a
new marriage one steps into freedom from mussi-
ness.   What one does I suppose and what you are
doing is to take a close comrad [sic] who understands the difficulties of everyday existence and
isn't fool enough to think they can be solved by reciting second rate poetry.

I am as sure as anything now that you are going to
have a life filled with fine spots and God knows we

are fools to ask or expect more than that. 37

I won't say anything about the woman struggle. You
know it.   I don't know whether or not you are like
me.   In me the struggle is intense.   I had thought
you had more reserve than I had.   Perhaps you
only cover up better.   I have to have a woman like
I have to breath[e].   I can't stand aside.   I have
to kiss, hold--get close to the mystery.   At any
price, in struggle and hurt I have to.

There is that thing in modern women. . . .   My own
failures have all been in that. . . a kind of jealousy
springs up.   There is something truer than any
woman knows through self.   That comes at all
times like a wall between. 38

As for women, my dear, our experience has been
not unlike others I have had with other women.
Much has been offered to me in the way of women,
in the flesh.   I have taken what I felt clean and
clear in the taking.   When I no longer felt that I
have stopped, sometimes only after much bitterness.   I have gone sometimes away from women
with fine bodies and fine minds and have gladly
taken women to whom I had no obligation because
to do so cleansed me like writing good prose. 39

Perhaps you do not understand at all.   The inner
thing in me is a clean boy running over the hills.
I turn to women because men are too concerned
with making money and overfeeding their lusts.   I
am stupid.   I forget that women are as much involved in the tangle as men.   So much of the time
I do not want hands on me but want to run clean
and alone.   I can't have that I know but like a silly
fellow I keep asking for it. 40

Of course I should have kicked him out.   It has
been my way.   I will never know whether it has
been right or wrong.   I have always fought and bit
and struck my way through, keeping after something.   I don't know whether it has been right or

not.   How can I know.   How can I know whether it
has been worthwhile. [41]

"Masculinity" [A fragment contained in a letter.]:

He lay on his back in a dentist chair.   The chair
was in a long hall.   There were many curtains.
He was young and strong and he laughed.   He threw
back his head and he laughed.

From behind the curtains, one by one, came women.   They crept along the floor, creeping slowly.
Her eyes shone and she kissed him. [sic.]

He slapped each of the women with his hand, a
ringing blow that echoed through the long hall.
Then he laughed.   Back he lay in the dentist's
chair and laughed.   The many curtains of the room
trembled and more women, naked, with shining
eyes came creeping, creeping.

He slapped them with his hand, a ringing slap.
Then he lay back in the chair and laughed.   "It
was [sic] always been so." he said.   "It will always be so."

Then (again) he laughed. [42]

I love to awake in the night and let my imagination
play over the person of another.

Women are sometimes very beautiful when sleeping.

It may be best not to awake them. [43]

Apart from E. [Eleanor] and you and a few, very
few women, women in general bore me. [44]

"A very dear friend of mine." [45]

Doubtless this is the most notable of all the descriptions of
Tennessee Anderson, coming as it does from the woman

whose first husband she married.   But there are many other
attestations to the high regard in which she was held.   Stuart Chase, who with his wife knew Sherwood and Tennessee
in the war years, thought of her as a leader[46] and found
that he admired her wit and strong character.[47]   Another
friend recalled her as witty, vital, energetic, charming, and
zestful.[48]   Her "poise, her quiet jollity, and her whimsical
cynicism" impressed one of Anderson's best friends.[49]   One
of her students thought her inspiring, noted her Bohemian
nature, and recalled her as one of the first women he knew
who smoked a lot.[50]   Miss Finley thought of her in this way:

> Tennessee Anderson I always admired very greatly.
> She was fair to other women and had a gracious-
> ness in dealing with others.   I knew her but slight-
> ly yet I always felt her great charm.   She was rath-
> er beautiful.[51]

Eunice Tietjens' daughter remembered that her mother appreciated her sense of obligation and courage.[52]   A friend
thought she was basically fine, in spite of long earrings and
arty clothes.[53]   Another woman remembered her as eccentric
in her dress, "inclined to floating scarves," but thought her
individualistic and that her clothes "expressed her soul."[54]

        Aside from these relatively objective sources, two
rather personally-involved people supply evidence as to her
nature.   The first of these is Tennessee herself, who left
a record in a set of letters to a friend.[55]   On one occasion
she confided, "I have had very little in my life of people
looking out for me.   It has been taken for granted that I was
quite capable of taking care of myself.   Of course I have
developed some technics but underneath I do so want...
thought and affection...."[56]   Perhaps her enforced self-reliance accounted for a certain aggressiveness: "I seem to be
quaintly old fashioned but when a person has been a skunk
to anyone I love while I wouldn't spit in their faces more
than once, I don't want to see them or have any connection
with them."[57]   Again she remarks dryly that a friend has
told her: "It isn't enough to do the right thing by other people.   You owe it to them too to see to it that they do the
right thing by you."[58]   But she could also write, "Blessings
on you for being hopelessly romantic.   I'm incurable myself
and want to have company and the ranks seem to be thinning
out."[59]   And then she could be mischievously rational:

        Two women from Evanston of the good and the

> beautiful and the true type are here.... Their en-
> thusiasm over your friend Westcott is so great they
> fairly oozed pools of sweetness. To bait them I
> impishly repeated rumors--to see them squirm--
> for which I humbly ask your forgiveness. Oh, it
> was so funny. [60]

Tennessee was teacher of music and dance, had been
a piano-tuner, became a sculptress, and was deeply interested in the theater. She stumbled onto sculpture through
her association with Sherwood, [61] and she was to say of it,
"It's absurd to get money [as she did occasionally] for doing
anything that is such fun." [62]   (See her prefatory figures in
Anderson's The Triumph of the Egg. [63])   Two of her comments on her sculpture reflect her wit and her unconventional
boldness:

> I also did a satire on fig leaves which is very fun-
> ny.   Five nudes clasping articles to their private
> parts--one a huge bouquet--a mask--a fan--a bunch
> of carrots and a heart....
>
> I did a high relief about 2 ft x 1-1/2 of a three
> quarters length nude negress--very buxom with
> arms akimbo.   In the background are 7 profiles of
> lusty bucks eagerly gazing at her.   I showed it to
> the Arts Club recently bringing down an angry
> press--obscene--belonged in a brothel, etc.   One
> defender said it was the only thing in the show with
> vitality. [64]

Though she was Sherwood's wife for eight years and
knew many artists of different kinds, it was not until 1928
that she wrote:

> Do go at that book.   I can't wait much longer to
> see it.   While I was West not being able to trail
> along sculpture appurtenances I did some writing
> and had a darned good time at it.   I never knew
> before that it could be much fun to string words
> together. [65]

Her writing just mentioned resulted in 77 long-hand
pages in a notebook left unfinished. [66]   One wonders whether
Anderson's own autobiographical writings may have conditioned
her effort, for it does have, in an embryonic way, some of
the puzzled, frank probing of his work.   It deals with death

and sex initiation and gives one a strong intimation of a
troubled and unsatisfactory road traveled, giving the basis
for the aggressiveness mentioned earlier.   One feels this
was a person who did things the hard way and who came
from a family similar to Sherwood's.

     She was born Tennessee Claflin Mitchell in Jackson,
Michigan, on April 18, 1874, [67] and her account of the factors surrounding her name are rather typical of the episodes
she relates:

>   Then there was the strange feeling about my name.
>   I knew without knowing that there was some taint
>   connected with it.   Sammy did tell me that I was
>   named for a bad woman but my mother said I was
>   named for a brave woman and that was confusing.
>   In my embarrassment when I started to school, I
>   called myself Tennie and later thinking it more
>   substantial Tennis.   I afterward learned that the
>   famous, or, as they were then generally thought,
>   infamous Claflin sisters--Virginia Woodhull and
>   Tennessee Claflin like Robert Ingersoll and the
>   mediums [--] had been guests at my grandfather's
>   house.
>
>   Their visit came just before my advent into the
>   world, my mother had an affection for the charm-
>   ing and spirited Tennessee Claflin--and then a
>   neighbor came to see the baby and tauntingly said--
>   "Even you I suppose wouldn't dare to name the
>   baby for 'your friend'. "
>
>   My mother said--"I like the name.   I admire the
>   woman and I shall and will. "   So Tennessee was
>   named without benefit of christening.

     It is interesting to note that she listed herself in the
Chicago city directory just after coming to the city as Tennis
C. Mitchell.

     Her father's character is suggested by the following
account:

>   My father was little more to me than another per-
>   son around the house, who sometimes expressed
>   his disapproval but never showed me any affection.
>   One day he put me between his knees on a high

cart while he drove a fractious young horse.   The
horse dove and reared.   I was frightened and
clutched my father's hands.   He said nothing but
got the horse under control, drove it up to a fence,
tied it, took me down from the seat quite unsus-
pecting, turned me over and spanked me.   He then
explained that what I had done was dangerous and
was one of the reasons men distrusted and despised
females.

She tells of arriving in Chicago and, having been told
she had perfect pitch, deciding to become a piano tuner, certainly a peculiar thing for a woman to try to do.   Her determination was stretched to the utmost by a series of refusals
on the part of other tuners to teach her.   But she did finally
find a man who would do it.

Of young men and women friends I had none because I hesitated to encourage the few contacts I
made for the reason that the setting[,] a home and
family[,] was lacking.   I finally looked my situation
squarely in the face and decided that I was cutting
myself off from this thing Life that I had set out
to meet.

With my changed attitude, when I saw men on the
street whom I had met in my few social ventures
and they asked me for luncheon I accepted.   But
usually when in their efforts to place me in the
social scheme I explained that I tuned pianos, their
attitude changed and there were often offers of
financial assistance.

She writes a good deal about her interest in men, and
it seems she is always rather puzzled by her relationship
with them.   These two passages will give the flavor of what
happened with the first man in whom she had a deep interest:

Soon I became conscious of a man, who was interested but never obtruded, who was protective without being patronizing, whom I knew could be my
friend.   He had social position that impressed me
--but he had what meant more--understanding.   He
belonged to that great number who have little interest or aptitude for business, a yearning for the
arts, and lack either a decided talent or the courage

to pursue them.   The type has always appealed to
me....

It came then without saying it in words we knew we
loved each other.   Owing to conditions in his life
we thought we ought not to marry.   I was divided
between very real agony and a very real sense of
relief, for something told me this was a valuable
and fine experience but not for all time.   My mind
and my emotions were at war and my person, the
battleground, suffered.   If this man went out of my
life--how would I know I could have the great experience that was so large a part of the literature
and art of the world.   I saw women to whom I knew
either love had come or that they had renounced it.
I could not become one of them.   Anyway, if marriage, which seemed only remotely possible, did
come, how could one be confident--of a lifetime
relationship without knowledge of the most important
element?

The man never broached the subject but I did.   He
said he could not take so great a responsibility,
that it might ruin my life.   I answered that if such
an experience between a man and a woman whose
love was beautiful and fine could ruin my life, I
was ready to have it ruined.

When Sherwood and Cornelia Anderson met Tennessee
at the home of Marjorie Currie and Floyd Dell, who thought
of her as having an atmosphere of the modern, [68] she became
the friend of both of them.   But eventually she became, for
a time, an object of near-adoration, if we may be guided by
what he wrote about her.   He was to tell Paul Rosenfeld, as
late as 1921, that she had a "certain thing about her that
makes her often almost too decent to be a woman at all. "[69]
Again he felt like "a crude woodsman that has been received
into the affection of a princess. "[70]

A certain almost unaccountable tentativeness and humility was felt:

I never go into Tennessee's house but I go a little
timidly, questioning.   I want to know how I am to
be received.   If ever I find her in the faintest way
not wanting me I shall merely run away.   Outwardly
I am strong and sure.   Inwardly I often quake hard

> enough. . . .   I am afraid no one will like me.   I
> have bad thoughts and feelings. . . people know noth-
> ing about.   I am sure they have left marks on
> me. [71]

Also, "I do not dare approach too close to Tennessee, make
her too close a part of my life because I do not want to take
into her life my greyness but to be where she is means
everything. "[72]

On the other hand, he felt that he was completely accepted, understood, perhaps even protected and indulged.

> Out from under a mess.   A fool woman came to
> town intent on going to bed of me.   Where do they
> get that queer little diseased gleam in their eye
> when they have that notion?   I climbed a tree.
> Then I ran along the treetops, leaping with hands
> and feet.   I threw nuts at her and cracked her
> head.
>
> Tennessee is unspeakably bully in such a situation.
> She does not become the wife.   What she does is
> walk blithely along and pay no attention.   Then
> when I have hit the lady with a large coconut and
> the milk streams down into her eyes, she winks. [73]
>
> There is a blessed flavor about understanding peo-
> ple--Tennessee is one of them.   She has bought
> me a little feather to wear in my hat.   She has
> bought me a golden yellow scarf. . . will buy my
> socks all splashed with purple and yellow. . . in a
> quite child-like way I have restored truth in the
> midst of ugliness. [74]

Reminiscing in 1930, he was to write:

> So I love again and work, and it seems to me I
> never loved before; and it is all strangely enough
> one thing, except that it seemed to me the others
> lost courage and wouldn't adventure any more. . . .
>
> Odd, isn't it, but that Tennessee came the nearest?
>
> She saw the thing--taking life so, with gusto, to
> the last drop.

> I used to take her sometimes to the very door, put
> her hand on the doorknob, but she always ran away
> like a frightened child. [75]

But Tennessee really did not always act the frightened
child.   A romantic episode from her manuscript involving her
with Edgar Lee Masters reads as follows:

> I had known a few yearners for the arts but none
> who worked creatively and felt himself dedicated to
> the arts.   He [Masters] said I had imagination.   I
> replied that I doubted it as I had never been deeply
> interested in fairy tales.   He said I belonged to
> the realistic school.   Many books came from him
> that I read avidly, because we would later discuss
> them.   It was my first real intellectual stimulus
> from personal contact.
>
> The man was married, but I heard from him and
> from others that the marital relationship had for
> years been only a formality.   There seemed to be
> no question of an intrinsic wrong in such a friend-
> ship, but there were conventions.   I argued that
> in my position I was deriving no benefit from the
> conventions, that I was alone and had no responsi-
> bility except to myself.   I felt confident to handle
> that, his situation was his own affair.   I liked my
> first taste of intellectual companionship and wanted
> more.
>
> My poet had been writing many years, had privately
> printed many books, but at that time received little
> recognition from the literary world.   About that he
> was bitter.   Mine were new and eager ears for his
> poetry, his bitterness and his hopes.   He took me
> into a new world of thought and I was flattered that
> an impetus for writing was coming in the wake of
> our relationship.
>
> My need was great for stimulating companionship,
> and sex was to me a part of an entireness which I
> knew was not in this relation.   So that when it
> ended and ended miserably I was desolated.   He
> told me that I was his source of inspiration that we
> must go together to Europe.   I argued that earning
> my living was my first necessity.   I could do noth-
> ing that would cut me off from that.   He turned all

the bitterness of an unappreciated poet and a man
whose vanity has been hurt against me and told me
that if I was too weak to rise to this my life would
be ruined.

His hatred became so intense that for years to see
him casually on the street affected me like physical
danger.   I trembled and ran into buildings to avoid
a meeting.   Several years later when we were in
a group and were introduced, I saw by his face
that the hatred had spent itself.   He asked "Are
you happy?" I replied, I have known much happiness but am not happy.   Are you? He looked away
and finally said, "No, I am neither happy nor do I
expect to be.   Happiness doesn't exist. "

One man had said a love experience would ruin my
life.   Another that the loss of it would ruin it.
Men and sex were confusing.

For some time I again had my life alone but only
tiring work and trying to keep the zest for reading
alive without the joys of sharing with another probably caused me unconsciously to put out feelers
for new friends.

It is truly a puzzling experience to read the 20 pages
that Edgar Lee Masters devotes to this relationship in his
autobiography.[76] He calls Tennessee by the name of Deirdre
in his recounting, and characterizes here as promiscuous
and scheming; himself, both bitter and defensive.   One familiar with Tennessee's life and the autobiographical segments
given above would certainly begin to see some related factors, but the accounts are different enough that one would
hardly be sure in the identification.   However, Masters wrote
to a scholar (through his wife) to identify Tennessee with
Deirdre of Across Spoon River. [77] Doubtless the precise
character of their relationship, which Masters says was at
its erotic height in 1909 and 1910 and affected him deeply
for three years, will never be established.   And doubtless
it need not be, for what is known with other data presented
demonstrates rather well that, at the time of her marriage
to Sherwood Anderson, Tennessee Claflin Mitchell was a person of many and varied experiences, some of them rather intense ones involving men.

In an interview with William Phillips, [78] Marco Morrow,

one of Anderson's long-time and close friends, said that Anderson had told him several years after 1916 that he had married Tennessee to protect her from a scandal involving Masters. The idea was that the Hearst newspapers were to print the story about Masters to get at Clarence Darrow. Morrow thought the story was one of Anderson's yarns. It does seem unlikely, but its significance for the present purpose is that it indicates that Anderson knew something of the relationship.

Cornelia has said that neither party was thinking of marriage when the separation was entered into in 1914. And it is understood that the divorce was requested when Sherwood and Tennessee realized they wanted to marry. This is easy to believe in view of the fact that the divorce was granted on July 27, 1916, and that the marriage took place on July 31, 1916.

Among Tennessee's interests was rhythmic dancing, and she had formed the custom of attending the dancing camp run by Alys Bentley at Lake Chateaugay, New York, of which more directly. In the newspaper account of the wedding the two participants were identified as "of Chicago, but at present members of the summer colony at Upper Chateaugay Lake." The newspaper article reported that "To add a touch of romance to the event the ceremony took place under an apple tree on the banks of the Chateaugay River near the Douglass Mill. The wedding party returned immediately to the camp after the ceremony. "[79] Local records show that the marriage ceremony was performed by Justice of the Peace M. J. McCoy and witnessed by Miss Bentley and her assistant, Edith Westcott. The record also gives such information as names of each person's parents, birthplace and age. Tennessee gave her age as 37 instead of 42, and Sherwood gave June 19, 1916, as the date of his divorce. [80]

Cornelia's friendship with Tennessee lasted until Tennessee's death in 1930. She had the children send presents on the occasion of the marriage, [81] and the honeymooning couple were received in her home in Michigan City. In the summer of 1917, Anderson, Tennessee, and Marion, his daughter, went to Chateaugay for a period together. [82]

One of Tennessee's friends has said that Cornelia and the children were, not surprisingly, devoted to her. Finding that seeing his former wife and children disturbed him, she took his place. Tennessee told this friend that she had a maternal feeling toward him and Cornelia admitted a similar reaction.

Thus, often on summer and autumn Sundays, Tennessee would go by electric train to Tremont to meet Cornelia and the children, who had come from Michigan City. Tennessee took clothing, food, and money and spent the day on the beach with them. Tennessee regretted that Sherwood would not meet this responsibility. [83]

There is evidence that Anderson was rather self-conscious at this time about his failure to support Tennessee:

> Tennessee is pretty well. It's too damn bad she has to go to work teaching because she married me who won't settle down and support a woman as a respectable man should. Lucile she has done some heads of Americans that are great. I get to talking to her about some imaginary character-- say Mrs. Windpeter Winters. We talk about her several days and then she takes some clay and there she is--very realistic vivid things. [84]

The two factors of art and work for Tennessee are again poised against each other in a variation on this theme:

> Naturally it makes Tennessee happy that you like her work and that Margaret likes it so much. She is unfortunately married to a man who can't support her so she has to make her own living. Therefore, she doesn't get time to work when she isn't tired. In other words, having found the impulses of an artist within herself, she is meeting the same situation that practically every American artist meets. [85]

Another phase of the same conflict, as it related to Tennessee, is seen in the Fairhope period:

> I persuaded Tennessee to be utterly reckless, chuck her job and income, and run off here with me.... For several years she has been a tired woman.... Tennessee suddenly began working in clay, and already she does really remarkable things. What new joy in life that approach towards beauty coming in a definite form out of herself has given her. [86]

There seems to be a half-humorous, rather unhappy note, as toward a person who unexpectedly becomes a competitor, thinly-masked by polite acceptance, especially in this instance:

> ...the trouble with her now is this. Down in Alabama she got some beautiful clay in her hands and turned out some remarkable heads. The result is that she doesn't want to be an honest working woman any more, but has the same disease that has caught the rest of us. She wants to sit under a fig tree by a green sea and have beautiful blacks bring her clay to be modeled.... Anyway the poor woman went and married me and is stuck to make her own living, and it's hell. She really has something smashing, I believe, in the clay thing. [87]

In Tennessee's obituary, her pride in being a "natural" artist was mentioned. Perhaps the following anecdote, though it is not especially convincing, reflects a little more of the suggestion that Anderson, fundamentally, was not happy with her achievement: Once, when she and Sherwood were sitting together on a mountainside, she unconsciously picked up a clod of mud and made a head. He was quite enraged to note it was of a man of whom he was jealous. She told this story to show how she had become a sculptress without training. [88]

Whatever else is known about this marriage, it is clear that it was unusual. Burton Rascoe recalled that Tennessee's apartment was on Division Street and that Sherwood was in the rooms on Cass Street. [89]

Amplification and correction are offered by this excerpt from an invitational letter to Frank:

> Come any time. There is a cat in my room on Schiller Street and a big table and typewriter for you. Tennessee's place is only two blocks away. You can write and wander about in the big loose town.... T. has a bed in her house for me. [90]

Schevill thought they agreed that each should come and go at will, that they hoped to practice the kind of Bohemian marriage, unfettered by requirements of fidelity and obedience, that was generally only talked about. [91]

A magazine article recorded that Tennessee earned

her own living and had her own apartment. Sherwood, living
in a shack in Palos Park, renting for twenty dollars a month,
was doing his own washing, housework, laundry. [92]   And
Anderson had a special note of explanation:

> And even this is misunderstood. I live away from
> this woman I have married. I go often to walk
> alone, to be alone. This also is misunderstood.
> Rumors run about. The woman is condemned be-
> cause of the loneliness in my life. She is made
> to seem hard, cruel and indifferent when she is
> only big. No want of mine is left unsatisfied.   In
> her love she like others, is willing to give all.
> I will not take it. Often I shut the door and go
> away. And she is condemned for that. [93]

Such satisfaction as is indicated above was certainly
reciprocated, for he could write three years later that she
"declares that I have given her the golden days of her life
these last two months. "[94]

However, the marriage did end in time, with considerable dissatisfaction on both sides, of which these items
will supply the flavor:

> One of the deep things T[ennessee] never realized
> was the harm in our relations to each other. Can
> you understand my saying, without my feeling her
> to blame, that these months away from her have
> done more to make me feel less assertive, com-
> bative, egotistical than I ever felt in her presence?
> Can you conceive of this being true and at the
> same time of my effect on her being equally bad?[95]

And in an undated letter fragment, recipient unknown,
he wrote, "I was granted my divorce from the woman with
whom I have been half living for several years...."[96]

>   *   *   *

> How people lose themselves who are not artists I
> do not know. Perhaps they--some of them--do it
> in love.

> To have a woman and possess her is a good deal.
> It isn't enough for an eager man. [97]

> I do not think there are many men of our day who
> have written much prose. . . .   I think very few men
> care.   I do.

> I care more than for any person.   That, at bottom,
> I dare say, is what has been wrong with me as a
> married man.

> Women do get me and then I lose them utterly.   I
> return to something else. [99]

> I have always been sure that none of the women
> were to blame when our marriage failed.   Any
> practitioner of the arts is a trial to live with. [100]

And perhaps the last word, mixing complaint and comparison, may be allowed Tennessee:

> The most amusing thing--I hear S feels that having
> lived with an artist and then being deserted has
> made me a sculptor.   I told Mrs. A. No. 1 whose
> reply was--He made me a school teacher and you
> a sculptor.   What a pity it is he doesn't work
> faster so he can do more for women.

> It's foolish of us to be down on him.   He's as he
> is, a very charming person--maybe it's too much
> to expect more.   That I did was my mistake.   I
> ought not to whine. [101]

It will be recalled that it was Tennessee who introduced Sherwood to the attractive surroundings of Upper Lake
Chateaugay in New York, at the northern edge of the Adirondacks.   The lake is still strikingly beautiful, and it was then
the site of Miss Alys Bentley's summer camp, now in ruins,
for women from the age of 16 up.   On three acres at the
shore of the lake were two main cottages and enough tents
to accommodate about fifty campers.   It was a "rhythm
camp, " emphasizing physical culture primarily through the
dance.   Evidently there was in addition some dietary fad-
dism. [102]

Apparently Sherwood spent most of the summer of
1916 and all of June, July and August in the vicinity of the
camp on Upper Lake Chateaugay.   A friend remembered that
he lived in a "tent house" with no heat of any kind in 1916

and so before his marriage came to her, the friend's, cabin
to sit in front of the fireplace and write when it was cold
and rainy.   She also recalled helping him "fix up his shack"
when he married Tennessee. [103]

In discussing his plans for the summer in a letter to
Waldo Frank on March 2, 1917 (JR), Anderson told him he
was going to live in a tent on a lake.   In another spring letter that year he told him "There will be a woods and a lake
but no people, except when we want to cross the lake to
them.   Instead there will be black shadows in the woods and
the flare of the furnace foundry at night." He directed Frank
to bring warm clothing as well as his bathing suit, some
soft shirts, and easy shoes. [104] During the summer he reported:

> Life goes straight on here.   I loaf and think.   The
> drive to work begins to stir in me but I put it
> away and wait.
>
> Had a fire in the tent and some of my manuscript
> got scorched. [105]

The Chateaugay experience evidently was a very interesting and enjoyable one, being in the extremely important
pattern for him of establishing contact with nature and exploring his own reactions.   He was not unaware of the camp,
however, as this echo indicates:

> ... cry back to the Bently physical attitude.   "Let
> Go." Sometime I shall become a God, a new John
> the Baptist crying in the wilderness and the burden
> of my cry shall be "Let go.   For God's sake, let
> go!"

The character of his emotional experience was strong:

> ...I find it nice to be alone in sight of the misty
> hills.   Today I ran into the woods.... I stretched
> myself out on the grass and sobbed like a woman
> for the glory and quiet of this place.   Deep in the
> ground my roots and my gods lie.   They are whis-
> pering to me. [106]

Looking back on that summer, he would write:

> As I have loafed and danced and waited in the sun

up here. . . a peculiar thing has taken place in me.
My mind has run back to the time when men tended
sheep and lived a nomadic life on hillsides and by
little talking streams.   I have become less and less
the thinker and more the thing of earth and the
winds.   When I awake at night and the wind is
howling, my first thought is that the gods are at
play here. [107]

So strong was their love for the place that Anderson
confided to Frank that Tennessee was thinking of buying "the
frame house on the upper road where we went up and stood
on the porch--the house back of the stone wall."[108]   This
could have provided a permanent base for the enjoyment he
found with Tennessee, whose coming he was anticipating for
"her quiet dignified companionship and for the thing in her
that understands these hills and these soft quiet nights better
than I."[109]

It was at Chateaugay that Anderson met Dr. Trigant
Burrow, a Baltimore psychiatrist who had a camp across the
lake from Miss Bentley's.   Dr. Burrow remembered particularly a day he spent with Anderson hiking and talking beside Rocky Brook "entirely along psychoanalytic lines."[110]
Anderson, in July, 1917, wrote his friend Waldo Frank:
"Some day I will tell you the story of my several long talks
with Dr. Burrow.   It all has an amusing and pathetic side."
Although Burrow originally thought he had met Anderson first
in 1915, he eventually agreed with another friend of Anderson's[111] that the first summer Anderson and Tennessee were
there was 1916.[112]   This dating is significant in that it
means the Winesburg stories, written in the winter of 1915-
1916, as will be seen, could not have been affected originally by any of these psychoanalytic conversations, evidently
in the summers of 1916 and 1917.   In an August, 1917, letter to Frank, Anderson added that he and Burrow had not
seen much of each other "and the purpose to sike [sic] me
faded out in one rather hectic talk on the matter."

As has just been seen, Anderson's original response
to Burrow's ideas was negative.   This may be seen as rather fully, though fictionally, developed in the story "Seeds"
in The Triumph of the Egg.   In the conversation with Burrow,
Anderson argued that human life was not a thing to be approached scientifically, and Burrow thought science offered
the only useful approach to the health and growth of sick personalities.[113]   The idea of "Seeds" is to present a

conversation between a narrator and a psychiatrist, in which
the allegation (page 23) is made that: "The thing you want
to do cannot be done. Fool--do you expect love to be understood?" This aroused the following comment in Burrow:

> Of Anderson I would say that socially he was one
> of the healthiest men I have ever known. His
> counter offensive in "Seeds" amply testifies to this.
> Indeed on this score many orthodox psychoanalysts
> might very profitably take a leaf from his book.
> Yes, I am the analyst to whom Anderson referred
> in this story. [114]

As perceptive as each man was, they did not immediately understand each other. It has already been seen that
Anderson did not originally value the relationship. Burrow
was to say, "I did not analyze Anderson. Our relationship
rested upon a quite unusual sympathy and understanding of
one another that was spontaneous, immediate," and phrased
his unusual admiration in this way:

> I do want to emphasize, moreover, that Sherwood
> Anderson was an original psychologist in his own
> right and, if he profited by any insights of mine,
> I also profited in no small measure by the excep-
> tional insight of this literary genius. [115]

But it took Anderson time to appreciate Burrow. In
August of 1917 he wrote: "Burrow has been a sharp disappointment to me. Put to the test he proved to have no gift
of companionship. The man wanted to reform, to remake
me; his attitude was like Dell's [Floyd Dell]. Tell me why
men constantly get the impression that I am a thing to be
molded."[116] By the end of 1918, however, he had changed
his view:

> I should have liked to see you in order to tell you
> how much of what you told me that summer up at
> the lake I have found to be true and how much you
> helped me by giving my mind new slants. The
> difficulty with me is that I cannot learn things by
> being taught but have to get them in my own way
> out of life. [117]

The next month he wrote that the "quarrel" they had
had did not go very deep and that he expected Burrow knew
it. [118]

At about the same time Burrow was writing him in unconscious refutation of the "reformist" allegation.   He told him he was much more interested in his understanding of life than of his changing it. [119]

Feeling Burrow's friendship and sympathy, Anderson confided his difficulties that fall:

> For weeks and months at a time now I find that the reserve of energy I have always had is gone. The long hours of work in an office every day begin to take the strength I need for my writing.
>
> As you no doubt know, there is no money to be got in writing the sort of books I write.   A copy of such a book is read by ten people to every one who purchases it.   The result is that the author gets little.
>
> In facing what I face now--that is to say, the possibility that I will have to give up the flight--my mind gropes about trying to see some way out. Surely I am willing to live in the very simplest way to accomplish what I want, but I do need some assured income every year.   I have three children who have to be supported.   In all I need from twenty-five hundred to three thousand a year to live. [120]

Two years later Anderson had developed the following evaluation of his reaction to Burrow:

> I have for so long a time been thinking of you as a successful man and that has made it difficult for me to approach you.   I am afraid too often I have been in my thought of you a little sarcastic.   My difficulty lay in the fact that I continually thought of you as one who thought they had found truth. What I thought to be your truth I could not accept for myself and perhaps I was angry at the thought you could accept it.   I have thought of the science to which you have given so much of your life as one that would very well do wonders in making life and its difficulties more understandable but that one person could in any way cure the evils in life for another seemed to me impossible.

> Perhaps I in some way wanted you to be an artist
> and to have an artist's point of view.   What twisted
> notion I had I can't get clear for myself.
>
> At any rate I know now...that all the thoughts I
> had of you these last few years have been unfair
> and untrue.   What a struggle must have been going
> on within you.   Will you forgive my stuffy think-
> ing[?][121]

Burrow, who was interested enough in literature to
have written plays, maintained his interest in Anderson and
his works for the rest of his life.   He wrote once that he
thought Anderson's work expressed what he had been trying
to do in his studies and practice.[122]   He was also to inform
Anderson that the mood of his work was more important and
attractive to him than the stories themselves.[123]   Finally,
in speaking of his own writings, mainly socio-psychoanalytic
theory, Burrow set forth ideas which show how close, at
base, his own motivations were to those of Anderson:

> You see, I did not personally write this thing.   It
> was, as it were, dictated to me, and I was in spite
> of myself forced to set it down.   I can't tell you
> how I stood out against it, just bitterly defiant.   It
> was life pushing itself through and my part was a
> sort of forced submission to it.   What is written
> here will be clear, I think, to the artist and that
> other form of response to the life-urge in man
> that is the farthest extreme of the artist's ex-
> pression--namely the artist who is unexpressed.   I
> mean the neurotic.[124]

Notes

1.   Memoirs, p. 381.

2.   Letter to Roger and Ruth Sergel, ca. May 11, 1931.

3.   Letter to Marietta D. Finley, Jan. 12, 1917.

4.   One of Anderson's cousins recalled a visit to Little
Point Sable of Irwin Anderson, who was notable for the
fanciful tales he told the children.   One of the adults
present at the time, according to the cousin, observed
that the old man was a "liar."

5.   Interview with Mrs. Cornelia Lane Anderson, Oct. 10, 1946.

6.   Ibid.

7.   Letter from Cornelia Lane Anderson, Oct. 18, 1962. In another note in this letter, Mrs. Anderson said, "I note you use the term cabin which is much more suitable than my word house."

8.   Oct. 1946 interview.

9.   Letter to Jay L. Bradley, Oct. 2, 1925 (JR).

10.   Oct. 1946 interview. A Christmas visitor had been Michael Carmichael Carr of the Dell circle in Chicago. Phillips, p. 29.

11.   Letter of Oct. 18, 1962.

12.   See Hansen, p. 122; Schevill, p. 79; Howe, p. 54-5.

13.   Howe, p. 54.

14.   Harry Hansen, Midwest Portraits, New York, Harcourt, Brace, 1923, p. 122.

15.   Letter of Oct. 18, 1962.

16.   Letter to William L. Phillips, April 26, 1949.

17.   Oct. 1946 interview.

18.   Letter to Waldo Frank, March 1917. The suggestion that Sherwood lived separately from his family is resisted by the statement of John S. Anderson, a son, that Sherwood had a "writing shack"; interview of April 6, 1962.

19.   Note intended to be her final, considered judgment with letter of Oct. 16, 1946.

20.   Ben Hecht, Marjorie Currie, Alexander Kowan, Michael Carr, Fannie Butcher, Margaret Anderson, Edna Kenton. The name "Marjorie Currie" is found in numerous citations spelled two different ways. The present writer has used one or the other solely according to source. See Appendix N. Dell was Miss Currie's husband.

21.   Cornelia Anderson Interview, Oct. 10, 1946.

22.   Ibid.

23.   Letter from Alma Schlif, financial secretary, Michigan City Public Schools, Oct. 29, 1962.

24.   Statements relevant to this divorce are based on documents reproduced and forwarded by the Clerk of the Circuit Court, Berrien County, Frank X. Duerr, Nov. 9, 1962.

25.   Letter to Waldo Frank, March 1917.

26.   Note with letter of Oct. 16, 1946.

27.   Mary Chryst Anderson, who married Robert L. Anderson; letter of Oct. 2, 1963.

28.   Letter from Cornelia to Sherwood, Feb. 21, 1929. It should be noted that letters from Cornelia to Sherwood would have been saved only through his interest.

29.   Letter from Sherwood to Mary Emmett, Nov. 3, 1938.

30.   Letter from Cornelia to Sherwood, May 9, 1923.

31.   Letter from Sherwood to Cornelia, April 25, 1926.

32.   Letter from Cornelia to Sherwood, Sept. 12, 1926.

33.   Letter from Cornelia to Sherwood, July 29, 1926.

34.   Letter from Mildred A. Smith, Michigan City, Ind., Oct. 26, 1962.

35.   Letter from Sherwood to Ferdinand Schevill, Jan. 16, 1929.

36.   Letter to M. D. Finley, Oct. 25, 1916.

37.   Letter to Bernardine Szold Fritz, undated, probably 1922.

38.   Letter to Charles Bockler, 1938?

39.   Letter to M. D. Finley, March 9, 1929.

40.   Letter to M. D. Finley, Nov. 1919.

41.   Letter to Karl, ca. 1927.

42.   Letter to M. D. Finley, Jan. 19, 1917.

43.   Letter to Carrow DeVries, Nov. 28, 1937.

44.   Letter to Mrs. L. L. Copenhaver, winter, 1935.

45.   Cornelia Anderson interview, Oct. 10, 1946.

46.   Letter of Nov. 25, 1962.

47.   Letter of Oct. 24, 1962.

48.   Letter from Mrs. Jean Allen, May 16, 1962.

49.   George Daugherty in an undated letter.

50.   Letter from Louis Sudler, May 14, 1962.

51.   Letter of May 31, 1962.

52.   Letter from Mrs. Jean Hart, April 6, 1962.

53.   Letter from Mrs. John Franklin Daniel, May 28,
1962.

54.   Interview with Dr. Alice Greenacre, spring, 1962.

55.   Bernardine Szold Fritz. These letters are in the
archives of the Library of the University of Chicago, and
quotations here are by permission of the Library.

56.   Letter from Tennessee to Bernardine, 1926?

57.   Tennessee to Bernardine, Sept. 4, 1926.

58.   Tennessee to Bernardine, Oct. 25, 1925.

59.   Tennessee to Bernardine, March 11, 1927.

60.   Tennessee to Bernardine, Aug. 30, 1925?

61.   "Until ten years ago, however, she had never modeled
so much as a mud pie, she declared once. And she also

said she never took an art lesson. " Obituary clipping from unidentified newspaper, probably <u>Chicago Tribune</u>, Dec. 27, 1930.

62.   Tennessee to Bernardine, 1926?

63.   New York, B. W. Huebsch, 1921.

64.   Tennessee to Bernardine, June 16, 1928.

65.   Tennessee to Bernardine, Sept. 11, 1928.

66.   The ms. may be examined in the Anderson Collection of the Newberry Library.   Also in the collection is a note, written in late 1929, by Tennessee to Sherwood, telling him a publisher has asked her if she will write her autobiography; she wants to know if he will mind being included.

67.   Letter from J. Richard Emens, attorney, Jackson, Mich. , Jan. 24, 1963.

68.   Letter from Dale Kramer, June 29, 1963.

69.   Letter of March, 1921.

70.   Letter to Waldo Frank, before May 21, 1918.

71.   Letter to M. D. Finley, Jan. 12, 1917.

72.   Letter to M. D. Finley, Jan. 26, 1917.

73.   Letter to Frank after Nov. 18, 1917.

74.   Letter to Frank, late Dec. 1917.

75.   Letter to Ferdinand Schevill, after July 13, 1930.

76.   <u>Across Spoon River</u>, New York, Farrar and Rinehart, 1936, p. 295-315 (Chap. XIV).

77.   William L. Phillips, May 25, 1949.

78.   Dec. 27, 1948.

79.   <u>Chateaugay Record and Franklin County Democrat</u>, Friday, Aug. 4, 1916.

80.   Record of Marriages, Chateaugay, New York, p. 35, No. 174.

81.   Mrs. Georgia Lane, Cornelia's step-mother.

82.   Interview with Miss Sue de Lorenzi and Phillips, May 17, 1949, in Phillips' unpublished dissertation.

83.   Mrs. John Franklin Daniel, letter of May 23, 1962.

84.   Letter to Lucile and Jerry Blum, Sept. 20, 1920.

85.   Letter to Waldo Frank, Nov. 18, 1921.

86.   Letter to Van Wyck Brooks, May 15, 1920 (JR).

87.   Letter to Jerry Blum, Nov. 12, 1920.

88.   Letter from Louis Sudler, May 14, 1962.

89.   Before I Forget, New York, Literary Guild of America, 1937, p. 344.

90.   Letter to Waldo Frank, ca. March 11, 1918.

91.   Schevill, p. 88.

92.   Anonymous, "The Literary Spotlight, VII: Sherwood Anderson," Bookman, April, 1922, 55:161.

93.   Letter to M. D. Finley, Jan. 26, 1917.

94.   Letter to Waldo Frank, ca. March 1920.

95.   Letter to Ferdinand Schevill, Dec. 16? 1923 (JR).

96.   In Anderson Collection of The Newberry Library.

97.   Letter to John Anderson, 1932.

98.   Letter to Burton Emmett, Nov. 10, 1930.

99.   Letter to Stark Young, ca. 1930.

100. "Dedication of the Memoirs," The Sherwood Anderson Reader, p. 688.

101.   Letter from Tennessee to Bernardine, 1926?   See
        note 55.

102.   Interview with Mrs. Marjorie Young Reilly, Aug. 21,
        1963.

103.   Interview with Miss Sue de Lorenzi, April 5, 1962.

104.   Letter to Waldo Frank, May 23, 1917.

105.   Letter to Frank, July 1917.

106.   Letters to M. D. Finley, Jan. 19, and June 1917.

107.   Letter to Frank, Aug. 27, 1917 (JR).

108.   Letter, June 1917.

109.   Letter to M. D. Finley, June 1917.

110.   A Search for Man's Sanity, New York, Oxford Univ.
        Press, 1958, p. 558-9.

111.   Miss de Lorenzi.

112.   Burrow, op. cit., p. 561.

113.   A Search for Man's Sanity, p. 39.

114.   A Search for Man's Sanity, p. 442.

115.   Ibid. p. 560 and 559.

116.   Letter to Waldo Frank, Aug. 27, 1917 (JR).

117.   Letter to Burrow, Dec. 31, 1918 (JR).

118.   Letter to Burrow, Jan. 1919.

119.   Letter from Burrow, Jan. 1919.

120.   Letter to Burrow, Sept. 15, 1919 (JR).

121.   Letter to Burrow, Sept. 11, 1921.

122.   Letter of April 11, 1933; A Search for Sanity, p. 269.

123.   Letter, July 20, 1937.

124.   A Search for Sanity, p. 58.

Mosaic XI

"That he shall know... "

I have been trying again to get back to entire absorbtion in some individual life, some little girl, or man, struggling along in life.... There are these crowds, masses of people. How can any one think of them in the mass. When you begin, with your eye to pick out individuals, wonder about them, it gets a little better.
to Roger Sergel, Nov. 2, 1938.

*   *   *

When I walk here in the country and see a man ploughing, say on a hillside field, I hunger to have the man know the beauty of the gesture, in himself and his horses, involved in the act of ploughing. I want him to know this in relation to earth, sky, trees, river, etc.
It may be that this is all we are after--that he shall know.
to John S. Anderson, July 1, 1935.

*   *   *

I wish I could say just what I want to say... something about a hope... that some day men may really begin to find each other again, this damn separateness through hate shown up for the nasty fake it is. Man's energy going into that.
to Roger Sergel, Dec. 14, 1938 (JR).

*   *   *

I am sure that all my writing has always been simply as an expression of my own feeling as an individual.
to Dwight Macdonald, June 14, 1939 (JR).

268

I want to be a wide-eyed boy, running about; a stern ready-
    handed man listening with quiet understanding at a
    street corner where two teamsters are quarreling con-
    cerning space for their wagons by a store door. A
    lover feeling with delight the blood that throbs in the
    finger-tips of the woman; a cold man full of hatred,
    sharpening a long knife for his enemy--a living thing
    in the world and a part of the world. I do not want to
    be a dead, dry thing, a writer mumbling over little
    words.

to M. D. Finley, Dec. 13, 1916.

*   *   *

I am pretty sure that writing may be a way of life in itself.
    It can be that because it continually forces us away
    from self toward others.   Let any man or woman look
    too much upon his own life and everything becomes a
    mess.   I think the whole glory of writing lies in the
    fact that it forces us out of ourselves and into the lives
    of others.   In the end the real writer becomes a lover.

to Carrow DeVries, Nov. 28, 1940.

*   *   *

The impulse that led me to write novels was the impulse for
    my own salvation.

from "Who's Who," Chicago Tribune,
May 31, 1919.

*   *   *

... having undertaken to write this story, that's what I'm up
    against, trying to do that.   I'm not claiming to be able
    to inform you or to do you any good.   I'm just trying
    to make you understand some things about me, as I
    would like to understand some things about you, or
    anyone, if I had the chance.

from "The Man Who Became a Woman,"
The Sherwood Anderson Reader, p. 144.

*   *   *

I thought that to understand men and women, get at the inner
    secret of them, was more important then to gloss over
    life.

to Mrs. L. L. Copenhaver, 1932.

Why should I care whether you, the young writer, have had
    your breakfast, whether or not you have money to pay
    your rent or buy a car? I care only that you may
    broaden my own vision, increase my own capacity to
    feel, add a little to my understanding of others.
                            to George Freitag, Aug. 27, 1938.

*   *   *   *   *

C. "Dear Brother"

> The development from the first two books [Windy
> McPherson's Son (1916) and Marching Men (1917)]
> to Winesburg was a natural flowering of the man. . . .
> Men like Burrow--all of us--merely "fortified,"
> as you may say: we did not inaugurate or even
> institute. . . or even lead.

This comment by Waldo Frank[1] comes from the person who
was foremost of all of Sherwood's friends in the period immediately preceding the appearance of Winesburg, Ohio. Having discussed Anderson's occupation and his marriages, we
may now turn to his associations with people generally, and
it seems valuable to consider what those relationships meant
to him.   It will be a process of experiencing the reverbera-
tions of the note struck by Frank.

Anderson's impulse to write grew out of his own
strenuous reactions to people and caused important modifica-
tions of his concerns with those in both close and distant
affiliation.   It was only natural that he would seek to know
other writers, and that he was both attracted and repelled
by them.   He tells Paul Rosenfeld: "Then you see I knew
no writers, no artists. . . .   When I began to know writers
and painters, I couldn't abide the way most of them talked."[2]
He wrote that he had expected, when he was not among artists, that they would be generous and understanding toward
other artists, that they would be less competitive than he
found them: "Life among us is so brief and so hurried that
to pause and snarl at each other is unspeakably dull."[3]

But he was able to write later:

> There were in New York and Chicago no end of
> people who were willing to talk to me, listen to

my talk, cry out for any good thing I did, condemn
with quick intelligence what I did that was cheap or
second-rate. Not one among them but had thought
further than myself, that could tell me a hundred
things I did not know. What a debt of gratitude I
owe to men like Paul Rosenfeld, Stark Young, Alfred Stieglitz, Waldo Frank and others, men who
have willingly taken long hours out of their busy
lives to walk and talk with me of my craft. [4]

Burton Rascoe saw another side to this coin, however:

Such was his profound belief in himself that this
belief precluded his active sympathy with the work
of any other writers, especially of any one working
in a different field from his own. Thus he may
profess in an amiable fashion that he likes the work
of Hecht, of Hergesheimer, of Waldo Frank, of
this one or that one he meets; but actually he not
only dislikes it and can't read it, but is very suspicious of it. He has hurt the feelings of many a
fellow writer by telling him, in effect, that in his
opinion the inquiring or hopeful writer wasn't honest
or sincere. A novelist should know better than to
ask another novelist what he thinks of his work:
in reply, if the questioned is truthful, he must
either admit that he considers the other fellow's
work bad or have doubts about the value of his
own work. And Sherwood has absolutely no doubts
whatever. [5]

Anderson, in his own mind, at least, seems to have
followed a wandering course in regard to such matters. In
early 1917 he could write:

My mind gropes and gropes here and I forget the
other groping minds. Then I meet people who are
thinking hard along some line allied to my own
thinking. I want to find out to what length these
men have gone, to feel my way a little along their
road. [6]

Later the same year he was to announce: "I have my own
understanding with the gods. With them I have agreed to
strip myself when the time comes; to throw off comrades,
lovers, happiness. I have driven a hard bargain. "[7]

Anderson was endlessly exploring the nature and meaning of people. Imagined people could interfere with the real ones:

> I am talking in riddles. It is because my mind is on the figure of a man walking on the streets of a town on a summer Sunday evening. I am about to write the story of what happened to the man.
>
> In passing I but wave a hand to you and the rest of the world. 8

And he could write, as he did to Frank, that he was full of the urge to write and that he thus had to stay away from people. 9

He finds, at another time, an "intense eagerness" to confront others; he finds confusion in "new people to love. "10 He can not understand a person's becoming an artist without a variety of experiences "in the thought of living life without ever once having a night of debauch. Great God, if I hold myself apart thus how am I ever to know a single man about me, how am I to love and understand?"11

He leaves record of the way in which particular people have fed his imagination. He says of one Alonzo Berners: "When I first became aware of the actuality of [him], I began to live in another, suffer in another, love another perhaps. "12 Or, in more detail:

> It was that way after my talk with the woman Friday and then Sunday I saw another woman at luncheon. She was in a group of people and I only talked to her casually. But I watched her intensely. I began to imagine and feel her reactions to life. At night my mind went on and I dreamed of her. A thousand little things I found out but I am tired. 13

The basic vitality and emotionality of his imaginative experience has been recorded in this way:

> There are certain days when one who is in the midst of the vigor of life feels himself capable of sustaining with a flourish any human experience. One walks along the street looking at people. He has a mad desire to take them all in his arms, to share with them the super-abundance of strength

he finds within himself.

> At such times one returns to a sort of savagery.
> The nuances of life seem trifling and not worth
> while.   He wants to move forward in a broad way
> like a river flowing to the sea.   He wants to lose
> himself in things primitive and real.   It is at such
> times that I realize that within me there is much
> of the primitive, the thing that could kill or save.
> The dreary time of asking questions passes and
> for a moment I stand forth, a naked man in a
> world clothed and choked by customs of habit and
> thought. 14

Relationships with others were tiring, enveloping, ex-
hilarating, confusing, saddening:

> I have been a little sad as is my mood nowadays
> when I walk through streets of houses where peo-
> ple live.   Perhaps I have thought too much about
> people and have wanted too much from them.

> One can't of course be impersonal in his attitude
> toward this pulsating, anxious thing in people that
> makes them pluck and cling like tight-fisted fright-
> ened children.   It is there and it has its basic
> truth too.   Perhaps I shall some day have the
> strength to come close and understand it.   I can't
> in any personal way now.

> Home I come confused.   A world of love has come
> in to strengthen me.   I cannot talk of it now.
> Everyone, everything the things people think and
> hope of me.   It is all beyond expression now.   It
> has made me love life intensely.

> Either I close the door altogether or else I open it
> wide, take the new person into my very inner con-
> sciousness.   I come out from such a talk feeling
> that I am tired, tired.   My mind has groped and
> delved into their inner thing.   I feel like one who
> has been running for a long time. 15

The intricacy and cost of relationships being thus quite

impressive to him, he was capable of this outburst:

> ... You want life cheap--at half price.
>
> This way ladies.   January sales of love and friend-
> ships and Truth.   To be sold quick to make way
> for the new spring assortment of goods--see other
> page for advertisement of the new love, the new
> friendships, the new truth.   Styles to fit the whims
> of all--Sold.
>
> Cheap.   Cheap.   Cheap. [16]

Stark Young described Anderson as a combination of
the "straightforward and contrived, of simple and disarming
sincerity and elaborate, canny pose."[17]   His flexible capacity
to adopt various roles was of great advantage in his passionately incisive researches into the nature of his fellow humans.
Rascoe thought Anderson preferred the company of "simple
and guileless" who would find him so seemingly interested
that they would yield up to him all their secrets, which gave
him material for his stories.   "People hurt by life, women
entangled with psychic conflicts, bruised, saddened and dis-
illusioned spirits find in him a consoler."   His intense interest in self-exploration has given him a "belief in the profound significance of all human life."[18]

Rascoe also found him "one of the most delightful of
entertainers," telling stories "curiously gay and comical,
not at all like the stories with somber overtones which he
writes," and highly enjoyable to those not "easily shocked or
embarrassed."

> His story of "Mama Geighen" is an epic now fa-
> mous in all the circles in which Anderson has
> moved.   It is a story about a huge, muscular
> Chaucerian woman who ran a countryside saloon in
> Wisconsin before prohibition and about how Anderson
> and a newspaperman who went with him on a fishing
> trip spent a Rabelaisian evening with the farmhands
> at Mame Geighen's place.   He has numerous such
> stories.... [19]

Howe suggests that Anderson carried on his friendships rather selectively, presented a different and appropriate
personality to each group he was in: "To the 57th Street
group he seemed the middle-class American who had lifted

himself out of a poisonous environment; to the Little Review
circle, a delightfully innocent primitive...to his advertising
friends, a man who would soon escape the drudgery of copy-
writing...."[20] Perhaps this kind of controlled efficiency
would account for another friend's summation: "Anderson
made friends easily but would often lose them as easily because of a certain abruptness in his relationships."[21] But
this could as well and probably better be accounted for by
relationships represented by the following account:

> In all the world there is nothing so sad as human
> relationships that have been ruined by a too quick
> and eager grasping at some immediate thing. To-
> day in the bright sunshine I have been walking about
> thinking of two old friendships, now quite ruined.
> My thoughts have been so sad that I have been al-
> most ill.
>
> The first of these was a woman from a country
> town. I won't go into detail as to how I met her
> but we became friends. She had a husband in her
> own place and they were engaged in business. She
> came her to buy goods but she was interested also
> in books. After her work was done she used to
> meet me and we spent hours together. The little
> details of her business interested me. I liked her
> homely absorption in details and her earnestness
> about things I did not think mattered. I talked to
> her of my own affairs, of my dreams and hopes.
> There was, I suppose, on her part, something
> clandestine about all this but it was delightful.
>
> Another woman I knew was English and very small
> and delicate. She was in a way the most intense
> person I have ever known. After seven years of
> not seeing her how sharply she still stands forth
> in my mind.
>
> And this woman also became my friend. She had
> a lover somewhere in England and often talked to
> me about him. We used to go away to the parks
> together in the evening. When it rained and was
> dark we ran along shouting and laughing. We
> wrestled and threw each other down on the wet
> grass.
>
> With both of these women I was finally swept into

> affairs more intimate.   In both cases that came
> about swiftly, quickly, without premeditation.
>
> And afterward, when we tried to resume the old
> life, to be quite simply and innocently friends we
> could not be.   I don't know why.   We were not
> really lovers.   We had betrayed each other.   For
> a while we tried to go on in a forced, self-con-
> scious way but it would not work.
>
> To-day I walked and thought of them.   One hates
> things that end so.   I was sad, half-sick with sad-
> ness. [22]

In considering Anderson's various friendships, the
number of even just the identifiable ones running perhaps
into the hundreds, there has been a temptation to catalog the
ones from this period in an appendix.   [Some sample lists
with the names of those who provided them: Stuart Chase:
Theron Cooper, Harriet Monroe, Mrs. Karsten of Hull House,
(letter of Nov. 25, 1962); Henry Blackman Sell: Carl Sandburg, Ben Hecht, Wallace Smith, J. P. McEvoy, Burton
Rascoe, J. V. A. Weaver, Edgar Lee Masters, Fanny Butcher, Wm. Marion Reedy, H. L. Mencken, Conrad Aiken,
(letter of Nov. 2, 1963); Marietta D. Finley: Marjorie Currie, Floyd Dell, John Emerson, Paul Rosenfeld, Van Wyck
Brooks, Waldo Frank, (letter of May 31, 1962); James Schevill: Ben Hecht, Michael Carr, Alexander Kaun, (Sherwood
Anderson, His Life and Works, p. 86.)]   The spirit and number of his personal observations of humanity would render
any very lengthy list, necessarily vastly incomplete, useless
or even misleading.   Instead, an attempt will be made to
present persons and groups about whom information has been
found and who seem to have been importantly involved with
him, and to discuss them in such a way as to have them
represent all his friends.   These friends created a large
part of the necessity of sacrificing his family life.   His people fed his writings, to which he was devoted as a means
toward compulsive self-examinations as well.   The restraints
and responsibilities would not allow the extemporaneous, ex-
hausting, unchartable self-indulgences which seem to have
become so necessary to him.

"My love for you is to me so fixed and sure a thing
that it delights me to toss it up in the air and catch it as a
boy would play with a ball. "[23]   This declaration by Anderson
was quite in keeping with the emotional tone of the friendship

between Anderson and Waldo Frank, who customarily used the
greeting, "Dear Brother," in their letters.   "Your brotherly
affection and understanding," Anderson was to write him, "is
the biggest thing I've struck since I became a writer."[24]
And Frank reported back his wife's having said that Sherwood
was the most helpful and understanding of his friends.[25]
Frank thought, in a letter in 1918, that what brought them
together was their "brotherhood, the fact that fundamentally
we see and take life the same way.   You know what I mean."
Each gave aid to the other in a lonely and difficult time.[26]
Frank: "I may have doubts about myself, but I have none
about Sherwood Anderson--and he thinks as I do: we are
both right, and it is true that there are few people in the
world who are as sane as we."[27]   Anderson, spring 1917:
"I am entirely uncommunicative but I keep thinking of you
and some other men in the world and am glad." As Frank
was to say, "We are the kindlers of fire in the dark night.
We are the seed of the spring in the cold winter."[28]   So
Anderson was to affirm, "I have been so influenced to good
by you.   I have never been influenced to anything second-
rate."[29]

But this friendship, strong and intimate as it was or
perhaps because of the passionate, egotistical natures of both
men, was to diminish.   Another friend has written, "Waldo
Frank he liked very much for a time."[30]   Even at its height,
Anderson would say, "He thinks of himself as one of America's big men and in that I suspect his vulgarity lies."[31]
And in a December, 1918, letter to Miss Finley he was capable of this candid appraisal:

> ...Waldo Frank's new novel...is ready to go to
> the publishers.   I wish I could make the man see
> how badly it is done but he is a good deal infatu-
> ated and my saying anything would do no good.
> The man has a genius for people and manages al-
> ways to get just the right people together.   Since I
> have come down here I have realized that this one
> man was responsible for the distinctive note of
> Seven Arts magazine.   As a writer he is impossi-
> ble.[32]

Frank's own epitaph was uttered later: "The friendship
faded a bit; it never died and it never turned into its opposite
or anything like that.   But it lost its enthusiastic overtures."[33]

When the friendship was at its height, after Anderson had become acquainted with Frank through the Seven Arts magazine, there was a certain camaraderie and humor in the relationship. Anderson wrote Frank that one of his letters to Anderson in care of John Emerson had only Emerson's name on it. Anderson reported this banter: "'It's mine,' I said [to Emerson]. 'He would never be calling you "beloved brother".' 'Well god damn it, it's addressed to me,' [Emerson] said handing it over."[34] At times Anderson was a little afraid of Frank's superior education, but then he boldly urged, "Let's shake off the culture of effete, offensive critics," he advised, "When you think of them be Rabelaisian. Fart at the moon." He was occasionally afraid his way of expressing himself was too crude for an Eastern esthete but when he reported he had two ulcerated teeth removed, he also commented: "Naturally my beauty is for the time ruined. However that may save some poor virgin from ruin."[35]

Fundamentally both Frank and Anderson were mystics, although perhaps they could not see it in themselves and each other. Frank thought creativity, including creative criticism, was emotional. He did not think himself uninterested. He warned Anderson against humbling himself too much, or failing to recognize his own intelligence and sensitivity.[36]

Anderson had a counterpart comment:

> I have on several occasions heard you curse your own education and I begin to understand why. I suppose for the most part, education consists in gathering confusing facts. Those facts divert and occupy the mind. The [sic] prevent a man's falling back on something buried deep within himself. . . .
>
> You see the real mind, the thing that is buried away in us must be a wonderful thing. I sometimes think that our minds really record every little thing we see and hear in life and that we only confuse and perplex ourselves by not trusting absolutely the knowledge that flows into us.[37]

The belief in a basically mystical approach to all the problems of life, particularly those related to art, was one of the strong bonds between them.

But undoubtedly the best thing about Frank was his

intense interest in and appreciation for Anderson's work. As
will be seen later, Frank, as editor of the Seven Arts, provided a prime outlet for Anderson's stories, in evaluating
which he said: "In the specific form of the short story he
seems to me, however, clearly the first among living writers."[38]   In his essay, "Emerging Greatness," in the November, 1916, Seven Arts, he gave great and favorable, but judicious, attention to Windy McPherson's Son.   "The significance
of Sherwood Anderson... is simply that he suggests at last a
presentation of life shot through with the searching color of
truth, which is a signal for a native culture." And Frank
grasped also the essential pattern of the fictional process as
Anderson knew it.

> ...he learned to venerate the truth that gushed like
> a hidden spring from his past life. He wrote more
> religiously. He went out into the world where he
> did penance for his bread with a new seeking con-
> sciousness. For he had learned that the world of
> his secret hours was after all the same as the one
> in which he worked. A world infinitely serious.
> He had found an escape, not from it, but from its
> superficial lies. Relief lay in the truth: in bring-
> ing it forth from life: in endowing it with form.
> A world he needed to create in order to feel
> clean. [39]

His very favorable attitude was otherwise expressed
in the figure of Anderson's books as a warming flame.   "It
helps prepare the muck heap for the great bonfire. Its value
lies in its inwardness, in its humble staging."[40] It was
very important to Anderson.   Frank assured him that what
seemed morbidity was actually the confusion of creative discovery in his work. [41]

As Anderson told his tales "with an odd double-look
in his eyes, as if one of them were wooing, the other sizing
up," to his appreciative listener, who was himself bursting
with reactions, projects, criticisms, it is no wonder these
two men visited each other in New York and Chicago and
spent precious time in the natural splendor of Lake Chateaugay.   All in all, this seems to have been the best-recorded
friendship of the period when Winesburg, Ohio was in the
making.

Frank confided to Anderson that, in the atmosphere of
"deadness and indifference" which seemed to be general in

the arts, he saw only two "artistic criticis, " Van Wyck
Brooks and Paul Rosenfeld.   For Brooks, as for Frank and
Paul Rosenfeld, Anderson embodied the fresh and promising
West for the Easterners who looked for a renaissance in
American letters.   When Anderson read Brooks' America's
Coming-of-Age (1915) in 1918 and, in the same year, his
Letters and Leadership (1918), consisting largely of the essays which had just appeared in Seven Arts, he was deeply
cheered and impressed, so much so that on September 14,
1918, he published in the Chicago Tribune (page 121) an article
entitled "Our Rebirth. "   In that article, he calls Brooks "a
man walking with a lengthy stride in the world of thought, "
one whose writings are concerned with "the giving of definite
voice to the hope of a distinctive American culture rising
out of the needs of Americans. "

Anderson relates in this article that he had felt there
was "something approaching a renascence going on in this
country" before the war broke out.   "The truth is that living
men with new faiths were growing up all over the country, "
he asserts and cites Lindsay and Sandburg as examples.
"The point, with the men I am writing about was that they
did not want to lose, in any sort of controversy, the sense
of the fact that corn grows in fields; that life is an intensely
interesting thing, and that they should be at the job of trying
to get the life directly about them expressed. "

Anderson further stated the movement has not been
killed by the war: "When the business overseas is polished
off it will be back on the job. "

> The point of real interest about Van Wyck Brooks
> is that he is a part of this movement.   He is the
> scholar with the fine spirit, who looks hopefully
> about him, refuses to be sentimentally optimistic
> about our failures, and prays for strength in us to
> carry on.

It was a pleasure to Anderson to look forward to seeing Brooks, whom he called "the most sustained and thoughtful mind concerned with criticism, "[42] when he went to New
York.   He was to write to Rosenfeld:

> And one of the most lovely things. . . is your recog-
> nition of my immense debt to the man Brooks.
> When you said that, my heart jumped with joy.   I
> have been so sore at him so often but deep down

in me I have always loved him so really. When I
began first to read him in Seven Arts his voice was
a great shout saying, "You are on the right road.
You may never get to the sacred city but your feet
are on the right road. "[43]

Even though Anderson could say, "In a way I respect
[Brooks' 'remarkable mind'] more than any other... in America. "[44] it is doubtless also true that "they were never close
friends. "[45] Anderson was delighted to lunch with Brooks and
report that "he never gave me a word of advice, "[46] but he
also had to speak of "what friendship you give, " even when
saying of it that "It is a thing that cuts across the darkness
and mist. "[47] He wrote to Frank on May 21, 1918, in uncomfortable terms of appreciation: "He will perhaps be more
fair than yourself in not having in him any warmth of affection for me. I do feel in him a solid and direct stab at
truth that I respect all the more because the things he says
bite so often and closely at me. " But as late as 1920 he
seemed to be searching in a puzzled, wistful way for a
missing reciprocity:

> I wonder if I make you feel what I'm talking about.
> In the first place, I wish you could know how much
> I have loved, do love, your mind. I've frankly
> banked on it more than the mind of any other
> American. Am I right in my secret belief that
> you, down at bottom, believe me, in my reaction
> to life--well, not nice? Can I--have I the privilege
> of cornering your mind so? [48]

But the man who had written Winesburg, Ohio could
always thrill to the recognition of a knowing and caring spirit
in the man who wrote:

> Life proceeds not by the burnishing up of existent
> ideals, but by the discovery of new and more vital
> ones, thanks to the imagination, which reaches out
> into an unknown whither the intelligence is able to
> follow by a long second. (Brooks, Letters and
> Leadership, p. 96.)

> For the creative impulses of man are always at
> war with their possessive impulses, and poetry,
> as we know, springs from brooding on just those
> aspects of experience that most retard the swift
> advance of the acquisitive mind. (Ibid. , p. 25.)

The great artist floats the visible world on the sea
of his imagination and measures it not according
to its own scale of values but according to the
values that he has himself derived from his descent
into the abysses of life.   (Ibid. , p. 40-41.)

But certainly no true social revolution will ever be
possible in America till a race of artists, profound
and sincere, have brought us face to face with our
own experience and set working in that experience
the leaven of the highest culture.   (Ibid. , p. 127.)

...to love life, to perceive the miraculous beauty
of life, and to seek for life, swiftly and effectively,
a setting worthy of its beauty--that is the acme of
civilization, to be attained, whether by the individual or by nations, only through a long and arduous
process.   (Ibid. , p. 117.)

Our life is like a badly motivated novel, full of
genius but written with an eye to quick returns; a
novel that possesses no leading theme, in which the
style alternates between journalese and purple
patches and every character goes its own ambitious
way, failing of its full effect. ("Young America, "
Seven Arts, Dec. 1916, p. 147.)

The third of three important friendships gained primarily through the association with the Seven Arts was that
with Paul Rosenfeld, who was not so close a friend so soon
but whose relationship was deeper for a longer time and
more devoted.   It was Rosenfeld who took Anderson to Europe as his guest in 1921, who wrote the major essay of the
Homage to Sherwood Anderson issue of Story the autumn after Anderson died, and who gave his name and a long critical
essay to The Sherwood Anderson Reader, published the year
after his own death in 1946.   After Anderson's death he was
the closest adviser to Anderson's widow, Eleanor Copenhaver
Anderson.

Something of the way Anderson differentiated these
three major friendships may be seen in this comment to
Rosenfeld written about 1921:

I emphasize this phase of myself to you Paul because you, Brooks, and Waldo were all brought up
in a different atmosphere.   I think your atmosphere

was as difficult as my own to penetrate, but it was
different. The New Englanders and the Jews have
always at least had the privilege of being serious.
You see I put Brooks among the New Englanders.
He may not have been born there but spiritually he
belongs there and has in his makeup the inner cold
fright of the New Englanders. That's what makes
it so difficult for me to feel warm and close to
him as I so often do to you and Waldo. . . .

Anderson was to write Rosenfeld that only in work and
in "the few people in whom I feel the power to love" could
he escape from fits of deep depression. "Among men I get
this from you and I do want you to know, Paul, that it en-
tails no demands. . . . I suppose I want you to love me
whether I deserve it or not. "[49] Rosenfeld, whose notable
career over three decades produced a considerable body of
well-regarded criticism on music, literature, and art, had
Anderson's respect as a judge of and connoisseur of the
creative arts: "I am so often humble before your sanity,
the clear beauty of the things you say and do. "[50]

The friendship was not particularly close till after the
Winesburg period, although in 1918, when Rosenfeld was suffering through an army stint, Anderson wrote to Frank about
a plan to visit him in camp. "He begged me to come and
offered to pay my RR fare. He can afford the expense of
course and he does need to be made to feel that we who are
not in will be carrying him along in our daily thoughts. "
The previous June he had commented that Rosenfeld should
not be allowed to think the army would kill him or drive him
insane. [51] On his part, Rosenfeld is reported to have had the
ability to draw out writers, artists, and musicians and to
help them to realize their highest potential. Anderson was
an exception to his usual pattern of fostering young artists
just beginning their careers, though he did need the help
Rosenfeld gave him.

Rosenfeld's account of a luncheon with Anderson at the
Yale Club in 1917, a few days after they met, contains essential elements of the relationship of the two men:

With an elbow on the cloth, one paw supporting his
head while the other occasionally and delicately
plucked at some grapes, my guest just regaled me
first with the tale of a female Falstaff up in Michigan [Mama Geighen], then with a strong recent

> impression of Randolph Bourne, "the only man
> whose political talk had ever interested him." I
> began telling him about another brilliant young fel-
> low, the pianist and composer Leo Ornstein: of his
> conception of universal sympathy as the possible
> goal of existence. "Still, how are you going to
> feel sympathy with policemen?" suddenly I asked,
> only half-jocose.... Hatred of those physical
> brethren, "New York's finest," was one of the ap-
> parently irreducible remnants of a childhood.
>
> Anderson leaned back, laughing, "Oh," he drawled,
> "I see them when they reach home at night. I see
> them taking off their boots. Their feet hurt
> them."[52]

The eastern intellectuals came into Anderson's life
through the Seven Arts, as has been indicated. He found his
way to that group through his friendship with a group of artists, to whom he was introduced by his brother, Karl, in
Chicago, some time in 1913 (accounts vary). The buildings
on the edge of Jackson Park, left over from the World's Fair
of 1893, were used as artist's studios by what became known
as the Fifty-Seventh Street Colony. When Anderson went back
to Chicago in February, 1913, he found himself a room near
this colony.[53]

The adjoining apartments of Floyd Dell and his wife,
Marjorie Currie, and probably others were the scene of many
gatherings of the rising generation of artists and critics.[54]
Dell was the literary editor of the Chicago Evening Post, his
wife a journalist. They often held Sunday evening parties at
which various writers read their latest work, something Anderson had been doing in Elyria. Anderson wrote very feel-
ingly of his gaining acquaintance with Marjorie Currie and
the way it seemed to open up the opportunity for him to find
comrades in the world of the arts.[55] That, he was to inform Roger Sergel, was the first place he had ever met
writers or artists.[56]

There was an atmosphere of ferment in these gatherings. One person referred to the "joy of intermingling pure
reason, anarchy and damfoolishness" that made the parties so
attractive.[57] Among other people who attended these parties
were both Cornelia Anderson and the then Tennessee Mitchell. The leadership of the Little Review came from this
group, and Anderson became known to the Seven Arts

through it.

A life-long friend, the University of Chicago professor, Robert Morss Lovett, has written three separate accounts of how he encountered Anderson at such a party in
1913 and heard him read. [58]   He recalls seeing him at Ernestine Evans' studio.   Anderson, he still thought in 1941,
was a house painter who came dressed in "house painter's
clothes" and "seemed the proletarian writer for whom we
were on the lookout. "   He seemed "grim and repressed" to
Lovett.

> He brought a manuscript that evening and read it
> to half-a-dozen hearers.   It was, as I remember,
> a very conscientious and detailed piece of narra-
> tive, reminiscent, I thought, of Theodore Dreiser
> and with something of Dreiser's power of sheer
> reality.   One of the listeners was Mr. Floyd Dell,
> who was so much impressed by its promise that he
> urged Anderson to go ahead.... [59]

Just how Dell came to know about Anderson as a writer is subject to differing accounts.   Dell thought his wife
showed him the manuscript of Windy McPherson's Son.   Frank
thought that Anderson "let slip his secret" in a conversation.
In any case, according to Karl Anderson, it was through
Dell that Anderson became a member of the Chicago group.
Suffice it to say that Dell was enough involved in the publication of Windy McPherson's Son for Anderson to call him
his literary father, to which Dell has reacted wryly, as will
be seen.

As Dell recalls being given the manuscript, he "then
and there" finished reading the book, and, curiously shaken,
"went out to look for its author. "   He found him a "tall,
keen, robust, laughing man, black-haired and blazing-black-
eyed, " a handsome fellow. [60]   Later he was to realize that,
although he had seemed healthy and happy, he was actually
in torment. [61]   Only recently he has written, in his disenchanted way, "I have always thought of Sherwood with affection.   In the old days I was shocked and disconcerted by his
childishly neurotic behavior.   I did not, as yet, know how
widespread childish neuroticism was among writers--but perhaps I should say, among members of the human race.   My
sympathies were with Cornelia. "[62]

Perhaps the reasons the Dell friendship did not survive

the Winesburg period are indicated in this statement by Anderson:

> There was a time when Mr. Dell was, in a way,
> my literary father.   He and Waldo Frank had been
> the first critics to praise some of my earlier work.
> He was generous and warm.   He, with Mr. Theo-
> dore Dreiser, was instrumental in getting my first
> book published.   When he saw the Winesburg stor-
> ies he, however, condemned them heartily.   He
> was at that time, I believe, deeply under the in-
> fluence of Maupassant.   He advised me to throw
> the Winesburg stories away.   They had no form.
> They were not stories.   A story, he said, must be
> sharply definite.   There must be sharply a begin-
> ning and an end.   I remember clearly our conver-
> sation.   "If you plan to go somewhere on a train
> and start for the station but loiter along the way,
> so that the train comes into the station, stops to
> discharge and then take on passengers and then
> goes on its way and you miss it, don't blame the
> locomotive engineer," I said.   I daresay it was an
> arrogant saying but arrogance was needed. 63

On the other hand, Dell included in Homecoming an episode which indicates that Anderson was willing to carica-ture him as a show-off.   He told Anderson not to dedicate his stories to him, as he had indicated he would, and con-sidered the friendship at an end. 64

Just what this problem relating to Dell reveals about Anderson may be viewed variously.   Certainly the reaction was defensive and rejecting.   As early as April, 1917, And-erson was writing to Frank, noting that "some one" on the Masses had "called down" Dell for his "trite and off-hand treatment" of "your book."   And he says of himself that he has been "getting sour and sour [sic] at the Dell kind of treatment of it."   In a letter of the preceding December 14th [JR], in referring to the story "Loneliness," which is included in Winesburg, Ohio, he told Frank: "There is a story every critic is bound to dislike.   I can remember reading it to Floyd Dell, and it made him hopping mad." 'It's damn rot,' says Floyd.   'It doesn't get anywhere'." Perhaps Anderson was the one who was "hopping mad." Dell has recorded that he was glad to see Anderson's work in Seven Arts, which he thought was better for him than The Masses. 65   Perhaps Dell was too frank or perhaps he did

not know how insecure Anderson felt and how bitterly dependent he was on the good will and help of others.   He found
that Anderson could not believe the favorable comment of his
friends. 66, 67

Dell seems to have been thicker-skinned than Anderson
and his comments seem to indicate that he expects people to
be able to stand unvarnished response; that he would be surprised to find Anderson, who is generally agreed to have
worn constantly a mask of confidence and bravado, negative
toward him is supported by a note, perhaps of 1920 or 1921,
in which he records the fact that Moon Calf had been influenced by strenuous criticism Anderson had given another
manuscript.   He also mentions specific points in connection
with another book. 68

> I have just been to lunch with Ben Hecht--the lad
> you abused so furiously.   You are quite right about
> him.   He is what you were five years ago only
> that you never did let yourself become so vulgar-
> ized.
>
> However Ben sees--every now and then--a thin
> streak of light.   He may not have the strength to
> follow it but anyway he sees it.   That's something.
> I go about every day with men who walk in abso-
> lute blindness. 69

The moderate esteem in which Anderson held Hecht was reciprocated.   Their associations began, evidently, soon after
Anderson returned to Chicago and joined the Little Review
group, and lasted till Anderson's death.   In his autobiography, A Child of the Century (1954), and as late as 1963,
Hecht wrote about Anderson in a tone of which the following
is representative:

> He was in his 30's, black-eyed, heavy featured,
> with a wiglike clump of black hair: not fat but
> soft-bodied.   He looked like an Italian barber but
> he exuded ego like a royalist.   It was no barber
> who spoke but a moony sort of Socrates.   His voice
> was full of caress and the smack of infinite super-
> iority.   To what?   To everyone who wasn't Sher-
> wood Anderson.   He held out a hand as he talked
> and fluttered it as if he were patting an infant on
> the head, the infant being his listener or, possibly,

the world. [70]

In spite of the fact that Hecht has taken delight in
telling outrageous and somewhat degrading stories about Anderson, presumably caused by a reaction to Anderson's patronizing manner, they were companions and friends in Chicago.   Vincent Starrett recalled meeting Anderson in a newspaper office when he was arranging for Hecht to review a
forthcoming book in the Chicago Evening Post. [71]   As will be
seen later, both Dell and Hecht wrote very encouraging, but
frank, reviews of his early Chicago novels.   In his book, A
Child Of The Century, [72] Hecht recalls his relationship with
Anderson.   Hecht says that in one period he and Anderson
tried collaborating on plays they attempted to write. [72]   He
invests Anderson with an almost hypnotic quality, which he
suggests led him to involvement against his better judgment.
"Of these and a hundred other tales Sherwood told about himself, I believed almost nothing.   But whether they were lies
or truths made no difference.   The man who told them was
full of a compelling salesmanship.   I sat always fascinated."
Perhaps quite annoyingly, Anderson would respond to Hecht's
adventures as a reporter "with a patronizing chuckle: Life
is more important than that.   And he would go off into a
dither of owlish words: 'Life is something precious.   You've
got to hold it that way.'"   Hecht almost grudgingly concedes:

> When he talked his features seemed to tremble
> with some inner delicacy of mood.   His writing
> contained a similar tremble.   Listener and reader
> both went from his presence with the sense that
> something superior and profound had been offered
> them--and not quite understood by their lesser
> spirits.   The effect on girls of those half-woozy
> and purring hints of hidden sublimities was ever
> greater than Sasha's Russian revolutionary songs. [73]

And then Hecht goes on to relate episodes intended to reflect
that idea that Anderson was, after all, only a human and not
a particularly pleasant or thoughtful one at that.

Anderson maintained tempered affectionate thoughts of
Hecht, "At that time in Chicago I knew a young Jew named
Ben Hecht, not yet a well-known writer, and sometimes he
and I went forth to do our cursing together."[74]   And, perhaps a little before the time of that writing: "The rest of
them in Chicago, except for Ben Hecht, now and then when
he isn't being a smarty are just talking.   The smartiness

will perhaps defeat Ben.   It may have already. "[75] Somewhat
later he could recall, "You know we were great friends in
Chicago, " adding that Hecht's mother thought "he should have
stuck to me and gone with me on my road. "[76]

The thought of Hecht, who had written him in 1938
that he certainly "would be glad to hear from you   at
any time, "[77] reminded Anderson, in writing his Memoirs,
that Ben had told him his "colossal egotism" would protect
him from the rigors of doubt, which Anderson evidently kept
hidden from him as well as he had from Dell: "You will
sail blithely through life, often doing terrible things to others
without at all knowing what you are doing. ...   When you are
pressed someone will always come to your rescue.   You will
always be going about wearing an air of modesty and even of
humility" (page 4).   Having tested himself with this remembered attitude, Anderson continues on the same page with
this rebuttal:

> Yet--what's wrong with this egotism?   If a man
> doesn't delight in himself and the force in him and
> feel that he and it are wonders, how is all life to
> become important to him?   The interest in the
> lives of others, the high evaluation of these lives,
> what are they but the overflow of the interest he
> finds in himself, the value he attributes to his own
> being?

Perhaps, though, it was just Ben Hecht's way.   In
his essay included in the "Homage to Sherwood Anderson"
issue of Story, [78] Hecht refers to Anderson as "This wattled
old Telemachus of letters" and "our Dostoevski of the corn
belts, " says he is dressed in something more like a gunny
sack than a suit, recalls his "boring the pants off" the listeners to his manuscripts in Chicago, but he also says that
Anderson "re-invented the American soul, " no one in his
time having written "as tenderly and deeply of small towns
and small people. "   Anderson is his old friend ("I can't take
these departures as lightly as I would wish") who was a sort
of "cross between a Yogi and a Lothario, " too shrewd to
"found a religion or wind up in jail for seduction. "

If Hecht had his misgivings about Anderson, so had
Anderson about Sandburg.   Several statements from 1917 record the character of restricted response:

> I have an undying faith in the long lovely sunset out

on the prairies and the wind whistling in the dry
corn at night. It puts something into a man. He
is sweetened by it. You know what I mean--the
thing you felt in Carl that night he stuck his head
in the room where Hecht and Rascoe were fighting
like alley cats. It's the thing Carl will lose if he
ever listens to too much talk which God be pleased
he won't. [79]

Two glimpses, written during the following April, are
additionally revealing:

I saw Sandburg the other night, and we had a long
evening together. He liked my songs very much,
and I liked him. There is something Scandinavian
about him, a suggestion of closed-in icy places.
Most of his verses do not sing, but he does. Ben
Hecht called him the poet who would not write poetry. [80]

Hecht also wrote:

In Sandburg's voice lived all his poetry. It was a
voice of pauses and undercurrents, with a hint of
anger always in it, and a lift of defiance in its
quiet tones. It was a voice that made words sound
fresh, and clothed the simplest of sentences in
mysteries. I had heard a cousin of that voice
speak out of Sherwood Anderson, but Sherwood was
garrulous and many-mooded. There was never
garrulity in Sandburg and there was only one mood
in him--a measured passion.... He spoke always
like a man slowly revealing something....

Sandburg's poetry always vibrated my heart. [Quoted
in A Child of the Century, p. 232 and 233.]

Thus something in Anderson kept him from catching all that
was there for others:

Carl Sandburg came to see me and read my songs.
He was lavish in his praise. The man is somewhat heavy, a cumbersome fellow with a good deal
of working-class prejudice and a gloomy Danish nature but very fine and sincere in his slow heavy way. [81]

Four years later he wrote Rosenfeld, ''I spent a day with Sandburg. He is really a beautiful thing--but there are limitations, sharp, terrible, unsurmountable.''[82]

Later he seemed to think Sandburg had gone commercial.   When he was in Reno, he told of going to the university and finding that "all the men who have made our life are
unknown to them.   They had heard faintly of Sandburg--be-
cause he gives his Shows.... "[83]   Christopher Sergel recalled
an episode in his home when he read a "character sketch"
Anderson had written in reaction to Sandburg, starting with
a line: "Carl Sandburg has become a professional peasant. "[84]
Also, he wrote to his teacher-friend, Trillena White:

> I am afraid you are entirely mistaken about Carl
> Sandburg.   He is really very shrewd and is very
> well-fixed.   It is true that for years poor old Carl
> had to go around the country putting on his show
> to make a living, but I am told the Woman's Home
> Companion paid him $30,000 for the portion of the
> Lincoln they published a few years ago.   The other
> day I had lunch with one of his publishers, who
> told me they had already sold forty thousand of the
> complete Lincolns at $20 each.   At 15 per cent
> you can figure that out yourself. [85]

And yet we are told that there was love between these
two.   Burton Rascoe told of Sandburg's habit of drawing an-
alogies that were inaccurate and unflattering.   He might,
compare a William S. Hart movie to Winesburg, Ohio, "whereupon Anderson's lips would quiver.   He would say nothing
for he loves 'Old Carl' with a profound affection"[86]   Only
two pieces of evidence of Sandburg's attitude have been found.
One is the poem, "Portrait (For S. A.),'" written, according
to a manuscript copy in the Anderson Collection, in 1918. [87]
In addition to paying Anderson the compliment of devoting a
poem to him or, as the title says, for him, these lines show
that Sandburg has noted him well.   They reflect the fact that
Anderson was deeply interested in capturing what he called
those of the outer fringe: the lonely, crazy man, the boot-
legger, Windy McPherson, the lonely woman.   Sandburg sees
him as the flamboyantly-dressed bohemian with the imposing
hair-do, the tweeds, the orange scarf.   The last stanza of
the poem deals with Anderson's struggle to be the sensitive
artist while sitting at a desk in a skyscraper in Chicago.

It has not been possible over the years to get any
comment on Anderson from Sandburg, but Miss Margaret
Sandburg, one of the poet's daughters, supplied the following very illuminating statement:

... The relationship between the two has always been described by my father as "good comradeship." He always adds to this, "but I was never as close to him as I was to Ben Hecht, and I was closer to Lloyd Lewis than to either of them, because of Lincoln." And this is easy to understand. But Anderson's contradictions are rather puzzling to me. His letters as edited by Howard Mumford Jones sound as though he did not appreciate my father's poetry or the Lincoln, yet his Memoirs call Chicago Poems "magical"....

My father, by the way, thoroughly enjoyed Anderson's story, The Egg. I have heard him say, many times, "An egg is a mysterious thing, an ancient thing. And there have been writers down through the ages, but only one man wrote a story about it--Sherwood Anderson." Then he would add with a reminiscent smile that took in the whole story, "And it's one of the best short stories in the English language." He liked the other works also, but about this one he was particularly enthusiastic. But though Anderson held his admiration as a novelist and a short story writer, as a weaver of words, and though he enjoyed his company and his wit and humor, he did not think much of his memory. In our copy of Anderson's Memoirs, on page 302, besides the chapter about Sandburg singing for Copeau, he has pencilled the words, "I don't remember this." If it had occurred, my father would not have written this, for he had a fantastic memory, though it is not what it used to be since a couple of years ago when he caught some kind of a virus in New York. [88]

With her comment, Miss Sandburg has kindly made available a transcript of a note, which she thinks was written "probably in 1917," referring to a poem, the full title of which is "The Four Brothers: Notes for War Songs (November, 1917)." It seems to erase any doubt that there was friendship and appreciation between the two artists:

The Four Brothers
  A magnificent thing Carl. It sings and it has sweep and bigness. Makes my heart jump to know we have a man like you in our old town.

> Would like to see you.   Can you have lunch with
> me tomorrow Wednesday.   Call me in the morning.
>   Wabash 3146
>   Sherwood Anderson. [89]

Both Ben Hecht[90] and one of Anderson's biographers[91]
indicate that Anderson met Theodore Dreiser in Chicago, but
the evidence indicates to the contrary.   Anderson says in his
Memoirs that it was years after 1916 (he published an appreciation of Dreiser in the April 1916 Little Review, 3:5) that
he met him and found out that "it was his word, given to the
publisher John Lane, that had got my first two books published" (page 334).   The following letters seem to clarify
both the meeting and publishing factors:

> Dear Mr. Dreiser:
>
>   I thank you a lot for your letter of today.   The
> book is in the hands of Mr. Mencken and as soon
> as he has looked at it I will ask him to turn it
> over to you.   I want it to go to the John Lane
> Company, so I can discuss it with them when I
> come to New York in February.
>
>   I hope I shall have the privilege of seeing you
> and becoming better acquainted at that time.
>
>   Yours very truly,

That letter, dated January 14, 1916, was followed
eleven days later by another, also addressed quite formally:

>   I am sending a copy of [a] letter received from
> John Lane Co. and a copy of my letter to Mr.
> Mencken.   What I said to Mr. Mencken in this let-
> ter would apply to you also, that is to say, that it
> looks as though I would not have to ask the favor
> I did ask of a busy man.   I count very much on
> seeing you and making your personal acquaintance
> in New York some time next month.

Subsequent evidence will show that Anderson evidently
did not make the "personal acquaintance" of Dreiser in New
York in February, 1917, nor until some time later.   That
he was deeply interested in Dreiser's work is made clear in
the one-page appreciation of Dreiser in the Little Review.
This statement, later used in conjunction with the dedication

of Horses and Men (1923) to Dreiser, refers to its subject in
frank but admiring terms.   Indicating that those who will follow the path his "heavy brutal feet" have broken will have virtues (as a sense of humor) which he does not have, it pays
homage to the "wonder and beauty of Theodore Dreiser."
It notes, as Anderson was characteristically to do, "his
heavy prose." It points out that those who come after him
"will never have to face the road through the wilderness of
Puritan denial, the road that Dreiser faced alone."

Too, Anderson rose to Dreiser's defense when The
Genius (1916) was attacked in Cincinnati as "lewd and profane." He wrote a letter to the Friday Literary Review of
the Chicago Evening Post:

> Until these people tackled Dreiser I, like most peo-
> ple, did not take them seriously. I don't know
> when I got the notion, but for years I supposed the
> Comstock type of man to be at least disinterested
> modern Don Quixotes intent on preventing virgin
> men and women stumbling into the facts of life.
> They are nothing of the sort.   Instead they are
> paid busy-bodies, fellows who must do things like
> this to justify their employment by whatever per-
> verse organization they work for....
>
> People do not have to read Dreiser's books.   The
> libraries, I presume, hide them away and only give
> them out to those holding certificates of soundness
> as to wind and limb.   There isn't, you see, a way
> by which one of this man's books can be any possi-
> bility get into the hands of the innocents this man
> Sumner is presumed to protect.   And if it did, they
> wouldn't be interested.
>
> The difficulty isn't there.   The crime lies deeper
> --it lies in administering this blow to the stoutest
> soul among us.
>
> Many of us here in America want Dreiser's books.
> We want him to go on writing.   We want to see his
> books on sale in the book stores.   If his outlook
> on life is grey we want that grey outlook. [92]

Early the next year he was again writing to Dreiser
to thank him for an invitation to visit, assuring him "you
may depend upon my doing so the first time I am in New

York, as I have long wanted to know you personally. "93   A
letter of the next month speaks adequately for itself:

> I must personally thank you for your illuminating
> article in Seven Arts magazine ["Life, Art and
> America," I:363-389 (Feb. 1917)]. It sets forth as
> nothing else I have ever read has set forth the
> complete and terrible fact of the wall in the shadow
> of which American artists must work.
>
> To many of us here in America the one really hope-
> ful note in our times is your own stout figure
> pounding at the wall.
>
> Our hats off to you, Captain. 94

In this Seven Arts article, Dreiser wrote (page 382):

> For, after all, as I have pointed out somewhere,
> the great business of life and mind is life. We
> are here, I take it, not merely to moon and vege-
> tate, but to do a little thinking about the state in
> which we find our selves.
>
> To me it is a thing for laughter, if not for tears:
> one hundred million Americans, rich (a fair per-
> centage of them, anyhow) beyond the dreams of
> avarice, and scarcely a sculptor, a musician, a
> poet worthy of the name.

Evidently the two men finally met in 1923, for Dreiser wrote the next year to say, "last year when I met you I
said this man is like his books that is [sic] capturing the
fancy of his readers. It is a groping, artistic, sincere personality. "95 Anderson answered by saying he was "damned
glad" to get Dreiser's letter. "In reality I doubt if you know
what you have meant to a lot of other writing men in America. When I wrote the thing in Horses and Men and the introduction to Free I had a strong feeling of fear afterward.
'Perhaps, ' I thought, 'he won't like it. '"96 As is depicted
in the account given on pages 333-337 in the Memoirs, Anderson stood in awe of Dreiser and found him hard to approach, as he thought others did, too. These comments to
a friend in 1924, seem to sum up his attitude:

> My first attempt to come a little closer to Dreiser
> was a failure. The same thing on him, used in

> Horses and Men, when published years ago in Little
> Review made him mad. The blessed old horse had
> just fallen in love with a new woman perhaps and
> it made him mad that I called him old, which he
> was, I fancy, always [Dreiser was born in 1871,
> Anderson in 1876]. . . . He is a silent, didactic old
> American who always seems to want to knock some
> one down--really sweet and sound at bottom
> though. [97]

In a letter of May, 1924, Dreiser had written: "But she
[Rose Suckow] isn't half as significant as is Sherwood Anderson of whom I heartily approve--the most original of them
all. "[98] If indeed the "old man" had been bothered by being
called old, he had, doubtless inadvertently, evened the score
by using the term "groping" for Anderson, an adjective which
never failed to disturb him.

There is no evidence that Anderson's admiration for
Dreiser ever flagged. In 1926 he was to say in a casual
newspaper interview: "He is really a distinguished literary
figure of our time in America. At times he appears heavy
and Germanic, but he has really a wonderful insight into
life. I am a great admirer of Dreiser. "[99] And he wrote
Dreiser late in his own life that his admiration for him had
been growing ever "since I first picked up the first book" of
his he had ever read. "I love your guts Teddy. " As a
postscript he added: "Anyway Teddy you are my Nobel Prize
man. "[100]

The admiration continued to be mutual. In his tribute
in the special Anderson issue of Story, Dreiser contributed a
whole page of very generous comment, including:

> Anderson, his life and his writings, epitomized for
> me the pilgrimage of a poet and dreamer across
> this limited stage called Life, whose reactions to
> the mystery of our being and doings here (our will-
> less and so wholly automatic responses to our en-
> vironing forces) involved tenderness, love and
> beauty, delight in the strangeness of our will-less
> reactions as well as pity, sympathy and love for
> all things both great and small. [101]

Another writer whom he met first through works and
later personally was Gertrude Stein, the pioneering expatri-
ate. When he went abroad with Paul Rosenfeld in 1921, he

found his way, through acquaintance with Sylvia Beach, owner
of that bookshop where American writers met in Paris,
Shakespeare and Co., to Gertrude Stein's apartment.   She
was delighted to see him because he told her how important
her work had been to his development and because, only two
years her junior, he was a successful writer, as she still
longed to be. [102]

Gertrude Stein wrote to Anderson, after he had returned to America, to see if he would write an introduction
to her forthcoming book, Geography and Plays.   "Of course
I would like that because as I told you, you are the only person who really knows what it is all about. "[103]   She was delighted with his ready acquiescence and with what he wrote.[104]
In his introduction, he recalled his brother Karl bringing
Tender Buttons[105] to his rooms, just at the time there was
"a good deal of fuss being made over it in American newspapers.   I had already read Three Lives [1909] and had
thought it contained some of the best writing ever done by
an American. "   Anderson reports his brother's comment:
"It gives words an oddly new intimate flavor and at the same
time makes familiar words seem like strangers.... " and then
he goes on to say that Miss Stein's work is "the most important pioneer work done in the field of letters in my time"
and that "these books of Gertrude Stein's do in a very real
sense recreate life in words. "[106]

It has been suggested that Anderson joined, originally,
in the laughter at Tender Buttons, [107] but his conversion, if
necessary, came quickly and certainly:

> Here was something purely experimental and deal-
> ing in words separated from sense--in the ordinary
> meaning of the word sense--an approach I was sure
> poets must often be compelled to make....   My
> mind did a kind of jerking flop and after Miss
> Stein's book had come into my hands I spent days
> going about with a tablet of paper in my pocket
> and making new and strange combinations of words.
> The result was I thought a new familiarity with the
> words of my own vocabulary.   I became a little
> conscious where before I had been unconscious. [108]

From this time on, as has been suggested, the friendship was very firm.   He gave letters of introduction to Gertrude to such people as Mr. and Mrs. Ernest Hemingway and
Cornelia Anderson when they went abroad.   The knowledge

of her influence on him, liberating rather than restrictive, had touched her deeply.

A somewhat more tenuous relationship may be examined between Anderson and Edgar Lee Masters. Daugherty said that they were not close friends but merely acquaintances in their occasional meetings at gatherings of writers and artists.[109] Masters could not recall where he first met Anderson, thought it might have been through Tennessee Mitchell, knew they saw each other infrequently, did not discuss The Spoon River Anthology with him.[110] Max Wald, one of the people who lived in the house on Cass Street with Anderson, recalled lending Master's book to Anderson soon after it was published (April, 1915); Anderson noted that Tennessee Mitchell knew the author and took it to his room to read. He returned the book the next morning, saying he had stayed up late reading it, had not been impressed.[111] According to Howe, he excitedly praised the book to his friends.[112]

Because both Spoon River and Winesburg depict life in a small middle western town, comparisons were natural. That Anderson must have been keenly aware of it, even before publication, is established by this note in "Notes on Names, " in the January, 1917, Seven Arts:

> Sherwood Anderson has written a series of intensive studies on the archetypes of the small Ohio town of which he is a native. He calls it "Winesburg. " The story in this issue ["The Untold Lie"] is the second of a series to appear in the Seven Arts; and others will follow. When the whole is gathered into a volume, America will see that a prose complement to E. L. Masters' "Spoon River Anthology" has been created.

One can only guess why the relationship between the two books and authors became a sensitive point; one recalls the Masters-Tennessee relationship. In any case, the assumed emotionality of it led to the following blatant error:

> So many critics have made the obvious comparison between "Winesburg, Ohio" and "Spoon River Anthology" that his publishers announce that Mr. Anderson's "Winesburg" stories appeared in magazines before Mr. Masters' work appeared.[113]

Masters' work had begun to appear in Reedy's Mirror in the
issue of May 29, 1914; the first Winesburg story to appear
was "The Book of the Grotesque, " in Masses for February,
1916.

    In several mentions in letters of 1918, Anderson dis-
plays his distaste for Masters. In speaking of his own poems and their possible failure, he says Masters might have
reached what he was trying for, but he has "too keen a
quality of hate. "[114] Then he says categorically:

> I do not know L. M. and have no pull to him, lone-
> ly as I sometimes am. I get the final notion on
> my mind that his successes have been founded on
> hatred. A burning hatred arose in him and gal-
> vanized his lackadaisical talent into something sharp
> and real. Then the fire went away and left the
> man empty. This is all a theory. I don't know
> the fellow. [115]

He further denigrates Masters, whom he continues to refer
to as L. M. , by saying he has probably "lost his grip" because he did not "stay among workers. " By going among
those who are idlers, he has come to mistake "meaningless
flattery" for "truth. " This is so grossly unfair and considerably unlike Anderson otherwise that it is difficult not to at
least entertain the idea that something personal lay behind
the attack.

    Included in the writers in whom Anderson had a deep
interest in this pre-Winesburg period are those whom he
could meet only through their books. He seems to have developed an intense interest in the Russian writers, for example, and a deep sense of vanity concerning them. He
wrote once that he discovered the "tales of defeated people"
by Gorki when he was "a young factory hand. "[116] He thought
of himself as having hungered to have the lives of people he
knew told in the accurate, sympathetic way of Gorki. Hecht
reported that Anderson had read Dostoevsky at 38 (after
September, 1914) and said, "If Dostoevsky came into my
room I would kneel before him. No one else. "[117] In 1921
he rejoiced that Hart Crane had discovered "the two books I
care for most, Karamazov and Possessed. ... However one
doesn't like this man, one loves him. I have always felt
him as the one writer I could go down on my knees to. "[118]
He told his Russian translator that he had "never found a
prose that satisfied" him until he found Tolstoy, Doestoevsky,

Turgenev, and Chekhov. [119]

> Two comments to Miss Finley are helpful in timing
his acquaintance with the Russians, though it is known he had
read their works in Chicago and Elyria:

> > There is no reason at all why Americanism should
> > not be seen with the same intensity of feeling so
> > characteristic of Russian Artists when they write
> > of Russian life. Our life is as provincial. It is
> > as full of strange and illuminating side lights. Be-
> > cause we have not written intensely is no reason
> > why we should not begin. [120]

To that indication of a general familiarity with the Russians
in 1916 may be added his statement that he was reading tales
of Pushkin for the first time in April, 1918. [121]

> Curiously, it seems to have concerned Anderson that
it might be believed he had actually read the Russians before
he began to write.

> > You note, Paul, that there was quite a joke about
> > myself and the Russians. Most of the critics spoke
> > of the influence the Russians had had upon me when
> > my stories first began to appear. As a matter of
> > fact, I had read none of the Russians at the time
> > this criticism was made and cannot now remember
> > just when I began to read them. [122]

Elsewhere, he is more evasive:

> > In later years, when my own name had a little got
> > up in the world as a teller of tales I was often
> > accused of having got my impulse, as a story-teller
> > from the Russians. The statement is a plausible
> > one. It is, in a way based upon reason. [123]

> But to Sergel he makes this highly-indicative revela-
tion:

> > I spent all those years floundering about. No ap-
> > proach I found satisfied me. Like other Ameri-
> > cans, from the beginning, I had to go abroad. I
> > was perhaps 35 years old [roughly 1911] when I
> > first found the Russian prose writers. One day I
> > picked up Turgenif's "Annals of a Sportsman." I

> remember how my hands trembled as I read the
> book.   I raced through the pages like a drunken
> man.
>
> Afterward in Tolstoi, Dostoevsky I found the same
> thing.   I did not want to write like these men.   The
> truth is I found in them the love of human life,
> tenderness, a lack of the eternal preaching and
> smartaleckness so characteristic of much western
> writing, nearly all of it in fact. [124]

Howe, pages 92-93, noted the similarities between Memoirs
of a Sportsman of Turgenev and Winesburg, Ohio: loosely-
bound but closely-related sketches, comprising episodic novels; dependence for impact less on dramatic action than on
climactic, lyrical insight; use of bland understatements to
provide ironic coda to the body of the tale.

    Yet Anderson could not feel comfortable about the re-
lationship, evidently felt it would mean his work was less
valuable if he admitted the relationship generally, for he was
to write:

> When I had grown to be a man, and when my sto-
> ries began to be published in the more reckless
> magazines, such as The Little Review, the old
> Masses, and later in The Seven Arts and the Dial,
> and when I was so often accused of being under the
> Russian influence, I began to read the Russians,
> to find out if the statement, so often made concern-
> ing me and my work, could be true. [125]

    Among American writers, Anderson had an intense in-
terest in Mark Twain and was wondering, as early as 1916,
why he was not included, with Whitman, among the "two or
three really great American artists."[126] He thrust himself, by
correspondence, into the very center of Van Wyck Brooks'
labors on The Ordeal of Mark Twain (1920).   His comments
to Brooks are importantly revealing of his attitude toward
other writers and toward his own art.

> I have myself understood the trenchant sadness of
> Lincoln, the rather childlike pessimism of Twain,
> the half-sullen and dogmatic insistence on the part
> of Dreiser on the fight with Puritanism and Whit-
> man's insistence on America.   I thought I under-
> stood these things, because I have lived in such a

> barren place, felt myself so futile, because I have
> really always felt a lack of strength to continue
> struggling in a vacuum and looked forward hopeless-
> ly to the time when some quirk of the mind would
> lead me to adopt some grotesque sectional attitude
> and spend myself uselessly on that.[127]

He told Brooks that he always thought of Twain as he did
with peculiar enthusiasm of George Borrow, for his honesty
and "wholesome disregard of precedent."

> As far as Twain is concerned, we have to remem-
> ber the influences about him. Remember how he
> came into literature. . . . It seems to me that when
> he began he addressed an audience that gets a big
> laugh out of the braying of a jackass. . . . There
> was tenderness and subtlety in Mark when he grew
> older.
>
> You get the picture of him, Brooks--the river man
> who could write going East and getting in with that
> New England crowd. . . and Howells did Twain no
> good.
>
> There's another point, Brooks, I can't help wishing
> Twain hadn't married such a good woman. There
> was such a universal inclination to tame the man--
> to save his soul as it were. Left alone, I fancy
> Mark might have been willing to throw his soul
> overboard and then--ye gods, what a fellow he
> might have been, what poetry might have come from
> him.
>
> The big point is this: it seems to me that this
> salvation of the soul business gets under every-
> body's skin. With artists it takes the form of be-
> ing concerned with their reputation as writers. A
> struggle constantly goes on. Call the poet a poet
> and he is no longer the poet.[128]

> Of course your book cannot be written in a cheerful
> spirit. In facing Twain's life you face a tragedy.
> How could the man mean what he does to us if he
> were not a tragedy? . . .
>
> America is a land of children, broken off from the

culture of the world.   Twain there, part of that.
There the coming of industrialism. . . .

Mark Twain was a factory child.   I am that.   I
can, however, stand back and look at him.   When
it would be second-rate and unmanly to weep concerning myself, I can think of him.   For his very
failure I love him.   He was maimed, hurt, broken.
In some way he got caught up by the dreadful cheap
smartness, the shrillness that was a part of the
life of the country, that is still its dominant note.[129]

I am struck with the thought that I would like to
have you believe that Twain's cheapness was not
really a part of him.   It was a thing out of the
civilization in which he lived that crept [in] and invaded him. . . .

Twain got more deeply [than Abraham Lincoln] into
the complex matter of living.   He was more like
you and me, facing more nearly our kind of problems.

Here I am going to confess something to you.   Whitman does not mean as much to me as do the other
two.   There is a pretense about him, even tricki-
ness. . . .

I am wondering if you might not profitably go to
Lincoln for a greater understanding of Twain and
Whitman.   There is something, a quality there,
common to the three men.

I get a sense of three very honest boys brought
suddenly to face the complex and intricate world.
There is a stare in their eyes.   They are puzzled
and confused.   You will be inclined to think Whitman the greater man perhaps.   He came closer to
understanding.   He lacked Lincoln's very great
honesty of soul.

Twain's way lies somewhere between the road taken
by the other two men. [130]

    Obviously, Anderson had a high degree of identification
with Twain.   He included in his profuse comments to Brooks

the fact that he had tried to "write a story concerning Twain. "
He said he had a copy of it in his desk.   "There is a character in the story, the old cheese maker from Indiana, that
I will sometime make the central figure in a real story.   He
is Twain's type of man. "[131]

Brooks was struck by Anderson's enthusiasm for Twain
and by the fact that he seemed to embody just these characteristics that Twain had when writing Huckleberry Finn: a
fresh, healthy mind, a true feeling of comradeship, a beautiful, new humility, a lovely generosity, and a proud, conscious innocence in his nature.   Further, after Brooks had
published the Ordeal, he found Anderson's criticism of its
shortcomings appropriate. [132]

An important influence on American literature, coming
in as something new, exciting, and powerful just as Anderson
was going from Elyria to Chicago, were the findings of Freud
and the other psychoanalysts.   Anderson's encounter with Dr.
Trigant Burrow at Lake Chateaugay touched upon the influence of Freud.   Perhaps a few more notes about relationships
with Freud will be in order.   Anderson devotes a portion of
his Memoirs (pages 243-245) to this subject:

> Freud had been discovered at the time and all the
> young intellectuals were busy analyzing each other
> and everyone they met.   Floyd Dell was hot at
> it....   Well, I hadn't read Freud (in fact, I never
> did read him) and was rather ashamed of my ig-
> norance.

Dr. Burrow thought, "It would be easy for the Freudian-minded
to see Freud as the inspiration to Anderson's work.   But...
Sherwood possessed insights into behavior, especially with
regard to the sexual determinants of it, which arose from
his own independent intuition. "   Burrow also used the expressions "amazing intuitive flashes" and "uncanny insight"
to refer to Anderson. [133]   Miss Finley said, "I discussed
Freud with him, and he knew a lot of the answers.   At least
he hit the high places in Freud. "[134]   Anderson has said,
Freud was being discussed all around him and an identifiable
Freudian outlook appeared rampantly in the Seven Arts,
Masses, and Little Review and in the writings of such people
as Dell and Frank, with whom he was so familiar.   And certainly what he heard had to have significance for his own intensive self-probings.   There can be no doubt that his works
fully exemplify what the Freudians were talking and writing

about.   His reaction to Burrow at Chateaugay shows how
prone he was to suspect the kind of oversimplification one
does find in "Freudians. "   He records an experience in the
Memoirs (page 245) of picking up a twig on a path while out
walking with a friend and breaking it in his fingers.   His
companion spoke to him of it, and Anderson reflected:

> It seemed he had found me out.   I was breaking a
> twig between my fingers, and obviously, he ex-
> plained to me, the twig was a phallic symbol.   I
> was wanting to destroy, the phallic in myself.   I
> had secretly a desire to be a woman.

At the very end of his life he was still resisting what he
thought was the over-readiness of the Freudians to superimpose symbolic meanings on what he thought were random actions.

This consideration of his fellows in the brotherhood of
literature and life has veered more and more into imperson-
alities.   Perhaps it will become ultimately so in turning to
a few suggestions on the importance of the writers of the
Bible to him.   He told Frank, "The Bible I have always
read. ... "[135]   He followed this statement with the remark:
"I'm writing a bible myself, or rather a New Testament
[published in 1927]. "   In a letter of the preceding year, in
which he is attempting to help Frank decide on the right title
for a book, he reveals one literary use for the Bible: "I
had some notion that by going back to the stories of Jacob
and Joseph and Saul I should get some word--an emerging
word--"   After considering rather carefully several possible
titles he says: "Tonight I'll spend an hour or two [groping]
in the old testament.   It will be odd if I do not find what
you want there. "[136]   Even a cursory look into Winesburg,
Ohio shows Anderson's deep involvement with religion and
Christianity and the Bible, but, of course, these had to be
in his own way and on his own terms.   He was a man who
did not belong to a church but had a continuing and deep concern over the idea that "We are all Christ and we are all
crucified. "

Before concluding this attempt to suggest which people
and groups had their impact on Anderson in this period, attention may be given to three group situations which have not
been discussed.   Mention has already been made of the rooming house at 735 Cass [now Wabash] Street, where Anderson
was living as early as the fall of 1914[137] on the second[138]

floor of a large red-brick house as "dean" of the "Little Children of the Arts," a group of otherwise-young artists and
writers.   In the middle of the bohemian North Side of Chicago, he wrote, among other things, the stories which became Winesburg, Ohio in the winter of 1915-1916.   He wrote
several versions of the event of what he considered his "first
real writing," which occurred in this room.   Probably somewhat fictionalized in the following personal letter version, [139]
this first real writing did represent a triumphant break-
through of artistic realization.

First, he noted he had done much reading and living
in the world of books.   "It is only after a long time that you
know that this is a special world, fed out of the world of
reality but not of the world of reality."

> And then, if you are a real writer, your moment
> comes.   I remember mine.   I walked along a city
> street in the snow.   I was working at work I hated.
> Already I had written several long novels. . . .   I
> was ill, discouraged, broke.   I was living in a
> cheap rooming house.   I remember that I went up-
> stairs and into the room.   It was very shabby. . . .
>
> I grew desperate, went and threw up my window.
> I sat by the open window.   It began to snow.   I'll
> catch cold sitting here."
>
> "What do I care?"   There was some paper on a
> small kitchen table I had bought and had brought up
> into the room.   I turned on the light and began to
> write.   I wrote, without looking up. . . a story called
> "Hands."   It was and is a beautiful story.

He got up finally and went out, full of a feeling of exhilara-
tion.   For several hours he wandered, not being able to remember later "all the foolish things I did that evening."
Then he went back to his room and read his story.

> It was all right.   It was sound.   It was real.   I
> went to sit by my desk.   A great many others have
> had such moments.   I wonder what they did.   I
> sat there and cried.   For a moment I thought the
> world very wonderful and I thought also that there
> was a good deal of wonder in me. [140]

The following letter will serve to suggest the kind of

people he knew at 735 Cass and his attitude toward them.   It
throws light on the preoccupation with the "grotesque" in
Winesburg.

> ... It is Sunday and I am alone in my room with
> the curtains drawn.   Here only two winters ago I
> began for the first time to live among people de-
> voted to the arts.   Our lives together did not work
> out but for a time how broken out with life the
> place was.   In the next room Mary lived.   Down
> the hall were Herman and little Max Grove.   Max
> Wald was in the next room.   Then came the end
> room with Betty and two others I have forgotten.
> The one was the mannish creature who was fat and
> used to put on a man's suit and wait for Mary in
> the hall.   She had great breasts and looked very
> funny in the man's clothes.
>
> Betty of course was courting Herman in those days.
> Max with whom he roomed went off to work in a
> railroad office at seven and one would hear Betty's
> little feet pattering down the hall.   She went to lie
> in bed with him for an hour and sometimes the
> hour extended all through the morning.   I took it
> for granted they were lovers and mentioned the
> matter casually in conversation with Mary.
>
> And after all it seems they were not.   Everybody
> was half starved and poorly fed and Herman was a
> mystic and no doubt in reality an intermediate.
> They merely wanted to lie down close to each oth-
> er, to be warmed a little by the faint heat of their
> sensuality.
>
> I suppose Betty was different.   She nearly died of
> it before they were finally married and passed on
> into something else.
>
> I must find a name for the lady of the fish-hooks
> and the man's clothes.   She was in love with Mary
> and suffered horribly.   She used to come into my
> room to smoke and talk.   In a way she was the
> most downright honest creature I ever knew.   Noth-
> ing was too blunt for her to hear and if her love
> was an unnatural thing it was a strong positive
> thing too.   She would have fought and died for it I
> am convinced.

Figure 5
Anderson photographed, evidently, at a party.
Chicago, ca. 1917. Photographer unknown.

I took her to dinner once in a fashionable restaurant. How funny she was. When I went for her I
found her rigged out in a great feathered hat and
she had on a terribly tight-fitting corset and high-
heeled shoes. Poor child, she thought that was the
way things were done. She wanted me not to be
ashamed of her but she looked like the keeper of
a house of ill fame. I wanted to laugh and to cry
too.

And Max Wald. I wonder how well you know him.
He is a study in tenseness; a violin string drawn
so tight so long that nothing but shrill high tones
can come from him. There is nothing of my man
of the corn fields about him. He also fell in love
with Mary and how tragically. He used to stand
for hours, tensely in the hall while she laughed or
talked with me or with someone else. I think he
was capable of murder then. For years he had
been a musician, striving to make a name for himself as the writer of delicate, beautiful little songs.
He threw it all overboard and began to write an
opera. . . something between ragtime and Wagner.
He had dreams of becoming the author of another
Floradora and becoming fabulously wealthy. Mary
was the beautiful lady in the castle. He would be
the knight coming out of the west, astride a great
horse, and followed by a long train of slaves, bearing jewels and perfumes and silks.

In the house then to dream a thing was to have it
become an actuality [emphasis supplied]. Every
one had a dream and talked of it as though it were
a fact already achieved. In the evening the house
reeked of dreams. Max played over and over the
songs from his opera, putting in and taking out
notes. One could hear the tramp of the camels
and the horses and the elephants coming softly
through deep sand, bring[ing] the treasure to lay at
the feet of Mary.

Little Max Grove fell in love with Betty's sister
who came on a visit from a place in Indiana. She
was a country school teacher. I used to see him
coming up the stairs, bearing a rose, held before
him as a priest would hold the sacrament. He
came occasionally to typewrite for me on Sunday

mornings and once when I brutally, and not understanding, kept him steadily at work for two hours
he fainted.   He was meagerly paid and I suspect
partially supported Betty and Herman.   There was
much pride among them.   Such things were whispered but not talked about aloud.   I was to them a
rich, capable, masculine thing--heavy and dangerous.   Poor little shadows!

Mary was the deep cause of misunderstanding between us.   She was lovely then--the born courtesan
in her first beauty and come out of innocent places.
She understood me, the hard working, rather stupid,
producing artist.   She understood them and their
shadow world.   She had a life of her own and she
could enter into the dark passions of the lady of
the fishhooks.

I have put Mary out of my door now and I hope she
never comes in again.   She is losing understanding,
demanding the price demanded by the working courtesan.   Then she could come to my door, knock
softly, enter, and stand poised, just for a moment,
in the deep shadows at the other side of the room,
the loveliest thing imaginable.

How really beautiful she was.   It wasn't physical
beauty.   It was instead something that cannot endure, something transitory, impossible.   Life had
to catch and destroy her.   She had to destroy herself.

And now I must stop talking of old things and go
back to my grinding work.   Max still clings to the
place.   He has become a little less tight but is
becoming bald.   Again he works at the beautiful,
delicate songs.   The place has become slipshod and
it is hard to keep alive the spirit of my room.
Presently I shall move away.

And I have not told you of the tall womanish man
who joined the British army or of Fedja, the
strange, the dead thing who came here to live and
who did actually die but I must go back to my
work. [141]

Another letter seems to capture perfectly the essence

of the process he was carrying on in the midst of a tantalizing, tortured, and strangely-beautiful life. It reveals a
compassionate yet semi-detached realization of the meaning
of life for others and therefore for himself:

> It was cold but I buttoned up my coat and went for
> a walk. All afternoon I had travelled through a
> country of cornfields. In the background the red
> trees. The city was empty. Down the ugly streets
> the wind ran throwing dust about. I went back to
> my room and lighted candles. In the room behind
> me a young girl lives. She is anxious to become
> acquainted. When I open my door hers creeps
> open. She stands looking at me.
>
> My mind is tumbling about and trying to fit itself
> in a mood of sustained work. That will come.
> You must of course know that the thing you want,
> the warm close thing, is the cry going up out of
> all hearts. Everyone in the world needs to love
> and be loved. I presume the lovely little thing in
> the next room--she is, I suppose, a clerk, wants
> that. [142]

As he looked out over the center of the complex of Chicago,
he considered the hopes and fears of these people and identified, perhaps unconsciously, in them his own puzzlement and
insecurity.

He wrote Frank of his room: "You can really work
here. My room on a side street is a secluded hole. "[143]
But Ben Hecht remembered that he enjoyed filling his room
with people and reading to them by candlelight. [144] On one
occasion he remembered that this "rugged-seeming man, "
who was really a "gentle, almost-womanish fellow, " had intended to read something from Windy McPherson's Son but
thought better of it. "So I'll read you some stories I've
written about a town called Winesburg, Ohio. They're not
really stories. They're people. "[145] And it was not only the
"young disciples" and the fellow members of the "outer fringe"
who came to 735 Cass, but also people like Carl Sandburg,
who came often and "played his banjo ad infinitum. "[146]

A totally different haunt which was of interest to Anderson was the Dill Pickle Club, opened in 1916 by a man
named Jack Jones, self-acclaimed safe-cracker, who had let
his hair grow, donned a flowing tie... but let Anderson tell it:

Are you a struggling poet, groping your way through
a dark and dreary commercial world?   Have you
written a prose masterpiece that some money-
minded publisher will not publish?   Are you an
eager young feminist longing to lift womankind into
a higher life?   Have you painted or sung or sculpted
or thought something that the dull minded world
does not appreciate?

What have you done?   What have you to say?   Jack
Jones and the Dill Pickle are looking for you.

Jack Jones is the father, the mother and the ring-
master of the Dill Pickle in Tooker alley, just off
Dearborn, north of Chicago avenue, on the north
side.

You may have visited the neighborhood.   There is
a charming little park just around the corner from
the Pickle.   It is filled with benches and trees and
the big, grim, wise looking Newberry Library looks
down on it.   Before Jones came to gather together
what he calls his "trained band of ants" the poor
homeless nuts lived with the squirrels in the park.
On warm Sunday afternoons they came forth in
droves.   One by one [they] climbed upon soap
boxes and talked to the sad-eyed loafers gathered
about.

Two years ago, Jones, the Pickler, arrived.   None
knew where he came from and you'll never find out
from Jones.   For a time he worked as a house
painter and ran the Pickle as a week end diversion.

The trade began to look up.   The nuts were gathered out of the park and to their amazement found
themselves in a big, comfortable room filled with
brightly painted chairs and a pulpit from which to
talk until they were weary.   Something happened
to them.

What happened is the secret of Jones.   The nuts
talked and everybody laughed.   In spite of themselves the nuts began to laugh.   "There it is.
Don't you see," said Jones, chuckling and wagging
his head, "the proletariat are just like the painters
and poets.   They'll laugh if you give them the

chance.   Even a skinny, long haired poet will laugh
if you give him a hand and a warm place to sit."

At that the Pickler might have been overlooked had
it not been for the highbrows.   Several months ago
our very best thinkers began to make their way,
rather sheepishly at first, into Tucker [sic] alley,
and now you are likely to find any one there.   The
street car conductor sits on a bench beside the college professor, the literary critic, the earnest
young wife, who hungers for culture, and the hobo.
Jack Jones is always in the background.   To every
guest he puts the same question.   "Are you a nut
about anything?" he asks.   "Don't you want to talk
to the Picklers?"

Jack Jones and the Dill Pickle are two bright spots
in the rather somber aspect of our town.   The
highbrows don't walk with Jones on Michigan avenue yet, but that may happen any day.   Pickle itself, he is now putting on a strictly artistic and
very literary affair every Thursday evening.   The
street car conductors and the nuts of the park
seem to be following Jones into this venture.   On
almost every Thursday evening the Dill Pickle
chapel is filled with devotees of the arts.   When
things grow a bit heavy and dull Jones cheers up
the children of the arts as he formerly cheered the
park hangers on.   Bright eyed, alert, filled with
good natured laughter and a born showman, Jones
and the Dill Pickles may go far.

It would be a delightful surprise if Jones the Pickler
should achieve in Chicago what Maurice Browne,
with his Little Theater, and all the more serious
minded yeomen who have tried so hard to make a
home for the arts among us, have failed to do.

In the meantime Jones isn't worrying.   If art wants
to come and make its home in the Dill Pickle he'll
be ready for it.   If things grow dull he'll chuckle
and try to stir up a row.   If you go to see him
he'll ask you the same question he asks everyone
else--"Are you a nut about anything?   Don't you
want to talk about the Picklers?   What have you
done?   What have you to say?"   Jack Jones and
the Dill Pickles are looking for you. [147]

It is evident that Andersoon took great delight in visiting 18 Tooker Alley, but it is not known whether he ever
performed, as did Ben Hecht and Maxwell Bodenheim. Perhaps he was delighted but not impressed, for Jones is said,
on the occasion of a lecture by a lady on "Men Who Have
Made Love to Me, " to have told him "I give them the high-
brow stuff until the crowd grows thin, and then I turn on the
sex faucet. "[148]

Another kind of association, involving an identifiable
group, was the ritual of the luncheons at Schlogl's (or possibly at a big table in the grill room at Marshall Field's),
which occurred once a week and involved, beside Anderson,
such people as: Carl Sandburg, Ben Hecht, Harry Hansen,
Burton Rascoe, Henry Blackman Sell, Llewellyn Jones, John
V. A. Weaver, Justin Smith, J. P. McEvoy, Keith Preston,
T. K. Hedrick, and Gene Markey.[149] Some of these men
were among the best literary friends Anderson had, and certainly his friendship with the reviewers created a better
newspaper climate when his works came out. Rascoe mentions his coming into town from Palos Park, his suburban
writing retreat for several years after the publication of
Winesburg, for this social occasion only.

This survey of some of Anderson's relationships,
friendships perhaps they might be called, many of them of
deep spiritual quality, a surprising number of life-long duration, all of them, whether captured in a voluminous correspondence or in his or other's memoirs or shaped into fictional format or in one of the many unrecorded explorations,
brought into being by his insatiable need to know himself
more fully through the penetration of the inner reality of
others, has not been intended to be more than suggestive.
Tortured as he often was, he was a person who mastered
very well the art of being attractive and interesting to others, no doubt largely through his great interest and understanding and, perhaps even more, through his need.

Notes

1.   Letter to William L. Phillips, March 23, 1949.

2.   Letter, ca. 1921.

3.   Letter to Waldo Frank, before Nov. 7, 1917.

4.   A Story Teller's Story, p. 394.

5.   Before I Forget, p. 431.

6.   Letter to Marietta D. Finley, Feb. 1917.

7.   Letter to M. D. Finley, Aug. 30, 1917.

8.   Letter to M. D. Finley, 1919.

9.   Letter after Oct. 29, 1917 (JR).

10.   Letter to M. D. Finley, Feb. 1917.

11.   Letter to M. D. Finley, Dec. 1, 1916.

12.   A Story Teller's Story, p. 260.

13.   Letter to M. D. Finley, Jan. 22, 1917.

14.   Letter to M. D. Finley, Nov. 23, 1917.

15.   From four 1917 letters to M. D. Finley: Nov. 6, Aug. 30, Feb. , and Jan. 22.

16.   Letter to M. D. Finley, Jan. 19, 1917.

17.   "A Marginal Note, " Paul Rosenfeld, Voyager in the Arts, New York, Creative Age Press, 1948, p. 195.

18.   Before I Forget, p. 430-1.

19.   Ibid. , p. 433-4.

20.   Irving Howe, Sherwood Anderson, New York, W. Sloan, 1951, p. 67.

21.   Letter from M. D. Finley, May 31, 1962.

22.   Letter to M. D. Finley, Jan. 8, 1917.

23.   Letter to Waldo Frank, after Aug. 6, 1918.

24.   Before Nov. 7, 1917.

25.   Oct. 29, 1917 (JR).

26.   Jerome W. Kloucek, "Waldo Frank, The Ground of His Mind and Art" (Evanston, Ill., Northwestern Univ., 1958, unpub. doctoral dissertation), points out that the years before 1920 were, according to Frank, "the crisis of my life."

27.   Letter, Dec. 7, 1917.

28.   Letter, Oct. 29, 1917 (JR).

29.   Letter after Aug. 6, 1918.

30.   Letter from M. D. Finley, May 31, 1962.

31.   Letter to M. D. Finley, June 1917.

32.   Letter to M. D. Finley, Dec. 1918.

33.   "Sherwood Anderson Documentary" (Part One), recorded by Radio Station WBAI, 1963.

34.   Letter after Aug. 6, 1918.

35.   Letters to Waldo Frank, spring 1918, June 5, 1918, and Jan. 4, 1919.

36.   Letter of Frank, 1918.

37.   Letter to Frank, Sept. 5, 1917.

38.   Salvos, New York, Boni and Liveright, 1924, p. 40.

39.   Our America, New York, Boni and Liveright, 1919, p. 139.

40.   In the American Jungle, New York, Farrar and Rinehart, 1937, p. 94.

41.   Letter from Waldo Frank, undated, 1917.

42.   Letter to M. D. Finley, Sept. 1918.

43.   Letter to Paul Rosenfeld, Jan. 1922.

44.   Letter to Hart Crane, Dec. 17, 1919 (JR).

45.   Letter from M. D. Finley, May 31, 1962.

46.   Letter to Waldo Frank, after Aug. 6, 1918.

47.   Letter to Van Wyck Brooks, May 31, 1918 (JR).

48.   Letter to Brooks, before Aug. 20, 1920 (JR).

49.   Letter, June 12, 1923.

50.   Letter to Paul Rosenfeld, Feb. 17, 1921.

51.   Letters to Frank, after Aug. 6, and after June 5, 1918.

52.   Reported by Schevill, p. 119-20.

53.   A Story Teller's Story, p. 223.

54.   A representative list: Theodore Dreiser, John Cowper Powys, Jerome Blum, Susan Glaspell, Edna Kenton, Arthur Davidson Ficke, Llewellyn Jones, Margaret Anderson, Robert Morss Lovett, Ben Hecht, Eunice Tietjens, Lucien Cary, Ernestine Evans.

55.   Memoirs, p. 339-40.

56.   Letter to Roger Sergel, March 26, 1928 (JR).

57.   Letter to George Daugherty, ca. 1924.

58.   New Republic, 89:103; English Journal, 13:531-9; Virginia Quarterly Review, 11: 379-88.

59.   Lovett, "Sherwood Anderson, " English Journal, Oct.

60.   Dell, Looking at Life, p. 80, and ms. review of Memoirs, p. 3.

61.   Letter from Floyd Dell to Dr. Stanley Pargellis, April 14, 1948.

62.   Letter from Dell, Feb. 5, 1964.

63.   Letter to George Freitag, Aug. 18, 1938.

64.   Homecoming, p. 274.

65.   Letter from Dell to Dr. Stanley Pargellis, April 14,

1948.

66.   Letter from Dell, Dec. 18, 1941.

67.   Letter from Dell to Dr. Pargellis, April 14, 1948.

68.   Letter from Dell to Anderson, on stationery of The
        Liberator, undated.

69.   Letter to Waldo Frank, Sept. 1918.

70.   "Letetia," Playboy, (July 1963), p. 124.

71.   Letter from Starrett, Nov. 20, 1962.

72.   Hecht; New York, The New American Library of World
        Literature, 1955; portions quoted from p. 212-30.

73.   Ibid.

74.   A Story Teller's Story, p. 253.

75.   Letter to Roger Sergel, 1924.

76.   Letter to Mrs. L. L. Copenhaver, fall 1936 (JR).

77.   Letter, Jan. 23, 1938.

78.   "Go Scholar-Gypsy," Story, Sept. 1941, p. 92-3. This
        was originally a newspaper feature article based on an
        interview just before Anderson started on his fatal trip to
        South America.

79.   Letter to Frank, Jan. 4, 1917.

80.   Letter to Waldo Frank, April 1917.

81.   Letter to M. D. Finley, April 17, 1917.

82.   Letter to Paul Rosenfeld, Feb. 17, 1921.

83.   Letter to Rosenfeld, 1924.

84.   "Sherwood Anderson Documentary," Radio Station
        WBAI, 1963, from taped recording in the possession of
        Mrs. Eleanor C. Anderson.

85.   Letter; May 22, 1940.

86.   Before I Forget, p. 438.

87.   In Smoke and Steel, New York, Harcourt, Brace, 1930, p. 174.

88.   Letter; July 2, 1964.

89.   Miss Sandburg says of this manuscript, which is in the possession of the Sandburg family: "Perhaps this should more properly be termed a note instead of a letter, but Anderson's large handwriting and wide spacing make it cover a whole page of typewriter paper. It is an exact copy--there is no salutation, no question mark after Wednesday. "

90.   "Letitia, " p. 124, places Dreiser and Anderson in the same room at a party.

91.   Howe, p. 64, says Dreiser's praise of a part of Windy McPherson's Son was a prized moment for Anderson at a 57th St. party.

92.   Chicago Evening Post, Sept. 15, 1916, p. 11.

93.   Letter, Feb. 26, 1917.

94.   Letter to Dreiser, March 2, 1917 (JR).

95.   Letter, Jan. 10, 1924.

96.   Letter to Dreiser, Mid-Jan. 1924 (JR).

97.   Letter to Roger Sergel, 1924.

98.   Letter to H. L. Mencken, May 12, 1924.

99.   Interview by T. H. Alexander, Nashville Tennesseean, ca. 1926.

100.   Letter, ca. Nov. 24, 1938.

101.   "Sherwood Anderson, " Story, Sept. -Oct. 1941, XIX:4.

102.   Elizabeth Sprigge, Gertrude Stein--Her Life and Work, New York, Harper, 1957, p. 125.

103.   Ibid. , p. 126.

104.   When the present writer appeared at Miss Stein's Paris apartment in 1946, he had only to mention his deep interest in Anderson to assure a very friendly reception.

105.   Of which a puzzled review appeared in the Chicago Evening Post for Aug. 7, 1914.

106.   "The Work of Gertrude Stein, " Geography and Plays, Boston, The Four Seas Company, 1922, p. 5-7.

107.   Howe, p. 95, and Daugherty, interview with Phillips, Feb. 22, 1949.   From Phillips' "Sherwood Anderson's Winesburg, Ohio. . . . "

108.   A Story Teller's Story, p. 359-367.

109.   Interview with Phillips, Feb. 22, 1949.   Found in Phillips' "Sherwood Anderson's Winesburg, Ohio. . . . "

110.   Letter from Masters to Phillips, May 25, 1949.

111.   Phillips, p. 89-90.

112.   p. 94-5; no source given.

113.   Anon. "Brief Mention of New Book, " Bookman, Sept. 1919, liix.

114.   Letter to Van Wyck Brooks, early April 1918 (JR).

115.   Letter to Brooks, May 31, 1918 (JR).

116.   Letter to Tass Agency, June 18, 1936 (JR).

117.   Chicago Evening Post, Sept. 8, 1916, p. 11.

118.   Letter to Crane, March 4, 1921 (JR).

119.   Letter to Peter Ochremenko, Dec. 1922.

120.   Letter to Marietta D. Finley, Dec. 21, 1916.

121.   Letter to M. D. Finley, April 1918.

122.   Letter to Paul Rosenfeld, Aug. 2, 1939.

123.   A Story Teller's Story, p. 47-8.

124.   Letter to Roger Sergel, after Dec. 25, 1924.

125.   A Story Teller's Story, p. 48.

126.   Letter to Frank, Nov. 6, 1916 (JR).

127.   Letter, May 23, 1918 (JR).

128.   Letter early April, 1918 (JR).

129.   Letter to Brooks, late April, 1918.

130.   Letter to Brooks, June 7, 1918 (JR).

131.   Letter to Brooks, early April, 1918. So far no trace of such a story has been found.

132.   Note to "Letters to Van Wyck Brooks," Story, Sept. - Oct. 1941, XIX:42.

133.   A Search for Man's Sanity, p. 561; and p. 442.

134.   Interview, Sept. 7, 1962.

135.   Letter, May 1919.

136.   Letter to Frank, after June 5, 1918.

137.   Letter from M. D. Finley, May 31, 1962.

138.   Also given as the third floor in some accounts.

139.   He appended a note at the end of the letter: "If you use this will you see that I get a copy?"

140.   Letter to Roy Jansen, April 1935 (JR).

141.   Letter to M. D. Finley, Jan. 14, 1917.

142.   Letter to M. D. Finley, Oct. 10, 1917.

143.   Letter to Waldo Frank, early 1918.

144.   Letter, Nov. 15, 1962.

145. A Child of the Century, p. 211.

146. Letter from M. D. Finley, Oct. 7, 1963.

147. "Jack Jones--The Pickler," Chicago Daily News, June
      18, 1919, p. 12.

148. Bernard Duffey, The Chicago Renaissance in American
      Letters, East Lansing, Mich., Michigan State College Press,
      1954, p. 256-7.

149. Memoirs, p. 251; Before I Forget, p. 365-6, 431.

Mosaic XII

"How many flashes of beauty..."

I have always understood horses better than men.   It's eas-
    ier.
                          from A Story Teller's Story, p. 266.

                    *   *   *

As for myself I have been a stormy cuss and perhaps still
    am that.   In the first place I had myself almost come
    to middle life before I really sensed what I waited to
    do.   I was full of ugly fighting resentments for what
    life had done to me.
                          to Karl Anderson, 1922.

                    *   *   *

I think that in myself I am prejudiced against the rich.   Per-
    haps I do not feel that they are any worse than the
    poor but that they have too great a handicap.   It is so
    difficult, if you are made to stand out a bit from the
    mass, not to assure yourself that it is all due to some
    special virtue in yourself.   All power of money or place
    therefore brings a kind of corruption, almost inevitable.
    The poor and the obscure escape, not because of some
    special merit but because their chances are better.
                          to Charles Bockler, Feb. 10, 1931 (JR).

                    *   *   *

Today I said something to you about friendship.   It was didac-
    tic.   I never write in this cock-sure didactic way but I
    am ashamed of it afterward.
                          to M. D. Finley, Dec. 21, 1916.

The country makes you so damn glad and full of love and the people generally so sad.

to Roger Sergel, Jan. 21, 1933.

*   *   *

I often see, being what I am, the whole life of some individual met, in a few seconds. I presume I'm what they call a genius. I don't know. It doesn't matter.

to Mary Emmett, 1935.

*   *   *

Just now--perhaps because I am not very well I am discouraged about my power to keep wrestling daily with the devil for a living and having power and strength enough to think and feel deeply in other directions. I can do one of the two things but am afraid cannot continue to do both.

to Waldo Frank, March 1918.

*   *   *

How many flashes of beauty had come to me out of American life.

from A Story Teller's Story, p. 409.

*   *   *

How rapidly my hair is graying and how diabolically young I am inside.

to M. D. Finley, Feb. 1920.

*   *   *

What is it that makes me always a bit more comfortable and at home among these folks of the outer rim. . . . It may be just a form of the protest in myself against organized society, as now organized but I do love a kind of defiance in such people.

to Ferdinand Schevill, March 2, 1933
(JR).

*   *   *   *   *

Chapter 9 (continued)

D.   A Certain Satisfaction

> I had discovered something.   I had discovered that
> I could, in writing, throw an imagined figure
> against a background of some of my own experiences
> --a thing all writers must do--and through the
> imagined figure get sometimes a kind of slant on
> some of my own questionable actions.
>
> I doubt that it ever reformed me.   It did give me
> a certain satisfaction. [1]

In examining the "imagined figure" as it is thrown against the background of life in a process culminating in Winesburg, Ohio, attention will be given first of all to the unpublished stories and novels which Anderson wrote.   Because it exemplifies very well how the relationship between business and art was to continue to be confusing and troublesome, the first of the unpublished items to be discussed will be a series of "country town stories" he told Frank the "Curtis crowd" wanted him to do. [2]   Anderson reports that he told the man he could not "write to order":

> But the damned cuss got an idea into my head.   I
> was a good deal tired and blue and began doing
> some small-town stories in a semi-light vein for
> my own amazement.   They fairly dance along, and
> I grin all the time I write.   The idea I have is
> whimsical and tremendously amusing.   In spite of
> myself I may do just what the cuss wants and make
> a little money. [3]

A little later he amplified the nature of his vision of this opportunity, which was much like many of the other "escape" efforts he initiated:

> The Curtis people approached me and I proposed
> to them that they send me on a two years literary
> pilgrimage to the cornfields.   I would like to find
> some publisher adventuresome enough to send me
> on a long walk, to last about two years among the
> farmers and the small town people of the middle
> west.   I want to pull out of business and go live
> among the people but don't want to make compro-
> mises.   I would produce stories sketches and arti-
> cles.   Don't like the flavor of the Curtis crowd
> but if I went for them would work for the Country
> Gentleman not the Post.   That would be better.
> Is there any other magazine, a little broad in its
> outlook that might be interested in such an idea?[4]

Frank's reply to this letter was both encouraging and wisely
frank.   After saying the Curtis offer is interesting, predicting that the idea for a "long walk subsidized will yet come
off," and judging that only the Curtis or Hearst people would
be able to provide the kind of backing called for, he warns:

> But I still fear me, that they would get cold feet
> when your stuff came in. ...   The idea of a liter-
> ary Odyssey through the West would appeal to
> them, doubtless--but your gospel of defeat, your
> golden discovery of unfinancial gods, your subtle
> revolutionary visions would give them the creeps if
> they begin to catch on.   You must remember,
> Sherwood, that there are mighty few, even among
> the elite, that understand you.   You are known in
> many circles as morbid--the usual term for the
> fresh and peculiarly lifelike in art.   And I'll be
> goddamned if I can see a traveling salesman read-
> ing you without chewing his cigar to bits![5]

The last word from either Anderson or Frank on this matter
is this note from Frank a week or so later:

> I think you are all wrong in your misgivings about
> the stories you are writing for the Curtis people.
> I only hope they sell and that you are at last free
> from bondage. [6]

All the evidence concerning Anderson's methods of
work indicates that he was constantly writing and destroying.
More than once he was to do 25,000 or 50,000 words on
something and then lose his taste for it.   The number of

stories he began or even finished and abandoned can only be imagined. Traces of several of these vanished stories give the flavor of Anderson's experiences with this aspect of serious and self-critical writing.

In a letter to a friend whose experience was evidently related to a story that Anderson called "Impotence":

> Out of that cry of yours in the letter regarding the two old people I have made a story I call impotence [sic]. Now that it is written I feel some delicacy about letting you see it.   There is this trick of yours of taking living personally that makes me hesitate.   For to take this story personally will hurt.

> Without appearing to do so I have made the girl of the story the central figure.   She lives in a house with her father, a tall, feeble quiet man.   Back of these two figures that represent Impotence are two people who represent force.   An old woman on whom they are dependent and a beggar she has picked up in the street.

> Now let me explain.   If you want to see the story I shall have to have an understanding with you first.   There is something gone out of my Marie that is not gone out of you.   You have a thousand things she has not.   I could not bear to have this story taken as an interpretation of your life.   That will have to be understood or I will tear it up and throw it to the winds.

> I couldn't bear not to write the story.   It had such tremendous possibilities. [7]

This letter serves as a balance with Anderson's other accounts of the writing experience, which tend to leave the impression that he wrote his stories in a non-calculated, emotional way.   The truth may well be that he wrote stories both passionately and rationally, and probably the mixture of factors is not assessable.   Anderson was at least capable of the process of conscious manufacture with full recognition of the source of the materials.   Nothing more is known of the structure of this story, and only two comments to Frank about it remain.   Both references are from letters which are not fully dated but which seem to be from 1917.   What is

assumed to be the first reference is: "Think I'll send you
the story called "Impotence" [doubtless for possible use in
Seven Arts].   It's a grewsome [sic] tale but you may want
it. "   And, doubtless later, is a rejoinder to Frank's criticism of it: "Your criticism of the story Impotence is just
words.   I'll make you cook me a dinner for that when we
get up in the woods. "8

He has a similar confidence about another story, of
which there is no other record.   "I am drunk with the inclination to write.   Such times come to me.   I have to keep
away from people, because every person I see is a big
story.   I have written a story called 'The Net' that is a
marvel.   It is one of the best things I have done. "9   And
later he reported that he was writing a story called "The
Pagan Jesus. "   And all that is known of it is that it was to
do "in a swift tale what Wells wanted to do when he wrote
'God, the Invisible King'. "10

In addition to these three named stories and, of
course, many others, Anderson had various novels he worked
on, three of which may be identified as coming from the
pre-Winesburg period.   Possibly his comments on Immaturity, which he attempted after writing at least most of the
Winesburg stories, are the most revealingly useful in terms
of insight into the artistic mind of Anderson, but more is
known about Mary Cochran and Talbot Whittingham, as will
be seen.   His first mention of Immaturity came at the beginning of 1917.   He was far enough into the idea of it to
write:

> My new novel will really move.   I had a splendid
> sense of grip on it.   The theme is broad, real,
> sturdy.   It is my kind of theme.   I shall call the
> book immaturity [sic].   Did I tell you the story,
> how the boy by a peculiar combination of circum-
> stances finds himself charged with promoting Amer-
> ican culture.   The boy has money, he has imagin-
> ation, he is really an artist at heart.   The story
> will concern itself with the story of a guest.   Many
> people will drift in and out.   I shall try to express
> somehow the terrible immaturity of America. 11

Perhaps a week or so later he gives a fuller, more intense
description, which shows that this book would have been, in
effect, a sequel to Winesburg, Ohio.   The latter was evidently a completed entity in his mind, if not in fact, though that

month brought the publication of only a fifth of the 24 stories
eventually published (See Appendix H.)

> The possibilities of my new book grow in my mind.
> In it I hope to strike away from the two scenes
> that have been characteristic in my books--the vil-
> lage and then this great western city. In this book
> I will stay in the small place. Factories come to
> Winesburg, Ohio. Beginning in the life of John
> Hardy [See "Surrender" in Winesburg, Ohio] the
> town becomes an industrial center. It grows into
> a small city. Life there will be much what it is
> in Canton or Columbus, Ohio--in Toledo or even in
> Indianapolis. After the hurried transition from an
> agricultural to an industrial community the children
> of the next generation come in. They go away to
> school and come back. Young men grow up who
> have crudely the idea of family. Something is try-
> ing to get itself established. There is a crude
> vague reaching out for culture.

> In this period Tom Hardy son of John Hardy a
> banker and industrial leader spends his life. He
> goes away and comes back. He falls in love and
> is married. He is divorced and adventures. And
> all the time he is striving, hoping, hungering,
> wanting.

> That is the background of my new book. In it I
> hope to strike at the terrible immaturity and crude-
> ness of all our lives. Back of it I hope to get a
> background of love. The theme is varied, it is
> intense and real. I appreciate it and approach it
> humbly and hopefully. As always when I come to
> a new book I am like a boy gone to live in a
> strange town. I walk through the streets seeing
> people, wondering who will be my friends. I am
> shy and afraid. At night I do not want to sleep
> but to think. My life here can mean so much or
> so little. I am in love with the possibilities of
> my life in this new place and afraid too. [12]

There is no information as to what kept him from
continuing with this well-formulated conception, but evidently
something did, for he wrote to Frank in August, 1917: "I
am myself gone at last into this novel that has been at work
in me for six months and every day I write some on it. In

two weeks now I will go back [from Lake Chateaugay, where
he had recently been married to Tennessee] to my work in
Chicago but I am not much afraid that that will interrupt the
flow of it. " So full of this book was he that he likened himself to a pregnant woman.   En route to Chicago, at the beginning of September, he found, "My new book goes steadily
and surely along.   All the time the theme grows on my mind.
I find myself working more slowly and painstakingly than ever
before so the job will be, no doubt a long one but I don't
care. "[13]   In two successive letters to Frank, obviously written immediately upon his return to Chicago from Chateaugay,
he refers to hard work on the book and mentions that he has
"the background laid in" and five chapters completed.

        Then reference to it must have stopped and possibly
work on it, too, for Frank had to ask in November: "How
goes Immaturity?"   And then he follows the query with characteristic optimistic assurance that it will be his best work
to date.[14]

        Seven Arts having succumbed, Anderson and Frank
were at this time very eager to start its successor.   Early
in 1918, in a letter anticipating the character of the hoped-
for new journal, Frank says he does not want to have only
short fiction in the new magazine, that he wants to publish
Immaturity serially.[15]   Possibly in answer but certainly subsequently, Anderson made this comment about the book, which
must serve as its epitaph, for there is no further mention:

        My Immaturity will not be the book you expected.
        It has gone insane--a really delicious, garrulous,
        heavy lame fellow with shaggy eyebrows is writing
        it.   If he is successful, as I pray the Chicago
        smoke gods he will be, the whole world will be
        puzzled to know what he is talking about.   Perhaps
        you--if the current sets your way--will some day
        hug the shaggy awkward advertising man, for a
        baked bean concern, who is writing the book, to
        your heart.   If you do not, some one, some time
        will.   God help us all.[16]

        Two other unpublished novels, "Mary Cochran" and
"Talbot Whittingham, " were very possibly written in Elyria,
though his secretary could remember only Windy McPherson's
Son and Marching Men.   Anderson discussed them with Hansen:

Those earlier novels really belong to a period of
my writing that is past.   I couldn't go back to
work over material conceived in one mood when
my whole writing mood has passed on to something
else.   The earlier books--before Winesburg--were
too deeply influenced by the work of others; my
own mood as a writer did not appear clearly
enough. ...   The books frankly were not good.

Anderson further told Hansen that he had not broken the books
up into stories (as the appearance in "Unlighted Lamps" and
"The Door of the Trap" of the Mary Cochran of The Triumph
of the Egg might have suggested) but that the characters did
remain alive in his imagination and "insisted" on being put
into a story. 17

Though "Mary Cochran" was not published, it is possible to consider something of what it was.   An appraisal of
it by a publisher's reader (Marietta D. Finley: see Appendix
J) is available, and from it can be learned something of the
book's content and intent.   The reader first judges that
"Sherwood Anderson has literally delved into the depths of
life and set forth a large, realistic, tragically awful and at
the same time ironically trivial piece of life. "

Mary Cochran, born in a quiet New England village
as the daughter of an actress and a typical old
country doctor, passes through the various stages
of her career under the sympathetic eyes of the
reader.   Her monotonous girlhood in the village,
absorbed by the doctor's routine of business, homely living and humdrum dying; then her life in a
middle western university, her friends there and
the impressions made upon her mind by the professor, who is irresistibly attracted by her charm,
and the poet to whose abnormal desire she unconsciously appealed; and then her entry into and her
life in Chicago with its temptations, its lonelinesses, its infinite restlessness that settles down
upon Mary as a cloud obscuring her vision and
yet still blindly attracting her. ...

This novel is indisputably an intensely realistic
portrayal of a woman's inner life, her emotions
and her primitive instincts at war with existing
conditions.   Sherwood Anderson has attempted
through the life-history of an ordinary woman to

show the development of a new class of woman in
the world--that the hope of the world lies in its
quiet obscure working women of the Mary Cochran
type. They are to look upon work as an end in
life and not as a single expedient taken up to bridge
over the years before their marriage day or to
enable them to drive a better bargain in the marriage market. Among them will grow up finally a
horror of selling out at any price and a passion
for independence.

The reader also noted that "Chicago typifying any big city
with its miriad [sic] people, its vice and vanity, its tragedies and comedies, is described with the same realistic, effective detail that is so marked in 'Marching Men'. "

The first recorded reference to this book by Anderson
is a retrospective one of 1916:

Some time ago the true solution of Mary Cochran
came to me. She could not of course have married Sylvester. That I think quite clear. In the
new draft [indicating a revision of perhaps an
Elyria or other early form, which is what happened
to Marching Men] Mary will be left with the realization that she has done a big thing in accepting
work as her way out. She might have had Sylvester too had she been able to realize beauty in herself. [18]

A year and a half later, "When I came to look at my novel
Mary Cochran, written several years ago, it didn't suit me.
I shall hold it back for more work. "[19] In the summer of
the next year, 1919, he tells Huebsch that he has looked at
it and found that he "wanted to rewrite it almost entirely. "
He refers to it as having been written "several years ago, "
thinks it can be greatly improved, and that he believes he
can have it ready early in 1920. [20] In a letter at the end of
that year to Paul Rosenfeld, he reveals that he has been trying to work when he could on "my Mary Cochran book, written a long time ago. " And his final reference comes when
he tells Waldo Frank:

The tales that are to make the Mary Cochran book
are waiting like tired people on the doorstep of the
home of my mind. They are unclothed. I need to
be a tailor and make warm clothes of words for

them. [21]

The reference to "the tales" might be a little confusing, but this becomes clearer when one recalls the reader's, Miss Finley's, reference to the "undeniably episodic plot" and the fact that two Mary Cochran stories were published later. Evidently, whatever form the original manuscript was in, he could not make the stories into a satisfying unity, as he did with Winesburg. In any case, his character's seeking for fulfillment, her loneliness, her restlessness, her puzzlement, her need for understanding all make her a blood sister of her creator.

There is confusion about the history of the manuscript of "Talbot Whittingham," even though a sizable amount of material relating to this character has been saved, a number of pages being the reverse side of the Winesburg, Ohio manuscript in the Newberry Library. Some have thought most of what is in the Newberry, aside from the Winesburg reverse sides, is reworking done in the thirties. Hansen reported that Floyd Dell had had the Whittingham manuscript. [22] But Dell has written that he saw only a sample of 15 pages on tablet paper. [23] It is therefore fortunate that, as in the case of "Mary Cochran," a reader's report on "Talbot Whittingham" (in full in Appendix K) is available for study.

Miss Marietta D. Finley was again the reader who prepared the analysis. She begins by referring to the book as a "daring analysis of a master-character and of the elemental impulses, motives and experiences from which the artist within him is evolved." Near the end of the paper she states her conviction that the novel could become "a masterly depiction of the artist in modern times."

> Granting primarily that the artist in the world is abnormal: that his sensual, intellectual and spiritual natures are constantly warning against one another; that it is only by a transition of the grotesque that true beauty is arrived at: and that if and only if we have enough logic and sympathy to grant these ugly facts, we may arrive at somewhat of an understanding of this Talbot Whittingham.

The writer's use here of the word "grotesque" is particularly exciting to the reader of Winesburg, Ohio, otherwise known as "The Book of the Grotesque." Later in the reports are two more references, neither quoting from the book but

obviously representing the artistic concept presented in it.
"This project--another futile attempt to give birth to the artist, to free himself from the grotesque--is carried out by
Talbot...[who] through her horrible yet beautiful death...was
brought through the lusts and grotesqueness of the world to
life and beauty. "

The struggle of Talbot, it becomes clear, is the
struggle of Sherwood, who became more and more the student
of the way life twists all humans away from what he considered to be their well-formed natural shapes and inclina-
tions.   It is no accident that Miss Finley would find that, in
this book

> Talbot's life in the city from a business view-point
> was that of a dreamer among men; from the art-
> ist's that of a man with the "seeing-eye" and the
> "poet-soul" among the sleeping and the dead men;
> men sleeping away ideals and dead to purpose and
> to the inner meaning of life.   The latent artist in
> him, stimulated by the miriad [sic] sights and
> sounds, beauties and horrors of the city, fought for
> expression while the physical lusts of the primitive
> man, responding equally to the same stimuli, fought
> with and well-nigh conquered the artist.

Talbot comes to see that for him "the quest for beauty (the
anti-grotesque, the dream of life as it could and should be)
was to be...the end in life. "   And Talbot is quoted: "After
this I shall know everything and I shall have my work.   I
shall quit this marching with the dead.   I shall have my
thing to do. "

This revolt in dedication to the desired pattern of life,
which became the focus of the lives of Talbot and Sherwood,
is summed up in a long quotation from the book:

> During the history of any race of men there are
> born many men and women who have the vision of
> perfection and beauty that is in the eye of the art-
> ist [emphasis supplied], but who can produce no
> beauty.   Hesitating these figures stand on the very
> threshold of existence.   Having quite clearly in
> mind the vision or the act that is beautiful they do
> not act but look into the distance, lost in dreams.
> To-morrow, they say, I shall go forward, tomor-
> row I shall sing this song, love this love, hew

from this sone [sic] a thing that is beautiful.   They
are not dullards, the waiters upon the threshold of
life.   In a way they keep alive the sense of beauty
in the hearts of men.   They are not dullards and
at the last they are not artists.   Theirs is the
story of the man with the five talents who returned
them unspent to the master and was rebuked by
him. ----at the last they must know that he who
does not dare defeat comes to no victory, and that
all of the beauty in the world from the figure of
the Christ to the verses of John Keats is but proof
anew that out of the defeat of the dreams of men
comes the beauty that is art.

Aside from the surface similarities, which the reader
can trace for himself, between the lives of Talbot and Sherwood, the following quotation from the manuscript identifies
the exact role Anderson was enacting in society, whether it
was in Chicago or Elyria: "From whatever angle he approached it the life of Talbot Whittingham was a delicious
thing to him.   Down in the city he would show himself the
tired faces and the empty, meaningless lives of modern men,
warning the boy within to keep hidden away from it all, safely concealed within the self-reliant, capable man. "

The creation of this book may well have marked the
point in his life when Anderson brought to a conscious statement his developing realizations that desire, frustration, revulsion, incongruity, suffering, determination, disjuncture,
and sacrifice were all part of the need of the artist and that
the role of the artist was his "thing to do. "   The interest in
Winesburg, Ohio is in "the people of the outer fringe, " the
suffering, helpless, defeated, frustrated people, and such a
one is Lucile Bearing, "a little school teacher from Indiana,
who with ambition and hope had come to Chicago. "   Only
through her death "did the artist in him stand forth unfettered
by the world and the people of the world.   This woman,
though defeated in her purpose and in her life was to Talbot
a subtle, indefinable inspiration. "   And such a one was Wing
Biddlebaum, and Louise Trunnion, and May Edgley, and
Will Appleton, and Mary Cochran, and Sam McPherson and
Beaut McGregor and Tar Moorehead and Sherwood Anderson.

Notes

1.   Memoirs, p. 266.

2.   Letter to Waldo Frank, before Nov. 7, 1917, probably in October.   In the <u>Memoirs</u>, p. 265, Anderson recounts this matter as a whole episode, in which "a man from the Curtis office," in effect asks for a novel recognizing business success, as describes the first part of <u>Windy McPherson's Son</u>.

3.   <u>Ibid.</u>

4.   Letter to Frank, before Oct. 29, 1917.

5.   Letter from Frank, Oct. 29, 1917 (JR).

6.   Letter, Nov. 7, 1917.

7.   Letter to Marietta D. Finley, Dec. 21, 1916.

8.   It would appear that this letter, now dated as Sept. 1917 by the Newberry Library Anderson Collection, was written in May or before in that year.

9.   Letter to Waldo Frank, after Oct. 29, 1917 (JR).

10.   Letter to Frank, April 10, 1918.

11.   Letter to M. D. Finley, Jan. 1917.

12.   Letter to M. D. Finley, Jan. 12, 1917.

13.   Letter to Frank, Sept. 3, 1917.

14.   Letter from Frank, Nov. 18, 1917.

15.   Letter from Frank, early 1918.

16.   Letter to Frank, spring 1918.

17.   <u>Midwest Portraits</u>, p. 122-3.

18.   Letter to M. D. Finley, Oct. 25, 1916.

19.   Letter to Van Wyck Brooks, early April, 1918.

20.   Letter, Aug. 23, 1919.

21.   Letter, ca. Dec. 4, 1919.

22.   Midwest Portraits, p. 124.

23.   Letter from Dell, Feb. 5, 1964.

Mosaic XIII

"Into channels of beauty... "

If he is an artist he tries to divert the energy arising from
his lusts into channels of beauty.... Any artist worth
his salt has always been full of lusts.
from "What Say!" Marion Democrat, undated.

*   *   *

Those who are to follow the arts should have a training in
what is called poverty. Given a comfortable middle-
class start in life, the artist is almost sure to end up
by becoming a bellyacher, constantly complaining because the public does not rush forward at once to proclaim him.
from A Story Teller's Story, p. 5.

*   *   *

... an artist is no less an artist for breaking the cake of
custom and giving us back our moral freedom.
to Ferdinand Schevill, May 7, 1929.

*   *   *

The real artist does not think of himself as such. He is a
man--a brother. His art is simply his way of talking
to himself and to his brother--a solemn, holy way he
tries, when he has something solemn to say.
to Waldo Frank, 1917.

*   *   *

There is a woman hidden away in every artist. Like the
woman he becomes pregnant. He gives birth. When

339

the children of his world are spoken of rudely or
through stupidity, not understood, there is a hurt that
anyone who has not been pregnant, who has not given
birth, will not understand.
                    to Mrs. L. L. Copenhaver, undated.

      *   *   *

And then, besides, I adore hotel life.   There is a grand
freedom to it.   I find that, when a man works intensely,
as I always must to work at all, he is likely to be
irritable, and even nasty, until he recovers.   You
simply pick up the phone in your room and tell the girl
at the switchboard that you are out, for 2, 3, 4 hours
as you choose.   Then you read, walk up and down,
take a drink, do whatever you can to try to make yourself human again.
                    to Roger Sergel, fall 1936.

      *   *   *

He goes into the institute here and sees pictures that have
been painted by heavens knows what perplexed, drinking, weeping, laughing old fellow of long ago.   He
wants to paint like that and he wants to save his own
soul.
                    to M. D. Finley, Dec. 1, 1916.

      *   *   *

What we need is men perfectly willing to go to hell!   We
want men courageous enough to start on the road to
art by saying to God, "All right then send me to hell.
That is your affair.   It is my affair to try and find
out and to express what I really feel. "
                    to M. D. Finley, Dec. 1, 1916.

      *   *   *

It is only as he feels everything others feel, meets the same
discouragement, has the same disillusionment, eats the
same food, makes a fool of himself like others, does
mean and generous things like others, that the artist
can work at all.   If there is a separation it lies in the
ability to occasionally go more out of himself, away
from self and into others. . . .   There are times when
self is thus thrown away and, as we all want to escape

from self, we envy him in doing it.... And I don't
think, really, we should be too sorry for the artist who
happens to be let alone, not recognized. Recognition
has its terrible side too and starvation isn't the [worst]
fate man has to endure.

to Mary Emmett, Nov. 1938.

*   *   *

I am interested only in what you may be able to contribute
to the advancement of our mutual craft.
But why not call it an art. That is what it is.
Did you ever hear of an artist who had an easy
road to travel in life?

to George Freitag, Aug. 27, 1938 (JR).

*   *   *

Read the history of all men who had devotion. In the end
perhaps a man can only remain devoted to the intangi-
ble. Nature serves the purpose and woman is sometimes an exquisite manifestation of nature. I would not
want you to miss that but can understand its confusion.

to John S. Anderson, 1926?

*   *   *

...In the end art is the essential thing, I think. It is so
difficult. The road is so long. Sometimes it is a
tremendous easement to center it on some other person. Women want that, of course. I do not believe
that, at bottom, they have the least interest in art.
What their lover gives to work they cannot get.

to John S. Anderson, 1926?

*   *   *

"True poetry is accidental, " I cried. "It is like a flash of
lightning revealing something in the darkness, a wide
stretch of cornfields or two lovers embracing beneath
a tree. It should always be buried in prose. We
should make an end of the term poet and recognize
only writers. "

to M. D. Finley, Dec. 10, 1916.

It is all curious enough, God knows.   I think this is true,
     that if you do at all good work, in any art, you begin
     to disturb people.   Closeness to life always hurts.
     Well, you do not want to hurt but these darts fly out
     from under your pen wounding people.   It takes, I
     presume faith, that in the long end it won't hurt and
     may perhaps even heal.
               to Miriam Phillips, fall 1935.

*   *   *   *   *

Chapter 10

"THE ROAD IS SO LONG"

A. Windy McPherson and the Little Magazines

When Anderson's contract with the John Lane Company
to publish Windy McPherson's Son was drawn up in February,
1916, he had published nine articles and stories since he left
Elyria four years before, and only one of these eventually appeared in Winesburg, Ohio. (A complete bibliography of his
publications from 1913 through 1918 is in Appendix H.) Attention here will be given to his magazine outlets, especially
the Little Review and Seven Arts.

Anderson was to write, years later, to a "little magazine" editor,[1] "I hardly know just how a good many of us
would ever have got any start at all but for such magazines.
All my early stories were published in magazines that were
fighting the same kind of battle that I am sure you are fighting." He also thought, in retrospect, that his first connection with literature was through Margaret Anderson (no relation) and the Little Review,[2] which was inaugurated in Chicago in March, 1914, "devoted to the interest of literature,
drama, music, and art."[3] Sherwood Anderson had an article, "The New Note," in the first issue and a continuation of
it, "More about 'the New Note'," in the April edition. The
new note, he pointed out, was really as "old as the world."
Simply stated, it is a cry "for the reinjection of truth and
honesty into the craft...." Aside from sounding a ringing
challenge for artists to "demand for themselves the right to
stand up and be counted among the soldiers of the new," he
gives this evidence of the formulation of one of his most
basic attitudes:

> ...I myself believe that when a man can thus stand
> aside from himself, recording simply and truthfully
> the inner workings of his own mind, he will be pre-
> pared to record truthfully the workings of other

343

minds. In every man or woman dwell dozens of
men and women, and the highly imaginative individual will lead fifty lives.... The practice of constantly and persistently making such a record will
prove invaluable to the person who wishes to become a true critic of writing in the new spirit.
Whenever he finds himself baffled in drawing a
character or in judging one drawn by another, let
him turn thus in upon himself, trusting with child-
like simplicity and honesty the truth that lives in
his own mind.

Anderson is, in effect, holding forth for a particular
fictional method. He says that the practice he recommends
induces a "partnership... between the hand and the brain of
the writer," causing the writer to be what he is trying to depict or criticize. Then he cautions that this fundamentally
emotional approach, which he prefers to that of the writer
who "looks outside himself for his material" (Zola, Howells
were two examples), does not always work and the person
may "run into barren periods when the brain and the hand do
not coordinate." In such periods, he recommends, the writer should drop his work and begin again "patiently making a
record of the workings of [his] own mind, trying to put down
truthfully those workings during the period of failure.... I
would like to scold every one who writes or who has anything
to do with writing, into adopting this practice, which has
been such a help and such a delight to me." In any case,
he felt this was the way of Whitman, Tolstoi, Dostoevsky,
Twain, and Fielding, whose work he admired and of whom
one could say the man revealed the workings of his own soul
and mind.

Another article in the first issue of the Little Review
was by Cornelia, [4] who encountered the literary group surrounding Floyd Dell and his wife with Sherwood. She thought
them "brilliant, scintillating. I got on and rode." Margaret
Anderson asked both Cornelia and Marjorie Currie to write
an article on a book[5] which had dealt with a German salon
figure of the early nineteenth century. Cornelia has said
that both she and Marjorie submitted what were in effect
reviews; excerpts were than pieced together and the article
was published under her name. [6] One important significance
of this article seems to be its indication of Cornelia's still
being actively in his circle of friends at that time. Presumably the real decline of the marriage started soon thereafter.

Even though the Little Review was tremendously important to Anderson as a publishing outlet at first (consult Appendix H), it became eventually impossible for him.   On the last day of the year of 1918, he wrote to Dr. Trigant Burrow: "The poor little magazine called the Little Review will be publishing in a month or two a tale of mine called The Triumph of the Egg I am particularly anxious to have you see. "   Then he wrote him in January, 1919 (JR), that he had withdrawn the story, saying the magazine had become "too dreadfully inartistic and bad, " and that he did not want his work in it any more, also bemoaning the dearth of outlets for his kind of work.   The story appeared in Dial in 1920.

The period from April, 1914, to December, 1915, was one of non-publication, but from that time on there was something appearing nearly every month.   In the winter of 1915-1916, as will be discussed more fully later, he began to visualize and create the Winesberg stories and their format. In the middle of 1916, when Anderson had written a lot of stories, when he had a publication contract for Windy McPherson's Son, when he was in the process of divorce and remarriage, the Seven Arts magazine entered his life and with it his three very important literary and personal friends, Waldo Frank, Paul Rosenfeld, and Van Wyck Brooks, of whom Waldo Frank was the closest.

It was Waldo Frank who wrote the very encouraging article, "Emerging Greatness, " in the first issue of the Seven Arts in November, 1916.   This was in reaction to Windy McPherson's Son, published in October.   In the opening issue the magazine carried this notice:

> During the summer months we sent out the following statement to American authors:
>
> It is our faith and the faith of many, that we are living in the first days of a renascent period, a time which means for America the coming of that national self-consciousness which is the beginning of greatness.   In all such epochs the arts cease to be private matters; they become not only the expression of the national life but a means of its enhancement.
>
> Our arts show signs of this change.   It is the aim of The Seven Arts to become a channel for the flow of these new tendencies: an expression of our

American arts which shall be fundamentally an expression of our American life.

We have no traditions to continue; we have no school of style to build up. What we ask of the writer is simply self-expression without regard to current magazine standards. We should prefer that portion of his work which is done through a joyous necessity of the writer himself.

As Llewellyn Jones, one of the Little Review group, editor of the "Friday Literary Review" for the Chicago Evening Post, said: "There the live American artist may bring his offerings."[7]

Anderson saw immediately the congeniality of this medium to his work and in mid-November, 1916 (JR), wrote to Frank as follows:

I sent you a little thing the other day that I believe you will like. Here is a suggestion....

I made last year a series of intensive studies of people of my home town, Clyde, Ohio. In the book I called the town Winesburg, Ohio. Some of the stories you may think pretty raw and there is a sad note running through them. One or two of them get pretty closely down to ugly things of life. However, I put a good deal into the writing of them and I believe they, as a whole, come a long step toward achieving what you were asking for in the article you ran in Seven Arts.

Some of the things have been used. Masses ran a story called "Hands" from this series. Two or three also appeared in a little magazine out here called the Little Review. The story called "Queer" you are using in December is one of them.

This thought occurs to me. There are or will be seventeen of these studies. Fifteen are I believe completed. If you have the time and inclination I might send the lot to you to be looked over.

It is my own idea that when these studies are published in book form they will suggest the real environment out of which present day American youth is coming.

On November 20, he wrote Frank again to thank him for a check and for "liking the story of the farm hands," ("The Untold Lie") which was to appear in the January, 1917, issue.   Referring again to the Winesburg group:

> The other day I wrote you a letter concerning a series of stories written last winter.   I am sending two for you to look at.   Personally, I like the Enoch Robinson thing ["Loneliness"] better than anything I have done.

In the November issue, previewing the next one, was this note: "Waldo Frank has written with deep insight of the works of Sherwood Anderson in this issue.   A story by Mr. Anderson, 'Queer,' appears in December."

The next letter to Frank gives a touching view of the feeling Anderson could have toward one of his stories, "Loneliness," the one he had told Frank he liked particularly. Apparently Frank did not choose it, for it was published only in the Winesburg, Ohio collection:

> Damn it, I wanted you to like the story about Enoch Robinson and the woman who came into his room and was too big for the room.
>
> There is a story every critic is bound to dislike. I can remember reading it to Floyd Dell, and it made him hopping mad.   "It's damn rot," says Floyd.   "It does not get anywhere."...
>
> Why do I try to convince you of this story?   Well, I want it in Seven Arts.   A writer knows when [a] story is good, and that story is good.
>
> Sometimes when I'm in New York, I'll bring that story in, and I'll make you see it. 8

In February he did visit New York and met the men who were publishing Seven Arts: "I like the Seven Arts group very much indeed.   They are generous and fine and listened to my provincial middle western point of view with interest."9   The editor, James Oppenheim, was to recall of this visit: "I had built an Anderson out of the stories, a shy sort of fellow, a little mussed, slipping against the wall so

as not to occupy too much space. Instead of that I looked
straight at an up-and-coming ad man with a stiff collar, and
a bit of the super salesman air. "[10]   And Anderson took inspiration from it:

> Truth is you see I was on a mountain top in a
> peculiarly impersonal way.   I felt like one who has
> worked his way through the breakers and cross
> currents close to the shore and has got out into
> the open sea.   I loved it all and I felt people lov-
> ing me.   Now I shall be able to go back to work
> with new courage and new understanding. [11]

Before he had gone to New York he had given Frank
this view of himself:

> I am not a hack writer in the sense that I have to
> depend on what I write for bread and butter, but I
> pay the price just the same.   Eight hours a day I
> have paid, working as an advertising writer these
> last five years [1913-1917], while trying to save
> verve force and courage enough to admit other writ-
> ing.   It has cost me dearly in fine work destroyed,
> rare projects gone wrong because of lack of
> strength to get on with them, and all that sort of
> thing.
>
> But why should I tell you of my woes?   It is an
> old tale in the literary world.   I will, of course,
> abide by what you can pay.
>
> At the same time I do reserve the right to point
> out that you are not taking real venturesome things
> in the magazine and that you edit only a little more
> closely than the ordinary magazine editors. [12]

Two months later, March 2, 1917 (JR), he wrote to tell
Frank that he wanted to build up his name as rapidly as
possible for the sake of book sales and declared, also:

> I'm damned, Frank, if I am going to let you pull
> and haul among my stories, taking the cream at
> $40 per.   It isn't fair, and you know it.   I will
> send you stories one at a time, and you will ac-
> cept or reject.   Forget the notion that there is no
> other market for these things.   I've got offers on
> my desk for them now.   I believe in Seven Arts

and want to swim with you, but there is no reason
why I should give you this unseemly privilege. You
may consider this an overt act, but I'm going to
stand on it. Now, damn it, man, behave.

The friendly battles over what should be submitted and what
paid for them in no way interfered with the high esteem in
which Anderson was held. In May he was referred to as
representing "the new generation in the West," as a "constant contributor," and "author of Windy McPherson's Son
and many authentic short stories." In September the editors
pointed out that his "many stories... have established 'Winesburg, Ohio' or the type of the Middle-western town."

When the sponsor, Mrs. A. K. Rankine, withdrew her
support in the fall of 1917, because the magazine objected
editorially to entrance into World War I, Anderson was greatly agitated. His letter on learning that the October issue
was to be the last one is full of questions and suggestions as
to how the magazine could or should be continued: "Can't
you and Brooks interest some one in the idea of buying the
property?" But he could also say: "It is strange that in
discussing all the dangers to Seven Arts we never thought of
her ladyship running away with the moneybags."13 The importance of Seven Arts registered so strongly with him that
at the end of 1918 he was searching for the June issue, the
only one he was missing. And then he wrote of the end of
the next year that he had had the complete set bound into a
book. "It is so caracteristic [sic] of me that now I read
Seven Arts for the first time. I have been reading your
[Frank's] articles. It is striking how often you have been a
voice for me...."14

There were, in this period, three other kinds of short
publication which must be mentioned before the creation of
his four books (Chapter 10) can be considered. The two
articles in Agricultural Advertising in February and March
of 1913 serve as sufficient reminder that he was a writing
advertiser during almost all of this time. "Rabbit-pen,"
which is the first identifiable story published, in Harper's,
in July, 1914, presents certain problems which it is still
hoped may be solved. Anderson indicates that he wrote it,
submitted it, and received word of its publication while still
in Elyria. This story has a real interest when it is seen
that it contains a heavy note of frustration and criticism.
Certainly one can see how it was written by the author of
"An Apology for Crudity," which appeared in the Dial and

the Chicago Daily News during November, 1917. In the
"crudity" article, Anderson lays stress on the idea that the
artist must live as people generally live and be concerned
with that life in their writings: "Your true novelist is a
man gone a little mad with the life of his times." Because
the character of his time is primarily industrial and is accordingly basically ugly, the beauty of modern writing will
come in its recording of the truth, he thinks. While "Rabbit-pen" is rather cultivated and domestic, it deals with a
crisis of sorts in an upper-class family, the mother failing
as a disciplinarian, being shown up by the German housekeeper, who is realistic, earthily effective, and who marries
the stableman. True, this is a highly-watered-down version
of the concern with the impulses of life as treated in "Vibrant
Life," for example, published in the March, 1916, Little Review, in which the sexuality leads to the picturing of a stallion on the cover of a farm magazine, and even becomes a
little melodramatic when rampant lust overturns a coffin.
But the same factors are a cocooned concern in "Rabbit-
pen," which opens with a minor but dramatic scene of death
in the rabbit pen. Sex, representing actual life, is seen as
violent, powerful, important in all of these early publications, and it will certainly be seen in the three novels and
a book of poems to which we now turn.

Windy McPherson's Son (September 1, 1916)

Sherwood Anderson had written Windy McPherson's
Son "one winter" in Elyria. Very probably parts of it were
among the things he read aloud to friends in his home there.
Certainly he took the manuscript to Chicago with him and
read from it. One of the main memories of his friends in
Chicago is his reading from his manuscripts, and Windy and
the Winesburg stories are the items recalled. He had been
trying to publish in Elyria. Indeed, reading aloud is a short
first step in that direction. It was through his reading to
his friends in Chicago and their eventual reading of the manuscript that the book was published. Cornelia said that they
went to the Ozarks at the beginning of the winter of 1913-
1914 on the strength of a publication agreement. Both Dell
and Hansen report an early acceptance of Windy. Howe
specifies that in 1913 Anderson sent this book to Alfred Harcourt, then an editor at Henry Holt & Company, who accepted
it with the proviso that "changes be made in its clumsy
style."[15] Cornelia thought the publisher "reneged," but all

other accounts indicate that Anderson would not accept revision.

When Dell, who first encountered the manuscript in the apartment of his wife, went to New York in the fall he learned from Harcourt that Anderson had agreed to have work done on it by a professional writer. Dell recalled that Sherwood spoke bitterly about a revision he had evidently paid a woman to make. Dell believed the typescript he took with him to New York to look for a publisher was the reviser's typescript, because it did not seem to be a manuscript in need of revision. 16 Because he saw in Anderson "not promise, it was accomplishment,"17 Dell, who believed thoroughly in its publishability, worked at his agent's task in New York. Dell offered it to various publishers, including Macmillan, which was the first to turn it down. "My impression is that all the publishers kept it a long time and were reluctant in passing it up."18 Dell eventually became discouraged over the prospects in the New York market and decided to send it to Grant Richards in London; "he wrote that if it were not for war conditions he would like to publish it; I asked him to send it to John Lane, who did accept it, publishing it through their American branch."19

The role of Theodore Dreiser in these negotiations is not clear, but that he was trying to help Anderson, though their correspondence indicates they had not met, is clear. On May 10, 1915, Anderson wrote to "Dear Mr. Dreiser," in care of John Lane Company, telling him that John Lane Company had written him with reference to Marching Men, which he reported was under consideration by Macmillan.

> I am writing you to thank you for your courtesy in suggesting me to the John Lane Company. I have some other novels finished but will not want to submit any of them to any one until the Macmillan Company make their decision.

As was noted earlier, after John Lane accepted Windy, Anderson wrote to Dreiser, saying he would not have to impose on him by getting him to read it. He wrote a similar letter, on January 21, 1916, to Henry L. Mencken.

Aside from whatever change the manuscript doctor made, Dell has written that he made one, too.

> I forget whether it was five or seven orphans that

Sam McPherson brought back to his wife. I thought
that was overdoing it.... I did not want to argue
with the author about it. I just cut one of the
pages in two with a pair of scissors, and pasted it
on a blank sheet of paper, so that the book ended
with Sam taking the three children to Sue; the rest
I put away in the drawer of my desk; the author
would do as he pleased about it when he read the
proof. And it was thus I sent the book to England.... I never told Sherwood what I had done
about his last chapter. [20]

According to the contract drawn up on February 28,
1916, between Anderson and the John Lane Company, he was
to furnish the publisher with a "full and complete" manuscript
of Windy McPherson's Son on or before April 1, 1916. He
agreed to give the publisher "first refusal" of three "full
length novels," the publisher to have an option to publish for
thirty days after the delivery of the manuscript. The author
was to get ten per cent of the retail price on sales up to
5,000; 12.5 per cent from 5,000 to 10,000; fifteen per cent
thereafter. On dramatic or motion picture rights he was to
get fifty per cent. [21] Jefferson Jones of the John Lane Company informed Hansen that the September 1, 1916, printing
was 2,500 copies, of which 1,000 were sent in sheets to
England. Encouraged by a good initial reception, the publisher printed 1,000 more copies in February, 1917. However, the demand stopped abruptly when 1,800 copies had
been sold. [22]

Within a month after Windy McPherson's Son had been
published, Anderson wrote an article in response to a request from The Chicago Daily News that he discuss it. [23] Most
revealing of his state of mind concerning the book is the following portion of that article:

As to my novel, Windy McPherson's Son, it isn't
a job of writing that comes up to my own ideas as
to what a novel should be. Perhaps I think it isn't
loose and disorderly enough to reflect the modern
American life. To do that it should read as the
elevated trains sound as they turn out of Van Buren
Street into Wabash Avenue. My people are not
enough alive. They are not enough American. I
have written and am writing other books. Perhaps
I shall do the job yet. Who can tell?

Otherwise he starts his essay by saying he believes "progress toward a vital American literature" could be made by allowing each new author to write half a dozen books and then sending him into exile, where he could neither talk of his books nor hear of them. He says no one can write effectively of his own work. "The nut of the thing lies in this--if you read my book and the characters seem real, living and vital to you, then for you it is a good book. If the people do not seem real, then for you it is a bad book."

He continues in the Daily News article to mention two major difficulties he thinks novelists face. "The novelist's art is a reflective art and there is no feeling for the reflective mood among us.". . . "And then we do not want to face the truth. No cry for truth goes up from us. From our novelists we demand only a rigid and unflinching sentimentality."

Of his attitude toward his reader he says:

> I feel like one who brings a troop of friends into your house, and I dare say I stand about a little anxious. I want you to like my people, to be interested in them, to take them into your lives and think about them. Perhaps you can solve the problems they meet and that I have not solved.

When he reads, he gets "the same kind of satisfaction that I get from looking back into the intimate things of my own life. If in their writing these men [specifically Fielding and Borrow] did not get to any definite place neither have I with my own life. It is enough that we are moving and living."

Hansen sums up rather well the attitude that underlies all of Anderson's artistic endeavor: "He was trying to apply his philosophy that life is not a mean thing to be tamed and held to hard and fast canons, but a beautiful, wild thing of ecstasies and dreams, something that must be lived deeply to be understood."[24] Anderson thought that the artist had a "rendezvous with purity" and that "to gain and hold purity in the midst of modern life is terribly hard. . . . One only succeeds occasionally, at odd moments, when one writes fervently, when one runs in the snow, when pure physical love finds natural expression, when one maintains friends in the midst of difficulty and misunderstanding."[25] He agreed with a quotation from Romain Rolland, which he had seen in Seven Arts, that it was important to achieve free, sincere, entire

self-expression, that originality and form must not rule, that
opinion must be fearless. [26] He thought he was "full of the
spirit of the times," realized that he could "be an American"
only by "remaining a part of the blood and spirit of all this
aimlessness," felt he had "a thousand beautiful children...
unborn" in him. [27] As will be noted, those ideas are as of
1916, several years after the time of writing but appropriate
to the time of publication of Windy. In retrospect he was to
say of the book that it was written in reaction against businessmen and with concern for "my former associates, the
workers," believing that he had been involved in "sentimental
liberalism": "For a time I did dream of a new world to
come out of some revolutionary movement that would spring
up out of the mass of people. "[28] In another statement Anderson wrote, "my own nature was in revolt against money
making as an end in life and the history of Sam McPherson
is the history of such a revolt." The later part of the book,
he adds, "represents my own floundering about in life. "[29]

Not surprisingly, the character of the book fits Anderson's avowed intentions quite well. While the book ostensibly
is about the rise and confusion in business of Anderson's
representative self, Sam McPherson, the local boy who made
good, it is, by indirection, deeply concerned with the artist
and his function and fate. John Telfer, the "high light" of
Sam's home town, Caxton, says "the artist is one who hungers and thirsts after perfection" (page 13). [30] The man of
genius "has a purpose independent of all the world, and
should cut and slash and pound his way toward his mark,"
again according to Telfer (page 69) who also bemoans the
fact that he failed to become "an artist fixing the minds of
thousands upon some thing of beauty or of truth" (page 71).
Sam, though he has no artistic desire at any time in the
book, is torn between his hunger for materialistic success
and the kind of self-realization which is part of the artist.
He believes "that all society had resolved itself into a few
sturdy souls who went on and on regardless" (page 73).

Part of the perfectionism implicit in the novel is the
expectancy of a discernible logic or pattern in existence,
something Anderson had relinquished sufficiently by the time
of its publication that he could write: "It is enough that we
are moving and living." Anderson uses Telfer to make the
occasion of Sam's mother's death an indication of how he
thinks problems should be treated logically. Briefly, instead
of going to the funeral and following the conventional pro-
cedures, Telfer sends Sam a note which contains the

statement: "In her memory I will hold a ceremony in my
heart. " Sam, who has devoted himself to the search for the
truth, is unhappily convinced that "all life was abortive, that
on all sides of him it wore itself out in little futile efforts
or ran away in side currents, that nowhere did it move
steadily, continuously forward, giving point to the tremendous
sacrifice involved in just living and working in the world"
(pages 277-278). In discussing millionaires, the narrator
informs the reader that "They wanted power and were, many
of them, entirely unscrupulous, but for the most part they
were men with fire burning within them, men who became
what they were because the world offered them no better outlet for their vast energies" (pages 232-233). Sam, additionally, feels there is maturity and manhood somewhere abroad
and wonders why he can not have it.

   Sam, who feels the lyrical impulses of the artist, is
depicted as unknowingly fighting a "battle in which the odds
were very much against the quality in him which wanted to
get out of bed to look at the snow-clad vacant lot" (page
139). He watches two bedraggled and exhausted Guinea hens
intermittently fighting and thinks they represent the "pointless
struggle" of man against the overwhelming backdrop of nature (page 292). Sam surveys the unsatisfactory scene and
is not without hope. He considers himself a new man and
declares: "I do not accept your ideas of life just because
you say they are good any more than I accept Windy McPherson just because he happens to be my father" (page 39). Quite
considerably later in his life Sam "began again to quarrel
with life and what life had offered him. He thought that always he would stubbornly refuse to accept the call of life
unless he could have it on his own terms, unless he could
command and direct it... " (page 333). When he revised the
ending of Windy, Anderson had the narrator say of Sam:
"Perhaps life wanted acceptance from him but he could not
accept" (page 344). The deviation between what Sam thinks
life could and should be and what he finds it to be provides
the tension which makes Sam run.

   In the book Sam is distracted from his enormously
energetic and ambitious business career by his marriage to
Sue. The marriage is given a very idealistic basis. Telfer
has taught Sam that sex and women are antithetical to man's
full achievement. In one of his formative discussions with
Telfer, he cries, "To Hell with women and girls, " as though
"throwing something distasteful out of his throat" (page 73).
If the events of the Elyria period, the fact of when the book

was written, and the disastrous effect upon his marriages of
his artistic drive all are kept in mind, the significance of
the principles enunciated for the union of Sue and Sam will
be inescapable.

> At bottom, his mind did not run strongly toward
> the idea of the love of women as an end in life; he
> had loved, and did love, Sue with something ap-
> proaching religious fervour, but the fervour was
> more than half due to the ideas she had given him
> and to the fact that with him she was to have been
> the instrument for the realization of those ideas.
> (Pages 221-222.)

At the moment when Sue decides to marry him, it seems to
Sam that "all the vague shadowy uncertainties that had, in
reflective moments, flitted through his mind, were to be
brushed away" (page 284).   Like her he wanted more than
the feel of another person in his arms.   Ideas rushed through
his head; he thought that she was going to give him some
bigger idea than he had ever known.

The idea Sue gave him "was one of service to mankind through children. "   She wanted Sam because she wanted
a man who would be the father of "children who do things. . . .
The idea seemed wonderfully simple and beautiful to Sam.
It seemed to add tremendously to the dignity and nobility of
his feeling for her" (pages 187-188).   Anderson reverses
Sam's attitude so that he thinks of his former attitude toward
women and sex as perverted.   "Sex is a solution, not a
menace--it is wonderful, " Sam tells himself.   Anderson adds:
"without knowing fully the meaning of the words that had
sprung to his lips" (page 191).

Furthermore, Sam tells Sue: "Marriage is a part, a
beginning, a point of departure, from which men and women
go forth upon the real voyage of life. "   And he says this
"peep into the great mystery. . . justifies us" (page 194).   After the marriage has partly run its course and after many
other adventures, Anderson has Sam consider the "unhealthy
hungry look" of sexual desire which he has seen and known.
"He wondered how much that eager aching hunger stood in
the way of men's getting hold of life and living it earnestly
and purposefully, as he wanted to live it, and as he felt all
men and women wanted at bottom to live it" (page 311).

The marriage is ideal.   The honeymoon, for example

is controlled and thoughtful, in a beautiful natural setting.
But when the joy of pregnancy appears, it brings with it
problems as well.   Sue, normally reasonable, has an hysterical reaction.   Even after Sam understands what is happening:

> Although they were together facing the first of the
> events that were to be like ports-of-call in the
> voyage of their lives, they were not facing it with
> the same mutual understanding and kindly tolerance
> with which they had faced smaller things in the
> past--a disagreement over the method of shooting
> a rapid in the river or the entertainment of a dis-
> agreeable guest.   The inclination to fits of temper
> loosens and disarranges all the little wires of life.
> The tune will not get itself played.   One stands
> waiting for the discord, strained missing the har-
> mony.   (Page 208).

After the catastrophe in their lives, Anderson comments in such a manner that it is possible to consider his
using, not in an obeisant, but an unconscious, or basic way,
the pattern of Greek tragedy:

> The blow given the plan of life so carefully thought
> out and so eagerly accepted by the young McPher-
> sons threw them back upon themselves.   For seve-
> ral years they had been living on a hill top, taking
> themselves very seriously and more than a little
> preening themselves with the thought that they were
> two very unusual and thoughtful people engaged
> upon a worthy and ennobling enterprise.   Sitting in
> their corner immersed in admiration of their own
> purposes and in the thoughts of the vigorous, dis-
> ciplined, new life they were to give the world by
> the combined efficiency of their two bodies and
> minds, they were, at a word and a shake of the
> head from Doctor Grover, impelled to remake the
> outline of their future together.   (Page 220.)

Anderson very gently but firmly envelopes Sam and
Sue in a drastic and ironic web.   They are noble, but they
are proud.   The tragedy is that Sue can not successfully
produce the children through which their lives were to gain
purpose, and after two desperate efforts they are forced to
stop trying.   The thought that they could not successfully
produce children never had occurred to them.   Anderson,

even though he can on occasion accuse himself of sentiment-
alism, is quietly very harsh about this matter.   Both Sam
and Sue are savagely hurt by what befalls them and take
years to recover, their lives perhaps being pulled together
at last with the children of someone else, and not a very
noble someone else, at the end of the book.   The essence
of Greek tragedy is that man controls little of his fate, and
Sam and Sue are exposed to the same lesson.   And Anderson
is presenting the picture through the lens of his own ambitions to superimpose his pattern on existence.

        Anderson was keenly aware of nature, even though
his concern was centrally the people who live in nature,
which he saw both as an unrelenting adversary and as possessing admirable beauty and power.   Fields of corn are
ubiquitously a matter of concern to Anderson; in this book he
sees them as "armies of standing corn which man had set up
in the fields to protect themselves against the march of piti-
less Nature...." (page 73).   But he also likes nature men-
acing:

> Now, lifting up his head, he looked about with de-
> light.   Trees in the grove in front of him bent and
> tossed in the wind.   The inky blackness of the
> night was relieved by the flickering oil lamp in the
> road beyond the graveyard and, in the distance, by
> the lights streaming out at the windows of the
> houses.   The light coming out of the house against
> which he stood made a little cylinder of brightness
> among the pine trees through which the raindrops
> fell gleaming and sparkling.   An occasional flash
> of lightning lit up the trees and the winding road,
> and the cannonry of the skies rolled and echoed
> overhead.   A kind of wild song rang in Sam's
> heart. (Page 26.)

It is not surprising that Sam grew into a man who would
watch Lake Michigan on stormy nights: "Great masses of
water moving swiftly and silently broke with a roar against
wooden piles, backed by hills of stone on earth, and the
spray from the broken waves fell upon Sam's face and on
winter nights on his coat... leaning upon the railing of the
bridge [he] would stand for hours... looking at the moving
waters, filled with awe and admiration at the silent power of
it" (pages 126-127).   Having in his consciousness such impressions as these, Sam believes that "we sprang from the
big clean new land, and yet the American cities are as ugly

and dirty as the older world metropolises.... Will mankind always go on with that old aching, queerly expressed hunger in its blood, and with that look in its eyes? Will it never shrive itself and understand itself, and turn fiercely and energetically toward the building of a bigger and cleaner race of men?" (Page 312.)

On the one hand the cleanness and power and pattern of nature were satisfactory, even inspirational. But Windy McPherson is used in the book to represent those natural phenomena, those human accidents, those normal, routine events and practices which can not be accepted. The evidence that Irwin Anderson separated himself from his first group of children and went on to make a new life is distinct. Whether he left his children or they rejected him or both participated in the widening of the gap is not known, but the latter seems probable. Irwin's new marriage, his new life in a different place was a matter of personal survivorship, perhaps. The negative attitude shown in this book was doubtless shared by Karl and perhaps most of the other children. Ray seems to have been living in Dayton when his father died there. Karl said specifically that he did not see him after his father left Clyde. There is no evidence of any relationship between Anderson and his father after the Clyde period, either. It must be recalled that Irwin was still living both when Windy McPherson's Son was written and when it was published and for several years thereafter. It is most likely that the old man never knew a book had been written about him, or rather using him as a point of departure for an analysis of life.

Long after he wrote Windy, Anderson wrote an article in which he said he had come to understand and accept his father. [31] The fact is that he had discovered his father quite early and completely and knew him quite well. He was in many ways almost a carbon copy of his father and must have known it. The main trouble with Irwin Anderson was that he hated routine; he was subject to impulsive desires to do things he wanted to rather than those that others needed him to do or that he said he would do. A capable workman, he simply could not be depended upon to get a job done, because he might not feel like working. He was a watcher and wonderer, too. He told stories that were not true because the reality did not suit him. As a parent he was completely irresponsible. In these and in other ways his bright, aggressive children, inexperienced with frustration and failure, found him unsatisfactory, perhaps despicable. A demanding Sam will not accept Windy McPherson. In the book he

degrades the father image unmercifully and even entertains
the desirability of destructive physical action. The braggart
Windy irresponsibly donates Sam's hard-earned money grand-
iloquently, as "one of the boys of '61'," for a Fourth of July
celebration, maneuvers his way into a degrading failure as
the incompetent bugler on the white horse in the parade.
Actually Irwin Anderson was a good enough musician to be
warned by his father as early as 1877 to be careful about
spending too much time with the band. Windy is a drunkard
and simply does not provide. The status of the actual Anderson family was considerably above the status Sherwood
assigned it in his "autobiographical" writings. There was
never any need, it seems, for the kind of physical attack
Sam makes on Windy when he leaves Caxton.

One reason for the intense negativity of the picture of
Windy, then, is that he is a scapegoat mechanism for the
attempt, unsuccessful, to exorcise those characteristics that
Anderson found to be undesirable and yet strong in himself.
Windy's trouble was that he lived first of all for himself. If
he ever considered others very much, it was not when Sherwood knew him. The extraordinary egotism which is an
essential of the artist's makeup is seen in Sherwood Anderson. Those who knew him, lived with him, worked with
him, loved him, all found that there was a core of his own
reaction and purpose which came first. His father was a
dreamer, a failure, a windbag. The son, who was very
much like him, had to make a poet out of the dreamer, an
independent critic of society out of the failure, and an imaginative artist out of the windbag. The use of the figure of
his father in this book is an articulation of a rather harrow-
ing struggle which continued for a major portion of his life.

A corollary to this denigration of his father is his
idealization of his mother, whom the evidence seems to show
was hardly the person of "keen observations on the life about
her" which would have awakened in him "the hunger to see
beneath the surface of lives." Rather than being a person
who saw beneath the surface, she was one who accepted the
pattern of the life of a mother in her day with rather remarkable placidity under the circumstances. Irwin Anderson
was something other than a good provider, and Sherwood reported he was unfaithful and made him, fictionally, an al-
coholic. Emma Anderson's solution seems to have been to
get the children to work hard to make up the difference.
Both the real and fictional mothers seem to have accepted
conventional religion. Emma Anderson was the Christian

woman in Clyde, and it was with his mother, Jane, that Sam
McPherson got his experience with religion, against which he
revolted.   Incidentally, it is not to be thought that Anderson
was unconcerned with, or negative to, Christianity or religion
generally.   He was opposed, however, to worship routines as
he found them.   He did not feel he could benefit from them.
There is a good deal of concern with the significance of the
Christ concept to man in Windy McPherson's Son.   There is
no evidence that Jane McPherson, or Emma Anderson, would
have encouraged any individualized probing.   If she were the
one who encouraged him to work, and she may not have
been, she was encouraging him in the most routine and un-
thinking of processes.   She seems to have been the customarily devoted, sympathetic, and reliable mother figure.   Anderson needed her, at least to some extent by default, when
he was a child.   He evidently needed women with a maternal
outlook all his life, as indeed many do.   But his need in
this area was greater than most.   In his role as an artist,
he was constantly looking for an angel, someone to make an
exception of him, to relieve him of the necessity of producing
and providing in the way required of others.   And it was, of
course, Emma who kept the home going when Irwin could not
be bothered.   And it seems to have been that Emma was
accepting and hard-working and completely sacrificed to her
family.   It should be noted that Sherwood, in the name of
art, permitted Cornelia to devote her life to his children,
though with less drastic results.

Lest it be thought that too much emphasis might be
placed on the relationship of Anderson's book to his family
life, attention is directed to the focus supplied by the title.
Sam McPherson is not solely himself.   He has to be considered as coming from an unacceptable and clearly identified source.   The book is not The Possibly Successful Struggle of Sam McPherson or The Son of Jane McPherson.   The
relationship to the non-performing braggart is emphasized.

The reader of Anderson must be struck with his sense
of paradox and ambivalence.   His treatment of Windy allows
the presentation of a good example of it: "There is a little
of Windy McPherson's grotesque pretentiousness in every
man and his son soon learned to look for and take advantage
of it. "   In his fully-developed concept of the grotesque, as
presented in Winesburg, Ohio, he explains that people become
grotesque by taking a truth and living with it too intensively.
As has been suggested, Anderson wanted to be the imaginative artist rather than the windbag.   He wanted to be a

mystic instead of an irresponsible individualist.   He was
motivated very deeply by his own desire to establish that
balance of factors which would enable him to escape being a
grotesque.   And he seems to recognize, in the midst of a
very bitter and negative remedial portrait of his father, that
the elder was at once the source of his own strengths and
his own weaknesses.

Another factor quarried rather directly from his own
experience and employed prominently in this book was that of
emotional reactions of such intensity as to involve a desire
to escape completely from the current situation.   The great
example of this was the Elyria "amnesia" attack.   Perhaps
the stamping on the straw hat in Clyde was a minor manifestation of the same thing.   When Sam nearly kills his
father, he finds that the "terrible and unexpected hatred had
paralysed his brain," and he finds himself some time later
fighting to "regain control of his mind" (page 95).   When
Sam hears malicious, untrue gossip about a friend, he
springs forward and knocks a man over an iron fence (pages
109-110).   The most violent reaction occurs when Sam, after
viewing his wife's miscarriage, runs wildly through the
streets of Chicago.   He thinks a passing policeman is going
to arrest him for the murder of his wife (who lives).   "Again
he stopped before a little frame drugstore on a corner, and
sitting down on the steps before it cursed God openly and
defiantly like an angry boy defying his father."   In his wan-
derings he spends some time riding in an empty coal car,
gets off somewhat bothered, sits on the earth, thinking,
among other things, "of the night when he had felt the throat
of his father between his fingers in the squalid little kitchen."
He sleeps on the open ground in a park, wakes the next
morning with a "strained, eager feeling like some one listening for a faint call out of the distance."   Finally, he stag-
gers, delirious, to his home and lapses into two weeks of
unconsciousness (pages 216-219).   Not quite so closely patterned after Anderson's own experience was the device which
provided the basis for the last hundred pages of the book.
At the very point of successfully concluding the consolidation
of his arms company with another, the pinnacle of his fantastic business success, Sam McPherson writes on a sheet
of paper: "The best men spend their lives seeking truth."

> He went to his apartment and packed a bag and
> from there disappeared saying goodbye to no one.
> In his mind was no definite idea of where he was
> going or what he was going to do.   He knew only

that he would follow the message his hand had
written.   He would try to spend his life seeking
truth.   (Page 255.)

The collection of random, rambling experiences which follow
is a panorama of the America Anderson knew and imagined,
much of which he had seen in his travels as a salesman.

There are, of course, many Clyde elements in Anderson's conception of Caxton, Sam's home town.   The book is
dedicated "to the living men and women of my own middle
western home town. "   "Sam felt that in a way he was a child
of Caxton.   Early it had taken him to its bosom; it had made
of him a semi-public character; it had encouraged him in his
money-making, humiliated him through his father, and pat-
ronised him lovingly because of his toiling mother. "   (Pages
107-108.)   After he has finished going through, car by car,
selling newspapers on a train which has stopped in Caxton,
"Off the last car dropped Sam McPherson, a smile upon his
lips, the bundle of newspapers gone, his pocket jingling with
coins.   The evening's entertainment for the town of Caxton
was at an end" (page 16).   It is Clyde as much as anywhere
he has in mind in one two-page arraignment which focuses
its attention on a "class of women" in every city and village,
"the thought of whom paralyses the mind. "   "They live lives
of unspeakable blankness. . . .   In these women there is no
light, no vision.   They have instead certain fixed ideas to
which they cling with a persistency touching heroism. . . .
They do not love, they sell, instead their bodies in the market place and cry out that man shall witness their virtue
because they have had the joy of finding one buyer instead of
the many of the red sisterhood. . . .   For the most part they
live and die unseen, unknown, eating rank food, sleeping
much, and sitting through summer afternoons rocking in
chairs and looking at people passing in the street" (pages
111-113).

Caxton does have its saving grace in the person of
John Telfer, whose original was identified earlier as John
Tichenor, the artist and intellectual in Clyde.   Telfer intro-
duces Sam McPherson to the artistic concept of life as opposed to the commercial, as was noted earlier.   And this
book even contains a version of the participation of Anderson
with Tichenor in Allatoona:

In the performance Sam had taken the role of a
drummer boy killed on the field of battle by a

swaggering villain in a gray uniform, and John Telfer, in the role of the villain, had become so in
earnest that, a pistol not exploding at a critical
moment, he had chased Sam about the stage trying
to hit him with the butt while the audience roared
with delight at the realism of Telfer's rage and at
the frightened boy begging for mercy.   (Pages 164-
165.)

Other Clyde echoes include the "ex-Caxton family
named Pergrin that had been in Chicago for several years,"
(page 122) obviously reminiscent of the Paden family.   The
threshing crew experience (pages 285-286) doubtless had its
original in Clyde days, possibly in that summer after the
Spanish-American War.   A sex-initiation scene (pages 63-65)
is like that found in many other books, notably in that the
female is the aggressor.   And he includes the anecdote of
"a fierce old woman" and the tramp and the rider, based on
his memory of his Grandma Myers (pages 88-89).[32]

A major part of the book occurs in Chicago, in which
he had lived and worked.   His experience laboring in a
warehouse near the lakefront is used (page 134) and his description of the vice district (pages 312-316) is a forerunner
of his greater concern with the same subject in Marching
Men.   As a financier, Sam has much to do with men like
Morris whom Anderson must have modeled on his colleagues
in the advertising business.   Chicago reviewers were quick
to note the way he portrayed their city.

There are other, relatively unimportant items, such
as the "young minister, who was a graduate of a Lutheran
seminary at Springfield, Ohio": his own Wittenberg.   Mary
Underwood represents the teacher-confidant, who might be
modeled on a Clyde teacher (no evidence) or on Trillena
White, the Wittenberg teacher with whom he maintained correspondence for several decades, but who seems never to
have been a close friend.   The "huge red-faced woman" encountered on a spree in Wisconsin may be some sort of relative to the "Mama Geighen," of whom all Anderson's friends
spoke.   "Something had to be stated out of me in Windy,"
he was to declare later,[33] and the overt evidence of the way
he ranged over the personal realities of his life in doing it
is impressive.

Windy McPherson's Son was published once again, in
1922, and something must be said of his revision of it at that

time. Just after its first publication, he admitted to Waldo Frank that he did not know "how to end a novel."[34] Dell is on record as having "cut one of the pages in two with a pair of scissors"[35] to reduce the number of children the character Sam would take home to his wife upon the occasion of their reconciliation.

The revision of pages 335-347 of the original edition, according to letters to Huebsch,[36] took place during 1921. He says in one letter that he and Sam "tiptoed out of the book," having "laid on the reader's doorstep a basket containing some three children picked up during one of Sam's periods of debauchery."[37] He says he wants to take the children back to St. Louis in the revised printing. But he did not change the basic events of the two chapters in Book IV at all. In both books the story deals with Sam's going to St. Louis, meeting a woman on a roistering boat trip, going about the town with her, and finally arriving at her home, meeting her two sons and a daughter. He gets the woman to sign the children over to him so that he can take them back to Chicago and Sue, his wife, whom he had not seen for several years. She accepts him and the children, and life is to go on. The revision added two pages to the book. It seems futile to detail the changes here, but it may be said they involved everything from minor emendations to insertions several pages long and excisions as long as several paragraphs. Approximately fifty per cent remained as it was. The addition of a net of two pages results in a generally better explanation of Sam's attitudes while the removal of two references to Tom Sawyer and Huckleberry Finn result in a less literary flavor.

Notes

1.   Robert J. Lowery, The Little Man; undated letter.

2.   Letter to Oscar H. Fidell, Jan. 9, 1933 (JR).

3.   Chicago Evening Post, March 20, 1914. Contributors whose names were noted: John Galsworthy, Floyd Dell, Margery Currey, Nicholas Vachel Lindsay, Llewellyn Jones, George Burnham Foster, DeWitt C. Wing, Arthur Davison Ficke, "and several others."

4.   "Some Contemporary Opinions of Rahel Varnhagen."

5.   Ellen Karolina Sofia Key, Rahel Varnhagen: a portrait. Tr. from the Swedish by Arthur G. Chater, with intro. by Havelock Ellis. New York, Putnam, 1913.

6.   Interview with Cornelia Lane Anderson, Oct. 10, 1916.

7.   Sept. 22, 1916, p. 11.

8.   Letter to Waldo Frank, Dec. 14, 1916 (JR).

9.   Letter to Marietta D. Finley, Feb. 20, 1917.

10.   Howe, p. 113.

11.   Letter to Finley, Feb. 20, 1917.

12.   Letter to Frank, Jan. 2, 1917.

13.   Letter to Frank, Sept. 1917.

14.   Letter to Frank, Dec. 12, 1919.

15.   Howe, p. 56.

16.   Letter from Floyd Dell, Feb. 5, 1964.

17.   Letter from Floyd Dell to Dr. Stanley Pargellis, April 14, 1948.

18.   Hansen, p. 119.

19.   Dell letter to Dr. Pargellis, April 14, 1948.

20.   Dell, Homecoming, p. 253. The search for the manuscript of Windy McPherson's Son has been a continuing one; there are many questions which study of it might answer.

21.   Photo copy of contract supplied by Bodley Head Ltd., successor to the John Lane Co.; Jan. 14, 1963.

22.   Hansen, p. 121.

23.   "People Who Write, " Chicago Daily News, Oct. 4, 1916, p. 11.

24.   Midwest Portraits, p. 116.

25. Letter to M. D. Finley, Jan. 16, 1917.

26. Letter to Frank, Nov. 6, 1916 (JR).

27. Letter to M. D. Finley, Nov. 27, 1916.

28. Letter to Paul Rosenfeld, ca. 1921.

29. Letter to Ben W. Huebsch, ca. Nov. 1921.

30. Windy McPherson's Son, New York, B. W. Huebsch, 1922. All page references in the present book are to this edition.

31. "Discovery of a Father," Reader's Digest, Nov. 1939, 35:21-25.

32. See A Story Teller's Story, p. 102, and Memoirs, p. 93-96.

33. Letter to Karl, ca. April 15, 1922.

34. Letter, Nov. 6, 1916 (JR).

35. Homecoming, p. 253.

36. July 5, Aug. 8, and Nov. 22, 1921.

37. Letter to Huebsch, Nov. 22, 1921 (JR).

B. Marching Men

Evidently both Windy McPherson's Son and Marching had been written in their first versions in Elyria. There is some evidence concerning revision of Windy, but considerably more dealing with changes in Marching Men. Which was written first can only be surmised, but Marching Men was published a year later, in September, 1917.

Burton Rascoe opened his review of the book by making the following reference to its composition: "He told me about this novel before it was published, how he had first written it five years ago and had subjected it to revisions so infinite that he had a month's fuel supply of it in manuscript before he finally dispatched one that pleased him and the publishers. "[1]

Soon after Anderson returned to Chicago from Elyria, he was following his familiar pattern of trying out his work on his friends. In the spring of 1913, Marco Morrow, who had been the editor of Agricultural Advertising, Anderson's first outlet, called George Daugherty, then in business in Michigan, to visit him in Chicago over the weekend. "I think Sherwood's got something. " The next Sunday Daugherty found Sherwood reading the manuscript of Marching Men to Morrow in the Sherman Hotel. Both friends liked the book. [2]

The book was receiving active consideration for publication as early as 1915. On May 10 of that year Anderson wrote to Dreiser, who had evidently mentioned the book to the John Lane Company, and informed him that "Mr. Marsh of Macmillan's has this novel under consideration. " Probably this opportunity was gained through Floyd Dell, who is reported to have had the book with him in New York that year and to have received this message from Anderson: "Send Marching Men to me, I am ready to do some patient sustained work on it. "³

Some time in this period, as she had of <u>Mary Cochran</u> and <u>Talbot Whittingham</u>, Marietta Finley wrote a reader's report of <u>Marching Men</u>, and this manuscript, though not dated, shows evidence of considerable revision. In the last two pages of her report, Miss Finley suggested possible improvement in the book. She suggested that:

> "Marching Men" needs a little revision and possibly a slight amount of condensing especially in the closing chapters, which, introducing as they do, two new figures--the Agitator and the Placid Friend --are too long in proportion to these characters' place in the action.... The last chapter, however, showing McGregor a father, owner of a small farm and outwardly content but with the old love of battle strong within him, is a clever contrast to his former stirring existence. ⁴

The characters of neither of the abstractly-named characters, the Agitator and the Placid Friend, can be found in the book. Nor is there any character which could be thought of in that way. So the section revolving around these two must have been excised or drastically revised. Also the "last chapter" is nowhere to be found. The book now ends with a chapter devoted to the reactions of David Ormsby and not picturing McGregor as more than possibly married. So the chapter relating to the latter must have been abandoned. Two other items which Miss Finley suggested eliminating, since she considered them "below the generally high tone" of the book: "the miner's jest concerning Nance McGregor and her son" and "the description of the student in Chicago university, " are to be found in pages 17 and 166 respectively of the published book.

It is in her discussion of what she calls "technical errors" that Miss Finley gives her most revealing clue as to the intensiveness of revision. "Frank Turner, " she points out, "who on Page 44 is blessed with two children, might object and justly, too, at an addition of two more on Page 52. " The references on pages 83 and 87 of the published book are in accord that the man had four children. In the same whimsical view, Miss Finley points out, "Again on Page 111 Margaret Ormsby is described as having brown eyes whereas on page 119 she has miraculously changed their color to black. " On page 203 of the book as published,

Margaret has brown eyes and on page 207 has eyes whose
color is not indicated. These two revisions seem to establish the fact that two pages of manuscript equal one of the
published book. But they show something much more striking: that much must have been done to develop the early
part of the book more fully. If the two-to-one relationship
of manuscript to book was maintained, the first reference to
the Turner children would be on page 22 of the book and the
reference to Margaret's eyes on page 55 or 56. They are,
instead, on pages 83 and 203, respectively. The one reference is 60 pages later in the book than might have been expected and the second is 150 pages later. A considerably
lengthy revision, whenever it happened, seems to be indicated.

However, there is more evidence than this to show
that Anderson labored long over this book. A manuscript of
the novel, one which is very close to the published version,
allows further study of Anderson's revision. [5] The work in
this form is a little less than half in typescript, appearing
to be the account from which the writer was working, to
which many emendations amounting to more than half the
book, had been made. The manuscript has literally hundreds
of corrections in spelling, changes in punctuation, and dele-
tions and additions of words and phrases.

Conclusions which might be drawn from study of the
manuscript are made less certain by the absence of two
factors. There is no indication who made all the corrections
in the manuscript. Anderson's longhand script is certainly
identifiable, but it is not all clear who made changes in
punctuation, for example. It has to be assumed that the
typescript was the original and the longhand the later version.
The typescript may even be the one the secretary prepared
in Elyria. If the manuscript of Windy McPherson's Son,
which some of Anderson's friends believe still existed at the
time of his death, could be found and studied, a sounder
analysis could be undertaken. It would be possible, for example, to compare paper, typewriter ink, pencil, various
markings. For the moment, it seems wiser to say that the
evidence shows conclusively that Anderson, before and during
the time of preparing Winesburg, Ohio, was no stranger to
revision.

Anderson, the evidence shows, was working on the
manuscript right up to the end of May, 1917, when he could
write, "'Marching Men' has gone on its way...."[6] On May

12, evidently re-examining the book for a last time, he wrote
to Miss Finley:

> Again as always when I read it I am aroused and
> stirred by the book "Marching Men." In a way the
> whole big message of my life is bound up into that
> volume. As I work it in my mind I recall the time
> when I began to work with it, crudely and brokenly.
> It was all a great song to me then, a big terrible
> song. I was not strong enough to hold it.... I
> walked at night praying. My mind from too much
> weariness stopped working once [evidently referring
> to the Elyria experience] and I was for a time a
> wreck, wandering as aimlessly as society is aim-
> less.

The next, short paragraph of that letter is, "Now the
story is beautifully simple. It will go far. It will start a
song in many hearts." But the book with its many values,
especially to those who value Anderson's work, has never
had a second edition. It was published in September in an
edition of 2,500 copies for a public which was disappointed
to find it had nothing to do with the war, as most books of
that day did, even when their titles were not so obviously
military. Because Windy had failed to sell in England, John
Lane refused to issue an English edition. [7]

Anderson continued to be concerned with the basic
idea for the rest of his life. Two decades after he wrote
the book, in the midst of his experience as an entrepreneur,
he expressed his concern for labor in this way: "I think
this notion of going to the factories for men's new religious
experience is so much the road of the future. I had the
conception myself long ago and tried to express it in Marching Men...." [8] At the same time he addressed the book
"To American Workingmen," he had this disenchanted view:

> Although I was but a young man I had already
> worked in factories in several cities and had lived
> in too many shabby rooms in shabby houses in
> factory streets. The outer surface of my life was
> too violently uncouth, too persistently uncouth.
> Well enough for Walt Whitman for Carl Sandburg
> and others to sing of the strength and fineness of
> laboring men, making heroes of them, but already
> the democratic dream had faded and laborers were
> not my heroes. I was born fussy, liked cleanness

and orderliness about me and had already been
thrown too much into the midst of shiftlessness.
The socialists and communists I had seen and heard
talk nearly all struck me as men who had no sense
of life at all. They were so likely to be dry intellectual sterile men. [9]

Not at all surprisingly, there is much concern with
order in Marching Men. In a bordello scene, "a great hatred
of the disorder of life" takes hold of McGregor, the main
character (page 104). [10] One of the notable events of a
miners' strike is the destruction of the carefully-planned garden of an Italian (page 39). McGregor's dream of the marching men is to have "a million feet rocking the world and
driving the great song of order purpose and discipline into
the soul of Americans." He feared, however, "that mankind
would go on forever along the old road, that youth would
continue always to grow into manhood, become fat, decay
and die with the great swing and rhythm of life a meaningless mystery to them" (page 178).

In a retrospective comment near the end of the book,
this most individualistic of men, McGregor, shows that he
sees another side of the coin, thinking of it evidently in
terms of the life he had lived in Chicago suburbia between
1900 and 1906:

It is difficult not to be of two minds about the
manifestation now called, and perhaps rightly,
"The Madness of the Marching Men." In one mood
it comes back to the mind as something unspeakably big and inspiring. We go each of us through
the treadmill of our lives caught and caged like
little animals in some vast menagerie. In turn we
love, marry, breed children, have our moments
of blind futile passion and then something happens.
All unconsciously a change creeps over us. Youth
passes. We become shrewd, careful, submerged
in little things. Life, art, great passions, dreams,
all of these pass. Under the night sky the suburb-
anite stands in the moonlight. He is hoeing his
radishes and worrying because the laundry has torn
one of his white collars. The railroad is to put on
an extra morning train. He remembers that fact
heard at the store. For him the night becomes
more beautiful. For ten minutes longer he can
stay with the radishes each morning. There is

much of a man's life in the figure of the suburban-
ite standing absorbed in his own thoughts in the
midst of his radishes. (Page 275.)

As was related earlier, Anderson says he wrote a
book or pamphlet called Why I Am a Socialist in the Elyria
period. And Cornelia indicated her knowledge of concern
with the subject. But this means of bringing order to the
world is dealt with quite skeptically in this book and in Windy
McPherson's Son as well. McGregor, as a boy, thinks "with
a sneer on his lips" of "the town socialist who was forever
talking of a day when men would march shoulder to shoulder
and life... should cease being aimless and become definite
and full of meaning" (page 13). Anderson has given this
character the apt name Barney Butterlips. In the midst of
a strike, another socialist, a "traveling... orator," begins
to talk of "the coming social revolution. As he talked it
seemed to McGregor that his jaw had become loose from
much wagging and that his whole body was loosely put together and without force" (page 142). All the evidence in
the two first novels is that socialism, as found institutional-
ized in the United States, was an empty fake.

According to Van Wyck Brooks, [11] Anderson said that
he conceived the idea of Marching Men while watching a
column of his fellow soldiers during the Spanish-American
War: national guardsmen from Clyde. He was certainly
thinking of their strike duty in the coal fields when he had
McGregor see the soldiers sympathetically as they held the
miners in check. "His blood was stirred by the sight of
them marching shoulder to shoulder. He thought there was
order and decency in the rank of the uniformed men moving
silently and quickly along...." (pages 40-41). Later, after
he has encountered the chaos of Chicago, McGregor recalls
the sight of the soldiers in his native Coal Creek. "They
were just ordinary men but they went swinging along, all as
one man. Something in that fact ennobled them" (page 130).
McGregor thought of the millions of workmen in Chicago and
other great cities "shuffling off along the streets to their
houses carrying with them no song, no hope, nothing but a
few paltry dollars with which to buy food and keep the endless hurtful scheme of things alive" (page 140). Evidently
the simple, but doomed, plan of McGregor to meet this
problem, "to just learn... to march," was based on Anderson's experience in, and observation of, the military.

Various Clyde aspects, other than the National Guard

experience, may be found embedded in this book, though it
does not recapitulate Anderson's life as overtly as <u>Windy
McPherson's Son</u> did.   The father figure is much changed.
Cracked McGregor is a responsible self-sacrificing man, who
is killed trying to help those trapped in a mine fire.   He is
a highly respected, if eccentric, worker.   Although Cracked
is much different from Windy, Beaut McGregor is able to
note, as Sam McPherson could have for opposite reasons.
"Like his father he was a marked man in Coal Creek" (page
26).   Perhaps this imaginative ameliorating of the parental
portrait may be related to Anderson's possibly unconscious
use of names.   When the portrait is closer to the original,
the names are very similar: McPherson has the same five
last letters as Anderson.   McPherson is also the most-
famed name in Clyde, possibly chosen ironically.   General
James B. McPherson, a native son killed at the battle of
Atlanta, is still honored through the Clyde highway and cemetery bearing his name (see Chapter 1, Note 75).   When the
Clyde echo became fainter, the name of McGregor was used,
retaining only the Scotch prefix.   Possibly Anderson never
thought of these factors, but they should not be ignored.

   The mother, Nancy McGregor, is much closer to the
portrait of his own mother, a thoroughly-approvable, hard-
working, sympathetic, self-sacrificing person, who thinks
only of her son's welfare.   The woman who does so much
for him in Chicago, Edith Carson, is congruent to this
mother-image, and he eventually marries her rather than
Margaret Ormsby, who needs a father so much she turns
back to the one she has after McGregor rather regretfully
rejects her for Edith.   As has been suggested earlier, the
maternal type of woman was to play a continuingly important
part in Anderson's life.

   One of the outstanding features of the book is the intensity of McGregor's hatred of his home town, Coal Creek.
His utterances concerning this feeling run like a refrain
through the first part of the book.   Twice he says he would
like to lead the town to an old mine shaft and push them in,
so he would watch them struggle and drown (pages 13 and
33).   He notes elsewhere his hatred of the "disorganized in-
effectiveness" of the life about him (page 44).   He cries out
to the people of the town: "I hate you because you are weak
and disorganized like cattle" (page 53).   As he approaches
Chicago, after leaving Coal Creek, he finds that his burning
hatred has set fire to his ambition.   "Coming from a community where no man arose above a condition of silent brute

labour, he meant to step up into the light of power.   Filled
with hatred and contempt for mankind he meant that mankind
should serve him" (page 64).   Long having wanted to, Beaut
McGregor leaves Coal Creek "full of hate" as a reaction to
a Mickey Finn given him by fellow workers in a livery stable.

> Like Nero he might have wished that all of the
> people of the town had but one head so that he
> might cut it off with a sweep of a sword or knock
> it into a gutter with one sweeping blow.   (Page
> 59.)

There is no evidence of his having such intense dislike
for Clyde or its inhabitants (just the contrary in some cases)
nor of his having such driving ambition when he left.   It is
certainly true that he followed the path of many others and
turned his back on his native place.   Both Sam McPherson
and McGregor have tremendous drive for self-realization,
though in totally different ways.   It seems Anderson must
have realized the same aspirations in himself as he ran his
mail-order paint business and created these characters.

Two more Clyde factors are the bicycle factory, in
which Anderson worked and which an advertising man is
promoted during the character, McGregor's, Chicago period,
and the livery stable, in which both Anderson and McGregor
worked.   Generally, however, it should be noted that Coal
Creek has many fewer similarities to Clyde than Caxton had.
It is in Pennsylvania rather than in the middle west.   It is
dominated completely by coal mining, while Clyde-Caxton had
both factories and agriculture.   Perhaps because he wishes
to concern himself with the problem of the working-man, he
chose in this town to focus its life on one over-riding industry, and he portrayed it in caricature.

Chicago, on the contrary, is portrayed rather metic-
ulously.   One of the major values of the book is the way it
gives the flavor and character of that city.   He refers to it
as a "maelstrom of misery and grim desperate want" (page
65) but cannot resist attempting repeatedly to capture its
fascinating and revolting features:

> ... Foul dust filled the air.   All day the street
> rumbled and roared under the wheels of trucks and
> light hurrying delivery wagons.   Soot from the fac-
> tory chimneys was caught up by the wind and having
> been mixed with powdered horse manure from the

roadway flew into the eyes and nostrils of the ped-
estrians. Always a babble of voices went on. At
a corner saloon teamsters stopped to have their
drinking cans filled with beer and stood about
swearing and shouting. In the evening women and
children went back and forth from their homes
carrying beer in pitchers from the same saloon.
Dogs howled and fought, drunken men reeled along
the sidewalk and women of the town appeared in
their cheap finery and paraded before the idlers
about the saloon door. (Page 76.)

In and out among the trees and on the green spaces
moved the people. Along the shores of a pond sat
men and women eating the evening meal from bas-
kets or from white cloths spread on the grass.
They laughed and shouted at each other and at the
children, calling them back from the gravel drive-
ways filled with moving carriages. Beaut says a
girl threw an egg shell and hit a young fellow between the eyes, and then ran laughing away along
the shore of the pond. Under a tree a woman
nursed a babe, covering her breasts with a shawl
so that just the black head of the baby showed.
Its tiny hand clutched at the mouth of the woman.
In an open space in the shadow of a building young
men played baseball, the shouts of the spectators
rising above the murmur of the voices of the people on the gravel walk. (Page 86.)

It is evening and the people of Chicago go home
from work. Clatter, clatter, clatter, go the heels
on the hard pavements, jaws wag, the wind blows
and dirt drifts and sifts through the masses of the
people. Everyone has dirty ears. The stench in
the street cars is horrible. The antiquated bridges
over the rivers are paced with people. The suburban trains going away south and west are cheaply
constructed and dangerous. A people calling itself
great and living in a city also called great go to
their houses a mere disorderly mass of humans
cheaply equipped. Everything is cheap. When the
people get home to their houses they sit on cheap
chairs before cheap tables and eat cheap food.
They have given their lives for cheap things. The

poorest peasant of one of the old countries is surrounded by more beauty. His very equipment for
living has more solidity. (Pages 100-101.)

Chicago is one vast gulf of disorder. Here is the
passion for gain, the very spirit of the Bourgeoise
[sic] gone drunk with desire. The result is something terrible. Chicago is leaderless, purposeless,
slovenly, down at the heels.

And back of Chicago lie the long corn fields that
are not disorderly. There is hope in the corn.
Spring comes and the corn is green. It shoots up
out of the black land and stands up in orderly
rows. The corn grows and thinks of nothing but
growth. Fruition comes to the corn and it is cut
down and disappears. Barns are filled to the
bursting with the yellow fruit of the corn.

And Chicago has forgotten the lesson of the corn.
All men have forgotten. It has never been told to
the young men who come out of the corn fields to
live in the city. (Page 156.)

Aside from his vivid observations, as exemplified in
the foregoing excerpts, Anderson shows evidence of reference
to specific and known experiences from the Chicago period.
He uses scenes in a warehouse, doubtless similar to the one
he worked in prior to his entrance into the Spanish-American
War, to show the ruthlessness and capability of McGregor.
A major sequence in the law career of McGregor deals with
the murder of a prominent citizen in a house of prostitution.
In the book it is "a young man--son of one of the city's
plunging millionaire wheat speculators" who is "found dead
in a little blind alley back of a resort known as Polk Street
Mary's place." A highly comparable case was that of Nath-
aniel Ford Moore, the twenty-six-year-old son of the Rock
Island Railroad family, who died on the night of January 8-9,
1910, in one of Chicago's better-known brothels after having
visited the internationally infamous Everleigh Club. There
was no court case like the one in Marching Men, but the
wild, vicious, and blatant immorality, with which both Mc-
Gregor and Anderson were concerned, was represented by
this case, which probably occurred just before the book was
written.

Asbury, a Chicago historian, indicates the crime wave in the city reached its crest during the last two months of 1905 and the first two of 1906, when Anderson was there to witness it; "the average citizen, and especially the average woman, was probably in greater danger of being robbed and murdered than any other time in the history of Chicago. "[12]

Additionally representative of his Chicago years is a sequence in which McGregor has dealings with an advertising man, John Van Moore, who is working out an advertising campaign for a bicycle manufacturer. Certainly the rather sardonic picture Anderson here paints represents his own work at Taylor-Critchfield. As he had himself gone to a night class in arithmetic at the Lewis Institute, Anderson has McGregor go to night classes, studying what are obviously more bookish courses than arithmetic, however.

In his discussions of marriage and sex with his friend, Turner, the barber and violin-maker, McGregor displays attitudes which must be relevant to the problems Anderson himself felt. It is evident he was feeling drawn to the matter of self-expression. His devotion to his writing had manifested itself in Elyria. Turner has left his wife and four children to start life anew in Chicago so that he could devote himself to what he wants to do--what his wife never thought mattered --the making of violins. As we know, Anderson finally made a choice between conventional family life and the pursuit of his artistic destiny. He has Turner say:

> I know men and women cling to their children. It's
> the only thing they have left of the dream they had
> before they married. I felt that way. It held me
> for a long time. It would be holding me now only
> that the violins pulled so hard at me. (Page 94.)

The following words may have been written in the original text or after the breakup of his marriage, but they certainly state the matter as it appeared to Anderson through Turner:

> You see I had to find an answer. I couldn't think
> of being a skunk--running away--and I couldn't
> stay. I wasn't intended to stay. Some men are
> intended to work and take care of children and
> serve women perhaps but others have to keep try-
> ing for a tone on a violin. If they don't get it it
> doesn't matter, they have to keep trying. (Page 94.)

The subject of the role of women in society and marriage
and how and why marriage comes about is given considerable
exploration in the relationship of Margaret and Edith and
McGregor.   All these matters certainly were very close to
his own immediate experience.

Later, when Winesburg, Ohio came out, much was
made of the way the work of Anderson was reminiscent of
Russian writers.   Anderson shows in this book, in a very
generalized way, that he was conscious of their work and its
character and impressed by it:

> And there was the marching song the Russian wrote
> for McGregor.   Who could forget it?   Its high
> pitched harsh feminine strain rang in the brain.
> How it went pitching and tumbling along in that
> wailing, calling endless high note.   It had strange
> breaks and intervals in the rendering.   The men
> did not sing it.   They chanted it.   There was in
> it just the weird haunting something the Russians
> know how to put into their songs and into the books
> they write.   (Pages 280-281.)

Two pieces of evidence remain as to his state of mind
after this book was published.   We are reminded how deeply
he felt himself invested in the fate of the work, which was
not reassuring, by his comment "I have recovered from the
depression that came with the inevitable pawing over of
Marching Men and am clear of it. "[13]

The following letter to the librarian of the Chicago
Historical Society, self-explanatory as it is, indicates his
vigor and aggressiveness after the publication of his first
two novels:

> I have really published two novels, both more or
> less intensive studies of present day Chicago life,
> and would be glad to present them to the Chicago
> Historical Society except that there is a matter of
> Principle involved.
>
> Really you know I suppose I have had already a
> hundred requests of presentation copies of both
> novels.   That means about two hundred dollars to
> me.   I am not a popular writer, at least the
> royalty checks from my publisher do not indicate
> that I am.   My books are seriously discussed by

our American deep sea thinkers but they are not
bought by the man in the street.

Now you do know that no one is so poorly paid for
his labor as the serious writer. I don't want to
take myself too seriously but it is a joke to me
that the Chicago Historical Society should want me
to give them a copy of "Marching Men." Make the
publisher give you one if you can. Don't tackle the
defenseless writer.

And please bear in mind this is not personal. I
don't blame you but I'll be hanged before I'll give
any institution a copy of any book I write.[14]

Notes

1.   Rascoe, "A Worth-while Chicago Novel," Chicago Daily
Tribune, Sept. 22, 1917.

2.   Daugherty interview, Feb. 22, 1949; Phillips, p. 26-7.

3.   Duffy, The Chicago Renaissance in American Letters.

4.   The reader's report is in the possession of the present
author through the generosity of Miss Finley.

5.   This manuscript, now in the Newberry Library in Chicago, was in the possession of Miss Marietta D. Finley
from some time in the Twenties until 1962. Miss Finley
had no information as to the exact time or circumstances
of its composition.

6.   Letter to M. D. Finley, May 25, 1917.

7.   Hansen, p. 121.

8.   Letter to Valenti Angelo, mid-April 1932 (JR).

9.   A Story Teller's Story, p. 141-2.

10.   Marching Men, New York, John Lane, 1917. All page
references in the present book are to this (the only) edition.

11.   The Confident Years, 1885-1915, New York, Dutton,

1952, p. 240.

12.   Herbert Asbury, Gem of the Prairie, New York, Knopf, 1940, p. 208.

13.   Letter to M. D. Finley, Nov. 1917.

14.   Letter from Anderson (on stationery of Taylor Critch-field Clague Co.) to Carolina M. McIlvaine, Librarian, Chicago Historical Society, October 3, 1917.

C. Mid-American Chants

In Chicago Anderson was associating with such people as Carl Sandburg and Harriet Monroe, whose <u>Poetry</u> office at 543 Cass Street, was less than two blocks away from Anderson's place at 735. Perhaps he was in the audience in the spring of 1914, at a meeting of poets and artists, to hear William Butler Yeats say:

> If America is to have great poets, they must be humble and simple. They must not stop to think whether they themselves are good or bad, but must express themselves as they are. They must give nature and themselves as they are, the evil with the good. Readers should encourage poets to lead lives of humility and simplicity. [1]

That he had been thinking seriously about poetry is evident from this comment of late 1916:

> The poetry of the old testament is ruined for me when a college professor has had it experimented upon and reprinted in blank verse. Do away with the term poet and we will have an end to writers building misunderstanding by lecturing of poetry in a hall. One might as well set up for a lover and deliver a series of talks on Love and Lovers. [2]

It may be imagined he wrote that, attacking as it does the idea of study and discipline as related to poetic expression, when he was in the process of making up his mind to try his hand at poems rather than stories. It would have been convenient to think there was no such thing as a "poet."

It is not known when Anderson began to write poems as well as stories and novels. But the effort which was to

result in <u>Mid-American Chants</u> evidently got started at or
near the beginning of 1917 and was deeply important by the
second month of that year:

> I cannot tell you how deeply this inclination to song
> has taken hold of me. Perhaps this is the thing
> you have felt in me and would not tell me about.
>
> Now that song has come I feel like one who has
> been climbing up a steep hill and has got out upon
> a broad, wind-swept place. In my prose I have
> been creeping toward rhythm and here in all of
> this realization of the terrible meaning and beauty
> of words that has not been realized. I will realize
> but a trifle of it but I will bring into song as I
> have into prose something middlewestern, something
> simple and if I can keep fairly pure, something
> also fairly pure.
>
> M. said to me once long ago that I was to express
> beauty breaking through the husks of life and that
> is true. If I can do anything at all it is by this
> road, keeping close, understanding, believing. [3]

The next record of his conception of this effort is
from April:

> About the songs. In them I see growing a great
> hungriness and through them I get for myself a
> sense of return to earthiness. Perhaps in my own
> way I will in the end populate the cornfields and
> the shadows by factory doors with mystery and
> faith so that sweaty men will look up from toil and
> feel on their faces the shadows of my gods.
>
> And by the road of song I go to the God myself.
> It is my answer to life that is too sordid, too
> hard, too pitiless.
>
> Perhaps, dear heart, I shall lead you, too. I
> shall take you perhaps to the dwelling place beyond
> the thought of clinging lips to where your gods
> dwell. There is unbelievable stoutness in me,
> dear. The march is long but I am on my way.
>
> Days of twisted people... songs not sung; things in
> a terrible twisted hush.

Then other days of happiness. [4]

In his foreword to the book, dated February, 1918, he expressed his belief that "a million men and women" were trying, as his poems did, to "express the hunger within." He thought his chants would "find an answering and clearer call in the hearts of other Mid-Americans. . . .   In Middle America men are awakening.   Like awkward and untrained boys we begin to form toward maturity and with our awakening we hunger for song"[5] (pages 7-8).   Several years later he was to recall, "The Chants were a making of new designs and emotions.   They helped mightily."[6]

In March 2, 1917 he had confidence enough that he could write to Frank [JR], "Oh, but these poems would make you sit up."   But he added coyly, "Now, lie low, little grey squirrel, you can't see them yet."   Three days later, however, he wrote admitting he could not resist sending Frank "two of my songs.   There are about twenty of them now.   I believe they get at a note."   Presumably in March he sent Frank typescripts of "Assurance" and "The Planting," which appeared in Mid-American Chants with minor emendations, and "Oblivion," which was not used and is thus reproduced here:

> 'T would be sweetest of all
> To hide
> Like a bird
> In a bush
> On a hill
> By a lake
> And think about beautiful women
> Walking on yellow sands.
>
> 'T would be bravest of all
> Never to look
> In the eyes
> Of beautiful death
> Like a man
> But to turn
> And run like a frightened boy
> Back to the womb and the mystery.

These poems are accompanied by a note: "Here are some of the songs.   Does Seven Arts want some of them."[7] Another undated note to Frank, again presumably from this same period, reveals both satisfaction and rejection:

> The songs sing to me.   They have carried me far.
> I am only sorry that Seven Arts does not want
> them, because it is the only place I ⌈at⌉this moment
> know for them.

Seven Arts did publish "From Chicago" and "Mid-American
Prayer" in its June, 1917, issue.   The only other poem of
which there is any specific mention in this period is "American Spring Song, " of which he wrote: "A few songs are
clear and strong... 'American Spring Song. '   Others not so
clear. "[8]

Also, during the spring of 1917, doubtless no later
than May, he found another outlet for his poetry.   In the
June issue of Others, [9] edited in New Jersey by Alfred Kreym-
borg, appeared "Song of the Soul of Chicago, " "Sang [Song]
Long After, " and "The Cornfields, " all of which were in-
cluded in Mid-American Chants.   All three of the poems in
Others had been edited when they appeared in book form.
The changes in "Song of the Soul of Chicago" and "The
Cornfields" were quite minor ones of punctuation and one
synonymic word.

But "Song Long After, " as it was corrected to read
in Mid-American Chants, had undergone much revision.   The
poem is addressed to the mother of Jesus.   In the Others
version (page 4), the opening and closing lines read as follows:

> Was that all you could do, Mary?
> Loving and giving--that's all right.

However, in Mid-American Chants (page 61) it reads this
way:

> Was that all you could do, Woman--loving and giv-
> ing?

The next line of the poem, in both versions, reads: "You
went pretty far.   I admire you for that. "   In Others, the
first person is maintained, as though Jesus were speaking:
"when I cried, " and "I wanted you then, " and "I was crucified for them. "   In the book this was changed to the third
person; "God knows / I wanted you then" became "God knows /
he needed you then. "   Because there is no comment by Anderson on this publication or other information concerning it,
conclusions about the changes made will have to be confined

to the speculative obvious.   But the changes do illuminate
Anderson as an artist who was capable of retrospective concern for his work and who did revise.

In addition to sending poems to Others and Seven Arts,
he had turned to Poetry, to whose editor, Harriet Monroe,
he wrote at the end of April: "Here is a spring song you
may like.   It may help to make up the group you are after. "10 It is not known when Miss Monroe had started to
take interest in collecting a group of Anderson's poems for
publication.   Doubtless the "spring song" was "American
Spring Song, " about which he had expressed himself as con-
fidently at the beginning of the month, for it was among the
poems published in Poetry in September.   The process of
deciding which of his poems to use evidently went on during
the spring and into the summer.   Presumably he had submitted more than were used, having had about twenty at the
beginning of March.   Anderson wrote Miss Monroe from
Lake Chateaugay early in July:

> The selection you have made suits me very well
> for my debut as a singer.   [Note June publication
> in Seven Arts and Others.   Possibly the magazines
> had not appeared.] I think the sequence you have
> named would be very good.   I trust you entirely
> for that.

The amount of $25. 00 for the six songs is ok. 11

Anderson was not certain what he wanted to call the
group of poems to be in Poetry.   First he sent an undated
post card requesting: "Call the group West Winds. "12
Another undated card said: "On second thought please call
the group of songs Mid-American Songs. " On July 9, the
same day Miss Monroe was answering him in Chicago, he
posted another card: "I really prefer Mid-American Songs
but do not think the matter of vital importance.   Do as your
judgment suggests. "13

His next message, evidently written a few days later,14
revealed he was interested in something far more important
than the title of the song-group, as much as he had fussed
over it:

> I hope you can use the verses in September.   I
> may issue a book of songs soon and would like
> ground broken through such good channels as Poetry

as soon as possible.

When he acknowledged receipt of his check from Poetry in
September, he also informed Miss Monroe, "You will be interested to hear that I am planning to of [sic] book of verse
or 'emotional prose' or whatever it may be called, sometime
this winter."[15]

Possibly in September, 1917, he wrote Frank an ex-
uberant insight into the status of his endeavor:

> Since I came back to Chicago [from Chateaugay] a
> madness has seized me. I do nothing but write
> songs. Like a big ugly bird I jump up on the rail
> of the bridges and sing. See this list.
>
> 1. Song of Theodore. 2. Chicago. 3. Song of
> the Break of Day. 4. The Cornfields. 5. The
> Strangers. 6. Manhattan. 7. A Visit. 8. A
> Lullaby. 9. The Beam. 10. Song of the Break
> of Day [sic]. 11. Revolt. 12. Night Whispers.
> 13. Hosanna. 14. Song of Cedric the Silent.
> 15. Song of the Love of Women. 16. Evening
> Song. 17. Song Long After. 18. Brief Barroom
> Songs. . . .
>
> But don't you tell anyone what I am doing. I am
> disguised as a truck driver, a man who owns a
> bird store, a fellow who opens oysters in a rest-
> aurant. They kill singers out here on suspicion.[16]

When the poems came out in Poetry,[17] Anderson reported to Frank:

> The poems. . . created some stir out here, and
> everyone abused me. Nevertheless I shall put
> them into a book. One of the newspapermen made
> a ten-shot. Do you remember the line "See the
> corn. How it aches?"
>
> He called me the chiropodist poet. I would publish
> the verses for one reason if for no other. It will
> give a rare opportunity to those who desire to flay
> me.[18]

Late the next month, presumably in reaction to Anderson's statement about his publishing plans, Frank asserted

his belief in the establishment of his position in publishing, additionally urging him to bring out his novel next rather than his poems. Anderson's answer was very direct and indicative:

> You are wrong about the songs. Your argument that I will make more progress by bringing out the novel is all right, but don't you see that I must snap my fingers at the world? That must remain a part of my creed. If a road leads to destruction, one must take it as a sporting proposition.[19]

His defensive and dogged attitude was also evident in an undated letter from about the same time to his brother Karl:

> The songs have brought the herds down on me. They offer just the opportunity for snappy, satirical comment that delights the souls of the newspaper editorial and paragraph writer. If Lane does not lose his nerve, I shall publish a book of them under the title Mid-American Chants. It will probably make me the most abused man in the country.

Abused or not, however, his creative impetus did not flag: "I have written until my hands tremble and I can hardly hold a pen."[20] And "John Lane Company, N.Y." and "Sherwood Anderson, Chicago, Ill." signed a contract for the publication of Mid-American Chants dated December 14, 1917. The book is said to have sold 200 copies[21] and had no second edition. On March 23, 1918, Anderson was predicting in a letter to Harriet Monroe that the book "should be set within two or three weeks." The first known review on April 17 fits that expectation.[22] Also, by April 19 he had written an apology to Miss Monroe for failure to get included in the book credit for the poems which had already appeared in Poetry: "The note to John Lane was written, put into my pocket and forgotten. Please forgive me."[23]

On the occasion of publication, Anderson began to make an assessment of the meaning of his experience and the degree of his success:

> I had an interesting experience with these songs and they have brought me in a way-greater personal satisfaction than anything that I have ever done. They are I presume illegitimate children

that have by some accident come to live in my
house.

At first no one liked them, then they began to make
headway.   I find that with certain people I care the
most about they have come to mean more than anything else I have done.   I really believe they will
be legitimated by time, and that you will also in
the end come to care for them. 24

Perhaps his putting Frank, above, on the defensive
was the result of this criticism from some time in 1918:

I read some of your poems aloud the other night,
and as I read them I felt their lack of form mili-
tate against them.   You would catch your reader
and then let him slip.   In very few of your poems
was there the solidity that maintains vision to the
interstices a lovely upright spirit that meant more
to me than the academic accomplishment.   I want
you to work hard at your stuff--harder--but I am
not going to shut my eyes to the beauty you are
bringing to life and to work.

In June Frank was more specific about his admiration
for the work, finding only few he did not give first rating.
He mentioned the poem about Stephen and "Song of Spring"
but indicated great difficulty in finding favorites, having fond-
ness for all the chants. 25

Such compliments were evidently rare enough, and
Anderson was able to feel that his songs would be "widely
abused and perhaps rightly. "26   Again he could predict, "My
songs will fall flat and go unnoticed" yet grudgingly concede
"They perhaps deserve it, " and then insist "they deserve
something better also. "27

Though Anderson wanted to think them his best effort,
and could write that the people whose opinion he valued most
highly thought them so, his poems did not evoke great enthusiasm from Frank.   In addition, he wrote Frank "I suspect Brooks of being reluctant about telling me how little he
respects them. "   On May 23, 1918 he wrote in an expostu-
lating way to Brooks, asking how he had failed.

In the chants I reached into my personal mutterings,
half insane and disordered, and tried to take out of

them a little something ordered. You should see
how I clutched at the ordered cornfield[s], insisted
on them to myself, took them as about the only
thing I could see.

His friend and fellow Chicagoan, Llewellyn Jones, literary editor of the Chicago Evening Post, entitled his review
"Nascent Poetry," and asserted "These chants are the nascent poems of an unterrified romanticist." He thought further that "Mr. Anderson is as well aware as you, dear
reader, that some of his lines do not make sense. They are
the inchoate verbal outcomes of inchoate feelings. To that
extent, of course, they are not art." Jones noted, too, that
some of the poems were "quite definite in form and content.
And probably Mr. Anderson is not unaware--if it be true that
he wrote them spontaneously--how his feeling has often forced
his words into the most orthodox of meters." Jones concluded:

> It is partly to confute Mr. Anderson's prefatory
> claim that he cannot sing--I should like to demon-
> strate to him that if he took the trouble to learn
> the art he could become a poet--.... There is
> very little--if any--free verse in the book at all.
> There is much lilting and lyrical verse.... He
> may learn the grammar of this--to him--new craft,
> if he will, and he read by poetry lovers. Or else
> his books of verse will live only to be pilfered of
> their poetic ideas and real feeling by smaller men
> who have the art which Mr. Anderson has not and
> lack the vitality which he has. [28]

Ben Hecht, another Chicago friend, began and ended
his review with the same sentences:

> Overwhelming thoughts had Anderson by the throat
> when he wrote "Mid-American Chants." And the
> thing he put to paper, the words and phrases, were
> the souls of these thoughts. "Mid-American
> Chants" contains the music out of which great po-
> ets fashion immortal poetry. [29]

Other highlights of Hect's colorfully frank comment
are as follows.

> Sherwood Anderson...has succeeded in revealing
> what is deepest and most fugitive in his soul

without giving it either color or form or what is
significant, intelligence....

Anderson's song will not bear inspection. Between
the lines he has written runs the urge of inarticu-
late passions. This urge cannot be seen nor can
it be read or even understood. It is like the face
of a woman raised and full of rapture, that asks
merely for an embrace. To interpret these songs
is to become forthwith a critical clown. For these
songs are not the carefully clothed and guided ideas
of lived inspiration. They are the expressions of
nothing. They are the thing itself, the soul of a
strong man revealed in an ecstatic pantomime.

What Anderson thought of the comments of Jones or
those mentioned of Hecht is not known, but one factor in
Hecht's review did call forth a curious response. Hecht had
written:

... Anderson exhibits finally as neither a poet nor
a thinker, but as a mystic, singing of corn fields
as mystics once sang of the Virgin's eyes....
Anderson brings to his song the profound and passionate incoherence of true mystics....

Anderson's response is given here in full for several
reasons. It indicates his feeling about the idea of being a
mystic. It gives him a chance to stick out his tongue at all
his critics. And it is an example of the "yokel humor"
which was well-known to his friends and of which a few examples are extant. This side of Anderson was evidently
seen most frequently by his advertising associates. Although
he did not always keep his sense of humor, he had an active
one which served him well most of his life, as in this disappointing situation, disappointing because he certainly wanted
and possibly expected much more encouragement than he got.
Under the heading "This and That" Anderson's comment, addressed to the Literary Editor of The Daily News, appears
as a letter signed by one "J. Smith." The present writer is
convinced, without documentation, that the author of this letter had to be Anderson. But all aspects of it are like Anderson and his attitude. Doubters are reminded that he wanted
to call his Poetry contribution "West Winds" and then referred to the quotation he approvingly presents:

Being what I am and not understanding only things

that are wrote out straight, I generally stay off the
book news.   But a while back the word "mystic"
over something signed "Ben Hecht" made me look
it over.   I just glanced it over as you may say,
but I thought if a fellow had got up a book like
"Mid-western Chance" it was the stuff for me, who
am always trying to get ahead and am a Mystic
Shriner besides.   Anyhow, I knew a barber supply
salesman named Ben Hecht and thinks I maybe this
was him.

So I looked over the article, as I say, and, of
course, this wasn't "Nosy" Hecht, like we used to
call him.   Then I got ahold of the book this Sherwood Anderson wrote, and I want to say, Mr. Editor, Anderson ain't no Shriner.   Or maybe he is,
but his book don't say so.

Then I borrowed my daughter Fanny's pocket Web-
ster and I find: "Mystic, mystical: Remote from
or beyond human comprehension, baffling human
understandable; unknowable. " Now, Mr. Editor, I
think you and this Hecht's done an injustice to Mr.
Anderson.   I read every one of them poems and,
barring what the printer done, not making the lines
come out even, I think they are good.   I don't get
the idea where you say he is unknowable.   Look
here, I bet he's just a plain hoss like me that
works his eight hours and smokes stogies and eats
over at the automatic.   I bet he goes to the games
and he is buying a bond on installments and is
married and lives out on Jackson boulevard.   You
can't put it over on me that he's remote from human understanding.   Every work was just like the
fellows in my shop waiting for seafoam uses, only
put together different, and he's copped some out
of the bible.   And that's where you can cop stuff
and get away with it, besides there ain't none better.

At that I don't mean to say he stole from the St.
James version.   But he seems to think like some
of them old fellows, so naturally he picks up their
lingo.   I mean what he says like this:

    "I will renew in my people the worship of
gods. I will set up for a king before them. A

king shall arise before my people. The sacred
vessel shall be filled with the sweet oil of the
corn.

"All the people of my time were bound with
chains. They had forgotten the long fields and
the standing corn. They had forgotten the west
wind. "[30]

I like that about the corn fields, Mr. Editor, and
don't you believe it baffles my understanding. God
knows ain't we sick enough of ear splitting "L"
roads and our tanneries and glue works, and ain't
they got a shoe factory now right across from the
Essex Arms, so my wife can't hardly hear the
canary? I asks her, I says, "Here's a fellow says
he'd like to get back to the cornfields. " And she
says, "Let's get somewhere, for the love of Mike,
this town is gettin' on my nerves. Read me what
the fellow says. "

So I read:

"Come, tired little sister, run with me.
Let's lie down on this hillside here.
Let our soft midwestern nights creep into you.
See the little things creeping, creeping.
Here, in the night, the little thing creeping...
Let's be creeping.
Let's be creeping. "[31]

Mr. Editor, I had to read pretty near the whole
darned book to that woman.

There was some that was unknowable, all right,
but then if reading poetry didn't take some work a
fellow might as well go to the movies all the time.
The main thing I want to say is I know a good
scout when I see one. I like to be talked to or
wrote at as man to man. When I was in the militia the officer for my money was the one who
yelled out, "Dress you big stiff on the end; dress
or I'll lam you plenty after parade. " And this
chap, Anderson, he has the same punch, though
politer. He makes me feel sort of gingered up
and more like I wanted to run the shop right and
besides not forget this burg ain't the only good spot
on earth.

And, by the way, there wasn't a word in the book
I had to look up in the dictionary. That's more
than I can say for Hecht's article.

Say, Mr. Editor, I wish you would send me a list
of things Mr. Anderson has wrote, and next book
he gets out please print it in full in your paper.
Thanking you, I am most kindly yours. 32

     In turning to an examination of the content of Mid-
American Chants, one might anticipate emphasis in it on
World War I, an outstanding fact of the nation's experience
during its composition. The extent of his artistic concern
may be realized after compiling a record of his non-literary
statements about the conflict, in which he had no personal
involvement. Though his attitude was essentially negative,
his first reference to it was optimistic:

To my mind people in general and particularly
women, get too close and personal a view of men
at war. I talked to Tennessee of it last night and
tried to make clear to her what I meant.

A thousand men are in a trench. Within an hour
they are to charge across on open space. To each
individual crouching there something happens. In
himself he has no courage for the task before him.
It is too terrible and hideous. But as he waits
something happens. A thrill runs through the mass
of men. Each individual is in an odd way infected
with the combined courage of all the men. This
of course needs elaboration. Perhaps I cannot
elaborate in a letter. You will be down upon me
with the horrors of war, starving children, etc.
Sometime when I see you I will talk to you of that
as I did with Tennessee. In a letter I can give
you one thought. In some one of my books I have
worked it out. I made a picture of trains coming
[into] the railroad stations in Chicago, and bearing
young men from the cornfields, strong bright eyed
young men, thousands of them, walking over the
bridge into the loop district and to spiritual death.
The bodies live but the thing that made them bright
eyed and eager dies. I should prefer my sons to
die in the war and terror of a Verdun.

But to get on with my thought. I see in fancy the

men of all those old countries going home. Can
you not sense such a scene, say in a Russian village and the men talking over and over their wonder stories? What a new sense of the world they
have!

And imagine a boy standing in the shadows of a
room at evening in a German village while the
fathers talk of Verdun. Do you not see that millions of such boys must get a new heritage of
beauty from that? Boys, you know, are right
when they are thrilled by the tales of war and are
not thrilled by the tales of the stock-exchange.

My notion is, you see, that the war will soon be
over and the world facing itself. Don't believe the
stories of ruin and anarchy after the war. Clerks
who agree that 2 and 2 make four have figured
that out. Trust instead the lesson men have got.
I tell you that youth will run all through the old
places. Poets and thinkers will arise, and the old
world will be sweetened by the storm, the very
air will be purer. It is inevitable. 33

    Within a few months, his certainty of the wholesome-
ness of the end result was shaken, as the following testifies:

Of course you know that if war comes it will mean
the practical death of all pure effort here in America just as it has meant that on the other side.
Perhaps our best men here will be blighted just as
theirs have been. Hatred and prejudice will be in
the saddle and we will have to wade thru a more
hopeless muddle of words and sentimentality than
has been brought on by industrialism. This kind
of war is I suppose, industrialism gone mad.

I had some dreams when the war began. I saw in
fancy men marching shoulder to shoulder and doing
big deeds. Instead as you know men have gone
into the ground and there are only the horrible machine guns and the deafness and the stench.

Well, I won't go on. Thinking of it has driven me
near to madness. 34

    In that same week two other letters gave other

indications of the deepness of the impact of the war prospects:

> If the war comes it will make me more and more
> religious. My mind leaps back over history seeing
> not the Caesars or Napoleons but Cromwell. I
> want a leader now for America who will have the
> courage to ask the people to pray and be sad.

> In the bigness of the things whirling and tumbling
> about our heads the little matter of whether I write
> or not is terribly unimportant. In some ways
> these last few days have made me love and respect
> something in my countrymen. I really believe they
> do not want to enter this terrible war. If war
> comes we shall have the other thing--hatred and
> all truth and beauty dying amid a jumble of words.
> But now, while we wait, in this hour we are splen-
> didly quiet. One must remember that in the days
> to come when we are all to be swung here and
> there by the wind of hideous words. 35

    Later that spring, after the United States had entered
the war, he had reached what was to be his most desperate
point:

> And I have no plans at all. The deep depression
> brought on by the war clings to all people. The
> whole human race is going through a dark place. 36

    By the fall, however, perhaps aided by his stay in
the lovely surroundings at Lake Chateaugay, he had rallied
strongly and could write:

> Every day I am more and more convinced that the
> war and all the distracting things that arise from
> the war are not going to upset me and the work I
> want to do. Now that I am back here and in
> things I know that it, with all its bad thinking and
> with all the distracting influences that are at work,
> is after all the same old clatter raised to a roar.
> Let it roar.

> Damn it man what has man an imagination for.
> [Is] he to be bluffed out by nations at war. In the
> midst of a whirlwind he can still conjure up men
> and women who have beautiful impulses and he can

live with them.

> In a thousand ways and at times you do not know
> if I live with you and others like you [who] have
> things to give me.   I make my thoughts exact
> against your more sager [sic] mind, I hear your
> voice saying much to me.

> We are going to do better work than we ever did.
> As the distractiong becomes more intense we will
> grip harder the things worth while.   Who is Pres
> W or any of the others of these men that they can
> by any act of theirs invade the place where we
> really work. 37

Also, shortly after the publication of Marching Men,
in September, 1917, he allowed himself to be quoted in the
New York Sun as being in favor of compulsory military service:

> Military service should be a great thing for the
> average American youth.   I would like to see more
> of them go into it, not for the sake of the country
> necessarily, but for the sake of the youth them-
> selves, said Sherwood Anderson. . . .   To live in
> one of the tented streets with a company of soldiers
> is exactly like living in a family where there are
> 100 to 150 children. . . .   A spirit of understanding
> of his fellow man comes to the individual soldier. . . .
> For myself I am a strong believer in compulsory
> military service. 38

In a letter commenting on Carl Sandburg's poem, "The
Four Brothers: Notes for War Songs (November, 1917), "
Anderson called it "magnificent, " noted that, "It rings and
has time. . . and bigness. " He made no mention of its content. 39   The "four brothers" of the four-page poem are
France, Russia, England, and "America. " Sandburg reviews the sacrifice of young men in the war, catalogs its
horrors, states that "a God who sees and pierces through,
is breaking and cleaning out an old thousand years, is making ready for a new thousand years. "40

Later, in a studied, determined attitude toward the
disturbance of war, he turned to history:

> As an antidote to the war I now read history.

Histories of Poland, Russia, Austria, Italy, France.
One gets a sense of the long line of events. The
present sinks into nothingness.

His sense of self-discipline was crystallized in this
way:

> To me dear friend it seems that the great thing is
> to keep alive the spirit of men at work in the more
> delicate and subtle things. The whole other busi-
> ness must as far as possible be treated as a right-
> minded elephant would treat the fact of a bee
> lodged in his ear. [41]

As he saw the war in the immediate past, he feared
for the devastating aftermath:

> People still feel that something has been gained to
> pay for the years of killing and ugliness and for a
> time words can still be manufactured to keep up
> the ugliness of the illusion. It will pass however
> and the sickening realization will come home to the
> man in the street. How he will stand it don't [sic]
> show. [42]

His essential pacifism is seen in this last recorded
comment, written during the following May:

> ... For nearly a week now I have been sitting in a
> room upstairs in a factory in Owensboro. Across
> the street in a school year a drill seargeant [sic]
> drills the school boys. Militarism has evidently
> come to America. When I think of the stark hor-
> ror of the terms imposed on Germany and the
> dreadful spectacle of hitting a fallen foe going on
> and on I am sick of civilization and wish I never
> had to go back to it. What has become of the old
> Anglo Saxon belief that it is cowardly to hit a man
> when [he] is down? [43]

Any consideration of his record of the war in his poetry must consider first of all that only seven of the forty-
nine poems in Mid-American Chants, for which he wrote his
Foreword in February, 1918, have any identifiable mention
of the great conflict. Five of the poems ("War," "Mid-
American Prayer," "We Enter In," "Dirge of War," and
"Night") are specifically and deeply concerned with it, and

one ("Industrialism") only peripherally; one ("Song of Stephen the Westerner") has a remote reference to conflict. The greater coverage in the book is on the industrial theme. Four of the poems ("War," "Mid-American Prayer," "We Enter In," and "Dirge of War") are grouped together, being in the fortieth through the forty-third positions in order of appearance in the book. "Industrialism" is twelfth and "Night" thirtieth. "Night," which is concerned only with the war, should have been with the other four if there were any careful effort to place all poems on the same subject together. As far as can be determined, there is no discernible system of order of arrangement of poems in the book. In any case, there is no identified "war section" in this book. It might be guessed that the four poems fell together naturally and that Anderson left them that way. The matter must be left that way in view of lack of evidence for a definite system of grouping and a failure to accomplish other groupings in other more fully-developed subjects.

Anderson thought his most important war poem was "Mid-American Prayer." On April 19, 1917, he wrote to Frank: "I am sending you enclosed in this letter a thing I just wrote this morning called Mid-American Prayer. This I believe strikes the note that I have been reaching for in this war matter." He went on to say, "It strikes me that this is the sort of thing that we need to have spread over the country," suggesting its publication in Seven Arts, suggesting additionally making it into a pamphlet to send out to the Seven Arts mailing list. "Also send it to the newspapers--then put it in the June number of Seven Arts." It did appear in the June, 1917, Seven Arts with "From Chicago."

The poem is in five free-verse stanzas. The narrator tells in the first stanza of his attempt to "find his way to gods" in communion with nature, particularly in "my cornfields that I loved." The second section refers to the way people have "lived in houses in cities and we forgot the fields and the praying.... I walk in the streets seeing my own well-clad body and my fat hands with shame." Next the "lean men fighting" connected with "the gods forgotten in the fields," and he concludes the third passage by declaring:

> My mind leaps forward and I think of the time when our hands, no longer fat, may touch even the lean dear hands of France, when we also have suffered and get back to prayer

The fourth part concerns itself with the way the old world may help the realization of the dream "that these fields and places, out here west of Pittsburgh, may become sacred places, that because of this terrible thing, of which we may now become a part, there is hope of hardness and leanness --that we may get to lives of which we may be unashamed. " In the last stanza, here reproduced, the essential message of rejection of the ugly conflict and the hope a brotherhood of all men is to grow out of it is stated:

> God, lead us to the fields now. Suns for us and rains for us and a prayer for every growing thing.
>
> May our fields become our sacred places.
>
> May we have courage to shake with our man's hate him who would profit by the suffering of the world.
>
> May we strip ourself clean and go hungry that after this terrible storm has passed our sacred fields may feed German, Jew and Japanese.
>
> May the sound of enmity die in the groaning of growing things in our fields.
>
> May we get to gods and the brotherhood through growth springing out of the destruction of man.
>
> For all of Mid-America the greater prayer and the birth of humbleness. [44]

The eight-line poem, "Night" is devoted to a statement of a sympathetic attitude toward the allied country, France, referred to in "Mid-American Prayer. " In the "longest, blackest, night of our lives, " "Dear France" is invited to "Put out your hand to us" (page 54).

"Dirge of War, " a twelve-stanza poem, has a simple message of rejection of the terrible conflict. In the first stanza the poet says "I did not think the end would come so/ soon. It has--goodbye. " Doubtless referring to a linkage between his statements and the development of America, he laments in the tenth stanza, "I was coming with America-- dreaming with America--hoping with America--then war came. " The last line is: "I pay my fare to hell--I die--I die" (pages 74-75).

In the interest of the reader's examining for himself the nature of this poetry and seeing at least some works other than by piece-meal reference, the two war-related poems of moderate length are now reproduced entire:

WAR

Long lanes of fire, dead cornstalks burning,
Run now--head downward--plunging and crying,
Hold hard the breath now,
Forward we run.

Out of Nebraska, on into Kansas, now the word
        runs,
Runs with the wind, runs with the news of war,
        crying and screaming.
Now the word runs.

Out on the low ridges, black 'gainst the night sky;
Farmers boys running, factory boys running;
Boys from Ohio
And my Illinois.

Questions and answers, over the land,
Questions that hurt, answers that hurt,
Questions of courage
That cannot but hurt.

Deep in the cornfields the gods come to life,
Gods that have waited, gods that we knew not.
Gods come to life
In America now.

WE ENTER IN

Now you see, brothers, here in the West,
        here's how it is--
We stand and fall, we hesitate--
It is all new to us,
To kill to take a fellow's life.
Uh!--a nauseous fever takes the light away.

Now we stand up and enter in.
The baseness of the deed we too embrace.
We go in dumbly--into that dark place.
The germ of death we take into our veins.

Do we not know that we ourselves have failed?
Our valleys wide, our long green fields
We have bestrewn with our dead.
In shop and mart we have befouled our souls.
Our corn is withered and our faces black
With smoke of hate.

We make the gesture and we go to die.
Had we been true to our own land our sweetness
    then had quite remade the world.
We now are true to failure grim.
We go in prayer to die.

To our own souls we take the killer's sin.
Into the waters black our souls we fling.
We take the chances of the broader dream.
Not ours but all the worlds [sic]--our fields.
We enter in.

These poems are sincere, idealistic as well as naive, inept, certainly undistinguished, and reasonably characteristic. To complete the record, two more items must be added. Consideration of the one entitled "Industrialism" allows emphasis to be placed on the fact that the war, for Anderson, was an element among many to be considered rather than an overriding consideration. Anderson was focused on the significance of the industrialization of the nation throughout his artistic life, and in this poem devoted to this process he indicates the way industry and war are linked. Two decades later the manipulations of munitions makers were a public matter. In this poem (on pages 31-32) he wryly exhorts his "grim Mistress," the goddess of the factory, to:

Awake and shake thy dusty locks.
Come and drive the soldiers to their toil.
A million men my mistress needs
To kiss
And kill
For her desire,
To-night--
Arise.

The war element is in even more remote perspective in "Song of Stephen the Westerner" (pages 38-40). In the customary process of the artist of recording, reiterating, exploring the process of life, Anderson has Stephen (a representative, of course, of himself) telling where he has come from, what he is doing, what is to become of him (and, of course, all of mankind). He is "of the West," "out of the creeping and straining." He has come "sweating and steaming out of the corn rows." The over-all process described the movement of man out of life in purely natural surroundings to the unnatural, complicated, undesirable ("My throat is sore with the dust of new cities") life in more complicated patterns. The account ends with the resolve:

> ...I shall build my/ home with great hammers.
> New song is tearing the cords/ of my throat. I
> am becoming a man covered with dust. / I have
> kissed the black hands of new brothers....

In the panoramic account of Stephen-man-Anderson he includes this passage:

> In my warm ignorance I lay dead in the corn rows.
> On the/ wind came names and cries. I squirmed
> and writhed. / I was frightened and wept. My fa-
> thers emerged from/ the corn and killed each other
> in battle.

Though he was unable to ignore the war, Anderson's poems seem from the first to have been absorbed with a basic reaction to nature, exemplified primarily by the growing corn. A letter of January, 1917, sets the tone <u>Mid-American Chants</u> continued to sound when published over a year later:

> Some day the strong race will come. Men will
> suffer and be unafraid. I went along praying. "My
> destiny is new." I said to myself[.] "I can be-
> lieve in beauty in the midst of this hububb. [sic]
> Down the wind comes the call of new men. It
> plays in the corn, in my corn, in the long corn
> fields.
>
> The corn fields shall be the mothers of men. They
> are rich with milk to suckle men. They will come
> sturdy and strong out of the west. You may prick
> them with spears. Their blood will run out on the
> snow but they are my men and shall survive.
>
> I am a little child and I weep. My hands are cold.
> I run along and blow upon them. But in me is the
> blood of strong men. A little I have endured and

shall endure. I am of the blood of strong men.
The milk of the corn is in me too.

Sweet, sweet the thought of new men.   I am cold
and run through the streets.   Sweet, sweet, the
thought of the new men. [45]

Before the collection was published, Anderson had
notice served on him that his lyric obsession with corn could
cause him difficulty.   The line "See the corn.   How it
aches" in "The Visit, " when it appeared in the September,
1917, issue of Poetry (page 285), gave one writer the opportunity to refer to him as "the chiropodist poet. "[46]   He expressed to Frank a stubborn determination to go ahead with
publication: "I would publish the verses for one reason if
no other.   It will give a rare opportunity to those who desire
to flay me. "   But he did change the poem.   In Poetry the
opening two lines are:

Westward the field of the cloth of gold.
It is fall. See the corn. How it aches.

And in Mid-American Chants (page 55) they are revised to
read:

Westward the field of the cloth of gold.
It is fall-see the gold in the dust of the fields.

The rest of the poem remained the same.

In a letter of early 1918 Anderson told Brooks, "Lane's
have decided to go ahead with my cornfield songs. "   The
emphasis on corn was even continued in the binding of the
book.   On the cover with the title and the name of the author
is the depiction of a ripe ear of corn, bursting forth from
its husk.

Two passages seem to explain the extreme multiplicity
of references to corn and cornfields in the book.   The first
is from the first poem, "The Cornfields" (page 11):

I am pregnant with song.   My body aches but do
not betray/ me.   I will sing songs and hide them
away.   I will tear/ them into bits and throw them
in the street.   The streets/ of my city are full of
dark holes.   I will hide my songs/ in the holes of
the streets.

In the darkness of the night I awoke and the bands
that / bound me were broken.   I was determined to
bring old / things into the land of the new.   A
sacred vessel I found / and ran with it into the
fields, into the long fields where / the corn rustles.

Into the cities the people had gathered.   They had
become / dizzy with words.   Words had choked
them.   They / could not breathe.

On my knees I crawled before my people.   I de-
based myself. / The excretions of their bodies I
took for my food.   Into / the ground I went and my
body died.   I emerged in the / corn, in the long
cornfields.   My head arose and was / touched by
the west wind.   The light of old things, awoke in
me.   In the cornfields / the sacred vessel is set
up.

   A less figurative recapitulation of his experience and
attitude is found in "Mid-American Prayer" (pages 70-71):

When I was a boy I went into the cornfields at
night.   I / said words I had not dared to say to
people, defying the / New Englanders' gods, trying
to find honest, mid-western / American gods.

And all the time the fields spread east and west.
An / empire was building. /
Towns grew up, factories multiplied. /
You see the corn had come into its own but that
[was?] destroyed too.

I and my men stood up but we grew fat.   We lived
in / homes in cities and we forgot the fields and
the praying /-the lurking sounds, sights, smells of
old things.

Now I am ashamed and many of my men are
ashamed. /
I cannot tell how deep my shame lies. /
I walk in the streets seeing my own well-clad body
and my / fat hands with shame.

   The regional (mid-American) character of Anderson's
view of his response to nature should not be overlooked.
These were "cornfield songs" and were especially in reaction

to the eastern part of the country. It will be noted that he
originally thought of calling the group of six poems published
in Poetry "West Winds" and then, seemingly to make his idea
more overt, he called them "Mid-American Songs. "

A sampling of the numerous, refrain-like references
to his dependence on the corn for inspiration and solace may
be given: "I am come to the face of the gods through the
cornfields" ("Song of the Beginning of Courage, " page 22);
"I am come sweating and streaming out of the corn rows"
(Song of Stephen the Westerner, " page 38); "Long, long ago,
when days were new, / Fresh born of cornfields, undefiled"
("Mid-American Prayer, " page 71); "I have heard gods whispering in the corn and wind/. . . . I have run back to gods,
to prayers and dreams" ("Assurance, " page 78); and "The
gods wait in the corn, / The soul of the song is in the land. /
Life up your lips to that" ("Song for Lonely Roads, " page
60).

Throughout the book there is an interest in nature
reverberative of his central focus on the corn.   This passage
perhaps helps to place the corn-worship in a broader frame.

I want falling light and an evening sky,
I want to sing my songs low crooning to the moon.
I want to bring gods home to sweating men in corn-
        rows and shops
When my songs sing. [47]

And in the "Song of the Bug" (page 77) he allows the bug to
address humans to express a need for the understanding of
the importance of non-human factors:

There is a certain dignity in my life if you
        could but under/
stand it,
You great bug that keep thinking such
        almighty thoughts,
Harsh to the little song of my kind
It would be well for you if you could understand
        that.

Perhaps before leaving the matter of nature-emphasis
in these poems, comment may be made, regarding the numerous
corn references, of an idea of one of Anderson's biographers[48] that "the chants reflect Anderson's wish to assert his
male certainty ('the milk of the corn is in me'). " The poem

from which the quotation was taken, "Hosanna," also includes
these lines (page 67):

> The cornfields shall be the mothers of men.
> They are rich with the milk that shall suckle men.
> The bearded men shall arise.
> They shall come sturdy and strong out of the
>   West.

. . .

> In me is the blood of the strong men.
> A little I have endured and shall endure.
> I am of the blood of strong bearded men.
> The milk of the corn is in me.

What the poem says is that the bearded men shall have been
suckled on the "milk of the corn." The "milk," it would
appear, is not to be thought of as a seminal metaphor. The
impression that these songs are not necessarily used for an
expression of masculinity is supported by the following passage, which finds the singer in a completely feminine role:

> Lying in deep grass my throat hurts
>   and my body aches
> I am with child to dreams.
> Cities new-build and all the squirming,
>   changing hoards of men
>   Press down on me.
> They press me deep into the ground. [49]

This poem also includes reference to the "male milk in my
breast." The Finley letter, quoted earlier, it may be recalled, said of the corn fields that they "shall be the mothers of men. They are rich with milk to suckle men." Thus
any "milk" reference to corn has to be examined carefully,
for it may be used either procreatively or nutritively, usually the latter. Further the "I" of the poems is always only
speculatively specifically Anderson. Sometimes he is speaking for midwesterners and sometimes for the whole human
race in the first person.

   The second poem in Mid-American Chants, following
"The Cornfields," is, no doubt by thoughtful choice, "Chicago," a poem which enunciates Anderson's concern with the
way of life in city streets as opposed to in the corn rows.
In "Manhattan" the poet writes, "From the place of cornfields

I went into the new places. " Having there suffered and known pain, the poet records (page 29):

> In the morning I arose from my bed and was
> healed [of the pain of the city.] To the
> cornfields I went laughing and singing.

In "Song to New Song" (page 47) the declaration is made that:

> As you [the singer of Chicago] float and wait,
>   uttering your hoarse cries
> I see new beauties in the standing corn,
> And dream of singers yet to come.

There is evidence that Anderson thinks of many Americans, presumably city-dwellers, as non-responsive to the message to be found in nature:

> We were the heavy ones, heavy and sure.
> The wind in the cornfields moved us not.
> We, the Americans, worthy and sure,
> Worthy and sure of ourselves.

But he could also be more optimistic about the influence of nature:

> In denser shadows by the factory walks,
> In my old cornfields, broken where the cattle roam,
> The shadow of the face of God falls down. [50]

Naturally the response of Anderson to city life was in terms of his observations of Chicago, where he had lived for approximately fifteen years when the poems about it were written.   Seventeen of the poems make distinct reference to city life, ten of them mentioning Chicago by name.   Two poems, "Chicago" and "Song of the Soul of Chicago, " are concerned entirely with reaction to the city.   "You know my city--Chicago triumphant--" he wrote, "factories and marts and the roar of machines--horrible, terrible, ugly and brutal. "[51]   In Chicago, too, were "many faces, drifting, perplexing, confusing, destroying, betraying, confounding. "[52] Then the city, as Anderson has it speak, makes immature claim to maturity, is forced to express its own weakness and paradoxicality:

> I am a little thing, a tiny little thing on the vast
> prairies.

I know nothing.   My mouth is dirty.   I cannot
   tell what
I want. . .

. . . Life is dying in men.
I am old and palsied.   I am just at the beginning
   of my
Life. 53

   There is irony in the title of "Song of the Soul of
Chicago, " which gives expression to a loutish Babbittry, as
exemplified by these lines (page 63):

I'll talk forever--I'm damned if I'll sing.   Don't
   you see
that mine is not a
singing people?   We're just a lot of
muddy things caught up by the stream.
You can't fool us.   Don't we know
ourselves?

Here we are, out here in Chicago.   You think
   we're not
humble?   You're a liar.   We are like the sewerage
   of our
town, swept up stream by a kind of mechanical
   triumph
--that's what we are.

   . . .

But say, bards, you keep off our bridges.   Keep
   out of our
dream, dreamers.   We want to give this democracy thing
they talk so big about a whirl.   We want to see if
   we
are any good out here, we Americans from all over
   hell.
That's what we want.

   Attendant upon the cruelty and ugliness of city life
was the scourge of industrialism.   Anderson had seen the
factories entering such villages as Clyde, found himself hating the factory work, saw in it the foe of creativity in man.
He expresses his reaction in a personification of Industrialism:

In the long house of hate,
In the long hours,
In the never-ending day;
Over the fields--her black hair flying--
My mistress
Terrible
Gigantic
Gaunt and drear. [54]

In this same poem, he looks back, as he was to do so characteristically to the village life of the past, and mourns.

Old knowledge and all old beliefs
By your hand killed--
My mistress
Grim.

In "Song of Industrial America" the interpolated refrain contains the repeated phrase, "Winter of song." The
questions are raised: "Can a singer arise and sing in this
world of smoke and grime? Can he keep his throat clear?
Can his courage survive?" Industry is pictured in this poem
as a "terrible, horrible flood turned loose"; above this torrent the artist is trying his "ringing voice." And the poem
ends with the sarcastic question, "Why the devil didn't you
make some money and own an automobile?" (Page 17.)

Anderson had shown concern for America's workers
in both Windy McPherson's Son and Marching Men. In "Song
to the Sap" he hopes to reach the "Men, sweaty men, who
walk on frozen reads/ or stand and listen by the factory
door." He refers (page 51) hopefully to a situation, in which
there will be:

From all of Mid-America a prayer,
To newer, braver gods, to dawns and days,
To truth and cleaner, braver life we come.
Lift up a song.
My sweaty men,
Lift up a song.

He can also rather desperately refer to hurling his songs into
the "mighty wheels of the engine." The poet is identified as
Cedric the Silent, "the son of Irwin and Emma." Cedric
must be strong and willing to give his life and his soul to
America. [55]

Although singers of the day may be "choked by the fury of the furnaces, " there are other singers yet to come. [56] The factors involved are poised against each other in the title of "Chant to Dawn in a Factory Town, " which includes the refrain, "I hail thee, O love, " meaning the dawn, and asserts that "Song is consuming the terrible engine of life" (page 56).

He was really more hopeful than his declaration in the opening sentence of the "Foreword" to Mid-American Chants suggests: "I do not believe that we people of mid-western America, immersed as we are in affairs, hurried and harried through life by the terrible engine-industrialism-have come to the time of song. " His diffident remarks, indicating that perhaps he could be the forerunner of some real poet to come, do not fit his real desire and hope:

> ...I wanted earth in me and skies and fields and rivers and people. I wanted these things to come out of me, or song, as singing prose, or poetry even.

> What else have I ever cared for as I have cared to have this happen. What women, what possessions, what promise of life after death, all that? I have wanted this unity of things, this song, this earth, this sky, this brotherhood.

> A race for a moment singing thus out of one throat. Is it not what I have wanted?

> For that would I not give, freely and gladly, all hope of such things as a future life, duty to society, to wife, to family, to all the white men's shibboleth? [57]

In Mid-American Chants (page 82), the concluding poem, "Song of the Singer, " gives the best summation of the way he saw himself as a poet, though numerous poems reflect fragments of the same concept:

> Drunken and staggering--
> Saying all profane things--
> Kissing your hands to the gods--
> In the night praying and whimpering
> Asking to sing and not singing--
> You--

My brother.

Beating upon it with fists--
Trying to shake it off--
Hoping and dreaming you will emerge--
My sister.

I wrap my arms about you that hunger.
In the long hair of my breast there is warmth.
I look far into the future beyond the
    noise and the clatter.
I will not be crushed by the iron machine.

Sing.
Dare to sing.
Kiss the mouth of song with your lips.
In the morning and the evening
Trust to the terrible strength of indomitable song.

The adjuration to "Kiss the mouth of song with your lips" is comparable to the line in "Spring Song": "Now, America, you press your lips to mine" (page 30). Anderson wrote a friend that he thought of his artistic experiences in terms comparable to copulation, and his poetry constantly makes use of sexual images. "I am pregnant with song" and "Now I leap and cry like a young stallion"[58] are good examples. The whole of "Song of the Mating Time" is devoted to the expression of poetic endeavor in sexual terms.

The following passages are representative of numerous references devoted to this basically emotional conception of himself in relation to his art:

I am come to the face of the gods through
    the cornfields.
Back to the work of my mother I go.
Ache-ache-ache and behold me.   Lay
    thy hot hands on my thigh. [59]

Do you not see, O my beloved, that I am
    become strong to caress the woman!   I
    caress
    all men and all women.   I make myself
    naked.

O my beloved--men and women--I come into your
presence.   It is night and I am alone and I come
to you.   I open the window of my room so that you
may come in.   I am a lover and I would touch you
with the fingers of my hands.   In my eyes a fire
burns.   The strength of my imagining is beyond
words to record.   I see the loveliness that is in
you hidden away.   I take something from you.
See, I embrace you.   I take you in my arms and
I run away. 60

In the soft night I have touched the bodies of men,
I have touched with rough fingers the lips of women,
I have become with child to all men,
I, master of life, embrace all men. 61

    In spite of the intensity of sexual images in Ander-
son's poetic consciousness, this book contains no identifiable
reference to any of his own experiences and few which appear to concern particular people or incidents.   The following poem, "The Stranger" (page 36), does seem to be concerned with a reaction to a specific woman:

Her eyes are like the seeds of melons.   Her
    breasts are thin
  and she walks awkwardly.   I am in love with
    her.
With her I have adventured into a new love.   In
    all the
  world there is no such love as I have for her.
I took hold of her shoulder and walked beside her.
    We
  went out of the city into the fields.   By the
    still
  road we went and it was night.   We were long
    alone together.
The bones of her shoulders are thin.   The sharp
    bone of her
  shoulder has left a mark on my hand.
I am come up into the wind like a ship.   Her thin
    hand is laid hold
  of me.   My land where the corn nods has
  become my land.
I am come up into the wind like a ship and the
    thin hand
  of woman is laid upon me.

Anderson has written much of the experience of being in love, as in the poem just quoted, but the following poem, celebrating the physical incompletion of such a relationship, is rather a rarity:

> Now you are dear to me,
> Now my beloved.
> You are the one I did not take.
> Even then,
> When my body was young,
> When the sweetness of you made me drunk,
> You are the one I did not take.
>
> All that is old came into me,
> The night by the bush and the stairs in the dark.
> Yours were the lips I did not kiss,
> Yours the love that I kept.
>
> Long and long have I walked alone,
> Past the cornfields and over the bridge,
> Sucking the sweetness out of nights,
> Dreaming things that have made me old
> and young,
> Since that night.
>
> Faring away down a lonely road.
> Now you must go, my beloved,
> Thinking your thoughts in the bitter nights,
> You that I loved and did not take. [62]

Another poem on this subject, which has the overt title, "Song of the Love of Women," treats it in a cryptic and generalized way. The following passage (page 37), which seems to catch the message of the three four-line stanzas, displays a yearning for a spiritual rather than a physical relationship:

> Come to me, sisters, come home to the corn-
>   fields--
> Long have I ached for you, body and brain.
> Have you nothing to offer but bread and your
>   bodies--
> How long must I wait for you, sisters, in vain?

As may be readily noticed, the factors of nature, sex, love, and religion were all interfused in Anderson's concept of life and his work. As he wrote in April, 1917:

In the forest amid old trees and wet dead leaves a
shrine.   Christ coming to life and life calling.
Lips to be pressed.   God in the winds as well as
the God that kneels and prays.   Let's be creeping.
Come away. 63

This reference is doubly valuable, for it may be imagined as
dating the poem, "Spring Song," which is a fuller development of the same ideas, using some of the same lines.   It
seems possible to decide the letter was written when Anderson was at work on a draft of the poem.

In the forest, amid old trees and wet leaves, a
    shrine.
Men on the wet leaves kneeling.
The spirit of God in the air above a shrine.

Now, America, you press your lips to mine,
Feel on your lips the throbbing of my blood.
Christ, come to life and life calling,
Sweet and strong.

Spring.   God in the air above the fields.
Farmers marking fields for the planting of the
    corn.
Fields marked for corn to stand in long straight
    aisles.

In the spring I press your body down on
    wet cold new-plowed ground.
Men, give your souls to me.
I would have my sacred way with you.

In the forest amid old trees and wet dead leaves,
    a shrine.
Men rising from the kneeling place to sing.
Everywhere in the fields now the planting of corn. 64

Although there is no evidence in any aspect of Anderson's life to support the idea of his following conventional
ideas of religion or Christianity--rather there are to the
contrary--the references in this poem to prayer and God and
Christ are echoed in other poems in this book.   The most
numerous references are to prayer, the outstanding of these
being in the title of "Mid-American Prayer" (pages 69-72),
which, it will be recalled, Anderson thought to be his most
important utterance on the war.   In this poem he makes six

references to prayer, which his letter indicates was not an
uncommon interest to him at this time. His poem says people generally have forgotten "the fields and the praying";
the speaker in the poem states "I go along here in Chicago
praying..."; the time is anticipated when the United States
will have suffered as France has and the population will have
gone "back to prayer"; in the cornfields "the old dreams and
prayers" will be recaptured; there is mention of "a prayer
for every growing thing"; and the concluding two lines of
the poem are in the mode of prayer:

> May we get to gods and the greater brother-
>   hood through
>   growth springing out of the destruction
>   of men.
> For all of Mid-America the greater prayer and
>   the
>   birth of humbleness.

     In general he seems to have thought of prayer in
terms of personal forces and excitement of the imagination,
as in the following lines, rather than in relation to deific
worship:

> You must get serious, now and then,
> In the night when it is dark and the wild winds
>   blow.
> I do. I weep and pray and have big thoughts.
> That's what makes life seem so strange and un-
>   believable... [65]

     Even though Anderson's conception of the deity seems
not at all to have been the definitive one he might have found
in the conventional worship of his day, which he seems
largely to have either rejected or ignored, a cluster of
references to God in these poems should be noted. Already
quoted in "Spring Song" was the mention of "The spirit of
God in the air above a shrine" and "God in the air above
the fields." In another poem are the lines:

> You see I am whispering my secret to you.
> I want you to believe in my insanity and
>   to understand
>   that I love God--[66]

In "Mid-American Prayer" (page 71) deity is looked to for
guidance and succor:

> God, lead us to the fields now.   Sun
> for us and rains for
> us and a prayer for every growing thing.
> May our fields become our sacred places.

More often, however, than he refers to God, Anderson refers to gods, examples of which have already appeared. An example of these two concepts appearing together is the following:

> Men, sweaty men, who walk on frozen roads,
> Or stand and listen by the factory door,
> Look up, men!
> Stand hard!
> On winds the gods sweep down.
>
> In denser shadows by the factory walks,
> In my old cornfields, broken where the cattle
>   roam,
> The shadow of the face of God falls down. [67]

Christ is specifically mentioned three times in these poems.   Once he uses "the lips of the dead Christ"[68] as a figure of whiteness.   In another the poet's mistress, Industrialism, waits beside the mill "To kiss the sword/ of Christ. "[69]   The third reference is a whole poem, "Song Long After, " addressed to a Woman, referred to as Mary in the version published in Others, considering imaginatively and inaccurately the scene in the "upper room" before the betrayal by Judas. [70]   The chief significance of these references is to establish his interest in and concern with the fate of Christ as a prelude to his use of this factor in Winesburg.

In view of the fact that the Mid-American Chants were written between the time he started Winesburg and the time he published it, it is not surprising that the poems have many elements in them which suggest the Ohio tales.   For example, Winesburg is primarily a protest against the way in which mankind fails to achieve its potential of beauty and happiness.   In one of the Chants (page 23), "Revolt, " Anderson writes: "By the/ howling of dogs in the silence the decay of men is pro-/claimed. "   Not only has man decayed from a better state, but, more important to Anderson, evidently, is the factor of undesirable restraint.   In one poem there is advice to be patient, an admonishment: "Burst not they hands, " the implication being that such bursting is costly and unpropitious, though an understandable

temptation.[71] Again there is notation that "The little flat
bands that bind my body were tense."[72] The creative process is directly recognized as a curative and corrective factor:

> I awoke and the bands that bind me were broken.
> I was
>   determined to bring love into the hearts of my
>   people.
> The sacred vessel was put into my hands and I ran
>   with
>   it into the fields. In the long cornfields the
>   sacred vessel
> is set up.[73]

The poet, as Anderson represents him, feels that the
"people of my time were bound with chains." The "Long
fields" and the "standing corn" and the "west winds," all in-
extricably intertwined with his excited reaction to nature,
had been forgotten by people to their detriment.

The way in which Anderson feels an impassioned involvement with the unfortunate person is reflected in several
passages. These two passages are indicative:

> Men, give your souls to me.
> I would have my sacred way with you.

> I have gone into the women's chambers, into the
>   secret places
> Of all women and all men I have gone. I have
>   made love
> to them. Before me in the chamber lies the naked
>   body
> of a woman. She is strong and young.[74]

As the "lover," he experiences "strength of imaginings...
beyond words to record." He sees "loneliness in you that
is hidden away."[75] He encourages the "faint little voices"
to "lift up." But he states, regretfully, "they are swept
away in the void...."[76]

It will be recalled that the factor of the grotesque had
appeared in his earlier prose writings. "American Spring
Song"[77] also makes use of this idea, so crucial in Winesburg:

> Under a bridge I crawled and stood trembling with
>   joy
> at the river's edge.
>
> Because it was spring and soft sunlight ran through
>   the cracks of the bridge
> I tried to understand myself.
>
> Out of the mud of the river's edge I moulded my-
>   self
>   a god,
> A grotesque little god with a twisted face,
> A god for myself and my men.

One poem and a passage from another show the influence in this book of the character studies which became
the content of Winesburg.   One feels the beginning of a
Winesburg episode in this:

> Now in this room, a face stands forth,
> A narrow face, with many shadows
>   hid 'twixt brow and chin.
> The face half turns,
> It tells its tale to me,
> Now down the drumming way of time it
>   goes and leaves me shaken here.
> Now women and tall men,
> My little brother who passed my way,
> Bestow a kiss on me.
> Turn quick they face, let what is old grow new.
> Strike in the darkness at the horrid lie. [78]

The following poem is a Winesburg episode:

> All the night she walked and dreamed on the frozen
>   road,
> Shy the insane one, feeling and thinking.
> All night she walked and wanted to kill,
> Wanted to love and kill.
>
> What did she want?
> Nobody knew.
> None of us knew why she wanted to kill.
>
> We were the heavy ones, heavy and sure.
> The wind in the cornfields moved us not.
> We the Americans, worthy and sure,

Worthy and sure of ourselves.

Tom killed his brother on Wednesday night,
Back of the corncrib, under the hill.
Then she ran to him, sobbing and calling,
She who had loved and could not kill. [79]

There is, of course, no way to measure the extent
to which Anderson had specific realities of his own life in
mind as he wrote his poems.   But enough can be identified
to make them worth mentioning.   No treatment of the book
would be complete without note of its dedication to his
daughter, Marion Margaret Anderson, then six years old.
There is no information of any kind about his reasons for
doing this.   It certainly may be assumed that the book was
not one she could read with interest or understanding.   It is
conceivable that the idea came to him as a means of showing
interest in the child, to make up for his absence from his
family.

A very different but equally intriguing reference is in
the poem, "Unborn" (page 53), here reproduced in its en-
tirety:

Swift across the nights a little cry,
Against the cold white night a stain of red.
The mood dips down,
The dull winds blow.
My unborn son is dead.

Perhaps this alludes to an unhappy experience of either his
first or second wife; present knowledge neither suggests nor
denies this supposition.

Any reader of Mid-American Chants will readily see
that the poems in the book are referent to Anderson's background of life.   Even the portions of poems which have been
given suggest it.   An unusual specific mention of his family
by name is found thus in "Song of Cedric the Silent" (page
19):

Like a guest I am come into the house,
the terrible house. / So gentle and quiet I came
they do not know me.   The / son of Irwin
and Emma I am....

A highly peripheral reference to his father is the line: "on the straw in the stables sat Enid the maker of harness. "80

In the poem on page 50, "Night Whispers," a glimpse
is seen of the poet thinking of his mother as a fellow sensitive sufferer of life, the mood he must have been in when
he wrote the dedication of Winesburg.

> Just midnight quiet and a sundered cloud, --
> mother I live--
> Aching and waiting to work my way through.

> You of the long and the gaunt--silent and grim
>   you stood
> Terribly sweet the touch of your hand--
> Mother, reach down.

> Grey the walks and long the waiting--
>   grey the age dust on the floor.
> If they whip and beat us, little mother,
>   need we care?

Between the summer of 1917 and the spring of 1918,
Anderson, it will be recalled, changed the words of "A Visit"
to avoid a newspaperman's jibe about the "chiropodist poet."
Examination of the Others text for June, 1917, the Poetry
text for September, 1917, and the text of Mid-American
Chants shows some other interesting editorial work, doubtless by Anderson. Minor changes include such things as
substituting the comma or the period for the dash or the
comma for the semicolon, changing line arrangement, and
two changes in capitalization. In a few cases a word has
been changed.

In three of the poems, however, there is indication
of more extensive change. The original Mary of "Song Long
After" becomes "Woman" and, more important, a first-per-
son monologue by Christ becomes a third-person account. 81
"Song of the Drunken Business Man" (page 64) is not changed
in meaning, but it is given a tighter structure through the
elimination of a refrain, which appears in four places in the
original, and the last stanza. Anderson relieved some of
the sentimental obviousness of the poem by dropping off a
last stanza which read as follows:

> Well, I'm tired. I ache. What's the use?
> I can't meet the note. I have a son.
> Let's go home. It's twelve o'clock.

I'm going to get that boy into West Point yet.

These four lines were probably the worst in a distinctly mediocre poem.

The two revisions in "Evening Song" show Anderson retaining his idea intact but attempting to rearrange it in order to improve its structure:

Poetry version:

My song will rest while I rest.   I struggle along.
     I'll get
back to the corn and the open fields.   Don't fret,
     love,
I'll come out all right.

Back of Chicago the open fields.   Were you ever
     there--
trains coming toward you out of the West--
     streaks of
light on the long gray plains?   Many a song--
     aching
to sing.

I've got a gray and ragged brother in my breast--
     that's a
fact.   Back of Chicago the open fields--long
     trains go
west too--in the silence.   Don't fret, love.   I'll
     come
out all right.

Mid-American Chants version:

Back of Chicago the open fields--were you ever
     there?
Trains coming toward you out of the west--
Streaks of light on the long grey plains--many a
     song--
Aching to sing.

I've got a grey and ragged brother in my breast--
That's a fact.

Back of Chicago the open fields--were you ever
     there?

Trains going from you into the West--
Clouds of dust on the long grey plains.
Long trains go West, too--in the silence
Always the song--
Waiting to sing.

Notes

1.   Chicago Daily News, March 2, 1914, p. 1.

2.   Letter to M. D. Finley, Dec. 10, 1916.

3.   Letter to M. D. Finley, Feb. 26, 1917. "M. " is believed to be Marion Bush, a friend of the early Chicago
period.

4.   Letter to M. D. Finley, April 9, 1917.

5.   Mid-American Chants, New York, John Lane, 1918.
All page references in the present book are to this edition.

6.   Letter to Paul Rosenfeld, presumably 1922.

7.   Note (undated) and typescripts are in the Anderson Collection of the Newberry Library.   Possibly other poems
accompanied the note.

8.   Ibid.

9.   4:3-6.

10.   Note marked by Miss Monroe "rec'd April 27, 1917. "

11.   This letter has on it Miss Monroe's stamp for July 9,
1917.   The poems were "American Spring Song, " "Song
of Stephen the Westerner, " "Evening Song, " "Song of the
Drunken Business Man, " "Song of Industrial America, "
and "A Visit. "   Poetry contained a note that Anderson had
published poetry in Others.

12.   The card has on it Miss Monroe's notation that she
answered it on July 9, 1917.

13.   The card is postmarked Merrill, N.Y. , the post office
for Lake Chateaugay, July 9, 1917.

14. Dated through Miss Monroe's notation: "July 14, 1917 Answd. H. M. "

15. Dated from Miss Monroe's notation: "No ans September 21, 1917. "

16. Undated letter (JR). Of the titles mentioned, only "Brief Barroom Songs" is not to be found in Mid-American Chants.

17. "Mid-American Songs, " Poetry, X (Sept. 1917) 281-291.

18. Letter of Sept. 17, 1917. Line quoted was eliminated from the text in Mid-American Chants.

19. Letter of Oct. 29, 1917, from Frank, and undated Anderson reply, apparently immediate.

20. Letter to M. D. Finley, Nov. 1917.

21. Howe, p. 22.

22. The review by Ben Hecht was on p. 9 of the Chicago Daily News.

23. Dated by Miss Monroe's note: "April 19, 1918. Rec'd. "

24. Letter to Frank, April 10, 1918.

25. Letters from Frank dated "1918, " and June 24, 1918.

26. Letter to Frank of early April 1918.

27. Letter to Frank, May 1918.

28. Chicago Evening Post, April 26, 1918, p. 10.

29. Chicago Daily News, April 17, 1918, p. 9.

30. From "The Cornfields, " p. 11-12, Mid-American Chants.

31. From "Song of the Mating Time, " p. 59.

32. Chicago Daily News, May 1, 1918, p. 12.

33. Letter to M. D. Finley, Nov. 27, 1916.

34. Letter to M. D. Finley, Feb. 5, 1917.

35. Letters to M. D. Finley; Feb. 1 and 3, 1917.

36. Letter to M. D. Finley, May 25, 1917.

37. Letter to Waldo Frank, Sept. 7, 1917.

38. Schevill, p. 90.

39. From copy of letter supplied by Miss Margaret Sandburg, the poet's daughter, Flat Rock, N. C. In a letter of July 2, 1964, Miss Sandburg dated the letter as "probably written in 1917."

40. Carl Sandburg, Complete Poems. New York: Harcourt Brace, 1950, p. 147. The poem appeared originally in Cornhuskers, 1918.

41. Letters to Waldo Frank, springtime and after Aug. 6, 1918.

42. Letter to M. D. Finley, Dec. 1918.

43. Letter to M. D. Finley, May 1919.

44. Mid-American Chants, p. 69-72.

45. Letter to M. D. Finley, Jan. 19, 1917.

46. Letter to Frank, September 1917.

47. "Song of the Middle World," Chants, p. 35.

48. Howe, p. 89.

49. "Song for Dark Nights"; Chants, p. 48.

50. "The Lover" and "Song to the Sap"; p. 49 and 51.

51. "Song of Industrial America"; p. 15.

52. "Song of the Break of Day"; p. 21.

53. "Chicago," p. 13.

54. "Industrialism"; p. 31.

55. "Song of Cedric the Silent"; p. 19-20.

56. "Song to the New Song"; p. 47.

57. "One Throat," Sherwood Anderson Reader, p. 227-8.

58. "The Cornfields" and "Song of the Mating Time"; p. 11 and 59.

59. "Song of the Beginning of Courage"; p. 22.

60. "Song of Theodore"; p. 27 and 25.

61. "Chant to Dawn in a Factory Town"; p. 56.

62. "Reminiscent Song"; p. 80.

63. Letter to M. D. Finley, April 17, 1917.

64. Mid-American Chants, p. 30.

65. "Song to a Western Statesman"; p. 76.

66. "American Spring Song"; p. 45.

67. "Song to the Sap"; p. 51.

68. "Chant to Dawn in a Factory Town"; p. 57.

69. "Industrialism"; p. 32.

70. p. 61. "Sang [sic] Long After," Others, (June 1917) 4:4.

71. "Rhythms"; p. 52.

72. "Song of the Awaking of Courage"; p. 22.

73. "The Cornfields"; p. 12.

74. "Spring Song" and "Song of Theodore"; p. 30 and 27.

75. "Song of Theodore"; p. 25.

76. "Song of Industrial America"; p. 16.

77.   Mid-American Chants, p. 44.

78.   "Assurance"; p. 78.

79.   "The Lover"; p. 49.

80.   "Song of Stephen the Westerner"; p. 39.

81.   Others, June 1917, 4:4.

Chapter 10 (continued)

D. Winesburg, Ohio

It was characteristic of Anderson to refer to the writing process in sexual terms: "I am always striving for the moment of copulation."[1] A friend who knew him when he was writing the Winesburg stories recalled, "He often said that the stories of the people in Winesburg fairly gushed from his pen. He wrote them rapidly and after re-reading for corrections would sometimes marvel himself at their graphicness."[2] Cornelia remembered his saying that he was "like a harp the wind blew through."[3]

Anderson's account of how he wrote the stories in Chicago is doubtless substantially correct.

> ...I wrote them all, complete in the one sitting. I do not think I afterward changed a word of it [the first story]. I wrote it off so, sitting at my desk, in that room, the rain blowing in on me and wetting my back and when I had written it I got up from my desk.
>
> The rest of the stories in the book were written on succeeding evenings, and sometimes during the day when I worked in advertising office. At intervals there would be a blank space of a week, and then there would be two or three written during a week. I was like a woman having my babies, one after the other but without pain. [4]

Another view of the time when he did "at last go out of myself, truly into others, the others I met constantly in the streets of the city, in the office where I then worked, and still others, remembered out of my childhood in an American small town,"[5] is supplied by Miss Finley:

Winesburg, Ohio was being written while he was
still in advertising and it was against the modern
industrialism and the dirt and smoke of Chicago.
He would go back to 735 Cass Street in the evenings
or sometimes he would sneak out on work for a
day or so--When he got to his room with the curtains drawn and the candles lighted on his big bare
table, the business world was shut out temporarily.
He was no longer at war with it. |He would begin—
to re-create the characters he had known best in
his days at home with his mother and brothers and
— sisters.| He once said that in those times he could
"see the glimmer of stars in the eyes of his neighbors" of those early days.   That was said in one
of his more romantic sentimental moods.   Realism
was forgotten for a time.

Winesburg was more of an "escape" for him probably than any of his other works.   He loved those people and wrote of them with love and understanding.
At that time he was going on business trips to
Kentucky and would stop over here in Indianapolis
whenever he could make it.   Always he would bring
one or two of his Winesburg stories and read them
to me to "see how they sounded. "   Several times
I gave him some unwanted criticism which he very
seldom took.   Usually he would leave with me a
typewritten carbon copy of a story.   These I kept
and once, I recall, he was camping out in the
Adirondacks at Chateaugay and there was fire in
his tent.   He lost some of the Winesburg stories
and asked me to send the copies I had. 6

Readers of Anderson encounter repetitious references
to his composition of "Hands, " which he felt was the story
in which he found himself as a writer and artist: "The pen
began to run over the paper.   I did not seek for words....
They seemed to leap out from my hand to the paper. "7
In all the accounts it is an intense, orgiastic experience,
followed by euphoria, and resulting in the discovery of a
complete and satisfying artifact.   It pleased him to think he
had never changed a word of it, but Phillips found that the
story had "extensive revisions of words and phrases" and
that the first five paragraphs as published in 1916 in Masses
differ widely from the first two paragraphs in Winesburg,
Ohio. 8

At the same time he thought of his work in highly emotional terms, he could, as has been noted, refer to the stories as "a series of intensive studies of people of my home town, Clyde, Ohio" and anticipate that "when these studies are published in book form, they will suggest the real environment out of which present day youth is coming. "[9] Cornelia has said she thought Anderson's writing had "no special social or literary purpose. "[10] And Anderson was to write, "When I wrote Winesburg, I had no social theories about the small town. I just wanted to get a picture of life in the small town as I felt it. "[11]

It is evident that, even though Anderson used at the end of 1916 the academic word studies to refer to these stories, he was not involved in any carefully-plotted analysis of Clyde or limited necessarily to Clyde. His concept of it did change. For example, when he wrote to Waldo Frank in November, 1916, he told him there would be "seventeen of these studies, " of which he believed fifteen were completed. By the beginning of 1918 he told Van Wyck Brooks, "I am going to publish the Winesburg tales, two dozen of them, in a book under the title Winesburg. "

There is much to surmise concerning just when the tales were written. Anderson told Frank in November, 1916, "I made last year a series of studies. " This could be taken to mean that he had written in 1915 the bulk of the fifteen stories which seem to have been completed by fall 1916. We know that the first story, "Book of the Grotesque, " was published in Masses in February, 1916, and "Hands" in the same magazine the next month. Only two other stories ("The Philosopher, " Little Review, June-July; "The Strength of God, " Masses, August) had been published by the time of his remark, though Frank did promptly publish "Queer" in Seven Arts for December.

It is possible that Anderson's Winesburg series was triggered by his encounter with Edgar Lee Masters' Spoon River Anthology, the portraits from which began to appear in May, 1914, and which was published as a book in April, 1915. Max Wald, who also lived at 735 Cass Street, recalled lending the book to Anderson soon after its publication, that he took it to his room that evening, returned it the next morning, saying that he had stayed up late into the night reading the poems and that he was "most surprised by them. "[12] Certainly someone in Seven Arts was conscious of a relationship between the work of Anderson and Masters, for in the January, 1917, issue, in which "The Untold Lie" appeared, an anonymous (Frank?) commentator, in the "Notes on Names" section, supplies this illuminating note:

> Sherwood Anderson has written a series of inten-
> sive studies on the archetype of the small Ohio
> town of which he is a native. He calls it "Wines-
> burg. " The story in this issue is the second of
> the series to appear in The Seven Arts; and others
> will follow. When the whole is gathered into a
> volume, America will see that a prose complement
> to E. L. Masters' "Spoon River Anthology" has
> been created.

On page 156 the same issue referred to the Spoon River Anthology as having "Some of the greatness of great art" in it.
The welcoming of comparison in that note has its counterpart
in this comment, made a few months after Winesburg, Ohio
was published:

> So many critics have made the obvious comparison
> between "Winesburg, Ohio" and "Spoon River An-
> thology" that his publishers announce that Mr. And-
> erson's "Winesburg" stories appeared in magazines
> before Mr. Masters' work appeared. 13

A sense of defensiveness and partisanship must have
been inspired by the comparison of the two works; the rejoinder above was ill-conceived and patently not true, but the
following remarks of Frank, published in 1919, speak well
of the independent greatness of Winesburg:

> The Spoon River Anthology marks the effect of our
> life-denying life: sin and disease and death.   You
> will find them no less in Winesburg.   But you will
> also find, impregnant in its words, the impulses
> of life.   Impulses which, in their material obsess-
> ion, made for the denial of impulse, tended toward
> death: but at their source were no less living,
> and after their release from the tyranny of the
> American perversion, shall live again.   Thus one
> finds in Winesburg the conflict of American life
> against its own rigid forms, the now upward stir-
> ring, the fierce passion of renewal.   Spoon River
> is static: Winesburg is dynamic.   Spoon River is
> the trampled and buried face of the American world:
> Winesburg is its heart. 14

Whether the idea of a collection of stories about a
small town was suggested by Spoon River or not, Anderson
seems to have continued to work on the book over a period
of years. There is little information as to precisely how he
went about it, but there are indications. For example, he
submitted the stories to editors a few at a time, usually one
at a time. After Frank had published "Queer" in December,
1916, and "The Untold Lie" the next month, Anderson wrote
him: "I am sending you another Winesburg story and hope
you will like it. The other story concerning the death of
George Willard's mother should not, I believe, be published
too closely on the back of the first story about her."[15]
There is a record of another installment going with a letter
to Frank, April 5, 1917: "I am sending for submission to
the magazine the little piece of rather colorful writing called
'Tandy Hard' and would like to have your opinion of it."
This story did not appear in Seven Arts. Further, Frank
did not see all the stories until the book was published, for
he was to comment on it in a letter: "There are other stories I didn't know: the two about the Minister and Kate Swift
and Willard. Why didn't you send these on the Seven Arts--
I'd have snatched them. Other tales that seemed fragmentary
alone here stand well buttressed and in their place complete."

That he was writing shorter works in the winter of
1916-17, presumably to add to those of the previous winter,
is undeniable. On December 21, 1916 he wrote Miss Finley:

> I like the more intensive things I am trying to do
> now rather than attempts at long novels. They fit
> better into the life I am leading. They are more
> true to my present impulses. I am trying to make
> up my mind not to labor heroically but to drift
> with life, seeing and putting down what I can.

And by the 15th of January he told Frank, "I have been rather open to the quick impressions that result in short stories this winter because I have not had a big job on." It
can be presumed that he thought of these stories consistently
as part of a larger whole. He wrote on November 23, 1916,
to Miss Finley, whom he was constantly showing his Winesburg stories:

> As you well enough know I have on now a big piece
> of work. It can be completed now only in a twisted
> and distorted way. I shall just write it blindly,
> pouring myself and my character into it when I can.

Then when I have leisure I will go back to it,
eliminating, changing and trying to make a book of
it.

(Four short efforts which seem to fit the description of "quick
impressions," sent to Miss Finley with dates of November
25, December 4, and December 5 [two items] in 1916, may
be found in Appendix N. Winesburg readers will see evident
similarities.) If he were referring to Winesburg, Ohio,
which is possible, it is interesting to recall that the pieces
which Frank saw as separates fitted well into the eventual
whole. Another possibility, however, is that he was thinking
of the abortive Immaturity, also set in Winesburg, as the
"big piece of work," for he was working on it in January,
1917.[16]

The fragments and stories and novel seem all to have
stemmed from the Clyde-Winesburg concept and may not have
been evolved quickly. In any case, the twenty-four-story
book had been evolved by the end of 1917.

However conscious or unconscious Anderson was of
form during the book's early stages, by the time he had
completed it, he considered its form one of his achievements:
"No one I know of has used the form as I see it and as I
hope to develop it in several books."[17] At the end of 1919
he told both Huebsch, his publisher, and Frank that he was
using the same format:

> Out of necessity I am throwing the Mary Cochran
> book into the Winesburg form, half individual tales,
> half long novel form. It enables me to go at each
> tale separately, perhaps when I am ready to do it
> at one long sitting. My life now is too broken up
> for the long sustained thing.[18]

The tales, woven about the life of one person, would be longer and more closely related to the central character than in
Winesburg, he told Huebsch. "It can be published in part as
a novel if you wish."[19] Later he was to point out:

> In the more compact novel form I have never been
> comfortable. A man keeps thinking of his own
> life....
>
> But life itself is a loose, flowing thing. There are
> no plot stories in life.

We are all controlled, constantly and deeply influenced by passing people, passing adventures.... 20

As late as September 12, 1938 he was to write Maxwell Perkins that he had decided "to return to a form I used
in Winesburg, Ohio.... I find myself curiously at ease in
the form. It seems to relate to life as I feel it. " He
expressed his ease, pleasure, and pride to his close friend,
Sergel:

> Sudden I decided to go back to the Winesburg form.
> That is really a novel. It is a form in which I
> feel at ease. I invented it. It was mine. "Why
> not use it, " I told myself. Since then I have been
> happier and am doing work I feel I can send to the
> stenographers. 21

The matter of form in his stories was the seeming
cause of estrangement between him and his "literary father, "
Floyd Dell, who had published the first Winesburg stories
and had helped get Windy McPherson's Son published. Evidently the Masses, after publishing two of Anderson's stories,
turned down subsequent ones through the vote of its editorial
board of 20 artists and writers. 22 Dell recalled that he suggested Anderson turn to Seven Arts, which did publish him
and paid him, 23 which the Masses did not. But Anderson
harbored a very negative memory of this, writing twenty
years later this biting account:

> Dell was at that time, I believe, deeply under the
> influence of Maupassant. He advised me to throw
> the Winesburg stories away. They had no form.
> They were not stories. A story, he said, must be
> sharply definite. There must be a beginning and
> an end. 24

Anderson remembered himself replying with what he considered necessary arrogance. His memory told him that both
Dell and "Mr. Henry Mencken, " having read the stories, declared them merely sketches. 25 It is curious to note that
the recorded comments of Dell and Mencken do not fit Anderson's recollection. Dell mentioned Winesburg, Ohio in a
magazine article and called it "a magnificent collection of
tales. "26 Mencken reviewed the book for the Chicago American, recognized it as one "of uncommon merit--well-order-
ed, thoughtful, original and alive. " He further noted, "I
saw these 'Winesburg' stories in manuscript fully four years

ago. They then seemed to me very remarkable, I was eager
to get them into type. But in the interval Anderson has
greatly improved them. "27

   The suggestions, explicit in Mencken's remark as in
Miss Finley's statements, that Anderson did revise these
stories, turns our attention to the surviving Winesburg, Ohio
manuscript, which is in the Anderson Collection of the Newberry Library. In the Memoirs (page 324) it pleased Anderson to remember the saving of it in this way:

> The book had been written on pages of a cheap tab-
> let. The manuscript existed only because a cer-
> tain woman, at the moment in love with me, had
> collected the scrawled sheets, thrown carelessly
> aside, and had saved them.

> So the manuscript had been saved, and later, when
> it began to have some value, I had managed--be-
> cause the woman who had saved it died--by lying
> to her sister, by telling the sister that the dead
> woman had only been keeping it for me, by such
> slickness I had got it back.

   However, according to six existing letters written in
January, April, and June of 1938 to three different people,
the manuscript was found in a box of old manuscripts in
Anderson's home in Marion, Virginia, in late 1937 or early
1938: "And by the way Paul I recently came across in a
box of old mms [sic] a complete origional [sic] mms of
Winesburg, partly in pencil, partly in ink.... "28 These letters support the statement which Anderson wrote as information to accompany the manuscript and which now lies in the
vault of the Newberry with it:

> The manuscript is all in the author's long hand
> script and most of it is on print paper. At the
> time these stories were written the author was
> employed as a copywriter in a Chicago advertising
> agency and the paper is no doubt that used for
> roughing up advertisements. It is likely the stor-
> ies were written two or three times, in the writer's
> room, in a rooming house on Cass Street in Chi-
> cago, or in hotels as he traveled about, visiting
> clients of his employers. It is the author's notion
> that the manuscript, which only showed up after
> many years, in a box of old manuscripts, is the

one prepared for the making of a fair copy by a
stenographer.

At the time these stories were written the author
had already published two novels and had made beginnings and scetches [sic] for others and some of
the manuscrict [sic] is on the back of sheets cover-
ed with these abandoned efforts.

Several years ago the author found, among some
other old papers, the pencil manuscript of one of
the Winesburg stories.... "Nobody Knows," and
presented it to Mr. Burton Emmett, but in the
complete manuscript, when it showed up, the same
story was there, in ink. How this came about the
author can't remember. One of the manuscripts
may have been misplaced at the time. The pencil
manuscript of the one story is in the hands of Mrs.
Emmett, whose husband was an enthusiastic collector.

In writing to Mrs. Emmett in April, 1938, about the
duplicate copies of "Nobody Knows," Anderson included the
comment that, "sometimes you see I have written stories
two or three times over." Frank was to recall that the first
of the manuscripts sent to him at Seven Arts were in long
hand but that "later, that was not so."29 The pencil, pen,
typescript, and carbon copies to which references have been
found seem to indicate something other than a smooth, effortless, and extemporaneous process of creation.

Phillips examined the manuscript at the Newberry
Library very carefully and found that, in it alone, Anderson
had made the following kinds of textual change: choice of
word, clarification of image, clarification of idea, varying
repeated descriptive phrases, following a preference for
monosyllables, lessening of auctorial intrusion, regularizing
series of prepositional phrases, and following a preference
for relative clauses rather than abstract nouns.   Phillips
also established that eighteen of the tales were written on
the backs of twenty-one separate fragments of manuscript,
primarily concerning Talbot Whittingham.30

The publication of the book, at one time called The
Book of the Grotesque,31 after the story which appears first
in the book and which was the first to be published, was not
without difficulty.   John Lane Company had the refusal of it

and was, evidently, not interested. There is no documentation concerning this phase of the matter. But it is known that, when he told Brooks that Lane was going to "go ahead" with Mid-American Chants, he also told him: "Then I am going to publish the Winesburg tales. . . . " One might guess then that he thought that Lane would publish the book. On April 10, 1918, he wrote Frank that "Winesburg will come along in the Fall. "

It can only be surmised that plans went sour, even though it is not known with whom they had been made. An exchange of letters between Anderson and his eventual publisher, Ben Huebsch, makes it clear that they had not even met before August of 1918. Anderson wrote Huebsch at that time: "So many of the fellows I know have spoken to me of you that I would like to come and call on you. " Huebsch replied immediately: "The same friends who spoke to you about me are probably the same ones who spoke to me about you. Since learning that you were in from New York I had hoped to meet you. "[32] Huebsch suggested a luncheon engagement for the next day, but Anderson's letter of a month later indicates no meeting had yet occurred:

> I would have called on you before this but have been running in and out of town and Mrs. Anderson has been to visit me. We have been sailing up and down the harbor, going to the top of the Woolworth Building and running out to look at pieces of New England. Wont [sic] you write and set an evening next week, when you will be willing to come and play with us. [33]

The light tone of this letter seems almost forced, particularly if other plans had fallen through. The fact remains that it took Anderson an unnecessary month to meet Huebsch when they were in the same city. Another curious item is that Huebsch thought he had given the book its title:

> I always had a tender feeling for that book, not only because it was the one which first gained you a wide audience, but because it marked the beginning of our relations and, incidentally, because I was its godfather, for you will remember that I proposed the title which it bears. [34]

By December, 1918, matters had progressed far enough that Anderson could write Huebsch, "I am glad you

like Winesburg. " He added, "From the first I have had the
hunch that you are the man I want to publish my stuff. " In
view of the facts, this seems to be of doubtful sincerity, and
so does the next sentence: "It is delightful to have a publisher you can have as a friend also. " This letter ends with
a promise that suggests continuing work or revision: "I
shall try to put something real into it. "[35] This letter was
followed by another which asserted, "I can't tell you how
glad I am that you are to be my publisher. "[36] On the last
day of the year he informed Trigant Burrow that the Winesburg tales would probably be published in March; the actual
date was in May.

The title of the book, when it was published, because
it used the name of an actual town in Ohio, confused many
people, and still does, into thinking Anderson intended to
write an account of existing people in a real place. Though
Anderson had been writing about Talbot Whittingham for
years, probably while still in Elyria, in Winesburg, this
locale was imagined, as were Caxton and Mirage (found in
manuscript). Anderson wrote to Huebsch, shortly after
Winesburg, Ohio was published, that he had encountered "an
interesting development, " the discovery that "There is a
Weinsberg [sic]. " He added, "I'll stay out of that place. "[37]
As late as 1940, he had to explain to a correspondent: "As
you know mine was a purely imagined town and I would be
much hurt if anyone there should think of it and its people
as having lived anywhere but in my imagination. "[38]

The real challenge to understanding does not concern
the relationship between the fictional and the real Winesburg
but rather between Winesburg and Clyde, which he thought of
as his "home town. " The attitude of Clyde residents is well
represented by this comment of a man who had lived there
as a boy and as a contemporary of Anderson: He noted that
Clyde and Winesburg both have a Buckeye Street, each a
barrel-stave factory, each a Duane Street, Clyde a Piety
Hill and Winesburg a Gospel Hill, and so on. He felt that
Clyde made a significant contribution to the book. [39]

Miss Evelyn Kintner in her unpublished study, "Sherwood Anderson: Small Town Man, " devoted considerable attention to the appearance of Clyde materials in Anderson's
works. She found that a good many Clyde names could be
recognized among the citizens of "Winesburg. " She even
found some characters which seemed to have been reproduced,
at least in part, from life. In the great majority of cases,

however, there is no evidence that either names or, much
less, "Winesburg" characters came from Clyde. Miss Kintner also reconstructed a map of "Winesburg" from the stories. She found many elements which coincide with the Clyde
map. One can not deny her conclusion (page 82) that this
"shows how vividly the physical features of his home town
were impressed on the writer Anderson's mind...." William
L. Phillips made a similar analysis, noting the same kind
of external correspondences that Miss Dinsmoor did. Putting
a study of the names of characters in <u>Windy McPherson's
Son, Marching Men, Mid-American Chants</u>, and <u>Winesburg,
Ohio</u> against a directory made from 1895 issues of the weekly
<u>Clyde Enterprise</u> brought only this conclusion: "the correla-
tion between the newspaper and literary names used by Sherwood Anderson is insignificant."[40]   The checking of Anderson's characters' names with the city directory of Clyde of
1887 yielded the same results. However, when the names
of Anderson's characters were checked against a Chicago
city directory for 1915-16, there was very high coincidence
of names.

In Appendix C will be found a most revealing letter
about Clyde, written by Anderson upon the occasion of a return visit in December, 1916. It reflects very well the way
his imagination must have played over the town and its people hundreds of times. This quotation seems most crucially
illuminatory of the process:

> I am sitting in the hotel office writing. I have
> barely gone to see anyone and have only walked
> through two or three streets. Why?--well because
> what I have already seen has awakened such a
> flood of memories that I am overwhelmed. I
> realize as I sit here that I could sit thus for
> hours--as long as life remained in mem [sic]
> writing of my people and the strange things that
> have happened to them. What real and living peo-
> ple they are to me. Even Jerry Donlin, the bag-
> gage man who I am told dropped dead of heart
> failure and who has just by chance come into my
> mind. His life is a living thing to me. I could
> write long novels concerning this sweet-hearted,
> profane Irishman and the <u>wonderful things my imag-
> ination helps me to believe went on in his head
> while he outwardly did not more than push baggage
> trucks up and down this station platform here.</u>
> [Emphasis supplied.]

Two comments show his concern, at least on occasion, with the problem of referring to specific individuals. He wrote Herman Hurd, his lifelong Clyde friend, to reassure him he was not in one of his stories:

> Be assured that I will do nothing of the sort. I did indeed have a caracter [sic] in a story I called Ben Hurd. . . having written the same into the story half unconscious of any connection with you but coming to realize that there might be a connection in the minds of others, had long since striken [sic] it out. [41]

In discussing with a friend, Maurice Long, of whom he said, "I have never quite forgiven him for dying, " he revealed a hesitancy to follow closely the more intimate aspects of reality in his fiction:

> As for using him in a novel or a story I may do it or I may not. Sometimes, in thinking about it, I have told myself that my feeling for him is too keen to be used. [42]

Nonetheless, there are people in Clyde who think they know just who Anderson was referring to in the various stories, and one Clyde family had reportedly marked the names of the supposed originals of characters in its copy of <u>Winesburg, Ohio</u>. [43]

Anderson's brother, Karl, understood the situation. "The characters in the book were suggested by certain personages in Clyde, but the stories were born of his imagination. " He reports one illustrative incident, Sherwood was recounting an incident to Karl and Irwin; noting an inaccuracy, Karl started to contradict Sherwood. The other brother, used to Sherwood's manner, urged that he not be interrupted: "I'd like to hear him tell it again to see what it would be like this time. "[44]

Anderson's comment, though characteristically inexact, must be seen as essentially valid:

> I myself remember with what a shock I heard people say that one of my own books, <u>Winesburg, Ohio</u>, was an exact picture of Ohio village life. The book was written in a crowded tenement district of Chicago. The hint for almost every character

was taken from my fellow lodgers in a large rooming house, many of whom had never lived in a village. The confusion arises out of the fact that
others besides practicing artists have imagination.
But most people are afraid to trust their imaginations and the artist is not. [45]

Or perhaps the confusion lies in calling the book Winesburg,
Ohio rather than Winesburg, Everywhere.

         In spite of the fact that care must be used in any at-
tempt to establish specific Clyde-Winesburg parallels, it is
possible to specify a few cases. The last words of the book
deal with George Willard leaving Winesburg, whereupon "his
life there had become but a background on which to paint the
dreams of his manhood." Sherwood Anderson certainly used
his life in Clyde, as well as other places, as a base for the
"dreams of his manhood." There is even a degree of simil-
arity between Anderson and Willard. They were both active,
sensitive people who left their home environments in a combination of revulsion and puzzlement to seek for better things.
George leaves on the westbound train, just as Sherwood did.
When Anderson bought his papers in Virginia in 1927, a note
in the Clyde Enterprise said that he used to "hang around the
shop" as a boy. However doubtful that may be, Anderson
was quoted in that article as saying: "At any rate something
I have always wanted to do I am doing." [46]

         There are two Winesburg stories for which Anderson
has recorded the specific inspiration, neither having to do
with Clyde. Anderson refers to the first as "one of many
experiences," and it could be taken to represent vestigial
remains of actual experience in Clyde and elsewhere:

         Stories do not come to me as definite facts. I
         remember once being on a train in a day coach and
         seeing a man run across a field. The gesture
         stayed with me and resulted years afterward in a
         story called "The Untold Lie".... [47]

Another example is as follows:

         Among the figures on the wall there had been one
         of a little frightened man. Perhaps it came out of
         some memory of my own, a face seen sometimes
         on the street, a story told by some man in a bar-
         room, as well as out of the experience that very

> day, the fat man calling me "Mabel," me calling
> him "Eva," and our suspiciousness in the eyes of
> other men, hangers-on in the cheap barrooms. But
> something else was mixed in it. Out of them
> seemed to speak the passionate desire of all people
> to be understood, to have their stories told, per-
> haps that the terrible isolation of their lives may
> break. I went to my table and began writing. The
> story is called "Hands".... [48]

Karl Anderson thought "Sherwood's preoccupation with
his long departed brother," Earl, was responsible for at
least some of the characters in Winesburg, Ohio. [49] Examination of what is known of Earl's tortured life makes it
seem quite possible that he could have suggested either El-
mer Cowley of "Queer" or Enoch Robinson of "Loneliness"
or both. Two documents are very helpful in providing a
basis for this kind of speculation. One is a letter, seemingly meant for Sherwood, since it refers to being mentioned
"in your latest book" (probably A Story Teller's Story) found
in Earl's pocket when he collapsed on the street in New York
and was, through his hospitalization, restored to his family,
from which he had separated himself thirteen years before.
Three quotations from it will suffice to give the resentful,
depressed tone of it:

> You may assume that this is from that silent one
> of whom we were all so fond and whom we could
> not help in the difficult matter of living....
>
> ...I think Karl had 100% parental OK upon his
> birth. I think each succeeding birth receives less
> with less favors [sic]. I myself got a parental OK
> upon my birth close to zero. I turned to mother
> for affection and got a cold shoulder. Probably
> she was so worn out with the effort of living that
> she had nothing left to give. I turned to each of
> the rest of the family in succession and got a view
> of their backs....
>
> What I mean to get at is this--I wanted affection
> or mental support of the family because it would
> have been beneficial to me. They withheld that
> affection and mental support because they thought
> that my existance [sic] was pure impudence because
> why go further. [50]

The other document is a manuscript of six typed pages written by Karl and entitled "Our Unforgettable Brother." It starts out by stating, as the article "My Brother, Sherwood Anderson" had done, that he wondered why Sherwood had not used the story of Earl, that he had asked Sherwood about it, that Sherwood had said, "For a long time I've mulled it over in my mind." The conclusion in the unpublished manuscript (page 27) is that, "He did write about Earl." The manuscript deals primarily with the time after the death of the mother, when Stella was keeping house in Clyde, providing a home for Earl and, presumably Ray, who is not mentioned in the account. The two boys in Chicago sensed that Stella thought Earl "had the best brains in the family." Sherwood took time off from his advertising soliciting to check up on Earl. He reported, on the one hand, "So far as I could see there was nothing unusual in the kid... just a big boned gawky boy... unnoticed when around and missed when gone." Then he added, "With a [sic] uncomfortable way of looking through you into the distance."

And then Sherwood told Karl of going with Stella to a high school entertainment at which Earl was to recite something Stella had drilled him on.

When Earl's turn came he stumbled on the steps going up to the stage. A boy, in front, shouted "Stumble bug" and a lot of others laughed. I had the anxious feeling that he was in a trance. Certainly he looked as if the present were unendurable ...turned and trudged away towards the rear. And he would have made his escape had not a woman run and turned him around... facing him towards his tormenting assignment. I saw now that his eyes were tightly closed and that he was feeling his way with his feet as a sleep walker moves to a particular spot. What I dreaded happened [sic] Earl plunged off the stage into the audience.... In an instant he had rolled himself back and was standing upon his feet. He calmly stood as if he were making new adjustments of a bad situation and unaware of the restless mirth in a space into which he gravely gazed. I saw that he shook his head and commenced to chew at his tongue. Well, now, I was prepared for the unexpected... as a torrent a rush of words came from him. He declared:

Figure 6.
The Children of Emma Smith and Irwin M. Anderson,
about 1886 in Clyde, Ohio.   Standing, Karl and
Stella. Seated, Sherwood, Earl, Ray and Irwin.

"Scented herbage from my breast
Leaves from you I glean"

His words were drowned in a howl of laughter....
Earl's fiasco was heavy on our spirits, and the going out the hall a penance.   We were like prisoners
walking along the town's streets.

Later, when Earl got home, Sherwood asked him,
"What the hell was the matter with you anyway?"
When Earl replied "with his husky resentment,"
Sherwood told Karl, "I had sense enough not to be-
lieve him.   I knew here was revolt and nothing
else. "

As a sequel to this incident, it is recounted that Earl
was a good baseball player.   "That kid brother of yours has
the making of a great ball pitcher. "   Then, one day, someone in the bleachers bellowed the quotation from the high
school recitation at him, and Earl untwisted himself from an
incompleted pitch, threw the ball on the ground, and walked
off the field, never to play again. 51

Certainly it was people like Earl about whom "The
Book of the Grotesque" was written.   Earl and Sherwood and
Karl and Stella and Irwin and Ray and Emma and Irwin Senior, among many others, were "mulled over" and crystallized
into a concept of the grotesque, which, as we have seen, was
mentioned as early as Windy McPherson's Son.

Now an examination may be made of the idea of the
grotesque as Anderson overtly recognized it in the process
of bringing it to flower in this book.   His emphasis on it,
is, first of all, a protest against the failure to find in life
what he most desired: "You see how it is.   One has the
sacred old thing...the dreams of love; and orderly movement
forward.   To put these things in words makes them seem
cumbersome and pretentious. "52   And "With the publication
of Winesburg I felt I had really begun to write out of the repressed, muddled life about me. "53   He wrote Burrow in
January, 1919, as the publication of Winesburg as anticipated, "You and I know that the big story here is the story
of repression, of the strange and almost universal insanity
of society. "   He added that the story need not be unpleasant
to right-minded men and women but that it "must be boldly
and subtly told and make its audience slowly. "   After giving
a summary of the episode (found in the November 25 passage

of Appendix K) about the farm boy who wanted to kill his father, "because he wanted the house to be quiet," he pointed
out to Frank:

> There must be things of that kind compressed and
> forced into the minds of boys raised in poverty in
> the West in the midst of woods and fields and in
> the midst also of that most terrible of all vulgar-
> ities, loose thinking and living. [54]

In commenting on the war, he gave an instance of how he
saw the twisting away from truth and reality, honesty and
truth:

> ...It seems to me that all the big radicals of the
> country have fallen before the fact of this war.
> In times of peace they have taken up a certain
> position, they have stood up for certain principles.

> Then came the war and it seemed to them that
> principles were put to the supreme test. They
> had braced themselves for a test. Oddly enough
> with their bracing came a tightening of the muscles
> of the mind. They had got hold of a truth you see
> and had become not thinkers but scientists. They
> are so very sure that two and two make four. In
> embracing their truth they have become grotesque. [55]

No reader of Winesburg would have to be reminded
of the use here of the exact words for "The Book of the
Grotesque," which had been published the year before.

Brooks thought of Anderson as "in search of the little
people he liked to write about, the 'obscure' people who, as
he put it, had given him life." Although he had wished to
escape from them at first, through his own material success,
a process very much part of his fictional life, his heart finally went out to "all the defeated people in the little wooden
houses." [56] He was to say, while in the very midst of composing the book,

> Men's fears are stories with which they build the
> wall of death. They die behind the wall and we do
> not know they are dead. With terrible labor I
> arouse myself and climb over my own wall. As
> far as I can see are the little walls and the men
> and women fallen on the ground, deformed and ill.

> Many are dying. The air is heavy with the stench
> of those who have already died. [57]

Winesburg was written out of compassion for the grotesques, himself at times included. He told Frank in a November, 1917, letter:

> The people hurried shivering along. I wanted to
> embrace them all, men and women. It seemed to
> me that within my old shell was room for them
> all, that there a fire burned at which they could
> all warm themselves.

His seemingly ineffective effort to do something for the "people of the outer fringe," as he called them and as he knew
himself to be, was characterized in this way: "During these
years I have been saying something over and over as into a
black night. 'These twisted ones have souls. Beauty lies
asleep in them'. "[58] As late as 1936 he was to write a close
friend, "I wish you would think again of the book of the Grotesque in Winesburg," mentioning "The white clear youth inside many persons. "[59] James T. Farrell has recorded his
reaction to Anderson's intense concern for the condition and
fate of humanity:

> His work was closer to my own areas of experi-
> ence. As a boy I had jeeringly been called, "Four
> Eyes. " Because of this and other experiences I
> had sometimes felt that I was a goof. Anderson's
> sympathy for the grotesque, the queer, the socially
> abnormal, evinced with feeling, sensibility, and
> simple humanity in Winesburg, Ohio struck imme-
> diate chords of response within me. [60]

The concern with Christianity in all of the books up
to and including Winesburg is doubtless obvious. And, as
Schevill has pointed out, part of this book is devoted to showing "that the moral values of Christianity in the village society have been distorted into the illusions which kill. "[61]
Burton Rascoe was to say of Anderson:

> ...He has a beautiful idealism, a great depth of
> poetic feeling; he is more religious than I have
> ever been, even though he has never been a Christ-
> ian, saying that "Christ was righter than any man
> I know of. " 'What we need in this country is more
> sorrow, more prayer, more reliance on something

outside ourselves, " he contended. [62]

It was at Christmas, 1917, that Anderson recorded his intense feeling of grotesqueness in that season:

> The very thought of Christmas fills me with pom-
> pous phrases. Don't you suppose that Christ on
> his cross laughed at the follies of men? [63]

And so Anderson's grotesques were presented to the
American public. He tried to remain as objective as possible
about reactions to his work:

> What an interesting comment on people the reviews
> of Winesburg will make. Do keep them for me.
> They begin to constitute something like an essay on
> present day American opinion. One has a feeling
> of standing aside and overhearing not his own life
> but the town life of his native village discussed. [64]

Innovational as they were, the stories in <u>Winesburg,
Ohio</u> got varied reactions, from near-adulation to scornful
denunciation. (In Appendix M are four representative reviews from contemporary Chicago papers.) In general Anderson seems to have maintained his balance and even, on
occasion, a certain sardonic humor. He wrote Huebsch:
"There was an ecstatic review of Winesburg in the September
Pagan. Suppose it has a circulation of about fifteen copies. "[65]
The review was probably the most extremely favorable ever
made of the book, a lyric statement by his poet-correspond-
ent, Hart Crane:

> The entire paraphernalia of criticism is insignifi-
> cant, erected against the walls of such a living
> monument as this book. ... The style is flawless.
> I know of no finer selection of "significant mate-
> rial, " combined with proper treatment and economy
> of detail. America should read this book on its
> knees. [66]

His very close friend, admirer, and editor, Waldo
Frank found the book miraculous, singing, sweet, a justifica-
tion. But he also told him that his style, good as it was,
could be improved through more care with language formalities. [67]

By May 27, 1919, Anderson was able to write Frank,

"The book has only been out a few days but already I have
had several letters of very deep appreciation for it...."
On September 15, he reported to Burrow, "The book has
been getting rather remarkable recognition even from those
who have fought me before." On December 4, Frank was
told, "I get instant and beautiful reaction from Winesburg."
And the next year he told his French translator, "Winesburg
continues to make headway in America and really strikes
deeper all the time."[68]

But, two decades after the publication of Winesburg,
Anderson had a rambling memory of bitter condemnation,
puritanical exclusion from libraries (including the one in
Clyde, it will be recalled), books actually burned, people
writing him of his uncleanness.[69] As he thought about characters he had created, he realized:

> They had lived within me. I had given a kind of
> life to them. They had lived, for a passing mo-
> ment anyway, in the consciousness of others beside
> myself. Surely I myself might well be blamed--
> condemned--for not having the strength or skill in
> myself to give them a more vital and a truer life--
> but that they should be called people not fit to be
> written about filled me with horror.[70]

The year after the book was published he saw the
problem in these terms:

> To me it seems a little as though one were per-
> mitted to talk abstractly of things, to use scientific
> terms regarding them, in the new dispensation, but
> when one attempts to dip down into the living stuff,
> the same old formula holds. A really beautiful
> story like "Hands," for example, is--well, nasty.
> God help us! Dozens of men have told me pri-
> vately they knew Wing Biddlebaum. I tried to
> present him sympathetically--taboo.[71]

Eventually, though, he was able to say, "the same critic who
had condemned them began asking why I did not write more
Winesburg stories."[72]

Anderson, eagerly hoping to find himself free of necessity of working in advertising and even more eagerly hoping to be free to write all that he found teeming in his imagination, could not help being interested in the sale of the

book. "Hope you are still getting some sales for Winesburg," he wrote Huebsch September 25, 1919, and followed
it with a reiteration of a feeling he had had for most of the
decade:

> I keep wondering why the devil I should have to
> spend so large a part of my life in writing fool
> advertisement [sic] in order to live. You dont [sic]
> know of some intelligent man or woman who wants
> to be a patron for an American artist, do you.

He ended that letter with this sardonic self-imprecation:
"Well little Sherwood the sun is in the sky and the winds
blow. If you dont [sic] like it why dont [sic] you be a
tramp. "

Evidently, sales were at least encouraging, not without frustration, and not enough to secure freedom. On November 30, 1920, discussing Poor White, he wrote Huebsch:
"I hope it will not get out of print at Christmas time as
Winesburg did. " In the fall of 1927 he wrote N. Bryllion
Fagin that Winesburg "was two years selling 5,000. "
Huebsch's records showed something less. Between May
and October 31, 1919, the book sold 1,754 copies. In the
next three periods of six months, the sales were 400, 375,
and 539 copies, respectively, for a grand total for the two-
year period ending May 1, 1921, of 3,068 copies.[73] Perhaps his statement to Fagin in 1927 that "It now sells 5,000
to 8,000 a year" may be considered factual.

Regardless of sales of books, marital relationships,
occupational demands, anything short of economic necessity,
Anderson had found in the course of writing the Winesburg
stories, specifically in writing "Hands, " his "thing to do. "
The impulses which led to the "studies" of his home town
which became the segments of Winesburg continued with him
for a quarter of a century into his fatal South American trip:

> What I would like to do is get up into some South
> American town, say of five to ten thousand people,
> settle there for a time and try to get to know the
> people of such a town, that is to say, not public
> figures but of the people, such as a man might get
> to know in any one of our towns, as far as possible
> getting to understand a little of their thinking and
> feeling, and trying to pick up the little comedies
> and tragedies of their lives, much as I have always

tried to do in relation to life in our own North
American towns. [74]

    The road that led Anderson to Winesburg, Ohio, and
was taking him to South America at the time of his death led
him into the hearts and minds of hundreds of thousands of
readers around the world, people of Winesburg, Everywhere
who recognized in him a man who made out of his experience
along the way a permanently significant record. Most of
these people knew nothing of literature in an academic or
historical way; they react to a perceptive and sympathetic
portrayal of life. Others, not a few and increasing in number, agree with the judgment that Winesburg, Ohio had set a
standard of judgment for the short story genre of its time.

Notes

1.   Letter to Roger Sergel, Dec. 1935.

2.   Letter from Marietta D. Finley, May 31, 1962.

3.   Interview, Oct. 10, 1946.

4.   Memoirs, p. 287-8.

5.   Ibid., p. 279.

6.   Letter of May 31, 1962.

7.   Letter to Charles H. Funk, Late May 1935 (JR).

8.   Phillips, p. 113.

9.   Letter to Waldo Frank, Nov. 14, 1916 (JR).

10.   Oct. 1946 interview.

11.   Letter to John Hall Wheelock, March 24, 1930 (JR).

12.   Interview of June 24, 1949; in Phillips, p. 89.

13.   Anonymous, "Brief Mention of New Book," Bookman,
Sept. 1919, p. lix.

14.   Our America, New York, Boni and Liveright, 1919, p.
144.

15.   Letter of Jan. 15, 1917.

16.   Letter to Frank, Jan. 15, 1917.

17.   Letter to Ben Huebsch, Nov. 12, 1919.

18.   Letter to Frank, ca. Dec. 4, 1919.

19.   Letter of Nov. 12, 1919.

20.   Undated note quoted by Schevill, p. 96.

21.   Letter to Roger Sergel, ca. Sept. 10, 1938.

22.   Letter from Floyd Dell to Dr. Stanley Pargellis, April 14, 1948.

23.   Anderson has reported in various places that he got $85.00 for all the Winesburg stories published. See letter to George Freitag, Aug. 15, 1938, in Anderson Collection, Newberry Library.

24.   Letter to George Freitag, Aug. 27, 1938 (JR).

25.   Letter to Freitag, Aug. 18, 1938.

26.   "American Fiction," Liberator, Sept. 1919, II:43.

27.   Undated clipping in Newberry Library collection.

28.   Letter to Paul Cullen received in Detroit, during the week of Jan. 19, 1938. Others are to Roger Sergel and Mrs. Burton Emmett.

29.   Letter to William L. Phillips, March 23, 1949.

30.   Phillips, p. 116.

31.   Letter from Floyd Dell to Phillips, Dec. 12, 1948.

32.   Anderson letter received, Huebsch letter sent, Aug. 23, 1918.

33.   Received by Huebsch, Sept. 21, 1918.

34.   Letter to Anderson, Sept. 21, 1936.

35.   Letter received Dec. 3, 1918.

36.   Received Dec. 12, 1918.

37.   Letter of June 14, 1919.

38.   Letter to Arthworth Smith, Aug. 1, 1940.

39.   Mr. F. Lauriston Bullard, Boston, Mass. Letter of April 18, 1942.

40.   James P. Moody, "Correlations between Names Found in Clyde Enterprise and Windy McPherson's Son, Marching Men, Mid-American Chants, and Winesburg, Ohio. "

41.   Letter of Jan. 7, 1939.

42.   Letter to Miss Ella Boese, June 19, 1937.

43.   Letter from Donald F. Mulvihill, Dec. 17, 1964.

44.   "My Brother, Sherwood Anderson, " p. 26.

45.   "A Writer's Conception of Realism, " The Sherwood Anderson Reader, p. 345.

46.   Specific date of this article is undetermined. It is, however, from the Clyde Enterprise and appeared sometime during 1927.

47.   Letter to John S. Anderson, July 16, 1936.

48.   "A Part of Earth, " The Sherwood Anderson Reader, p. 327.

49.   "My Brother, Sherwood Anderson, " p. 27.

50.   Copy of letter supplied Nov. 10, 1964, Mrs. Anne Poor, formerly secretary to Mr. Karl Anderson, Westport, Conn.

51.   The manuscript on which this account is based and from which the quotations are made was in the hands of Mrs. Anne Poor, in December, 1964; the present author has a photo copy. It is now in the possession of Mr. James B. Anderson of New York, who has given his kind permission for use of the writings of his father.

52. Letter to M. D. Finley, May 29, 1917.

53. Letter to Serge Ochremenko, Jan. 1923 (JR).

54. Letter of May 21, 1918.

55. Letter to M. D. Finley, May 29, 1917.

56. The Confident Years, p. 528.

57. Letter to M. D. Finley, Dec. 2, 1916.

58. Letter to M. D. Finley, 1921.

59. Letter to Mary Emmett, July 1, 1936.

60. James T. Farrell, Reflections at Fifty, New York, Vanguard Press, 1954, p. 165.

61. Schevill, p. 103.

62. Before I Forget, p. 345.

63. Letter to M. D. Finley, Dec. 26, 1917.

64. Letter to Huebsch, received July 28, 1919.

65. Letter of Nov. 12, 1919.

66. From the September, 1919, Pagan magazine, as quoted in Phillips, p. 4.

67. Undated letter of 1919, probably preceding May 27.

68. Letter to Gaston Gallimard, undated, 1920.

69. Letter to Freitag, Aug. 27, 1938.

70. A Story Teller's Story, p. 123.

71. Letter to Brooks, before Aug. 27, 1920.

72. Letter to Freitag, Aug. 27, 1938.

73. Huebsch statement rendered to Anderson, May 1, 1921. On 2,500 of these copies Anderson got a royalty of 10 cents per copy and on the remaining 568 a royalty of

19. 2 cents each, a total of $359. 05.

74.   Letter to Robert Littell, Dec. 5, 1940. Anderson died in Colon, Panama Canal Zone, on March 8, 1941, having been taken off the ship in which he was en route to South America.

Chapter 10 (continued)

E.   Primarily for My Benefit

The following self-portrait was written especially by
Anderson for the Chicago Daily News, July 10, 1918, page
12, and is here reprinted with permission.   Demonstrating
as it does his capacity to understand himself and his fellow-
artists, it has been chosen as the note on which to conclude
this consideration of him:

> How can a man who has taught himself to see the
> drama in the lives of others see anything but drama
> in his own life?

> I swear to you I am a hero to myself.   There are
> days right here in Chicago when, in spite of the
> needs of millions of other men and in spite of
> cornfields, trees, grass, and every other living
> thing, I am convinced that the sun has come up
> primarily for my benefit, that people I meet laugh,
> weep and talk in order that I may see a little the
> play of emotions on their faces and that all the
> factories are run in order that I may note the color
> of black smoke from the chimneys against a morn-
> ing sky.

> You have, I assure you, no conception of the ex-
> traordinary vanity of the writer unless you happen
> to be one yourself.

> How could it be otherwise.   The circumstances of
> our lives are too dull to be borne.   One has to lie
> about them.

> As to the facts of my own existence--if I were to
> recite them to you they would not be true.

A few weeks ago you ran just such a sketch as
this under Quin Hall's cartoons of Joseph Hergesheimer. He declared his life a dull routine of
inaction. He was but fabricating a cast iron lie
when he said so. I have read some of his stories
and I know.

Put the case down as hopeless. You can't get the
truth concerning himself from a writer. The thing
can't be done.

With this preface I would--did space permit--be
delighted to go on and tell you a thousand things
concerning myself. I would tell you touching tales
of my early poverty, my heroic struggle to acquire
learning, my keen sympathy with the men and
women who, like myself, are caught and held in
the trap of industrial life.

I would go on in this way for days and months.
My talk of myself would grow into volumes and
still my hurtful vanity would not be satisfied.

I tell you it can't be done. You will never get any
writer to tell you the truth concerning himself.
That is a thing--take any word for it--that is impossible.

Be satisfied with my bold statement--it is the
truth--I am a hero to myself. The only time I am
barred out of that is when I read a criticism of
one of my books, and I am going to save myself
that humiliation in the future by refusing to read
criticism of my works. [1]

Notes

1. At least sometimes he was able to confront criticism
    with a crusty humor: "My favorite critic is a woman
    named Ethel Colson who is literary editor of the Herald
    Examiner here. She has a middle-class mind and is con-
    vinced I am dirty-minded. Whenever I print a book she
    says that of me. I know where she stands. She is at
    least honest. " Letter to M. D. Finley, May, 1918.

Mosaic XIV

"I simply stayed at home. . . "

You spoke of the story "Hands" in Winesburg, and it just
   happens that the particular story was the first one I
   ever wrote that did grow into form.   I remember well
   the thing happening.   I had been struggling with it and
   other stories and at last, one rainy night. . . I was living
   in a little Chicago rooming house. . . it came clear.
      I remember the feeling of exultation, of happi-
   ness, of walking up and down the room with tears flowing from my eyes.
      It was a kind of coming out of darkness into light.
      And I do not believe that, when it happens as,
   the feeling that comes is one of pride in achievement.
   For the moment form is achieved the thing goes entirely
   out of you.   It no longer exists in you or as a part of
   you.   It is rather like a child, born of a woman, that
   begins, at once, to have a life of its own, aside from
   her life.
                    to Norman H. Pearson, After Sept. 13, 1938 (JR).

                  *   *   *

I think that you may note that most of the characters in all
   my stories are working people.
                    to Gilbert Wilson, Oct. 12, 1937 (JR).

                  *   *   *

I knew as I sat down at my desk that morning, determined
   again not to impose myself, to let the story I was trying to write write itself, to be again what I had always
   been, a slave to the people of my imaginary world if
   they would do it, making their own story of their own
   loves, my pen merely forming the words on the paper. . . .   I knew that what I had been through, in such
   an absurd and childish form, letting myself again be a
                              458

victim to old fears, was nevertheless the story of like experiences in the life of all artists, no doubt throughout time.

> from "The Sound of the Stream," The Sherwood Anderson Reader, p. 373.

*   *   *

I have never been one who can correct, fill in, rework his stories. I must try, and when I fail must throw away. Some of my best stories have been written ten or twelve times.

> from "The Sound of the Stream," The Sherwood Anderson Reader, p. 362-63.

*   *   *

In my stories I simply stayed at home, among my own people, wherever I happened to be, people on my own street. I think I must, very clearly, have realized that this was my milieu, that is to say common everyday American lives. The ordinary beliefs of the people around me, that love lasted indefinitely, that success meant happiness, simply did not seem true to me.

> to George Freitag, Aug. 18, 1938.

*   *   *

We poor tellers of tales have our moments too, it seems. Like great generals sitting upon horses upon the tops of hills and throwing troops into the arena, we throw the little soldier words into our battles.

> from A Story Teller's Story, p. 66.

*   *   *

...I'm trying again... a man has to begin over and over... to try to think and feel only in a very limited field, the house, the street, the men at the corner drug store.

> to Roger Sergel, May 1939.

*   *   *

I get no chance at all for long periods of uninterrupted thought or work. I can take my character into my consciousness and live with it but have to work in this fragmentary way. These individual tales come clear

and sharp.   When I am ready for one of them it comes
all at one sitting, a distillation, an outbreak.
                    to Ben Huebsch, Nov. 12, 1919.

                    *   *   *

The men employed with me, the business men, many of them
    successful and even rich, were like the laborer, gam-
    bler, soldiers, race track swipes I had formerly known.
    Their guards down, often over drinks, they told me the
    same stories of tangled twisted lives.
            How could I throw glamour over such lives.   I
    couldn't.
                    to George Freitag, Aug. 18, 1938.

*   *   *   *   *

PART TWO

Family Addenda

I: SOMETHING SPECIAL IN HIS LIFE

In previous discussion of his mother and father almost all available authentic information concerning Anderson's infancy and early childhood has been presented. There is, however, one curious item that will bear mention.

Sherwood Anderson's birth date has been generally accepted as September 13, 1876. Almost equally well established is his birthplace, Camden (Preble County), Ohio. But Anderson never had any official record of his birth and used an affidavit of Mr. James Gift when he needed proof of the time and place of his entering the world. [1] The fact is that the record of Sherwood's birth was available all the time in the Preble County records and in his father's Civil War pension records. The failure of any one to find his birth record in Preble County is due to a peculiar quirk, which can be pointed out but not explained.

There can be no doubt that Anderson was born in 1876 in Camden. One of the best pieces of substantiating evidence is in the Clyde school record, which says he was eight in the fall of 1884. The directories show his father lived in Camden in 1875 and 1878, and doubtless the family was there between those years. But the name of the child born to I. M. Anderson and his wife, Emma Smith Anderson, on Sept. 13, 1876, in Camden is given as Lawrence. [2] According to the record, that was the name supplied by the county assessor on June 13, 1877. Since Lawrence and Sherwood[3] are names not at all similar, it does not seem likely that the assessor might have confused the two names in any way. But, if it was not a mistake on the part of the assessor, the name must have been dropped very early, for there is absolutely no record of it other than this one. If Anderson had known of it, he could have had his birth record when he wanted it. Furthermore, it seems impossible that he could have foregone the pleasure of mentioning it. How appropriate the idea of the double name would have been to his concept of a multiplicity of personalities within the individual!

462

When Sherwood was born, his father's business had at least not reached the point of failure.   Camden was in an area of "fine farming country" and "an important grain center. "[4]   Irwin Anderson was probably still in business for himself when he went to Caledonia, and it seems that he had not lost his business until the end of the Caledonia period or beginning of the Clyde period.   According to a playmate, [5] the Anderson children seemed happy, well-fed, and were seldom ill.   "They were nice children; our parents wouldn't have let us play with them otherwise. "

Anderson has recorded his consciousness of Camden in various ways.   It was "one of those towns through which father and mother had trekked when they were first married. "[6]   He admitted to the editor of the Camden newspaper: "I am afraid there is very little I can tell you about my connection with Camden, Ohio.   My father, I believe, was a small harness maker there.   I believe he had a shop.... What happened to my father and why he left Camden I do not know. "[7]   In 1939 he wrote, "I never went there until about two years ago when Eleanor and I were driving North and spent part of a Sunday afternoon in the town. "[8]   He also told Cullen his belief that his father moved shortly after his birth in Camden to Caledonia, where he set up another shop.   He recalls being taken on the occasion of his Camden visit to the "house of my birth, a very charming little brick house [actually of frame construction] occupied by a very old woman who remembered my mother and father. "   The woman was Mrs. Mary Pierce, who recalled later: "He rested in a chair you occupy... and when I showed him the house he remarked, 'Mother's cooking stove must have set about here. ' But he made few references to his father. "[9]

The thought of his father in that time could arouse exuberance:

> He was in the saddlery and harness business and you cannot fail to catch the flavor of that.   There would be a little shop on the town's main street with a leather horse collar hanging on a peg over the sidewalk before the door.   Inside there would be shiny new harnesses hanging on the shop walls and, in the morning when the sun crept in, the brass and nickel buckles would shine like jewels. [10]

More frequently he struck a less appreciative note. He told Simpson, "Father was an improvident man and we did a good deal of moving from place to place. "[11] He alludes to the idea of moving to escape bill collectors and possibly getting financial aid from his family, adding, "However, I know little of his people and only have this notion because I cannot conceive of his having earned it or of his having made it by his shrewdness. "[12]

His most extensive reaction to his early childhood and Camden in particular is in Tar. In the foreword to this book he says he "...determined to try to tell the story of his own childhood..." The problems and reactions related to that effort are discussed for eighteen pages, at the end of which he reports that "...it was only after I had created Tar Moorehead, had brought him into my own fancy, that I could sit down before my sheets and feel at ease."

The following excerpts from the foreword to Tar catch the essential spirit of his imaginative processes in this case and many others:

> Tar Moorehead was born in the town of Camden, Ohio, but when he left there he went in his mother's arms. As a conscious human being he never saw the town, never walked in its streets and later when he grew to manhood he was careful never to go back. (Page 4.)

Anderson reveals that the character Tar-Sherwood discarded all realistic features of the place when he thought of Camden:

> He thought of it as his own town, the product of his own fancy. Sometimes it sat at the edge of a long plain and people of the town could see from the windows of their houses vast expanse of earth and sky. Such a place to walk in the evening, out on the grassy plain, such a place to count the stars, feel the evening wind on the cheek, hear, coming from the distance, the little sounds of the night. (Page 5.)

> As a man Tar sometimes lay in his bed in a city and thought of Camden, the town in which he was born and which he never saw and never intended to see, the town filled with people he could understand and who always understood him. (Page 6.)

Tar kept the town of Camden as something special in his life. Even when he had become a grown man and was called successful he clung to his dreams of the place. (Page 9.)

He knew the people in every house along the little streets, knew all about them. They were what he had dreamed people were like when he was a small boy. The men he had thought brave and kind were really brave and kind; the little girl he had thought lovely had grown into a beautiful woman.

It is coming closer to people that hurts. We find out people are like ourselves. Better, if you want peace, keep far off, dream about people. The men who make a romance of life are perhaps right after all. The reality is too terrible. (Page 10.)

Notes

1. Mr. Stephen Coombs, Abingdon, Va.; letter to author, Jan. 21, 1942.

2. Record of Births, Preble County, Ohio, Vol. 1, p. 126.

3. Mrs. Eleanor C. Anderson has stated her husband told her he was named Sherwood after one of his mother's favorite teachers; conversation of April 8, 1962.

4. Morgan, Directory of Preble County for 1875, p. 170.

5. Interview with Mrs. Alice Irey, Marion, Ohio.

6. A Story Teller's Story, p. 103.

7. Letter to Ray Simpson, Camden, from Chicago, Dec. 12, 1921.

8. Letter to John Paul Cullen, from New York, Feb. 7, 1939 (JR).

9. Undated clipping, probably from a Dayton, Ohio, paper, in file of Miss Eleanor Jones, Camden, April 17, 1962.

10.   A Story Teller's Story, p. 103.

11.   Letter of Dec. 12, 1921.

12.   A Story Teller's Story, p. 103.

II: ON PARENTAL PORTRAITS

It was Van Wyck Brooks who pointed out, "This father, who appears in so many of his books, was Anderson's
greatest creation, side by side with the mother of the family
who saved the household by desperate ruses. . . . "1

Anderson himself has made several comments which
must be held in mind while considering his parents and what
they meant to him, both artistically and otherwise:

> Suppose it please my fancy to have a certain kind
> of father or mother. That is the great privilege
> of being a writer--that life may be constantly re-
> created in the field of fancy. But my brothers,
> reputable men, may have quite different notions of
> how these worthy people, my parents and theirs,
> should be presented to the world. . . . 2

> . . . it has amused me sometimes in talking with
> some of my brothers, to see how poorly my con-
> ception of our father and mother fitted into their
> conceptions. "Why, I dare say, the woman you
> have pictured is all right. She is very interesting,
> but she is not my mother as I knew her, " they
> say. 3

> When, for example, I wrote of my own father and
> mother, I depicted people my brothers and my sis-
> ter could not recognize.

> "Anyway, " I said to myself, "I have made a picture
> of my father and mother--They were my father and
> mother as I felt them. "4

It is in the exploration of the portrait of his father,
Irwin Anderson, that the true ambivalence of Anderson's

attitude toward his realistic materials may be most dramatically explored, as exemplified in the following pages.

Notes

1. The Confident Years, p. 530.

2. Foreword to Tar, p. x-xi.

3. "A Writer's Conception of Realism, " The Sherwood Anderson Reader, p. 338.

4. "Introduction to the Memoirs, " The Sherwood Anderson Reader, p. 696.

III: ONE WHO ENJOYED THIS LIFE

James Anderson, Sherwood Anderson's paternal grand-
father, was brought to Adams County, Ohio, in 1807 from
Cumberland County, Pennsylvania, by his father and mother,
Robert and Elizabeth Dickey Anderson. He had been born in
Cumberland County on March 1, 1796.[1]

A land purchase of October 3, 1808, gives approxi-
mate verification of the 1807 date of the arrival of the Robert
Anderson family in Ohio. On October 3, 1808, "Robert Anderson of the County of Adams" bought from Daniel and Betsy
Neff of Montgomery County, Ohio, "300 acres" near West
Union for "$1,500 current money of the U.S.A."[2] Any one
searching Adams County records for traces of the Anderson
Family is in danger of being confused by the fact that there
were several Anderson families in the county. But any doubt
as to whether this was the right Robert Anderson who bought
the land mentioned above is removed by an examination of
the auction sale of part of that same property on December
16, 1847.

Robert Anderson had died on February 9, 1841, when
he was 75.[3] In 1847 the administrator of his estate, his
son, James, was ordered to sell at public auction 226 acres
of the property already mentioned. Beside James and Robert's widow, Elizabeth Dickey Anderson, who died on November 20, 1859, at 83,[4] other heirs mentioned in the will
include Robert Anderson, Benjamin D. Anderson, Joseph N.
Anderson, and members of Leach, Baird, Denning, and Mc-
Clane families. The Andersons may have been sons or
grandsons, and those with the other names may have been
either married Anderson daughters or their children. At
any rate, these heirs presumably shared the $1,638 which
constituted the proceeds of the sale.[5]

On July 10, 1834, "Robert Anderson sen. and Elizabeth his wife" sold approximately 100 acres of their farm
to James Anderson for $300.[6] On March 2, 1868, James

sold the same property for $4,000.[7] The price set by the
parents seems very reasonable; presumably they were helping
James to set himself up on a farm.   James had married
Miss Mary Baird on June 2, 1831,[8] when he was 35 and she
about 25.   On May 27, 1820, a James Anderson had bought
"one yoke of oxen, yoke for oxen, three draught chains,
three axes, 4 hoes, 1 plough, sixteen hogs" for $40 from
one Thomas H. Haskell.[9] Sherwood's grandfather was then
24 and would very appropriately have been accumulating farm
equipment.

According to Evans' and Stivers' History of Adams
County (page 505; see Note 1, present section) and a Trotter
graveyard headstone, Mary Baird Anderson lived only till
May 7, 1840, at which time she was in her thirty-fourth
year, but this was not before she had borne her husband
six children (See Appendix B).   On November 7, 1844, James
Anderson married Isabella Bryan Huggins, a widow with two
children.   By her he had three children, the first of which
was Irwin McLain Anderson (b. August 7, 1845).   Apparently
the arrangement was a successful one, for "Mr. and Mrs.
Anderson reared three sets of children without a jar.   They
all got along happily together.   Mrs. Anderson had the same
happy and genial disposition as her husband. "

The biographical sketch of James Anderson in the
Evans and Stiver county history is quite laudatory.   He is
pictured (page 504) as one who "enjoyed this life and made
it more pleasing to those around him. "

...James Anderson may have had fits of bad temper, but the writer never saw him in one or ever
heard of him having one.   He was always brimful
and running over with good humor.   He always persisted in looking at the bright and cheerful side of
things and was always ready to laugh and make
those about him laugh.   Trouble rolled away from
him like water rolls from a duck's feathers....
He was [at fifty] a man to drive away despondency
and lift the world up.

But the fact that "he had the keenest sense of humor
of any man of his time in the county" did not interfere with
his meeting and performing "all the serious duties of life as
a man and Christian should. "   A "most earnest and conscientious man" for all his love of a good story, "He was anti-
slavery. "   First a Whig and afterward a Republican, he was

brought up an Associate Reform Presbyterian, in which faith
he was an elder for thirty years. He was "honest and honorable in all his dealings" and "was not the man to worry himself to make money. " "As a farmer, he lived comfortable
and easy. "

As evidence of his capability and popularity his record
in the militia is cited:

On June 26, 1838, he was commissioned by Governor Vance as a Major of the First Cavalry Regiment, First Brigade, Eighth Division of the Ohio
Militia, and on August 1, 1839, he was commissioned by Governor Shannon as Lieutenant-Colonel
of the same regiment. When it is remembered that
he was elected to those positions by those who knew
him best the honor will be appreciated.

In 1862, he was elected Captain by the "Squirrel
Hunters" and took his company to Aberdeen [Ohio,
across the river from Maysville, Ky.] to repel
Morgan's Raid.

Very often in county histories one finds the praise
most often showered either on men prominent in the county
when the history was prepared or upon their ancestors.
Too, the hardy pioneers come in for idealization. But it
seems safe to say that not one direct descendant of James
Anderson was alive in Adams County when the Evans-Stivers
account was prepared; at least, Irwin Anderson, who had
been out of the county over thirty years, was the only other
member of the family who was accorded a biographical
sketch. James Anderson was perhaps an early settler,
since his father had brought him to the Ohio country only a
year or two after West Union was laid out in 1806. But his
biographer mentioned the time of his coming to the state only
incidentally. Consequently the only conclusion is that the
county historian considered James Anderson a truly noteworthy
character, and one who reads his record must agree he was
not without distinction in his time and place.

In 1866, after the death of his mother in 1859, James
Anderson moved to Sardinia, Ohio, where he died on May
11, 1886, aged 90, survived by his widow. It was while he
was living in Sardinia, on August 24, 1877, that James wrote
the only surviving letter between him and his son, Irwin.

Aside from the assistance it renders in dating the departure of Irwin's family from Camden, the letter allows a
fuller view of the personality of Sherwood's grandfather Anderson.   James, then 81 years old, does not take up the occasion of his letter immediately.   Rather he concerns himself first with comments on the length of time between letters, everyone's state of health, and the fun of taking an ex-
cursion ride on the newly-completed railroad to Winchester,
ten miles away.

In the opening line of his letter, James refers to the
fact that a letter from Irwin has arrived that evening and
that he has immediately thought it necessary to "sit down to
answer. "   The urgency of answering lay in the fact that Irwin
had informed his father that he was going to move.   The old
man says he is sorry his son "cannot get a situation nearer
to us, " points out that "if you go far away we may never
meet agane [sic], " mentions his desire to see "Ema [sic]
and the little ones, " and fears that the children "will not remember anything about their Grandpa and Grandma. "

He could not resist, in concluding, some fatherly advice "if you do go, " he tells him to "trust God and keep his
commandments, " to be "obliging [and] gentle to all, " and to
"remember that time is money and that you will never be able
to get a home by blowing the horn and spending your time
with the Band. "

When James Anderson died, he left a substantial estate.
It has already been noted that he received $4,000 for a piece
of property in 1868.   The terms of the will probated on June
30, 1886, are such that no exact value of the estate is stated.
There were four next-of-kin residing in Ohio, according to
the probate record.   These were Isabella Anderson, Sardinia,
widow; I. M. Anderson, Clyde, son; Benjamin D. Anderson,
Sardinia, son; and William Anderson, Aberdeen, grandson.
To his widow James left the family house and lots 40 and 41
in Sardinia and $1,652 in notes, including one dated Sept.
17, 1870, on "Irvin" Anderson for $150.   Interest on two
notes on Benjamin D. Anderson for $100 each was declared
discharged by the will, which further provided that the notes
and all other property were to pass into the hands of Benjamin D. Anderson on the death of the widow.   "This bequest
to B. D. Anderson is made in consideration of his care and
provision during the time he has lived with us and with the
understanding that he will continue to live with us as hereto-
fore while we live. "[10]

If examined carelessly, the will might seem to contain a deliberate slight to Irwin. But it must be borne in mind that, according to the Evans-Stivers account, at least two of James' children by his first wife and the widow of another and his last-born child by Isabella were alive as late as 1900. It is true that James might have eased up on Irwin's note a little, but it is equally true that Benjamin Dickey was the only one of at least five living children to be made an heir, apparently because he had stayed on the homestead and made a home for his aged parents during their declining years.

Information such as the foregoing never appears in any of Anderson's works and apparently was not in his mind or possession. He once wrote an inquirer that, "The truth is, that my knowledge of our family genealogy is so vague that I can hardly answer any of your questions definitely."11 He suggested asking his brother, Karl, for the desired facts.

Karl wrote later in life that he had passed up a chance to buy the Evans-Stivers history of Adams County. Evidently he had a disturbing partial memory of the time when Evans visited his school friend, Irwin Anderson, in Clyde. "Often in the passing years I spoke to Sherwood of my search for a book of unknown title." Later Karl and Ray found the Evans history.12

When Karl mentioned the half-remembered book to Sherwood, "Often I was told to forget it. It's the bunk, he would say." Later, Karl says, Sherwood "cast out his enigmatic notion of humble background. Conquered his Lincoln complex." Then Sherwood, too, "went in search of the unknown book."

A note prepared for biographical purposes shortly after Sherwood's death shows that Karl never mastered the family history, possibly being conditioned more than he would admit by Sherwood's attitude:

> Father was born near Ironton, Ohio. [Actually West Union, two counties farther west.] The first of his people came from the north of Ireland just after the American Revolution. He was said to have eleven sons. [James did have eleven children of both sexes, counting the two of his second wife by her previous marriage.] These things were unimportant in Sherwood's mind. He dismissed them

as inventions.... [13]

Sherwood seems never to have been interested enough in the factual material to examine it, though Karl suggests he eventually wanted it. Karl gained acquaintance with it but could not retain possession of it as a serious record. He was still troubled by the problem when he wrote to Eleanor, Sherwood's widow: "I think the biographical sketch is OK.... Although I still resist the thought of Sherwood just rising from the dust and with no background at all."[14]

Notes

1.   Nelson W. Evans and Emmons B. Stivers, History of Adams County, Ohio. West Union, Ohio, 1900, p. 504.

2.   Records of Adams County Recorder, vol. 6, p. 352.

3.   From inscription on gravestone in Trotter graveyard near West Union, Ohio.

4.   Ibid.

5.   Records of Adams County Recorder, vol. 28, p. 89.

6.   Ibid., vol. 17, p. 43.

7.   Ibid., vol. 45, p. 31.

8.   Adams County Marriage Record for 1831, p. 258.

9.   Records of Adams County Recorder, vol. 11, p. 84-5.

10. Record of Wills, Brown County, Ohio, vol. 8, p. 432-36.

11. Letter to John F. Kendrick, Chicago, from New Orleans, July 10, 1925.

12. Letter from Karl Anderson to R. A. Huggins, Xenia, Ohio, July 17, 1946.

13. Letter from Karl Anderson to the Encyclopedia of American Biography, June 7, 1941.

14. Letter from Karl to Eleanor C. Anderson, "Saturday p. m. , " ca. June, 1941.

IV: THE ITALIAN GRANDMOTHER

Much more is known about Anderson's paternal grandfather, James Anderson, than about his paternal grandmother, Isabella Bryan Huggins Anderson. The situation is just reversed in the case of his maternal grandparents. Practically nothing is known about William H. Smith, but of Margaret Austry Smith Myers one may draw a fairly complete picture.

Margaret "Oystry" and William H. Smith were married in Butler County, Ohio, on December 22, 1851, by a Justice of the Peace.[1] On December 4, 1857, that marriage was "dissolved and held for naught." On October 1, 1852,[2] Margaret Smith bore her first child, Emma Jane. According to the divorce plea, she was abandoned "without support and without cause" by her husband in March, 1854. On May 10, 1854, her second child, Mary Ann, was born. From then until the time of the divorce she supported herself and her children through her own industry and the help of her parents; the whereabouts of William H. Smith remained "unknown and not discoverable." Karl Anderson wrote that "Her first husband, named Smith... a school teacher, deserted my Grand Mother and went back to England where he came from."[3] When the marriage was dissolved in 1857, Margaret Smith was given the custody of her children and the right to $300 in alimony, which it is doubtful that she ever collected.[4]

Although the divorce decree does not specifically grant Margaret Smith's request that her maiden name be restored, she must have taken the fact that the marriage was "held for naught" as permission to use it, for Margaret "Ostracy" was married to Lewis Maer on March 29, 1858, by a Rev. Edward W. Hood.[5] By this marriage she had one daughter, Margaret, born March 1, 1859. Maer died of cholera in Oxford, Ohio, in September, 1861.[6] The account of his death as Karl recalled it was that "her second husband... was killed by a bolt of lightning while standing under a tree."[7] Though Mrs. Myers, as the name is now spelled, lived until June 30, 1915,[8] she did not marry a third time.

476

She was born in Germany on Sept. 10, 1830,[9] and her granddaughter, Miss Nellie Finch, in whose family she lived for thirty-two years, understood the family came to the United States from near Berlin when Margaret Austry (note earlier spellings) was perhaps three or four years old, the ship landing in New Orleans. Possibly Margaret Austry's parents were living somewhere in Butler County when they aided the daughter with two small children and a defaulting husband. A brother, Henry Austry, lived many years in St. Joseph, Mo.

It was his grandmother Myers whom Anderson romanticized so thoroughly. As late as 1938 he stated of her:

I tried to make a picture of my maternal grandmother in A Story Teller's Story. She was from Austria and had come to this country at an early age. I have the impression that she came from that part of Austria nearest Italy and was Italian. I have no way of knowing when she first came to America. She was married, I was told, four times and had children by all four of her husbands. All four of her husbands died before she did. Also I do not know the various places in which she lived but I have the impression that she was all of her life a country woman. She last lived with my mother's one sister at Oxford, Ohio.[10]

One gathers from the above that Anderson came to believe his account of his maternal grandmother was accurate. His brother Ray used to complain to him of calling their grandmother Italian when she was actually German. But Sherwood had apparently decided this grandmother was the source of the Italian blood he wanted to think was in the family. One has only to read the following paragraph and reflect on the fact that, as Miss Finch reports, she was all her life a staunch Presbyterian to realize again how little reality meant to Anderson when his imagination had been stirred:

She the dark evil old woman with the broad hips and the great breasts of a peasant and with the glowing hate shining out of her one eye would be worth a book in herself. It was said she had shuffled off four husbands and when I knew her, although she was old, she looked not unwilling to tackle another. Some day perhaps I shall tell the

tale of the old woman and the tramp who tried to
rob the farm house when she was staying alone;
and how she, after beating him into submission
with her old firsts, got drunk with him over a bar-
rel of hard cider in a shed and of how the two
went singing off together down the road.... [11]

This is the same woman who did housework for a living and has been described as "prudish, nasty-nice." She
was neurotic, suspicious, volatile, and easily-offended, a
difficult person to live with, but above all she was abundantly
moralistic. As a Presbyterian church member she was
shocked at the fact that her son-in-law, in whose home she
lived more than three decades, did not attend church and
mentioned his shortcoming to him frequently. [12]

One can imagine the impact of the arrival of this
actively unhappy grandmother would have on the Andersons
when she arrived late on a Friday evening to stay because
no one else could stand her. Sherwood, approaching eleven,
drank all this in, stored it and doubtless other impressions
in his memory, and eventually recorded the following impression:

Had I not seen and did I not then sharply remember that old grandmother from the southeast of
Europe, she with the one eye and the quick, dark
and dangerous temper! There were possibilities
of cruelty in her. Once she tried to kill my sister with a butcher knife, and one could think of her
as killing with a laugh on her lips. Having known
her one could easily conceive of the possibility of
life in which cruelty had its place too. [13]

Beyond what one gathers from the marriage and divorce records, one has only the following statement from
Sherwood as information about the maternal grandfather: "I
know nothing at all of my maternal grandfather except that I
was told he was a laborer named Smith and that he was
killed by a falling tree in clearing land." [14]

Karl wrote his niece, Stella's daughter, that his grandmother's name was Austry and that her first husband, the
father of Emma Smith, was an Englishman by the name of
Smith.

He had gone to the German province of Hessen-

Darmstadt as a tutor and there married a daughter of the family named Austry. There seems to have been some objection to the marriage, in any event, the [sic] came to this country and settled at Oxford, Ohio. This marriage was apparently of short duration and only one child was born of this union, my mother.

Just when this German grandmother married a man by the name of Myers, I do not know, but of that union there was born, I seem to remember, two daughters. One was Aunt Maggie, whom I never knew, and the other, whose given name I do not know, married a man by the name of Jones who lives or lived somewhere in the far West.15

The briefest comparison of the factual, available record with this account of Karl's shows that Sherwood had, in the attitude of his brother, ample precedent for a lack of respect for factuality. That Stella also could share in this attitude is shown in the following comment by Karl:

There can be doubt of my Grand Mother Myers being Italian as Sherwood called her. Her maiden name was Austry.... I think it is inadvisable to change her nationality to German. Sherwood called her that [Italian] so often. I think he got that from an obsession my sister, Stella, had as a young woman. Stella and I like my mother were of latin coloration. In a while she held tenaciously to the thought that we had Italian blood in us. Often have I been told that she was German, that Grand Mother. It doesn't matter what she was except that it is inescapable that she was a problem.16

Notes

1. <u>Butler County Marriage Records</u>, vol. 3, p. 132.

2. Date shown on gravestone in McPherson Cemetery, Clyde; and substantiated by Emma Anderson obituary in <u>Clyde Enterprise</u>, May 14, 1895.

3. Letter to <u>Encyclopedia of American Biography</u>, June 7, 1941.

4. Code Record Butler County, vol. 5, p. 412-3.

5. Butler County Marriage Records, vol. 3, p. 288.

6. Interview with Miss Nellie Finch, Oxford, Ohio.

7. Letter to Encyclopedia of American Biography, June 7, 1941.

8. Health Department, Hamilton, Ohio.

9. Ibid.

10. Dinsmoor, p. 63; letter of June 24, 1938.

11. A Story Teller's Story, p. 7.

12. Interview with Miss Finch.

13. A Story Teller's Story, p. 102.

14. Dinsmoor, p. 63; letter of June 24, 1938.

15. Letter to Margaret Hill Schroeder, Hinsdale, Ill., April 19, 1951.

16. Letter to Encyclopedia of American Biography, June 7, 1941.

V: FINE IN EVERY WAY

Little enough is known of the girlhood of Emma Anderson, but it will be useful to an understanding of her as the wife of Irwin and mother of Sherwood. Her obituary in the Clyde newspaper reports she was born on October 1, 1851, near Oxford, Ohio.[1] Presumably this date, which is used on the Clyde grave marker, is correct.

Emma's early years were difficult ones for her mother. When Emma was 17 months old, her mother, who was about to give birth to her second child, was deserted by her father. Left to her own devices with two infants, the mother must have known many hardships, perhaps not the least of which was the necessity of turning to her parents for aid. Her two children were five and three when she obtained her freedom to establish a new life. Probably she had already embarked on her career of doing housework by that time. The procedure would have been to go into some household where she could work and keep her two small children, probably in a farm home, and work for room and board and perhaps a little pay. Her circumstances would have been not much more than adequate.

Perhaps it was with a view to the marriage to Lewis Maer in March, 1858, that Margaret Smith obtained her divorce in December, 1857. At any rate, the new marriage may very possibly have seemed the welcome beginning of a new and more secure life for her and her children. It seems reasonable to assume that she was happy in her marriage and in the birth of her third daughter in March, 1859. Regardless of the character or intentions of the new husband, of whom almost nothing is known, he turned out to be no better provider than the first, for his death in September, 1861, left his widow in a worse position than she had occupied before. For she had now three children instead of two, and one was not yet three years old.

What help Margaret Maer (later Myers) got from

481

others is not known, but it can not be thought that the problems in providing for herself and her three small girls were
few. She seems to have gone back to working for any family
that would have her and her children.

As soon as they were old enough, the children were
sent into other families. They were not on the basis of
"bound girls, " as Anderson said his mother was, [2] but instead the arrangement was less formal and probably much
more charitable. Just how old Emma was when she left her
mother is not known, but she is said to have gone into the
home of Mr. and Mrs. James I. Faris, near Morning Sun,
Ohio, "as soon as she was able to work. "[3] The only specific
information about her for this period is the statement in her
obituary that "She united with the Methodist Church at Oxford
in 1865. "[4] Her sister, Mary, used to tell her daughter[5]
that she lived in eighteen different homes from the time she
was six until she was twelve. Allowing for possible exagger-
ation in the number of homes lived in, one finds in that
statement two important indications. Mary left her mother
when she was six. Probably Emma left her mother at the
death of her stepfather, when she was nine. In addition,
Mary was so impressed with the difficulty and uncertainty of
her early life in strange families as to comment on it often
and emphatically to her daughter, Mrs. Ormes.

Perhaps it is safe to assume that Emma went into the
Faris home at the age of nine or perhaps a little later and
stayed there continuously until her marriage, for she left the
Faris family to marry Irwin. [6] Emma's experience with the
Faris family was probably happier than that recorded by her
sister, for Mrs. Beaton said her mother thought very highly
of Emma and often spoke well of her after she had gone.
Mrs. Faris said Emma was "fine in every way, was kind
and a good housekeeper. " Mrs. Beaton was only three years
old in 1873, when Emma married Irwin, but she reported
that the family recollection of her was a very pleasant one.

Karl's testimony is corroborative of the happiness of
Emma's relationship with the Faris family:

> As to the question of my mother being indentured
> after my grandfather Smith escaped from his some-
> what tempestuous wife, or as Sherwood refers to
> mother as a bound girl, I have remembrance of the
> many letters she received from a Mrs. Faris, with
> whom she lived in girlhood, they were always

written in a spirit of a mother's tenderness and I
am sure her girlhood was very happy. As a con-
firmation of this I have in my possession a daily
diary written by my mother as the evidence of her
happy life and of her attendance at the girl's academy at Oxford, of this there is no doubt. 7

Probably she had been with the family some time when
her marriage occurred, for it was at the Faris farm-home,
which is about a mile south of Morning Sun, that the marriage took place. Miss Finch understood that it was a "nice
home wedding, " and Mrs. Beaton recalled hearing her mother
talk of "giving a reception for Emma. "

Notes

1.   Enterprise, May 14, 1895, p. 3.

2.   A Story Teller's Story, p. 7.

3.   Interview with Miss Finch.

4.   Enterprise, May 14, 1895.

5.   Mrs. Myrtle Ormes, Pendleton, Ind.

6.   Miss Finch; and Mrs. William Beaton, Oxford, O. ,
     daughter of Mr. and Mrs. James I. Faris.

7.   Letter to Margaret Schroeder, April 19, 1951.

VI: A COLLECTOR OF TALES

Though the childhood of Emma Smith was turbulent, she grew to adulthood in the wholesome, hard-working, friendly atmosphere of the Faris household. It was as a young woman of almost 21 years who had known both the uncertainty attendant on her mother's experiences and the security of work among friends, a young woman of beauty and sweetness of disposition, that she entered her marriage with Irwin McLain Anderson.

For many of the details of Irwin Anderson's youth one must turn to the account of Nelson W. Evans, co-author of the Adams County history mentioned earlier. Irwin was the only child of James Anderson to have a biographical sketch of himself in that county history. Since Sherwood Anderson made his father out to be a kind of ne'er-do-well and since he never reached any appreciable worldly success, an explanation of the biographical sketch is naturally sought. An item in the Clyde, Ohio, paper goes far toward supply that explanation: "Capt. N. W. Evans, of Portsmouth, stopped here last Friday on his way home from Put-in-Bay to spend a few hours with his old schoolmate, I. M. Anderson. "[1] The newspaper item is evidence that I. M. Anderson's biographer had known him forty years or more when he wrote of him for the volume that came out in 1900. Although it has been possible to verify some of what Evans wrote, if he had not thought enough of his friend to record what he did when he did, information concerning the youth of I. M. Anderson would now be almost completely lacking.

Evans says Irwin Anderson was born in West Union on August 7, 1845. Since Irwin's army record says he was eighteen when mustered into service on August 10, 1863, and since August 7, 1845, is the birth date on the record at the Dayton Soldier's Home, this date seems established beyond doubt. [2]

From the account of James Anderson one learns that

484

Irwin grew up in an apparently happy and comfortable family of eleven children of mixed parentage. Irwin apparently grew up on his father's farm just outside the town limits of West Union and went to school, Evans says, "in the old stone schoolhouse where the house occupied by John Knox now [1900] stands..." as apparently Evans did himself.

No records of any West Union schools of pre-Civil War days exist; consequently, there is no specific information about Irwin's early schooling. The first record which pertains to Irwin specifically is that of his enlistment in the infantry in the Civil War. Evans, who was a first-lieutenant in Company G with him, has summarized his military career (page 677) in these words:

In June, 1863, he enlisted in Company G, 129th O. V. I. , and served until the eighth of March following. He enlisted August 25, 1864, in the Seventh Ohio Cavalry, and was mustered out with the company, July 1, 1865. In both services he was in campaigns about East Tennessee. He was in the affair at Cumberland Gap on September 9, 1863; in Burnside's campaign against Longstreet that fall and winter. He was engaged in the siege of Knoxville in the Fall of 1864, and was in the battle of Franklin and Nashville, Tennessee; Pulaski, Tennessee; Plantersville and Selma, Alabama, in 1865.

The official army record differs from the Evans-Stivers account in that it has Anderson enrolling in Company G on July 20, 1863. Additionally it tells that Anderson was a private and was mustered in and out of service in Company G at Camp Cleveland, Ohio. Once more a private in the cavalry company, Anderson was mustered in at Ironton, Ohio, and mustered out at Nashville, Tenn. [3] On the occasion of his first enlistment he was five feet, nine inches tall, of dark complexion, having black eyes and hair, and by occupation a farmer. [4]

Of the activities in general of Company G, Evans has this to say (page 354):

On August 10, 1863, it was sent to Camp Nelson, Ky. On August 20, 1863, it started on the march to Cumberland Gap, where it arrived September 8, 1863. On the ninth of September, 1863, Gen. Frazier surrendered the Gap with 2, 400 prisoners

and the 129th was relegated to garrison duty there
with scouting. Dec. 2, 1863, it was sent to Black
Fox Ford on the Clinch River, where it had a
skirmish with Longstreet's army, with occasional
skirmishes until he returned to Virginia. The
regiment then returned to Cumberland Gap, whence
it was sent home at the expiration of its service....

This company did some hard marching, much
starving, and was under fire several times, but
fortunately no one out of the company was wounded
or killed [but six died in service], though the rebels
lost sixty-five killed or wounded in making the
charge at Black Fox Ford....

One also gains from Evans a view of the activities of
Company F in the Seventh Cavalry:

The hardest fought battle ever participated in was
Franklin, Tenn. At Rogersville, Tenn., the regiment met its first serious losses by capture. The
captured men suffered greatly in Libby and Ander-
sonville prisons. One of the most deplorable events
which occurred during the service of the regiment
was the explosion of the steamer, "Sultana," April
27, 1865, on the Mississippi River near Memphis,
Tenn. Several members of this regiment had been
paroled at Vicksburg and were on their way home
when the explosion occurred in the night and several hundred men lost their lives.

Major General Upton in General Order No. 21,
issued at Edgefield, Tenn., in 1865, highly compliments this the last campaign of the war, reciting
the conduct of the division of which the seventh was
a part, he says: "In thirty days you have traveled
600 miles, crossing six rivers, met and defeated
the enemy at Montevalle, Ala., capturing 100 prisoners; routed Forrest, Buford and Rhoddy in their
chosen positions at Ebenezer, capturing two guns
and 300 prisoners; carried the works in your front
at Selma, capturing thirteen guns and 1,100 prisoners, five battle flags, and finally crowned your
success by a night assault on the enemy's entrench-
ments at Columbus, Ga., where you captured 1,500
prisoners, twenty-four guns, eight battle flags with
vast ammunitions of war; April 21, you arrived at

> Macon, Ga., having captured on your march 300
> prisoners, thirty-nine pieces of artillery and thir-
> teen battle flags. Whether mounted with the saber
> or dismounted with carbines the brave men of the
> Third, Fourth, and Fifth Iowa; First and Seventh
> Ohio and Fourth Missouri triumphed in every con-
> flict. " (Pages 357-358.)

As a youth of 18 and 19 years, it may be concluded,
Irwin Anderson saw a lot of fighting and heard a great deal
more, though he entered the war as a private and retired
from it unwounded and still a private. But, when the rest
marched, starved, and fought, there is no reason to doubt
that he did, too. In all, young Irwin Anderson served during
the Civil War a little more than sixteen months. It is hardly
a surprise he had stories to tell when he came back; he had
seen a good deal to tell about. If later he is seen as an
imaginative gaffer whose mind is constantly focused on events
of twenty and thirty years before, that situation may be understood better in terms of an oration delivered in the Methodist Episcopal Church in West Union, on September 2, 1865.
This memorial address, which was delivered by Captain Nelson W. Evans, was published as a booklet of about a dozen
pages, and the assumption is that at least a certain group
agreed so heartily with its sentiment as to want to preserve
and circulate it.

Captain Evans, the friend who later wrote of Irwin
Anderson, declared the war heroes "fought in the light of a
full blaze of a meridian sun. Their patriotism was not hatred, bigotry, fanaticism; it was reason, conscience. They
saw the end from the beginning; they had calculated the cost;
they admitted no doubtful issue. "[5]

But Captain Evans spoke not only of the dead; he had
remarks very directly intended for the living:

> And the survivors? What of them? They have re-
> turned, bronzed by the fierce heat and fire of many
> battles. They have brought their honorable cre-
> dentials--their scars--many of them disabled for
> life. They constitute the glorious church of heroes.
> They have received the baptism of blood on a score
> of battle fields. They have returned to us from
> the jaws of destruction, from the "mouth of hell. "
> They danced at the high carnival of Death; they sat
> at his banquet; they drank his health and dashed

their goblets in his face. They have fought the
demons of darkness, and the deadly arrows have
hurtled harmlessly from their armor. They have
entered the "valley of the shadow of death, " plucked
the "olive branch of peace, " and brought it back to
us. They have earned the gratitude of unborn millions; they have crowned themselves with eternal
honors. Since they have passed through the ordeal
of fire, and blood, and leaden death, privation and
pestilence, they seem to belong to a higher order
of beings. Since their return from the Sinais of
the Republic, where the Lord of hosts spake great
truths amid the thunders of battle, their faces seem
to shine with a sacred light.

We would do well to heed their teaching. . . . 6

One can only surmise that Irwin Anderson either heard
or read this oration, but the chances of his having done
either one or the other are good. It had been written and
delivered by a friend, and it dealt directly with the most important experience of his life. One can be sure that he
would have felt its terms appropriate and justified, for the
spirit of that speech is the spirit of the G. A. R. , an organization in which Irwin Anderson was active to his dying day.
The flattering acclaim of the speech would be hard for a
youth of nineteen to resist. From just such unrestrained
flights of rhetoric Irwin Anderson may have contracted a very
persistent and affecting condition.

However seriously Irwin may have taken the acclaim
showered on him and his fellow veterans at the war's end,
he soon entered a new and different atmosphere. For in the
next year he was attending the Xenia Female College. The
evidence of this is quite sound. Evans-Stivers on (page 677)
says: "After the war was over, he went to school in Xenia,
Ohio, in 1865 and 1866. " The 1865-66 catalogue of the Xenia
Female College lists Irwin M. Anderson of West Union as
one of about fifty "Gentlemen" enrolled. 7

Just why Irwin was sent to that institution is purely a
matter of conjecture, though speculation is not altogether un-
guided by facts. James Anderson may have felt Irwin needed
cultural and spiritual guidance after being exposed to the
rigors of warfare as a youth. Too, he may simply have
wanted to help Irwin to a little education with a view to
establishing him economically. Since one can hardly imagine

Irwin's asking to be sent to this particular institution, it must
be noted that it was United Presbyterian, which would have
suited James. The Associate Reform Presbyterian was one
of two sects which united to form the United Presbyterian
group. "Health, Energy, Promptness, Industry and Earnest
Systematic Application are essential to success at school and
after life," proclaims the catalogue, and it is not impossible
that James felt Irwin needed bolstering in some of these respects. Certainly he did later. The institution had devotion-
al exercises every morning, two prayer meetings a week,
and Bible classes; each student was required to attend the
church of his choice "on Sabbath." The trustees declared
openly their "aim to make the Institution a Christian Home,
where comfort, health, morals and mind will receive attention."

Everything indicates James Anderson would naturally
conclude he could not err in sending Irwin to Xenia. But it
must not be overlooked that Irwin's sister, Martha, was a
first year student in the "Female College" during the year
1865-66 and that a Stella Anderson of Xenia was in the
"Preparatory Department" that year. Martha would have
lived in the dormitory with the other female students from
outside Xenia, but Irwin would have been housed in some
suitable household in Xenia. That makes one wonder if Stella
Anderson were not some relative to Irwin and Martha; if so,
perhaps Irwin stayed with that family, possibly that of an
uncle. The possibility seems a little greater when one recalls that Irwin's daughter, though named Estella, was generally called Stella.

Some fragments of information about Irwin's year at
Female College reached Sherwood and aroused him to inquiry.
Accordingly, Karl was to write:

> I believe I can throw some light on my brother,
> Sherwood Anderson's seeking from you, some in-
> formation of the early life of his father. Why he
> came to Xenia with his belated curiosity.
>
> As to his father Irwin Anderson ever having lived
> in Xenia that I am not sure. Certain, I am, that
> he talked of being there, of in his youth knowing
> Whitelaw Reid. Stories that had no reality, he was
> given to, facts of his imagination. He was the
> [father]... of six artists and writers, I among
> them... Sherwood the most renowned. [8]

The reference to Reid and Karl's reaction to it are
revealing of Irwin's credibility rating with his son. Reid, a
foremost American citizen of his time, was born in Xenia
in 1837 and was serving as American ambassador in London
at the time of his death in 1912. Two years after his graduation from college in 1856, he took control of the Xenia
News, which he operated until 1860, when he became deeply
involved in Lincoln's campaign for the presidency and subsequently left Xenia to become one of the outstanding chroni-
clers of the Civil War. Though he was no longer in Xenia
when Irwin arrived to go to school there, he was certainly
one of its more illustrious products, and, as one who was
additionally well-known for his writings about the war, he
most certainly would be a personage well-known to Irwin.
Irwin very probably did know people who had known Reid.
If Reid visited there while Irwin was there, it is possible
Irwin could have met him. Irwin wrote that he was "traveling between 1865 [properly 1866 at earliest] and 1870. " Reid
travelled through the South just after the war and published,
in 1866, After the War: A Southern Tour. Karl thus dis-
misses as "facts of the imagination" a story which had at
least a chance of accuracy. The father was fully established
as a story-teller rather than a reliable informant.

There is no way to be sure of Irwin's reaction to
scholastic life. One may guess that he did not like it; at
least, it was not continued beyond that year. For Evans
relates, "He then located in Mexico, Missouri, and was in
the west and southwest from 1866 to 1870. " What he did
there and why he went is not known. A step-brother, George
Washington, James' first child, may have died in Webb City,
Missouri. His widow and children lived there in 1900, according to Evans-Stivers. A remote possibility is that Irwin
went to Missouri because of his contact with soldiers in the
Fourth Missouri Cavalry Regiment while he was with the
Seventh Ohio. Whatever other reasons there may have been,
though, perhaps the one which underlay the others was that
he was a young man who had known adventures and wanted
more. He had got into the South with the army; perhaps he
had heard tales about the Southwest. On his Declaration for
Pension, Irwin was required to list "several places of residence since leaving the service. " For this period he wrote
simply: "1865 to '70 traveling from '70 to '77 Preble
County Ohio. "9 Perhaps his going away was in reaction to
the restrictions of the school year. Doubtless he collected
more tales to tell. It is strange Sherwood did not recall
any tales of the Southwest.

Whatever else is true of Irwin's travels in the South-west, it is safe to say that they did not make his fortune. The note mentioned in James' will was dated September 17, 1870; in 1886 the $150 was still not repaid. Perhaps this money was borrowed on his return to Ohio to enable him to enter business for himself as a saddler and harnessmaker. Where and when Irwin learned the harnessmaker's trade can only be guessed. The first real evidence that connects him with that trade indicates he was in business in Morning Sun, Ohio, in 1872. "I. N. " Anderson is listed in a business directory for 1872-73 and one in that town who deals in "saddles and harness. "[10]

When Boni & Liveright asked for biographical information to send to John Taylor of Encyclopaedia Britannica, part of Sherwood's brief reply was: "My father, Irwin Anderson, was, I have heard him say, a North Carolina man--the son of a planter. Have never looked up his people. "[11] Except for partial, sporadic, and ineffectual efforts, he never did.

Notes

1.   Enterprise, July 20, 1897, p. 3.

2.   Any birth records in Adams County of that date perished when the court house burned in 1910. Pension records agree on the birth date.

3.   Letter from The Library of Congress, Legislative Reference Service, Oct. 17, 1941.

4.   Declaration for Pension, May 18, 1912.

5.   Capt. N. W. Evans, In Memoriam: A Tribute of Respect to the Memory of the Deceased Soldiers of Adams County, Ohio, an address... delivered at the Methodist Episcopal Church, West Union, September 2, 1865; Cincinnati, O. , Achilles Pugh, Ohio, 1865, p. 9.

6.   Ibid. , p. 11.

7.   Sixteenth Annual Catalogue of the Xenia Female College for Collegiate Year 1865-6; Xenia, O. , Kinney and Milburn, 1866, p. 11.

8.   Letter to R. A. Higgins, Xenia, O. July 17, 1946.

9.   Filed at Connersville, Ind. , on May 18, 1912.

10. Williams' Ohio State Directory for 1872-3, Cincinnati,
     Williams & Co. , [1872?], p. 227.

11. Letter; New Orleans, Oct. 7, 1925.

VII: THE MUTUALLY ATTRACTED

It is certain that Irwin was in the vicinity of Morning Sun as early as November 14, 1871, because on that date he was received into the Hopewell United Presbyterian Church by "Profession of Faith."[1] The Hopewell Church, still standing in 1942 but abandoned, was in between the towns of Morning Sun and College Corner, though closer to the former, and ministered to residents of both towns and the surrounding countryside.

It seems possible that this church may have been the hub of the romance between Irwin Anderson and Emma Smith, for the Faris family attended the Hopewell Church; although Emma had joined the Methodist Church in Oxford, she may very possibly have attended the Hopewell Church with the Faris family.

Irwin was a handsome man and probably made a dashing figure in the little town of Morning Sun, the population of which in 1872 was 135. After all, he was a Civil War veteran, perhaps at times a hero, a traveler to what is still the glamorous Southwest, a man with a year of schooling, and one established in an honorable trade. One of Emma's descendants has ventured to say that she was fascinated by him.

Emma, as her photograph shows, was a handsome woman. She does not seem to have had much opportunity for education, but she has been described as kind and capable. Those who knew her later have been unanimous in speaking of her as intelligent, industrious, and possessing a certain charm. She may well have possessed as much attraction for Irwin as he may have had for her.

Sherwood's own impression is that, "He found her in a farm house when he was by way of being something of a young swell himself and she was a bound girl; and she was then beautiful--beautiful without the aid of shadows cast by a

493

kerosene lamp. "[2]

On March 11, 1873, the marriage of Irwin M. Anderson and Emma Jane Smith was solemnized by Rev. Joseph MacHatton of the Hopewell Church. [3] As indicated before, the ceremony is said to have taken place at the Faris farm home with a reception following. [4] Irwin is on record as stating that he and Emma were married on March 11, 1873, at College Corner. [5]

It is likely that an early consequence of the marriage was Emma Anderson's joining the Hopewell Church by "Profession of Faith" on August 21, 1873. [6] The memberships of both Irwin and Emma Anderson were dismissed to Camden, Ohio, (Preble County) on June 14, 1874, [7] at which time it may be presumed they moved to Camden so that Irwin could set up his shop there.

Though no record of his birth has been found, Karl Anderson, their first child, gives his birth date as Jan. 13, 1874. [8] In that case he must have been born in Morning Sun before the parents moved to Camden.

Other children born to these parents were Stella (April 13, 1875), Sherwood (Sept. 13, 1876), Irwin M. (June 18, 1878), Ray Maynard (May 21, 1883), Earl (June 18, 1885), and Fern (Dec. 11, 1890). [9]

Notes

1.   From a transcript of Hopewell Church records in keeping of Reverend Edward Paxton, College Corner, O. , made by Reverend Paxton, Oct. 1942.

2.   A Story Teller's Story, p. 39-40.

3.   Preble County Marriage Records, vol. 3, p. 354.

4.   It should be mentioned that a transcript of Hopewell Church records made by Rev. Paxton places the date of the marriage at March 16, 1873, and Emma Smith's residence as College Corner.   The evidence of Mrs. William Beaton and George Faris and the Preble County Record seems more reliable.   The Hopewell Church record agrees the ceremony was performed by Rev. Joseph Mac Hatton.

5. Bureau of Pensions Questionnaire, May 13, 1898.

6. Transcript of Rev. Paxton. See above, note 4.

7. Ibid.

8. Who's Who in America, 1942-3 ed. This date is corroborated by a statement filed by Irwin Anderson with the Bureau of Pensions on May 5, 1898.

9. Deposition of Irwin M. Anderson on April 12, 1915, for Pension Bureau records.

VIII: "I. M. ANDERSON, HARNESS"

The Hopewell Church record allows the inference that Irwin Anderson moved with his wife and infant son to Camden in June of 1874. It is certain that he was established in the harness business there in time to be included in a Preble County Directory, the preface of which was dated July 28, 1875.[1] In that directory (page 173) he was listed as one dealing in "Harness &c" in Camden and was represented by an advertisement (page 62) about 1.5 by 3.5 inches in size. According to the advertisement, he was a "Manufacturer and Dealer in Harness, Saddles, Bridles, Collars, Whips, &c," of which he had a large stock "always on hand." These items were "of the Best Materials" and sold at "lowest Cash prices." Fine harness was a specialty.

Morning Sun to Caledonia: Chronology

Evans-Stivers[2]	Irwin Anderson[3]	Place
		Morning Sun
1870-1877	1870-1877	Preble Co: Camden
1877-	1877-1879	Richland Co. : Mansfield
1880-1883	1879-1883	Marion Co. : Caledonia

The tabular chronology presented herewith provides an over-all summary of where Irwin Anderson, and presumably the rest of his family, lived from 1876, the year of Sherwood's birth, until the removal to Clyde. The leaving of Camden is dated almost perfectly by the following item in a Camden newspaper of September 1, 1877: "I. M. Anderson will leave here in a few days for Independence., O. , where he will engage in business."[4] But where he went and what he did is not clear. Evans-Stivers says specifically that, "In that year [1877] he located in Mansfield, Ohio, and worked for

496

the Aultman-Taylor Company. "5   The likelihood of his working in this farm-machine factory, one of the largest in the
country, is heightened by his father's use of the word situation.   The Camden item had it as engage in business, which
is probably the impression he wanted to leave after having
his own shop in Camden.   No trace has been found of an I.
M. Anderson in either of the towns called Independence in
Ohio.

   The problem is complicated by the fact that Anderson
is not listed in the Mansfield directory for 1877-8 (not surprisingly) or for the next one issued, for 1881-2.   But a
Mansfield directory, the preface of which is dated June 26,
1883, has "Anderson, Irwin M. , harness maker. "6   The
directory shows further that Irwin Anderson was boarding
with one Joe W. Bell, who was in the saddlery hardware
business.   Anderson was not listed in the harnessmaker category of the business directory.   His working for Aultman-
Taylor, whenever he did it, would mean he had gone out of
business for himself.   Ray Anderson, in a note appended to
a copy of material from the Evans history, says categorically,
as a correction, that "the Anderson family did not live at
Marion, but at Caladonia [sic], Ohio, from 1880 to 1883. "

   Mansfield is only thirty miles from Caledonia; thus
his boarding in Mansfield, to work in the factory, while his
family lived in a smaller, possibly more economical, town,
would be understandable.   It is possible that Irwin worked
in the Mansfield factory at different times between 1877 and
1883, possibly in relationship to the declining fortunes of his
own business.   The idea of his boarding in Mansfield is
strengthened by the fact that Herman Hurd could not recall
that the Andersons ever lived in Mansfield. 7

   The references given above seem to establish beyond
question that Irwin M. Anderson left Camden in September,
1877.   Yet a directory for 1878-9 mentions "I. M. Anderson,
harness" as residing in Camden. 8

   Wherever Irwin took his family from Camden, the
impression given by Sherwood of his father's tiptoeing out of
town ahead of his debts has been widely circulated.   It may
be noted now that his leaving Camden was a published fact.
Many have repeated Sherwood's statement that no two children
in the family were born in the same town.   Both Stella (or,
Estella, as the record has it) and Sherwood were born in
Camden. 9   A story told in Camden10 has it that Irwin skipped

out of the nearby town of Fairhaven owing a bill for leather.
Mr. Coombs even had pointed out to him a house where Mr.
Anderson lived in Fairhaven. There is no evidence to prove
this story, and the chances are it may have persisted only because of the support given it by Sherwood's account. One
need only note that a "D. B. Anderson, " a dealer in "Saddles and Harness, " was listed as living in Fairhaven in a
business directory for 1875-6[11] to realize how the story probably got its start.

According to Mr. James Gift, who worked for Mr.
Anderson when he had his shop in Camden, he made friends
easily. Mr. Gift made the halters, which "M, " as Irwin
was called, did not like to do. He was a kind employer and
was recalled as one who liked to tell "glowing tales of his
own experiences. " During his spare moments he sat in the
rear of the store and practiced on the alto horn, which he
played in the village band. At one time he taught a Sunday
school class.[12] The Preble County Directory for 1875 lists
the personnel of the "Camden Cornet Band, " but Irwin Anderson is not included. He may have joined later. Mrs. Elizabeth Pierce, who lived in the house the Andersons occupied,
the north half of a double house at 142 South Lafayette Street,
said she was told Irwin taught a Methodist Sunday school
class. C. E. Morlatt was to recall many years later that
he had been in Irwin's Sunday school class and that he took
part in an oyster supper in the Anderson home, put on by
Irwin as a treat.[13]

Morlatt further stated that Irwin "worked hard to support his family. " There is much other evidence to indicate
that he was a known and respected business man in Camden.
A note on page 1 of The Eaton Register, July 30, 1874, observes that "J. [sic] M. Anderson, Esq. , is one of the most
enterprising harness dealers in Western Ohio. He is doing
an extensive business. " This rather obvious business puff
was doubtless born of courtesy to an advertiser, and that
Irwin Anderson was. In available copies of the Camden Herald and the Eaton Register and Eaton Democrat, published in
the nearby county seat, in the period between June 3, 1875,
and August, 1877, it has been possible to find 96 separate
insertions of ads for Anderson's business. It may be assumed there were more, for the files are not complete. Of
those found, the following, which occupied a space of one and
three-eighths column inches and which appeared weekly in the
Eaton Register between June 3 and December, 1875, is representative:

For the Best and Cheapest

SADDLES & HARNESS

Go to J.[14] M. Anderson, North Main Street, Camden, O., where will always be found a full stock
of everything in the saddlery line, made of the best
material by experienced workmen, at less figures
than any other house in Southern Ohio.

Call and see. My work will show for itself.

I. M. Anderson

That Irwin had a certain status in the town is suggested by this squib (page 4) by the editor, Will R. Hart-
pence, of the Camden Herald, June 16, 1877: "We visited
the Devil's Backbone [still a local scenic spot] last Sunday,
in company with Dr. Stephenson and Mr. Anderson...." Examination of a succession of issues of the Herald supports
the assumption that Mr. Anderson was Irwin M., the dealer
in saddles and harness.

Later, in Clyde, Irwin Anderson became a painter.
Possibly a suggestion as to the beginning of his learning that
trade is found in the fact that, in Camden, he seems to have
been a business neighbor of O. P. Brown, who styles himself as "House, Sign, and Carriage Painter" and "Grainer,
Glazier and Paper Hanger." His business address is given
as "North Main Street," as was Anderson's. In the Camden
Herald for the period of June to August, 1877, the ads for
their two establishments were next to each other.

Whenever he moved to Caledonia, Irwin rented a shop
building and a house. The family may have lived in more
than one place, but one informant felt certain that Irwin was
always punctual in paying his rent. He recalled that "M...
played in the band," was a "great story teller," and that he
"might have gone on a little toot once in a while."[15]

A woman who was a girl when the Andersons lived in
Caledonia[16] recalls Irwin Anderson as a harnessmaker who
worked hard, was smart, and "spent his money on drink in
saloons." "Because he drank up most of the money, neighbors would help out with gifts occasionally." According to
her, "The only fault any one ever found with the Andersons
was that he drank up his money." She said definitely that

the family moved from Caledonia to Clyde. Another informant[17] remembered playing with Karl and Stella, but of Irwin she recalls only that, "They say he was dissipated in
Caledonia." This acquaintance believed the Anderson family
lived in Caledonia from about 1880 until 1883. She based her
dates on her recollection of playing with the Anderson children.

Notes

1.   B. F. Morgan, Directory of Preble Co., Ohio, for
      1875 ..., Eaton, O., 1875.

2.   History of Adams Co., Ohio, p. 677-8.

3.   Declaration for Pension, May 18, 1912.

4.   Camden Herald, Sept. 1, 1877, p. 4.

5.   History of Adams County, p. 677.

6.   A. Bailey, comp., The Herald's Directory to Mansfield,
      Ohio, 1883-4; Mansfield, Geo. U. Harn & Co., 1883, p.
      28.

7.   Hurd interview, Clyde, Nov. 10, 1962.

8.   Williams' Ohio State Director for 1878-9; Cincinnati,
      Williams and Co., [1878?], p. 79 and p. 504.

9.   Record of Births, Preble County, O., vol. 1, p. 112
      and p. 126.

10.   Mrs. Elizabeth Pierce, Camden, and Mr. Stephen
      Coombs, Abingdon, Va.

11.   Williams' Ohio State Directory for 1875-6, p. 503.

12.   Statements of Mr. James Gift in an interview of June
      30, 1938, reported by Dinsmoor, p. 5-6.

13.   Undated clipping, probably from a Dayton, O., paper,
      in a file in the Camden town library, April 12, 1962.

14.   The ad had J. M. for the insertions of June 3, 10, 17,

24 and was changed to I. M. on July 1.

15. Mr. C. S. Geddis, Caledonia; Sept. 1, 1938; reported by Dinsmoor, p. 7.

16. Interview with Mrs. Alice Irey, Marion, O.; a good friend of Stella's, she corresponded with her until as late as 1891.

17. Miss Mary Curl, Marion.

IX: A MOST ESTIMABLE LADY

The dedication of Winesburg, Ohio is to "My Mother, "
"Whose keen observations on the life about her first awoke
in me the hunger to see beneath the surface of lives. . . . "

Something of Anderson's attitude toward his mother
when he had grown to manhood may be grasped from the following two quotations:

> Mother was tall and slender and had once been
> beautiful. She had been a bound girl in a farmer's
> family when she married father, the improvident
> young dandy. There was Italian blood in her veins
> and her origin was something of a mystery. Per-
> haps we never cared to solve it--wanted it to re-
> main a mystery. It is so wonderfully comforting
> to think of one's mother as a dark, beautiful and
> somewhat mysterious woman. [1]

> A mother, after her death, or after you no longer
> live with her, is something the male fancy can play
> with, dream of, make a part of the movement of
> the grotesque dance of life. Idealize her. Why
> not? She is gone. She will not come near to
> break the thread of the dream. The dream is as
> true as the reality. Who knows the difference?
> Who knows anything? [2]

Anderson admitted in those passages his tendency to
think of his mother imaginatively. Facts already presented
throw some light on the operation of Anderson's imagination
on the memory of his mother. Others which may now be
brought forth make the picture clearer.

Anderson pictured his mother as putting up a gallant
and silent struggle against poverty in Clyde. Mrs. Ormes
summed up her aunt's difficulties as she understood them by
saying, "She had a man that depended on her. " Anderson

has said of the hardship she endured:

> If, in later life, I was sometimes to be called a
> "red," even a communist, which of course I never
> was, it was because every working woman I saw
> reminded me of my mother coming into our little
> frame house on a winter day after hanging a wash
> out on a line, her clothes frozen to her body, the
> look of patient suffering on her face. 3

Working women, he notes elsewhere, had large families, led
hard laborious lives. 4   He wrote to Rosenfeld, "I presume I
shall never in my life see a working woman without identifying her with my mother. "5   The theme of "Death in the
Woods" was continuingly in his mind, the matter of the woman who spent her life feeding men and animals.

In the Memoirs Anderson said it must have been about
the time his father became a painter that his mother began
her "career as a washwoman. "

> She had worked all of her life, even from child-
> hood, for others, a childhood and young girlhood
> of washing dishes, milking cows, waiting on tables,
> a kind of half servant in a house of strangers to
> her own blood, only, after marriage and the com-
> ing of her children, to become a washwoman.

He remembered a "kind of shame" he and the other children
felt at having to collect and deliver the clothes. 6   Anderson
had a "kind of hatred" toward his father in his youthful
years.   But, if Sherwood and the other children bitterly resented their mother's hardships, it is Anderson's opinion
that his mother did not.

> ... it was only after I had become a mature man,
> long after our mother's death, that I began to ap-
> preciate our father and to understand somewhat his
> eternal boyishness, his lack of the feeling of re-
> sponsibility to others, his passion for always play-
> ing with life, qualities which, I have no doubt, our
> mother saw in him and which enabled her, in spite
> of the long hardship of her life with him, to re-
> main always a faithful, and for anything I ever
> heard her say, a devoted wife. 7

Surely, if she could continue to love her exasperatingly

improvident husband, who "flew in and out as a bird flies in
and out of a bush"[8] and who returned days or months later
with some token of his stewardship, her capacity for love
was indeed great. Anderson has represented her as smiling
on the return of her husband after one of his trips. When
he could presume to say that he was going to provide for his
children,

> ...She'd never say a word about the weeks and
> months he'd been away, not leaving us a cent for
> food. Once I heard her speaking to a woman in
> our street. Maybe the woman had dared to sympa-
> thize with her. "Oh," she said, "it's all right.
> He isn't dull like most of the men in this street.
> Life is never dull when my man is about."[9]

If Anderson's mother did not complain bitterly of her
treatment, which many women would consider themselves to
have a perfect right to do, it was because of three considerations. As Anderson pointed out, she always had worked.
It seems certain that she was a woman of pride. And she
was obviously devoted to her family. As bad as conditions
apparently were at times, and there is no way of knowing
exactly how bad or good they were, her children lived
through it and managed to hold their heads up in the village.
It may well have been devotion to the children rather than
appreciation of the novelties of the father that made her keep
silence. Although her picture makes one feel that she was
"quiet and sweet," as Kintner (page 36) summed up the Clyde
impression of her, Anderson remembered times "when she
grew angry and fell into one of her silences."[10]

Anderson wrote Dinsmoor in 1939 that the experience
in his life he remembered with greatest pleasure was that of
his mother coming to his bedside at night. This may be
taken as being at once a signal of his enjoyment and his lack
of objectivity in reminiscing of her. In A Story Teller's
Story (pages 9-11) he gives this recollection: three of the
Anderson boys slept in one bed; the youngest automatically
slept nearest the window. It was a trial of strength between
the other two boys to see who would get the inner-most,
warmest position. At the sound of his mother's footsteps on
the stairs, the struggle stopped. The boys knew their mother
would want them quiet. They did as she expected, knowing
her "well-you'd-better" look. It was their habit to obey
her silent control. But when she got to the room she had
not come just to see that all was quiet. She had warm fat

to rub on the boys' chapped hands. Sherwood remembers his
mother as a woman who could control and caress, the first
according to need and the second, as the opportunity arose.

Part of the uncomplaining determination which Anderson's mother showed may have come to her through her religion. Her joining the Hopewell Church has already been
mentioned. Though she did not join the First Presbyterian
Church in Clyde until March 6, 1892, when Stella joined,[11] she and Stella have been described as constant at-
tendants at the church. "She was an active member of the
church and performed her duties in it. Mrs. Anderson was
a devout Christian if there ever was one."[12] As one pro-
fessing faith in the announced principles of the Presbyterian
religion, she may very possibly have felt it her natural lot
to work and suffer in this life to her greater glory in the
one to come. But Anderson was to report there was "no
Christian forbearance in her." As she sat on the edge of
the bed rubbing her children's frost-bitten hands, he heard a
"kind of smoldering fire in her words."[13]

It is not to be thought, however, that Mrs. Anderson
became enclosed in a wall of silence and suffering. She has
been called "a good conversationalist, easy to get along with,
very friendly with every one." "Every one who knew her
was her friend."[14] Though the task of making both ends
meet and taking care of a large family was hard and restrict-
ing, she found time to be friendly, and the consensus in
Clyde seems to be that she was a woman of sweet disposition.

An item in the Clyde paper allows a view of character
of Mrs. Anderson and shows again how Sherwood's imagination could transmute an incident. First, Anderson's account:

> There was a barrel sunk in the ground and once we
> had a terrible tragedy at the spring. Someone had
> carelessly left the cover off the barrel and a small
> neighbor child, one of the children of Wyatt, the
> town drayman, a little thing just beginning to totter
> about, went down there and fell into the sunken
> barrel.
>
> The child was drowned, and mother going for a
> pail of water found it, and I remember vividly the
> sight of my mother, the tiny white body of the
> child in her arms, her own face white, the water

running from the little child's clothes and leaving
a dark trail in the dust of the roadway. Mother
must have screamed for there were the Wyatts,
running out of their house and also screaming.

It was a cry taken up along the street, women
running out of houses, cries and sobs, the whole
street aroused. Someone had run for the drayman
and presently here he came, standing up in his
dray and lashing his horses, the dray followed by
the buggy of a doctor.

The doctor, was, however, too late and I perhaps
remember the tragedy so clearly became it seemed
to me at the time that mother was, in some way,
the central figure among the screaming sobbing
women gathered about the door of the Wyatt house.
She had uttered one wild cry and then had remained
silent, and having delivered the dead child into the
arms of its mother, had come quietly back to our
house to resume her place at the washtub. 15

With his account may be compared that found in the Clyde
newspaper:

Last Saturday afternoon, Charley, five year old
son of Mr. and Mrs. M. B. Wyatt, while playing
alone at the old Indian spring near the home of
his parents on Spring street, in some manner fell
into the spring, and when a few minutes later he
was found life seemed to be extinct. Not more
than five minutes before his mother and the neighbors had seen him in the street. It would appear
that he must have stubbed his toe while playing at
the spring and pitched in head first, as his head
was in the water when he was found, and a bruise
on the forehead indicated that he had struck his
head on stones in the bottom of the spring, the
blow stunning him so that he was unable to escape
from the few inches of water into which he had
fallen.

A neighbor lady who lives nearest the spring was
the first to discover the boy, and she was so
frightened that she simply pulled him out of the
water, laid him on the grass and fled to the house,
instead of trying to resuscitate him. Finally

> somebody told the distracted mother that her boy
> had fallen into the spring, and she, thinking it was
> the big spring farther from the street, rushed
> thither and not seeing her son she plunged into the
> water supposing his body to be there. It was not
> until then that she was made aware of the real
> place of the accident. She at once ran and picked
> up the boy, but strength failed her before she
> reached her home and neighbors had to carry both
> her and the body of her son. Such a length of
> time had then elapsed that all that all efforts to
> resuscitate the child proved unavailing.[16]

There can be no doubt that the drowning to which the accounts refer is the same in each case.[17] But Anderson has changed his mother, who must have been the "neighbor lady" who found the child, considerably. In his account she utters only one cry and then takes the dead child to his mother. In the newspaper account her fright is so great that she is kept from effective action. One learns, too, from the incident that Mrs. Anderson was capable of becoming overcome by a situation in the worst feminine tradition; she was not always resolute, resourceful.

Another child whose death gives insight into Emma's method of meeting emergencies is Fern Anderson, the last of the children to be born (Dec. 11, 1890) and the first to succumb (Dec. 9, 1892). The Enterprise reported the little girl's death of "congestion of the brain" and noted she had been ill for a week: "... the parents thought nothing serious was the matter and failed to call a physician until two hours before the child died, when too late to save its life."[18] Karl, it may be noted, returned to Clyde from Cleveland for the funeral.[19]

The death of his mother was an event that made a considerable impression on Anderson, then a youth of 18. He has written of it in both A Story Teller's Story and Memoirs and with some inaccuracy. In the former (page 25) he spoke of "a mother who is to die, outworn and done for at thirty--...." The notion that Anderson's mother died when he was fourteen has gained currency; the correct date of her death in Clyde, however, was May 10, 1895[20] when she was 42 and Sherwood 18. This conflicts, too, with the statement that she died on a "wet dismal fall day."[21] The county death record says Mrs. Anderson died of "consumption." Mrs. Ormes understood it was "hasty consumption."

Anderson said that "There was a cold that immediately ran into pneumonia and in a few days our mother was dead."[22]

The death of the woman whom Anderson was to remember as "tall and gaunt and silent"[23] may be documented through references in the Clyde Enterprise, which reported on April 30, 1895 that she was lying "very ill at her home on Spring avenue" and was "not expected to recover."[24] On May 7 she was reported on page 3 as "lying unconscious today, and her death is a matter of a few hours at best." Ironically, in the paper for the day she died, May 10, appeared on page 2 the news that "Mrs. I. M. Anderson, who was several times reported to be dead within the last few days, is considerably better today."

In her obituary (of some 150 words) it was noted that she "had been lying ill for several weeks," and she was a "faithful, consistent Christian," and "a most estimable lady" who left "many friends." In the same issue of the newspaper appeared a "Card of Thanks": "We desire to express our heartfelt thanks to all who so kindly assisted us during the illness and after the death of our loved one. I. M. Anderson and Family."[25]

It may be noted that Anderson had a tendency to think of himself as a child when it was in connection with his mother's sudden death. As late as December 21, 1940, he was to write to Karl, "well you know Karl our own mother died when we were all so young--...." Karl was able also to recall the event in these terms: "Mother had died swiftly, mysteriously, without warning."[26] The fact that he was in attendance when she died is borne out by a seven-page letter to her postmarked only April, 1895, which he devotes primarily to an account of a wedding in which he had participated. In it also he tells his mother he is coming home to stay for a while.

The significance of Anderson's mother's life to his own may be viewed variously. He suggests on the one hand that her departure from the family was an irreparable and notable loss: "The spirit of the household had fled. It had gone down into the ground with the body of the woman out of whose living body had come five strong sons [and two daughters]."[27] In writing of his mother to his brother, Earl, he touches on the subject "women who are not loved," allowing the suggestion that she is one of these and saying that such women "have to pass on the seeds of destruction to their children. "[28]

He uses his mother's memory as a focus of his own acute and continuing sense of rebellion against life as he experienced it. The thought of her fingers "flying, flying, trying to earn food to raise five sons" came to him. "And that day was one of those on which I rebelled. "[29] He declares that he had written all his life to make it clear that just such unjustly-treated people did exist.

Waldo Frank had the impression that Anderson's mother was a kind of "heroine" to him. He reports Anderson telling his friends of her loneliness, her "uncompanioned" toil, her many children,[30] her lack of recognition in the town. "He tells the amazement of them all when, at his mother's death, the whole village followed bareheaded to the grave. The neighbors had been too much harried themselves to see her much, to help her any, during her life and yet she had gone forth, the spirit of her silence, and filled the village.... "[31]

Another observer[32] thought his mother contributed much to improve his personal stability and his desire to succeed, held back by his hatred of his father. Miss Finley also believed that he repudiated his wives when they failed to live up to the ideal of his mother.

Notes

1.   A Story Teller's Story, p. 7.

2.   Dark Laughter, p. 90.

3.   Memoirs, p. 118.

4.   "Father Abraham: A Lincoln Fragment, " The Sherwood Anderson Reader, p. 533.

5.   Letter, Aug. 14, 1936, in Letters of Sherwood Anderson, p. 361 (JR).

6.   Memoirs, p. 26. Hurd confirmed that Mrs. Anderson did washings; interview, Nov. 10, 1962.

7.   Ibid. , p. 27.

8.   A Story Teller's Story, p. 54.

9.   Memoirs, p. 47.

10. A Story Teller's Story, p. 8.

11. Church records in possession of Mrs. John Becker, Clyde, O.

12. Judge S. S. Richards, Clyde.

13. A Story Teller's Story, p. 11-12.

14. Ibid.

15. Memoirs, p. 50.

16. Enterprise, May 2, 1889, p. 3.

17. Marve B. Wyatt is listed in the Clyde Directory for 1887 as a "drayman, res[iding] e[ast] s[ide] Spring Ave s[outh] Cherry."

18. Enterprise, Dec. 10, 1892.

19. Ibid., Dec. 17, 1892.

20. Record of Deaths, Sandusky County, O., vol. 3, p. 41, entry no. 19.

21. A Story Teller's Story, p. 83.

22. Memoirs, p. 75.

23. "Who's Who," Chicago Tribune, May 31, 1919, p. 13.

24. Page 3. Another item in the same paper says that "Carl" has arrived from Chicago, "being called here by the fatal illness of his mother."

25. Enterprise, May 14, 1895, p. 3 and 2.

26. A Story Teller's Story, p. 82.

27. Ibid.

28. Letter to Earl, from Grant, Va., Aug. 19, 1928 in

Letters of Sherwood Anderson, p. 159 (JR).

29.   "The Life of Art, " The Sherwood Anderson Reader, p. 325.

30.   Karl was to write: "The only abundance in our home ...was the ever-increasing number of children. "   "My Brother, Sherwood Anderson, " p. 6.

31.   Waldo Frank, Our America, p. 142.

32.   Letter from Marietta D. Finley, May 31, 1962.   Her friendship between 1914 and 1933 resulted in nearly 300 letters from Sherwood to her.

X: THE LOVABLE, IMPROVIDENT FELLOW

Whatever Irwin was doing in Mansfield in 1883, he did not stay there long. Clyde public school records show that Karl, Stella, and Sherwood were in school in Clyde in the fall of 1884. Mrs. Anderson's obituary, in the Clyde Enterprise, says the "family moved to Clyde in March, 1884." Anderson says his father had "gone broke and his harness shop was gone."

> We had moved northward to the town of Clyde, father now became a maker of harnesses for farm horses, a mere workman in another man's shop. . . .
>
> In Clyde he soon lost his place in the harness shop. It may have been due to one of the periods of depression, the two men who owned the shop, the brothers Irwin, compelled to retrench, no more work coming in, no new harness being sold, or it may have been father's fault, his work neglected, he running off to some reunion of Civil War veterans or perhaps gone into one of his periods of drinking when he could not work. 1

Herman Hurd, a friend of Sherwood from boyhood till death, said that Irwin Anderson worked for the Ervin Brothers. 2 In the Clyde paper during the eighties the Ervin Brothers, harness manufacturers and dealers, ran ads similar to the ones Irwin had in Preble County. The job Irwin Anderson took in Clyde was an indication that his fortunes were still waning. When he lost his job with the Ervin Brothers, matters became still worse. Anderson describes the winter his mother was pregnant with his brother Earl as "our hardest one." Since Earl was born on June 18, 1885, this might have been the winter of 1884-5, the first one spent in Clyde. Anderson says, unsympathetically, his father had become at this time a wandering sign painter. "Painting the sign announcing mother's willingness to become a seamstress may have set off the artist in him." 3

A little later, according to Anderson, the family had begun to "prosper a little":

> Now father had become a house painter. He had
> begun to speak a new language. There was much
> talk of the fine art of mixing house paint, of how
> the brush should be held in the hand. At the time
> there was a great passion for what was called
> graining. The trick was to make pine look like
> oak, oak like cherry, cherry like walnut. Father
> had acquired an outfit of graining tools and practiced
> on the doors and walls of our house. He spread
> a dirty brown mixture over a panel of one of the
> doors and got out his tools. He advanced upon the
> door, made certain flourishes with his hand. The
> paint was to imitate the grain of some particular
> wood. [4]

There can be no doubt that painting became I. M. Anderson's main occupation, for a directory of Clyde for 1887 describes him as a "House and sign painter" living on the "e[ast] s[ide] of Race St. n[ear] South St."[5] A directory for 1890-91 says he was a "painter."[6] On his record at the soldier's home in Dayton, Ohio, the occupation given is painter. His stepson[7] says he did painting and paperhanging while he lived in Connersville, Indiana. Apparently Irwin saw that he could no longer earn a living at harnessmaking and made during the middle eighties the change to the trade he was to follow the rest of his life. It is interesting to note that, in spite of the obvious decline of his father's trade, Karl was to recall, "While attending school I had been apprenticed to a harness maker, for my father was insistent that I have a trade, and naturally favored his own."[8]

One Clyde resident[9] remembered that he did paperhanging as well as painting even then and had a cart on which was painted "I. M. Anderson." Mr. John Becker, a tailor in Clyde, recalled that Mr. Anderson did a satisfactory job of papering his shop. Another man remembered his buying wallpaper and paints in a local drugstore.[10] A newspaper item mentions the fact that "Major Anderson is displaying his artistic taste with the brush at Fremont this week upon Pickett's new green house."[11]

A newspaper item of 1892 refers to the same type of work:

I. M. Anderson, who has been working at Toledo, has returned to Clyde, and will confine himself to house painting here and in Fremont. He will begin making Doctor Harnden's new house pretty this week. [12]

It is evidently one of his working trips to Fremont to which Emma Anderson refers in her letter to Stella: "We are all well but pa. He is miserable. He gave out at Fremont. only staid two days[.] has been working at [the property of] Hartly Alton."

A man who was in Company I with Sherwood recalled Irwin as a "board-fence artist" who painted advertising on board fences along the highway. [13] It is this activity to which Sherwood referred when he told of the three older boys going out with the father in a spring wagon. Apparently Sherwood drove while the father supervised the work of Karl and Irwin. The consent of the farmer was to be obtained before the fence could be painted. If the farmer did not consent, the fence was painted by stealth. As Anderson has said, "What a delicate tinge of romance spread over our common-place enough business!"[14] Herman Hurd recalled an incident in which the older Anderson boys were painting with their father, but Irwin was telling stories about the Civil War instead of working. Sherwood threw his brush to the ground, swearing never to paint for him again.

A fair summary of Irwin Anderson's occupational status in Clyde is contained in the words of an old Clyde resident:

He did any kind of painting work and went out through the country soliciting work. He did good work when he worked but was fond of taking numerous vacations on impulse. He had the ability to do a good job and did do it. But he was as apt to quit in the middle of a job as at the end. He was not shiftless but a ne'erdowell. He was not, and did not care to be, employed steadily. He destroyed the possibility of continuous employment by drinking. [15]

One woman remembers Irwin Anderson as "jovial" and "the biggest liar that ever lived." He was a "ne'erdowell but very bright." "He would be here a day and then gone for weeks. Then he might return with money, and the family would have a good time.   He was very erratic as a provider. "16   The man whose shop he papered concurred that "The Major drank quite a bit and did little for his family. "   He said Irwin played a cornet in "Miller's City Band, " the forerunner of the Silver Cornet Band, a later organization, in which he did not play.   He was a "great talker and liked to tell stories. "17

Perhaps the most concrete piece of evidence concerning Irwin Anderson in Clyde is in the form of an item appearing in the Clyde paper in 1887:

Major Anderson, of Race Street, is an old soldier. He can testify to the music there is in a bullet. He can tell you what pleasures and privations there are in camp life.   His experience in being taken prisoner, and escaping in the darkness is interesting.   He now has another chapter, where he was the prisoner, but failed to escape.   Such was his experience last Tuesday evening, when he returned home and found his loving family prisoners in the hands of about forty of the Piety Hillyers.   A strong guard stationed on the outside cut off his escape, and he willingly gave himself up to an evening of enjoyment with his friends.   A pretty set of cane seated chairs was left, a gift from his friends.   It [the party] was enjoyed by all, barring one accident which befell Mr. Anderson.   He was crossing the street from Neighbor Tuttle's with a teakettle of hot water, when he stepped into an open ditch, spilling the hot water and scalding his right arm severely.   This ditch was opened some time ago, to repair a string of tile, and has been left open some twenty rods or more, to the great danger of life and limb.... 18

Apparently considerable pain went with the pleasure of the surprise party, for two weeks later the paper reported, "Major Anderson has not been able to perform a day's work since his fall into an unclosed ditch.   He has suffered great pain, nearly all the skin from the elbow to the hand coming off. "19

There are several different aspects of the importance of the account of the party and gift.   For one thing, mention is made of Irwin's propensity for telling stories about the Civil War, of which more may be said a little later.   Then

there is very clear indication that Irwin and his family were
very definitely accepted as part of their neighborhood group;
as many as forty people were willing to come to a party in
their honor, and there was the gift of cane chairs to give
more substantial token of their regard. The significance of
this lies in its indication that Sherwood was not adhering
strictly to the facts when he wrote that his father was an
"outlaw" in Clyde. [20] A third element is that Sherwood must
have had this incident in mind when he pictured his character
Tom Appleton as scalding himself with the hot coffee while
preparing a surprise party for a neighbor. [21] The way this
incident was twisted is perhaps indicative of Anderson's
whole treatment of his father in his fiction, principally in
Windy McPherson's Son, which seems to have been a deliberate effort to debase the memory of his father. [22] In the
actual incident Irwin Anderson's accident was unfortunate and
painful and came while receiving the friendly attention of his
neighbors. In "The Sad Horn Blowers" Tom Appleton spills
the coffee on himself purely as a result of his own officious-
ness and clumsiness. One may cite in this connection the
incident in Windy McPherson's Son (pages 30-32) which has
Windy McPherson getting to be parade marshal, riding forth
on a snow-white horse to blow the bugle. He refuses to
consider the fact that he can not play the instrument. At
the great moment Windy can make the bugle emit only "a
thin piercing shriek followed by a squawk." Actually Irwin
could play several brass instruments[23] and there is no likelihood that Irwin would have made such a spectacle of himself. This is not to say that Irwin did not know failure and
frustration. Probably he did. But the facts about Irwin
Anderson simply remind one again that the facts served only
as a springboard for Sherwood's imagination.

One might be tempted to write "embittered imagination," for Windy McPherson is a ludicrous character, perhaps a wry caricature of Irwin. Miss Jeanette Paden was
conscious of what she called the resentment of Irwin's sons
toward him. But in the section of the Memoirs called "Discovery of a Father"[24] Anderson related a story of how he
became reconciled once and for all to his father's lack of
dignity. Probably the reconciliation was not as simple as
that related in "Discovery of a Father." Doubtless the resentment continued until after the Elyria period, during which
Windy McPherson's Son was written.

Anderson wrote Miss Dinsmoor that the bitterest disappointments of his boyhood were with his father. He cited

an example of one sort of thing that caused his disappointment:

> I went once into the country with him and we stayed
> over night at a camp where there were several
> men and women gathered. This was on the shore
> of Lake Erie and there must have been fishing,
> and there, during the night, I discovered that my
> father was having an affair with one of the women
> and was being untrue to my mother. 25

Elsewhere he was to temper this attitude: "Father,
in his own way, was devoted to mother. "26

Later, Anderson was able to write, "Poor man, he
never did get over loving women. ... "27 and to describe his
father as

> ...a journeyman harnessmaker of the old days...
> a lovable, improvident fellow, inclined to stretch
> the truth in statement, loving to swagger before
> his fellow townsmen, not adverse [sic] to losing
> an occasional battle with the demon rum--on the
> whole, a dear lovable, colorful no-account, who
> should have been a novelist himself. 28

But that appreciation for the father came "afterward,
a long time afterward":

> My father's drinking made our family poor, often
> we suffered extreme poverty, but afterward, a
> long time afterward, I did not blame him.   Life
> was dull to him.   Drink, I think, inflamed his
> imagination.   He used to sing and tell marvelous
> stories to us children when he was drinking. Sober,
> he was often dull and heavy.   In his cups he gath-
> ered us about his knees.   He would read some old
> tale and expound it.   He read us Robinson Crusoe
> and some of the Shakespearean comedies.   He
> imagined himself Falstaff, although he was lean,
> not a fat man.   He walked up and down the floor.
> There was no butter in the house.   For weeks
> sometimes we lived on corn meal mush.   Man
> does not live by bread alone, he said. ...

> How many charming memories I have of the
> man. ... 29

Perhaps one or two of what must have been "charming memories" may be mentioned. Because of his lack of dignity, "perhaps when he was drunk," the children snubbed the father. He gathered up a package of papers in the attic, burned them sternly in the yard, and announced then they were the deeds to the business district of Cincinnati, their now-lost inheritance. [30]

> I remember that my father, a man given to outbursts of picturesque cursing, used to sometimes startle us children by some pronouncement as this (some neighbor had perhaps won his disfavor): Damn his hide. I hope he has to live all the rest of his days in a pie factory with a muzzle on, he cried, shaking his fist at the neighbor's house. [31]

It is true that "much later" Anderson expressed himself as being content with his father. "One need not waste too much sympathy on his family. Although he was never what we called in our Ohio country 'a good provider,' he had his points and as one of his sons I at least would be loath to trade him for a more provident shrewd and thoughtful father."[32] An even more positive phase of appreciation is found in the following statement: "I think my own father did, for all his faults, of which I myself have more--teach his children a kind of self-reliance. 'Use your imaginations. Stand on your own feet'."[33] On the other hand, he is moved to say that his father was not one "with whom one spoke of children," and that his father existed "but vaguely" for him.[34] Years later he was still puzzling over the insecurity of his youth, writing to a friend, "Suppose some one who knew how... a father, had provided for me, making me safe. Wouldn't I have worked very much the same. I don't know."[35]

Irwin Anderson's vocation in Clyde, when he followed it, lay in some phase of painting. His two main avocations focused on his army experience and amateur theatricals. A third, his playing in a town band, has been mentioned, but little is known about it, except that in 1877 his father thought he was overdoing it. (See Appendix C.) Of the first two information is more plentiful.

In A Story Teller's Story (pages 31-46 and 57-72) Anderson wrote at length of his father's story-telling and of his relating highly imaginative accounts of his Civil War experiences. Apparently he liked to allow his imagination to play

with his memories and delighted to recount tales both factual
and fictional.

> He had been a soldier on the Northern side and
> evening after evening, when I was a small boy,
> other soldiers came to sit with him.

> They were all talkers, story tellers.   There was
> a little green lawn before our house.   They lounged
> and sat there, some with their backs against the
> front wall of the house.

> The point is that they sat there and talked, always
> of the war.... 36

It was perhaps while listening to some such session
that Sherwood Anderson got the idea his father had been "a
ruined dandy from the south,"37 a notion he was to repeat
many times and finally to contradict very briefly. 38   Anderson's perpetuation of the legend of his father's Southern birth
is perhaps as much proof as is needed of the charm his
father's stories could have for him.

Judge Richards recalled that Irwin "used to like to
swap stories on army matters.   He used to talk about the
Civil War a great deal.   He was a fluent talker with a great
fund of anecdote. "   Mr. Hayden remembered him as single-
handedly putting down the rebellion "to hear him tell it.   He
told things that he thought were the truth, but he was often
just romanticizing. "

Anderson has described his father as a man "who
loved a parade, bands playing in the streets and himself in
a gaudy uniform somewhere up near the head of the proces-
sion";39 and a woman in the Women's Relief Corps of the
G. A. R. in Clyde recalled that he was always out on Memorial Day or any occasion sponsored by the G. A. R. post or the
women's auxiliary. 40

The records of the Eaton Post of the G. A. R. , to
which Irwin Anderson belonged in Clyde, are not to be found,
but items in the Clyde paper indicate he was officer of the
guard in 1890, chairman of the committee in charge of the
Memorial Day observance in 1895, adjutant of the post in
1896 and 1897, and one of two delegates to the state encampment in Mount Vernon, Ohio, in 1898.   His name appears in the paper signed to various notices connected with

such matters as attendance at Memorial Day services, providing audience for "Washington, the Christian Statesman, "
installing officers of Sons of Veterans, and memorializing
the virtues of a deceased brother veteran. [41]

Perhaps his most prominent role came in arranging
for the Memorial Day "exercises" of 1895. A notice of
April 30 tells of the adopting (at the last meeting of the
Eaton G. A. R. Post) of a report detailing such things as the
grand marshal for the day, the decoration of soldiers'
graves and the bringing of flowers therefore to the cementery,
the participation of "all civic and military societies" in the
parade and the "Memorial services" at the McPherson cemetery in the afternoon of May 30.   After Emma Anderson's
death on May 10, an article of fourteen column inches appeared (on May 17), giving full plans for Memorial Day.
It was signed by I. M. Anderson, J. B. Sprague, and Sex-
ton Duley, in that order.   On May 31, the Enterprise had
the following page 1 comment on the handiwork of Irwin and
his friends:

> Never was Memorial Day more fittingly or elabor-
> ately observed in Clyde than it was yesterday.
> Every business place on Main Street was decorated
> in honor of the occasion, and from many private
> residences hung the red, white, and blue. Busi-
> ness was suspended in the afternoon, and an im-
> mense throng turned out to assist in honoring the
> dead soldiers at McPherson Cemetery.... Take
> it all in all...the committee of arrangements in
> charge of the affair are to be congratulated.

Mr. Fred Stevens, his stepson by his second marriage,
noted he was very active in the G. A. R. throughout the latter
part of his life in Indiana and that he "went through the
chairs several times. "

An activity related to his G. A. R. interest was the
American Protective Association, a secret anti-Catholic organization, which flourished in the nineties.   When Council
64, of Clyde, was formed in September, 1896, I. M. Anderson, aided by some of his G. A. R. buddies, incorporated it
"for the purpose of taking better care of the money lately
willed" it by a man who "gave his estate 'to the end that
American institutions and a pure and undefiled religion may
be fostered and maintained in the country'. "   The writer of
the news story commented: "Now don't laugh because such

men as the above have undertaken to 'foster and maintain' a 'pure and undefiled religion'. "[42]

Irwin Anderson's interest in amateur theatricals was very closely connected with his interest in the G. A. R. and can be rather well documented. But perhaps it would be well to consider first Sherwood Anderson's account of his father's theatrical experience. "Once he actually set up as a showman. With a man of our town, named Aldrich, who owned a broken-down horse and a spring wagon he went forth to strut his own little hour on the boards. " The spirit of that recollection informs the whole of Anderson's account of his father's touring country school houses to present a magic lantern display and a song-and-dance routine. [43] Sherwood said elsewhere, "As a public figure, he had to content himself with the exercise of an art in which he was as bad, I fancy, as any man who has ever lived. " The father would rehearse his act upstairs while the family downstairs tried to ignore his activities. Anderson described his singing and dancing as "like a scar in my memory of him. "[44]

No other information of Irwin's activities with the magic lantern and song-and-dance has been discovered, but Evans-Stivers notes (around 1900) that "Mr. Anderson takes a great interest in army organizations. For four years he has been engaged in preparing entertainments for various Grand Army Posts. He possesses considerable talent, and has been very successful in his work. " The only play of this type about which anything is known was called "Old Glory in Cuba, " its author anonymous. The play, which seems to have been produced only during the Spanish-American War period, is known to have been given around Ohio by amateur groups under Mr. Anderson's supervision: in Clyde on November 17 and 18, 1898; Republic, December 2, 1898; Attica, December 17, 1898; Bellevue, January 24 and 25, 1899; and Genoa, at an unknown date probably about this time. [45]

Of the production of the play in Clyde the following report was made:

> Old Glory in Cuba, the Spanish-American war drama presented by local talent at Terry's opera house Thursday and Friday nights for benefit of Grand Army and Relief Corps, drew a large audience, and the proceeds were about $55. The play was quite realistic and well rendered. Mr.

Anderson having drilled the members of the caste
[sic] to a high degree of excellency. Mr. Anderson himself was very effective as Hiram Lawton,
and the other members of the company--Harkness
Miller, Will Sergeant, Ralph Hines, Minnie Jackson and Elsie Donaher--all acquitted themselves
with much credit. [46]

Mr. Anderson not only directed the play but also had
the part of the villain. What was the play about? What
sort of play was it? From a synopsis in the two-column
advertisement in the November 17 issue of the Enterprise
(page 3) one can get information which shows it to be a
super-patriotic melodrama. Act I takes place in the New
York office of one Hiram Lawton, where it is enacted that
Lawton's plan to ruin one Adams, the hero, has failed.
Three years pass before Act II, which "sees Bridget get in
her work on the Spaniards with her broom. There is an
attempt to arrest Adams, who cries, 'Who tears down that
flag, does it over my dead body'. " In Act III Adams is
arrested by the Spanish as an American spy. He is to be
shot "on the count of three. " "Just before the third count
May throws the flag around Adams and cries, 'Fire on that
if you dare!'" In Act IV the Americans find refuge in a
ruined monastery. Sampson's fleet arrives. There is a
conflict, and the Spaniards are vanquished. The play ends
with the playing of The Star Spangled Banner. The advertisement advised "The Play is Grand, Glorious, Pure and Pat-
riotic!"

This home-grown skit was used for money-raising
purposes by the veterans' organization with which Anderson
was connected. The fact that the two Clyde performances
brought $55 in ten-, 15-, and 20-cent admissions shows that
it served its purpose. How Anderson came to be put in
charge of such skits is unknown, but the chances are that he
liked the applause and the publicity and talked his way into
it. If his experience in this type of endeavor extended over
years, as Evans said, he must at least have been able to
please his particular public.

One story that is told in Clyde should be mentioned
for the record, though it is hard to explain. Mr. Harkness
Miller, who played the part of Adams in the Clyde performances, recalled in an interview that Irwin got drunk by
drinking alcohol from the spirit lamps used to light the stage
and fell on his face on the stage during the performance.

Miss Kintner heard the same story from another source; yet
the Clyde paper seems to have been satisfied with his performance. Either "the Major" had an unusually good press
or an unnecessarily bad reputation.

One other review of "Old Glory in Cuba" may be
quoted for some interesting items in it.

> The citizenry of Genoa and those outside of town
> who attended the play at Opera Hall Friday and
> Sat. evening, Women's Relief Corps made arrange-
> ments with Mr. I. M. Anderson of Clyde, an old
> soldier and veteran actor, to play "Old Glory in
> Cuba, " great Spanish-American war drama. Mr.
> Anderson proved himself to be a good judge of
> character as was shown by the selection made of
> persons to act the different parts in the play. In
> the cast of characters, Mr. Anderson was Hiram
> Lawton, and showed himself familiar with the play
> and the stage. While he is some fifty years old,
> on the stage he is taken to be a young man. Time
> has touched him with lightest fingers, having worked
> but few wrinkles in his brow. [47]

Another undated clipping, in the possession of Mrs.
Margaret Brindle, this from the Leipsic (Ohio) Free Press,
contains what may be the only other known review of a stage
performance (not "Old Glory in Cuba") by Irwin Anderson:

> Widow McGinty was seen for the first time in this
> city, and under the direction of Maj. Anderson,
> the home talent comprising the cast, done their
> part to a finish. The Widow is a character of
> peculiarities, and was carried throughout in a way
> that caught the large audience from start to finish,
> winning rounds of applause. The Major as Mul-
> doon, with his inexhaustible store of Irish wit, and
> his quaint and easy manner of delivery, proved
> himself to be master of the role he played. The
> show was a mirth provoker throughout, and the
> storm of applause that greeted each act would have
> made a Booth or a Barratt [sic] green with envy.
> The Major is a clever and accomplished artist,
> and gives you the worth of your money in fun
> wherever seen. The different characters were all
> well filled showing the performers to be more than
> novices of the business.

Sherwood's reactions to his father's theatrics are
varied. At one point,

> It seemed to me then that he was always showing
> off. Let's say someone in our town had got up a
> show. They were always doing it. The druggist
> would be in it, the shoe-store clerk, the horse-
> doctor, and a lot of women and girls. My father
> would manage to get the chief comedy part. It
> was, let's say, a Civil War play and he was a
> comic Irish soldier. He had to do the most absurd
> things. They thought he was funny, but I didn't. [48]

Again he could remark, "As I write this I am remembering
that my father, like myself, [49] could never be singly himself
but must always be playing some role, everlastingly strutting
the stage of life in some part not his own. "[50]

Anderson later thought that he had instinctively wanted
to be a story-teller. "Having listened to the tales told by
my father, I wanted to begin inventing tales of my own. "[51]
"My father was a rather famous story-teller... and I very
much admired that quality in him. "[52] He realized, eventually, that his father was not just a windbag, that the Civil
War was his paint pot and his imagination the brush for
painting his pictures, his mechanism, and that of others, for
escape from the humdrum of village life. "And he did have
a fancy for escape as I myself have always had. "[53] It
seemed to Anderson later that he had "found his father" while
he was still in Clyde. "For the first time I knew that I was
the son of my father. He was a story-teller as I was to
be. "[54]

The confusion over what he thought of his father continued through the years. It was echoed by the confusion
over what he thought of himself, as will be seen. On the
one hand, his father gave too much credit, could not refuse
it. "I thought he was a fool. I had got to hating him. "
When his mother laughed with the others, he went away to
cry. [55] It puzzled him to find his mother seemingly accepting his father's empty "grand gestures. " At the same time
Herman Hurd could say he never detected any antagonism on
the part of the family toward the father, [56] Marietta Finley
reported, "All I ever got from Sherwood was that he disliked
his father. He was bitter about his father. Just said he
was no good. "[57]

At the same time Sherwood could believe his father had a "never-dying faith" that he was "appointed to be the bearer of lovely things to obscure people,"[58] he writes quite sardonically of an incident in which his father's contribution to a move from one house to another, a "compelled" move, was to make the exhausted children take the regular straw out of their ticks and put in some "special straw" he had provided. And "as we lads tramped wearily up the stairs with the refilled bags," their mother stood "smiling--a little resentfully perhaps," and their father said grandly, "There is nothing too good for my kids."[59]

As a man sitting in front of the fire, he was one who "always managed to keep himself supplied with the little comforts of life."[60] Usually "a gay dog," he could, "the rest of us suddenly silent," sing "'Over the Hill to the Poor House'."[61]

> My father lived in a land and in a time when what one later begins to understand a little as the artist in man could not by any possibility be understood by his fellows. Dreams then were to be expressed in building railroads and factories, in boring gas wells, stringing telegraph poles. There was room for no other dream and since father could not do any of these things he was an outlaw in his community. The community tolerated him. His own sons tolerated.[62]

Perhaps only one remaining comment is needed: "I have perhaps lied now and then regarding the facts of his life but have not lied about the essence of it."[63]

Notes

1.   Memoirs, p. 19-20.

2.   Kintner, p. 42.

3.   Memoirs, p. 21.

4.   Ibid., p. 26.

5.   Directory of Clyde and Vicinity, Clyde, O., A. D. Ames, Book and Job Printer, Jan. 1, 1887, p. 18.

6. Williams' Ohio State Directory, Cincinnati, [1890?] p. 251.

7. Mr. Fred Stevens, Alpine, Ind.

8. "My Brother, Sherwood Anderson," p. 6.

9. Mr. John Hoffman, according to Kintner, p. 43.

10. Interview with Mr. Albert Hayden, Tiffin, O.

11. Clyde Enterprise, July 28, 1887, p. 2.

12. Enterprise, Aug. 11, 1892, p. 3.

13. Interview with Dr. William A. Holtz, Tiffin, O.

14. A Story Teller's Story, p. 3-5.

15. Judge Richards interview.

16. From interview with Miss Jeanette Paden, Clyde.

17. From interviews with Mr. John Becker and Herman Hurd.

18. Enterprise, March 17, 1887, p. 3.

19. Ibid., March 31, 1887, p. 3.

20. A Story Teller's Story, p. 26.

21. "The Sad Horn Blowers," Horses and Men; New York, B. W. Huebsch, 1923, p. 251-55.

22. When Karl Anderson read this passage, he wrote the following note: "It is more than a probability Sherwood's (as well [as] that of his brothers) youthful embarrassment by the antics of a playboy father was the source of later judgment of him, rather than a 'deliberate effort' to debase his father's memory."

23. According to an interview with Mr. Fred Stevens.

24. Page 45-49, earlier published in Reader's Digest for November, 1939. Also in The Sherwood Anderson Reader, p. 698-703.

25. Letter of June 24, 1938; Dinsmoor, p. 63.

26. A Story Teller's Story, p. 39.

27. "Country Town Notes," Vanity Fair, May 1929, p. 63.

28. Quoted in Bookman, May 1917, p. 307.

29. "Country Town Notes," loc. cit.

30. A Story Teller's Story, p. 87-8.

31. "Notes on Standardization," Sherwood Anderson's Note-book, p. 145-6.

32. A Story Teller's Story, p. 47.

33. "Country Town Notes," Vanity Fair, May 1929, p. 126.

34. A Story Teller's Story, p. 417.

35. Letter to Roger Sergel, Chicago, winter 1935.

36. "Virginia," Vanity Fair, Aug. 1929, p. 66 and 74.

37. A Story Teller's Story, p. 3.

38. In the Memoirs, p. 46, Anderson says his father was constantly changing his background in tales, so convincingly that Sherwood would have believed him if he "hadn't known he was born in Southern Ohio." This same brief statement occurred originally when the story was first published in the November, 1939, Reader's Digest. Interestingly, on p. 246 of the Memoirs (pub. in 1942) Anderson says his father came from North Carolina.

39. A Story Teller's Story, p. 383.

40. Interview with Mrs. Mollie Harnden, Clyde.

41. Enterprise, Jan. 16, 1890; Nov. 15, 1895; Jan. 7, 1896; Feb. 18, 1896; May 22, 1896; May 13, 1897; June 16, 1898.

42. Ibid., Sept. 6, 1886, p. 4.

43. A Story Teller's Story, p. 25-30.

44. Ibid., p. 73-75.

45. Enterprise, Nov. 17, 1898, p. 3; Dec. 1, p. 3; Dec. 22, p. 3; Jan. 19, 1899, p. 3; and an undated clipping from the Genoa Times. Attica, Bellevue, Republic, and Genoa are all in the Clyde vicinity.

46. Ibid., Nov. 24, 1898, p. 3.

47. This is an undated clipping from the Genoa (Ohio) Times. It is now in the possession of Mrs. Margaret Brindle, Lockland, O. having been owned by her mother-in-law, Mrs. Minnie Stevens Anderson, until the latter's death in 1939. Mrs. Brindle's first husband, Harold Anderson, who was born in 1903 and died in 1928, was Irwin's last-born son.

48. "Discovery of a Father," The Sherwood Anderson Reader, p. 698.

49. Compare Elizabeth Prall Anderson's observation that he was always playing a role; letter to Hans W. Poppe, Sept. 15, 1947.

50. A Story Teller's Story, p. 21.

51. Ibid., p. 94.

52. "A Writer's Conception of Realism," The Sherwood Anderson Reader, p. 341.

53. A Story Teller's Story, p. 59-60.

54. "Discovery of a Father," The Sherwood Anderson Reader, p. 703.

55. Ibid., p. 699 and 698.

56. Nov. 1962 interview.

57. Sept. 7, 1962 interview.

58. A Story Teller's Story, p. 33.

59. Ibid., p. 56.

60. Ibid., p. 32.

61. "The Sound of the Stream," The Sherwood Anderson
    Reader, p. 369-70.

62. A Story Teller's Story, p. 26.

63. Ibid., p. 383.

XI: IRWIN'S SECOND MARRIAGE

According to his stepson, Mr. Fred Stevens, Irwin Anderson went to Connersville, Indiana, about 1900. Irwin put down in his Declaration for Pension that he had lived in Fayette County, Indiana (Connersville), since 1899. Newspaper items concerning his activities with amateur dramatics show he was in Clyde in 1899. So it is likely that he went to Connersville from Clyde. Mr. Stevens said Irwin met his widowed mother, Mrs. Minnie Stevens, at the old Barton House in Connersville, where both roomed and boarded. They married on March 13, 1901[1] and had a son, Harold, born in Connersville on March 21, 1903.

The picture Mr. Stevens gave of his stepfather is an interesting one, partly because Irwin seems to have been somewhat changed in his second marriage. Mr. Stevens never knew Irwin to drink to excess and found him "pretty much of a home man. " "The only time he'd be away from home was to do work or to attend a lodge meeting. " He provided well for his wife, according to his stepson, who praised his "extremely fine temperament. " Mr. Stevens, himself a paperhanger, always enjoyed working with his stepfather.

In Connersville Irwin continued his interest in the G. A. R. and amateur theatricals. He seemed to Mr. Stevens quite familiar with Shakespeare. "He said he played in East Lynne in San Francisco when the seats sold for no less than $5. "' This is as much as to say Irwin's imagination went with him to Connersville.

He was a "great talker" and entertainer, "telling Jewish and Irish stories in dialect. " "On a job he'd entertain as much as he'd work. " He talked little about the Civil War but would talk if questioned. He used to talk a lot of an "Uncle Dick" [probably Irwin's brother, Benjamin Dickey Anderson] in California.

Irwin told Mr. Stevens he had traveled with the

O'Brien Circus and played in its band for five years. This statement belongs in the same category with a statement in a clipping in the possession of Mrs. Brindle datelined Manchester, Ohio, April 24, 1919: "[Irwin Anderson] had one of the important roles in East Lynne with Maggie Mitchell and played that part for five years." Since Mr. Stevens had seen contracts issued to Irwin when he was in the theater, it must not be considered impossible that he had some experience on the stage. But the character of it is entirely uncertain. The only time he could have had such experience was in the period between 1866-1871, when he was reputedly in the Southwest. Maybe he was in both theatrical and circus companies at times, but the statements referred to above seem at best exaggerations. The O'Brien Circus may be O'Brien's Six Shows, which Odell[2] mentions as being in New York in 1873. Maggie Mitchell was a featured performer on the New York stage from 1866 to 1871, one learns from Odell, but she is not mentioned as playing East Lynne, her specialties being Little Barefoot, Fanchon, and The Pearl of Savoy. Her leading man was almost always her husband, J. W. Collier.

On January 12, 1914, Irwin Anderson was admitted to the soldiers' home in Dayton, Ohio. There until his death on May 23, 1919, he stayed, making trips every two weeks or so to Connersville. He seems to have been active until his last days, according to Mr. Stevens, for he was training school children for Memorial Day exercises at the time of his death. Irwin's son, Ray, who lived in Dayton, wrote Karl that their father fell from a ladder while painting at the soldiers' home, and two weeks later he died of a brain hemorrhage.[3]

Karl displays his own resentment (shared by at least one other member of the family) of his father's eventual separation from his first family in two surviving notes. In an article about Sherwood, he observes that "a year after" his mother's death "our father had married again; I never afterwards saw him again."[4] To his niece he wrote a reminder that "Undoubtedly Stella [her mother] told you of our father's 'dereliction' a year or so after mother's death."[5] When it is recalled that Emma Anderson died on May 10, 1895, that Irwin left Clyde apparently in 1899, and that his second marriage took place on March 13, 1901, after nearly six years of being a widower, it seems that Karl's shortening of the interval so drastically indicates his dislike for the man, the event, or both.

528

Notes

1. Declaration for Widow's Pension, July 7, 1919.

2. George C. D. Odell, Annals of the New York Stage, New York, Columbia Univ. Press, 1937, p. 361 and 373.

3. Karl Anderson in annotation of manuscript: William A. Sutton, "Sherwood Anderson's Formative Years, 1876-1913," unpub. Ph. D. dissertation, Columbus, Ohio State Univ., 1943.

4. "My Brother, Sherwood Anderson," p. 7.

5. Letter of Karl Anderson to Mrs. Schroeder, Sept. 4, 1951.

XII: EMMA ANDERSON: PRE-CLYDE

Understanding of the life of Emma Anderson before her residence in Clyde is closely tied to what is known of Irwin. The confusion over the Mansfield-Caledonia residence is, of course, unresolved. Thus only a brief glimpse of Mrs. Anderson in Camden and Caledonia may be obtained. Mr. Gift recalled her as "a small, neat, pretty woman who occasionally pushed a baby carriage to her husband's shop...."[1] Mrs. Irey of Caledonia, whose mother was a friend of Mrs. Anderson, remembers her chiefly as one struggling to keep the family going under adverse circumstances: "Her efforts made her children as good as any one's." Mrs. Irey's mother often went to the Anderson home "to help," especially when a new baby (Ray) came. Because of his "negligence" with regard to providing for his family, Mrs. Irey's mother was hostile toward I. M. Mrs. Irey says Mrs. Anderson was tall and slender like her husband, the Andersons making a "nice couple."

Notes

1. Dinsmoor, p. 5.

PART THREE

Appendices

Appendix A

SHERWOOD ANDERSON'S IMAGINATION

Now there are two distinct channels in every man's
life. We all live on two planes. There is what we call
the world of reality and there is the somewhat unreal world of imagination. These roads do not
cross each other but the road of the imagination
constantly touches the road of reality. It comes
near and goes away. All of us are sometimes on
one road and sometimes on another. I think that
we are all living more of our lives on the road of
the imagination, or perhaps I had better say in the
world of the imagination, than in the real world. [1]

Perhaps the best starting point for an exploration of
that "world of imagination" is the "world of reality." For
that real world is very definitely the germ of the unreal one
in Anderson's mind. He has said, "The work of any writer
and for that matter of any artist in the seven arts should
contain within it the story of his own life. "[2] Anderson believed that the imagination must feed constantly on the fact
in nature in order that the imaginative life remain significant. In fact, "the imagination must feed upon reality or
starve. "[3]

The teller of tales, Anderson pointed out, lives in a
world of his own. In his normal life among other people he
is quite different from what he is when he sits down to
write.

While he is a writer nothing happens but that it is
changed by his fancy and his fancy is always at
work. Really, you should never trust such a man.
Do not put him on the witness stand. [4]

Anderson explained further that his fancy was "a wall
between myself and the Truth. " There was a world of the
fancy into which he plunged constantly and out of which he

536

seldom emerged completely. This had something to do with making life the great adventure he called it at the end of the <u>Memoirs</u>.

> I want every day to be absorbingly interesting and exciting to me and if it will not, I, with my fancy, try to make it so. If you, a stranger, come into my presence there is a chance that for a moment I shall see you as you are but in another you will be lost. You say something that starts my fancy working and I am off. 5

The ever-active fancy was clearly visible to Anderson as the enemy of factual truth. The implications of this fact to the biographer will be touched on more fully later, but one may include here a single significant quotation from the Foreword (page xvi): "Like every one else in the world I had so thoroughly re-created my childhood in my own Fancy that Truth was utterly lost. "

One may note the phrase Anderson used to qualify his use of the imagination. He appears here to think that he was "Like every one else" in that respect. The student of Anderson is not likely to be misled by this note. It was Anderson's will to view the world about him sympathetically but he was essentially egocentric as an individual and certainly so in his use of the imagination. He explained his own use of the imagination in meeting or dodging his personal problems, but he again put his statement in terms which imply that this is what the average human would be expected to do:

> When you are puzzled about your own life, as we all are most of the time, you can throw imagined figures of others against a background very like your own, put these imagined figures through situations in which you have been involved. It is a very comforting thing to do, a great relief at times, this occasionally losing sense of self, living in these imagined figures. This thing we call self is very often like a disease. It seems to sap you, destroy your relationship with others, while even occasionally losing sense of self seems to give you an understanding that you didn't have before you became absorbed. 6

Put in simplest terms this is the psychological

mechanism of "escape" that Anderson has described. Apparently it was a process very familiar to him, one which he presumed to be familiar to most people. But Anderson did not always use his imagination just to escape unpleasant or puzzling reality. There is at least the imaginative life which was familiar to him from early life and under ordinary circumstances. He wrote that he played as a lad with fanciful scenes as other boys played with brightly-colored marbles. From the beginning there was the realm of "grotesque fancies" opposed to his "actual life. "[7] And books, as one might expect, were chiefly used as imagination-fodder. Books always fed his "dreams, " Anderson said, for he was one who "always lived by his dreams" and could "often get as much fun and satisfaction out of a dull book as a so-called brilliant or witty one. " Indeed, "The books like life itself are only useful to me in as much as they feed my own dreams or give me a background upon which I can construct dreams. "[8]

The construction of the "imaginative" world on the basis of the "real" world was a very conscious and serious process to Anderson. In his essay, "Man and His Imagination, " he gave a rather detailed discussion (pages 48-53) of how real people and real events became changed into other people and other events which seemed to the imaginer to have meaning. As soon as the attention of the writer (Anderson said this happened to all writers and, for that matter, all people) was attracted to a certain person or series of circumstances, the imagination began "to play. " There was no particular volition involved, no reason for it. As Anderson might have said, "a thing happened. "

It is no wonder that Anderson was shocked to be called a realist when his work was first noticed. The following quotation is typical of Anderson's attitude toward realism:

> I do not know what reality is. I do not think any
> of us quite know how much our point of view and,
> in fact all of our touch with life, is influenced by
> our imagination. [9]

However, one is not to think that the operation of the imagination is directionless and irresponsible. Once one has begun the transformation of events, persons, and places by using the imagination, one must not interfere with the sure but mysterious workings of the fancy. The integrity of the imagination must be maintained or all is lost. This was a point Anderson felt it necessary to emphasize:

> What is not generally understood is that to do vio-
> lence, to sell out a character in the imaginative
> world is as much a crime as to sell out people in
> the real world. As I have already tried to say,
> this imaginative world of ours, the imaginative
> lives we live, are as important to us as our real
> lives. They may be more important. 10

The understanding of the relationship between the
"real" and "imaginary" worlds in Anderson's life is vital to
an understanding of Anderson. For that reason it seems
wise to recapitulate that relationship in the simplest possible
terms, happily supplied by Anderson himself. In remarks
prefatory to the Memoirs he stated specifically that he did
not want to write about his "apparent life. " Instead he
wanted to use his life "only as a springboard. " Anderson
stood in awe of the integrity of the subjective or "imaginative" life, but his basic attitude toward the factual or "real"
life was one of disregard when desirable or necessary. Any
concern for the "real" life was usually brought about by
necessity, very often was disposed of as an onerous duty.
If one thinks of Anderson in his own terms, he is seen as a
diver into the "imaginative truth" of life. As a good diver
he must give concern to the state of the springboard, but
that is only a means to an end. It is the dive in which Anderson is finally interested.

When one considers the nature of Anderson in these
terms, it is easy to realize that he would be grossly miscast
as his own factual biographer. Yet it is not entirely surprising that unwary readers have assumed Anderson's statements about his life in the "real" world to be autobiographical. Anderson has explained how it happened:

> The imaginative world in which he [the writer] is
> for the time living has become for him more alive
> than the world of reality can ever become. His
> very sincerity confuses. Being unversed in the
> matter of making the delicate distinction that the
> writer himself has such a hard time making, they
> call him a realist. 11

Anderson recognized that he was his own biographer
only in a spiritual or imaginative way. He took pains on
more than one occasion to make definite allusion to his

disregard for physical facts. In one place he wrote:

> One of these conflicts between myself, as I live in
> fancy, and myself as I exist in fact, that have been
> going on in me since I was a child had now started.
> It is the sort of thing that makes autobiography of
> the half-playful sort I am now attempting, so dif-
> ficult to manage. [12]

In preparing his reader for the same type of situation, in
the "Foreword" to Tar (page xviii), he wrote, "As I have
suggested, when it came to writing of myself, I, the teller
of tales, would be all right if there were no living witnesses
to check up on me. "

There is enough evidence to allow the supposition,
however, that the factual unreliability of his autobiography
became a difficult if not touchy matter for Anderson. It
has been seen that Anderson was aware that some of his
readers were "confused. " Anderson probably felt he could
hardly explain the situation more clearly than he had in the
nine-page preface to Tar, which is devoted to that point.
The number of references made here to "Man and His Imagination" shows that discussion to be appropriate. One notes his
reference to his autobiography as of the "half-playful" sort
in A Story Teller's Story, and one finds him saying that any
living witnesses who could check his story "will also have
changed the actual happenings of our common lives to suit
their own fancies, " an observation not without basis in fact.

He may have been led to a variety of feelings, including anger, disappointment, and apology, by the tendency
in his readers to compare his account with the facts. In
one case he offered mock-apology for not being strictly factual:

> Now it happens that my friends and relatives have
> already stood much from me. I am forever writ-
> ing of myself and dragging them in, re-creating
> them to suit my fancy, and they have been a fore-
> bearing lot. It is dreadful really having a scrib-
> bler in the family. Avoid it if you can. · If you
> have a son who has a leaning that way hurry him
> into industrial life. If he becomes a writer he
> may give you away. [13]

In "Man and His Imagination" (page 49) he wrote that

he had been amused sometimes to find how poorly his concept of his father and mother, for example, fitted that of
his brothers. Probably it was not always amusing, for some
of his relatives have suggested in interviews that he was
either stupid or malicious for picturing his relatives as he
did. These people may possibly have forgotten that he
wrote, "My own belief is that the writer with a notebook in
his hand is always a bad workman, a man who distrusts his
imagination. Such a man describes actual scenes accurately,
he puts down conversation accurately. "14

Finally, one should understand that there is much to
indicate that Anderson's misstatements of fact concerning
his life were also partly unconscious. As early as 1924 he
pointed out his capacity for becoming utterly oblivious to the
factuality of incidents:

> How often later, when I became a man of business,
> I did in fancy some shrewd or notable act that was
> never done in fact at all, but that seemed so real
> that it was difficult not to believe in it as a
> fact. . . . [A] story several times repeated became
> a part of the history of my life and nothing would
> have later so amazed me as to have been com-
> pelled to face the facts of the conversation and the
> figure I had cut in it. 15

And in 1938 he declared himself "hesitant" about giving information concerning his life:

> I am a little hesitant about answering because any
> answer I may be able to give to your questions
> will necessarily be vague. There is so much of
> the information you ask for that I simply do not
> have. I have rather an idea that the man Windy
> McPherson, of the novel Windy McPherson's Son,
> is a fairly good picture of my father and that the
> mother in A Story Teller's Story and in Tar are
> fairly good pictures of my mother.

> I should, however, say something about another
> difficulty in answering such questions. One who
> has dealt for years with imagined figures has great
> difficulty in separating fact from fancy. 16

Notes

1.   Anderson, "Man and His Imagination," in Centeno,
     Auguste, ed., The Intent of the Artist, Princeton, N. J.,
     Princeton Univ. Press, 1941, p. 44.

2.   Ibid., p. 58.

3.   Ibid., p. 87.

4.   Anderson, "Foreword," Tar, xii.

5.   Ibid., xvi.

6.   "Man and His Imagination," op. cit., p. 64.

7.   A Story Teller's Story, p. 119.

8.   Ibid., p. 155-6.

9.   "Man and His Imagination," op. cit., p. 49.

10. Ibid., p. 58.

11. Ibid., p. 69.

12. A Story Teller's Story, p. 257.

13. "Foreword," Tar, p. xi.

14. "A Note on Realism," Sherwood Anderson's Notebook,
     p. 75.

15. A Story Teller's Story, p. 257-8.

16. Letter of June 24, 1938, to Miss Mary Helen Dinsmoor;
     quoted from p. 62 of her work.

Appendix B. GENEALOGY. 1. Children of James Anderson

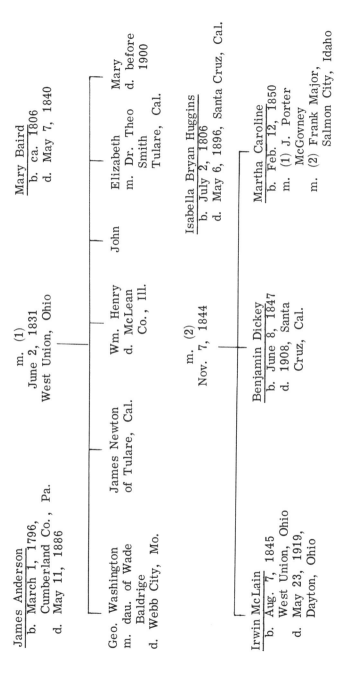

James Anderson
b. March 1, 1796,
   Cumberland Co., Pa.
d. May 11, 1886

m. (1)
June 2, 1831
West Union, Ohio

Mary Baird
b. ca. 1806
d. May 7, 1840

Geo. Washington
m. dau. of Wade
   Baldrige
d. Webb City, Mo.

James Newton
of Tulare, Cal.

Wm. Henry
d. McLean
   Co., Ill.

John

Elizabeth
m. Dr. Theo
   Smith
   Tulare, Cal.

Mary
d. before
   1900

m. (2)
Nov. 7, 1844

Isabella Bryan Huggins
b. July 2, 1806
d. May 6, 1896, Santa Cruz, Cal.

Irwin McLain
b. Aug. 7, 1845
   West Union, Ohio
d. May 23, 1919,
   Dayton, Ohio

Benjamin Dickey
b. June 8, 1847
d. 1908, Santa
   Cruz, Cal.

Martha Caroline
b. Feb. 12, 1850
m. (1) J. Porter
       McGovney
m. (2) Frank Major,
       Salmon City, Idaho

2. Children of Margaret Austry Smith Myers

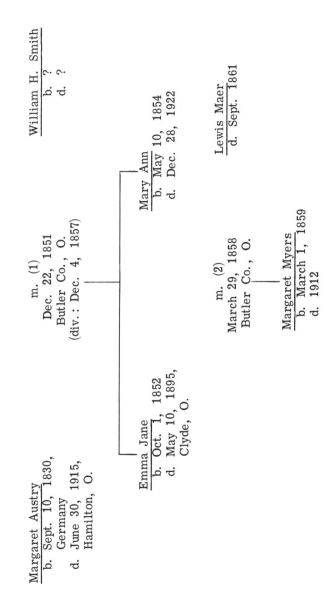

Margaret Austry
b. Sept. 10, 1830,
    Germany
d. June 30, 1915,
    Hamilton, O.

William H. Smith
b. ?
d. ?

m. (1)
Dec. 22, 1851
Butler Co., O.
(div.: Dec. 4, 1857)

m. (2)
March 29, 1858
Butler Co., O.

Emma Jane
b. Oct. 1, 1852
d. May 10, 1895,
    Clyde, O.

Mary Ann
b. May 10, 1854
d. Dec. 28, 1922

Lewis Maer
d. Sept. 1861

Margaret Myers
b. March 1, 1859
d. 1912

3. Children of Irwin McLain Anderson

Irwin McLain Anderson
b. Aug. 7, 1845
   West Union, Ohio
d. May 23, 1919
   Dayton, Ohio

m. (1)
March 11, 1873
Morning Sun, Ohio

Emma Jane Smith
b. Oct. 1, 1852
d. May 10, 1895
   Clyde, Ohio

Karl
b. Jan. 13, 1874

Stella
b. Apr. 13, 1875
   Camden, O.
d. 1917

Sherwood Berton
b. Sept. 13 1876
   Camden, O.
d. Mar. 8 1941

Irwin M.
b. ca. 1878

Fern (?)

Raymond M.
b. ca. 1883

Earl
b. ca. 1885
d. Mar. 1927

m. (2)

Mrs. Minnie Stevens
b. ca. 1870
d. Aug. 1939

Harold
b. March 21, 1903
d. July 18, 1928

4. Children of Sherwood Anderson

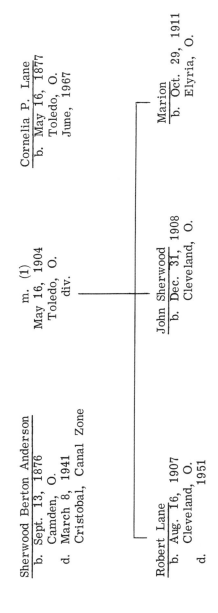

Sherwood Berton Anderson
b. Sept. 13, 1876
   Camden, O.
d. March 8, 1941
   Cristobal, Canal Zone

m. (1)
May 16, 1904
Toledo, O.
div.

Cornelia P. Lane
b. May 16, 1877
   Toledo, O.
   June, 1967

Robert Lane
b. Aug. 16, 1907
   Cleveland, O.
d.   1951

John Sherwood
b. Dec. 31, 1908
   Cleveland, O.

Marion
b. Oct. 29, 1911
   Elyria, O.

Appendix C

ANDERSON'S LETTER ABOUT CLYDE

[This letter, the only document which records the way Anderson allowed his imagination to play over his memory while visiting Clyde, was written to Miss Marietta D. Finley of Indianapolis, on December 7, 1916. As was normal in his correspondence to her, there is no salutation. The place, the "little hotel office" in Clyde, from which the letter was written, has not been located exactly. Original in the Newberry Library. On May 27, 1962, Herman Hurd examined this letter with the present author and made comments which are interpolated in brackets.]

December 7, 1916.

How tremendously our American small town life has changed in twenty years. I went to my home town in Ohio yesterday and spent three hours there. It is a pretty town lying some ten or twelve miles back from Lake Erie. When I was a boy there the town was isolated. To go to Fremont or to Bellevue, eight miles away was to take a journey. Factories had not come in and the people were engaging in farming, the selling of merchandise or in the practice of the crafts in the old sense. Two carpenters met on the streets in the evening and talked for hours concerning the best way to cut out a window frame or build a door. Now doors and window frames are made in big factories and shipped in.

I came into town by electric car from the East. We stopped at a switch and two big motor trucks bearing merchandise passed us. Automobiles driven by sons of men whom I once knew went whirling by.

As soon as I arrived in town I felt sad and lonely. I stood on a corner looking about. The section of town where the car stopped used to be a desolate spot unlighted and with

547

weeds and bushes growing in the empty lots [Main St. north
of railroad tracks]. Now it is all built up with neat, ugly
working men's houses.

Romance dwelt about these corners then. The old
town long before my day, had consisted of a few houses
scattered along the road where the electric car runs now.
When I was a boy these houses and one or two decayed brick
buildings that had been stores were empty and deserted.
Weeds grew high in the vacant lots. To the north stretched
the open farming country. At night when I carried papers
I went shivering along this road.

A girl came to town from a village called Castalia
half way down to the lake. I fell in love with her, an innocent boyhood love. But, although she was young she had
already had lovers. How vividly I remember the evening
when I found this out. She let me know because she wanted
me to be her lover. She met me on Main Street and we
walked down into this dark place. She took off her cloak and
laughed. "Kiss me" she whispered.

That was a night for me. I was full of pride and
shame too. I remember with what a strange mixed feeling
I later went home.

Well, I walked up the street, my head singing with
old memories. In the old brick house across the street
lived Dr. Duse [Dr. Luse] who made liver pills and sold
them all over the country. He had a daughter [Minnie] who
went to Boston and became a singer. She used to come
back home in the summer wearing such fine clothes that we
all looked upon her with awe. She was lonely and would
have flirted with our young fellows but they were afraid.
She seemed too grand and far away for them.

Here on a corner lived big "Mac" [McPherson Robin-
son] with his grandfather [who worked for Hurd's grandfath-
er]. He was a tremendously tall boy and became a baker.
How strong his hands were. He used to save all his money
until he had achieved twenty or thirty dollars and then go to
another town on a debauch. When the money was gone he
came home and went quietly to work. [Hurd did not recall
this.] Later he found employment on the railroad and became a steady, working fellow. He is there now I suppose.

I am sitting in the little hotel office writing. I have

hardly gone to see anyone and have only walked through two
or three streets. Why?--well because what I have already
seen has awakened such a flood of memories that I am overwhelmed. I realize as I sit here that I could sit thus for
hours--as long as life remained in me writing of my people
and the strange things that have happened to them. What
real and living people they are to me. Even Jerry Donlin,
the baggage man who I am told dropped dead of heart failure
and who has just by chance come into my mind. His life is
a living thing to me. I could write long novels concerning
this sweet-hearted profane Irishman and the wonderful things
my imagination helps me to believe went on in his head
while he outwardly did no more than push baggage trucks up
and down this station platform here.

So here I sit and my hand shakes with excitement.
Names flood in upon me. Waxy Sellinger [a little older;
played ball], Pete McChine; Ed [George] Douglas. Percy
Welsh [Ed Welsh, ball player, gardener]; Tough McCreary
[Frank McCreery, "boy about town"]; Turkey Clapp [Irving
Clapp, substantial citizen, on school board]; Ben McHugh
[ran a saloon].

Why go on? I could write three hundred of such
names and each name a story, a great book filled with
strange things.

The girls were not so well named. I remember only
a vague and meaningless jumble of Jennies and Mables and
Minnies. And oddly enough the women I see passing the
hotel here do not look interesting. What dull, heavy faces.
There is no beauty in them whereas the old men, tottering
about are in some way almost beautiful. Things have happened to them. Adventures have come in, whereas one
feels that adventure has not come to these women who were
once girls and my playmates. I feel that the young women
growing up are better than the women who went before but I
do not feel that the young men who go into the factories are
the equals of their fathers who went into the fields and the
old hand-crafts.

I will not go on about my town. Some day when I
am in a reflective mood I will write more of my visit--the
memories awakened and the thoughts I had.

In as much as I have abused women I will end by
telling of a woman who lived here in my time of whom I

have often thought.   There was something splendid about her.

Maria Welling [Julia Welker] came here from Sandusky.   If you could sit beside me now I could point out the
building where she once ran an hotel here.   [Empire House,
way station for Cleveland, Columbus, Lakeshore.]

Maria had been a keeper of a house of ill repute ["I
heard that too, one time"].   She married a gambler and they
both came away to this town determined to settle down and
be quiet respectable people.

There was nothing of the hypocrite about Maria.   If
she was ashamed of her past life she kept it to herself.
Here she came and settled and while her husband [Frank
Welker] ran the bar and the office of the little hotel she did
the cooking and made the beds.

Soon the place began to shine under her labors.
Trade came and money was made.   Girls were employed to
work in the dining room of her hotel and she made money.

Now you know how it usually is with girls in the dining room of a country hotel--well it wasn't that way with
Maria's girls.   I was a newsboy then and used to bring the
evening paper to her kitchen door.   Often I was invited in
to have a generous cut of one of Maria's pies.   Sherwood
liked her awful well.

And there I heard her talk, plainly and frankly to her
girls; not once but dozens of times.   She didn't scold.   That
wasn't Maria's way.   She knew things and she told them
things.   No moralizing, no windiness; just plain straight
talk.   'I know.   I've been over the road.   If you could beat
the game I'd say so.   You can't."   She told them over and
over.

One evening I remember Maria talked to me, ex-
plaining what she meant by her talk with the girls.   I
strolled by her place homeward bound after my evening's
papers were delivered [and] Maria's voice called.   I found her
sitting in the darkness at the back door of her kitchen and
she made a motion for me to sit doown beside her.

She put her big hand on my shoulder and talked.   I
won't attempt to tell what she told me but it was all about
the life she had been in.   To me she talked as she did to

the girls.

"You stay away.   It's rotten, " she cried.   "You're a clean boy and I want you to stay away from girls.   Just mind this.   Don't you pay and don't you have anything to do with as takes pay.   It will bring you sorrow and it brings sorrow to women but don't let it be with you the sorrow of paying or to any woman you ever know the sorrow of taking pay. "

Her voice broke and she drew me down until my head lay on her breast.   "I'd rather been a slut on the street because I was naturally bad and wanted loving than to have been what I was for money, " she said brokenly.

Appendix D

ELYRIA DOCUMENTS

I. Amnesia Factors.

The notes that I said were kept during the amnesia trip were not a record of what Mr. Anderson actually did but of what he thought he did or impressions he got. They were patently a picture of his state of mind.

I don't think he knew anything of what he'd written or of what the newspapers said until years later. I had the notes and clippings, and when he said he did not want to see them, I put them together in the bottom of an old trunk.

In 1939 or perhaps 1940 I was about to dispose of them without rereading, but I wrote him asking if he now wanted to see them. He said yes, so I sent them on without opening the package. He never commented on them to me.

The fact of the existence of the notes is for you only. Since I mentioned them, I want you to know that they were not a conventional record.

I am sure you will be convinced that the amnesia is real, and that is what I want.

The above quotation is a note included with a letter from Mrs. Cornelia Lane Anderson to the present author, October 16, 1946. This was a commentary on previous remarks, recorded in an interview with her in her apartment in Marion, Virginia, on October 10, 1946: "He kept track of his whole adventure on a tablet. That was interesting to the doctors, who told him if he'd just lie there in the hospital and think through the whole experience, he would not have to fear recurrence. He did finally get every link."

552

The Secretarial Note

Anderson says that he dictated a note to his secretary for Cornelia before he walked out of his office to Cleveland. What follows is a note found in the files of the Anderson Collection in the Newberry Library, possibly the one; although this as yet is not confirmed, it does seem consonant with his mental state as otherwise expressed in this period. It is in an unknown hand and it is written on the long axis of a sheet 8 1/2" by 4".

Cornelia:
There is a bridge over a river with cross-ties

before it.   When I come to that I'll be all right.

I'll write all day in the sun and the wind will blow

through my hair.

Sherwood.

The Amnesia Letter

Completely authentic and crucial to the understanding of the Elyria crisis is the letter, referred to above by Mrs. Anderson as "The notes that I said were kept during the amnesia trip. . . . " the text of which is herewith reproduced. The seven pages of lined notepaper with the envelope in which they came now are in the Anderson Collection of the Newberry Library.   The envelope is addressed to "Cornelia L. Anderson/ Pres. / American Striving Co. / Elyria O. "   The postmark is of Cleveland, Ohio, Station B, dated 5 p. m. , Nov. 30, 1912.   Three written notations appear on the front of the envelope.   In the upper left hand corner: "Getts Bros. "; along the lower left margin, starting at the left: "5 a. m. , " written three times; roughly parallel to the right margin of the envelope, starting about one inch from the right bottom margin, the note: "Phone Ryan. "   There is no information as to who made these notes or when or why. The present writer thought "Getts Bros" and the "5 a. m. " notations appeared to have been on the envelope when it was sent.   Possibly Mrs. Cornelia Anderson knew.

The back of the envelope contains two postmarks related to the receipt of the letter in Elyria.   The first is the

typical round mark: "Elyria, Ohio, Dec. 1, 7:30 A., 1912."
An elliptical mark to the right of the first, which is almost
exactly centered on the flap, reads: "Received 1."

When it is recalled that Anderson left Elyria on the
afternoon of Thursday, November 28, and that he was hospitalized in Cleveland on the evening of Sunday, December 1,
it is seen that the markings on the envelope establish that
the notes represent a record made by an amnesia victim
during the first two of four days of wandering, posted during
his wandering, and received by his wife before the amnesia
attack was concluded. Anderson did not see the record until
more than twenty years later.

The notes are written on the short axis of seven
sheets of 4" by 8" lined note paper, on one side only.

Page 1:

        Lenard - Saw Mrs

        Lenard - Lenard -

        Elyria. Told her

        I was g going to

        Elsinore - T Pow-

        ers Elsinore.

[A heavy, three-inch line separates the above,
which is in a much larger hand, from what follows, which is in a smaller version of the same
hand. In each case a line of transcript equals a
line of the original manuscript.]

        Why do the children cry. They
        are everywhere underfoot. Among
        them ran yellow dogs with brown

Page 2:

        dirt stuck on their backs. The
        dogs howl and the children
        cry. At night the dogs

Why do the children cry. They are everywhere underfoot. Among them are yellow dogs with brown dirt streaks on their backs. The dogs howl and the children cry. At night the dogs howl and the children cry and your head hurts. There are so many children and so many dogs and so many long streets filled with dirty houses. If one dares ask he

howl and the children cry
and your head hurts. There
are so many children and
so many dogs and so
many long streets filled
with dirty houses.

If one does ask he
could find Cornelia but if
you ask the people they
will hit you. Mrs. Leonard
had a book in her hand
and tried to hit me
with it. There is a place
near Bedford. A child that
cried looked at a man
with a pipe in his mouth
who growled like a yellow
dog. I tried to drink
some beer but it was
bitter and the room was
full of men who would
have hit me but I
ran.

Page 3:

Why does a man stand
in a field shooting a
gun - I crawled in a
big tile and he didn't
see me. It was cold
at night. Think of Elsinore
Why are men so proud of
a house - They walk
around it and take
pictures
Writing don't hurt your
head. Its just being
hit with things
Ask Cornelia about the
men and the houses.
Tell Robert I saw a
man chewing tobacco. It
made his mouth nasty

Page 4:

           Elsinore - Elsinore
           Elsinore - Elsinore.
           Get to Elsinore.
           T Powers Esinore.
           River at Elsinore.
           Bridge at Elsinore
           Elsinore Water Works.
           T Powers head hurt
           also. went to Elsinore.
           They hit T Powers. One
           after another they hit
           him. like you.
           They put his name
           on a wall - near
           Elsinore.
           They didn't mean to
           hurt anyone. They
           didn't mean to hit
           you. Keep thinking of
           that and walk. Dont
           talk to anyone. Dont

Page 5:

           Hit any one. Give Robert
           Piece of corn - tell
           him how it grows.
           Dont let them hit
           him. After while
           your head wont hurt
           Walk and keep still.
           Go to Elsinore.
           Hamlet - Elsinore. -
           Cornelia - am hidden.
           No one knows - Dont
           tell
           I didn't want to fish
           in the river. Why
           did they hit me
           There were so many
           negroes.

Page 6:

           to look at. Another man

had his mouth full of dry
crackers.   Thought it made
my head hurt I laughed
To Elsinore.

Page 7:

3600
5000
14

16000

1111

Elsinor

The Dictation at the Hospital

At the hospital in Cleveland, Anderson dictated the
following statement, in which he attempted to recall the
events of November 28 to December 1.   The original is in
the Anderson Collection of the Newberry Library.   The paper is from a lined tablet, 4" by 8".   The amanuensis is
not known.   A line of type is equal to a line of the original
manuscript.

Page 1:

Went into an orchard &
gathered corn & apples -
Ate   "   &   "
Brought away corn to
show Robert & many apples
Left orchard.   Went across
street car track & along
way down a road & into
a wood gully.   Built
fire & tried to smoke but
head hurt & couldnt -

Went along & it got dark
Came to tiles.   Didnt get
into it.   Sat on it.   Near
a lumber yard town or

edge of city. Realized
where I was & tho't I'd go home
in daylight - and struck
off into country for home -
(Rocky River?) Got long
bean to show Robert - Dogs

Page 2:

Kept coming up - (all kinds)
Went south west to little
town (Dover!) got loaf of
bread in store. Rested on
bridges. Tho-t dam
Should be taken out of river
Woman in store.

A Dog Parallel

The following excerpt from Tar (page 213) is included
for the way it seems to fuse the persistent memory on which
"Death in the Woods" was built and the dog factor in both
the "amnesia letter" and the "hospital dictation. "

When one of the dogs came to where the old woman
sat with her back against the tree and had thrust
his nose close to her face he seemed satisfied and
went back to run with the pack. All the Grimes
dogs did it at some time, during the evening, before she died. Tar Moorhead knew all about it,
afterwards, when he grew to be a man, because
once in a wood on another winter night he saw a
pack of dogs act just that way. The dogs were
waiting for him to die as they had waited for the
old woman that night when he was a child. When
it happened to him he was a young man and had
no intention of dying.

II. Letter of December 8, 1916.

The following letter, the full text of which is given
here, was written to Miss Marietta D. Finley of Indianapolis.
It is dated "December 8th-----1916. " It has no greeting,
as many do not of the nearly 300 letters he sent Miss Finley. The content of this letter and others written in the

same period shows he was traveling. The letter may or may
not have been written from Chicago, probably not. It is in
Anderson's typescript, having many strike-outs, strike-
overs, and inked corrections. In this copy, spelling, spacing and punctuation have been reproduced. Corrections of
errors have not been reproduced. The original typescript
was double-spaced.

For nearly seven years now, ever since I
began writing---and I count any happiness I have
had in life as beginning when I began to scribble
---I have had one thought constantly in mind. The
thought has left me at times but has always come
back. It must come back. There is death in
forgetting.

And now I come to express that vague
thought it is unspeakably difficult. I want to try
to remember the relation of myself to my time.
and place. That is it. It sounds in written words
self-conscious and foolish but as my time and
place is neither beautiful nor inspiring I feel myself capable of embracing the thought and I do embrace it.

It seems to me that if I lived in France
now, and had been born a Frenchman I should remain silent. My own terrible ignorance, a somewhat superficial quality in me and the life about
me, would keep me silent among the great voices
of France or of Russia. I would be there a quiet,
rather studious man perhaps given to scribbling in
secret.

And here I have allowed myself to speak.
Nearly all of the qualities of the Americans of my
time are embodied in me. My struggle, my ignorance, my years of futile work to meaningless
ends---all these are American traits. If I fail to
get at anything approaching real beauty so have my
times and the men of my times failed. [end of
page 1]

Yesterday I came through Elyria where I
was in business as a manufacturer for five years.
I arrived in the evening and all day as I sat in the
train or talked to men in another town there was a

peculiar tightening of the muscles of my body. My
feet did not want to touch the soil of Elyria. That
is the truth.   I was too terribly unhappy there.
For five years there I fought a meaningless battle
for a meaningless end.   I tried to make money,
become rich.   The experience ended in a convulsion that touched the edge of insanity.

        Yesterday in a book I read the writer [who]
talked of convicts in a Russian prison. He spoke
of the terrible punishment of giving men meaningless work to do.   "Make a man carry dirt from
one place to another and then caryy back and he
will inevitably become insane. " the writer said.

        And I did just that for five years in Elyria.
Other men were doing it there, Americans are doing it everywhere.   We are all insane.   The men
of the industrial age will always be insane.

        It was evening when I got to Elyria and
rathere dark and cold.   My train did not go further
and I had to get out and wait a half hour for
another train.   My body was cold and I shivered.
None of the people who stood about me knew me
and I was glad of that.   I stood in the deep shadow
by the station and waited.   The soul within me was
weary with old memories.

        Just acrosse the track from where I stood
was the factory building where I employed myself
striving to get rich.   For a little time I made
money and then the seeds of failure that have always been
        [Anderson's spacing]
in me began to take root in the industry I was trying to manage.   Uh, the memory of those years!
I tried hard to be cunning, to be shrewd.   I must
have lied and boasted and cheated prodidgiously.
All day and every day the thing went on like an
insane nightmare.   At night I [end of page 2]

tried to heal myself.   Sometimes I got drunk.   At
other times I walked alone through endless streets
of small frame houses.   I crept away into the
open and lay down on the ground in the fields.   I
wept, I swore, I worked myself into new fits of

enthusiasm concerning the thing I was doing.

How many laughable sides there are to that long struggle in which I was engaged. My wife thought me insane. She had always considered me a little twisted in the head and who can blame her? It was her fate to live with me in my terrible time and to know nothing of what went on in my soul and I could not understand what went on in her either. In the house we looked at each other with unseeing eyes. Now and then tenderness swept over us and we sat in the darkness of the house late at night and wept.

In my second year her I began to write. I wrote Windy and Marching Men her and the writing saved me from insanity. Night after night I crept away to my room to write. I was without education and training. The thought came to me---"I am an intensification of the spirit of my times." I whispered to myself. "As I am ignorant so are all my brothers ignorant, as I am now terribly sad, on the point of madness so will all America some day be (sad) to the edge of insanity."

There was a woman worked in my office who was the daughter of people here. At night she stayed in the office and typed what I had written. She was strong, full of virility and honest. Sometimes when she had typed what I had written and we were trudging homeward up the dark track she would put a hand on my arm and speak in a low voice. Tears would come into her eyes, "It would be wonderful if you could get clear of all this." she said

During the day when the others were about this woman continually bustled about. There was a good deal to the tom-boy about her and she was always tearing her clothing. At the noon hour she would [end of page 3]

run into the yard and begin wrestling with one of the boys from the factory. When finally the affairs of the company became desperate and I, seeing the money entrusted to me by others, slipping away, I could not sleep at night, she watched me with motherly solicitude. One morning my mind became a blank and I ran away from Elyria, scurrying across fields, sleeping in ditches, filling my pockets with corn from the fields that I nibbled like a beast. I would have been afraid even of her then. I was afraid of everything on human form. When, after several days of wandering my mind came into my body and I dragged myself weary and yet glad of my final defeat into a hospital in a strange town and slept, the touch of her honest, broad hand awakened me. I sat up in bed ready to cry out, eager to express to her my joy at being back among the living but only the bland walls of a new strange place confronted me. I had begun a new life and there was something complete and final in the low voice that whispered as I turned again to sleep. "You must leave all that life and everything that has been a part of that life behind you."

III. The Infuriating Interview.

By far the most curious of all the articles concerning Anderson's "amnesia" is that which appeared last. It is apparently an account of an interview with both Mr. and Mrs. Anderson and was published in the Cleveland Evening Telegram, page 1, on December 6, 1912.

Cleveland, O., Dec. 6--As soon as he recovers from the trance into which he placed himself, Sherwood Anderson, Elyria manufacturer, in Huron Road Hospital, will write a book of the sensations he experienced while he wandered over the country as a nomad.

Anderson who disappeared from his home Thanksgiving eve, was found in a drug store at E. 152nd street and Aspinwall avenue last week, and taken to Huron Road hospital. For days he wandered gypsylike over the countryside, while in a strange trance. He knew his identity, but could not disclose it; he wanted to return home, but could tell no person of his desires; he knew where he lived, but could not speak the name of the city.

He knew who he was, what he was doing, where

he was going and what he wanted to do, Mrs. Anderson said, but he could not tell any person or do
what he wished. Yesterday he recalled the last
thing that happened during that strange adventure.
Mr. Anderson through deep thought threw himself
into the trance. It is dangerous, but it will be a
good story and the money will always be welcome,
said he.

Mrs. Anderson has referred to this (in a letter of
November 18, 1946) as "the purported joint interview between
us and a reporter... a man who dubbed himself as a free-
lancer came to the hospital and stood in the hall talking fantastic nonsense. Instead of choking him, I thought I was being astute in telling nothing he could quote.... The next
day came the article containing what he had said. I faced the
angry doctors and told them my lame tale, which, in their
relief at finding their patient had not been interviewed, they
accepted pityingly, I suppose...."

IV.   "The Lost Novel" Parallel.

Attention of the reader is drawn to the story. "The
Lost Novel" (Scribner's Magazine, September 1928, vol. 84,
pages 255-258). as it offers an excellent example of the way
Anderson played his imagination over real events, this time
his relationship with Cornelia in his artistic crisis in Elyria
and Chicago. The reader of this account may want to get
the story to examine the way locale is changed, time se-
quences are rearranged and foreshortened, reactions simpli-
fied or tempered, the artifact in question being changed from
real to imaginary.

But the essence is saved; the meaning of the trans-
cendent artistic experience and the devotion of the artist save
it.

Some several particulars may be worth quoting here.
"Because he was writing he of course, neglected his job, his
wife, his kids.... No woman can quite bear the absolute
way in which a man who has been her lover can drop her
when he is at work.... And they [artists] are absolutely
ruthless about throwing direct personal love aside.... Such
tenderness of understanding--of her difficulties and her limitations, and such a casual, brutal way of treating her--per-
sonally.... He kept on writing. He said it was the most

intense writing he ever did or ever hoped to do. Hours and hours passed. He sat there on that bench writing like a crazy man. . . . He said that all the love he had in his being went into that novel. "

The closing lines of the story are perhaps the most tellingly appropriate ones of all for Anderson, who was constantly impressed or oppressed with a feeling of separation from the reaction patterns of others (paradoxically, and again typically, when he was able to think of himself as a man representative of the spirit of his times):

> Of course, when he said it he laughed.

> I do not believe there are too many people in the world who will know exactly what he was laughing about.

V.   The Many Marriages Particulars.

In Anderson's novel Many Marriages, which does not generally recreate or depend on his life-situation in Elyria, several particulars are reminiscent.

> 1.   The foreword is devoted to discussion of the difficulty of moving out of an undesirable situation, the frustration of the ambivalent attitude: "Are you sane or are you insane? Why this whirlpool of thoughts within your brain, a whirlpool of thoughts that, as you now stand hesitant, seem to be sucking you down and down into a bottomless pit? "

> 2.   John Webster, the central figure, is manufacturer of washing machine who undergoes "a certain revolution" in his life. He is "thirty-seven or eight years old" to Anderson's thirty-six.

> 3.   The room of John Webster has a garden scene, as did Anderson's in Elyria.

Appendix E

MISCELLANEOUS TRAVEL REFERENCES

Among the materials available for attempted recon-
struction and study of Anderson's life are what may be called
miscellaneous travel references. Perhaps the most interesting of these is found in a letter to Waldo Frank, May, 1919.

> When I worked as a roustabout on the docks at Buf-
> falo one winter long ago I lived in a house where
> the only books they had were Shakespeare. How
> they got there God knows. A young chap from
> Iowa had the next room. We layed [sic] abed all
> day Sunday after getting piped together on Saturday
> night. When we staggered in late at night we
> nabbed the books and carried them upstairs. The
> door was open between the two rooms. The house
> was old and dismal. For an hour I read the roll-
> ing, lovely free verse and then he took a turn. We
> went through everything, got it into us.

This reference raises questions as to how highly-fic-
tionalized it is. It arouses memories of the type of experience referred to, this time as a factory hand in Erie, in
"The Sad Horn Blowers." These references and others, recurrent but unsubstantiated, establish the fact that Anderson
liked to think he had at one time been an itinerant factory
worker and laborer. It is impossible so far to document
this time or these times in his life. His rooming house
references could have been created in the image of the
places where he lived in Chicago. His imaginative grasp
and self-conviction were sufficient that he certainly was able
convince himself he had had experiences which actually had
only suggested themselves to him. At least, he asserts that
he had experiences for which there is no substantiation available, and one can imagine his chuckling over any one's attempting to verify them.

Another significant aspect of this reference is the Shakespeare reading. One is reminded of the way his mind turned to Shakespeare for its escape symbolism in his Elyria amnesia. He liked to refer to himself as uneducated, untutored, unschooled. He seemed to react both apologetically and proudly against the established academic traditions. He was both attracted and repelled by the fact that Waldo Frank, for whom this anecdote was written, was a highly-educated man. The suggestion presents itself that this episode may have been manufactured in the interests of impressing Frank with Anderson's cultural gains in the school of hard knocks. The correspondence with Frank reveals that Frank was capable of undertaking a project to go west and live on a farm, something for which he was completely unprepared, in the interests of confronting life. Suppositional as the idea of Anderson's fictionalizing this for Frank's benefit may be, it fits the basically proud spirit of Anderson and certainly does not violate what is known of Anderson's failure to recall at all accurately what the facts of his life were.

If the episode is factual, perhaps another reference, if factual, is related to the time when it might have happened:

> One night, years before, when I was a young laborer beating my way westward on a freight train, a brakesman had succeeded in throwing me off the train in an Indiana town. I had remembered the place long afterwards because of my embarrassment--walking about among people in my dirty torn clothes and with my dirty hands and face. However, I had little money and after I had walked through the town to a country road I found a creek and bathed. Then I went back to a restaurant and bought food. [1]

One notes that this young laborer was going westward and that, for both episodes to be true, he had to travel eastward, too. One of the only time periods into which these "years ago" experiences could have fallen was the Clyde period roughly between 1893 and 1896, when he went to Chicago. If so, they were brief trips. The present writer has doubts about their authenticity. No one else seems to have been aware enough of them to mention them.

Another kind of travel is reflected in two other references.

> I used to go to Elkhart years ago, walk in the
> streets there at night. At that time I wasn't doing
> what I wanted to do and was very unhappy. I
> walked about in Elkhart in dark streets and past
> dark houses. I was very unhappy....[2]

> Indeed I do know a great deal about Terre Haute,
> Indiana.... A good many years ago, before I be-
> came a writer, I used to go to Terre Haute myself
> on business....[3]

Visits to these cities are representative of many that
he made to states adjacent to Chicago in his work in the advertising business. One would also suspect they might be
timed as in the 1900-1906 period in Chicago, but his "years
ago" is sufficiently vague as to discourage attempting chronology. Perhaps the main effect of these references will be
to remind students of Anderson of his wide acquaintance over
the area, of his many visits to many cities in it, and that
there are doubtless people who know a good deal about him
still living in the area. However, as his particularizations
of places in his novels and stories are the distillation of
many experiences and memories of many places throughout
the midwest, so perhaps are these scattered mentions of
towns and places in his letters. His mention of wandering
the streets of Elkhart at night makes it sound like a regular
haunt, something that seems unlikely in view of his never
living near enough to make it convenient. It may be that he
had occasion to be there often at some crucial emotional
juncture, for there are many examples of his tendency to
walk in times of stress, in both town and country.

Notes

1. A Story Teller's Story, p. 336.

2. Letter to David Virgrin, Oct. 5, 1939.

3. Letter to Mrs. Lucile Vaughan Payne, Sept. 24, 1940.

Appendix F

SHERWOOD AND HIS BROTHERS AND SISTER

With one notable exception, Anderson seems never to
have wanted to write directly about his four brothers and his
sister, though they are mentioned to some extent in his
"autobiographical" accounts. The reader has seen that any
such accounts are completely unreliable. There is information about the relationship between Anderson and his siblings,
and it seems appropriate to have it on record.

The one he wanted to write about was Earl, who was
nine years younger than Sherwood, and a very unhappy person, as it would seem. It will be recalled that Earl was the
unsuccessful one, whom everyone tried, without positive result, to help. He severed communications from the rest of
the family, apparently without notice, and was gone for ten
years or more, to be projected back into the family in 1926
on the occasion of a stroke, which disability gave place to
his death in March, 1927.

The arrangements for the care of Earl devolved upon
Karl, but Sherwood was more than usually concerned over
his brother's life. In 1935 he was to write to Karl:

> I have long wanted to do a book of some sort,
> based on Earl, and have got into it, a rather crazy
> book I call Brother Earl, an attempt to get at
> something in his life, what it meant, etc. I have
> already, in the last two months, got down some
> fifty thousand words of it. [There is no record of
> the existence of this manuscript.]

> Of course I have given him a new background, dif-
> ferent parents, in a different position in life but
> yet, in some way, I hope, having the essence of
> his background too. [1]

It is rather impressive that Earl was able to intrude this much on the highly-individualized working-out of Anderson's personal and artistic destiny. Remarks quoted earlier show that he thought of Earl at times as a self-pitying ineffective combatant in an aggressive family group, made so by the necessity to scratch for a living. He was capable of romanticizing his family in these terms: "A common sense of pride in our cleverness held us together."[2] As a matter of fact, the family does not seem to have had a sense of closeness. Earl's seclusion of himself from the rest, apparently mostly through a sense of personal inadequacy, is only an extreme example of the way in which every one went his own way.

Probably the closest relationship was between Sherwood and Karl, who wrote and published an essay with the revealing title, "My Brother, Sherwood Anderson." Karl was the first born and was readily successful in his chosen field. He went first to Cleveland, then to Chicago, and generally taught the rest of the family by his example what they were capable of. By 1909, a Sandusky County history paid him this tribute:

> Karl Anderson, who has his studio in New York, is another Clyde boy who has achieved fame and fortune as an artist. He is now recognized as one of the best illustrators in the county.[3]

On the occasion of Karl's engagement, Sherwood graciously wrote to the fiancée that he had long hoped to be able to live near his brother (in New York at that time), but he was also to write in 1922:

> I had a letter from a man in New York asking me to write something of you. I've tried. The difficulty, as I have tried to say in the little thing I wrote, is that brothers always have difficulty getting into the position of friends. The little flashing adventures of life that make up that part of our lives upon which we later feed and live are not told to brothers. Just why I don't know. It happens to be a fact.[4]

There is no record of the effect that such a declaration might have had on the elder brother, but the pride Karl had in Sherwood is amply revealed in the following statement:

In the environment tightly gnarled, among unimag-
inative folk, dependent upon agriculture for a living,
it may appear surprising that the Anderson children
should early have shown something of the fire of
the poets; something also that could evaporate. I,
the oldest, took up painting. Stella, who later became an occasional contributor to religious publications, was a year younger than myself. Next was
Sherwood, then Irving [Irwin] who had an inclination to be an artist but became a business man,
then Raymond, who took up newspaper work, and
Earl, who studied art in Paris.... 5

The article in which this reference occurred was published because of Sherwood's international recognition, and
the list recognizes that fact. Sherwood had once written
Karl, "I am writing what I damn please!" And it seems
that it was Sherwood's capability of doing that and getting the
public to accept it which made Karl yield the palm to his
younger, less conventional brother. In his correspondence,
Karl makes frequent reference, sometimes quite bitter, to
the "mugs" he is doing as a materialistically successful portrait painter.

As a restrained, very decent man he kept his envy of
his brother's success within bounds and rejoiced moderately
in it. When he died, he left behind him the manuscript of
a novel6 which has been described as not autobiographical
but rewarding for what may be gleaned from it of Karl's attitude toward his family. Karl left evidence in his writings
that he had great affection and respect for his mother. 7

Mrs. Poor's way of presenting a point of difference
between Karl and Sherwood is: "...he always was annoyed
that Sherwood did write the family down and accused him of
trying to give himself a Lincolnesque character. Karl felt
that his mother entrusted the family honor and responsibility
to him so he resented it when Sherwood wanted a 'common
man' background. " Though he felt this way toward Sherwood
on this point, they still maintained a strong relationship.
And not the least of what they had in common was their
idealization of their mother and their disappointment in their
father. When Earl died, Sherwood revealed their closeness
in this note: "I am on my way to Clyde Ohio to help bring
my poor brother--who died just as I was getting off the boat.
Karl and I are taking him back to bury him beside mother. "8
Here were Karl and Sherwood working together evidently

without Irwin and Ray, the two others still living, to put Earl
lovingly in a place of honor.

As has been stated earlier, Stella and the younger
children went to Chicago about 1900, when Irwin, the father,
seems to have resigned his responsibility. Karl, we are
told, felt that the care of the family fell to him, on his
mother's death. Stella's daughter understood that Stella had
made a deathbed promise "to keep the family together. "9
Mrs. Schroeder also recalled that Karl had given "$1,000
to the family in Chicago after his mother's death. " It seems
that Karl, who was pursuing his rising career, and Stella
cooperated to care for the two younger children particularly.
Chicago directory records seem to indicate that Irwin worked
as soon as he got to Chicago.

A close relationship between Karl and Stella is indicated by the fact that in 1894 "Miss Stella Anderson pleasant-
ly entertained about thirty of her friends on Tuesday evening
in honor of her brother Carl, who is home from Chicago for
a short time. "10 By this time Stella had been the valedictorian of her high school class in 1891 and had taught in the
local schools for two years, though "Miss Stella Anderson,
formerly of D Grammar No. 1, was not an applicant this
year [1894].... "11 Perhaps she did not re-apply because of
her mother's failing health.

Sherwood was to recall his sister ambivalently. "You
know she was a peculiarly eager one with a world of energy.
One of the sort who graduated from high school at 14 [really
16]. "12 And "My sister, when she was alive had a mania
for what she called 'doing something for the world. ' It
destroyed her. She got into a queer fantastic notion that she
was a kind of representative of Christ on earth. "13 He
could not see that her interest in changing the conditions of
life on earth was different from his own only in the form it
took.

Neither Irwin nor Ray maintained close contact with
Sherwood, as far as can be determined. When Earl's illness brought him back to the family, it brought about a re-
union which gave occasion for Karl to paint a picture of Earl,
Sherwood, and Irwin. Irwin was for many years a manager-
ial employee of The American Can Company in Baltimore,
Maryland. Ray did newspaper work and evidently was in
Dayton, Ohio, for some time, seemingly at the time of his
father's death in the veteran's home there in 1919. When

the present writer was taken to see Ray, while he was visiting Karl in Westport, Connecticut, in 1946, it was at a grocery store where Ray was working as a clerk. He said he could not understand why any one would be doing research on Sherwood's writings.

All of Irwin and Emma Anderson's children are now deceased.

Notes

1. Letter to Karl Anderson, late April, 1935. There is no evidence of a manuscript which could be this one.

2. A Story Teller's Story, p. 53.

3. Basil Mack, Twentieth Century History of Sandusky County, Ohio, and Representative Citizens. Chicago, Richmond-Arnold Pub. Co., 1909, p. 319-20.

4. Letter to Karl Anderson, ca. April 15, 1922.

5. "My Brother, Sherwood Anderson," p. 6.

6. The property of Karl's son, James.

7. Letter of Jan. 13, 1964, to author, from Mrs. David L. Poor, Westport, Conn., formerly Karl Anderson's secretary.

8. Letter to M. D. Finley, March 1927.

9. Interview with Mrs. Margaret Hill Schroeder, Hinsdale, Ill.; June 1962.

10. Clyde Enterprise, Aug. 9, 1894.

11. Enterprise, June 14, 1894.

12. Letter to Mary Emmett, June 26, 1936.

13. Letter to M. D. Finley, May 1918. Stella's sudden death, in the course of an operation, came in 1917.

Appendix G

THE CHILDREN OF SHERWOOD ANDERSON

To avoid the erroneous conclusion that Anderson devoted himself so completely to the pursuit of his personal artistic destiny that he lost interest in his children, it seems desirable to include some notes about his relationship with them.

As has been pointed out, three children were born to Sherwood and Cornelia between 1907 and 1911 in Cleveland and Elyria. The children and their mother were on friendly terms with all of their step-mothers. Sherwood's second wife, Tennessee Mitchell, was a friend of Cornelia's before the divorce of Cornelia and Sherwood, during the marriage of Tennessee and Sherwood, and after the divorce of Tennessee and Sherwood. Cornelia had the children send wedding presents when Tennessee and Sherwood were married, and Sherwood and Tennessee visited Cornelia and the children on their honeymoon. In the succeeding summer, Cornelia and the children went to Lake Chateaugay with Sherwood and Tennessee. Cornelia, although not having met Elizabeth Prall, the third wife, spoke very well of her. And Eleanor Copenhaver Anderson and Cornelia, who both lived in Marion, Virginia at the same time during one period, were on friendly terms until Cornelia's death in June, 1967.

These facts are related as a background for realizing that, unlikely as it may seem, throughout his irregular life, for a part of which he willingly absented himself from his family circle, Anderson maintained contact with, interest in, love for, and provided partial, if erratic, support for his children. After the breakup of his first marriage in the period 1914 to 1916 (when the divorce and the marriage to Tennessee took place), Anderson remained conscious of his responsibility to his children, even if he did not allow the thought to constrict his own activities materially. In his correspondence may be found reference to letters to Roger

Sergel (December, 1923) and Waldo Frank (after March 2, 1917) to the effect that he has three children he must provide for. To Sergel he confides that he "cannot" live where his children are and that he sees them only two or three times a year.

Occasionally there were moments like this one:

> T[ennessee] and I went [from Chicago] last Sunday for the day with the children [in Michigan City, Ind.]. Robert had made a puppet theater that was really wonderful. In the late afternoon when the light failed they gave a show. It was a strikingly nice thing they had done. All the family seemed happy. Mimi [aged 7] has begun to pass out of infancy and become a little girl. It seems to me that Cornelia is happier and is learning better how to handle her life.[1]

A letter of 1920 refers to having "Christmas with the kids."[2] Even though in a letter a decade later he was to say his home situation in Clyde had left him confused about Christmas,[3] he asked the committee in charge of the Dial Magazine Award to postpone the dinner planned in his honor so that he could stay in Chicago to be with his children during the holiday.

A long-time friend and observer of Anderson, a person who visited in Cornelia's home in Michigan City and who displayed an intense interest over a period of years in the welfare of the children, wrote this summation of Anderson's relationship to them:

> Of Anderson's three children, Robert, John, and Marion, I feel that he loved John the most deeply because he could identify with him best. John's very quietness intrigued Anderson greatly. Bob was a different personality and Anderson, though he cared for him, resented his quick smartness, as he called it. Bob's nature was, so Anderson felt, just like his own worst side. Anderson, however, did not realize clearly enough that he let his preference to John be felt by Bob.
>
> Marion or Mimi as they called her was a girl and fathers are wont to like their girl children best. Mimi got along with her father always.[4]

Correspondence in the Anderson Collection in the Newberry Library supports the general conclusion that Anderson
corresponded with his children with interest and with love
from their school days onward. Similarly the correspondence
with Cornelia, mostly about affairs related to the children,
extends into 1938. There seems never to have been any
cessation to the relationship among the five people until his
death.

On the occasion of his separation from his second
wife, Tennessee, he discussed his plans for his family with
his friend, Ferdinand Schevill:

> My dream is something like this--to take my chil-
> dren, one by one, as they graduate from high
> school and have each live with me for a year or
> two. Naturally I do not want them to be restricted
> by the outlook of a middle western industrial town
> like Michigan City.

> On the other hand, their mother, Cornelia Ander-
> son, has given her life for them and in a position
> much more difficult than TM knows anything about
> was very fine and splendid.

> I want, if possible, to be able to enlarge her life
> now. If the city is to take the children I want her
> to be a part of their later life too. [5]

Finally he was able to establish himself in Virginia
and, by 1930, he was able to create an arrangement by
means of which he made over to his son, Robert, the two
papers he had bought and operated in Marion, Virginia. The
worth of the papers was considered to be $15,000. Robert
paid the other two Anderson children $5,000 apiece, for their
shares in the patrimony. [6] Robert, with time out for military service, ran the papers until his sudden death in 1951.
John has pursued studies as a painter, now is a college
teacher of art, and has one of his father's paintings hanging
in his living room. Marion and her husband have jointly
operated a newspaper in North Carolina for several decades.
Mrs. Cornelia Anderson lived in the same town as her
daughter until her death in 1967.

An additional statement by Anderson about his children
may be supplied:

I shall try to be as philosophical as I can
about the children--do for them all I can.
They in turn will have to be what they can.
What they make themselves.
More than all what fate makes them. [7]

He compliments Paul Rosenfeld on "other subtle things
I did not know you knew, the escape from the dominance of
women and children,"[8] and in so doing identifies a basic conflict in both his personal life and in his relationship
between himself and his art. It seems to be to the credit
of all concerned that the conflicts both within and around the
artist were weathered, not without suffering but with love,
respect, understanding, and pride.

Notes

1. Letter to M. D. Finley, Jan. 1919.

2. Letter to Jerry Blum, Dec. 24, 1920.

3. Letter to Charles Bockler, Dec. 25, 1930.

4. Letter from M. D. Finley, May 31, 1962.

5. Letter to Schevill, Jan. 27, 1924.

6. Letter to Burton Emmett of March 11, 1930, and letter
   of Jan. 20, 1933, to Paul Rosenfeld.

7. Letter to M. D. Finley, dated only 1927.

8. Undated letter, prob. early 1920's, to Rosenfeld, in Paul
   Rosenfeld, Voyager in the Arts, p. 210.

Appendix H

SHERWOOD ANDERSON PUBLICATIONS, 1913-1918

1913

"Making It Clear, " Agricultural Advertising, Feb. 1913, 24:16.

1914

"The New Note, " Little Review, March 1914, 1:23.

"The Rabbit-pen, " Harper's, July 1914, 129:207-19.

1915

"Sister, " Little Review, Dec. 1915, 2:3-4.

1916

"The Story Writers, " Smart Set, Jan. 1916, 48:243-48.

"The Novelist, " Little Review, Jan. -Feb. 1916, 2:12-14.

"Book of the Grotesque, " Masses, Feb. 1916, 8:7.

"Hands, " Masses, March 1916, 8:5, 7.

"Vibrant Life, " Little Review, March 1916, 3:10-11.

"Dreiser, " Little Review, April 1916, 3:5.

"The Struggle, " Little Review, May 1916, 3:7-10.

"Blackfoot's Masterpiece, " Forum, June 1916, 55:679-83.

"The Philosopher, " Little Review, June-July 1916, 3:7-9.

"The Strength of God, " Masses, Aug. 1916, 8:12-13.

"Queer, " Seven Arts, Dec. 1916, 1:97-108.

Windy McPherson's Son, October, 1916.

1917

"The Untold Lie, " Seven Arts, Jan. 1917, 1:215-21.

"Mother, " Seven Arts, March 1917, 1:452-61.

"From Chicago, " Seven Arts, May 1917, 2:41-59.

"Mid-American Songs, " Poetry, Sept. 1917, 10:281-91.

"The Thinker, " Seven Arts, Sept. 1917, 2:584-97.

"An Apology for Crudity, " Dial, Nov. 8, 1917, 63:437-8.

"An Apology for Crudity, " Chicago Daily News, Nov. 14, 1917, p. 13, cols. 1-4.

Marching Men, Sept. , 1917.

1918

"Chicago Culture, " Chicago Daily News, Feb. 20, 1918, p. 7, cols. 7-8.

"Seeds, " Little Review, July 1918, 5:24-31.

"The White Streak, " Smart Set, July 1918, 55:27-30.

"Here's Looking at You" (self-portrait), Chicago Daily News, p. 12, cols. 3-4.

"Senility, " Little Review, Sept. 1918, 5:37-39.

"Our Rebirth, " Chicago Daily Tribune, Sept. 14, 1918, p. 10, cols. 5-7. (Review of Van Wyck Brooks' Letters and Leadership).

"An Awakening, " Little Review, Dec. 1918, 5:13-21.

Mid-American Chants, April 1918.

Appendix I

PERIODICAL PUBLICATION OF WINESBURG, OHIO
STORIES

"Book of the Grotesque," Masses, Feb. 1916.

"Hands," Masses, March 1916.

"The Strength of God," Masses, Aug. 1916.

"Queer," Seven Arts, Dec. 1916.

"The Untold Lie," Seven Arts, Jan. 1917.

"Mother," Seven Arts, March 1917.

"The Philosopher," Little Review, March 1917.

"The Thinker," Seven Arts, Sept. 1917.

"An Awakening," Little Review, Dec. 1918.

Appendix J

READER'S ANALYSIS OF MARY COCHRAN

(The text which follows is an estimate of the publishability of
Mary Cochran, prepared between 1917 and 1919 by Anderson's Indianapolis friend, Marietta D. Finley. Miss Finley
had been a reader for Bobbs-Merrill Co. but did not prepare
this report for that or any other publisher.)

"Mary Cochran"---Sherwood Anderson.

In the interpretation of "Mary Cochran" Sherwood Anderson has literally delved into the depths of life and set forth
a large, realistic, tragically awful and at the same time
ironically trivial piece of life. "Mary Cochran" is a girl of
mediocre attainments, not beautiful, not intellectual nor re-
fined yet possessing that indefinable charm that Marriott calls
"woman"--not a feminine woman but the idea, woman, per-
sonified. It is this subtle essence, in [its] gradual development, its seeking for expression, that holds the reader's attention through all the intricate windings of Mary Cochran's
checkered career.

Mary Cochran, born in a quiet New England village
as the daughter of an actress and a typical old country doctor, passes through the various stages of her career under
the sympathetic eyes of the reader. Her monotonous girlhood in the village, absorbed by the doctor's routine of business, homely living and humdrum dying; then her life in a
middle western university, her friends there and the impressions made upon her mind by the professor, who is irresistibly attracted by her charm, and the poet to whose abnormal
desire she unconsciously appealed; and then her entry into
and her life in Chicago with its temptations, its lonelinesses,
its infinite restlessness that settles down upon Mary as a
cloud obscuring her vision and yet still blindly attracting her.

It is in Chicago that the woman ultimately awakens to a realization of herself--of the infinite yearning within her for a companion, a man who will understand her every feeling, who will respond to her every desire and above all take away forever that impending spirit of restlessness.

It is the seeking to satisfy this longing that makes Mary the victim not only of convention but of her own nature. Thinking to fulfill all her hopes she engages herself to one Duke Yetter in whose office she is working and whom she had known as a boy in her own village. Duke Yetter with all the instincts of the primitive man, glories in his possession of the woman. Not satisfied, however, with accepting the courtesan type as her standard Mary then seeks (comradeship) the ignoring of sex, and here not only convention but her own nature revolt. Sylvester Hunnicutt the emotional experimenter, seeks to prove to Mary that they two can be comrades, talking sensibly, acting sensibly and ignoring all else. Sylvester succeeds but Mary--Mary's restlessness becomes more unbearable than ever.

And so passes Mary Cochran's life in Chicago--a life filled with steady, monotonous work, requiring the utmost of the woman's mental and physical power to accomplish, and now and then an emotional climax comes upon her, wracks her with wild desire and a craving for love, for home and children and then on goes the steady whirr [sic] of existence, of labor.

True, "MARY COCHRAN" is a sex novel to a certain degree, but what novel especially depicting a woman, who, though outwardly more restrained, is nevertheless more keenly alive than man to sex attractions and antagonisms, can in any sense be a sincere portrayal of life if it does not deal, normally, with this natural force? This novel is indisputably an intensely realistic portrayal of a woman's inner life, her emotions and her primitive instincts at war with the existing conditions. Sherwood Anderson has attempted through the life-history of an ordinary woman to show the development of a new class of women in the world --"that the hope of the world lies in its quiet obscure working women of the Mary Cochran type. They are to look upon work as an end in life and not as a single expedient taken up to bridge over the years before their marriage day or to enable them to drive a better bargain in the marriage market. Among them will grow up finally a horror of selling out at any price and a passion for independence."

Through all the passing phases of her life, her inter-course with men and women, her instinctive emotional passions and her ultimate marriage with Hunnicutt, this idea is slowly evolved--the new women-workers of the world.

As a background for this character-study, which, though presented by a man, is notwithstanding, set forth with a deep and broad sympathy, --Chicago typifying any big city, with its miriad [sic] people, its vice and vanity, its tragedies and comedies, is described with the same realistic, effective detail that is so marked in "Marching Men."

With its undeniably episodic plot, its many characters who have a way--not altogether sanctioned but infinitely natural we must admit, of slipping into the plot and out again forever, with its vivid though sketchy descriptions of city-streets, "Mary Cochran" carries a human appeal together with an underlying truth that will stand a hearing and will, to thinking people at least, prove saleable.

Appendix K

READER'S ANALYSIS OF TALBOT WHITTINGHAM

[The text which follows was, as Appendix J, produced by
Marietta D. Finley and under the same general circumstances. Miss Finley has said that she had the Whittingham
manuscript in her keeping for a period of time.]

Talbot Whittingham. ------Report.

It is no easy matter to pass judgment on this novel,
this daring analysis of a master-character and of the elemental impulses, motives and experiences from which the
artist within him is evolved. Granting primarily that the
artist in the world is abnormal; that his sensual, intellectual
and spiritual natures are constantly warring against one
another; that it is only by a transition of the grotesque that
true beauty is arrived at; and that if and only if we have
enough logic and sympathy to grant these ugly facts, we may
arrive at somewhat of an understanding of this Talbot Whittingham.

Sherwood Anderson has laid for a background to Talbot, the boy, a stuffy little apartment in New York City
where "in the evening would come an indiscriminate lot of
art hangers-on, young minor poets who had forgotten to wash
their hands, singers with sad eyes and painters with long
jaws and an inclination to become excited and resentful if the
names of other painters living or dead, were brought into
the conversation." In this abnormal, sickly atmosphere Talbot, the son of an umbrella-thief and a musician, who as-
pired to holding a salon where young art might be duly appreciated, lived for twelve years. At the end of this time
Talbot, forced by circumstances over which he had no con-
trol--namely the disappearance of his thief father and his
mother's discovery of her affinity in the person of a wealthy
Breakfast Food man--left New York for a small town in Ohio

584

where lived his mother's patron, one Billy Bustard, to whose
tender mercies his fond parent now entrusted him.

Talbot's life in Mirage was typical of hundreds of village boys. Possessed of and [sic] active imagination, a bold
fearlessness and everlasting swagger he at once assumed the
leadership of boys and aroused a friendly interest in the men
of the town. Toward Billy Bustard, the town's little baker
and his own benefactor, Talbot affected a supreme and
haughty indifference, though the pathos of Billy's narrow,
cringing, colorless life roused the boy's tenderness as well
as his contempt.

Here Talbot lived in idleness, enjoying to the utmost
all village-life, growing strong and vigorous as a healthy
young animal and acquiring a knowledge and a keen insight
into men's motives, a crude, somewhat skeptical but sturdy
philosophy of life. At last, however, came the day of reck-
oning. Talbot, in whom the seeds of the domineering, all-
demanding artist were even in boyhood, sprouting gloriously,
had domineered over fearful little Billy, snatching his live-
lihood from the long-suffering little baker. Now in turn
Talbot was to be the victim of brute force in the shape of
Tom Bustard, the baker's strong, brutal father. The boy
against the man and by a lucky turn of fortune the boy's
strength of will, his sheer hatred of the brute won and Tom
Bustard was killed by the hand of Talbot. Killed in defense
of Billy, his benefactor was the villager's report. True the
old man was threatening his son but what cared Talbot?--
fortune was but shielding him by appearances. Such was
the foreordained necessity toward the evolution of the artist.

The boy had gained his badge to manhood and he must
move on. The law is unalterable and Talbot dimly knew and
obeyed the Law. To the big city then the boy turned and
here for a time he was but a spectator of the multitudes,
thronging the streets of Chicago. "From whatever angle he
approached it the life of Talbot Whittingham was a delicious
thing to him. Down in the city he would show himself the
tired faces and the empty, meaningless lives of modern men,
warning the boy within to keep hidden away from it all, safely
concealed within the self-reliant, capable man."

Talbot's life in the city from a business view-point
was that of a dreamer among men; from the artist's that of
a man with the "seeing-eye" and the "poet-soul" among the
sleeping and the dead; men sleeping away ideals and dead to

purpose and to the inner meaning of life. The latent artist
in him, stimulated by the miriad [sic] sights and sounds,
beauties and horrors of the city, fought for expression while
the physical lusts of the primitive man, responding equally
to the same stimuli, fought with and well-nigh conquered the
artist. From one revolting experience to another we follow
Talbot with a sickening dread that the outcome will be chaos.
Through one night, when Talbot, drunk with wine from without and with life, in its manifold grotesqueness from within,
we follow the man, watching as he insanely clutches at human
beings from out the dense fog that clouds the city; watching
as he fights with a desire to take human-life, to spill blood
and by so doing to cleanse and clarify his struggling vision.
Then comes an equally distraught idea to buy and sell out a
cemetery thereby making "the dead bury its dead[.]" This
project--another futile attempt to give birth to the artist, to
free himself from the grotesque--is carried out by Talbot
and his friend, Turner who together have been working profitably in the Advertising business. The cemetery project
also fails and Talbot weeps nor yet knows why.

Not until the death of Lucile Bearing,--a little school
teacher from Indiana, who with ambition and hope had come
to Chicago on the same train with Talbot, did the artist in
him stand forth unfettered by the world and the people of the
world. This woman, though defeated in her purpose and in
her life was to Talbot a subtle, indefinable inspiration. To
her, in fancy, he brought the best of himself, his purest and
highest of love and art and through her horrible yet beautiful
death Talbot Whittingham was brought through the lusts and
the grotesqueness of the world to life and beauty. Watching
Lucile Bearing's brave meeting with death, with victory
through defeat Talbot "knew that the quest for beauty was to
be for him the end in life.["] "After this I shall know everything and I shall have my work. I shall quit this marching
with the dead. I shall have my thing to do."

This then, in brief, is the story of Talbot Whittingham. Sherwood Anderson has without doubt evolved a character-study of strength and power. Any mention of the numerous minor characters and minor plots running in and out
of the novel has of necessity been omitted in relating the
structural character, Talbot. Some of these characters,
however, are splendidly executed. Billy Bustard, the little
baker of Mirage, is a character who through his deafness,
his cringing desire for popularity and his pathetic miserli-
ness, will long be remembered. The village setting abounds

in characterizations; some clever and some revolting in their
coarseness. In his Chicago interpretation, the author's love
of minor characters--and they are deservedly loved because
well-done--has well-nigh run away with itself. The multi-
tudinous array of characters overwhelms the reader, be-
wilders him and leads him far away from the workings of
fate upon Talbot, the central figure. Granted that Talbot
may have come into contact with them all, that his fine
sensibilities were effected [sic] by each one of them, nevertheless the reader's mind cannot assimilate them and they
therefore become obstacles to the clear perceptions. Take
for example a few of these characters, draw them with boldness and leave a little leaway [sic] for the reader's imagina-
tion--it will respond and the effect will be gained by a dose
and not a paralyzing overdose of the stimulant. For instance, the characters of Lucile Bearing, the girl in the
dance-hall, Adelaide Brown and perhaps one casual meeting
will suffice to secure the desired effect. There you have
typical characterizations and the other women, though they
may be mentioned, should not be dwelt on as individuals.

These women I have mentioned are some of the best
character-work in the book. Lucile Bearing in her plea for
the artist in woman and her revolt against woman's fate is
a character of the greatest appeal and strength. Adelaide
Brown is also a good portrayal of a society woman with an
inborn craving for vivid experience not to be felt in a walled-
up social caste.

Talbot Whittingham has great potentialities. Though
crude in many places, vague and blurred in others, faulty
in construction at times it is nevertheless worth cutting-
down, reworking and perfecting. At the first reading I felt
this to be nearly impossible, but on a second and yet a third
reading I have reversed my decision. With careful remodel-
ing, a clear eye toward proportion and some judicious cutting
the novel will become a masterly depiction of the artist in
modern times. Some conscientious scruples come into my
mind as to this book's moral value. Keeping before the
reader, constantly the thought that it is the revelation of the
artist not the ordinary man, it losese [sic]--except possibly
for keen thinkers who are intellectually toughened--any force
as a moral or immoral propaganda. It is the disecting [sic]
table of the artist and has a forceful influence only as such.
Saleable to the majority I doubt if it will ever be, but to an
interested, keenly alive, moderately large public it will win
in favor, espescially [sic] on second reading. Any book with

such a philosophy must gain an ultimate audiene [sic].

"During the history of any race of men there are born
many men and women who have the vision of perfection and
beauty that is in the eye of the artist, but who can produce
no beauty.   Hesitating, these figures stand on the very threshold of existence.   Having quite clearly in mind the vision
or the act that is beautiful they do not act but look into the
distance, lost in dreams.   To-morrow, they say, I shall go
forward, tomorrow I shall sing this song, love this love,
hew from this sone [sic] a thing that is beautiful. "   ["]They
are not dullards, the waiters upon the threshold of life.   In
a way they keep alive the sense of beauty in the hearts of
men.   They are not dullards and at the last they are not
artists.   Theirs is the story of the man with the five talents
who returned them unspent to the master and was rebuked
by him. --At the last they must know that he who does not
dare defeat comes to no victory, and that all of the beauty
in the world from the figure of the Christ to the verses of
John Keats is but proof anew that out of the defeat of the
dreams of men comes the beauty that is art. "

Appendix L

"QUICK IMPRESSIONS" IN LETTERS TO M. D. FINLEY, 1916

Chicago--November 25, 1916.

I went to lunch with Danaghay, a heavily built man who walks awkwardly. He stumbles along, banging against you and while you are crossing the street with him it is necessary to be on the alert lest he knock you under a passing car.

Danaghy [sic] is an Irishman but his people have lived in America through several generations. His father was a very poor farmhand working on a farm near the town of Dayton, Ohio. He was a very religious man and driven to desperation by poverty and the burning zeal within him that could not get itself expressed [and] he finally went insane and died in an asylum.

Danaghy [sic] had one brother, a slight tubercular fellow who became a newspare [sic] man and went to Kansas City. There he lived for several years, being unable to work most of the time. A passing indiscretion resulted in a loathsome disease and he died suddenly. During the last year of his life he was almost constantly abed and there is a very fine story concerning the loyalty and thoughtfulness of his fellow newspaper employees. These men, who are poorly paid and many of whom have wives and families, came every evening to the room of the dying boy. The wives who knew the disease from which he, at the end, suffered came in their best dresses. They brought delicacies and wine. A little pale girl with red hair who had a place as stenographer in the newspaper office sang songs. One of the reporters always stayed through the night. When the boy died they made up a purse to pay the expense of his burial.

My friend, the heavy awkward brother, has begun to rise in the world. He writes advertisements for a company

manufacturing automobiles. He is a devout student of Niet-
sche [sic] and often stops on a busy street to breakforth into
a violent declaration against the influence of Christianity.
"Jesus huh!" he will cry, waving his awkward hands about.
"Who is this Jesus--a weeping, wailing little intermediate!
He appealed to pity. There is no such thing as pity. Man
is ruled by superman. It is right that it should be so."

When Danaghy [sic] was a boy living with his father,
the farmhand, he knew poverty of the worst sort. He talks
of his youth with touching simplicity and directness. What
wonderful pictures he has made for me.

There is one of a night in the farmhouse. It was
late fall and the boy with his father had been digging potatoes all afternoon. It was cold and the boy's bare hands
were split and cracked. The father worked in silence except
that he occasionally muttered a prayer. When night came
on they carried the potatoes into the barn. The boy was too
tired and cold to eat and at once went to bed.

In the bed he lay with his face to the wall, all hud-
dled into a ball, trying to get warm. His body was fevered
and his brain extraordinarily alive. The bed hadd [sic] been
made of a great bag filled with straw. It crackled when he
moved. A wind arose and rattled the boards of the house.
All that night his father prayed. He had gone to bed in the
next room but almost immediately kneeling on the floor cried
out to God. "Oh Father" he cried. "Do not let me remain
here in this obscure place. My soul is afire with zeal for
Thy service. Make me a shepherd fit to lead Thy flocks.
Put the fire of eloquence into my mouth. Give me burning
words to say. Lead me to the place Thou hast assigned to
me."

Toward midnight the boy arose. Creeping to the door
that separated the two rooms he looked at his father. The
moonlight, coming in at the window made the figure stand
out clearly. He was clad in a shirt and his legs were cov-
ered with black hair. The soles of his feet were black from
the dirt of the fields. My friend, Danaghy wanted to kill his
father that night. The idea got into his fevered brain and he
had to force himself to return to bed. A heavy yoke, such
as is used when oxen are harnessed to a wagon lay on the
floor by the door. He reached down and took hold of it.
"I will kill him who is God's servant and then I will be
hanged for it and go to hell." he whispered to himself and

the fever of his passion was so strong in him that the effect
of it left him ill for several days.

Since Danaghy [sic] has grown into a man he has married and has several children. Two of his sons are in college. His wife, a tall quiet woman with black eyes, is like
his father, inclined toward the religious life. Donoaghy [sic]
has little to do with her. He goes to his home often and
mutters prayers at the table when he is there for dinner.
He even subscribes to the support of a suburban church but
the home and the wife have in reality nothing to do with his
life.

In the city this man has made a number of strange
friends and with these he laughs, talks and delivers himself
of his pronouncements against religion, marriage and the other accepted institutions of our civilization. I see him often
in the company of a young Hebrew musician who has a shrill
voice and a French laboring man who works at the stock
yards but comes often to dine with Danaghy at some cafe in
the evening.

Columbus, O. Dec. 4, 1916.

I am in the station waiting for a train. A little mid-
dleaged woman in a brown velvet dress had the berth opposite me in the sleeper out of Chicago. I saw her in the
station there as we stood waiting by the gate in the train
shed. She was with a man who must be her lover. He was
tall and had blue eyes. He looked like a laborer who has
managed to rise out of the ranks of labor. Perhaps he is
an inventor working in steel. His hands were broad and
strong and about the nails I could see, in the strong light,
traces of machine oil.

I stood behind the couple in the train shed. He kept
patting the little woman on the arm and saying, "Never mind,
I will see you again soon." The woman wept and kissed the
sleeve of his coat.

This morning at Columbus another man was waiting
for the woman. He is small and nervous and has red eyes
and nose. He is surely her husband. They had breakfast
together at the station and I sat at the same table. He ate
greedily and with his mouth full of food scolded. "What did
you want to stop in Chicago for?" he asked. "Why didn't

you come on home?"

        The woman was pale and looked old. When she drank
coffee her hand trembled. "Ah, home! Be quiet. You talk
too much." she said.

        An old soldier who wears a long grey beard sits be-
side me as I write. He is smoking a cheap cigar that does
not burn evenly. It is singeing his mustache. He is angry
and keeps spitting and swearing but he does not throw the
cigar away.

December 5, 1916
[Tiffany 1]

        I know a man here who is now forty years old. For
fifteen years we have been acquainted and he occasionally
comes to visit me. Of recent years I have seen him but
seldom and until last night he has not been in my room to
sit for an hour's talk for more than six months.

        My friend's name is Alfred Tiffany and he comes
from Indiana. When he was a boy his father ran a saw mill
and wood yard in the town where they lived. He had one
brother who has now become a farmer.

        When young Tiffany first came here to the city there
was something very fine and delicate about his character.
I knew him well then and often in the evening we walked and
talked together. For a time he was a great hero to me.
One spring he threw up his place as clerk in a wholesale
shoe house and went west on an adventure. How well I remember that evening. I boarded a street car and went with
him to Hammond, Indiana. It was a warm rainy night and
we went along the tracks and crouched in the shadow of a
fence. When a freight train came along he climbed aboard.
I sat in the darkness and wept because I could not go also.

        For a year he stayed in the west and when he came
back got a place in the office of a well-known advertising
man. Gradually a change took place in his nature.

        It was during the year after he had come from his
western adventure that I enjoyed my friend the most. I had

also become and [sic] advertising writer and we met often
at lunch but that didn't count.   I lived then as I do now just
outside the business district on the north side and he came
often to dine with me.   How fine and upstanding he was.   We
had both of us, small salaries and we cooked the dinner over
a small oil stove.   There would be tea and cakes and perhaps eggs or bacon; then pipes and talk.

        Alfred talked fervently.   He walked up and down the
room with his eyes shining and his shoulders thrown back
telling me of nights spent in the company of tramps at the
edge of some village in the west; of long days spent in western wheat fields; of a girl in men's clothes who once rode
all day with him in an empty car and a hundred other adventures.

        Alfred has changed.   He was here in my room last
night and I could have wept when he went away.   At forty
life and the old love of life has almost gone out of him.   In
his hour of ease now he is nervous and his eyes that once
sparkled with excitement roam listlessly about.   He has
acquired a dozen vulgar little habits.   He picks at the lobe
of his ear with his finger nails.   When he talks he puts his
hand before his mouth and laughs shyly.   He dresses in expensive clothes and wears shoes made by a fashionable shoe-
maker but he no longer is the handsome fellow who came
from the western adventure and who used to strut before me
telling of the things he had done and intended to do.

        Alfred is making money.   That is the trouble with
him.   He has listened to the talk of getting on that goes on
among the men here.   He still believes in a childish sort of
way that presently he will be rich and will go adventuring
again, not realizing that the last fifteen years have made a
different man of him.   Now his adventures, if he adventures
at all, will be the adventures of his class.   He will go with
an actress to dinner at the Blackstone.   Some night when he
has been drinking a woman of the town will give him a disease.   He will begin soon to grow fat and bald.   He will
know the headwaitress at the most expensive eating places
but he will not know how the wind scolds and talks among
the dry corn blades in the western fields at night or how the
heart of a boy thumps as he crouches by a fence in the darkness of a rainy night, waiting to leap aboard a passing
freight train and go bravely away into the unknown.

December 5, 1916
[Tiffany 2]

It is ten o'clock and has begun to rain. Every one
has gone away. Only one candle is burning and the wind
tosses the flame so that the grease falls on the table. I am
thinking of Alfred Tiffany who was here last night. I must
tell you a tale of him in his earlier days, tell it in memory
of the part of him that was my friend and that has died; tell
it in memory of the beautiful boy who is becoming a successful man.

There was a girl came here from England who was a
designer of gowns. She did not look in the least English but
was small and dark. Like the emperor of Germany she had
a withered arm that she kept always concealed.

This woman was in some way related to the advertising man for whom Alfred worked when he had just come home
from his adventures as a tramp. They met at a dinner given
for ten or twelve people in a north side restaurant.

In those days Alfred was always excited. His straight
young body was a store house of energy. The people at the
table were members of our American middle class, people
who had money. They talked and drank heavily in a dull effort to be lively and engaging.

Alfred looked at the little English girl beside him and
began to talk to her. He grew confidential and told her of
an adventure that came to him one evening out west. Something in her sharp little face awoke a vein of sadness in him
and the sadness made him talk well. He was capable of being sensitive to people then. He told her of a girl he had
seen in a farmhouse in North Dakota. He had stopped there
for the night, had helped do chores about the farm for his
supper and lodging and as darkness came on sat with his
back against the wall of the barn looking across the fields.

A woman came to be [sic] barn to milk the cows.
She was about thirty and had broad shoulders. When she
saw Alfred she stopped and smiled.

The night was warm and Alfred continued to sit in the
darkness by the barn. He heard the milk striking against
the sides of the tin milk bucket and the voice of the woman.
She passed him again, going to the house. [A]nd then all

was quiet.

Hours passed and the young man did not move. He had been told he could sleep on the hay in the barn loft but he did not feel like sleep. Suddenly in the darkness he saw something white and the voice of the woman called softly, "Young man[,]" she called. "Young man[.] Where are you?"

The farm woman in the white night robe sat down beside Alfred on the ground and put her hand into his. It was roughened by toil. Nothing happened. Presently she whispered and made him understand why she had come. The farm house was isolated and she was terribly lonely. In touching Alfred's hand she felt she touched the hand of the world. She had crept out of bed, where her husband slept and had risked the whole future of her life as a wife by her action.

This simple tale told by the Alfred of long ago had a strange effect upon the English girl. She fell in love with him. He did not know that at the time but he found out later.

One day Alfred got a note from the English girl inviting him to go with her for a two days vacation with some friends who had taken a house for the summer on the eastern shore of the lake. "My Aunt and her two daughters are there[,]" the note said. "We will go on the boat Friday evening. I have been there before so I will make all arrangements. You have but to come to the dock at the foot of Dearborn Street. My brother who lives here will take me to the boat. All arrangements will be made. You have but to walk up and down on the dock until I come. Write me if you intend to go. "

The details of that evening on the boat with the English woman as told by Alfred long ago have passed from my mind. I remember that he had no notion of making love to her, had not thought of such a thing but that she had so arranged as to make love-making almost inevitable. She had only engaged one state room and as soon as the brother went away she took Alfred aboard the boat and told him. He was worried and spoke of the danger to her, of his fears that she might be seen by someone who knew her, that she might become with child and so forth. She only laughed and stroked the sleeve of his coat with her well hand.

There must have been something tremendously touching and unforgettable about that love-making. I remember
vividly the figure of my friend standing in my room later
and talking of it and the picture he made of himself sitting
on a stool beside her berth, holding her thin little hand
while he looked through the port hole at the night over the
sea[.] "She sobbed and sobbed[,]" he said. "with her well-
hand she clung to me and almost forced me to get into bed
with her. When I yielded she wept with joy. Later I found
out that she wanted to have a child, was ready to risk everything to bring that about. She knew I would never make love
to her again and she had fallen in love with me. She wanted
everything to take that night. When she sobbed in such a
broken hearted way it was partly from depth of feeling but
it was mostly from fear that the terrible, beautiful, for-
bidden thing she wanted would not come to pass. "

It seems to me that Alfred Tiffany has grown old,
that he is dead. I do not blame him. I do not believe he
has killed himself. I think modern American industrial life
has done it. Perhaps his mind was not strong enough to
resist the insidious daily suggestion borne into his ears by
thousands of voices around him. Perhaps the thing he had
in him long ago when the farm woman came to sit beside
him and when the English girl tried at one swift sudden
stroke to win a child from him had to be lost.

I know nothing of the reasons for the change in Alfred. I only know he is changed and that I hope not to see
him again. Last night I asked him again of the English girl
but he wanted to talk of one evening he had spent at the
["]Bismark [sic] Gardens. " "I have forgotten! Did she have
the child? " I asked. "Why do you harp on that? " [sic]
The woman was a fool and so was I then. I almost decided
to marry her. It might have turned out a regular mess.
I'm glad enough to forget it. Why not let it alone? "

Appendix M

CHICAGO REVIEWS OF WINESBURG, OHIO

1. "The Unroofing of Winesburg, Tales of Life that Seem Overheard Rather than Written, " The Friday Literary Review, Chicago Evening Post, June 6, 1919, page 11, column 3.

Sherwood Anderson once published a short story in Harper's Magazine, of which I remarked in a brief note that it betrayed the hand of the novelist rather than that of the short story writer--and I was afterward told by its author that he wrote it on a bet that he could get it accepted by Harper's. He had simply taken the kind of characters that he knew how to portray and immersed them in enough of a plot to make the thing "go" for magazine story purposes.

But when Anderson did produce two novels it became evident that his genius ran to the episodes, after all, rather than to the novelistic form. His first novel, "Windy Mc-Pherson's Son, " began with a splendid character delineation and then took the son--perhaps not so well realized a character as the father--thru a number of episodes. And "Marching Men" consisted purely of a character well limned and then made the central figure in what was, after all, only one great episode.

Now comes a volume of short stories, connected in place and in person, "Winesburg, Ohio, " and it is increasingly evident that one's judgment of Anderson's story in Harper's Magazine is in part right. Anderson is not a short story writer in so far as that implies a man who can handle the form of the short story. His metier is rather the--to qualify what alone would sound like a trifle--significant episode. Here, for example, are a number of episodes in the lives of dwellers in a small Ohio town, in a country where farming and berry-growing and merchandising occupy the

people.   They have no form in the sense of artifice--a bad
sense in which to use the word, however.   To be more accurate they have no pattern.   Artistic form they have in that
each episode in its outer garb reflects and presents some
emotional reality.

It was in one of Barrie's early books that I first read
the remark, which other people have also made, that genius
is the ability to prolong one's childhood.   Sherwood Anderson
has in these pages given a remarkable proof of his power to
hold in a realm of the mind more intimate than memory the
very feel of what his own youth must have been and the inner
aspects also of all the youth, the age, the whole psychic
atmosphere of this Ohio town.   He has not merely remembered the peculiarities of the townsfolk and made stories of
them, he has in a manner peculiar altogether to himself
managed to stay in the center of each little town tragedy or
comedy--and he tells you about it.   He does not write these
stories--the writing seems an accident.   A writer would
have patterned and transformed the tales.   Sherwood Anderson lets you overhear him telling the tales--telling them to
himself or to the moon, very often.   What writer would tell
you a story with this content?   A drunkard comes to Winesburg and, sitting before the hotel, bestows a name--Tandy--
a symbolical name which he has made up to represent an
ideal for a woman--upon a little 7-year-old girl who is sitting on her father's knee.   He has missed love, and he tells
this child that he might have loved.   Then he goes away, but
the child, taken by the name he has bestowed upon her, in-
sists upon its possession.

How slight and fugitive and unimportant that is in
prose.   And yet what a significant poem Mr. Anderson has
made out of the telling of it.   And most of the tales in this
book have that strange air of seeming consequence that only
life has, that conscious art strives so hard to avoid.   More
than once, for instance, Mr. Anderson shows us an "affair"
brewing between some village man and maiden, and then a
tremor of the soul or an almost imperceptible zephyr of circumstance intervenes.   And the story as the reader had tried
to imagine it in advance fades away.   Nothing is left but the
revelation of some living soul's thought and feeling for a
brief time.

Cooped up in this small Ohio town with no outlets for
spiritual endeavor and only more or less accidental outlets
for passion it is not surprising that sex repression and sex

outbursts should play a relatively large part in the dramas
--or should, to be more exact, create whirlpools of drama
out of the quiet currents--of Winesburg life. So the reader
must not be surprised to meet that sort of thing frankly
treated in Mr. Anderson's book. (The author will pardon
my warning to the timid, I am sure.)

Once or twice in the course of these tales I wondered
if the plowmen and the small souls of the town would gener-
alize "life" as a force that had them in its grip as Mr. Anderson has them do. It has seemed to me rather that such
an expression as "tricked by life" or that boy's reaction who
stole, was ashamed of his reaction and then said: "It is all
right to be ashamed and make me understand new things, "
savors of a more thought-out and aggressive self-conscious-
ness than these people would be likely to exhibit. But perhaps we may safely take Mr. Anderson's report in the matters. For if he has fabricated his tale in anything else than
the merest scaffolding, he has done so in a way that no other American author and few British writings have done. In
fact, his honesty is just as human as that of Tchekoff at his
most sympathetic--although there is none of the Russian's
conscious short-story art.

So far, then, we have in this book Sherwood Anderson's best work. In emphasizing its most characteristic
quality I have neglected to add that the author is sometimes
visible, and does criticize life from his own point of view
in the course of his tales. But one's main impression of the
book is not derived from that, but from the actual souls who
wander so aimlessly and with so random and revealing greatness as one sees them thru his window--uncurtained with so
careless a gesture--in the firmament over Winesburg.

Llewellyn Jones

2. "Winesburg, Ohio" by Burton Rascoe, The Chicago Daily
    Tribune, Saturday, June 7, 1919, page 13, columns 1-
    2. Reprinted by permission of the Chicago Tribune.

Comparison of Sherwood Anderson's new book, "WINES-
BURG, OHIO, " and "The Spoon River Anthology" is rather
inevitable, possibly so inevitable that it may be questioned

whether the analogy is entirely legitimate. The prevailing
tone of Mr. Anderson's prose tales and of Mr.
Masters' mephitic monologues is gray; both books are concerned with
life in small midwestern communities a couple of decades or
so ago; and in each there is a very justifiable recognition of
the motivating force of sex in the life of all sentient creatures, among whom is not included, of course, the hurt and
vegetative organism of an eastern paper who referred to love
as portrayed by Mr. Anderson as "obscene acts. "

But to press the likeness further would, I think, lead
into the difficulties encountered in the linking of any two
quite dissimilar things. The temperaments of the two men
are widely at variance and their literary method is no less
so. Mr. Masters says, in short, "Here are human beings
for you! What embeciles [sic], groveling, hopeless vermin
they are!" Mr. Anderson says in effect[,] "Here are the
human beings of whom I am one. Even our errors, our
grossest weaknesses have about them something of tragic
beauty. Are we not worthy of your sympathy no less than
of your disgust? Isn't it possible that you, too, are one of
us--a human being for whom unhappiness means frustrated
desire, to whom life is a perturbing mystery, in whom there
is a spiritual impulse to be 'good' which is plagued and
balked by a natural urgency at times to be otherwise?" Into
the soul of Mr. Masters the iron has sank; he is bitter, re-
proachful, and removed. In Mr. Anderson there is fraternal
pity and a lonely tender feeling of participation in human
destiny.

Of course, both Mr. Masters and Mr. Anderson are
right.... They are right for life itself is a point of view;
and one's enjoyment of life and literature is dependent upon
the catholicity of one's tastes, one's capacity for partaking
of it and benefiting from points of view differing from one's
own.

_____

Than with "The Spoon River Anthology, " it seems to
me that a comparison of "Winesburg, Ohio" with the Russians,
Chekhov and Dostoevski, is a more suitable one. Unques-
tionably, Mr. Anderson's book will offend a great number of
readers, many of whom are quite willing to admit that Chekhov and Dostoevski, being Russian, are great and significant
writers. These people, too, it is likely, are among the
numerous derogators of our native literature who frequently

ask why America does not produce writers of the caliber to
be found abroad.   The answer is that for the most part
America does, and in far greater numbers than the reading
public is entitled to; for the closer an American approxi-
mates the literary excellence of Europe, the more shameless
is the nation's neglect of him.

Mr. Anderson's unified series of stories in "Winesburg, Ohio," possess actually for Americans not only a
higher literary value than any one volume of Chekhov, but
in interpretation and relation of a phase of our national life
of far greater importance to us than the stories of Russian
life in Chekov's day can ever be.   If I was asked to name
half a dozen contemporary indigenous products of American
literature for translation abroad, I should name Mr. Anderson's book as one of them.   The Russian life that we read
about in translations from Chekov was a thing of the past
even before war; it relates to conditions vastly changed even
before the fall of czarism.   The American life Europeans
would read about in a translation of these Winesburg stories
obtains in a certain degree in every small town throughout
the United States at the present time.

Mr. Anderson has in this book eclipsed the excellence
he achieved in his novel, "Windy McPherson's Son." Its
form is something of an innovation; he has, with much the
continuity of a novel, written a series of complete short
stories in which the same characters recur at different
times.   As a result we have the fluid illusion of life, together with the heightened drama of it, the relation of character in crucial flashes instead of by arduous development,
the selection of incident without the detail that is part of the
method of the novel, a group portrait of a community in an
interwoven series of stories.

It is to Mr. Anderson's artistic credit, too, that he
frequently suggests rather than depicts; that he respects the
imaginative faculty of his reader by refusing to be explicit
wherever overtones of emotion are already involved by the
reader; that he is selective, indefinite and provocative instead of inclusive, precise, and explanatory.   He, one of the
most personal and subjective of writers, has in these stories
achieved a fine effect of impersonality.

His personal ethics or beliefs obtrude, I think, but

once, and that is the one unconvincing and manufactured story in the book--the story of the preacher who at night peeped through the window of his study into the bedroom of the pretty school teacher and afterwards delivered impassioned sermons on human frailty and temptation.

These stories are practically all concerned chiefly with the sex life of the inhabitants of the Ohio-village--of the doctor, the bartender, the school teacher, the young reporter, the hired girl, the bumpkin lad, the village "sport," the woman hater--of every one in this drab community, where there was little incentive to sublimited [sic] desire, and where emotion was all the more intense for being defeated and repressed at every turn.

There the rigid old Puritan ethic, to which this community owes at once so much of good and evil, was an ineradicable and saving instinct and yet an instinct constantly at war with the instinct for mating; the conflict itself produces drama of an intensely poignant kind, romance of effective and realistic beauty. The awakening of sex in the idealistic youth; the harassing desire for love and companionship that obsessed the lonely school teacher, the simple surrender of the ignorant young girl; all these constantly recurrent incidents of life are told with sympathy, skill, and sincerity.

Mr. Anderson is frequently crude in his employment of English, he has not a sense of word values; but he has an intense vision of life; he is a cautious and interpretive observer; and he has recorded here a bit of life which could rank him with the most important contemporary writers in this country. He may not be, as some one called him, the American Dostoevski, but he is the American Sherwood Anderson.

3. "Sherwood Anderson," Chicago Daily News, June 11, 1919, page 12, columns 5-6. Reprinted with permission from the Chicago Daily News.

It is so easy to make comparisons. Really, of course, nothing into which the human element has gone is very similar to anything else. But there are certain general

likenesses, and perhaps I may be pardoned if I compare
Sherwood Anderson with some of his fellows.

Anderson; Theodore Dreiser; Willard Huntington
Wright. Read "A Man of Promise"; read "The Genius";
then read "Windy McPherson's Son. " There is some uncanny
insight into the secret coigns of the soul, the same almost
fiendish dexterity in hounding out the most furtive thoughts;
the hidden wishes that man hesitates to admit even to himself. Wright, however, always remains cruelly unaffected
by the spectacle, he devotes himself to his task as would a
great surgeon, and one is awed by the skillfulness of the
beautiful, cold blooded perfection. Dreiser goes to the other
extreme; he feels so deeply about the whole affair; he is
blinded, as it were, by his tears so that you feel sometimes
as though the knife had slipped and was cutting Dreiser himself.

Anderson is perhaps, halfway between the two. He
does not become so worked up that he is seized with Dreiser's almost hysterical incoherence nor has he Wright's icy
detachment. He pities, the business hurts him, yet the job
must be done, and he does it with precision.

Such a piece of work is "Winesburg, Ohio, " Anderson's latest volume. In this collection of sketches and short
stories Anderson has gone far beneath the surface of a small
town's life, and has penetrated to the seething heart of it.

To the casual observer there is nothing nastier, nothing more hopeless than the American small town which has
"gone to seed. " The town which boasts my alma mater had
a population of about 2, 000 in 1812. One hundred years
later, in 1912, this town contained only 1800. And I was
told by the principal of the high school that out of fifty girls
in his graduating class that year no fewer than five were in
what the euphuists [sic] call "an interesting condition. "

Our casual observer sees in such a town merely a
disgusting, degenerate group of "rubes. " Anderson knows
and understands these people. He shows you the tortured
consciences, the thwarted hopes and dreams, the magnificent
potential energy conquered by insidious inaction that keeps
them all in the same old rut, despite their longings. What
you get in "Winesburg, Ohio, " is a panorama, with minds
in place of houses.

What Dostoievsky, Andreyev, Gogol have done for Russia Anderson has done for America. But the Russia of those writers is manifestly out of date; it is a Russia of the days of serfdom. Anderson's Winesburg is the small town of today, this minute.

I put the proposition to you; Compare Sherwood Anderson with those admittedly great Russian interpreters, and see if you consider Anderson as great as they.

There has always been great hue and cry over "the great American novel." "Why does nobody arise to produce it?" "Why have we no true interpreter of America?" and what not. Edgar Lee Masters approaches it with "Spoon River," but he has not made good the promise he showed, and apparently never will if his "Doomsday Book" is a sample of his future output. Dreiser, great though he be, is nevertheless too illiterate and too sentimental. Wright has not enough true feeling. But Anderson--If the great American novel ever arrives, he will bring it.

By
J. V. A. Weaver

4. "Civilian Communique," Chicago Daily News, September 3, 1919, page 6, columns 4-5. Reprinted with permission from the Chicago Daily News.

Chicago Illinois--"Don Euriguez mi amigo muy querido." Have a look at Sherwood Anderson's "Winesburg, Ohio." Here's a fine rainy afternoon of gossip set down in the pat phrases of the sewing circle and the party whirl. Here's a record of what the members of the ladies aid society always wanted to know about the real reason for Mrs. Applegate's visits to the doctor's office and what led to the engagement of the girl around the corner who paints and powders.

And little else.

Sherwood Anderson's friends claim for this "Winesburg, Ohio" the force of what questionable translations from the Russians are supposed to be[:] typical literature of the country where it is always house cleaning time. Not so! In "Winesburg, Ohio" Anderson falls short of being a Maumee Tchekoff by at least three murders, two criminal assaults and a suicide.

Other friends ballyhoo that from this source will come "the great American novel. " Nonsense! If such stuff makes the great American novel we have that precious volume already in the latest report of the psychopathic hospital, and the history of the world has for its author Dr. P. von Kraft-Ebing.

Anderson has nosed out from the Winesburg population the subjects most intriguing to the psychophysical, the juggler of weird neuroses. He describes their least pleasant symptoms in the terms of Little Red Riding Hood.

In fact so labored is his simplicity that at the beginning one gets the picture of a patient, plump uncle telling his nieces and nephews long fireside stories. But no uncle would attempt these Winesburg gossipings as bedtime tales for juveniles--not even in this day when the "adults only" sign lures our youngsters to a broader if not a higher education.

The collection of small town sketches calls to mind the deplorable Jukes family, still the favorite of the barking statistician to prove the hereditary horrors made possible by the mating of a thoroughly undesirable male to even a less desirable female. All this revealed in a style marred by hefty platitude--for instance, the sententious declaration that railroads[,] newspapers and other developments have made quite a difference in this country since the civil war. Another instance, the observation that after all country folks and city folks think and speak a great deal alike.

It is marred, too, by tricks having the feel of laziness. He falls back from the work of establishing characters with a futile wish for the pen of a poet or the assertion that it really would take an entire novel to do justice to the subject in hand.

Despite these faults of delivery and craftsmanship there are splendid bits in the book--the simple report of youth in his first "romance" for one; the cruel irony of the two tales, "The Strength of God" and "The Teacher" for another. Larded with the whiskey platitudes are encouraging

slices of writing streaks here and there, which one hopes indicate what Anderson really can do when he rolls back his
sleeves and dashes off the American novel his friends are
megaphoning.

But always it goes back to the same monotonous level.
Always it returns to a decadent exposure of strange neurotics
and the search for the wen and the wart on the face of humanity. The only young woman in the village left by Anderson and the Winesburg males is the daughter of the town
banker. Not a surprising fact to one acquainted with the
chastity of such young ladies through the pages of Horatio
Alger and Oliver Optic.

It is palpable that in drafting such a criticism as this
one bends over invitingly to a Chaplin kick from those who
will look upon it as raving puritanism.

But this is not written in shocked indignation. One
who has scanned the report of the Chicago vice commission
--1911--the volume was the gift of a bishop--one who is
familiar with the analysis of Dr. William A. Hammond; one
who has witnessed a private exhibition of the censor's movie
cutouts--such a one will not shrink from "Winesburg, Ohio,"
except per chance in ennui.

And as an evidence of friendliness and good wishes
for future Andersonia, it is suggested that Anderson devote
himself next time to some Illinois town. A traveling insur-
ance man once informed me that the insanity rate on the
Illinois prairies is higher than in any other state in the union.

Wallace Smith

Appendix N

COMMENT OF FLOYD DELL

(Mr. Floyd Dell graciously agreed, though harassed by illness, to read that part of the manuscript of The Road to Winesburg which specifically dealt with the relationship between him and Anderson. The following two illuminating letters resulted. Page references are to manuscript.

July 16, 1964
[first letter]

Dear Sutton:

I have read an account of the way some Russian academicians dealt with a map of Bering's explorations. There was another map, quite different, and the Russian academicians, following what is said to have been their standard procedure drew up a map which combined the Bering map and the other map as far as possible, and replaced both to some extent with a third map which was betwixt and between them. Bering's map was a true map, the other map was a false map, and the academy concoction was a preposterous fabrication. So far as I can judge by the pages you send me, you have worked in the spirit of those dead-and-gone Russian academicians. You (apparently) don't take my account of certain events, you prefer Sherwood's account, and you jumble them up.

It may be true that Sherwood was introduced to a group of artists in Chicago by his brother Karl in 1913; but I never heard this; you don't name the artists in Chicago to whom Karl introduced him. (Jerome Blum is the only artist in the list of nine persons called representative in a footnote on your p. 17 [note 54, end of Ch. 9, Sect. C.]) Margery Currey's name was spelled this way, not as it is in your text and Lucian Cary's name this way. (I hope you don't

607

regard Sherwood's misspellings as sacred.) Incidentally, the apartments of Margery Currey and me were not adjoining, being around the corner from each other. I have read a letter written by Harriet Monroe about a party in my studio at which Arthur Ficke read his sonnets; but I had forgotten the party, and I think I am right in saying that it was not a custom of the writers I knew to read their latest writings at parties; and I don't believe that Sherwood ever read any of his writings at a party while I was in Chicago. (This was a custom of French writers, never of American writers.)

May I suggest that "an atmosphere of ferment" in these gatherings is an unfortunate phrase?

I think that Sherwood became acquainted with the Seven Arts group after coming to New York and not through the Chicago group. This Seven Arts group acquaintanceship may have come about simply through my suggesting to Sherwood that he send his things to that magazine. (I knew Randolph Bourne, Waldo Frank, and others of the Seven Arts group.) But Sherwood was subsequently anxious to disavow any ties with me and he would probably not have agreed that I had anything to do with his Seven Arts fame.

Surely Robert Morss Lovett has mixed his dates in regard to Anderson's seeming to be "the proletarian writer for whom we were on the lookout." This "proletarian" business dates from a later time than 1913. And if Lovett in 1941 still thought that Anderson had been a house-painter, then he could think anything about anybody.

"Just how Dell came to know about Anderson as a writer is," you say, "subject to different accounts." This, if you don't mind my saying so, is not good English according to my notions. Be that as it may, surely "Dell thought" should be "Dell thinks it likely that Margery Currey showed him" etc. And "Frank thinks" etc. I feel some amazement at the idea that the writing of a long novel should be a "secret." You presently go on: "Suffice it to say that Dell became enough involved in the publication of Windy McPherson's Son for Anderson to call him his literary father******"

What do you mean, "enough involved in the publication" of Windy? Publication was long delayed, and the idea of my being his "literary father" began in the summer of 1913, as his other remarks show. Here, apparently, you are trying to say and at the same time partly deny that I

got his first novel published. The way it comes out, you
indistinctly mumble that I had something to do with the book's
publication. A little later, on top of p. 70, you quote Sherwood (letter to Freitag, 1938) as saying of Dell: "He, with
Mr. Theodore Dreiser, was instrumental in getting my first
book published." I take it that you believe this statement of
Sherwood's. Take note then that I deny it. I have published
a clear and detailed account of my finally sending the MS of
Windy to John Lane, who accepted it. Dreiser did not come
into it, except that Lane was publishing or going to publish
Dreiser. At some time after that transaction, Sherwood decided to alter the facts and have Dreiser get him a publisher.
He began to tell people that it was Dreiser who got Windy
published. This wasn't true. It was one of Sherwood's
transmogrifications of fact to suit his neurotic purposes.
And you try to combine my recital of fact with Sherwood's
falsehood. It won't do. You can't say that Peary and Dr.
Cook somehow between them discovered the North Pole. You
have to decide which story is true and recognize that the
other story is false. In a wishy-washy way, you try to hang
on to Sherwood's falsehood without quite rejecting my account.
No, it won't do. If you seriously doubted my statement, you
could have written to John Lane. But you wish to accept
Sherwood's account. You can't do so with my permission.
In my review of Sherwood Anderson's Memoirs, in Herald-
Tribune Books, April 12, 1942, I wrote: "Most of the facts
reported in his memoirs, so far as I have knowledge of
them, are confused, distorted, or simply untrue. He never
could distinguish facts from fancies; he freely fictionized his
own life and that of other people, not only in fiction as such
but in accounts about people under their real names." And
I quote from this same book of Memoirs: "When I deal in
facts, at once I begin to lie. I can't help it." This review,
as published, is one of the main documents to be used in any
account of my friendship with Sherwood, if it is to bring in
my testimony. Another main document is my piece "On Being Sherwood Anderson's Literary Father," as published in
the Newberry Bulletin. You are mistaken in thinking that
you can ignore these documents. You do not have the privilege of turning aside from them and quoting other letters
and scraps. The penalty of evasion is that your account
looks fishy and raises the question: "What are you trying
to do?" Something, apparently, besides tell the truth, but
why not just tell the truth? It is all too plain that Sherwood
told fanciful lies about himself and others. You can't successfully hush it up. You don't have to believe him when he
invents things, tells lies--you are duty bound to spot his lies.

Is your judgment really so poor that you can't tell when
Sherwood is lying?   It is not true that when I read the
Winesburg stories stories I "condemned them heartily. "   It
is not true, it is absolutely not true, that I advised him to
"throw the Winesburg stories away. "   Again, top of p. 21,
letter of Anderson to Waldo Frank.   It is not true when he
wrote: "I can remember reading it to Floyd Dell, and it
made him hopping mad.   'It's damn rot, ' says Floyd.   'It
doesn't get anywhere'. "   All this happened in Sherwood's
mind--never in reality.   Let me say categorically that I
never spoke or wrote like that to Sherwood about his writing.
Is that clear?   Floyd never said or wrote to Sherwood about
this story or any other, saying: "It's damn rot. "   Never,
never.   Sometimes these neurotic falsifications of Sherwood
have some relation to facts.   I wrote to Sherwood that in an
editorial meeting, when some story of his was read aloud,
it was voted down, and I summarized some criticisms in the
statement "They say it doesn't get anywhere. "   This criticism
indicates that a story is a certain type of story--the type that
came to be associated with the name of Checkhov, especially
as compared with the Maupassant type, which came to a
point that was dramatic and important.   Sherwood chose to
take this criticism as my criticism; he wished to blame me
for the refusal of The Masses to publish any more of his
stories (after "Hands").   And he wrote back to me saying
something like this: "The story gets to where it is going
but you aren't there to meet it. "   There is a muddled version of that retort in the letter to Freitag, top of p. 20--
"If you plan to go somewhere on a train, " etc.   In this muddled form the retort seems meaningless, though Sherwood
refers to it as "arrogant * * * but arrogance was needed. "
In that same letter I am quoted as saying that in a story
there must be a beginning and an end.   Now at that time I
was eagerly and earnestly reading the stories of Checkhov
and trying to formulate in my mind (and sometimes in print)
what their particular values were.   When I discussed those
stories with Sherwood (or anybody else) I was likely to say
that I was inclined to agree with Aristotle in thinking that a
story or play should have a beginning, a middle, and an end.
I still feel that way and am likely to say so.   But I know
now and knew then that some other people preferred the other
kind of story.   Did I ever advise Sherwood or anybody else
to throw stories away that they had written?   No.   Never,
never.   You, Bill Sutton, evidently believe that I talked and/
or wrote that way to Sherwood.   You are mistaken.   You
seem inclined to believe anything Sherwood wrote about me.
I think you should be more careful.   Perhaps you just don't

know the way some people distort facts. I described the way
Sherwood did so in my piece in the Newberry Bulletin, especially with regard to his coming to parties at Margery Currey's Studio. I heard of his giving accounts to various persons of hearing people inside saying "Sherwood will never be
a writer." (I do not invent these people nor what they told
me.)--You quote from a letter to Waldo Frank in which Sherwood sympathizes with him on account of what he refers to
as Dell's "trite and offhand treatment" of Waldo's novel. No
quotations are given from this review. I would bet a nickel
that quotations would not show anything either trite or offhand
in my treatment of Waldo's novel.

I am puzzled by some of your sentences which are,
in position, introductory to quotations but which do not have
the relation suggested by their position. On page 21 you
say, "Perhaps Dell was too frank, as possibly suggested by
this situation"--but what follows seems to me not to have
any possible relation to frankness (it is about a writer, making money). On bottom of p. 21 and top of 22 is your comment on Sherwood and me, in which Anderson's violent and
preposterous attack on me in the pseudo-dedication is referred to as a "negative" response--a strange wording which,
so far as I can see, comes from your unwillingness to see
Sherwood's behavior in simple and familiar terms--it has to
be fancied up. "Negative" response indeed! My remarks
came too late to be of use to you, but that is not my fault.
Your thesis may very well have merits which compensate for
its faults. In any case, I suppose that your mistaken ideas
about Sherwood and me are too deeply rooted for these brief
comments to eradicate. Some day, I expect you will learn
what a certain type of person (such as Sherwood) is like; the
experience will be painful, but perhaps a bit less so because
you will remember that Floyd Dell told you this a long time
ago, only at that time you couldn't believe him. You will be
fortunate if you are the type of person who, having been
treated badly, can call it quits rather than come back to be
treated badly again and again. It may be that I am mistaken
about your being prone to victimization by a certain kind of
"genius." But I am not mistaken about matters within my
own experience that I clearly remember.

Best wishes,

Floyd Dell

July 23, 1964
[second letter]

Dear Sutton:

Yes, you may use my letter about Sherwood Anderson
and me as an appendix or in any other way you wish.

If its publication helps to make Anderson better understood by those who write about him I should be pleased but
surprised.

This is the first time I have seen any letters from
him purporting to quote me.   I would have said "not true"
if I had seen them before.   But I have heard many reports
of things like that said by Sherwood about me.

Despite these things, I remember Sherwood as a very
attractive and likeable fellow.   I enjoyed his company and
conversation very much that summer of 1913.

Yours,

Floyd Dell

Appendix O

COMMENTS OF WALDO FRANK

(Mr. Waldo Frank wrote the following after reading the pages
of the manuscript of The Road to Winesburg dealing specifically with the relationship between him and Anderson.   Since
the effect of the relationship is reflected in many other parts
of the book, Mr. Frank is not reacting here to the total
impression created.)

July 30 64
Truro, Mass.

Dear Professor Sutton,

I've read the pages you sent me.   I do not know exactly what comment you wish me to make.   Everything you
cite from the letters is doubtless faithfully rendered and yet
the final effect is false.   This was inevitable, since a collection of details necessarily fragmentary does not add up to
the organic whole.   Thus, the comment in (37) is certainly
out of focus.   To place it properly in context would have required far more extended treatment.   There was much that
simply could not be said, given the time and the place.   A
biography or a full consideration in literary criticism would
have had to include the works of the two men and their characters; and above all (since your subject is S. A.) his shifts
of judgment, according to the nature and opinions of the
specific correspondent.   For A. had a way of playing his
friends off, one against the other.   (All this, of course, I
left out in the WBAI interview.)

I hope you have good luck with your book and find a
Publisher for it.

sincerely,

Waldo Frank

613

BIBLIOGRAPHY

Books

1. Anderson, Sherwood, Dark Laughter, New York, Boni and Liveright, 1925.

2. Anderson, Sherwood, Harlan Miners Speak, New York, Harcourt, 1932.

3. Anderson, Sherwood, Hello Towns, New York, Liveright, 1929.

4. Anderson, Sherwood, Horses and Men, New York, Huebsch, 1923.

5. Anderson, Sherwood, Letters of Sherwood Anderson, edited by Howard Mumford Jones and Walter Rideout. Boston, Little, Brown, 1953.

6. Anderson, Sherwood, Many Marriages, New York, Huebsch, 1923.

7. Anderson, Sherwood, Marching Men, New York, John Lane, 1917.

8. Anderson, Sherwood, Mid-American Chants, New York, John Lane, 1918.

9. Anderson, Sherwood, Perhaps Women, New York, Liveright, New York, 1935.

10. Anderson, Sherwood, Puzzled America, New York, Scribner's, 1935.

11. Anderson, Sherwood, Sherwood Anderson's Memoirs, New York, Harcourt, Brace, 1942.

12. Anderson, Sherwood, Sherwood Anderson's Notebook,

New York, Boni and Liveright, 1926.

13. Anderson, Sherwood, The Sherwood Anderson Reader, (Edited by Paul Rosenfeld), Boston, Houghton, Mifflin, 1947.

14. Anderson, Sherwood, A Story Teller's Story, New York, Huebsch, 1924.

15. Anderson, Sherwood, Tar: A Midwest Childhood, New York, Boni and Liveright, 1926.

16. Anderson, Sherwood, Triumph of the Egg, New York, Huebsch, 1921.

17. Anderson, Sherwood, Windy McPherson's Son, New York, John Lane, 1917 [(c) 1916]; and Huebsch, 1922.

18. Anderson, Sherwood, Winesburg, Ohio, New York, Huebsch, 1919.

19. Anderson, Tennessee Mitchell, Untitled autobiographical fragment of 77 pages in the Newberry Library.

20. Asbury, Herbert, Gem of the Prairie, New York, Knopf, 1940.

21. Axline, Henry A., Adjutant General's Report...., Norwalk, O., Laning Printing Co., 1897.

22. Bailey, A., The Herald's Directory to Mansfield, Ohio, 1883-4, Mansfield, O., Geo. U. Harn, 1883.

23. Brooks, Van Wyck, The Confident Years: 1885-1915, New York, Dutton, 1952.

24. Brooks, Van Wyck, Letters and Leadership, New York, Huebsch, 1918.

25. Burrow, Trigant, A Search for Man's Sanity, New York, Oxford University Press, 1958.

26. Dell, Floyd, Homecoming, New York, Farrar and Rinehart, 1933.

27. Dell, Floyd, Looking at Life, New York, Knopf, 1924.

28. Dinsmoor, Mary H. "An Inquiry into the Life of Sher-
    wood Anderson as Reflected in His Literary Works,"
    Unpublished M. A. Thesis, Athens, Ohio, Ohio
    University, 1939.

29. Directory of Clyde and Vicinity, Clyde, O., A. D.
    Ames, 1887.

30. Duffey, Bernard I., The Chicago Renaissance in Amer-
    ican Letters, East Lansing, Mich., Michigan State
    College Press, 1954.

31. Evans, Nelson W. and Emmons B. Stivers, History of
    Adams County, Ohio, West Union, O., E. B. Stiv-
    ers, 1900.

32. Evans, Capt. Nelson W., In Memorian: A Tribute of
    Respect to the Memory of the Deceased Soldiers of
    Adams County, Ohio..., Cincinnati, O., Achilles
    Pugh, 1865.

33. Farrell, James T., Reflections at Fifty, New York,
    Vanguard Press, 1954.

34. Fifty-fourth Annual Catalogue, Wittenberg College, 1899-
    1900, Springfield, Springfield Pub. Co., 1900.

35. Frank, Waldo, In the American Jungle, New York, Far-
    rar and Rinehart, 1937.

36. Frank, Waldo, Our America, New York, Boni and Liv-
    eright, 1919.

37. Frank, Waldo, Salvos, New York, Boni and Liveright,
    1924.

38. Hansen, Harry, Midwest Portraits, New York, Har-
    court, Brace, 1923.

39. Hecht, Ben, A Child of the Century, New York, New
    American Library of World Literature, 1955.

40. Howe, Irving, Sherwood Anderson, New York, Sloane,
    1951.

41. Howe, James G., Annual Report of the Adjutant General,
    Columbus, O., Westbote, 1895.

42.   Key, Ellen Karoline Sofia, Rahel Varnhagen: a Por-
       trait, New York, Putnam, 1913.

43.   Kintner, Evelyn, "Sherwood Anderson, a Small Town
       Man," Unpublished M. A. Thesis, Bowling Green,
       O., Bowling Green State University, 1942.

44.   Kirkpatrick, Judson and J. Owen Moore, Allatoona,
       New York, French, 1875.

45.   Kloucek, Jerome W., Waldo Frank, the Ground of His
       Mind and Art, Evanston, Ill., Northwestern Univer-
       sity, 1958, unpublished doctoral dissertation.

46.   Lorain County Directory, Elyria, O., Globe Publishing
       Co., 1910.

47.   Mack, Basil, Twentieth Century History of Sandusky
       County, Ohio...., Chicago, Richmond-Arnold, 1909.

48.   Masters, Edgar Lee, Across Spoon River, New York,
       Farrar and Rinehart, 1936.

49.   Meek, Basil, Twentieth Century History of Sandusky
       County, Ohio and Representative Citizens, Chicago,
       Richmond-Arnold Publishing Co., 1909.

50.   Moody, James F., "Correlations between Names Found
       in Clyde Enterprise and Windy McPherson's Son,
       Marching Men, Mid-American Chants, and Winesburg,
       Ohio," unpublished paper, Muncie, Ind., Ball State
       University, 1963.

51.   Morgan, B. F., Directory of Preble Co., Ohio, for
       1875..., Eaton, O., Morgan, 1875.

52.   Odell, George C., Annals of the New York Stage, New
       York, Columbia University Press, 1937, IX.

53.   Official Roster of Ohio Soldiers in the War with
       Spain...., Published by Authority of the Ohio Gener-
       al Assembly, no publisher, 1916.

54.   Phillips, William L., "Sherwood Anderson's Winesburg,
       Ohio: Its Origins Composition, Technique, and Re-
       ception," Unpublished doctoral dissertation, Univer-
       sity of Chicago, 1950.

55. Rascoe, Burton, Before I Forget, New York, Literary
    Guild of America 1937.

56. Rosenfeld, Paul, Port of New York, New York, Har-
    court, Brace, 1924.

57. Rosenfeld, Paul, Voyager in the Arts, New York,
    Creative Age Press, 1948.

58. Sandburg, Carl, Complete Poems, New York, Harcourt,
    Brace, 1950.

59. Schevill, James, Sherwood Anderson, His Life and
    Work, Denver, Colo., University of Denver Press,
    1951.

60. Scribner, Harvey, Memories of Lucas County and Tole-
    do, Madison, Wis., Western Historical Assn., 1910,
    I.

61. "Sherwood Anderson Documentary" (Part One), re-
    corded by Radio Station WBAI, 1963.

62. Sixteenth Annual Catalogue of the Xenia Female College
    for....1865-6., Xenia, O., Kinsey and Milbrey,
    1866.

63. Sixth Ohio Volunteer Infantry War Album [of] Historical
    Events.... of the Spanish-American War..., ...by
    Capt. L. W. Howard, Toledo, O., Bee Job Print,
    n. d.

64. Sprigge, Elizabeth, Gertrude Stein: Her Life and Work,
    New York, Harper, 1957.

65. Who's Who in America, 1942-3, Chicago, Marquis,
    1942.

66. Williams' Ohio State Directory for 1878-9, Cincinnati,
    Williams [1878?]

Articles

1. Alexander, T. H., Interview with Anderson, Nashville
   Tennesseean, undated ca. 1926.

2. Anderson, Cornelia Lane, "The Development of the
    Mark in English Literature Until the Beginning of
    the Seventeenth Century," The College Folio [Mather
    College, Cleveland, O.] January, 1900, pp. 105-9.

3. Anderson, Cornelia Lane, "Some Contemporary Opinions
    of Rahel Varnhagen," Little Review (March, 1914).

4. Anderson, Karl, "My Brother, Sherwood Anderson,"
    Saturday Review [of Literature] (September 4, 1949).

5. Anderson, Karl, "Our Unforgettable Brother," unpub-
    lished manuscript about Earl Anderson.

6. Anderson, Sherwood, "About Cleverness," Agricultural
    Advertising, November, 1903, X:56, 8.

7. Anderson, Sherwood, "About Country Roads," Agricul-
    tural Advertising, November, 1903, X:56, 8.

8. Anderson, Sherwood, "About Inquiries," Agricultural
    Advertising, November, 1903, X:56, 8.

9. Anderson, Sherwood, "About Suspicion," Agricultural
    Advertising, November, 1903, X:56, 8.

10. Anderson, Sherwood, [Adventuring], Agricultural Adver-
    tising, February, 1913, [2]:16.

11. Anderson, Sherwood, "Advertising a Nation," Agricul-
    tural Advertising, May, 1905, XII:389.

12. Anderson, Sherwood, "An Apology for Crudity," Chicago
    Daily News, Nov. 14, 1917, p. 13.

13. Anderson, Sherwood, "An Apology for Crudity," Dial,
    Nov. 8, 1917, 63: 437-8.

14. Anderson, Sherwood, "An Awakening," Little Review,
    Dec., 1918, 5:13-21.

15. Anderson, Sherwood, "Blackfoot's Masterpiece," Forum,
    June, 1916, 55: 679-83.

16. Anderson, Sherwood, "Book of the Grotesque," Masses,

Feb. , 1916, 8:7.

17. Anderson, Sherwood, "Boost No. 1, " Agricultural Advertising, June, 1903, X: 54, 56-7.

18. Anderson, Sherwood, "The Born Quitter, " Agricultural Advertising, March, 1903, X: 18-19.

19. Anderson, Sherwood, "The Boyish Man, " Agricultural Advertising, October, 1904, XI: 53.

20. Anderson, Sherwood, "A Business Man's Reading, " Agricultural Advertising, The Reader, October, 1903, X: 17-19.

21. Anderson, Sherwood, "Chicago, A Feeling, " Vanity Fair, October, 1926.

22. Anderson, Sherwood, "Chicago Inspirations, " Agricultural Advertising, April, 1903.

23. Anderson, Sherwood, "Chicago Culture, " Chicago Daily News, Feb. 20, 1918, p. 7.

24. Anderson, Sherwood, "A Christmas Thought, " Agricultural Advertising, December, 1903, X: 50-51.

25. Anderson, Sherwood, "Country Town Notes, " Vanity Fair, May, 1929, p. 63.

26. Anderson, Sherwood, "The Discouraged Man, " Agricultural Advertising, July, 1904, XI: 43-4.

27. Anderson, Sherwood, "Discovery of a Father, " Reader's Digest, November, 1939, 35: 21-25.

28. Anderson, Sherwood, "Doing Stunts, " Agricultural Advertising, April, 1903, X: 12-14.

29. Anderson, Sherwood, "Dreiser, " Little Review, April, 1916, 3: 5.

30. Anderson, Sherwood, "Fairs, " Agricultural Advertising, October, 1903, X: 17-19.

31. Anderson, Sherwood, "The Farmer Wears Clothes, " Agricultural Advertising, February, 1902, IX:6.

32.   Anderson, Sherwood, "Finding Our Work," Agricultural
      Advertising, May, 1903, X:20-21.

33.   Anderson, Sherwood, "From Chicago," Seven Arts,
      May, 1917, 2:41-59.

34.   Anderson, Sherwood, "Fun and Works," Agricultural
      Advertising, July, 1903, X: 22-23, 26.

35.   Anderson, Sherwood, "The Fussy Man and the Trim-
      mer," Agricultural Advertising, December, 1904,
      XI: 79, 81-2.

36.   Anderson, Sherwood, "Golden Fake," Agricultural Ad-
      vertising, August, 1903, X: 22, 24-5.

37.   Anderson, Sherwood, "Golden Harvest Farmer," Agri-
      cultural Advertising, August, 1903, X: 22, 24-5.

38.   Anderson, Sherwood, "Golden Harvest Manufacturers,"
      Agricultural Advertising, August, 1903, X: 22, 24-5.

39.   Anderson, Sherwood, "The Good Fellow," Agricultural
      Advertising, January, 1904, XI: 36.

40.   Anderson, Sherwood, "Hands," Masses, March, 1916,
      8: 5, 7.

41.   Anderson, Sherwood, "Here They Come," Esquire,
      (March, 1940).

42.   Anderson, Sherwood, "Here's Looking At You," (self-
      portrait), Chicago Daily News, July 10, 1918, p. 12.

43.   Anderson, Sherwood, "The Hot Young'Un and the Cold
      Old 'Un," Agricultural Advertising, September, 1904,
      XI: 24-6.

44.   Anderson, Sherwood, "In a Box Car," Vanity Fair
      (October, 1928).

45.   Anderson, Sherwood, "It's a Woman's Age," Scribner's
      Magazine (December, 1930).

46.   Anderson, Sherwood, "Jack Jones--The Pickler," Chi-
      cago Daily News, June 18, 1919, p. 12.

47. Anderson, Sherwood, "Knock No. 1," Agricultural Advertising, June, 1903, X: 54, 56-7.

48. Anderson, Sherwood, "Knock No. 2," Agricultural Advertising, June, 1903, X: 54, 56-7.

49. Anderson, Sherwood, "The Laugh of Scorn," Agricultural Advertising, February, 1903, X: 13-16.

50. Anderson, Sherwood, "The Liar-A Vacation Story," Agricultural Advertising, May, 1904, XI: 27-9.

51. Anderson, Sherwood, "The Liar-A Vacation Story," Agricultural Advertising, June, 1904, XI: 27-9.

52. Anderson, Sherwood, "The Lightweight," Agricultural Advertising, March, 1903, X: 18-19.

53. Anderson, Sherwood, "The Lost Novel," Scribner's, September, 1928, 84: 255-8.

54. Anderson, Sherwood, "Making It Clear," Agricultural Advertising, February, 1913, 24: 16.

55. Anderson, Sherwood, "The Man of Affairs," Agricultural Advertising, March, 1904, XI: 36-8.

56. Anderson, Sherwood, "The Man and the Book," The Reader, December, 1903, III: 71-3.

57. Anderson, Sherwood, "Man and His Imagination," in Centeno, Auguste, editor, The Intent of the Artist, Princeton, Princeton University Press, 1941.

58. Anderson, Sherwood, Manuscript statement about Winesburg, Ohio Manuscript, now kept with manuscript in vault at Newberry Library, Chicago.

59. Anderson, Sherwood, "Men That Are Wanted," Agricultural Advertising, December, 1903, X: 50-1.

60. Anderson, Sherwood, "Mid-American Songs," Poetry, September, 1917, 1: 281-91.

61. Anderson, Sherwood, "More About the New Note," Little Review, April, 1914, 1: 24.

62.   Anderson, Sherwood, "Mother," Seven Arts, March,
      1917, 1: 452-61.

63.   Anderson, Sherwood, "The New Job," Agricultural Ad-
      vertising, February, 1903, X: 13-16.

64.   Anderson, Sherwood, "The New Note," Little Review,
      March, 1914, 1: 23.

65.   Anderson, Sherwood, "The Novelist," Little Review,
      Jan. - Feb., 1916, 2: 12-14.

66.   Anderson, Sherwood, "Office Tone," Agricultural Ad-
      vertising, July, 1903, X: 22-3, 26.

67.   Anderson, Sherwood, "Of No Value," Agricultural Ad-
      vertising, April, 1903, X: 14.

68.   Anderson, Sherwood, "The Old and the New," Agricul-
      tural Advertising, December, 1903, X: 50-1.

69.   Anderson, Sherwood, "On Being Published," Colophon,
      (1930) (not paginated).

70.   Anderson, Sherwood, "Our Rebirth," Chicago Daily
      Tribune, Sept. 14, 1918, p. 10.   (review of Brooks'
      Letters and Leadership)

71.   Anderson, Sherwood, "Packingham," Agricultural Adver-
      tising, April, 1903, X: 12-14.

72.   Anderson, Sherwood, "People Who Write," Chicago
      Daily News, October 4, 1916, p. 11.

73.   Anderson, Sherwood, "The Philosopher," Little Review,
      June-July, 1916, 3: 7-9.

74.   Anderson, Sherwood, "Portrait," Bookman, (May, 1917).

75.   Anderson, Sherwood, "Push, Push, Push," Agricultural
      Advertising, February, 1903, X: 16.

76.   Anderson, Sherwood, "Queer," Seven Arts, Dec., 1916,
      1: 97-108.

77.   Anderson, Sherwood, "The Rabbit Pen," Harper's, July,
      1914, 129: 207-19.

78. Anderson, Sherwood, "The Sales Master and the Selling Organization," Agricultural Advertising, April, 1905, XII: 306-8.

79. Anderson, Sherwood, "Seeds," Little Review, July, 1918, 5: 24-31.

80. Anderson, Sherwood, "Self-Portrait," Chicago Daily News, July 10, 1918, p. 12.

81. Anderson, Sherwood, "Senility," Little Review, September, 1918, 5: 37-39.

82. Anderson, Sherwood, "The Silent Men," Agricultural Advertising, February, 1904, XI: 19.

83. Anderson, Sherwood, "Sister," Little Review, Dec., 1915, 2: 3-4.

84. Anderson, Sherwood, "The Solicitor," Agricultural Advertising, August, 1904, XI: 21-4.

85. Anderson, Sherwood, "Song Long After," Others (June, 1917).

86. Anderson, Sherwood, "The Story Writers," Smart Set, Jan., 1916, 48: 243-8.

87. Anderson, Sherwood, "The Strength of God," Masses, Aug., 1916, 8: 12-13.

88. Anderson, Sherwood, "The Struggle," Little Review, May, 1916, 3: 7-10.

89. Anderson, Sherwood, "The Thinker," Seven Arts, Sept., 1917, 2: 584-97.

90. Anderson, Sherwood, "The Traveling Man," Agricultural Advertising, February, 1903, X: 13-16.

91. Anderson, Sherwood, "The Traveling Man," Agricultural Advertising, April, 1904, XI: 39-40.

92. Anderson, Sherwood, "Twenty Years in Figures," Agricultural Advertising, October, 1903, X: 17-19.

93. Anderson, Sherwood, "Twenty Years in the West,"

Agricultural Advertising, October, 1903, X: 17-19.

94.   Anderson, Sherwood, "Undeveloped Man, " Agricultural Advertising, May, 1904, p. 31-32.

95.   Anderson, Sherwood, "Unfinished, " Agricultural Advertising, May, 1903, X: 20-21.

96.   Anderson, Sherwood, "Unfinished Contracts, " Agricultural Advertising, February, 1903, X: 13-16.

97.   Anderson, Sherwood, Untitled Item, Agricultural Advertising, April, 1903, X: 14.

98.   Anderson, Sherwood, Untitled Item, Agricultural Advertising, May, 1903, X: 22.

99.   Anderson, Sherwood, "The Untold Lie, " Seven Arts, Jan. , 1917, 1: 215-21.

100. Anderson, Sherwood, "Vibrant Life, " Little Review, March, 1916, 3: 10-11.

101. Anderson, Sherwood, "Virginia, " Vanity Fair, August, 1929, pp. 66, 74.

102. Anderson, Sherwood, "We Would Be Wise, " Agricultural Advertising, January, 1903, X: 45-6.

103. Anderson, Sherwood, "What Henry George Said Twenty Years Ago, " Agricultural Advertising, October, 1903, X: 17-19.

104. Anderson, Sherwood, "What Say? " Marion Democrat, undated.

105. Anderson, Sherwood, "The White Streak, " Smart Set, July, 1918, 55: 27-30.

106. Anderson, Sherwood, "Who's Who, " Chicago Tribune (May 31, 1919).

107. Anderson, Sherwood, "Why I Write, " Writer, December, 49: 363-4.

108. Anderson, Sherwood, "Why Men Write, " Story, January, 1936, 8: 2, 4, 103, 105.

109. Anderson, Sherwood, "Work in the Dark," Agricultural Advertising, July, 1903, X: 22-3, 26.

110. Anderson, Sherwood, "The Work of Gertrude Stein," Geography and Plays, Boston, The Four Seas Company, 1922.

111. Anonymous, "American Fiction," Liberator (September, 1919).

112. Anonymous, Announcement, Seven Arts, November, 1916, unpaginated.

113. Anonymous, "Brief Mention of New Books," Bookman, September, 1919, L:ix.

114. Anonymous, "The Literary Spotlight VII: Sherwood Anderson," Bookman, (April, 1922), p. 307.

115. Anonymous, "Long-Critchfield Banquet," Agricultural Advertising, May, 1905.

116. Anonymous, News Article about William Butler Yeats Appearance in Chicago, Chicago Daily News, March 2, 1914, p. 1.

117. Anonymous, "Notes on Names," Seven Arts, January, 1917, unpaginated.

118. Anonymous, Untitled, Bookman, May, 1917, p. 307.

119. Anonymous, "Whitelaw Reid," The National Cyclopedia of American Biography, New York, James T. White, 1932, XXII.

120. Brooks, Van Wyck, "Letters to Van Wyck Brooks," Story, Sept.-Oct., 1941, XIX: 42.

121. Brooks, Van Wyck, "Young America," Seven Arts, December, 1916, p. 147.

122. Chateaugay (N.Y.) Record and Franklin County Democrat, August 14, 1916.

123. Dell, Floyd, "American Fiction," Liberator, September, 1919, II: 43.

124. Dreiser, Theodore, "Life, Arts and America," Seven
     Arts, February, 1: 363-89.

125. Dreiser, Theodore, "Sherwood Anderson," Story, Sept. -
     Oct., 1941, XIX: 4.

126. Finley, Marietta D., Publisher's Reader's Report on
     Marching Men (for Bobbs-Merrill Co.), unpublished.

127. Finley, Marietta D., Unpublished reading report for
     Bobbs, Merrill Co. on "Mary Cochran" manuscript.

128. Finley, Marietta D., Unpublished reading report for
     Bobbs, Merrill Co. on "Talbot Whittingham manu-
     script.

129. Hecht, Ben, "Go Scholar Gypsy," Story, September,
     1941. pp. 92-3.

130. Hecht, Ben, "Letitia," Playboy, July, 1963, p. 124.

131. Hecht, Ben, "Mid-American Chants," Chicago Daily
     News, April 17, 1918, p. 9.

132. Hecht, Ben, Untitled article, Chicago Evening Post,
     Sept. 8, 1916, p. 11.

133. Jones, Llewellyn, "Nascent Poetry," Chicago Evening
     Post, April 26, 1918, p. 10.

134. Jones, Llewellyn, "The Unroofing of Winesburg," Chi-
     cago Evening Post, June 6, 1919, p. 11.

135. Jones, Llewellyn, Untitled, Chicago Evening Post,
     Sept. 27, 1916, p. 11.

136. Lovett, Robert Morss, "Sherwood Anderson," English
     Journal, October, 1924, 13: 531-9.

137. Lovett, Robert Morss, "Sherwood Anderson," New Re-
     public, January 25, 1936, 89: 103-5.

138. Lovett, Robert Morss, "Sherwood Anderson, Ameri-
     can," Virginia Quarterly, Summer, 1941, 17: 379-88.

139. Rascoe, Burton, "A Worthwhile Chicago Novel," Chi-
     cago Daily Tribune, Sept., 1917.

140. Rascoe, Burton, "Winesburg, Ohio," The Chicago Daily
      Tribune, June 7, 1919, p. 13.

141. Smith, Wallace, "Civilian Communique," Chicago Daily
      News, Sept. 3, 1919, p. 6.

142. Weaver, J. V. A., "Sherwood Anderson," Chicago
      Daily News, June 11, 1919, p. 12.

143. Wright, Donald M., "A Mid-Western Advertising Man
      Remembers," Advertising and Selling, December 17,
      1936, pp. 35 and 68.

631

Jones, Jack: 313-4, 323
Jones, Jefferson: 352
Jones, L. P.: 46
Jones, Llewellyn: 315, 318, 346, 365, 390-1, 597-599

Kahn, Otto: 46
Kansas City: 589
Karsten, Mrs.: 277
Kastorp, Mr.: 44
Kaun, Alexander: 277
Keats, John: 588
Kellogg, Paul A.: 51
Kendrick, John F.: 474
Kenton, Edith: 234
Kenton, Edna: 261, 318
Kentucky: 219, 429
Key, Ellen K. S.: 366
Kimbel, Frank: 199-200
Kintner, Evelyn: 45-7, 438-9, 504, 523, 525-6
Kirkpatrick, Leonard: 91
Kloucek, Jerome W.: 317
Knoxville, Tenn.: 72
Komroff, Manuel: 208
Kowan, Alexander: 261
Kramer, Dale: 264
Kuhn, Mrs. Oliver: 44

Lake Chateaugay, N.Y.: 196, 222, 251, 255, 280, 305-6, 331, 386-7, 396, 423, 429, 574
Lake Erie: 517, 547
Lake Michigan: 358
Lane, (Mrs.) Georgia: 163, 265
Lane, John: 351, 609
Lane, Margaret: 198
Lane, Robert H.: 133
Lankes, J. J.: 160
Laughter: 51
Leach Family: 469
Leipsic, Ohio: 523
Leonard, Mrs.: 193
Lerner, Daniel: 161
"Letitia": 319-20
Letters and Leadership: 225, 282
Lewis Institute: 56, 87, 92
Lewis, Lloyd: 293

Liberator, The: 319
"Life of Art, The": 511
Lillard, George Ann: 234
Lincoln, Abraham: 293, 473, 571
Lindsay, Vachel: 281, 365
"Literary Spotlight: The, VII: Sherwood Anderson": 265
Literature: 217
Littell, Robert: 455
Little Point Sable, Mich.: 198-9, 234, 260
Little Review: 276, 285, 288, 294, 302, 305, 343, 345-6, 350, 430
Liveright, Horace: 228
London: 351
"Loneliness": 287, 347, 442
Long-Crutchfield Agency: 132, 143, 151
Long, Maurice: 440
Loos, Anita: 58, 222, 228
Lorain County Directory: 169
Lord, Charles: 200, 202
"Lost Novel, The": 564
Love: 160, 414, 459
"Lover, The": 425, 427
Lovett, Robert Morss: 286, 318, 608
Lowery, Robert J.: 365
Luse, Dr.: 548
Luse, Minnie: 548

Macaulay, Thomas Babington: 131
MacDonald, Dwight: 86, 161, 227, 268
Macmillan Company: 351, 368
Magazine: 219-20
"Making Good": 132
"Making It Clear": 578
Mama Geighen: 275, 284, 364
"Man and His Imagination": 538, 540, 542
"Man and the Book, The": 130
"Manhattan": 407
Manning, Mrs. Jane: 201
Mansfield, Ohio: 496-7, 500, 512, 533
"Man Who Became a Woman, The": 47, 269
Many Marriages: 565

202, 228, 459, 529
South America: 450-1
Spoon River Anthology, The:
299, 430-1, 599-600, 604
Sprague, J. B.: 520
Spriggs, Elizabeth: 320
Springfield, Ohio: 41, 80, 87,
92-7, 101, 364
"Spring Song": 412, 415-6,
426
Squire, Ira H.: 48, 173
Squire, S. H.: 199-200
Standards: 118
Starrett, Vincent: 289, 319
Steele, W. A.: 228
Stein, Gertrude: 297-9, 320-1
Stenographers: 201
Stevens, Fred: 520, 526, 530
Stevenson, Robert Louis: 129-
30
Stieglitz, Alfred: 47, 203, 207,
272
St. Joseph, Mo.: 477
Stories: 458
Story: 283, 290, 297, 320,
322
Story Teller's Story, A: 14,
18-9, 28-9, 34, 46-8, 52,
56, 58-62, 81-2, 84-6, 90,
148, 150, 185, 196, 203,
206-8, 216, 227-8, 316,
318-9, 321-2, 324, 339,
367, 380, 442, 459, 465-6,
477, 480, 483, 494, 504,
507, 509-10, 518, 526-9,
540-2, 568, 573
Story-telling: 25, 43, 52, 85,
161, 163, 181, 206-8, 230-
2, 275, 284, 359, 524
"Story Writers, The": 578
Strain: 182, 188
"Stranger, The": 413
"Strength of God, The": 430,
579-80, 605
Striking miners: 39
"Struggle, The": 578
Style: 180
Subsidization: 327
Success: 84, 150, 459
Success pattern: 126-8
Sudler, Louis: 263, 265
Suicide: 210, 216
"Surrender": 330

Sympathy: 285
Szold, Bernardine Fritz: 262,
264, 266

Talbot Whittingham: 329, 331,
334-6, 369, 436, 584-8
"Tandy Hard": 432
Tar: 25-6, 29-30, 36, 464,
468, 540-2, 559
Taylor-Critchfield Co.: 196-7,
214, 378
"Teacher, The": 605
Telfer, John: 354, 363
Tender Buttons: 298
Terre Haute, Indiana: 568
Terry, Miss Florence: 183-4,
200, 204
Thanksgiving: 216
Theatrics: 24-5, 521-4, 530-1
"Thinker, The": 579-80
Three lives: 298
Tichenor, John B.: 24, 363
Tietjens, Eunice: 243, 318
Tiffany, Alfred: 592-6
Tiffin, Ohio: 526
Toledo, Ohio: 66-9, 133-6,
143-4, 196, 514
Tolstoi, Leo: 129, 300, 302,
344
Tom Sawyer: 365
Tragedy: 357-8
Travel: 566-8
"Triumph of the Egg, The":
244, 332, 345
Turgenev, Ivan: 301-2
Twain, Mark: 302-5, 344

"Unborn": 420
Union Pier, Mich.: 236-7
United Factories Co.: 151-5,
165-7, 169
United Presbyterian: 489
University of Chicago: 286
"Unlighted Lamps": 332
"Unroofing of Winesburg, The":
597
"Untold Lie, The": 299, 347,
431-2, 441, 579-80
U. S. T. Minnewaska: 72

643

Xenia, Ohio: 489-90